THE GÖTTINGEN DOGMATICS

Instruction in the Christian Religion

THE GÖTTINGEN DOGMATICS

Instruction in the Christian Religion

Karl Barth

Edited by Hannelotte Reiffen

Translated by Geoffrey W. Bromiley

VOLUME I

WILLIAM B. EERDMANS PUBLISHING COMPANY
GRAND RAPIDS, MICHIGAN

First published as *Unterricht in der christlichen Religion*
by Theologischer Verlag Zürich
Copyright © 1990 by Theologischer Verlag Zürich

First English edition copyright © 1991 by Wm. B. Eerdmans Publishing Co.
255 Jefferson Ave. S.E., Grand Rapids, Mich. 49503

Printed in the United States of America

Library of Congress Cataloging-in-Publication Data

Barth, Karl, 1886-1968.
[Unterricht in der christlichen Religion. English]
The Göttingen dogmatics: instruction in the Christian religion/
Karl Barth; edited by Hannelotte Reiffen;
translated by Geoffrey W. Bromiley. — 1st English ed.
p.   cm.
Translation of: Unterricht in der christlichen Religion.
Includes bibliographical references and indexes.
ISBN 0-8028-2421-8
1. Theology, Doctrinal.   I. Reiffen, Hannelotte.   II. Title.
BT75.2.B3413   1991
230'.044—dc20   91-9780
                                                       CIP

Contents

Translator's Note   vii

Preface   ix

Abbreviations   xii

Karl Barth's First Lectures in Dogmatics:
Instruction in the Christian Religion   xv
by Daniel L. Migliore

Introduction   1

§ 1   The Word of God as the Problem of Dogmatics   3

§ 2   Preaching as the Starting Point and Goal
of Dogmatics   23

Chapter 1   The Word of God as Revelation   43

§ 3   *Deus dixit*   45

§ 4   Man and His Question   69

§ 5   God: Father, Son, and Holy Spirit   87

§ 6   The Incarnation of God   131

§ 7   Faith and Obedience   168

Chapter 2   The Word of God as Holy Scripture   199

§ 8   The Scripture Principle   201

Contents

§ 9   Authority   227

§ 10   Freedom   250

Chapter 3   The Word of God as Christian Preaching   263

§ 11   Pure Doctrine   265

§ 12   The Dogmatic Norm   280

§ 13   Dogmatic Thinking   298

Chapter 4   The Doctrine of God   315

§ 14   Introduction: The Material and the Task of Dogmatics   317

§ 15   The Knowability of God   325

§ 16   The Nature of God   351

§ 17   The Attributes of God   375

§ 18   The Election of Grace   440

Indexes   476

I   Subjects   476

II   Names   483

III   Scripture References   487

Translator's Preface

Barth's first attempt at dogmatics claims interest for two reasons. Historically, as the *Urdogmatik,* it gives evidence of Barth's earliest thinking. Materially, it is the only larger dogmatics that he ever completed. Naturally, had Barth lived, the final materials would have differed as widely from the first proposals as did those of the volumes in which comparison is possible. Yet there is enough similarity, particularly in basic structure, to show along what lines his thought was moving. In addition, this early course, tentative as it was, can very well stand as a dogmatics in its own right. Thus scholars will welcome this edition for the insights that it gives into Barth's development, especially where *Christliche Dogmatik* as well as *Church Dogmatics* may be consulted. Furthermore, all who have an interest in theology may profit from Barth's discussions even when they will not agree with them, as Barth himself would often disagree with himself in his maturer deliberations.

The present translation offers the text of the lectures in full according to the excellent Swiss edition in the *Gesamtausgabe (Collected Works).* Latin passages have been translated or paraphrased, however, to make for easier reading. For this reason the index of Latin terms has been dropped as superfluous. There has also been some reduction of extended references in the notes; students can check these out for themselves in the Swiss original. Readers should also be aware that Barth often uses his own scripture translations. The three volumes of the original have been compressed into two. After some consideration it has been thought good to give the work the main title *The Göttingen Dogmatics.* Barth, of course, avoided the title "dogmatics" after his conflict with the Göttingen faculty, and he had already moved to Münster when he taught the final section. Nevertheless, the series does represent Barth's first dogmatics at the climax of his Göttingen professorship, and it is not inappropriate, therefore, to call it *The Göttingen Dogmatics,* forerunner of the abortive *Christliche Dogmatik* of Münster and the magisterial *Church Dogmatics* of Bonn and Basel.

Geoffrey W. Bromiley

Preface

When Karl Barth became Honorary Professor of Reformed Theology at Göttingen in 1921, he devoted his first years to historical lectures on the Heidelberg Catechism, Calvin, Zwingli, the Reformed Confessions, and finally Schleiermacher. Only then did he decide to lecture on dogmatics. In his introduction to the new edition of H. Heppe's *Reformed Dogmatics* in 1935 he expressly tells us about the problems that faced him in carrying out his intention. He was firmly convinced that holy scripture must be the master in an evangelical dogmatics and that there must be a specific link with the Reformers.[1] He found in the Reformers and the older orthodox a dogmatics that had both form and substance, that was oriented to the central directions of the biblical witness to revelation, that also attempted a worthy continuation of the teaching of the early church and sought to protect and cultivate continuity with the medieval scholarship of the church.[2] Barth came to see that Protestant dogmatics had been an orderly and sober affair, and he cherished the hope that it might become so again if it could regain its obviously lost nerve and return to a strict churchly and scientific attitude.[3] This was the presupposition of his own dogmatic work. In volume II of the Barth-Thurneysen letters we find many references that show how carefully Barth prepared his lectures.[4]

I might also refer to the battle that Barth had to fight with the Lutheran theological faculty about the title of the lectures. The faculty

---

1. Heppe, p. vii (1958 edition); ET (1950), p. v.
2. Ibid., p. viii; ET p. vi.
3. Ibid., p. viii; ET p. vi.
4. Cf. Barth-Thurneysen, *Briefwechsel*, II (Zurich, 1974), esp. pp. 243ff.; ET *Revolutionary Theology in the Making* (Richmond, 1964), pp. 166ff.

insisted that he lecture only on *Reformed* dogmatics. Barth refused to do this.[5] The issue went to the Minister of Culture at Berlin, and Barth lost.[6] Under compulsion he thus chose the title "Instruction in the Christian Religion." Regarding this title, before beginning his first lecture, he told his students that it needed some explanation. It posed the question whether he was thinking of lecturing on religious pedagogy. This was not so. Put into Latin *(Institutio religionis christianae),* the title was the same as that of Calvin's chief work. But Barth was not going to expound Calvin. He proposed to lecture on dogmatics, and the title was nothing more or less than a cover which took into account the fact that within the present theological faculty only Lutheran dogmatics could have the general title of "dogmatics." Barth's dogmatics, in accordance with his background, office, and theological convictions, would obviously have to be Reformed dogmatics. But he was not prepared to announce the course as such because he did not see why he should call in question the ecumenical character of his lectures by a confessional tag which would run contrary to the history and nature of the Reformed church and its theology. The covering title that he had chosen, with its allusion to Calvin, was a compromise. It simply had academic significance, no more. Having yielded to necessity with the announcement, he would not come back to the title again. For his own part, the title of the first session was "Prolegomena to Dogmatics." (Barth made this introductory statement on the first page of his manuscript.) The title is retained in the *Gesamtausgabe (Collected Works)* in order to distinguish these lectures from his later *Christliche Dogmatik* and *Church Dogmatics.*

The present edition is based on the manuscript in Barth's own hand. Marginal notes that Barth did not put in the text have been incorporated with the other notes which provide references to the secondary literature used by Barth. Mistakes in style and construction have been corrected or noted. Necessary additions are put in square brackets. The orthography is most faithful to the original but the punctuation has been modernized. Underlinings in the manuscript are printed in italics. For easier reading some reparagraphing has been done.

I am grateful to Pastor Hans Theo Goebel for putting his class notes at my disposal. These contain some interesting extemporaneous additions that are included in the notes under N. For help in tracking

---

5. For his reasons, see ibid., p. 213; ET p. 166.
6. See ibid., p. 250; ET p. 182.

down quotations thanks are due to many teachers and students, especially Professor Hans Georg Geyer, Mrs. Johanna Clauss, and Dr. Beroald Thomassen. I am also grateful to Mr. Volker Eschen and Pastor Holger Finze for assiduous help with the proofs and indexes. Finally, I owe a great debt to Dr. Hinrich Stoevesandt for invaluable assistance in editing the text and notes.

Bonn, October 1984   Hannelotte Reiffen

Abbreviations

Bartmann	B. Bartmann, *Lehrbuch der Dogmatik* (Freiburg im Breisgau, 1925)
Bavinck	H. Bavinck, *Gereformeerde Dogmatiek,* 4 vols. (Kampen, 1906-1911; 6th ed. Kampen, 1976)
BSLK	*Die Bekenntnisschriften der evangelisch-lutherischen Kirche* (Göttingen, 1930; 6th ed. 1979)
BSRK	*Die Bekenntnisschriften der reformierten Kirche,* ed. E. F. K. Müller (Leipzig, 1903)
CCSL	Corpus Christianorum, Series Latina (Turnhout, 1953ff.)
CF	F. Schleiermacher, *The Christian Faith,* 2 vols. (repr. New York, 1963); ET of *Der christliche Glaube,* 2 vols. (2nd ed. 1830)
ChD	Karl Barth, *Die christliche Dogmatik im Entwurf,* I (Zurich, 1982)
CR	Corpus Reformatorum (Berlin, 1834ff.)
CSEL	Corpus Scriptorum Ecclesiasticorum Latinorum (Vienna/Leipzig/Prague, 1866ff.)
CW	*Die Christliche Welt*
DS	*Enchiridion Symbolorum,* ed. H. Denzinger and A. Schönmetzer (36th ed. 1973)
ET	English translation
Haering	T. Haering, *Der christliche Glaube (Dogmatik)* (Stuttgart, 1906); ET *The Christian Faith,* I (London, 1913)
Hase	K. von Hase, *Hutterus Redivivus oder Dogmatik der evangelisch-lutherischen Kirche* (10th ed. Leipzig, 1862)
Heppe	H. Heppe, *Die Dogmatik der evangelisch-reformierten Kirche* (Eberfeld, 1861)

Heppe-Bizer	H. Heppe, *Die Dogmatik der evangelisch-reformierten Kirche,* rev. and ed. E. Bizer (2nd ed. Neukirchen, 1958); ET *Reformed Dogmatics* (repr. Grand Rapids, 1978)
Inst.	J. Calvin, *Institutio Religionis Christianae* (1559), CR, XXX (Brunsvigae, 1869); ET *Institutes of the Christian Religion,* 2 vols., LCC, XX-XXI (Philadelphia, 1960)
Kaftan	J. Kaftan, *Dogmatik* (3rd-4th ed. Tübingen/Leipzig, 1901)
Luthardt	C. E. Luthardt, *Kompendium der Dogmatik* (4th ed. Leipzig, 1873)
LW	*Luther's Works,* ed. J. Pelikan and H. T. Lehmann (St. Louis/Philadelphia, 1955ff.)
MPG	J.-P. Migne, *Patrologiae cursus completus,* Series Graeca (Paris, 1857ff.)
MPL	J.-P. Migne, *Patrologiae cursus completus,* Series Latina (Paris, 1841ff.)
MS	Manuscript
Müller	*Die symbolischen Bücher der evangelisch-lutherischen Kirche,* ed. J. T. Müller (10th ed. Gütersloh, 1907)
N.	Material in the notes based on the class notes of H.-T. Goebel
Nitzsch-Stephan	F. A. B. Nitzsch, *Lehrbuch der Evangelischen Dogmatik,* ed. H. Stephan, 3rd ed. (Tübingen, 1912)
PhB	Philosophische Bibliothek
RE	*Realencyklopädie für protestantische Theologie und Kirche* (3rd ed. Leipzig, 1896-1913)
RGG	*Die Religion in Geschichte und Gegenwart* (1st ed. Tübingen, 1909-1913; 3rd ed. 1957-1965)
SC	Sources chrétiennes (Paris, 1941ff.)
Schaff	P. Schaff, *Creeds of Christendom,* III (6th ed. New York, 1919)
Schmid	*Die Dogmatik der evangelisch-lutherischen Kirche,* ed. H. Schmid (4th ed. Frankfurt a.M./Erlangen, 1858); ET *The Doctrinal Theology of the Evangelical Lutheran Church* (Philadelphia, 1899)
Schmid-Pöhlmann	*Die Dogmatik der evangelisch-lutherischen Kirche,* ed. and rev. G. Pöhlmann (Gütersloh, 1979)
Schweizer	A. Schweizer, *Die Glaubenslehre der evangelisch-reformierten Kirche,* I (Zurich, 1844)
STh	Thomas Aquinas, *Summa theologica,* Paris edition

Tappert	T. G. Tappert, *The Book of Concord* (Philadelphia, 1959)
TBl	*Theologische Blätter*
TBü	Theologische Bücherei
WA	*Luthers Werke*, Weimarer Ausgabe (1883ff.)
Wendt	H. H. Wendt, *System der christlichen Lehre* (Göttingen, 1906)
ZST	*Zeitschrift für systematische Theologie*
ZTK	*Zeitschrift für Theologie und Kirche*

Karl Barth's First Lectures in Dogmatics: *Instruction in the Christian Religion*[1]

DANIEL L. MIGLIORE

I. Barth's Three Cycles of Dogmatics

While the *Church Dogmatics* is widely recognized as Karl Barth's definitive theological work, it is less well known that he actually taught three cycles of courses in dogmatics during his lifetime. His production of church dogmatics thus began not in Bonn in 1931, or even in Münster in 1926, but in Göttingen in 1924.

The initial cycle of dogmatics, offered during his first academic appointment at the University of Göttingen, ran from the summer semester of 1924 through the summer semester of 1925 (the cycle was completed with an abbreviated course on eschatology in the winter semester of 1925 in Münster). Barth's proposed title for these lectures set off a small controversy. As an honorary rather than a regularly appointed professor, and as the only Reformed theologian on the Göttingen faculty, Barth met resistance from his Lutheran colleagues when he made known his plan to lecture on dogmatics. They contended that Barth's appointment was specifically to teach *Reformed* theology, and their view was upheld when Barth appealed the case to the authorities in Berlin. As a result, Barth renamed his lectures *Unterricht in der christlichen Religion (Instruction in the Christian Religion)*, an obvious allusion to John Calvin's classic statement of Christian theology, *Institutes of the Christian Religion*. Nevertheless,

---

1. I would like to express my thanks to Dr. Hinrich Stoevesandt, editor-in-chief of the *Karl Barth — Gesamtausgabe*, who read an earlier draft of this essay and offered helpful suggestions.

Barth always considered this title an "alias,"[2] and in his first lecture he defiantly told his students that, despite the legalities surrounding the catalogue description of the course, his use of the Calvin title was a compromise and that on the first page of *his* manuscript was the title "Prolegomena to Dogmatics."[3]

The dispute about the title was a matter of principle for Barth. In his judgment, strictly speaking there can be no such thing as Reformed or Lutheran or Roman Catholic dogmatics. In principle and in intention there can be only Christian dogmatics pursued within a particular confessional tradition (cf. *Göttingen Dogmatics*, 12.II.293).[4]

Although the Göttingen lectures, delivered to a class of about sixty students, created excitement from the beginning, Barth resisted the urging of his friends to publish his work as soon as possible because he wanted more time to refine his ideas and his distinctive approach. Hence after his move to the University of Münster he offered a second cycle of courses in dogmatics from the winter semester of 1926 through the winter semester of 1927. The prolegomenon of this cycle was published in 1927 under the title *Die Christliche Dogmatik in Entwurf, 1. Die Lehre vom Worte Gottes, Prolegomena zur Christlichen Dogmatik.*[5] Intended to be a three-volume project, it was discontinued after the initial volume because Barth became convinced that he had still not clarified sufficiently his theological method and intentions. Apart from the prolegomena, the Münster dogmatics is still unedited and unpublished.

Barth's third and final cycle of lectures in dogmatics began in Bonn in 1931 and, after his expulsion from Germany by the Nazi regime, continued in Basel from 1935 to 1961. This last cycle of lectures was published as the multivolume but incomplete *Die Kirchliche Dogmatik (Church Dogmatics).* As publication of the Göttingen lectures amply documents, Barth's final cycle of dogmatics incorporated the earlier ones, even if he also thoroughly reworked, corrected, reorganized, and greatly expanded the material.

Until recently the Göttingen lectures in dogmatics remained in

---

2. See K. Barth and E. Thurneysen, *Briefwechsel* (Zurich, 1974), II, 231.

3. See the Preface by Hannelotte Reiffen above, pp. ix-x.

4. Hereafter, references to the *Göttingen Dogmatics* will be cited in the text by section, subsection, and page, except for references to the second volume of this set (not yet translated), which will be cited only by section and subsection.

5. A new critical edition of this volume, prepared by Gerhard Sauter, appeared in 1982.

manuscript form in the Barth Archives in Basel. Edited by Hannelotte Reiffen and Hinrich Stoevesandt, they are being published in three volumes in German as part of the vast collected works of Barth *(Karl Barth — Gesamtausgabe)* and will be available to the English-language theological world in this two-volume set published by Eerdmans. These lectures not only provide exceedingly rich new material for understanding the development of Barth's thought but also offer a remarkably original, lively, and "reader-friendly"[6] summary of Barth's early theology whose interest and value exceed that of being merely an initial stage of the later *Church Dogmatics*. The clarity, passion, originality, struggle, candor, and humor exhibited in these lectures will establish a permanent place for them in the history of twentieth-century theology.

II. Preparation for the *Göttingen Dogmatics*

When Barth left his pastorate in Safenwil, Switzerland, in 1921 to take up his new academic post in Göttingen, Germany, he was not optimistic about his chances of success. He wrote to his friend Eduard Thurneysen: "I dare not even *think* about having to lecture three or six or eight hours each week."[7] "I just can't imagine myself in the situation and cannot think that I will be anything but a great failure."[8] Barth was not expressing false modesty in these statements. His epochal commentary on Romans — undertaken in disenchantment with what was then called "modern theology" and in search of an entirely new theological foundation for ministry in the church — had signaled the end of a theological era.[9] Yet it is one thing to dismantle a dominant theology; it is another thing to replace it with a better theology. Barth did not know whether he could move from deconstruction to reconstruction. Moreover, he was fully aware that he was not adequately prepared for his new responsibilities. In letters to Thurneysen, Barth is frank about how poor his knowledge of theological texts was as compared with that

---

6. See Dieter Schellong, *Theologische Literaturzeitung* 112 (1987) 614.

7. Barth-Thurneysen, *Briefwechsel* (Zurich, 1973), I, 483.

8. See Eberhard Busch, *Karl Barth* (Philadelphia, 1976), p. 124.

9. Barth, *Römerbrief* (Bern, 1st ed. 1919, 2nd ed. 1922); ET of 6th ed. (only slight changes from the 2nd ed.) *The Epistle to the Romans* (London, 1933; repr. New York, 1980).

of Göttingen colleagues like Emanuel Hirsch. He knew that he had much catching up to do. "What am I doing?" he writes in response to a question of Thurneysen, "I am studying."[10]

Although appointed Professor of Reformed Theology, Barth did not begin immediately to lecture in dogmatics. Before plunging into that task, he wanted to learn more about classical and Reformation theology. Much later Barth would muse about why he had been chosen for the Göttingen chair in Reformed theology in view of the fact that the first edition of the *Römerbrief* was not strongly marked by Reformed themes. He concluded that perhaps he was considered qualified for the position because he had at least shown that he intended to wrestle seriously with the witness of scripture.[11]

Aware of his need to study classical theological texts, especially of the Reformed tradition, before launching his own dogmatics, Barth offered courses during his first several semesters on the Heidelberg Catechism, Reformed Confessions, Calvin, Zwingli, Schleiermacher, 1 Corinthians, Ephesians, and 1 John. He "burned the midnight oil" in his struggle to familiarize himself with "the mysteries of specifically Reformed theology."[12] When he began to read Calvin seriously, he found him "a waterfall, a primitive forest, a demonic power, something straight down from the Himalayas, absolutely Chinese, strange, mythological; I just don't have the organs, the suction cups, even to assimilate this phenomenon, let alone to describe it properly."[13]

In early 1924 Barth began intensive preparations on his first lectures in dogmatics. "I shall never forget the spring vacation of 1924. I sat in my study at Göttingen, faced with the task of giving lectures on dogmatics for the first time. No one can ever have been more plagued than I then was with the problem, could I do it? and how?"[14] At this juncture Barth found unexpected help in Heinrich Heppe's *Reformed Dogmatics* (a collection of texts on all the loci of dogmatics from the sixteenth-, seventeenth-, and early eighteenth-century Reformed theologians) and in the parallel compendium of Lutheran sources by H. Schmid. Heppe, said Barth, was "out of date, dusty, unattractive, almost like a table of logarithms, dreary

---

10. Barth-Thurneysen, *Briefwechsel,* II, 29.

11. Busch, *Karl Barth,* p. 123.

12. Ibid., p. 129.

13. Ibid., p. 138.

14. Barth, "Foreword," in Heinrich Heppe, *Reformed Dogmatics* (London, 1950; repr. Grand Rapids, 1978), p. v.

to read, stiff and eccentric on almost every page I opened."[15] Yet Barth persisted and was impressed by the seriousness, discipline, and depth of the treatment of theological issues by the old Reformed scholars, and by their awareness of theology as a discipline of the church. As we shall see, while open to instruction from the old Reformed theologians, Barth was not uncritical of them. They became for him a doorway into the expanses of the Reformed theological tradition and beyond that into the riches of patristic, medieval, and Reformation theology.

In a letter to Thurneysen from this period, Barth wrote: "All day long I am reading pell-mell hundreds and hundreds of pages: Heim, Thomas Aquinas, Fr. Strauss, Alex. Schweizer, Herrmann."[16] He continued to work at this feverish pace throughout the production of the *Göttingen Dogmatics.* Sometimes he grew dizzy from the intensity of his reflection.[17] His labor pursued him even into his dreams.[18] He looked upon these first lectures in dogmatics as an "experiment," surrounded by all sorts of dangers and suspicions. He reported that on one occasion at 3:00 A.M. he had to conclude that what he had written for the next morning's lecture on the covenant was all wrong. So he had to excuse himself from lecturing as though he were sick.[19]

Although the work was demanding, the *Göttingen Dogmatics,* like the *Römerbrief,* leaves the impression of having been written by someone who has made an important discovery.[20] This is displayed in the rapid movement of thought, in the forceful language, and in the many new and bold ideas. Spice is added by Barth's parenthetical comments to students and by his lively sense of humor (e.g., he describes the doctrine of the inerrancy of the Bible, including the Hebrew vowel points of the Old Testament text, as "an exhibit from the darkest corner of the orthodox chamber of horrors" [9.III.235]; he contends that analogies of the Trinity are ballast thrown from a balloon 10,000 feet up, not attempts to throw sandbags 10,000 feet high [5.II.108]; for Barth God's Yes and No are not

---

15. Ibid.

16. Barth-Thurneysen, *Briefwechsel,* II, 243; partial ET, cited here and wherever possible: *Revolutionary Theology in the Making: Barth-Thurneysen Correspondence, 1914-1925* (Richmond, 1964), p. 176.

17. Barth-Thurneysen, II, 319.

18. Ibid., 222.

19. Ibid., 303.

20. Barth speaks of having written the *Romans* commentary with "a joyful sense of discovery" (p. 2).

like the constant up-and-down movement of a hyena in a cage [18.IV.470]; with regard to divine attributes like eternity Barth comments, "If I were the theologian of negation that I am rumored to be, I could hold a perfect orgy here" [17.IV.435]; in speaking of God by the way of eminence, Barth cautions that "Feuerbach is again peeping through the window here" [17.IV.399-400]).

Barth was frankly surprised by the direction in which his thinking increasingly moved. "After much head shaking and astonishment, I agree with orthodoxy on almost all points and hear myself lecturing about things that I would never have dreamed could really be true when I was a student or when I was pastor in Safenwil. I am excitedly waiting how the whole will look to me when I can get some distance from it after it is finished."[21]

Aware that he was once again swimming against the stream, Barth knew that he could expect applause from neither the critics nor the admirers of his earlier writings. "I often sigh under the awareness of the complete isolation of the whole undertaking."[22] With typically self-deprecating humor, Barth wrote to Thurneysen shortly after the conclusion of his lecture cycle: "In the final hour of eschatology I explained that according to Thomas in addition to the aurea given to all the righteous there are other aureolae for marytrs, virgins, and — church teachers. I fit into none of these categories. Indeed, even whether I will receive the common aurea is more than worrisome and questionable."[23]

III. Dogmatics in the Service of Preaching

At the very beginning of his Göttingen lectures Barth repeats a prayer that Thomas Aquinas used as a superscription for the *Summa Theologica:* "Merciful God, I ask that thou wilt grant me, as thou pleasest, to seek earnestly, to investigate carefully, to know truthfully, and to present perfectly, to the glory of thy name, amen" (1.I.3). Barth's only emendation is that the

---

21. Barth-Thurneysen, *Briefwechsel,* II, 328-29.
22. Ibid.
23. Ibid., pp. 406-7.

prayer for God's grace has a place not only at the beginning but also in the middle and at the end of the project of a dogmatic theology.

Beginning his lecture series with prayer is no empty, pious gesture for Barth. He insists that dogmatics has never been "child's play" (1.I.5); it has always been a "mortally dangerous" undertaking (1.I.3). This was no doubt also true for classical theologians whose works display such remarkable confidence, joy, and beauty. In the modern era, however, the dogmatic task is far more burdensome (1.I.4). Pursued in a time of extraordinary distress and perplexity in the church, it has become "laborious, unsatisfying, and difficult" work (11.I.269). For us, Barth says, dogmatics is done not as "an end in itself, nor for the joy of scholarship, but because it is bitterly necessary" (12.I.281). He has only scorn for the theologians who avoid the difficulty and danger of serious theological reflection either by remaining mere academic spectators of the theological task or by plunging thoughtlessly into practice. Both spectators and activists seek escape from the "Damocles' sword" that hangs over the head, the "pistol at the breast" of the person who must answer the inescapable questions of dogmatics: *What* will you say? and What will *you* say of God? (1.I.6).

According to Barth, "dogmatics has to serve the church" (11.III.276). More specifically, it serves the ministry of the Word of God (13.II.312). It starts with "the concrete situation of preachers mounting the pulpit steps" (8.I.201). The commission to proclaim the Word of God is a fearful task and creates anxiety and doubt. "The world does not know what real doubts are, real collapse, really being at one's wits' end, real destructive criticism" (3.IV.65).

Barth's decisive break with liberalism around 1915 had occurred not out of any desire to form a new school or to construct a new system of theology; "it arose simply out of what we felt to be the '*need and promise of Christian preaching.*'"[24] In a letter to Thurneysen during the first few weeks of the Göttingen lectures, Barth states his intention always to come back "with stubborn persistence and from all directions to the situation of the preacher in the pulpit."[25] He is convinced that those who feel no responsibility for the fact of Christian proclamation can have no serious interest in the dogmatic task (14.I.316).

The determination to reorient the discipline of dogmatics to the

---

24. Barth, *The Word of God and the Word of Man* (London, 1928; repr. Grand Rapids, 1935), p. 100.

25. Barth-Thurneysen, *Briefwechsel,* II, 252; ET *Revolutionary Theology,* p. 183.

task of church proclamation is everywhere evident in the Göttingen lectures.[26] In the very first sentence Barth defines dogmatics as "scientific reflection on the Word of God" (1, summary statement, 3). Still more specifically, it is "the science of the principles of Christian proclamation" (14, summary statement, 314), "the science of Christian preaching" (16.III.364). Dogmatics is not the science of God (*scientia de Deo*), nor of religion, nor of faith. And it is not to be confused with homiletics, which is the science of the practice of preaching. Dogmatics is the science of the principles and norms of Christian proclamation (14.I.315).

In a celebrated exchange of letters with Barth in 1923, Adolf von Harnack accused the author of the *Römerbrief* of being a "despiser of academic theology" and of wanting to turn the professorial chair into a pulpit.[27] In his *Göttingen Dogmatics,* however, Barth emphasizes the difference as well as the intimate relation of dogmatics and preaching. While a dogmatics that might not also function as Christian preaching alongside what it properly intends would be a "God-forsaken dogmatics" (1.III.16), the primary purpose of dogma and dogmatics is not to preach but to provide a critical test of preaching. Dogma and dogmatics are needed because "in every age the church's preaching has been sick" (11.III.277). Dogmatics exists for the sake of responsible Christian preaching. It provides criticism and guidance regarding the content of the Word of God. Thus dogmatics stands both under and over proclamation: *under* it because dogmatics has its origin in proclamation and "must yield to it as the moon does to the sun" (1.III.18), and *over* it because as a human act, proclamation needs critical examination, not just by any norm but by the norm of the Word of God (14.I.319).

Another way of describing the relationship of dogmatics and preaching is to say that Christian preaching provides the "raw stuff" of dogma and dogmatics (2.I.24). Or to use a different analogy, dogmatics stands to Christian preaching as the Platonic Socrates stands to the rhetorician Gorgias (2.I.25). It asks about the basic principles and presuppositions of Christian proclamation not out of purely theoretical interest but because of the very practical need to help preaching keep to its "own proper point" (2.I.27). Yet while emphasizing the practical goal of dog-

---

26. This determination remains a constant in Barth's later work. See Hinrich Stoevesandt, "Wandlungen in Karl Barths Theologischen Verstandnis der Predigt?" in *Evangelische Theologie* 47 (Nov./Dec. 1987) 536-50.
27. See Busch, *Karl Barth,* p. 147.

matics, Barth refuses to reduce the dogmatic task to providing content for next week's sermon. Dogmatics is not the stuff of preaching and education in the church but "academic exercises that we must have done before we can preach and teach" (17.III.385). Preaching, like every responsible human act, requires critical reflection; it can therefore be done well only if there is awareness of the basic principles that inform it (2.I.30).

Thus Barth sees dogmatics as the attempt to clarify the "commonplaces" *(loci communes)* of the community of faith, words used again and again in the Christian community and especially by Christian preachers, such as God, creation, providence, sin, guilt, Christ, reconciliation, and faith (11.III.278). Theology reflects on these words, shows how they must be used, with what meaning and in what context, with what presuppositions and consequences. Arising out of this work are dogmatic statements, formulas, summaries, dogmas in the widest sense of the word. Dogmas provide rules and canons for preaching.[28] Barth pleads with his students not to empty their theological notebooks on their poor congregations (11.III.276). Dogmas "have no place in the pulpit, but pastors in the pulpit should give evidence that they know them by their silent adherence to them. They should preach nondogmatically but with a solid dogmatics behind them" (11.III.278).

For example, the doctrine of predestination should be familiar and well-considered by the Christian preacher since it is "the death of all Pelagianism and semi-Pelagianism" (18.IV.475) and since our talk of God becomes more accurate when it is clear that God is free to elect and to reject. That is, good preaching will be permeated by this "esoteric doctrine" of the Reformed tradition that aims to give glory to God alone. At the same time, Barth advises his students to avoid presenting the doctrine of predestination "too often or expressly" in preaching (18.IV.475).

There are numerous other examples of Barth's understanding of dogmatics as having a regulatory function for preaching rather than providing material to be preached: all Christian preaching should be informed by the recognition of God's incomprehensibility (15.II.359); it is a basic rule of preaching that the realities of sin, suffering, and death may under no circumstances be interpreted as essential elements of the created order (19.III); a proper understanding of the classical doctrine of the anhypostatic human nature of Christ helps to guard against ideological interpreta-

---

28. Cf. George Lindbeck's idea of doctrines as rules of Christian grammar in *The Nature of Doctrine* (Louisville, 1984).

tions of his humanity (28.II); no Christian sermon can speak rightly of the benefits of Christ if the mystery of his person is not presupposed (29.I).

Thus while Barth sees preaching and dogmatics as closely related, he also emphasizes that they are distinct activities. Christian preaching is edifying speech; dogmatics is scientific examination of this speech. Of course, by themselves the human words of dogmas and dogmatics can no more guarantee that our talk of God will be true and effective than can any others words of ours. Only God can truly speak the Word of God; only the Holy Spirit can make the work of dogmatics helpful. But this does not alter the fact that there is in fact better or worse doctrine, and that the doctrinal task of the church should be approached as a serious responsibility. "Just for this purpose dogmatics exists" (28.I).

The intimate bond between dogmatics and preaching in the *Göttingen Dogmatics* is built into the very organization of the material. After the three chapters of prolegomena which analyze the threefold form of the Word of God as the norm of all Christian proclamation, Barth orders the material topics of dogmatics into four chapters based on "the logical content of Christian preaching" (14.II.320). Christian preaching has to do with the Word of *God* which is addressed to *humanity* and which tells of God's gift of *reconciliation* in Christ and of our *salvation* in him. Thus the four parts of dogmatics are: the doctrines of God, humanity, reconciliation, and salvation. Originally, Barth intended to deal with eschatology as material that like the prolegomena would stand outside the regular order of topics and would function like a "great exclamation point" to all that preceded.[29]

Not surprisingly, in his lectures Barth sometimes alludes to his own experience as preacher in Safenwil to support what he says. Regarding the difficulty and risks of Christian preaching, he tells his students: "Take as much or as little as you like of what I am here presenting to you, but believe me — *credite experto* — that this venture and its difficulty are no joke. You will perhaps be having a quiet laugh at the sentence which recurs so monotonously: 'Christian preachers dare to talk about God.' But in a few years your own path will lead into this impasse. I know what I am about when I keep repeating this statement" (11.I.265).

Many years later, no longer able to continue his theological work, Barth would express joy and satisfaction whenever he was told that many

---

29. For Barth's modification of this plan before the end of his lecture cycle, see 27.I.

pastors were reading and finding help in the *Church Dogmatics*.[30] For the later Barth, too, theology should not be ashamed of "the unavoidable affinity between all genuine theology and preaching" (*CD* IV/3.2, 802).[31] But this affinity of his dogmatic work with the preaching task is even more readily apparent in the Göttingen lectures. Theology has its "starting point and goal" in preaching (cf. the title of § 2). Apart from the "fact of preaching," from its need and promise, dogmatics would fall apart "like a house of cards" (20.IV).

IV. The Theme: God Is God

The *Göttingen Dogmatics* is divided into seven chapters, the first three devoted to prolegomena (the doctrine of the three forms of the Word of God), followed by four chapters on the major doctrinal loci of God, anthropology, reconciliation, and redemption. Each of the chapters is divided into several sections, with thirty-eight sections in all. Every section begins with a thesis or summary statement *(Diktatsatz)* that students were expected to take down verbatim. This format was common in German Protestant theology at least since Schleiermacher, and Barth continued to make use of it in all three cycles of his lectures in dogmatics.

At the center of Barth's pioneering work is the affirmation of the deity of God over against all comfortable, bourgeois distortions of the God attested by scripture. Barth's decisive turn from the old liberalism that he had learned in his university years and had espoused in his early ministry was registered as early as 1916 in his programmatic statement: "We should begin at the beginning and recognize that God is God."[32] The declaration "God is God" runs like a great fugal theme with many variations through the *Göttingen Dogmatics*. That God is God means that God is the living, free, gracious, and righteous Lord. All that we think and say about God and the world must take into account that "we are human and not God" (7.IV.197).

The claim that God is God bears first and foremost on the meaning of revelation. God does not cease to be the living Lord in revelation and

---

30. Busch, *Karl Barth*, p. 488.
31. References in the text to the *Church Dogmatics* (*CD*) will be by volume, part volume, and page number.
32. Busch, *Karl Barth*, p. 90.

become an object we can manipulate. God remains the hidden subject of every moment of the event of revelation. According to Barth, this is the key to the doctrine of the Trinity: it expresses the "inalienable subjectivity of God" in revelation. In his preparation for his first course in dogmatics Barth had realized the crucial importance of the doctrine of the Trinity. "A Trinity of *being,* not just an economic Trinity! At all costs the doctrine of the Trinity! If I could get the right key in my hand there, then everything would come out right."[33] And then came his discovery: "I understand the Trinity as *the problem of the inalienable subjectivity of God in his revelation.*"[34] As Father, Son, and Spirit, God is the source, the objective content, and the power of the subjective realization of revelation. The doctrine of the Trinity is for Barth "the dogma of all dogmas . . . the doctrine of God's subjectivity in his revelation" (5.II.103).

The theme of God's living reality and lordship is sounded again and again. The doctrines of election and *creatio ex nihilo* declare it in their distinctive ways. So too does the ancient christological doctrine of the anhypostatic (or, positively expressed, enhypostatic) human nature of Christ. As Barth understands this doctrine, it affirms that the humanity of Christ is no exception to the canon of the priority and sovereignty of God in relation to creatures. The same concern to honor the mystery and inexhaustibility of God is evident in Barth's discussion of the attributes of God. He insists that it must always be clear that the attributes ascribed to God are subordinate to God, and not God to them (17.II.383). Infant baptism is for Barth another vivid reminder that God is God, that God loves us in "absolute one-sidedness," establishing a covenantal relationship with us out of sheer grace (30.II).

Thus in every doctrine of Christian dogmatics, from revelation to eschatology, Barth wants to make clear that "God remains subject and does not become a predicate of history" (36.IV). All the central doctrines of the faith are interpreted to give God alone the glory. As already noted, Barth begins his dogmatics with a prayer of Thomas Aquinas asking God for assistance so that all may be said and done *ad laudem nominis tui,* "to the glory of your name" (1.I.3). Appropriately, the final paragraph of his chapter on eschatology is entitled, "The Glory of God" (38).

"God is God" — this is the theme of the *Göttingen Dogmatics* (5.I.88; 5.III.113; 5.III.120; 6.II.134 and n.5; 16.IV.368-69; 18.II.446;

---

33. Barth-Thurneysen, *Briefwechsel,* II, 245; ET *Revolutionary Theology,* p. 176.
34. Ibid., p. 254; ET p. 185.

35.V; etc.). For Barth, the Lutheran *sola fide* is sound and good theology, but it is best understood in the light of the "stubborn and exclusive" Calvinist *Deus solus* (18.III.464) and *soli Deo gloria* (7.IV.195). Yet the familiar rule of Reformed theology, "the finite is not capable of the infinite," would be misunderstood if it were not qualified at once by the affirmation, "the infinite is capable of the finite" (20.II). Both statements aim simply to uphold the *soli Deo gloria,* which does not exclude but includes us ("God would not be God if we were not also there, if his Word were not put in our hearts and on our lips" [11.I.270]).

As expounded in the *Göttingen Dogmatics* and later in the *Church Dogmatics,* the theme "God is God," far from being an empty tautology, is a "hymn" (16.III.369) with multiple meanings. Barth's elaboration of the theme is already imbued with the "Chalcedonian imagination" that will characterize his later work.[35] That God is God means that God and creature are different and are never to be confused ("without confusion or change"); but it also means that God is free to establish genuine communion with the creature ("without separation or division"); furthermore, it means that the relationship between God and creature is always asymmetrical, always one in which God has the initiative and the priority.

Finally, there are unmistakable political and cultural ramifications of recognizing that God is God. All other claimants to deity must give way, all other objects of allegiance must take second place or disappear altogether. "Knowledge of God," Barth contends, "means *eo ipso* the most radical twilight of the gods. Olympus and Valhalla are emptied out and become secular. Their inhabitants become successively weaker as ideas, demons, ghosts, and finally comic figures" (17.V.428). "There is only one God. No statement is more dangerous or revolutionary than this for all mythologies and ideologies" (ibid.).

V. Dialectic and Analogy

In his lecture on "The Christian's Place in Society" (1919), Barth described the work of theology as like the impossible task of painting a bird in flight.[36] This vivid image aptly depicts the kind of dogmatics Barth tries to present in the Göttingen lectures. It also captures the intent of his

---

35. Cf. George Hunsinger, *How to Read Karl Barth* (London, 1991), p. 85.
36. Barth, *Word of God and Word of Man,* pp. 282-83.

dialectical method. He wants to speak of God who is indestructibly subject, who is knowable but not comprehensible, who is the living, free, and sovereign God.

In another essay from this period, "The Word of God and the Task of the Ministry" (1922), Barth distinguished among three ways of speaking of God.[37] The first is the way of dogmatism or orthodoxy. Barth applauds the "taste for objectivity" in this approach, but thinks that it confuses our descriptions of God with God himself, and that it becomes coercive when it demands that people give up thinking and simply say yes to what they are told.[38] The second way is mysticism or self-criticism. This way calls us to surrender to God, to become as receptive as the Virgin Mary, even to die to self. All this is true, Barth allows, but he objects that the negation of humanity is not in itself the revelation of God.[39] The third way is the way of dialectic, and Barth considers it "by far the best." In dialectic the living truth of God that cannot be named directly is appropriately acknowledged by a continuous movement of thought between the Yes and the No, the glory and the concealment of God.[40]

A dialectical understanding of revelation marks Barth's treatment of all the loci of the *Göttingen Dogmatics* and is apparent on virtually every page. The dialectic is not that of Hegelian logic with its triumphant synthesis of thesis and antithesis, but the dialectic of the hiddenness of God in the event of revelation. God's revelation is always *hidden* revelation, always grounded in God's free grace alone. But equally true, God's hiddenness is *revealed* hiddenness and is not to be identified with the inaccessibility of supposedly transcendental realities. God truly reveals Godself, yet without ceasing to be hidden, without ceasing to be the free, living Lord. God freely becomes an object for our knowledge while yet remaining indissolubly subject. In revelation God is knowable but never comprehensible.

Barth uses the term "dialectic" in several senses in the *Göttingen Dogmatics.* (1) There is the *dialectic of concepts* that cannot be thought without each other. Possibility and impossibility, necessity and contingency, and autonomy and heteronomy would be such dialectical pairs. By itself this dialectic of concepts is theologically inadequate since God cannot

---

37. Ibid., pp. 199ff.
38. Ibid., p. 202.
39. Ibid., p. 205.
40. Ibid., pp. 206-7.

be imprisoned in any conceptual scheme. If God were subsumed within a conceptual dialectic, however sophisticated, the relationship between God and the world would be symmetrical and reversible, and the world in its contingency would be as necessary to God as God is to the world (cf. 20.III).

(2) There is, further, the *dialectic of existence* or the dialectic of inner-worldly antinomies. Barth calls this a "relative dialectic" (19.III). We experience happiness and unhappiness, beauty and ugliness, joy and pain, war and peace. We see freedom and necessity, teleology and dysteleology at work in the creation (19.III). While God's Word is addressed to us *within* these dialectics of existence, it cannot be equated *with* them. Not the problem of inner-worldly antinomies but the far greater antinomy of God and the world is the problem on which the dogmatic theologian has to work (20.III).

(3) For Barth the term "dialectic" refers primarily to the *dialectic of revelation,* to God's twofold word of grace and judgment, of Yes and No, of God in human form, of God's hidden revelation and revealed hiddenness. Theology has to do with this "dialectic of revelation and not just any dialectic" (17.III.394).

(4) There is, finally, *dialectic as a theological method* or at least as a way of theological reflection. Dialectical thinking recognizes that God is always subject and cannot be made into an object. "Dogmatic dialectic is nothing other than genuine, open, honest dialogue, with no confusion between me and the other, between this side and that, between object and subject. The aim is a purification of what I think and speak about God by what God thinks and speaks" (13.II.310 n.16). Our thinking and speaking of God must be in continuous movement from one inadequate concept to another, seeking all the while to allow the Word of God to define all our concepts, giving God the glory as we acknowledge both our incapacity and God's steadfast promise (cf. 13.II.311). Such dialectical thinking belongs to the worldly, human character of dogmatics. Only in heaven will we no longer need dialectical thinking (13.II.312).

In the *Göttingen Dogmatics* Barth offers a dialectical rereading of the Reformed theological tradition. The center of this dialectic is the revelation of the hiddenness of God and the corresponding emphasis on the radical freedom of the gracious God in all relationships with the world. "Precisely in his revelation God is the hidden God" (6.II.135). The "diacritical element" of revelation is that it occurs in hiddenness (18.II.446). Whether we think of the human word of preaching, or the human witness of the Bible, or finally and decisively of the crucified Jesus, the revelation of God is indirect, hidden, never something that can be immediately read off empirical reality. The Word became flesh. In Jesus Christ crucified, God meets us in "complete incognito" (18.II.446). "God's hiddenness, his alien work, meets us in Christ, and finally and supremely in the crucified Christ, for where is God so hidden as here, and where is the possibility of offense so great as here?" (15.III.335). This hiddenness of God is for Barth a theological reality and not simply an epistemological limitation. "God is hidden . . . not because of the relativity of all human knowledge, but because he is the living God" (6.II.135).

What Barth calls dialectical thinking marks his treatment of every doctrinal locus. It is present in his discussion of the three forms of the Word of God. It is at work in his doctrine of the Trinity, which expresses the indissoluble subjectivity of God in both the objective event of the incarnation and in the subjective response of believers to that event. Dialectic is also evident in Barth's reinterpretation of the doctrine of election, according to which for every person in every moment there is the double possibility of faith or unfaith, and yet finally the "decision between the two possibilities does not lie in our hands but in God's" (18.II.451). Barth's discussion of the divine attributes holds in dialectical tension the communicable and incommunicable attributes, God's being for us and God's being in Godself. The living and inexhaustible reality of God must be described by the attributes of both personality and aseity. One cannot speak rightly of God by saying only one word, even if that word is love. To speak rightly of God one must contemplate one reality but say many things (17.II.383).

The dialectic of revelation is also apparent in Barth's anthropology. Just as revelation is the revelation of the hidden God, so it is addressed not to the public human being but to "the *human*" in people, to the arcane, hidden human being, to the *homo absconditus* (4.I.70). It is hidden humanity, not humanity in its all-too-superficial piety, morality, culture, nationality, and bourgeois or proletarian status, that is addressed by God's Word.

Most decisively, of course, christology requires dialectical reflection. In his state of humiliation Christ is present under the opposition of revelation and hiddenness (36.III). All knowledge of Christ is dialectical knowledge. Christian theology has to watch with special vigilance over the "dialectical character of its christology and soteriology. . . . Were it to give this up, it would also give up no less than revelation itself" (36.III). This is the reason for Barth's frequent criticism of every naive life-of-Jesus theology. "The life of Jesus does not in itself impart the knowledge of God. In itself it is instead a riddle, a mystery, a veiling" (15.III.334). Jesus of Nazareth is revelation only as the humanity united with the Word of God.

According to Barth, the hypostatic union of divine and human natures in Christ is the prototype of every relationship of God and creature (20.II). All dialectical thinking in Christian theology has its central reference point here. Nevertheless, each doctrine has its own special weight, and each demands dialectical reflection. In every dogmatic statement rightly understood "everything is to be said" (20.I) and yet said with a different emphasis. While God's Yes to us is in itself "an undialectically true and valid word" (35.II), all our words this side of the eschaton are "broken, dialectical words" (35.III).

Many errors in theology, Barth insists, can be subsumed under the heading of "premature eschatology" (35.II). While Christian hope anticipates a presence of Christ that is not dialectical but simple and direct truth (36.III), our present life in Christ is deeply hidden and our present theology must be thoroughly dialectical.

All these exercises in dialectic are no "useless scholastic triflings" for Barth (17.V.437). As he explains in his letters, his dialectical approach arose in response to the ethical crisis of the time.[41] It was a means of resistance to the easy identification of God with popular movements and dominant ideologies in contemporary culture. Dialectic is the attempt to respect God's freedom, mystery, and hiddenness in all of God's relations with the world. To speak of an action of God without acknowledging its worldly incognito would mean that God had ceased to be God (20.II).

Thus for Barth there is a particular "logic of revelation" (20.II), and this logic is common to the whole of dogmatics. Dialectic is that logic or way of thinking appropriate to the subject matter *(die Sache)* of revelation. For Barth, the coherence of dogmatics is not to be found in a particular doctrine. What holds dogmatics together is that in every part the revealed mystery and incomprehensibility of God is acknowledged.

---

41. In a letter to Thurneysen (Barth-Thurneysen, *Briefwechsel*, II, 589), Barth writes that his dialectical theology was not cooked up in some theoretical brew but arose as a furious attack on the ethics and sensibility of the older generation. For Barth the declaration of support for the war policy of Kaiser Wilhelm II in 1914, signed by ninety-three German intellectuals, including many of Barth's former teachers, was a "shaking of the foundations" that showed the hopeless compromise of liberal exegesis, ethics, theology, and preaching with the dominant cultural ideology. See Busch, *Karl Barth*, 81.

The final word is not ours but God's. Theology must allow itself to be controlled by its object (16.III.372). In all loci of theology, from prolegomena to eschatology, the *gloria soli Deo* must find its place (cf. 20.III).

While the language of dialectic is very prominent in the *Göttingen Dogmatics,* readers may be surprised to discover that analogical thinking also flourishes. Contrary to the reigning model of the development of Barth's theology, it is much too simplistic to talk of the pre–*Church Dogmatics* period as the period of dialectic that was then replaced by the period of analogy.[42] No doubt passages can be found in the *Göttingen Dogmatics* where Barth claims that there is *no* analogy with the action of God in Christ (cf. 5.II.109). But in fact, three forms of analogy may be identified in these lectures.

(1) There are negative analogies, or what might be called instances of an *analogia crucis.* Barth speaks of human experiences of limitation and, above all, of the inescapability of death as events that may become negative analogies of the mystery, inaccessibility, and hiddenness of God. Such experiences of negativity are not in themselves events of grace but mark the place where the possibility of God's grace becomes conceivable in its inconceivability (35.V). "We stand deeper in the No [of God] than in the Yes. . . . The 'night side' of existence is better able to be bearer and medium also of the divine Word than its 'sunny side' " (19.III). Barth even suggests that the real purpose of a proof for the existence of God (and the necessary critique of this project) is to lay bare the analogy — but only the analogy — of our helpless human condition to Christ's experience of God-forsakenness (15.IV.349; cf. 357).

(2) There are also positive analogies in the human sphere of faith to what God does. Human beings do not possess revelation or stand in unbroken continuity with it. Nevertheless, human action may become an analogy to the divine action; the free act of faith corresponds to the divine act of free grace (5.I.94). An analogy of the creature to the Creator belongs to the original intention of God for human life (23.II). What Barth introduces here is the equivalent of the *analogia fidei* developed at length in the *Church Dogmatics.*

---

42. Hans Urs von Balthasar, *The Theology of Karl Barth* (New York, 1972), is a prominent representative of the interpretation of Barth's theology as falling into discrete periods of dialectic and analogy. But see the fine dissertation by Bruce McCormack, "A Scholastic of a Higher Order: The Development of Karl Barth's Theology, 1921-1931," Princeton Theological Seminary, 1989, which makes use of the Göttingen lectures in dogmatics to provide a new understanding of the development of Barth's thought.

(3) Because God is faithful, there are also analogies among the gracious acts of God. Barth repeatedly draws an analogy between the relationship of the three forms of the Word of God and the communion of the persons of the Trinity (1.III.15; 2.III.37; 11.I.270). He also speaks of an analogy between God's creation of the world, the conception of the Incarnate Word by the Holy Spirit, and the resurrection of the dead (19.II). According to Barth, the parousia of Christ stands in analogy with the incarnation although it is also something entirely new (36.III). We might call this use of analogy by Barth the *analogia magnalium Dei*, "analogy of the mighty acts of God." In numerous places in the *Göttingen Dogmatics* Barth affirms analogies among classical Christian doctrines. Here again continuity may be seen with the later *Church Dogmatics*, where Barth affirms in countless ways that God is faithful. As E. Jüngel paraphrases a central theme of Barth's doctrine of God: God corresponds to Godself *ad intra* and *ad extra*.[43]

(4) Not clearly present in the Göttingen lectures is the use of *analogia relationis* that will later play a very important role in the *Church Dogmatics*. Thus Barth does not interpret the man-woman relationship as a central element of the meaning of being created in the image of God or as an analogy of the intratrinitarian relationality of God.

For Barth, whether the theologian speaks dialectically or analogically, the subject matter of theology is the mystery of God who is the indissolubly free and gracious subject. Theological thinking must thus be dynamic, self-critical, always open to reform, in continuous movement. It is as difficult as painting a bird in flight. It is like crossing a stream, leaping from one stone to another, keeping in movement so as not to fall into the water (cf. 11.I.266). Whether we refer to the event of Jesus Christ, or to scripture as witness to the revelation in him, or to Christian preaching as the church's witness to revelation based on the witness of scripture, revelation is always an event, an act of sovereign grace (cf. 11.III.275).

In Barth's judgment, it is not the word "dialectic" that is important. Indeed, he advises his students neither to be intimidated by the word nor to use it too frequently (13.II.309). He obviously fears that it has become a mere slogan rather than one useful theological tool among others.[44] He does not spend much time defining his own uses of the term. What he

---

43. Cf. Eberhard Jüngel, *The Doctrine of the Trinity* (Grand Rapids, 1976).
44. See Michael Beintker, "Unterricht in der christlichen Religion," *Verkundigung und Forschung* 30/2 (1985) 145-49.

considers most important is to realize that in theology, as in preaching, "we must not ossify or freeze anything here. We must not make anything into a block or stock" (11.III.275). Theology has no final solutions. It must always be disturbing, unsettling, and eccentric, like the deliberately asymmetrical front window in many Franciscan churches (3.I.50).[45] Or in another striking metaphor: "Theology is like a sphinx, which even after one has done what one is responsible for doing, still lies there a riddle in the sand, and faces eastward without betraying its final mystery" (20.II).

VI. Barth's Use of Reformed Orthodoxy

As previously noted, in his preparation for the *Göttingen Dogmatics* Barth found unexpected help in the work of the old Reformed theologians. Their influence is evident almost everywhere in the lectures, from the order of topics to the fine distinctions that are often drawn. In his advice to his students regarding their independent reading in the field, he urges them under no conditions to begin with modern theology. Even if later they should decide to endorse the way of Schleiermacher that has dominated all subsequent theology, they should know what they are doing. They should at least have worked through the older dogmatic tradition. Barth specifically recommends the Breviloquium of Bonaventura; Melanchthon, Zwingli, and Calvin among the Reformers (Luther is not mentioned!); and the compendiums of Protestant scholastic theologians by H. Heppe (Reformed) and H. Schmid (Lutheran) (1.IV.21-22).

In the Göttingen lectures Barth refers repeatedly to his mentors in the Reformed tradition as "the older writers" (1.IV.21), "our older Protestant predecessors" (15.IV.344), "the older Orthodox" theologians (ibid.), "our forefathers" (345), "our older Protestant fathers" (16.I.355), "the older dogmaticians" (18.III.456). Indeed, he cites them far more often than either Calvin or Luther. Barth not only takes the Reformed scholastics seriously, but finds their theologoumena impressive despite their "baroque garb" (17.II.379).

But while he often employs the categories and distinctions of the scholastics, he does not slavishly follow them. Wishing that theology today could regain something of the "remarkable objectivity and perspicacity"

---

45. An example well-known to Barth was the Barfusser Franciscan church in Basel, now a historical museum.

of the "masters of the old theological school" (17.III.386), he nevertheless
tries to say better what they intended to say, and not infrequently diverges
explicitly and sharply from their positions. While Barth considers continuity with the Reformed school a mark of his theological method (18.III.456;
cf. 12.II.292-93), this does not mean for him a "repristination of the older
Christian or Reformed dogmatics" (12.II.294). What he is after is something quite different from mere repetition of the Reformed traditions
(18.III.456). His aim is to explore to what extent the lines drawn by the
elders are necessary and right (21.II). The material must be thought
through again and from the very foundations. While respect is owed to
the teachers of the church, their work cannot be simply repeated. True
dogma is not something given but something sought (2.IV.39). Received
dogmas are only preliminary stopping points in what is a continuing task
of theological reflection within the church. According to Barth, it is
necessary initially to suspend the validity of any given dogma in order to
test it and see to what extent it can be established anew (ibid.). Even the
decisions of Nicea and Chalcedon are in principle open to correction
(9.IV.247).

A representative list of Barth's differences from Reformed orthodoxy
can be readily assembled, even if adequate discussion of them would
require far more space than is available in this essay.[46]

(1) The order of loci of the *Göttingen Dogmatics* follows closely, but
by no means unthinkingly, the order of the old Reformed dogmatics
summarized by Heppe. Like the old Reformed theologians, Barth begins
with the doctrine of revelation, but what a difference his doctrine of the
threefold form of the Word of God makes! Barth has already dealt with
the doctrines of the Trinity, the incarnation, and the work of the Holy
Spirit *before* he comes to the doctrine of scripture. Other significant
changes in the order of loci include: placing the doctrine of the covenant
of grace (the only covenant!) before the doctrine of sin (§ 24); and bringing
together baptism and calling, and the Lord's Supper and perseverance
(§§ 30, 33).

(2) Barth observes that the older Reformed theology had no prolegomena, or only the most primitive kind. This is, he thinks, actually a mark of
a classical age of theology: it is free to get on at once with the study of its
subject matter without spending excessive time on questions of method and

---

46. See McCormack, "A Scholastic of a Higher Order: The Development of Karl
Barth's Theology."

possibility (6.I.133). In Barth's judgment, however, "we do not live in a classical age of theology" (1.IV.18), and prolegomena are necessary "for us poor moderns" (6.I.133) who have become uncertain of the presuppositions of this discipline and how one proceeds in it (1.IV.18). No one can simply repeat the work of Thomas and Calvin as though epochal changes had not occurred in Protestant theology since 1600. "We are not allowed to imagine that we are at another point in history, and inevitably such imaginings can never be more than that" (1.IV.19). Barth admits that he acquiesces to the modern requirement of prolegomena only under protest, but he nevertheless acquiesces. To do otherwise would be to forget that dogmatics "must be part of a conversation; it must be open to discussion" (1.IV.20).

(3) Barth argues that the distinction between natural and supernat-ural revelation began to play an ever more important role in Protestant theology from the end of the sixteenth century. Included in natural rev-elation were the voice of God in nature, conscience, the moral light of nature, the religious sense, the virtually universal knowledge of the exis-tence and unity of God, and the creation and governance of the world by God. Such natural revelation was considered a good and useful "narthex" to authentic Christian revelation, and old Reformed theology in particular placed great value on this initial edifice of theology. Of this project of natural theology Barth says, "For my part, although I am Reformed, I want no part of it" (5.I.91). Barth thinks that Calvin was far more cautious on this topic than his successors in the Reformed tradition. Calvin spoke of the reality of natural revelation in the first chapters of the *Institutes,* but in dialectical fashion he strictly subordinated natural knowledge of God to revealed knowledge of God and unfolded his theology as if there were only the latter (5.I.92).

(4) In Barth's view the old Reformed theology tended to reduce doctrine to a formula or a system of formulas. Of a piece with this "fatal error" was the "deplorable" reduction of holy scripture to a book of inspired propositions (11.III.274; 8.II.217). The doctrine of verbal inspira-tion in late Protestant orthodoxy did "incalculable damage" because it obscured the paradox of the hiddenness of God's revelation (3.III.58). "To deny the hiddenness of revelation even in scripture is to deny revelation itself, and with it the Word of God" (3.III.59). Long before the Enlight-enment, Barth judges, orthodoxy itself had begun the process of histori-cizing revelation, which made it subject to human control.

(5) Probably the most striking departure of Barth from the old Reformed theology comes in his doctrine of election. He sharply criticizes

the orthodox doctrine of the double decrees of God and particularly its notion that "certain individuals" have been ordained from all eternity to salvation and "certain others" foreordained to damnation. This construal of the doctrine of predestination was present, Barth thinks, only at the margin of Calvin's theology but assumed a central place among his followers. The idea of "certain individuals" elected and reprobated was "the worm in the timbers of Reformed orthodoxy," or, to change the metaphor, "the Trojan horse" that brought down the holy city of Ilion (18.III.455). It led to the "mechanization" of the doctrine of election, and reduced it to determinism or fatalism. According to Barth's interpretation in these early lectures, election has to do with the triumph of God's freedom, the freedom God has in every moment in relation to every person to say Yes or No. This, he thinks, represents the "true intentions" of the classical tradition (ibid.). The doctrine of election says that it is in God's hand alone to hide or to reveal Godself, to exercise judgment or grace (24.I).

(6) Barth contends that the old school of Reformed theology had only a "naive dialectic" at work in its doctrine of God. Its logic was: *of course* God is inconceivable; *however,* God has now revealed Godself and is knowable in this self-revelation. This naive dialectic bases the inconceivability of God only on human capacities and limitations and thus opens the way to the Feuerbachian critique of theology as secret anthropology. For Barth, on the contrary, God remains inconceivable precisely in revelation. Barth explains that his criticism of the Reformed tradition on this point has the purpose "not to change the intentions of the school but to pursue them along the same lines and with inner necessity" (16.II.356).

(7) Continuity and discontinuity with the old Reformed tradition are also evident in Barth's doctrine of the attributes of God. While he takes over the distinction made by orthodoxy between incommunicable and communicable attributes, he reverses their traditional order and arranges them in dialectical pairs. A continuous movement of thought is thus achieved. Furthermore, in his doctrine of the attributes of God Barth is able to presuppose his earlier treatment of the doctrine of the Trinity, whereas in orthodoxy the doctrine of the attributes of God was placed before the doctrine of the Trinity.

(8) While agreeing that the doctrine of the covenant is part of the "family estate" *(Stammgut)* of Reformed dogmatics, Barth takes vigorous issue with two developments within the Reformed tradition regarding the covenant. The first is the distinction, introduced by Cocceius, between a

covenant of works and a covenant of grace. Barth calls this a "fatal historical moment" (27.III) that laid the groundwork for a dualistic understanding both of revelation and of God's covenantal relationship with humanity. For Barth the idea of a covenant of works with Adam before the fall is a disastrous mistake. "Pelagianism was not worth recommending as a possibility even for paradisal humanity" (24.IV). The second unfortunate development in Reformed orthodoxy is the introduction of an understanding of revelation as a sequence of stages (27.III). This contributed to the historicization of revelation in later theology. "Although not intended in this way, it actually worked as a decisive compromise with the Enlightenment and Pietism" (24.I). The distinction between a "covenant of nature" and a "covenant of grace" represents a corruption of the Calvinist tradition (27.III).

(9) Barth stands solidly in the Reformed tradition in insisting that faith and obedience are inseparable and that justification and sanctification are equally important gifts of grace. But he sets himself firmly against the tendency toward legalism and arrogance in the Reformed tradition. Barth sees the problem rooted in the effort of later Reformed orthodoxy to view rebirth as an event that continues developmentally through time. This encourages the view that sin becomes less and less a factor in Christian life. However, "the *homo peccator* may not disappear at any point. Otherwise God and grace also disappear" (30.IV). Connected with the developmental model of sanctification is the idea of the cooperation of God and humanity after the first moment of conversion in which God alone is at work. In response to every form of synergism Barth asks: Is there any moment in which the canon "To God alone in the highest be the glory" would no longer be in effect? (30.V).

(10) Barth also departs from the way taken by the old Reformed theologians in eschatology. He sees two primary errors here. First, there is the general error of allowing eschatology to become detached from the rest of dogmatics. As a result, eschatology fails to be properly integrated with and controlled by the center of dogmatics which is God's free grace in Jesus Christ. The second error is more specific: eschatology was spiritualized; it no longer had as its center the resurrection of the body and the transformation of this world. The old eschatology thus tends to be speculative, a kind of "hot-air balloon flight" (38.I).

As this brief summary indicates, Barth's attitude to the old Reformed tradition is deferential yet critical. He approaches the old theologians respectfully and encourages his students to do the same: "I see no reason why we should not listen to them. Let us try to think with and after them" (20.II; see also 6.IV.167). Yet his appropriation of the tradition is critical and reconstructive. He thinks *with* and *after* but not infrequently also *against* old Reformed orthodoxy.

VII. The Debate with Lutheran Theology

From the first pages of the *Göttingen Dogmatics* Barth engages in an intensive debate with modern Protestant theology. Its cardinal error, he thinks, has been to begin with the human rather than with the divine subject. Consequently, modern theology is like a clock that is constructed so that its hands move counter clockwise (4.IV.82).

Yet while this opposition to liberal Protestant theology and its "Copernican revolution" (1.II.9, 11) is pervasive, in fact Barth's most frequent dialogue partner in these early lectures in dogmatics is not the Schleiermacherian, Ritschlian, or Hegelian traditions but orthodox Lutheran theology. Several reasons may be suggested for this fact. First, as a Reformed theologian in the predominantly Lutheran theological faculty at Göttingen, Barth found himself in a distinct minority and had to make a case for the Reformed tradition (we recall the conflict that he had with the rest of the faculty over the title of these lectures). Second, Barth drew extensively from two orthodox Protestant texts in preparing his lectures: H. Heppe (Reformed) and H. Schmid (Lutheran), and it is not surprising that the debates of these scholastics were alive for him as he worked out his own position. Third, Barth found Lutheran orthodoxy a better partner for serious theological reflection than neo-Protestantism. Interestingly, when Barth left Göttingen for Münster, where there was a strong Catholic faculty, his respectful engagement with Catholic theology and especially his opposition to the doctrine of the *analogia entis* became more explicit than had been the case at Göttingen.

Barth summarizes the decisive marks of the Reformed theological school which informs his own dogmatics as follows: (a) Formalism rules in fundamental theology. By this Barth means that the Word of God as attested by scripture in the church is always to be the basis of what is considered normative. Stated negatively, the norm is not to be sought in some particular doctrine abstracted from the whole witness of scripture. (b) God is always given the priority in the relationship between God and humanity. The salvation of humanity is included in giving God glory rather than God's glory being defined solely in terms of the salvation of humanity. (c) Within the doctrine of God, the emphasis is on the subjectivity, freedom, and majesty of God. God is never to be considered an object at our disposal. (d) In christology, too, the emphasis is on the freely gracious act of God whereby God and humanity are united in one person. (e) Equal weight is given to the religious *and* ethical aspects of the subjective appropriation of revelation, or in other words, to faith *and* obedience (12.II.294).

In developing his own Reformed theology Barth takes issue at numerous points with his Lutheran colleagues.

(1) For Lutheran theology the doctrine of justification by faith is the *articulus stantis et cadentis ecclesiae*. It is the material principle of theology, and dogmatics becomes "the logical unfolding of the basic principle and its individual parts" (13.I.300). Barth thinks this leads to a relationship to scripture and revelation in which the chief content is already known in advance. Certainly in Lutheran dogmatics the doctrine of justification has monopolized attention (19.I). Barth wants to avoid setting his dogmatics on the summit of a single dogma, and quite emphatically refuses to assign this position to the doctrine of election (19.I). For Barth "the center and object of Christianity, of Christian proclamation, and of Christian dogmatics is God in his revelation. It is in God that all the threads of dogmatics come together, not in one of the particular truths that must be taught on the basis of this revelation. It should never happen that one of them, whichever it may be, is presented in such a way that it swallows, as it were, the others, so that everything else becomes only a help for one favorite idea" (20.IV).

(2) According to Barth, whereas Lutheran theology says faith is the appropriate human response to grace, Reformed theology says faith *and* obedience. God not only justifies sinners but also sanctifies them. "We cannot have knowledge in relation to God without action" (7.I.172).

(3) Barth finds himself in disagreement with Lutheran theology both in the placement and in the content of the doctrine of election. In Lutheran dogmatics this doctrine is commonly set just before or after the doctrine of justification. (Barth fails to say that Calvin also placed election in the context of the Christian life in the 1559 edition of the *Institutes!*) So located it leads, in Barth's view, a thin and "shadowy existence" (18.I.444). He argues that its proper position is in the doctrine of God and before the doctrine of creation, to make it clear that election is the first and decisive thing which must be said about the living God, viz., that whether as believers or unbelievers we are in God's hands (18.IV.445).

VII. The Debate with Lutheran Theology

As Barth understands it, the Lutheran doctrine of election turns on the distinction between the antecedent and the consequent will of God. By antecedent will God wants all to be saved. But God's consequent will is to elect all those whom he foresees will avail themselves of the grace which has been acquired for them in Christ. By contrast, Barth follows the Reformed tradition that contends that our faith must in no way be considered a cause of our election (18.III.463).

(4) While the concept of covenant has relatively little importance in early Lutheran theology, for Reformed theology it is as basic for a sound anthropology as the doctrine of election is for the Reformed understanding of God. From the beginning humanity is set within the definite order of covenantal relationship with God. For the Reformed tradition even in paradise humanity is God's covenant partner. Both before and after the fall, humanity is dependent on God's grace and is heir of the divine promise of eternal life in communion with God. From this perspective even humanity in paradise is a "wanderer between two worlds" (24.III). Unlike the orthodox Lutheran view that considers humanity to have need of eternal life only after the fall, the old Reformed theologians interpret the tree of life in the garden as a visible sign of the promised fulfillment of the covenant. So, Barth quips, even in the garden of Eden Adam held to a strictly Reformed doctrine of the sacraments! (24.III).

(5) The most important differences between Lutheran and Reformed theologies are in the doctrines of christology and sacraments. Barth sees the differences in christology in this way: Lutheran theology is interested more in the *result* of the union of God and humanity (hence the considerable attention given to the *communicatio idiomatum*); Reformed theology, on the other hand, places its primary emphasis on the *act* or event of the union (hence the stress on the hypostatic union as an act of God's sovereign grace). According to Barth, the intent of the much-debated *extra Calvinisticum* is to guard the mystery of revelation and the freedom of grace as well as to affirm the true humanity of Christ (6.IV.159-60). For Reformed theology neither nature nor history, even in the incarnation, is in itself revelation; nature and history can become predicates of revelation only in act, only in event, only in the Holy Spirit (16.III.366).

(6) Similarly, the Reformed tradition as interpreted by Barth contends that the sacraments have no inherent power to confer grace. They do not convey anything by themselves; they are signs of the grace of God given in Christ by the power of the Holy Spirit. The sacraments are signs and seals of the covenant of grace in Jesus Christ. "They give assurance.

They are the ground of the knowledge of reconciliation. But the ontological ground can only be God in Christ through the Holy Spirit" (30.II).

(7) According to Barth, the different emphases of Lutheran and Reformed theology continue all the way to eschatology. For Lutheran orthodoxy the bodies of the saints have the properties of spirituality, invisibility, and illocality. This is judged by the Reformed as a disguised denial of corporeality (38.I).

Behind this sustained and often intense conversation with Lutheran theology in the *Göttingen Dogmatics* is Barth's conviction that serious theology will in some sense always be school theology. "We cannot do dogmatics in a vacuum" (12.II.293). To recognize the place of various schools of Christian theology is simply to recognize that all appropriations of Christian revelation are partial and that revelation cannot be exhaustively expressed by any single theology. Emphasis on the school character of theology fits into Barth's dialectical conception both of revelation and of responsible thinking about revelation. We simply do not have the single word which will say the whole truth about God and ourselves in the light of revelation. We must use two words, or more precisely, many words, to speak of the God who can be known but never comprehended. Schools of theology are necessary but need not be sources of schism in the church. On the contrary, they should serve the fullness of the proclamation of the church.

Barth freely acknowledges that his dogmatics has a decidedly Reformed profile and that it strictly emphasizes the difference between God and humanity in their communion. "I realize," Barth tells his students, that "this is not for everyone." But he adds: "There has to be this strictness somewhere in Protestant theology" (17.III.396).

Barth's insistence on the importance of responsible school theology may have more contemporary significance than is apparent at first glance. In current theological discussions distinctions of classical theological schools (Catholic, Lutheran, Reformed, etc.) are not as prominent as they once were. Yet schools of another form are evident, based mostly on social location or communal experience in which the importance of class, race, and gender is emphasized. The future health of Christian theology may well depend on recognizing both the legitimacy and the responsibility of various theological schools within the common theological task of the church. If theological schools are willing to enter into serious and respectful conversation and resist the temptation to become church-splintering factions, they may serve as sources of mutual correction and enrichment. That is surely the intent of Barth's dialogue with Lutheran theology in the *Göttingen Dogmatics*.

VIII. Different Accents of the Prolegomena

While Barth's critical and creative use of the old Reformed theology in his *Göttingen Dogmatics* merits close study, it is the relationship between these lectures and the later *Church Dogmatics* that will be of greatest interest to readers. My comments on this relationship in this essay must necessarily be brief and can serve only to identify some points where new lines of inquiry have been opened by the publication of Barth's *Urdogmatik*.

As previously noted, Barth's organization of the *Göttingen Dogmatics* following the prolegomena is based on what he calls the "logical content" of Christian proclamation (14.II.320) — God, anthropology, reconciliation, and redemption. His ordering principle has a phenomenological component and is thus somewhat different from the one employed in the *Church Dogmatics*. The latter also develops a fourfold division of the material after the prolegomena, but the ordering principle is now the reality of God *ad intra* (*CD* II/1-2) and the acts of God *ad extra:* creation, reconciliation, and redemption (*CD* III/1-IV/4 and the projected vol. V). A surprise in the order of the first dogmatics is that creation and providence are formally taken up within the doctrine of God. An equally conspicuous difference between the earlier and later order of loci is that, unlike the *Church Dogmatics,* the *Göttingen Dogmatics* has no chapters (or even sections) devoted specifically to theological ethics, although Barth repeatedly underscores the bond between faith and obedience (see esp. § 7).

A basic methodological principle at work in all cycles of Barth's dogmatics is that a very particular *petitio principii* ("begging the question") is necessary in all theological inquiry. Prolegomena must thus "borrow" from the material content of dogmatics proper rather than attempt to establish principles independent of this content (4.IV.81; 6.I.132-33; cf. *CD* I/1, 42).

As far as the content of the prolegomena is concerned, in both the Göttingen lectures (chaps. 1–3) and the *Church Dogmatics* (I/1-I/2) the centerpiece is the doctrine of the threefold form of the Word of God as revelation, holy scripture, and Christian proclamation. Some differences, however, are evident.

(1) In chapter 1, on the Word of God as revelation, Barth begins with a section on *"Deus dixit"* (§ 3) and follows with a section on "Man and His Question" (§ 4). The latter is especially interesting since Barth here takes quite seriously the fact that human existence, whatever its surface appearances, is riddled with questions about God and human life. Indeed, he notes that in many of the catechisms of the Reformed tradition, human questions are given a kind of pedagogical precedence over the word of revelation. This

might seem at first glance to legitimize a simplistic question and answer method of correlation in theology. But Barth argues to the contrary that all our serious questions about God and ourselves in fact presuppose the event of revelation and are only meaningful in its light. Humanity would not ask about God if God had not already prompted the questions. Revelation awakens new questions rather than merely giving answers to questions we already have (7.IV.194). The deepest questions are not those of public humanity but of *arcanum* or secret humanity, "the *human* in people" (4.II.70). "Those who ask the right question about God show that they already know God's answer" (4.IV.84). "Believers are not secure people. They are those who first know what questioning means" (4.V.86). While the treatment of the issue of the relationship of human questioning and revelation in this section of the Göttingen lectures is perhaps less methodologically precise than the parallel section of the *Church Dogmatics* (I/1, 187-247), it nevertheless invites rather than forecloses further reflection.

(2) Another notable difference between the prolegomena of these two cycles of Barth's dogmatics is the relationship of what he calls the possibility and the reality of revelation. In the *Göttingen Dogmatics* Barth inquires into the "objective possibility of revelation" in the incarnation (6.II.140), and speaks of the miracle of faith and obedience by the power of the Holy Spirit as the "subjective possibility of revelation" (7.I.168). Barth's line of inquiry proceeds as follows: If God is hidden in revelation, what "must" be the conditions of the possibility of such an event? According to Barth, God "must" become human so as to encounter us objectively as an I; the union between God and humanity "must" be a strictly dialectical union, etc. (6.II.138ff.). But having pursued the inquiry into the conditions of possibility to its conclusion, Barth then "lays down his arms and openly confesses" that this apparent a priori line of reasoning is in fact — like that of Anselm of Canterbury in *Cur Deus Homo?* — an a posteriori construction (6.II.141-42, n.16). The reality of this possibility is presupposed; it makes no sense to prescribe what is possible and impossible for God. Thus Barth says that his intent all along has been only to clarify the reality of the incarnation in Jesus Christ. (According to the editor, Barth added a question mark in red pencil in the margin of his manuscript alongside his statement, "The provisionality of human existence makes revelation necessary" [24.III]).

By contrast, in the *Church Dogmatics* Barth avoids all possible confusion about his intentions by speaking first of Jesus Christ as the objective reality of revelation before considering him as the objective possibility of revelation (*CD* I/2, 1, 25). The same order is followed with respect to the Holy Spirit as the subjective reality and subjective possibility of revelation (*CD* I/2, 203, 242). Barth's Anselm book of 1931 gave him the opportunity to clarify what he argued were Anselm's and what were certainly Barth's own deepest intentions even in the Göttingen lectures.[47]

(3) Still another difference between the prolegomena of the Göttingen lectures and those of the *Church Dogmatics* is that the former explicitly endorse a dialectical way of thinking in theology. As we have seen, reference to theological dialectic is prominent in the *Göttingen Dogmatics* and is listed as one of the distinguishing marks of dogmatic thinking in § 13. "Before God human thoughts *become* dialectical" (13.II.311). In Barth's view, dialectic is a useful tool, even a gift of God, to be used for the glory of God, not for mere play (13.II.312).

Strikingly, in the parallel passage in the *Church Dogmatics* (I/2, 853ff.) dialectical thinking is not mentioned at all. Yet in different words the same point is made: that God is subject and not object, that knowledge of God cannot be reduced to a system, that all of our categories and words are human, and that we must recognize again and again that "God is God" (*CD* I/2, 880). While it is true that the *term* "dialectic" recedes in the *Church Dogmatics* whereas the language and use of analogy become increasingly prominent, nevertheless it must be emphasized that in the *Göttingen Dogmatics* dialectic and analogy coexist, and that what Barth understands by analogy in the *Church Dogmatics* includes the dynamic of what he earlier called dialectical thinking and speaking of God.[48] Dialectical thinking is unmistakably at work in the *Church Dogmatics* in the relationship between the Word of God and human words; in the pairing of the perfections of God as the One who loves in freedom; in the relationship between creation and covenant; in the narrative of God's self-humiliation and human exaltation; in the tensive bond between justification and sanctification; and in numerous other ways.

IX. The Doctrines of God and Humanity

In the doctrines of God and humanity, which comprise chapters 4 and 5 of the *Göttingen Dogmatics,* there are a number of interesting points of

---

47. Barth, *Fides Quaerens Intellectum* (Zurich, 1931); ET *Anselm: Fides Quaerens Intellectum* (repr. Cleveland, 1960).

48. See Stoevesandt, "Wandlungen": "Barth's style of thinking never became undialectical" (p. 536).

comparison and contrast with the treatment of these subjects in the *Church Dogmatics*. I will touch briefly on three.

(1) In the Göttingen lectures Barth provides an extensive discussion of the attributes of God. He orders them in two sets: considering first the communicable attributes, or attributes of the revealed personhood *(Persönlichkeit)* of God, and then the incommunicable attributes, or attributes of divine aseity and concealment. Taking up the attributes always in pairs, he considers under attributes of personhood: life and power, knowledge and will, and love and blessedness; and under attributes of aseity: unity (and uniqueness), eternity and omnipresence, and immutability and glory. For Barth all the attributes must be specifically defined in terms of the unique reality of God. The statements "God is love," "God is power," and "God is life" are not convertible. God is "wholly other" *(ganz andere)* love, power, and life (17.IV.402ff.).

In *Church Dogmatics* II/1, §§ 28-31, Barth again develops the doctrine of the perfections of God, as he now prefers to call them, in dialectical fashion. God is described as "One who loves in freedom," and the perfections of divine loving — grace and holiness, mercy and righteousness, and patience and wisdom — are discussed prior to the perfections of divine freedom — unity and omnipresence, constancy and omnipotence, and eternity and glory. While insistence on the priority of the attributes of divine personhood (cf. love) to those of divine aseity (cf. freedom) and treatment of the attributes in dialectical pairs are points common to the *Göttingen Dogmatics* and the *Church Dogmatics,* careful study of each of the attributes in their respective contexts will show distinctive emphases. For example, there is no hint in the *Göttingen Dogmatics* of the theme of the beauty of God that Barth will include in his discussion of the glory of God in the *Church Dogmatics* (II/1, 650-56).

(2) Among the most intriguing points of continuity and discontinuity between the *Göttingen Dogmatics* and the *Church Dogmatics* is the doctrine of the electing grace of God (18.I-IV.440ff.; cf. *CD* II/2, §§ 32-35).

In both works the doctrine of election is taken up within the doctrine of God rather than as a subtopic of providence (as in many scholastic theologies) or within the doctrine of the Christian life (as in Calvin). Moreover, in both cases Barth flatly rejects every Pelagian or semi-Pelagian resolution of the relationship of divine grace and human freedom. God is never passive. A spectator God is not God (18.III.452).

Further, in both cycles of dogmatics Barth repudiates the doctrine of double predestination interpreted as God's election of certain individuals to salvation and God's reprobation of certain others to damnation. Again, in both cases Barth expresses preference for the supralapsarian position (18.III.468). Finally, in both cases Barth insists with Calvin that Christ is the mirror of election (18.III.471).

But there are also striking differences. In the *Göttingen Dogmatics* Barth deals first with rejection as the negative counterpart or foil of election. In the *Church Dogmatics* this order is reversed. According to the earlier treatment, God is identified as the ground of the possibility of both the human yes and the human no to God's revelation. Election is interpreted actualistically; it expresses the freedom of the living God in relation to human beings at every moment rather than referring to a divine decision in the distant past. But although Barth repudiates every "symmetrical" relationship of election and reprobation in the *Göttingen Dogmatics* (18.III.460), he describes reprobation as God's "holding back," i.e., God wills *not* to will the possibility of faith. Barth here adopts the older Reformed doctrine of *praeteritio* or God's "passing over" those who are not elected (18.III.456).

All this is worked out quite differently in the *Church Dogmatics* (II/2) where Barth's revised doctrine of election focuses with unprecedented intensity on Jesus Christ as the electing God and the elected human being, the one in whom all humanity is both elected and rejected. Also, whereas in the *Göttingen Dogmatics* the communal dimension of election remains undeveloped (indeed, the emphasis is on the triumph of God's glory in the actual double possibility "for each of us at each moment" [18, summary statement, 440]), the priority of the community over the individual is a prominent feature of the doctrine of election in *Church Dogmatics* (II/2, §§ 34, 35).

(3) There are two notable differences between the *Göttingen Dogmatics* and the *Church Dogmatics* in the doctrine of humanity.

First, in the Göttingen lectures no mention is made of the relationship of male and female as the clue to the meaning of our creation in the image of God. Nor is there any development of the theme of a super- and subordination of man and woman, as there is in one of the most controversial sections of the *Church Dogmatics* (III/4, 116-240). (The super-/subordination theme in Barth's theology would thus appear to have several phases: [a] absent in the *Göttingen Dogmatics;* [b] considered a result of the fall in *CD* I/2; [c] presented as part of the meaning of being created in the image of God in *CD* III/2 and III/4; [d] grounded in the trinitarian being of God in *CD* IV/1.)

Second, in the *Göttingen Dogmatics* the doctrine of sin is treated in the context of the doctrine of humanity and prior to the doctrine of reconciliation. In the *Church Dogmatics,* by contrast, sin is taken up strictly within the context of the doctrine of reconciliation. Sin is defined as the opposite of what God does in Christ: human pride in contrast to God's self-humiliation; human sloth in contrast to God's elevation of humanity to partnership with God; human falsehood in contrast to the true witness to God made by Christ. "Only when we know Jesus Christ do we really know that man is the man of sin, and what sin is, and what it means for man" (*CD* IV/1, 389). Of course, there is evidence in the *Göttingen Dogmatics* that Barth is already moving in this direction. Thus he places a section on the covenant of grace (§ 24) before the sections on sin (§§ 25, 26). And when he begins the doctrine of reconciliation, he insists that the doctrines of God and humanity are not mere "preparations" for the doctrine of reconciliation but must be completely saturated with the truth of this doctrine (27.I).

Nevertheless, the doctrine of human sin in the *Göttingen Dogmatics* is worked out without explicit benefit of christology. Barth even states at the conclusion of his analysis of sin that the appropriate final word in the doctrine of humanity is that there is a hell and that it is for all of us without exception (26.IV; 27.I). Whereas in the Göttingen lectures Barth says that in anthropology "seen apart from Christ and the redemption completed in him, we have to hold to revelation as condemnation" (26.I), in the *Church Dogmatics* no such "apart from Christ" is permitted. The logic of the development of the doctrine of sin in the *Göttingen Dogmatics* has affinities with the very pattern Barth will later criticize so sharply in the *Church Dogmatics:* first stating the problem of sin, and then giving the decisive answer to it in the doctrine of the incarnation and atoning death of Jesus Christ (*CD* IV/1, 359).

X. Changes in Christology

A careful comparison of the christologies of the *Göttingen Dogmatics* and the *Church Dogmatics* would require far more space than is available here. We can only briefly mention a few points that invite further exploration.

(1) Barth's early dogmatics are best described as theocentric or

trinitarian rather than simply christocentric. Indeed, readers may be surprised by the sharp criticism of christocentrism in theology found in these lectures. There are at least two reasons for this criticism.

The first is Barth's suspicion of all proposed material principles of dogmatics that tend to replace the scripture principle of Reformed theology with a system centered on one doctrine or idea. "We have already had an anthropocentric, a theocentric, a christocentric, and a staurocentric theology. I believe I could promise to build up a similar kind of theology on the basis of baptism or eschatology, but I want no part in this Protestant proliferation" (14.II.319).

The second reason for Barth's criticism of christocentrism is that he associates it with the life-of-Jesus theology of the nineteenth and early twentieth centuries. His theme is that "*God* is always the subject. . . . *God* is subject even in what we try to say about him [Christ]" (3.III.61-62). "To honor heroes, even the man Jesus of Nazareth, is to deny revelation, for it forgets the *Deus dixit*, the divine nature in Christ, to which alone honor and worship belong" (62). Barth insists that the name Jesus Christ is no "magic formula" (4.III.79). Even this word is not the word of reconciliation if humanity rather than God is its subject. Questioning the movement in modern dogmatics toward an "ever more ardent" christocentrism that concentrates on the life of Jesus, or on his religious personality, rather than on the crucified and risen Lord as did Paul and the Reformers, Barth argues that dogmatics must "dare to be less christocentric" (5.I.91).

The positive meaning of a "less christocentric" dogmatics for Barth is a more trinitarian dogmatics. "I regard the doctrine of the Trinity as the true center of the concept of revelation." (Barth goes on to say that he could also agree that the doctrine of the incarnation, properly understood, is the nucleus of all Christian theology [6.I.131].) These warnings in the *Göttingen Dogmatics* against certain kinds of christocentrism help to underscore the fact that for Barth, early and late, christocentrism was theologically sound only in a trinitarian context.

(2) In the *Göttingen Dogmatics* Barth advances a theological argument for the virgin birth that he would later consider flawed. He rejects, of course, the view that the miracle of the virgin birth was necessary because of a supposed connection of original sin with sexual concupiscence. The real meaning of the virgin birth is not the absence of the sexual act but the removal of the male in God's beginning of the new humanity. "World history," Barth writes, "is not for nothing male history. Economics, politics,

art, and science, with some exceptions . . . , are male affairs. The creative shaping of things, the personal fashioning of existence, as far as the eye can see, is a male privilege" (6.IV.163). According to Barth, it is *this* man that must be replaced if the new Adam is to be born. He is not allowed to function here in the typically masculine attitude of the *paterfamilias,* the lord and ruler.

Barth goes on to argue that under the conditions of sin what is called personhood is constituted by the refusal to live by grace alone. Hence our sinful person cannot be the subject of the new creation. "The removal of the person is the removal of the male, his ejection from that role as creator." With the removal of the human person what remains is "human nature as such, man in himself, the impersonal substratum of history, man as creature, not creator. The bearer of human creatureliness is the female" (6.IV.164). Barth hastens to add that woman, too, is a sinner. She participates in this event only as a vessel that must receive a new content. Noncreative humanity, represented by Mary, is "the human possibility that stands over against the impossible possibility of God and can become an organ for God as God's miracle makes her this" (ibid.).

Two comments on this passage are necessary. First, in certain respects Barth is ahead of his time in acknowledging the evil of patriarchal domination of history and culture. But in the effort to lift up the sheer grace of the incarnation, Barth's argument stereotypes male and female as creative and noncreative respectively. Human nature must be purely receptive in relation to God's grace and salvation. Hence what is "typically male" must be removed in order that a new humanity may arise.

Second, Barth comes close to ascribing to the noncreative female a natural possibility, a point of contact in humanity for the working of divine grace. However, his comment that Mary is able to be an instrument of God only "as God's miracle makes her this" shows that he in fact does not intend to posit a natural human capacity for grace in women any more than he does in men.

In the *Church Dogmatics* Barth states clearly that "human nature possesses no capacity for becoming the human nature of Jesus Christ, the place of divine revelation" (I/2, 188). He now acknowledges his earlier failure to avoid leaving the impression that the virgin birth is a condition of the new beginning for humanity rather than its sign. (While he is specifically referring here to the *Christliche Dogmatik* of 1927, the retraction would hold as well for the parallel passage in the *Göttingen Dogmatics*.) Barth now wants to dispel all suspicion of attributing a natural capacity or openness for grace (an error he thinks is common to Schleiermacher and Roman Catholic Mariology).

Furthermore, in his discussion of the virgin birth in the *Church Dogmatics* Barth does not dwell on the different social roles traditionally assigned to male and female. The important distinction, he now argues, is between supposedly sovereign and self-creative humanity on the one hand, and humanity that is receptive to God's grace on the other. Still, he counsels the church to hold to the sign of the virgin birth as a witness to the limitation of humanity and its sin that is at the same time a witness to the "limitation of male pre-eminence" (I/2, 194).

(3) There are also important differences between the *Göttingen Dogmatics* and the *Church Dogmatics* with regard to the offices of Christ and the nature of his atoning work. While the building blocks of Barth's highly original christological architectonics in the *Church Dogmatics* are already present in the Göttingen christology, the latter lacks the imaginative interweaving of the offices, natures, and states of Christ, as well as the detailed interest in the gospel narrative found in the former. An obvious difference in the two dogmatics is the order of the offices of Christ: prophet, priest, king (*Göttingen Dogmatics*); priest, king, prophet (*Church Dogmatics*).

In the Göttingen lectures Barth does not question the concept of satisfaction. He is very clear that no conditions are to be attached to God's gracious work in Christ. Against Anselm Barth argues that we cannot say in advance what must happen in order to reconcile sinners with God. It is impossible to establish "a general rule" about how God and humanity can come together (29.IV). One must simply start from the *consummatum est, satisfactum est.* Following Calvin, Barth contends that the necessity of the atonement rests solely on God's good pleasure.[49] Yet despite his reservations about Anselm's doctrine, Barth describes the work of Christ in terms of satisfaction. "I recapitulate: *satisfaction,* because obedience, because in Christ's life and death there takes place what must unavoidably happen for the maintenance of the covenant, what we do not have the freedom to do: the willing humiliation of humanity, acknowledgment and confession of sin, solidarity not with the Pharisees but with the tax collectors, taking and bearing the wrath and punishment of God which must be for the sake of sin. That is what Christ has done" (29.IV).

In the *Church Dogmatics,* on the other hand, Barth calls the concept

---

49. Calvin, *Institutes,* II, 12, 1.

of satisfaction "doubtful" and prefers to speak instead of what is sufficient *(Genugtuung)*. What is sufficient is the destruction of the sinful person and the introduction of the new person reconciled to God. The passion and death of Christ were necessary "not out of any desire for vengeance and retribution on the part of God, but because of the radical nature of the divine love" (IV/1, 254).

According to Barth in the *Göttingen Dogmatics,* Lutheran and Reformed theologies give different answers to the question for whom *(pro quo)* satisfaction was accomplished in Christ. For Lutheran theology the satisfaction was offered for each and every individual, no one being absolutely excluded. God's intentions are gracious to all. If the satisfaction does not become effective for all, the cause lies only in the sinner and not in God. Orthodox Reformed theology, however, makes a distinction. Christ has suffered sufficiently for all, but this is efficacious only for the elect. A distinction is thus made between the potential and the actual power of Christ's sacrifice. God's will to reconcile only the elect is the meaning both of the incarnation and of the sacrifice of Christ.

Barth applauds the Lutheran intention to honor the greatness of God's love and concedes that the Reformed position seems by comparison hard, partisan, and even gruesome (29.IV). Nevertheless, he prefers the Reformed position because it holds to the "monergism of grace" (ibid.). By the express negation of a universalist theory of the atonement, the Reformed position secures the character of this event as free grace, "as a special, particular divine work that is not self-evident and must not be rationalized" (ibid.).

While Barth aligns himself with the Reformed emphasis in the doctrine of the atonement, he endorses the teaching that Christ died "only for the elect" with the reservation that the divine election does not mean a fixed, closed number of those elected and those rejected. Readers may justifiably wonder, however, whether Barth's position on the scope of the work of Christ in the *Göttingen Dogmatics* is convincing. He is content finally to answer the question *pro quo* with the statement, "the Lord knows his own" (29.IV).

In the *Church Dogmatics,* Barth's understanding of the scope of the work of Christ takes a very different form. In *CD* II/2 he reconstructs the doctrine of election so that all persons are both elect and reprobate in Christ. In him grace has triumphed for all. When Barth turns to the doctrine of atonement in *CD* IV/1, he rejects the view that Christ did not die for all persons but only for a limited number as a "grim doctrine," which he thinks does indeed follow logically from Calvin's conception of predestination (IV/1, 57). Jesus Christ has died and has risen for all.

(4) In the *Göttingen Dogmatics* Barth does not take up explicitly the question of who is the subject of the vicarious suffering of Christ. Does God suffer in the suffering and dying of the incarnate Lord? According to the old orthodox theologians, the suffering that accomplishes our reconciliation is not to be ascribed to the divine and human natures in the same way. "It is Christ's human nature that suffered for us, not the divine which cannot suffer and die. But the divine nature added weight to the passion. . . . We ascribe the passion to the human nature, but the efficacy of the passion to the divine."[50] Barth does not contest this view, and seems to share some of its presuppositions (cf. 17.IV.408).

In the *Church Dogmatics,* Barth insists that in the light of the reconciling work of Christ, God is not exclusively "active in contrast to all suffering" (IV/1, 186). God's immutability does not stand in the way of his self-humiliation. God is not the prisoner of a concept of deity that excludes predicates like obedience, subordination, and suffering as alien to God. Barth can even say that there is a particular truth in the teaching of the early Patripassianists. Indeed, "primarily it is God the Father who suffers in the offering and sending of His Son, in His abasement" (IV/2, 357). This teaching is a novum in comparison with the discussion of the passion of Christ in the *Göttingen Dogmatics,* and yet it also stands in continuity with the spirit of the earlier work. In both cases Barth intends to follow to its end the "strangely logical final continuation of the history in which [God] is God" (IV/1, 203).

XI. Baptism and the Lord's Supper

In the Göttingen lectures Barth takes up the sacraments at the beginning and end of the doctrinal complex that has to do with the appropriation of salvation (30.I). Instead of postponing discussion of the sacraments until after consideration of the Christian life as did the old Reformed theologians, Barth links baptism to calling *(Berufung)* and the Lord's Supper to perseverance *(Bewahrung).* He notes that this reordering of topics, whose effect is to surround Christian life with the sacraments, is "a severe departure from the usual order of teaching in the old dogmatics,"

---

50. So Wendelin, cited in Heppe, *Reformed Dogmatics,* pp. 465-66.

but is necessary in order to clarify the meaning and importance of the sacraments (30.I). In Barth's view, the modern problem of the immanence of God, which neo-Protestantism has tried to resolve with its emphasis on religious consciousness and experience, is properly addressed by a right understanding of the sacraments.

Baptism for Barth is the sign of God's including us in the covenant of grace and calling us to discipleship prior to any action on our part.

There could not be a stronger theological defender of infant baptism than the Barth of the *Göttingen Dogmatics*. He interprets infant baptism as a powerful witness to the free grace of God "without and against our will and understanding" (30.II). Infant baptism occurs in "absolute one-sidedness." Properly understood, all baptism has this meaning: our reconciliation is grounded not in our faith, piety, or morality, but in the free grace of God in Jesus Christ. "Do we find ourselves, whether as children or as adults, in regard to this real ground of reconciliation, in any different situation than that of howling and kicking infants?" (30.II). A corollary of Barth's theology of infant baptism is his criticism of the practice of confirmation, which he thinks badly undermines the authentic meaning of baptism, since it implies that a valid baptism depends upon the response of faith.

When we turn to the treatise on baptism in *CD* IV/4 (fragment), Barth's position has changed dramatically. He is no longer convinced of his earlier arguments. "The strongest [argument for infant baptism] — I myself used it for some decades — is that infant baptism is so remarkably vivid a depiction of the free and omnipotent grace of God which is independent of all human thought and will, faith and unbelief. . . . There is something in this" (IV/4, 189). But Barth now contends that if this argument is valid, then with equal justification adults and whole nations might be compelled to enter the church, as happened at certain points in the Constantinian era.

The central concern of the later Barth, however, is for a proper understanding of divine and human activity, grace and freedom all along the line in theology, and not least in the doctrine of baptism. Whereas his earlier concern had been primarily for the recognition of the deity of God and the sovereignty of God's grace, his emphasis now is that the grace of God is not totalitarian.[51] "The omnicausality of God must not be construed as His sole causality" (*CD* IV/4, 22). God is indeed "indissolubly

---

51. On this shift of emphasis, see esp. Barth, *The Humanity of God* (Richmond, 1960).

subject," but the activity of this subject does not reduce human beings to mere objects. Grace liberates and empowers us to become "responsible subjects" (26). The act of baptism thus bears witness to the primacy of divine grace, to the faithfulness of God made known in Jesus Christ. Yet it is a genuinely free human response of faith and obedience to the grace of God, a binding confession, made in prayer for God's grace, wherein the freedom of this grace is honored (2). Since baptism marks the commencement of the life of responsible Christian discipleship, it should take the form of adult baptism. "It is human action which simply responds to divine action. Nevertheless, it does so in an appropriate way. It reflects this action. It is thus a pre-eminent human action" (143). In line with this theology of baptism in *CD* IV/4, Barth now acknowledges that the "ancient ecclesiastical error," the "irregular practice" of infant baptism, does indeed call for a supplemental rite like confirmation (188).

Barth's doctrine of the Lord's Supper in the *Göttingen Dogmatics* is linked to the theme of perseverance. The basic question he raises is whether there is any real continuity in the Christian life. This question is prompted by the fact that in the doctrines of justification and sanctification, which Barth locates between the doctrine of calling (and Baptism) on the one hand and the doctrine of perseverance (and the Lord's Supper) on the other, he speaks of God's action as "lightning-like," breaking into the life of the elect perpendicularly from above (33.I). Does this radical actualism of grace mean that there is no real continuity in the life of the reconciled person? Does the eventfulness of grace mean sheer discontinuity? Is there no reconciled *being*?

A recurrent criticism of Barth's theology, early and late, is that his understanding of grace is occasionalistic. Has not Barth collapsed being into act with the result that no real continuity of human existence is allowed? Barth agrees that humans exist in unbroken temporal duration, and that the grace of God must be related somehow to this temporal structure of human existence. Hence there must be a grace of perseverance. But for Barth, this grace too must be an ever new action of God. Here as in every other moment of the appropriation of salvation, "God is and remains subject" (33.I). Barth finds the Westminster Confession's phrase "perseverance of the saints" ambiguous because it is not first we but God who is faithful and who perseveres in relation to us. God's faithfulness is the great Nevertheless! over against our unfaithfulness (33.I). If we persist in the habit of grace and do not lose it, this is not primarily our doing — it is the result of God's faithfulness.

If we go on to ask what is the basis of our knowledge of our continuity in faith, it would be a correct but incomplete answer to refer to God's Word and Spirit. For there is a concrete analogy of this act of Word and Spirit in our world of embodied human existence. This is the sacrament of the Lord's Supper that attests the constancy and perseverance of God's grace and hence the continuity of the life of faith. "The Lord's Supper is the last word on the question of the continuity of the appropriation of grace" (33.II). The Lord's Supper is repeatedly celebrated; it is the sacrament of the promise that God's grace is new every morning, the sacrament of the command to obey this God who is Lord of every moment of our life.

Barth affirms the "real full presence" of Christ and the "real full self-communication" of Christ in the Lord's Supper. He understands the doctrine of the Lord's Supper in the Reformed tradition as basically occupying the middle ground between the spiritualistic and Zwinglian interpretations on the one hand and the Catholic and Lutheran interpretations on the other. But the Reformed position is not a static point midway between opposite poles. It is a highly dynamic and dialectical point. A right understanding of this sacrament depends on both a proper distinction and proper binding together of sign and thing signified (*Zeichen* and *Sache*).

Thus, on the one hand, Christ and sign are to be distinguished; Christ is not imprisoned in the sign. Barth's emphasis on the freedom and initiative of God persists in his doctrine of the Lord's Supper. God is God: God remains indissolubly subject in the event of the Lord's Supper as elsewhere. Hence the sign remains sign. In itself it is always ambiguous and creates offense to those who have eyes but do not see and ears but do not hear. There is an analogy between this sacramental ambiguity and hiddenness, and the ambiguity and hiddenness which also characterize the incarnation, the scriptural witness, and the preaching of the Word of God.

But this is only one side of the dialectic. The sign is no mere symbol of a presence of grace available always and everywhere. This sign is not exchangeable for another. The sign remains sign, but by the power of the Spirit it truly and effectively attests the grace of God in Christ, really confirms his presence to us. This particular sign has been chosen by God, and in the power of the Spirit serves as the means by which the reconciled receive assurance and confirmation. Barth expresses it this way: "As certainly as the bread is broken here before your eyes, and the wine is separated from the bread, so certainly has my body been broken on the cross for you. Again, as certainly as I give the holy signs of my body and blood to you to eat and drink, so certainly shall you also take part and have communion in my very body and blood" (33.II).

In the *Church Dogmatics* Barth intended to take up the doctrine of the Lord's Supper in the context of the ethics of reconciliation. As in the *Göttingen Dogmatics* it was to have completed the doctrine of the Christian life just as the doctrine of baptism served as its beginning. After a "presentation of the various practical aspects of Christian life under the guidance of the Lord's prayer," the doctrine of the Lord's Supper was to have been treated as a "conclusion and crown . . . as the thanksgiving which responds to the presence of Jesus Christ in His self-sacrifice and which looks forward to His future" (*CD* IV/4, ix).

There are certainly strands of continuity between the sketch of the Lord's Supper in the Göttingen lectures and the very brief description of its proposed treatment in the *Church Dogmatics*. On the basis of Barth's revision of his doctrine of baptism, we may assume that he would have given greater emphasis to the celebration of the Lord's Supper as also an act of our free gratitude that corresponds to God's gracious work of reconciliation. Hence more attention would have been given to the ethical implications of this act than is done in the earlier dogmatics. Nevertheless, this new emphasis would surely have been coupled with the continued affirmation of the freedom, initiative, and faithfulness of God in preserving and sustaining the Christian community in the praise and service of God to which it is called.

XII. Revisions in Eschatology

The seventh and final chapter of the *Göttingen Dogmatics* contains the doctrine of redemption *(Erlösung)* or eschatology. Since Barth did not live to write the fifth volume of the *Church Dogmatics* that was to deal explicitly with this doctrine, the final section of his earliest dogmatics holds special interest and will be carefully examined by readers for clues as to how Barth might likely have unfolded his eschatology in his magnum opus.

In Barth's view, it was an unmitigated disaster for dogmatics when eschatology was allowed to become a "suspicious little final chapter next to other things" (35.Intro.). "A dogmatics which has not seen and respected the eschatological character of revelation from the beginning will necessarily stand before closed doors here" (ibid.). Christian truth is "from the beginning eschatological" (35.III). There is an echo here of what Barth had stated so powerfully in the second edition of the *Römerbrief:* "If

Christianity be not altogether thoroughgoing eschatology, there remains in it no relationship whatever with Christ."[52] It is one of Barth's recurrent criticisms of nineteenth-century Protestant theology that it was responsible for a "de-eschatologization" of Christian doctrine.

Barth begins by contrasting Christian eschatological statements with other ways of speaking about the future, specifically what he calls the historical-sociological, the geological-astronomical, the parapsychological, and the ontological eschatologies. What distinguishes Christian eschatology is that its affirmations about the future, like all affirmations of Christian dogmatics, are based on the Word of God as it addresses us in the threefold form of Jesus Christ attested by scripture and proclaimed by the church. Thus Christian eschatology is interested primarily not in "last *things*," but in the *Person* who is coming (chap. 7, Intro.); it is motivated not by curiosity but by fidelity to the Word of God; and it is not idle, speculative knowledge but essentially personal address to us which claims our faith and obedience.

The basis of Christian hope for Barth cannot be some aspect of our created being, as is postulated by the doctrine of the immortality of the soul. Nor can we claim that since we have been created and preserved by divine grace, God will necessarily bring us to fulfillment and grant us eternal life. A guarantee of hope can be found neither in ourselves nor in some necessity in God to rescue us from death and to redeem history from ultimate meaninglessness. The love of God is no abstract principle; the living God loves in freedom. "Just as God does not owe us our being and existence, so God owes us nothing beyond that, nothing at all" (35.I). There is a firm basis for Christian hope only in the event of God's grace in Jesus Christ for rebellious sinners. "God has so loved the world that he gave his only begotten Son. Christian hope rests on the basis of this extravagant *so*" (35.II).

Barth describes the content of Christian hope in three sections: the presence of Jesus Christ (§ 36); the resurrection of the dead (§ 37); and the glory of God (§ 38). As object and content of hope the presence of Jesus Christ is his presence in *status exaltationis* (36.III). While there is an analogy between the parousia and the incarnation, between Christ in the state of exaltation and Christ in the state of humiliation, the parousia is no mere copy or repetition of the incarnation. It is "something really new" (36.I). The dialectic of revelation and hiddenness characterizes God's self-disclosure in history. Many errors in theology have been the result of trying to achieve a "premature eschatology," of Christian hope being unable to

---

52. Barth, *Romans*, p. 314.

wait and pretending instead to be already at its goal. The object and content of hope is what we do not yet possess: the parousia, the undialectical, unparadoxical coming of Christ, without opposition of form and content, end and means, eternity and time (36.III).

Since human beings are persons only in the unity of body and soul, redemption must mean more than immortality of the soul; it must also include resurrection of the body. "Something other than bodily resurrection does not come into consideration when we speak of resurrection in the sense of redemption, of completed reconciliation" (37.III). Indeed, Barth contends that embodiment is "the end of the way of God" (35.III).[53] *This* body must be transformed; *this* world must be renewed. Not that humans cease to be human and become something else after death, perhaps angels. In redemption, marked by the resurrection of the body, "humanity does not become God. God remains the Creator, and humans remain creatures" (37.III). In the resurrection human beings become true subjects of all the predicates which on this side of the parousia can be attributed without qualification only to Jesus Christ.

For Barth the end of God's mighty acts is the glory of God. Even in its final word, Christian doctrine reminds us that God remains the Lord and subject of Christian proclamation. "God is the subject, and creation, reconciliation, and redemption are for his glory" (38.II). Redemption does not occur solely or primarily for the sake of humanity. "God's glory alone can constitute the satisfying conclusion of Christian dogmatics if it is to be something other than just a worldview" (38.II). Yet the glory of God is not antithetical to the glorification of the people of God. The glory of God includes rather than excludes the salvation of humanity. God comes to glory in the realization of a people who see God as God is *(visio Dei)* and who love God as God wants to be loved *(fruitio Dei)*.

There are unmistakable similarities between the eschatology of the Göttingen lectures and the discussions of Christian hope in the later volumes of the *Church Dogmatics*. In both cycles of dogmatics, Barth's interpretation of hope is christocentric. In the early dogmatics we find: "The new presence of Jesus Christ is in fact the content, the whole content, the one and all of Christian hope" (37.I). And in the *Church Dogmatics*: "The Christian hopes in Jesus Christ, in Him alone, but in Him confi-

---

53. Cf. Jürgen Moltmann's discussion of the thesis of Friedrich Oetinger: "Embodiment is the end of all God's works," in *God in Creation* (San Francisco, 1985), pp. 244ff.

dently. For He alone, but dependably, is the origin, theme and content of Christian hope, as of Christian faith and love" (IV/3.2, 921-22).

Moreover, both early and late, Barth interprets Christian hope in a holistic and inclusive manner. He is critical of all narrow otherworldliness in eschatology. He wants to avoid every "hot-air balloon flight of eschatological speculation" (*Göttingen Dogmatics* 38.I), which he thinks was a constant danger of the older eschatology. That hope has a communal as well as a personal dimension is also a consistent theme in both works. In the earliest dogmatics Barth contends that the hoped-for community is not reducible to the marital relationship, the family, or the nation. Only the church, the *communio sanctorum,* is the community anticipated by Christian hope — no other (38.I). Similarly, in the *Church Dogmatics* Barth drives home the point that Christian hope is not the pursuit of a private cause (IV/3.2, 930). Christians cannot have any concern for their own glory; their hoping, as well as their believing and loving, is directed beyond themselves (930-31).

Finally, both in the *Göttingen Dogmatics* and in the *Church Dogmatics* Barth insists that there are signs of the kingdom of God here and now, but warns that these signs must never be confused with what they signify. We must never allow ourselves to be taken prisoner by any great historical event or movement, whether the Roman Empire, the Roman church, socialism, or the cause of one's own people. It can be legitimate, Barth claims, to find in socialism, or some other promising historical development, a sign of the millennium of Christ (as Barth himself had been inclined to do during his years in Safenwil). But one must never affirm the sign for its own sake; one's fear and love are appropriately directed only to God (36.V). Similarly, in the *Church Dogmatics* and in the posthumously published fragments on *The Christian Life,* Barth allows that there are "intimations" of the ultimate in the penultimate events of history (*CD* IV/3.2, 937); there are parables of the kingdom in history, human actions that are kingdom-like.[54]

What is the difference between Barth's earlier and later interpretations of eschatology? The answer would seem to be that in the *Göttingen Dogmatics* Barth speaks of life in hope more dialectically. Eschewing all "premature eschatology" (35.II), Barth emphasizes that Christians are still in the midst of conflict and are not already at the goal. Corresponding to his interpretation of the doctrine of election in these lectures, Barth declares that there is an eternal damnation as well as an eternal salvation, that God is both merciful

---

54. Barth, *The Christian Life* (Grand Rapids, 1981), p. 266; see also Barth, *Community, State, and Church* (New York, 1960).

and righteous. In whom will God demonstrate the one, and in whom the other? asks Barth. This final question of dogmatics is far from speculative; it is addressed personally to each of us (38.II).

In the reflections on eschatology in the *Church Dogmatics,* on the other hand, the atmosphere has changed. The emphasis is on the confidence, patience, and cheerfulness of the expectation of Christians, not of course as something grounded in themselves but only in God through Christ (IV/3.2, 902). Indeed, Barth now explicitly distinguishes between Christian hope and what he calls a "dangerous dialectic" with its "twofold, ambivalent, equivocal future" (907). This emphasis in the *Church Dogmatics* corresponds to Barth's more radically christocentric doctrine of election and his unequivocal rejection of a doctrine of limited atonement (918). While the later like the earlier Barth refuses to adopt a doctrine of apocatastasis, he insists that on the basis of the superabundant grace of God made known in Jesus Christ, no a priori limit can be set to the extent of God's redemptive work in him. "The Christian expectation of the future cannot be uncertain, nor unsettled, nor sceptical, but only assured and patient and cheerful expectation" (909).

XIII. Summary

While a precise assessment of the place and significance of the *Göttingen Dogmatics* within the development of Barth's theology must await detailed studies by many scholars, several points seem to be beyond dispute.

(1) Barth commenced the task of dogmatic construction much earlier than has been assumed by many who knew his work only from the *Römerbrief* and his early essays on the one hand and from the *Church Dogmatics* on the other. We are now able to see much more continuity in Barth's development than before. A neat division between a dialectical period and a period of analogy, with the book on Anselm, *Fides Quaerens Intellectum,* as the decisive turning point, is no longer compelling.

(2) While we can now see more clearly than before that there is a deep, coherent logic that informs Barth's theology, early and late, we are also made more aware of his remarkable freedom to modify, correct, refine, and develop his central theological vision.[55] In the *Göttingen Dogmatics*

---

55. Cf. E. Jüngel, "What is systematic about [Barth's] theology is that it resolves to make progress precisely by constantly correcting, or else completely changing, its direction," in *Karl Barth, a Theological Legacy* (Philadelphia, 1986), p. 27.

he is conscious of engaging in an experiment and is not entirely sure how it will all turn out. This open, experimental spirit would continue to characterize his work in the *Church Dogmatics,* the content of each part volume being known in advance "only to the angels in heaven" (*CD* IV/2, x-xi). Early and late, Barth invites theologians to take the risk *(Wagnis)* of fresh and energetic reflection on the Word of God, to have the boldness and the freedom to "begin again at the beginning."

(3) We see a Barth in the *Göttingen Dogmatics* who tenaciously does theology — indeed, defines theology — in relation to preaching and pastoral praxis. Not only the numerous asides to his students about their future pastoral responsibilities but also the rich metaphors and images which he employs testify that his theology at this stage is still very close to concrete pastoral responsibility. Something of this sensibility may be lost in the great expanses of the *Church Dogmatics,* although the intimate relation between theology and preaching remained an axiom for Barth to the end.

(4) Finally, the question will have to be raised whether the movement from the pastorate in Safenwil to the teaching of dogmatics in Göttingen, Münster, Bonn, and finally Basel did not involve certain losses as well as gains, whether Barth was able to prevent a slide toward the systematization of revelation, a one-sided christocentricity that Barth himself was critical of in earlier years. Did not the theology of the later Barth, for example, develop an inflexible and one-sided description of the order of the relationship of man and woman that seems determined more by the constraints of system than by the deepest logic of the Christian gospel? Or again, was the theology of the later Barth itself threatened by the danger of de-eschatologization, a "premature eschatology" as he earlier described it, that could be corrected only by a renewed awareness that the people of God and the whole creation still groan and sigh for the completion of God's redemptive activity?

With respect to these and many other questions, theology today must go its own way even where it remains indebted to Barth. His stature as a theological colossus of the twentieth century is not in doubt. Yet he is honored best not by mechanical repetitions of his work but by theology that dares "to begin its work again at the very beginning" (1.II.13).[56] This is precisely what we see Barth himself doing in his first lectures in dogmatics in Göttingen.

---

56. Cf. Barth, *Evangelical Theology,* p. 146.

INTRODUCTION

The Word of God as the Problem of Dogmatics

The problem of dogmatics is scientific reflection on the Word of God which is spoken by God in revelation, which is recorded in the holy scripture of the prophets and apostles, and which now both is and should be proclaimed and heard in Christian preaching. "Prolegomena to dogmatics" is what we call the attempt to achieve a basic understanding of the theme, the necessity, and the course of such reflection.

I. Dangers and Questions

The present course is envisaged as the first and introductory part of a series on dogmatics that will stretch over three semesters. It was significant that Thomas Aquinas put at the head of his *Summa Theologica* the prayer: "Merciful God, I ask that thou wilt grant me, as thou pleasest, to seek earnestly, to investigate carefully, to know truthfully, and to present perfectly, to the glory of thy name, amen."[1] If there is any mortally dangerous undertaking on earth, any undertaking in which we have reason not only at the beginning but also in the middle and at the end to take the last resort of invoking the name of the Most High, then it is that of a *summa theologica,* a dogmatics, and I must add that in our day and our situation such a prayer will have to be made out of materially much deeper distress

---

1. For this prayer, see *STh,* p. 12, under the heading: Devota oratio ante studium dicenda quam ipsemet S. Thomas composuit, ac Leo XIII Pont. Maximus indulgentiis ditavit.

and perplexity than in the time of Thomas. The manner in which Thomas pursued dogmatics leaves the impression of a holy, lofty, beautiful, and joyful work of art. Not for nothing he gives the doctor of the church a heavenly halo along with the virgin and martyr.[2] But for us, presenting and studying dogmatics is a burden, a burden that we cannot and may not and will not avoid, but still a burden. We are a generation that has to learn again, sometimes even by name, what are the presuppositions that a Thomas, an Augustine before him, and a Calvin after him could quietly take for granted.

Dogmatics as a work that praises its master[3] flourishes only against a specific background. I might list the presence of a Christian church that we do not have to build or support but that edifies and supports us; a living concept of the office and task of a church teacher; acquaintance with a generally or widely recognized Christian message; self-evident acceptance of a qualified and differentiated authority; not least the personal knowledge of serious, disciplined dealings with God; a knowing and fearing and loving of his name that claims our human existence.[4] How little acquainted we are with these things without which no one can really do dogmatics! How artificial, empty, and useless our work will be if we try to do dogmatics without these presuppositions! But how gigantic is the task of even gaining some glimpse of them from afar! "Dogmatics" denotes a place where all the inner and outer difficulties of theology assemble and emerge, the place which almost all those have in mind who cleverly or foolishly sigh over theology and theologians, the place which in spite of all the assurances of prudent negotiators and advocates calls into question the validity of our stay at the university and even perhaps of our whole existence, the place which we theologians try as hard as we can to avoid by fleeing to history or practice. Is not the word "dogmatics" an ominous one, a bogey that causes the children of light [cf. Luke 16:8] as well as the children of the world to shudder? Not arbitrarily might we not think of the dark and musty wigs of the 17th century on the one hand and head-shaking natural scientists on the other? Dogmatics and the youth movement — an unheard-of and insulting combination, is it not? Does not the study of dogmatics hold out the same promise only as efforts to square the circle or find the philosopher's stone or invent perpetual motion?

---

2. Ibid., III, 96, 7.
3. Cf. Schiller's *Das Lied von der Glocke* (1799), v. 7.
4. See Ps. 9:10; Mal. 4:2; Ps. 5:11-12; etc.

Will we not willingly forgo the doctor's halo in our anxiety whether dogmaticians can get to heaven at all and whether they can even be credible figures here on earth?

As regards all this, I can only note first that the task of dogmatics, whether put early or late, has always placed students in an anxious, precarious, and, as already stated, dangerous situation, and it will always do so. A scholastic of the renown of Bonaventura called his dogmatics a poverty-stricken bit of human scholarship,[5] and I do not think he was merely asking for gentle treatment. Even behind the proud structure of Thomas, if appearances do not deceive, there may be seen more anxiety, difficulty, and even dread than the first impression of a secure and tidy work might suggest. And one has only to look at Calvin's face to be convinced that it was not an easy thing, or child's play, to write dogmatics in the Reformation period. As I have shown, we today undoubtedly face extraordinary difficulties. But the task is posed for us as for previous generations. None of the laughter or head shaking of our contemporaries and none of our faintheartedness ought to keep us from at least recognizing the task. And when we do so, we shall have to address it in some way.

Let me say something about that which has always made the task of dogmatics dangerous, and always will. We can do theology as those who out of interest, or as willing or unwilling participants, but at any rate objectively, are investigators of religion in general and of Christianity in particular, immersing ourselves in the thinking of a Lao-Tse or a Buddha or a Paul or a John, and with more or less enthusiasm learning the teachings of a Luther or a Schleiermacher. There is nothing dangerous or suspect about this if we at least know how to walk warily around the burning bush [Exod. 3:2ff.]. This is just one aspect of scholarship like any other, and on these academic pastures, and in good company, one can spend one's life most honorably. Again, we can study theology as practice. In this case we do not merely investigate; we also speak, and we say very impressively and clearly and convincingly and winningly — what? We can find this out too. With the help of the Bible and other good books, we can always say something with reference to human needs and from the fount of our own experience. The great question in practical theology is the "how." Happy are those who have found an answer either at university or by practice. There is nothing dangerous or suspect about all this. But there comes a

---

5. *Sancti Bonaventurae Breviloquium*, ed. K. D. Hefele (Tübingen, 1845), p. 21 (Prooemium): *pauper portiuncula scientolae nostrae* (or *paupercula scientiola nostra*).

point — and no theologian can evade it — at which theology does become dangerous and suspect. This is the point where the twofold question arises: What are *you* going to say? Not as one who knows the Bible or Thomas or the Reformers or the older Blumhardt, but responsibly and seriously as one who stands by the words that are said: *you*? And *what* are you going to say? Not how impressively or how clearly or how well adapted to your hearers and to the present age — these are all secondary concerns — but *what*?

You? What? These are the questions of dogmatics. We have to consider the fact that "in some way" we have to speak about *God*. The questions put a pistol at the breast of theologians and through them at that of the public. If these questions are right, it is not just a matter of the so-called religions and religious personalities of distant times and countries which we can keep at a distance, knowing either nothing or not much about them. In our own midst a commission has been given whereby certain people have to speak, and they have to speak, mark you, about *God*. And it is not a matter of indifference, or of chance or caprice, what they say. This "what" is an unsettling question, a sword of Damocles that hangs over them and obviously, therefore, over all of us. This "what" means that in what is said about God there is truth and error. Is it not clear how many *fatal* possibilities await theologians when they face the dogmatic question? Perplexity and admission of total ignorance might be the result when historical investigators and bright practical theologians move on to the answering of the dogmatic question. Serious mistakes and illusions, priestly arrogance and impatience, might follow when they do this. One can well understand why even theologians prefer an undogmatic Christianity. What things might come to light if they were suddenly to answer the dogmatic question in this general sense! How rightly do those sigh who honestly take up the matter, and how right they are again to sigh about the results of their exertions!

Dogmatics means striking a balance, and this is hard when we are not sure whether we are not already bankrupt. And who can be sure and not afraid when constantly faced by those questions: You? and What? In my view this is the sinister thing about dogmatics in every age. Every dogmatician is a rider on Lake Constance,[6] and the same applies to every theologian, for every theologian has to be a dogmatician. And in this regard theology simply shows how it stands with all of us. I repeat, we are not

---

6. Cf. G. Schwab's ballad "Der Reiter und der Bodensee" (1826).

Thomas or Calvin. We have to relearn the most rudimentary presuppositions that are needed to answer the question. We can take only the smallest steps. We have every reason, as we embark upon this science that is so difficult both in general and in detail, to keep in view the last resort to which I alluded at the outset. This must be our first prolegomenon.

II. Dogmatics as the Science of Dogmas

I must first point out that my definition of dogmatics in the thesis, that is, "scientific reflection on the Word of God," does not deviate very greatly from the modern theological tradition. In comparison with it I will show how many of my respected predecessors have defined dogmatics. According to Schleiermacher dogmatics is the science of the relationship between a Christian church-community and the teaching which is valid in a given time,[7] that is, the science of the epitome of states of Christian piety expressed in words.[8] According to A. Schweizer dogmatics is the scientific presentation of the evangelical Protestant faith at its present stage of development.[9] According to Luthardt it is the science of the nexus of dogmas reproduced from the religious faith of Christians.[10] According to R. Rothe it is the coherent scientific presentation of the principles in which a specific church-community has expressly and authentically stated its pious consciousness in concepts.[11] According to R. Lipsius it is the scientific presentation of Christian faith from the standpoint of Christian faith and for those who hold it, so that they may see what is its content and its most suitable expression.[12] According to F. Nitzsch (Stephan) it is the scientific presentation and vindication of the evangelical Christian faith or the content of its consciousness in contemporary forms of thought and speech,[13] or the scientific self-understanding of the educated among believers, or of believers among the educated (i.e., theologians), concerning the

---

7. F. Schleiermacher, *Der christliche Glaube* (1821, 1830), I, § 19; ET *CF,* I, § 19.
8. Ibid., § 15.
9. A. Schweizer, *Die Christliche Glaubenslehre nach protestantischen Grundsätzen,* I, 2nd ed. (Leipzig, 1877), p. 2.
10. Luthardt, p. 6.
11. R. Rothe, *Zur Dogmatik* (Gotha, 1863), p. 14.
12. R. A. Lipsius, *Lehrbuch der evangelisch-protestantische Dogmatik,* 2nd ed. (Brunswick, 1879), § 1.
13. Nitzsch-Stephan, § 1, p. 1.

essential content and validity of Christian faith.[14] According to Kaftan it is the science of Christian truth believed and confessed in the church on the basis of divine revelation.[15] According to Herrmann it is the search for clarity concerning the origin and validity of our own religion.[16] According to Haering it is the science of Christian faith.[17] According to H. H. Wendt it is the scientific grasp of the whole of Christian doctrine and its elevation to a single system of belief.[18] According to Troeltsch it is a consistent presentation of Christian faith on the presupposition of actual changes in the religious consciousness and the life of the world as a whole.[19]

The unquestionable agreement between the theological tradition recognizable in these formulas and the definition that I have attempted seems to lie first only in the concept "science." Wendt, whom I take to represent this modern theology, defines this concept as follows. We describe as scientific a knowledge in which we diligently apply every method to establish the objective truth of knowledge.[20] He then defines it more strictly as a coherent and freely critical knowledge which has the logical grounding of all knowledge as its aim. I myself would equate "scientific" and "objective," objectivity being the closest possible adjustment of knowledge to the distinctiveness of its object. The most fitting means to establish objective truth, the most certain way to achieve coherence in knowledge, the freest critical norm, and the most logical grounding of all knowledge will in every field of science be the truth itself, which we do not have to produce but which is given to us. If, then, the means of knowledge, the coherence, the criticism, and the grounding must be determined by the distinctiveness of the object in dogmatics, this does not preclude its scientific character but includes it. With this proviso I can adopt Wendt's definition at every point. Dogmatics is not fiction. It is not a free outgush of sentiment. It is not tendentious speech. It is science. To this extent I am in agreement.

But then dissent begins. It consists of the fact that I take over an older dogmatic tradition and call dogmatics reflection on the Word of

---

14. Ibid., § 2, p. 4.

15. Kaftan, § 1.

16. W. Herrmann, *Dogmatik* (Gotha, 1925), § 5. This volume came out only posthumously. Barth was using the lectures "Dogmatik I" of 1908.

17. Haering, p. 9; cf. p. 7; ET p. 4; cf. p. 6.

18. Wendt, Part I, pp. 14-15.

19. This definition is based on the Heidelberg lectures "Dogmatik I" of 1908.

20. Wendt, p. 2.

God, whereas all those other definitions speak more or less expressly of faith, religion, or the religious consciousness, sometimes with an explicit limitation to present-day faith. The tradition behind them does not date only from Schleiermacher. It goes back by way of Pietism to Protestant orthodoxy. Not to Zwingli and Calvin, one must say, in spite of the bad impression that might be made by a first glimpse of titles like *Commentary on True and False Religion* or *Institutes of the Christian Religion.* We have only to read the first pages of these books to be convinced that we do not have here a theology of religious consciousness. What God is, we of ourselves know as little as a scarab knows what a man is, Zwingli tells us. It would be Luciferian and Promethean arrogance to want to know what God is in any other way than through God himself.[21] Calvin, too, will link the knowledge of God directly to self-knowledge only insofar as insight into our poverty, nakedness, and ruin through the fall compel us to ask after God.[22] To this extent, but only to this extent, can human awareness of God be the object of theology for Calvin. It seems to be in English Presbyterianism that we are to seek the source of that tradition. In Franeker at the beginning of the 17th century it found a champion in the Englishman Amesius, the teacher of Cocceius. For him, living to God through Christ, religion, and the cultus were the themes of theology.[23] The Lutheran Abraham Calovius took the same line in Wittenberg in the second half of the century, finding the object of dogmatics in those who are being brought to salvation.[24] Schleiermacher's Copernican revolution, which the formulas that I have quoted reflect, was the culmination of an older development rather than the initiation of a new one. He gave classical and even canonical form to a view which from those beginnings had come to increasingly more forceful expression throughout the 18th century, the view that theology in general and dogmatics in particular is the science of religion, the science of statements of pious experience such as is found in the Christian church, a view which achieved repristination later in theologians like Luthardt,[25] and which has even left traces in such ruggedly independent thinkers as J. T. Beck and A. Schlatter.[26]

---

21. *Huldrici Zuingli Opera,* ed. Schuler-Schulthess, III (Turici, 1835), p. 157; CR, 90, p. 643.

22. *Inst.* I, 1, 1.

23. Cf. Bavinck, I, p. 11; for specific references cf. *ChD,* p. 115 n. 23.

24. Ibid.

25. Luthardt, p. 3.

26. Cf. J. T. Beck, *Einleitung in das System der christlichen Lehre oder Propädeutische*

Far from adopting this view, I oppose to it the view that I find expressed in Luther's saying that God's Word — and no one else, not even an angel — must establish articles of faith;[27] and if not an angel, then certainly not I, a man with my pious experience. I also find it expressed in the statement of Ursinus that dogmas are things we must believe or obey because God commands them, so that the principle behind every theological dogma is: *Deus dixit.*[28] I also find it expressed in the saying of S. Maresius, the contentious opponent of Cocceius, to the effect that the doctrine of true religion is disclosed to us by God to his own glory and our salvation. God is the author, the final end is his glory, and the secondary end is our salvation.[29]

By way of explanation, I must point out that my definition of dogmatics as reflection on God's Word is not a definition of theology as the science of God.[30] In my view the modern objections to this latter definition are right, namely, that it confuses dogmatics with a metaphysics that has become impossible since Kant, and that it does not give faith its proper place in fixing the object.[31] Thomas already defended his thesis that God is the subject of this science with a reference to its principles. These are the articles of faith, and faith, which for Thomas is naturally not just a subjective concept, is from God.[32] Thus only insofar as God speaks through faith, according to this master of a metaphysical theology, can a science that concerns itself with articles or dogmas be a science of God. Campegius Vitringa (d. 1722) has left a fine definition of a theologian as one who speaks the truth about God to the glory of God.[33] I can adopt this so long as we understand by "truth" the Word that God himself and God alone has spoken, so that the correlation of God and faith is not destroyed or restricted by the interposition of a truth that we humans have rationally or irrationally established, but is secured by an intervening *Deus dixit.*

Nevertheless — to return to the modern tradition — the recogni-

---

Entwicklung der Christlichen Lehr-Wissenschaft (Stuttgart, 1838), pp. 48ff.; A. Schlatter, *Das christliche Dogma* (Stuttgart, 1906), e.g., p. 14.

27. Schmalkaldic Articles, II, 2; *BSLK,* p. 421.40-41; Tappert, p. 295.

28. Bavinck, I, p. 5. For the true origin of this statement, which is wrongly ascribed to Ursinus, cf. *ChD,* p. 65 n. 8.

29. See Schweizer, p. 40.

30. On this term cf. *ChD,* p. 118 n. 31a.

31. Cf. Kaftan, pp. 6, 94, 108.

32. *STh* I, q. 1, a. 7, i.c.

33. Schweizer, p. 140.

tion of this correlation does not mean a Copernican reversal of the divine and human subjects. It is hard to see why the commonly adduced saying of Luther that faith and God belong together[34] should entail modern fideism or religionism. On the contrary, in the intervening statement which establishes the correlation of God and faith that is rightly so important to modern theology (i.e., the statement *Deus dixit*), God is obviously the subject, not man. If God were not the speaking subject who creates faith by his Word, then what could he be but the object of a scholarly metaphysics? We must be on guard lest with the Ritschlians we deny out of hand that he might perhaps be this as well, but that is another question. If they are right with the positive side of their thesis — with the demand that dogmatics has to speak about God primarily in relation to faith — it follows ineluctably, if we are not to fall into the arms of Feuerbach at the very first step, that in this relation we must think of God as the subject. But we must then express this already in our basic definition of the discipline. That is what I am trying to do when I call God's own speaking the problem of dogmatics.

I can put this differently and more materially. Let us accept provisionally, if not without reservation, the common Protestant definition of faith as trust. We need not understand this as sentimentally or emotionally as is often done. Trust has a secondary legal meaning. It can denote the leaving of property in trust, or the agreement by which this is done (as in a pro-forma sale), or the security given in a mortgage.[35] We need to remember that the Reformers constantly relate trust to promise.[36] We shall then realize that the legal meaning is a vital one. As an action, or as the agreement behind it, or as the receiving of a security for the agreement, trust always stands in relation to the word given by someone else. This word does not express the trust, nor is it a symbol of the meeting of the minds. That would be complete nonsense. No, trust relates to the word, which is its basis and origin, its raison d'être. At times the given word can evoke no trust, but trust is logically and materially impossible if it does not relate to a given word. To speak plainly, faith always relates to something that is believed, whether as a human action (the faith with which we believe), or as a confession stipulated in thoughts and words (the faith

---

34. Large Catechism, in Müller, p. 386; *BSLK*, p. 560.25ff.; cf. Tappert, p. 365.
35. Barth bases all this on K. E. Georges, *Ausführliches lateinisch-deutsches Handwörterbuch*, I (Hanover/Leipzig, 1913), col. 2754-55.
36. Cf. Apologia Confessionis Augustanae, in *BSLK*, p. 225.42-48; Tappert, p. 157.

which we believe), or as a pledge or deposit (faith as the gift of God, as the living presence of the Holy Spirit). There is always a relation. God has turned to us in such a way that we can answer only with faith (and how else could he do so if God is God and we are as we are?). We may not give this answer, but when we do it is an answer to God, an answer to this confidential turning and address of his. The address is not an expression of faith. Faith, if it is faith, finds its generative basis in it. Faith assents only to what is revealed by God, Thomas tell us.[37] If dogmatics is to speak about God, and if as Protestant dogmatics it can do so only in a correlation of God and faith, then there is no doubt that it must find its first, primary, and principal theme in this generative basis, in this confidential turning and address of God, without which faith is nonsense. If not, then openly or secretly it sides with Feuerbach in viewing God as the product of faith instead of vice versa.

I can finally link the demonstration of my thesis with a little discussion of the word "dogmatics" such as is usually given in the first section of books and lectures on this discipline. It is well to remember that the word "dogmatic" was at first an adjective which the 17th century related to the word "theology" in order to make a distinction from ethical or moral theology. Obviously the noun "theology" shows us what is distinctive about both disciplines. If we understand the noun according to its generally accepted etymology as *logos peri tou theou* (the knowledge of God), then so long as we do not again confuse theology and metaphysics, as used to be done, we come up against the same insight as we did when we began with faith, namely, that this *logos peri tou theou* can be only a relation to a *logos tou theou,* to God's making himself known. If we reject the possibility of a science of God in the sense of philosophical or metaphysical speaking about God, then speaking about God can refer only to an original speaking by God,[38] or to the impress of the knowledge of God that God himself has revealed to us in his Word.[39] Ethical theology is then an attempt at the understanding of human life from the standpoint of this Word originally spoken by God. Dogmatic theology is the materially prior attempt to grasp this standpoint of the Word of God. The word "dogma" points us imperiously to this fact. Such translations as

---

37. *STh* II/2, 1, 1. Marginal note: "*Mel.* Apol. Art. 4 (Müller, p. 96!)." (*ChD,* p. 22, gives the quotation; cf. *BSLK,* p. 171.11-16; Tappert, p. 114.)

38. Second Helvetic Confession, II; see *BSRK,* p. 170.29-30; Schaff, p. 832.

39. Bavinck, I, p. 20: "our knowledge of God in dogmatics can be only an impress of the knowledge of himself that God has revealed to us in his Word."

"doctrine" or even "expression," "view," or the like do not really get its true sense. Whether referring to a philosophical, political, cultic, or theological dogma, the ancients always had in view a position that was necessary and could not be debated, a first principle that had certainly to be discovered and promulgated but that had not in any sense to be invented or established or validated. Even the most rigid orthodoxy has never contested the fact that in every dogma we have to distinguish between content and expression, between essence and form, between what is human and transitory on the one side, what is divine and eternal on the other. But this does not alter the possibility that there are dogmas, that there are in our own case standpoints and principles which are grounded in God's Word and which are therefore necessary. Theology betrays itself if, insisting on the word *doxa* (view or opinion), it denies this; if, after it has been historical theology and before it can become moral theology, it is not prepared consciously and expressly to be dogmatic theology.

Scientific dogmatics as distinct from dogma is the attempt to discover (note, not to establish or produce but to discover) these necessary standpoints. Earlier discoveries and promulgations will naturally demand its most attentive consideration, but even if the authority of the whole of the early church or of some specific church stands behind them, this will not prevent it from beginning its work again at the very beginning with no absolute presupposition apart from the Word of God in which dogmas are grounded and from which they necessarily follow. Only as reflection on God's Word can it really be the science of dogmas. This appeal to the highest court distinguishes it in principle from the history of dogmas, which considers their rise and history, and from symbolics, which deals with the dogmas confessed and acknowledged by the present-day churches. Because it investigates the principles which ought to enjoy authority throughout the church, it derives the scope of its investigation from the Author in whom alone this authority finds its legitimate source. The church and its decisions are not valid in or of themselves, no matter how old they are or how unanimously or solemnly they are proclaimed. Just as we found in respect of faith, their validity lies in their relation to him who can give authority because he has it. For the holy Christian church whose Head is Christ is born of God's Word, in which it also abides, and it hears not the voice of a stranger.[40] With this movement back to first principles, which dogmatics must make afresh with every step, the authority of its

---

40. Zwingli, in *BSRK,* p. 30.9-11 (Bern Theses, 1528, I); Schaff, p. 208.

statements stands or falls. With good insight into what dogmatics has to be as the science of dogmas, Kaftan has postulated that it has to relearn how to speak in an absolute tone.[41] True, Bavinck replied, but dogma and dogmatics cannot achieve these absolute tones in their own name or power, but only because and so far as they stand on the authority of God and can appeal to a *Deus dixit*. The weakness of dogmatics is precisely that it believes so little in this *Deus dixit*.[42]

III. Reflection on the Word of God

In a secondary introductory subsection I would like to say more explicitly what I mean by "reflection" on the Word of God. First, I must say something about the addition I have made to "Word of God" in the thesis of this first section: "which is spoken by God in revelation, which is recorded in the holy scripture of the prophets and apostles, and which now both is and should be proclaimed and heard in Christian preaching." You can see compressed in this addition all that I am trying to say this semester in the form of prolegomena to dogmatics. For this reason any supporting or expounding of the addition would anticipate my whole series. At this point I can only show logically and grammatically what is meant.

I am distinguishing the Word of God in a first address in which God himself and God alone is the speaker, in a second address in which it is the Word of a specific category of people (the prophets and apostles), and in a third address in which the number of its human agents or proclaimers is theoretically unlimited. But God's Word abides forever.[43] It neither is nor can be different whether it has its first, its second, or its third form, and always when it is one of the three it is also in some sense the other two as well. The Word of God on which dogmatics reflects — I need only refer to the common formula to show the point at issue — is one in three and three in one: revelation, scripture, and preaching — the Word of God as revelation, the Word of God as scripture, and the Word of God as preaching, neither to be confused nor separated. One Word of God, one authority, one power, and yet not one but three addresses. Three

---

41. Kaftan, p. 23.
42. Bavinck, I, p. 25.
43. Isa. 40:8; 1 Pet. 1:25.

addresses of God in revelation, scripture, and preaching, yet not three Words of God, three authorities, truths, or powers, but one. Scripture is not revelation, but from revelation. Preaching is not revelation or scripture, but from both. But the Word of God is scripture no less than it is revelation, and it is preaching no less than it is scripture. Revelation is from God alone, scripture is from revelation alone, and preaching is from revelation and scripture. Yet there is no first or last, no greater or less. The first, the second, and the third are all God's Word in the same glory, unity in trinity and trinity in unity. I will not go on to say with the Athanasian Creed that those who would be saved must think thus of the Trinity,[44] for as yet I have only said and not shown that this is so and why it is so. But I think that this statement, which must simply stand until it can be confirmed[45] or not in the course of our discussion, will be enough to show what I have in mind when I call the object of the reflection which is the dogmatic task the Word of God.

I must add two observations. (a) At this third point I have tried to indicate that God's Word is to be regarded as a living, actual, and present factor, the Word of God which now both is and should be proclaimed and heard. Now! Should be! Note in these expressions first of all the movement, the qualified temporal element, the turning from past to present denoted by them. The Word of God is God's speaking. It is ongoing as Christian preaching. It is not ongoing as revelation in the strict sense. It never took place as such. The statement "God revealed himself" means something different from the statement "revelation took place." Revelation is what it is in time, but as the frontier of time, remote from us as heaven is from earth. Nor is God's Word ongoing as holy scripture. It is in time as such. It took place as the witness given to revelation. But in itself it is a self-enclosed part of history which is as far from us as everything historical and past. Our experiences are not a continuation of those of the prophets and apostles. Theoretically one might declare the continuation of the biblical canon to be possible (e.g., if two lost epistles to the Corinthians were found again, or if an ecumenical council received the *Didache* into the NT). But this would not be an ongoing of scripture, only an extension of the concept of scripture, or of what the concept

---

44. Athanasian Creed: "And in this Trinity none is afore, or after other; none is greater, or less than another . . . the Unity in Trinity, and the Trinity in Unity . . . He therefore that will be saved, must thus think of the Trinity."

45. Barth uses *erwahren* here in the sense of *bestätigen*.

means. All conceivable extensions of scripture would still belong to the past, not to the present. They would not be a step out of the past into the future. But as Christian preaching, which proceeds from revelation and scripture (as the Holy Spirit proceeds from the Father and the Son),[46] the Word of God is ongoing. It is present. Naturally, in, with, and under Christian preaching, revelation and scripture are present too, but not otherwise. In this regard we are not restricting the term "Christian preaching" to sermons from the pulpit, or to the work of pastors, but including in it whatever we all "preach" to ourselves in the quiet of our own rooms. The only point is that outwardly or inwardly this must be a speaking, a mediated addressing and hearing of the Word of God from revelation and scripture. It is on account of Christian preaching, the Word of God today, that we take up the question of the Word of God and that theology in general and dogmatics in particular are a concern. It is from Christian preaching that we recognize God's Word and for the sake of it that we must recognize it, for there is no knowledge here that does not immediately and once again have to become recognition, a relearning from the very beginning. It is also Christian preaching that constitutes the office of the theologian, not as the mastery of human words over God but as the service rendered to God's own Word, the ministry of the Word of God. This is where we shall have to start in § 2, which will bring us closer to the heart of the matter.

(b) What follows for dogma and dogmatics from our concept of God's Word as one and threefold? First and very plainly some forceful negations. Dogma and dogmatics are not in any event either revelation or scripture, not even the most generally accepted dogma (e.g., the existence of God) or the best and most brilliant dogmatics, not even when they quote biblical texts, for holy scripture in the strict sense is the totality of the prophetic and apostolic witness and not a single text as such, not even the text that "God is love" [1 John 4:8] or the like. Insofar as they are not, they are not God's Word, and in principle they are thus of a lower rank. Dogma and dogmatics, apart from what they are as such, may also be Christian preaching. Thus the reciting of the Apostles' Creed in worship, where it still takes place, is undoubtedly meant also as a constituent part of liturgical kerygma, not as this alone, but also as this. And a dogmatics which along with its specific aim does not also function as Christian preaching is an extremely God-forsaken dogmatics. But as such

---

46. Cf. the clause added to the Nicene Creed in the West in A.D. 589.

dogma and dogmatics are not Christian preaching and therefore they are not God's Word. "An article of faith is a *perception* of the divine truth, to which it tends," according to the definition of Thomas.[47]

What, then, are dogma and dogmatics? Obviously their dignity, significance, and role are derived and therefore critical. We have already seen and shown that a dogma is a principle or viewpoint that is born of God's Word and won from it. Over against the triune Word of God it is thus a second and independent thing, a human word which lives only in relation to the first thing and which is thus unquestionably secondary. As a human word it is qualified by that relation. Hence it is not a human opinion or a symbol of things that are humanly inexpressible. It is a symbol that has been set up because God has spoken something definite. Yet it is still a symbol (you are aware that this is the term the churches use for their confessional summaries), a human word and not God's own Word, neither revelation nor scripture nor (as dogma) preaching. As a human word it stands unconditionally under the caveat and shadow and even the judgment of God's Word. In relation to its dogma, the church both rightly and necessarily maintains a certain final reserve. "I beg you, where I have not understood aright the scripture that I treat of here, to help me to a better understanding, but from the same scripture," is Zwingli's plea when he promulgates the 67 Articles in 1523.[48] This reservation with regard to dogma, which frequently occurs in Reformed confessions, is grounded in the matter itself and must be established already at this point.

But what is the point of this secondary thing? What is the point of dogma? What is the point of the church's enterprise that we call *dogmatizein,* dogmatics — the effort to establish dogmas, the principles and viewpoints that arise necessarily from God's Word? Dogma and dogmatics are obviously not necessary for God's Word as revelation and scripture, for the eternal Word or the Word of past testimony. They are necessary for the ongoing and living Word, for Christian preaching. This is a gift and task. We can have a responsible part in it, and we are theologians for this reason. Christian preaching is also a human act which has constantly to be performed. We cannot perform this act without reflection: What is Christian preaching, and what, then, is God's Word? Dogma, and dogmatics as its ongoing discovery, give us guidance and direction as we answer the question of this "what." They set up border-

---

47. *STh* IIa, IIae, q. 1, a. 6 sed contra (quoting Isidore of Seville).
48. *BSRK,* p. 2.13-18.

posts and anchor buoys. They tell us what will do and what will not do, what we may say and what we may not say if what we say is to be Christian preaching. They do so, not for any reasons, and not finally out of regard for the spirit of a given time, but on account of the command of God[49] from which they themselves come. If I may take a not wholly congruent parallel from political life, dogma and dogmatics do not represent the legislative branch (which is God's Word) or the executive branch (the church as the bearer of the kerygma) but the judicial branch, the supreme court. As a critical authority dogma and dogmatics stand above Christian preaching, which may not escape their service (not their lordship) insofar as preaching is a human act that needs a norm. Yet they also stand under it, for they have their origin in it and must yield to it as the moon does to the sun insofar as preaching, proceeding from revelation and scripture, is itself God's Word. We shall have to come back to this twofold relation between dogmatics and preaching in § 2. In what has been said we have at least provisionally shown how they belong together in principle and what their purposes are.

IV. Conclusion

We may conclude with some specific statements about the theme of the semester. I have called it *prolegomena* to dogmatics. Others usually give to the discussions attempted here, or those like them, the title "Dogmatics I." They then establish the dogmas — or however else they may formulate the task — as "Dogmatics II," something which I myself plan to spread over two courses.

The fact that an introduction to dogmatics is generally regarded as necessary, at times in the form of a so-called philosophy of religion, is a symptom that we do not live in a classical age of theology. A science needs prolegomena when it is no longer sure of its presuppositions, when it has to reach agreement on them, when it has to work at showing with what right and with what means it can do what it wants to do, when it does not any longer, or, more hopefully put, when it does not yet understand the self-evident things with which any science commences. Of the 611 *quaestiones* of his *Summa theologica* Thomas Aquinas devoted only one to a discussion of sacred doctrine as such. With qu. 2

---

49. Quoting Bavinck, I, p. 5.

he plunged into the middle of things under the heading "The Existence of God." Melanchthon, Zwingli, and Calvin acted similarly. They were so sure of their cause that they hardly thought it worth the effort to devote more than a few pages to the concept and method of their science. To the extent that theologians increasingly lost sight of their theme and became unsure of their cause, beginning the tragic retreat which in the theology of Schleiermacher ended with total capitulation, there flourished introductions, prolegomena, debates about scripture, inspiration, revelation, miracles, religion, and reason, and apologetic efforts to establish and justify the discipline and its theme. Not for nothing it was Schleiermacher who wrote the most famous and indeed the classical introduction to doctrine.[50] This is an enterprise that necessarily arises out of the situation in which theology, and especially Protestant theology, finds itself. The less people have to say, the more zealously they must *pro-legein,* that is, precede what they should really say with excuses and explanations and adjustments. It is not that as individuals modern theologians are wanting in faith, or that they have not plunged deeply into the Bible or the confessions, when the poverty of their witness comes to expression in their need for prolegomena. The theologians of the 19th century who took the path of repristination had no less need of *pro-legein* than those who took the path of speculation and mediation. Even a J. T. Beck, whom one cannot accuse of any real lack of directness or of any conscious assimilation to the spirit of the time, regarded it as necessary to write an *Einleitung in das System der Christlichen Lehre oder Propädeutische Entwicklung der Christlichen Lehr-Wissenschaft.*[51] The rise of what is called religious philosophy, in which both right-wing and left-wing theologians took part with the same zeal, is simply another manifestation of the same need and concern.

This is a situation that no one can escape. I myself neither can nor wish to do so. We can none of us simply reverse the change that came about in Protestant theology around 1600 and act like a Thomas or a Calvin. We are not allowed to imagine that we are at another point in history, and inevitably such imaginings can never be more than that. We adjust under protest, but we still adjust. This is my view. I know that among modern dogmaticians Schlatter, following the classical model with no such imaginings, jumps headlong into the development of dogmatics

---

50. *Cf.* §§ 1-31.
51. Cf. n. 26 above.

after only two short introductory sections.[52] But I have my own reasons for not following his example. In my opinion dogmatics must be teaching as well as doctrine. It must be part of a conversation; it must be open to discussion. This is not true of Schlatter's dogmatics even though it has many great advantages which are perhaps connected with this. In my view Schlatter's dogmatics is like his exegesis. Those who are not ready to stay by him through thick and thin will probably be thrown off on the very first page, neither hearing nor seeing, and as the racehorse gallops away they may watch it with respect and astonishment but they will not really learn anything. If I am right, we are not yet ready for this method.

My own position with regard to it is this. We are obviously today at a great distance from the origin and theme of dogma and dogmatics. If in spite of this we venture on a dogmatics, we must accept the fact, second-rate and decadent though it may undoubtedly be, that instead of drawing straight *from* the subject we must first speak *about* the subject, reaching an understanding with those to whom we speak (or for whom we write) about the point from which we are doing dogmatics, the meaning of the enterprise, and the way in which we are doing it. This does not mean that we are doing apologetics like the older or more recent supernaturalists, or that we are borrowing principles from a philosophy of culture as Schleiermacher did,[53] or that with many modern thinkers we are discussing the essence or truth of the Christian religion,[54] or the essence of religion, or the essence of Christianity,[55] or that we want to be numbered among the so-called religious philosophers. I propose to do none of these things. After what I have said in the first subsection of § 1 you will not expect me to do so.

But I want to say something by way of reply about why I think of dogmatics as I do. Our task is not simply to present dogmatics or to listen to it. We have to study dogmatics together. And for us today, as things now are, that also means that we have first to work back to a point where *dogmatizein* is possible. And if we cannot accept as a basis this resignation to the plight of the age whose children we are, then we are free to edify and to console ourselves with the thought of Kant, whose prolegomena to a future metaphysics that might take the form of a science were first a

---

52. A. Schlatter, *Das christliche Dogma;* the first main section follows after § 1 on the subject and § 2 on the arrangement.

53. Cf. the first three main sections of the Introduction to *CF* (cf. n. 50 above).

54. Cf. Haering, pp. 25ff., 64ff., ET pp. 35ff.

55. Cf. Nitzsch-Stephan, pp. 72ff., 139ff.

testimony to the poverty that he found in philosophy (or that philosophy made apparent through him), but then also a demand that all who might take up metaphysics would begin their work by regarding all that had previously happened as though it had not happened, and first raise the question whether metaphysics was possible at all.[56] No matter how we take it, this was certainly not a second-rate or decadent statement, but a fruitful and forward-looking and decisive one. Dogmatics, too, needs a Kant that will bear a final witness to its poverty and at the same time produce the decisive prolegomenon that will make all prolegomena superfluous, as they were for a Paul or a Luther. But it is self-deception to think that they are superfluous for us, and we are not going to be guilty of this self-deception.

The content of these lectures I have already mentioned in discussing the main concept "the Word of God." I propose to devote three chapters to revelation, scripture, and Christian preaching, and by means of these concepts I hope to make plain to you what are the theme or origin, the concept or necessity, and the way or method of dogmatics. There are some books and lectures on dogmatics in which, under the heading of prolegomena or introduction, a more or less express history of dogmatics is offered, for example, in Hase's Hutter redivivus, the dogmatics of Luthardt and of Ebrard, the primer of F. Nitzsch (Stephan), and the *Gereformeerde Dogmatiek* of Bavinck, while H. H. Wendt is content to give a list of books arranged according to the different periods and movements.[57] We for our part cannot think that the latter method is enough, but in my view the former represents a separate scientific task — a good one and a beautiful one, but one that I cannot trust myself to discharge in passing.

As regards your private study of dogmatics, I cannot advise you to begin with modern writers. Even though you may later decide to go along with the great Schleiermacherian revolution which characterizes almost all modern dogmatics, my urgent recommendation is that you should know what you are doing when you take this course, having first learned and considered the unreconstructed dogmatics of the older writers, for example, the medieval dogmatics of Bonaventura (Breviloquium), the reformation dogmatics of Melanchthon, Zwingli, and Calvin, and the dog-

---

56. I. Kant, *Prolegomena zu einer jeden künftigen Metaphysik, die als Wissenschaft wird auftreten können* (1783), in *Gesammelte Schriften*, IV (Berlin, 1911), p. 255.

57. Hase, Locus III, §§ 19-27; Luthardt, pp. 24-58; J. H. Ebrard, *Christliche Dogmatik*, 2 vols. (Königsberg, 2nd ed. 1862, 3rd ed. 1863), I, pp. 44-115; Nitzsch-Stephan, pp. 21-63; Bavinck, I, pp. 90-179; H. H. Wendt, pp. 8-11.

matics of orthodoxy as collected by Schweizer or Heppe in the case of the Reformed, Hase or Heinrich Schmid in the case of the Lutherans.[58] In a second introductory section I myself must first say something more about the special relation between dogmatics and that with which my whole train of thought will culminate, namely, preaching.

---

58. On the *Breviloquium* see n. 5 above. On Melanchthon, see *Loci communes* (1521), in Melanchthon's *Werke in Auswahl,* II/1, ed. H. Engelland (Gütersloh, 1952), pp. 163ff.; ET LCC, XIX (Philadelphia, 1969), pp. 18ff.; also *Loci praecipui theologici* (1559); *Werke in Auswahl,* II/1, pp. 164-352, II/2, 353-780. On Zwingli see n. 21 above. On Calvin, see *Institutes.* On the Reformed, see Schweizer; Heppe; Heppe-Bizer. On the Lutherans, see Hase; Schmid; or Schmid-Pöhlmann.

§ 2

Preaching as the Starting Point
and Goal of Dogmatics

The divine address to which dogmatics reflection must relate directly is preaching, that is, the proclamation of the Christian church which has its basis in revelation and scripture. This reflection is twofold. It involves first the hearing of the Word of God which is actually spoken in this proclamation, and it then involves the task of truly speaking the Word of God in this proclamation. Both take place as we work back from preaching itself to the underlying scripture and revelation. Dogmatics is the methodical execution of this movement. The theses that are established in the process are dogmas. A dogma achieves symbolical status when the church or one of the churches publicly recognizes it.

I. The Point of Dogmatics

In § 1.II we tried to understand dogmatics as the science of dogmas, that is, as investigation of the basic statements that are grounded in God's Word and that proceed from it. But what is the point of dogma or dogmatics? We already asked this question in § 1.III. We must return to it and to the answer we then gave. This answer related dogma and dogmatics to Christian preaching, and to this preaching as in the first instance a human act. The question of valid principles obviously has as its presupposition the presence and expression of theses and groups of theses that both deserve and need to be traced back to norms. This phenomenon of Christian *speaking*, whether by Christianity, in its name, for its extension or establishment, or however

23

we might put it, is as it were the *raw stuff* of dogma and dogmatics. As such it is our methodological starting point. Phenomenologically, the origin and meaning of dogmatics is the fact that there is talk either by the Christian church or, as we might put it more cautiously for the time being, in the Christian church. The Christian church begins by listening to the address of the prophets and apostles, which was not babbled, or mimed, or put to music, or danced, but spoken and written in statements and groups of statements. Why precisely *this* specific address? Not for its own sake nor for the sake of its bearers, the prophets and apostles, but because in and through it the church thinks it perceives another address, that is, revelation, and through the kerygma, through the revelation perceived in the kerygma, the Word of God. It adopts this address, the original kerygma, not mechanically, not repetitively in simple copying or recitation — this also takes place and at the right point it has its own significance — but primarily by its own responsible thinking and speaking, not passively but actively as it sends out the original witness as its own witness.

To be sure, the church is also a fellowship of spirit and of faith. It is a fellowship with a distinctive orientation, a fellowship of the sacrament. But what always makes it the church, what distinguishes it from any other fellowship of faith and spirit and distinctive orientation and sacrament, is the vital link between this very specific hearing and making heard, the Word which it receives and passes on. To generate faith God has instituted the preaching office, giving the gospel and the sacrament, so that through them as means he might give the Holy Spirit, who works when and where he wills in those who hear the gospel.[1] Yet the preaching office that God has instituted is still a historical, human, conditioned entity. The instruments that are put in its hands, the audible and the visible Word, are still a human word, with the implied concealment of the divinely posited reality. When the church receives the Word, the question has to arise: To what extent is the address that takes place in Christian preaching identical with the address that took place through the prophets and apostles, with the revelation that gave rise to the prophetic and apostolic kerygma? To what extent is it the *Word of God?*

This is where dogma and dogmatics come in. For reflection is necessary here, an investigation of the meaning or concealed reality within the very ambiguous phenomenon of Christian speech. As an earthly entity, as human action (which it also is), Christian preaching cannot evade the

---

1. Augsburg Confession, Art. 5, in *BSLK,* p. 17.2-7; Tappert, p. 31.

task of this reflection, just as the rhetorician Gorgias cannot evade the questioning of Plato's Socrates.[2] The Christian rhetorician might also be a Gorgias. He is at least under orders to consider each Saturday whether he might not be a Gorgias. The question arises then, and is put to all human action as such: Do you know what you are doing? Only in subjection to this earthly necessity, only in the process of reflection on what we are doing, can we discover justification for the glory of our action and above all a new and better mandate for it. The action that comes into question is Christian speaking. I emphasize, Christian *speaking*. This is where *dogmatizein* begins. To the degree that the Christian church is something other than the fellowship of hearing and speaking God's Word,[3] to the degree that it is, for example, a free society of like-minded souls, to the degree that it participates more or less adequately in all kinds of educational and cultural work, to the degree that it includes in its activity the sacred dance and reverent silence, the mystery play and the Christ or Luther film, it still cannot escape the task of reflection, and it must take note how this turns out. But it does not need dogma and dogmatics, for *this* reflection relates to the Christian church to the degree that it can and should intend to *speak*. Dogmatics is very specifically reflection on this speaking with reference to the Word of God, namely, how far the Word of God is, or is meant to be, identical with it.

You will realize that this definition of the stuff of dogmatics differs somewhat from what you might read or hear elsewhere, and I suspect that it might at first be rather strange to you. It seems to be more in accord with the modern need for immediacy to begin with the pious consciousness of Schleiermacher,[4] or the inner life of Herrmann that is freed by encounter with an overpowering fact,[5] and to work these statements into a system. It seems to be more Christian to plunge with Frank into the experience of regeneration and conversion in the well-meant hope that this will lead to the theology of the Formula of Concord (which in our case might be the theology of Dort),[6] or to plunge with J. T. Beck into the substance of

---

2. The edition of Plato's *Gorgias* used by Barth was that of O. Apelt, in PhB, 148 (Leipzig, 1914).

3. Marginal note: "It is! 1 Cor. 12; Rom. 12!"

4. *Cf.* §§ 3, 6, etc.

5. W. Herrmann, *Christlich-protestantische Dogmatik,* in W. Herrmann, *Schriften zur Grundlegung der Theologie,* ed. P. Fischer-Appelt, ThB, 36 (Munich, 1966), I, pp. 340, 346.

6. For the text of Dort cf. *BSRK,* pp. 843-61; Schaff, pp. 581ff. Cf. F. H. R.

Christian doctrine which has made its way into us as a spiritual possession, which has become dynamically immanent, and which is to be raised up from faith to knowledge.[7] It seems to be more comprehensive to look with A. Schweizer at the believing consciousness of the Christian church as its subjective appropriation of what it is objectively offered,[8] and richer and more exciting to divide revelation with Troeltsch[9] into three elements: (a) the primitive classical period and the personality of Jesus; (b) the ongoing revelation of historical development that one might call tradition; and (c) the present experience in which what is handed down historically becomes inner revelation in a new way by individual and personal appropriation, that is, present illumination and experience. And it seems to be most cosmic and liberating to read what Schlatter says when he points out that "the field that dogmatic work has to traverse is as broad as God's revelatory action. We are oriented to the *totality. All* the divine action that embraces and determines our consciousness demands our attention, both *nature* and Christ, both *abnormal* processes and normal. The concept of God contains directly the thesis that *all* being relates to God and manifests his power and will in some way. *Nothing* is totally insignificant, then, for those who stand before the question of God. The more God's working may be seen by us in *all things,* the richer is the content of our concept of God, and the surer its basis."[10]

If by contrast I find in preaching a direct point of contact for dogmatic reflection, in the preaching that we may or must hear and that we ought to engage in, I sympathize with you if at first you probably think that this is paltry or clerical or intellectualistic. In favor of this definition I would advance four considerations.

A first argument for it is that the construction of dogma and dogmatics today and for us must be done at root only as it has always been done in history. It would simply not be true to maintain that in the 2nd, 4th, and 16th centuries dogma arose as some pious feeling or consciousness of faith made statements about itself as a volcano throws out lava or the sea mussels, simply to express or represent or impart itself from

---

Frank, *System der christlichen Wahrheit,* 2nd ed. (Erlangen, 1885), p. 1; ET *System of Christian Certainty* (Edinburgh, 1886), p. 1.

7. J. T. Beck, *Einleitung in das System der christlichen Lehre,* pp. 8-9.

8. A. Schweizer, *Die Christliche Glaubenslehre,* I, § 18, p. 60.

9. Heidelberg lectures "Dogmatik I" of 1908, p. 82. Cf. also E. Troeltsch, *Glaubenslehre . . .* (Munich/Leipzig, 1925), p. 20.

10. A. Schlatter, *Das christliche Dogma,* pp. 13-14. The italics (except the first) reflect Barth's underlinings.

the standpoint: "I believe and therefore I speak" [cf. 2 Cor. 4:13]. Such statements, which might include those of Beck about the substance of doctrine, or those of Troeltsch about threefold revelation, or Schlatter's concept of God that relates him to all being, would then have taken the knotty form of constructs like the Nicene Creed, the Formula of Concord, or the Confession of Dort, whereas we today would have to adopt different forms more suited to our own day. A view of this kind would at best do justice only to the genesis of Christian *preaching* (its historical and psychological genesis, of course). But in no case can dogma be viewed genetically as merely a spontaneous, unrelated production of faith or of the thoughts of faith. Its presupposition is the fact of preaching, of different kinds of preaching, so that the question has arisen in the church that there might be on the one hand a preaching that is pure and correct and true, and on the other hand a preaching that is muddied and perverted and false. Agreement on what is true and false, the principle by which to understand God's Word, is dogma, which Basil in the 4th century was already distinguishing explicitly from the kerygma, that is, from preaching.[11] Dogma is the critical court which confronts the believing or superstitious "statements" of preaching — to accept this for a moment. Dogma is not itself a "statement" but a decision about statements, their norm. This is why it takes such a strictly dialectical form (obscure and hairsplitting, as people usually say when they do not grasp what it is all about). This is why it rightly leaves an impression of contentiousness and rigidity (things that the church needs in its economy at a certain point!).

The same applies to dogmatics. As a free presentation of faith or revelation, as a "statement" about God or the miracles of the inner life, a dogmatics of 600 pages with chapters and sections and definitions and deductions — for heaven's sake, what kind of a monstrosity do dogmaticians think they are! But as scientific reflection on Christian speaking, as a service that is rendered to this greater and freer and more natural activity, preparing and guiding and regulating it, so that it does not lose its own proper point, dogmatics can pass muster, for it can accept with humor the taint of scholasticism that clings to the concept of dogmatics. In my view an objection to the above-mentioned definitions of dogmatics is that they sever the connection with earlier dogmatic work, so that we cannot understand them in the light of dogmatic history. I for my part, relating dogmatics to preaching, want to *restore* that connection.

---

11. Basil of Caesarea, *De Spiritu Sancto*, XXVII, § 66, SC, 17, p. 236.

Second, my proposal has the further advantage that no long inquiry is now needed into the stuff of dogma and dogmatics. The statements and groups of statements on which dogmaticians reflect and which they have to reduce to theses are already given, whether they be good or bad, Protestant or Roman Catholic, liberal or orthodox, appropriate or inappropriate. Preaching goes on from pulpits and in the streets, oral and written. We can never complain of[12] any lack of raw material of this kind, and those who live in isolation may listen to themselves with a fine sense of awe, like Schleiermacher.[13] The work of reflection on the Word of God in all this Christian tumult, the work of establishing principles in the ocean of unfounded statements which is all around us and in which they are one of the waves — this is the work that dogmaticians must do. But it is not their task as such to ensure that in it all there is an echo of the first kerygma, and in this kerygma an echo of revelation, no matter how confused and distorted it might sound. Dogmaticians are working on something given when they reflect on God's Word. What is given is the wonderful song of praise of the Christian church as we may hear it each dear Sunday or even each weekday.

This unconditional presence of the material I regard as an advantage of my definition over the others quoted. The pious consciousness of Schleiermacher, or the inner life of Herrmann, or the experience of regeneration in Frank, or the believing experience of the Evangelical Church in Schweizer, or the threefold revelation of Troeltsch, or the relation of God to all being that Schlatter so finely and truly describes — I have nothing against these, but I think that if we are referred to them, then as dogmaticians we might be left pitifully in the lurch on more than one day in the year, for the pious consciousness is not by a long way as communicative as appears in Schleiermacher, and God's revelatory work in all things is not so evident as one might conclude from the words of Schlatter. How can we arrive at fundamental theses if we finally have no theses to begin with? In particular the richness of what Troeltsch calls present illumination and experience seems suspiciously to leave a great deal wanting. But the Christian church does speak; there can be no doubt about that. Once we turn to this, material for reflection is truly present. It is superabundant. There is too much of it.

---

12. Barth has *an* here; the editor corrects it to *über.*
13. Barth is alluding to Schleiermacher's *Monologen;* cf. PhB, 84 (Leipzig, 1902), p. 7; ET *Soliloquies* (Chicago, 1926), pp. 10ff.

The third advantage of my proposal is that one can see at once what is the point of dogma and dogmatics quite apart from making a confession merely for the sake of a confession. Why is there this concern to express scientifically the so-called statements of faith? Why does there have to be a confession? Much appeal is made to the need to think, but is this an adequate reason for dogmatizing? I have yet to see anyone whose need to think is satisfied by the offerings of dogma and dogmatics! Are not the unused dogmatic notebooks which gather dust in, I wager, almost every manse an eloquent proof that even serious and zealous theologians (not to speak of nontheologians) do not know what to make of the dogmatic work that was once done for them and directed to them. Why not? Because they do not see to what it relates, to what it should constantly relate. Things would be different if the material of dogmatics were identical with their own material, but from the standpoint of what it ought to be; if the material to which dogmatics relates as reflection on God's Word were preaching, not the preaching that we hear but the preaching that we want to give or ought to give. The church speaks, and it is a serious question (never settled) whether it is speaking correctly, whether all this Christian talk is to the point, especially when (through understanding or misunderstanding, through human folly or divine providence or both) people are forced to engage in Christian speaking. What is meaningful here and what is meaningless? What should we say and what for God's sake should we not say? What can we do, and what can we avoid, so as not at least to get in the way of God's Word with our own word? Homiletics does not provide the answer to this truly practical rather than academic question. Dogmatics does. What is needed is the discovery of basic principles, and to find these by way of reflection on the Word of God is the work of dogmaticians.

The fourth advantage that I claim for giving dogmatics a twofold relation to preaching is that it avoids a misunderstanding that we do not find in the theology of the Reformation or the early church, namely, that dogmatics burdens the consciences of Christians with propositions that they have to believe, or accept as true, if they are to be saved — a possibility against which the whole zeal of especially W. Herrmann's theology was directed,[14] and the contesting of which today is the true religious nerve

---

14. Cf. W. Herrmann, *Der Verkehr des Christen mit Gott* (1886), 4th ed. (Stuttgart/Berlin, 1903), pp. 180ff.; ET *Communion with God* (New York, 1906), pp. 214ff.; idem, *Ethik* (1901), 4th ed. (Tübingen, 1909), pp. 99ff.

in the theology of Paul Tillich, which is anti-orthodox at all costs.[15] This whole assault, which has some justification insofar as dogmatics really claims to represent the orthodox Christian faith, becomes pointless once dogmatics is set soberly and objectively in relation to preaching. Dogma and dogmatics cannot be a matter of telling people (even theologians!) what they must believe. The Word of God saves, not faith. If dogma is made a norm for believers,[16] as it has almost inconceivably been regarded from the very earliest theology, then the relation is reversed, and faith is stamped as a saving work. This ought not to be. For this reason I must still follow my teacher Herrmann in this regard, and even give unconditional assent to Tillich.

Yet recollection of the genesis of dogma has led us to look at things differently. Dogma does not relate to faith but to what faith says. It does not lay down what faith has to say. The question of the "what" is far too serious to be answered by rules. Preaching is not the same as dogma. But in order to be correct teaching, pure dogma, it rests on reflection, and there can be no reflection without the recognition of basic principles. These principles are not to be adopted or accepted with a sacrifice of the intellect. They are to be known; we are to know them, to recognize them for ourselves. This is why we study dogmatics and not just symbolics. But in this case the objection to dogma, dogmatics, and orthodoxy falls away. It can exist only when theologians, like almost all modern theologians, do not see the particular place in the whole economy where these things belong, where they cannot cast that feared shadow, but where they have their own right and necessity along the lines just described.

II. Preaching

Partly to explain and partly to sharpen the focus I must add a recollection to what has just been said. Christian preaching is the point to which dogmatics must be directly related because in it, as already established in § 1.III, we are to see God's address now, today. This thesis, on which the other rests, is not self-evident, least of all at the present time and for us.

---

15. Cf. P. Tillich, *Rechtfertigung und Zweifel* (1924), in *Gesammelte Werke*, VIII, ed. R. Albrecht (Stuttgart, 1970), pp. 85-100, esp. pp. 88 and 97.

16. On this expression cf. *ChD*, p. 52 n. 36; Schmid-Pöhlmann, p. 74; Schmid ET pp. 92ff.

II. Preaching

It has now become a most unusual consideration, common only in the language of edification, to say that people go to church to hear God's Word — no, they go to hear Pastor So-and-So — or to say of the pastor that his task is to proclaim God's Word — no, it is to offer his expositions, meditations, applications, and demands! I need hardly say that the devastating lack of tension and dynamic, the lukewarm tediousness and irrelevance of Protestant worship, is closely connected with the disappearance of this consideration. The lack might be concealed or reduced by good preachers, but let us not be deceived: the ship is leaking even though the best preachers might be at the pumps. There is no lack of good preachers and sermons, but a lack of sermons that are meant to be God's Word and are received as such — a lack of *qualified* preaching.

The best preaching is as such an equivalent to the kerygma that the Roman Catholic church offers every day in the form of the sacrament of the altar. According to the conscious and universal view of this church, that sacrament is the living Word of God today, the daily renewal, presentation, and offering of what took place at Golgotha. We might regard it as an aberration from the true line of the Christian church that sacramental action as the bearer of God's Word should crowd into the background in this way the personal, oral, responsible witness to the truth. But we have the right to protest against it only if our own pastors and their congregations are swayed by the consideration that the Word of God is at issue in that which the Reformers put in place of the sacrament of the altar. Again, we might object that extreme unction is materialistic, that it is sacramental magic, but it is at any rate intended and regarded as word, as a true and powerful self-proffering of God, and friendly religious sayings in the same situation, being meant only as such, are a poor substitute for it. If the presupposition is lacking, the advantage of Roman Catholicism is *unmistakable*. The sacrament as the visible Word of God[17] is simply more and better than the finest or most eloquent Protestant address as such if it does not have this character. If the call for more liturgy that is being sounded in our churches simply means that Handel's Largo must be listed among the Protestant means of grace, or that with almost shameless modesty we drop the sermon for the Paradise Play,[18] because these

---

17. Cf. Augustine, *Faustum Man.* 19, 16; CSEL, 25, 513.
18. Cf. *Spiel vom Sündenfall. Paradeisspiel aus Oberufer bei Pressburg 14. Jahrhundert*, ed. K. J. Schröer (Leipzig, 1917). For what Barth has in view cf. B. K. Röttger, "Gesungene Dichtung," *CW* 38 (1924) 518.

have at least as much or more to say than the pastor with his sermons, is not all this a by no means silent and even a very loud admission that with its loss or forgetting of God's Word Israel is conceding the victory [1 Sam. 4:10-11]? Perhaps Roman Catholicism will have to make progress in other ways — and there are signs that it is doing so — before the modern Protestant churches see clearly this cancerous sore, the unqualified nature of their proclamation.

Naturally, none of us has the power to restore this consideration merely by bold assertion. We can do only three things. (1) We can try to see the problem, to awake from the strange delusion of our slumbers that things can go on in this way, not to let ourselves be lulled by the opinion that we can be helped by good sermons or what is substituted for them. (2) We can try to deal with the prejudices that stand in the way of the consideration that preaching is and ought to be the Word of God. (3) We can see and hear what is to be seen and heard along the lines of this equation and act accordingly. I will not return to the problem.

As regards the prejudices, the most important is the question whether equation of preaching and God's Word is not itself an aberration from Protestantism, a catholicizing transmuting of the divine into something material, finite, and human. To this I reply: On the contrary, the Reformation orientation which took precisely this direction the most sharply, the church of Zwingli and Calvin, maintained this equation loudly and definitely from the very outset. The preaching of God's Word *is* God's Word; this is how the heading of the second section of the Second Helvetic Confession runs, and it then goes on to say that whenever God's Word is proclaimed in the churches by regularly called preachers, we believe that *God's* Word is proclaimed and is received by believers. No one, then, should either invent another Word of God or expect one from heaven.[19] The parallel Lutheran statement is that of J. Gerhard, who says that it is one and the same Word of God whether it be presented to us in spoken or written form.[20] From this confident assertion may we not at least ask whether there are not words which, although they are human words and mere words like any others, are also more than that on account of the knowledge or recognition to which they lead, on account of their impar-

---

19. Bullinger's *Bekanntnuss Dess waaren Gloubens unnd einfalte erlüterung der rachten allgemeinen Leer uñ houptarticklen der reinen Christenlichen Religion . . .* (Zurich, 1566), p. 1; ET Schaff, p. 832.

20. Schmid, p. 20; Schmid-Pöhlmann, p. 42; Schmid ET p. 41.

tation of truth from one person to another. The fact that they are human does not entail a humanizing of the divine. From the very first Protestantism has involved a belief that the Logos takes human shape in spoken human words. It has always reckoned with this possibility. That is beyond question. If some do not recognize the word that is spoken today as such, they are not following the Reformers but the Baptists, and they should ask themselves whether, with their rejection of God's Word in preaching, they are not secretly denying it in holy scripture and revelation as well.

But, some might say, how can we theologians come to speak God's Word in *our* words? Or, some congregation might say, how can we come to hear God's Word in the words of this or that pastor who has nothing to offer us, or in the words of all pastors, none of whom we trust? The answer to the theologians is that precisely with the question the possibility of a right answer comes into view if they are serious, if they are not just trying to evade the issue, and it is in order to seek this answer that they should study dogmatics among other things. And the answer to the public may again be put in the words of the Second Helvetic when it says that we should have regard to the Word that is proclaimed and not to the ministers who proclaim it. These may well be wicked and sinners, but the Word of God is still true and good.[21] If we expected to hear God's Word more, we would hear it more even in weak and perverted sermons. The statement that there was nothing in it for me should often read that I was not ready to let anything be said to me. What is needed here is repentance by *both* pastors and congregations.

But the question then arises: Why specifically is the church's preaching God's Word? Might not other human voices proclaim this Word too, and do they not do so by common experience? Does not God speak through *nature* too, through *history,* through Handel's Largo and all kinds of good *art?* And can we say that God does not speak directly to people today? No, we cannot, is the obvious answer. As Calvin says,[22] God is not tied to such aids or such inferior means, and as the East Frisian preachers, who were deeply affected by this conviction, say similarly,[23] God's work is not tied to ours. As we have already said, nothing stands in the way of taking the idea of preaching broadly, more broadly than Bullinger and Calvin did. The general breakup of the Christian body simply compels us to do so today. If I were to say that God's Word may be heard only in the

---

21. *Bekanntnuss Dess waaren Gloubens,* p. 1; ET Schaff, p. 832.
22. Gallican Confession, Art. 25, in *BSRK,* p. 228.1-2; ET Schaff, p. 374.
23. 1528 Confession, Art. 6, in *BSRK,* p. 931.10-11.

preaching of a regularly inducted pastor in an official Reformed church, this would be narrow-minded. I would thus strike out the "only" and say that I accept the preaching of the Reformed church first, but also that of the Lutheran, United, and Methodist churches, and I expect to hear God's Word as well from the Irvingites, the Christian Catholics, and the Salvation Army. I am also glad to have heard God's Word in Roman Catholic preaching. I will open my ears wide to be convinced that God's Word might even come through voices that belong to no church, that are perhaps directed against every church, that have nothing to do with what we call religion, and yet that I have to listen to if I am not to be disobedient to the heavenly voice [cf. Acts 26:19]. I hope I am ready at any time to be open to God's Word as in fact it may be spoken to me also in nature, history, art, and, who knows, even my own heart and conscience. All this is true (we have, of course, still to speak about it in principle). Nevertheless — we have to add, and again in the words of the Second Helvetic — we leave all that to God's omnipotence. We are speaking here of the general and usual means of enlightening and converting people as God has given them to us by his decree or command or by example.[24] Or, as the Confession says later, God in his omnipotence might himself gather and claim a church without any means, but he has preferred to deal with us through means, that is, through human ministry. Thus, when we ascribe the instruction and teaching of people to the secret power of the Holy Spirit, we do not thereby negate or invalidate the church's ministry.[25]

In my view the important point is not whether we draw the circle of what we call Christian preaching more broadly or more narrowly. What counts is (a) that it really is a circle with a center, and (b) that we take seriously what takes place within this circle. It would be undisciplined to infer from the actual presence of wider possibilities that there does not exist between these distant possibilities and those that are close or closest to hand not an absolute but a relative and important distinction, namely, that we resolutely stick to the latter, or at least start with them. That the Word of God based on revelation and scripture might meet us in a green forest or a symphony concert is a remote possibility that has to be pondered rather more carefully than usually happens when it is maintained. Many modern pagans might be messengers to a church which has largely forgotten its calling. This we do not rule out. Yet we have to weigh it from case

---

24. Art. 1; *Bekanntnuss Dess waaren Gloubens*, p. 2; Schaff, p. 832.
25. Art. 18; ibid., p. 39; Schaff, pp. 875-76.

to case. It is also very possible that I might find Christian preaching in a Roman Catholic church. There are certain presuppositions for this that are lacking among modern Protestants. Yet first of all I must notice where I myself am deliberately and purposefully addressed as a baptized Christian who is set under God's Word. This place is *my own* church. Striking out the "only" does not mean that this is not the center of my attention. Theologians are not forbidden — indeed, they are commanded — to look further afield, but for them particularly this does not mean that they are not charged to look first at what they should hear and say and reflect on in *their own* church. We do not really help a church's preaching by so swamping it with other inquiries that we do not take it seriously. We do so by again learning from the congregations and pastors to take it very seriously, to take it absolutely seriously as *the* possibility of the Word of God which, like others, is *given* us as the center of the circle. To take it seriously, however, is to take it as *God's Word,* as God's Word in the present for the future, grounded in God's Word in the past from which we come (i.e., holy scripture), and in the eternal Word of God (i.e., revelation). This is what we must see and hear and do again. This is, to put it more cautiously, the thought to which we must again accustom ourselves, the thought which is absolutely constitutive for hearing and receiving God's Word.

This does not mean that congregations must say Yea and Amen to all the words of their reverend pastors. Pastors are sinners. They are unprofitable servants with all their words even though they do all that they are under obligation to do [cf. Luke 17:10]. Nevertheless, they are servants of the Most High [cf. Dan. 3:26]. They speak in his name. They carry out his commission, which is a reality even today. No matter how well or how badly they do it, this is the presupposition of listening to them. This does not mean that when pastors speak officially, then with their words they enjoy a sense of papal infallibility.[26] On the contrary, they know fear and trembling whenever they mount the pulpit. They are crushed by the feeling of being poor human beings who are probably more unworthy than all those who sit before them. Nevertheless, precisely then it is still a matter of God's Word. The Word of God that they have to proclaim is what judges them, but this does *not* alter the fact — indeed, it *means* — that they have to *proclaim* it. This is the presupposition of their proclaiming it.

---

26. Cf. the definition of papal infallibility in the *Pastor aeternus* of Vatican I (7.18.1870); DS, 3074.

Criticism of preaching does not end, then, with this presupposition, neither that of the pastors nor that of the congregations. On the contrary, it begins with this presupposition — not, of course, the complaining, unfruitful criticism of congregations, not the useless charge that "it has nothing to offer me," not the sorry self-criticism of pastors, not the equally useless confession that "I have nothing to say," but on both sides fruitful, positive criticism, which is true *krisis,* which is differentiation, which leads from the appearance to the reality, from the form to the substance, or in this instance from the words to the Word within the words, and then back again to new and better and more suitable words. This criticism of preaching is the work of dogmatics. For this reason dogmatics is basically a concern of all Christians and not just of theologians. Theologians must take the lead in this work of penitence — which is dogmatics. That is still true. Yet the presupposition of this criticism is the principle that preaching is God's Word no less than holy scripture or revelation — God's Word in the present. Without this presupposition, the criticism is pointless.

III. Reflection

I must now say something more concrete about reflection itself. I said in the thesis that it is a working back from preaching to the underlying scripture and revelation. Preaching is the reproduction, the spontaneous adoption of the biblical witness to revelation. Christian preachers are second-rank witnesses. They are not prophets, nor apostles, but witnesses. As witness, preaching relates directly not only to scripture but also to revelation. As scripture is the Word of God in time and history, and as such the presupposition of the church and its preaching, revelation is the eternal Word of God. Both together are the basis of Christian preaching.

At this point we must take up again the definite distinguishing and linking of scripture and Spirit which was so important to the older Protestantism, especially the Reformed. The Spirit makes revelation as present and close to us as history does holy scripture, not, of course, without holy scripture, but in it and by it, and yet in it and by it it is the Spirit making revelation itself present and close. Scripture can be holy scripture, the Word of God, only through the Spirit, through revelation, which attests, presents, and expounds itself in scripture. We shall have to say much more about this distinction and linkage. Here we need say only that God's Word today as a common work of scripture and Spirit is not something abstract but something concrete — the preaching of the Christian church. Preaching arises neither out of the mere letter of scripture nor out of direct spiritual illumination without scripture, an eternal and timeless view of things.[27] In neither case would preaching be God's Word. In the former case it would a historical reference, in the latter a work of the imagination. Where scripture bears witness to revelation and revelation to scripture, there we have Christian preaching and there the Word of God — I repeat, no less, no less significantly or adequately, than in scripture or revelation. The triunity of the eternal, the temporal, and the present in God's Word no more means a distinction of steps or grades or values than does the triunity of Father, Son, and Spirit in God himself.

Preaching, of course, is God's Word in human words, concealed by the total inability of everything human to attain to this object, just as God's Word in scripture is concealed by the separating distance of everything historical, by Lessing's "ugly ditch,"[28] and just as God's Word in revelation is concealed by God's inaccessibility, by his incomprehensibility, which does not cease but becomes very great in his revelation. And as the Word of God in revelation demands that we pay heed to scripture if we are to hear it, and as the Word of God in scripture demands that we obey the Spirit and revelation if we are to understand it, so the Word of God in Christian preaching demands that we search and investigate scripture and revelation if we are to accept and speak it as God's Word. If the background and economy of God's Word cannot be seen behind the poor human words of preaching, if these are not tested against their twofold background, if they are not understood better than they are stated, if they are not constantly criticized and corrected against that background, if they are not both judged and oriented in the light of what they are really supposed to be saying according to revelation and scripture, if for both speakers and hearers they are not in the movement started by recognition of the Word in the words, then they are never anything more than poor human words and they are useless, perhaps most of all if they are fine and impressive preaching, just as the sick at the pool of Bethesda[29] remained sick if they had no one to put them in the water when the angel stirred

---

27. Barth uses here the term *species aeternitatis,* which he took from Spinoza (cf. *Ethica* 2,44.2; 5,22; 5,29), and which is common in Kierkegaard and the early Barth.

28. G. E. Lessing, *Über den Beweis des Geistes und der Kraft* (1777), in *Werke,* VIII, ed. G. Göpfert (Munich, 1979), p. 13; ET *Theological Writings,* ed. H. Chadwick (Stanford, 1956), p. 53.

29. Barth had "Siloah."

it [cf. John 5:2ff.]. Dogmatics must render the church the service of seeing that its preaching has always been sick. It is not self-evident that God's Word should be truly heard and spoken in it. Dogmatics must lead it back to that movement by summoning it to reflection, by reminding it of its origin and purpose. It does this by literally taking it at its word, by understanding it better than the pastors who engage in it do, by uncovering its relations to the past, by bringing out as clearly as possible its links to its origins, by underlining, completing, and clarifying the reference that preaching itself makes either well or badly, and therefore, by keeping always either critically or consentingly to that which is actually being said among us, making both speakers and hearers aware more powerfully, perhaps, than previously of the scope of what they are saying and hearing. This is a modest ministry which is not even to be compared with the glory of the ministry of the Word itself. It is also a dangerous ministry, as we said at the outset. Yet it is a ministry that has to be performed, and allowing for the fallibility of all things human, it *can* also be performed.

IV. God's Word and the Church's Human Word

Little need be said about the final statements of the thesis. I gave to the methodical movement back from revelation to scripture the name of dogmatics. This working back is reflection on God's Word in the church's human word. It is methodical. It might be done chaotically, in guerrilla fashion, in individual bursts, and one must say at once that often infinitely more has been accomplished this way than in books and lectures that deal with the whole. Reflection on scripture and revelation, on God's Word above, behind, and in the sermons one hears or preaches, when done in terms of isolated thoughts or from specific standpoints or for particular reasons, is irregular dogmatics, a little of which all of us secretly do and which we ought to do boldly, especially if we are pastors. If only we stick to the subject matter, it will always be rewarding even though we never become great dogmaticians, which is not in any case necessary. When we do it, however, in the long run we will finally begin to look at the whole and methodical reflection will commence. This is dogmatics proper, regular dogmatics, dogmatics as a science, which is needed to give backbone[30] to irregular dogmatics. Even historically true dogmatics developed out of

---

30. Barth used a Swiss form here, *Rückgrat* in the masculine.

free dogmatics. The usual procedure for individuals is that the methodical work of their teachers will stir them to think on their own, then on their own two feet they will move on to what is probably rather chaotic independent inquiry and investigation, and they will end with some more or less clear conception of methodically arranged dogmatic thinking. We should not overvalue the methodical element in dogmatics, for all our plans are merely ventures, but we should also not undervalue it, for tackling the whole is better than stopping with half-truths, even though much of the work that is only half or quarter done may be in fact more productive than many a finished work because of its inner worth.

The concept "dogma" is debated. Most people adopt only my third sense, that is, the dogma which has become a symbol or which a church has adopted as such. I ask myself whether this really does justice to the older usage. Even as late as the 16th century we still find references to unofficial or private or heretical dogmas. A statement that might be regarded as wrong could also be called a dogma. This is in keeping with the nature of the case. As we said earlier, dogma differs from *doxa*. It is not something that is humanly established, posited, or maintained. It is something that is discovered, acknowledged, and promulgated. It is the statement underlying Christian statements, derived from the Word of God. But the dogma of which we say *this* is not given; it is sought. Even acknowledged articles of faith are only an approximation to it. What is given is not unchangeable and infallible dogma but the dogma that in principle is changeable, reformable, and in need of supplementation. A given dogma, a principle that is stated and laid down in Greek or Latin or any other language, is as such only a formula in which dogmatic reflection, reflection on the Word of God, done by any person, has provisionally come to a halt and reached a conclusion. But all new dogmatic reflection means that movement has begun again from the very source. It thus means that the validity of the previous formulation, the given dogma, is for the time being suspended again and must be established afresh. Note how in Thomas dogmatics sought clarity on the whole sum of theological truths from the existence and triunity of God to the most detailed matters of the angelic world and the orders of human life. These become the object of *Quaestiones* which can be answered only after regard is had to all the objections that Thomas himself can bring. Note that the classical form of Protestant dogmatics, too, is the play of question and answer in the catechism, which embraces everything as though nothing were for the time being fixed. This manner of instruction has the material significance of winning in order to have.[31] Even for children it is not fundamentally a matter of repetition but of knowledge. In fact, dogma follows the ongoing Word of God in Christian preaching. New proclamation results in new consideration of revelation and scripture, new discovery of the most ancient truth, new criticism of what is preached, and therefore new formulation, new dogma.

From the wealth of given dogma, true or false, old or new, general or detailed, there arises the dogma that is made a symbol by the confession of the church or a church. Only very few dogmas become dogma in this sense of a principle which the fellowship of the teaching church, or one such fellowship, recognizes and promulgates as conformable to revelation and scripture, as flowing from God's Word. Dogmatics always has to reckon with the possibility that one dogma has undeservedly not become a symbol whereas another has perhaps undeservedly achieved this rank. When among other things[32] dogmatics makes and emphatically establishes such critical judgments, its service to the church has the direct form of cooperating in its confession. And I need hardly say that for the church's own sake this linking of dogmatic scholarship with the given confession of a church must not involve any obligation to stick with any given formulations. As dogmatics relates to the church's preaching, recognizing its starting point and goal, it will obviously acknowledge rather than question the special dignity of the dogma of the church, or of a particular church. How far it will do this will be considered separately in a later section.

It may be noted here that in this regard the dogmatics of present-day Protestantism has been more or less left in the lurch by its churches. For the most part they do not say what church dogma is, or they do so only with enigmatic brevity, or by means of a cheap and very general reference to the confessional writings of the Reformation. They act like Nebuchadnezzar among his wise men when he wanted them to tell him not only what his dream meant but also what it was [cf. Dan. 2:1ff.]. In face of the embarrassed mumbling or total silence of the modern churches about their basic statements, dogmaticians can only surmise that finally the churches do not want any dogmatics, that they simply wish to preach, and go on preaching, as though the church were all right if only it could go on preaching, and did not want any reflection on God's Word, which might

---

31. See J. W. von Goethe, *Faust*, I, V.683 (Night).
32. This *u.A.* might be *u.U.*, i.e., "in some circumstances."

bring unrest to both the pastors and their flocks. If this is so, then the answer is that dogmatics must not respect these "*un*dogmatic slumbers" of the church — to invoke once more the shades of Kant[33] — but look out for the vital interest of the church, even *against* the church. The vital interest of the church may be summed up again in the old war cry that the Reformers understood better and more profoundly than the humanists who first raised it: Back to the sources!

---

33. Cf. I. Kant, *Prolegomena zu einer jeden künftigen Metaphysik,* in *Gesammelte Schriften,* IV, p. 260. In the preface to the *Prolegomena* he acknowledges that David Hume aroused him from his dogmatic slumbers and reoriented his researches in the field of speculative philosophy.

CHAPTER 1

THE WORD OF GOD AS REVELATION

§ 3

Deus Dixit

Christian preachers dare to speak about God. The permission and requirement to do so can rest only on their adoption of the witness of the prophets and apostles that underlies the church, the witness which is to the effect that God himself has spoken and that for this reason, and with this reference, they too must speak about God. This assumption can arise only because they take it that God's address is directed to them as well. It means that with fear and trembling they recognize God as the true subject of the biblical witness and their own proclamation.

I. Daring to Speak about God

Christian preachers dare to speak about God. This is the given fact with which we start. Think of some sermon you liked, perhaps the one, I assume, that you heard yesterday. Recall, if you would, the sorriest murmuring or the crudest shouting or the worst idealistic moralizing or the most dubious claims to supernatural power that you have heard in your lives under the name of preaching. Or recall, as I hope you can, the instances of Christian witness which have given you — you are sure — an irresistible impression of authority and richness, of spirit and truth. Or imagine that you yourselves are the preachers — as you will be in a few years — and that it is Sunday morning and that on paper or in your head there is some material — we will not say how valuable or valueless — and that with this you have to go into the pulpit and present it to a more or less Christian public. In some such way you stand before the fact that I

45

have in mind, namely, that certain people have dared, or dare, or will dare to speak about God. Theologians are people who speak about God, we have stated already.[1] Perhaps only in a few vague sentences shortly before the Amen; perhaps only as if they were saying: Please excuse me if I briefly say something about the main thing; perhaps in a mystical or orthodox-mythological veiling so that people cannot tell whether they really mean God when they say "God"; perhaps with all kinds of open substitutions, for example, between God and various other gods; perhaps, to satisfy the linguistic refinement of the declining West,[2] in intentional avoidance of pronouncing the word "God" and using instead all kinds of old or new hyperboles, even, it may be, "the Unconditioned."[3] Or perhaps in the very first words, unhesitatingly and confidently, convinced and convincingly, dynamically and powerfully, they may say "God." Either way, however, they dare to speak about God. Let us not inquire too closely how they think about this final thing about which they obviously speak or want to speak. Let us grant — we are all sinners [Rom. 3:23] — that they really mean God by what they say. From their elevated station they make state-ments which demand *faith* from their hearers — an attitude which is obviously fitting only in relation to God. They make assertions about the final *truth* not only in existence but above it. They claim to give the profoundest answer to the profoundest human question. They place before the I of the hearers a *Thou* whom they cannot overlook or dissolve or transcend. Is this Thou the friend or foe of the I, its life or death, most near to it or most distant? At any rate, it is a Thou confronting it.

Preachers dare — and it is no wonder that we are not sure whether they themselves believe what they are saying — they dare as though the history of philosophy had ended with the most satisfying or at least the most definite result — they dare to take the whole world, nature which is so incommensurable in all its dimensions and perspectives, the sphinx of past history and the mystery of future history, the riddle of the individual and the never-ending crisis of abstract thought, destiny, guilt, and death — they dare to bracket all these things and deal with them from outside by tossing out such words as eternity, assurance, victory, forgiveness, righ-teousness, Lord, and life, as though they could and should do so. This, at

---

1. Cf. C. Vitringa, in Schweizer, p. 340; see above, p. 10.
2. An allusion to O. Spengler's *Decline of the West*.
3. German Idealism used this term in both its philosophy and its theology, and P. Tillich gave it increasing importance in the 1920s; cf. *RGG*, V, 2nd ed. (1931), col. 1350.

any rate, is what they do, and no homiletical or theological stupidity, ineptitude, or perversion can alter the fact. Either as conscious thinkers or those who simply repeat what they have heard and learned from others, they do so boldly, knowing what they are doing insofar as this is possible, or they do so with great uncertainty, either saying it explicitly in blunt words or implicitly but in such a way that it is more or less unavoidable that the inference should be made from their words. They do it. They dare to speak about *God.*

The recognition that we have here a venture seems to me to be the beginning of dogmatic wisdom. A venture is an enterprise in which we realize that there are many things against the possibility of its success. In our case, there are not just many things but all things. The "dare to" is much too weak an expression for what theologians are doing. If we speak about the obstacles that stand in their way, at the university we usually think especially of the difficulty of knowing the God about whom we speak, of grasping conceptually the truth of the object of what is or should be said by preachers. The modern theology and philosophy of religion which starts with pious experience or faith, so far as I can see, has reached the more or less agreed conclusion, for all the differences in detail, that grasping God as truth is possible only on the condition of the presence of certain presuppositions in those who grasp it. If we follow, for example, the exposition of Wobbermin, we need only stand in the basic act of religion and we are in a relationship of which one of the poles is the primal reality of the certainty and validity of all reality (namely, the experiencing I). That the other pole, then, does not lie in an illusion or fiction of human thought, but in ultimate and supreme reality itself, is a rationally compelling conclusion.[4] God is the source of the feeling of absolute dependence, as Schleiermacher had already argued.[5] According to L. Ihmels, the certainty of Christians about God stands or falls with the certainty about themselves. As Ihmels says, it is in the strict sense a self-certainty. The specific content of Christian experience guarantees the truth of its statements as the idea of religion, our divine destiny, comes to light and fulfilment in it.[6] According to H. Scholz, the fact that religious experience is categorically incomparable and nonderivable makes it possible to main-

---

4. G. Wobbermin, *Systematische Theologie nach religionspsychologischer Methode,* II (Leipzig, 1921), p. 456.

5. *CF,* § 4.4.

6. L. Ihmels, *Die christliche Wahrheitsgewissheit . . . ,* 2nd ed. (Leipzig, 1908), pp. 367-68.

tain as at least philosophically possible and honestly conceivable the basic judgment of religion that God exists even though we must leave open the possibility that materially this might be a mistake.[7] According to Heim, the conceptual possibility of the certainty of faith rests on the fact that the subject, which is put out of the region of the objective when it is no longer conceivable to knowledge, is taken up into the region of the non-objective and has a share in God's perception of the whole.[8] We can easily reduce all these modern trains of theological thought to Descartes's proof of God, to which Wobbermin and Scholz make explicit appeal.[9] Because the idea of God exists in us, therefore God exists in himself. The only difference is that the moderns do not speak of an innate idea of God but of an achieved experience of God, and thus substitute "so far as" for "because." Even if we accept the relation of the conclusion to the object, the theologians mentioned present it only as a conditioned relation, and more than one of them refers expressly to a circle.[10]

I for my part lay my finger on the subjective side that is everywhere taken as given. What does grasping mean even in this conditional sense when I as the one who does the grasping must first meet the condition of positing myself in my religious experience as the one pole of the primal reality of all knowledge and validity, or of knowing myself as one who possesses the specific content of Christian experience, or one who has an incomparable and nonderivable experience, or who can put off an objective consciousness of the self like an old coat and share in God's own knowledge of all things? If these fulfilments of the concept of experience are meant seriously, do they not go far beyond the concept inasmuch as we do not usually experience such things? How can I see even the possibility of any such positing of the object when this kind of demand is made upon the subject? And what becomes of the positing of the object if this demand on the subject is not meant as seriously as it sounds, and as it is surely meant to be, in all these formulas?

Problems to the right of us and problems to the left of us! Have I really posited *God* as the object if my experience as the subject, supposedly real and given, is the only basis of this positing? Is not the God who is posited thus

---

7. H. Scholz, *Religionsphilosophie,* 2nd ed. (Berlin, 1922), pp. 307ff.

8. K. Heim, *Glaubensgewissheit, eine Untersuchung der Lebensfrage der Religion,* 3rd ed. (Berlin, 1923), p. 273.

9. G. Wobbermin, *Systematische Theologie,* p. 455; H. Scholz, *Religionsphilosophie,* p. 310.

10. L. Ihmels, *Die christliche Wahrheitsgewissheit,* p. 372; and esp. G. Wobbermin, *Systematische Theologie,* pp. 7ff., 55ff.

something other and smaller than God himself, one object among others, a part of the world, no matter how incommensurable or exalted? Conversely, have I posited myself as the subject when the categories in which my supposed experience is described are taken seriously, and can thus be regarded as an adequate reason for positing God, or does not this way of positing myself — this is particularly plain in Heim — shatter any real concept of a true and given human subject? Is it not really a venture (even Scholz uses the term)[11] and more than a venture to speak about God if this is how it stands with the possibility of knowing God, if we either do not know God, or if it is not we who know him? Quite apart from the fact that preaching about God wants to be something very different from speaking on the basis of a *possible* knowledge. What Christian preachers say presupposes *real* knowledge of God. Let us be careful from what source we take this!

But the difficulty of knowing the God of whom Christian preaching speaks is only the one side of the venture at issue. We must not undervalue this side. It is not relevant merely at the university, where *ex officio* we usually look at things from the standpoint of the so-called worldview. Yet I would not call it the vital question of religion, as Heim does in the subtitle of his book. The problem of speaking about God can and must be considered from other and no less important and dangerous angles. Let us assume that in the matter of knowing God everything is in order. We may then go on to ask where we are to find the courage to give expression to this knowledge. When we speak about God, we toss into the world the statement of a fact which the world may regard only as a beautiful but impractical dream. We know this. We have to know it. If in the place of God we were to put an idol, if we were to proclaim almighty Eros, or the wonder of infrasensory life, or a German god like Wotan, or the spirit of progress, then we would still have to expect the rivalry of the principalities and powers of this aeon. But when we really know God, we know that he is above all gods, that he cannot be confused or equated with any, that he is not in competition with the greatest or the smallest things that are called divine in nature or history or culture or civilization. How lonely are those who dare to speak about God, how far removed from the broad way of the many or even the quiet paths of the finest and noblest among us.

Again, those who speak about God demand faith from their hearers. They demand the presence or establishment of the same condition under which they have set themselves. They cannot be content if people simply

---

11. H. Scholz, *Religionsphilosophie*, p. 309.

let them talk, if they simply listen, if they are simply interested. The attention, gratitude, and willingness that they must seek is the specific and unheard-of one of faith. Those who speak about God want to set people before God, to claim them for God, to save their souls, to win them. What a golden age of naivety it is when people think that this is possible, when they think that they can appeal to all kinds of obvious successes in this regard, when they triumphantly read away the doubt expressed in the gospel whether the Son of Man will find faith on the earth when he comes [Luke 18:8]. When this age passes, when especially people learn to know themselves better, then we encounter unbelief, which might even be devout unbelief, the obstinate resistance of the I that does not want to be born again [cf. John 3:4ff.], the universal flight from God's kingdom which is best seen in a highly Christian form, the Judas Iscariot that is like a wall in all of us. But then even with this insight we must still speak about God.

Perhaps you still do not see why I call the matter a venture in this respect. You will learn this later. Again, those who speak about God must find a need in people that they do not perceive along with all their other needs. They must teach them to ask so that they can give them an answer. They must plunge them into the depths so that they can really lead them to the heights. They proclaim to them a peace that the inhabitants of no city or village would call such but which startles them if they have any inkling of what it is all about. To speak about God does not fit in with what they are and do even in their best moments. To speak about God is to set up in human society and order and custom that which is symbolized by the unsymmetrical window at the front of many old Franciscan churches,12 an echo, a corrective, a reminder of eternity, the great divine disruption to which alone we may attach our hope. Those who speak about God, who really speak about him, will have to accept much odium, much responsibility, much conflict of conscience, much temptation to confuse human and divine sorrow [cf. 2 Cor. 7:10] or God's anger at sin with their own anger at others and themselves. It is a venture, and more, to go where all that is unavoidable, and the problem of a worldview is a small one compared to the question how we can have the courage to do it. Not everyone is born a "knight of faith" like Kierkegaard,13 and unfortunately

---

12. Barth was familiar from childhood with a good example of such a 14th-century church in Basel.

13. For this phrase see Kierkegaard's *Fear and Trembling* (Princeton, 1954), p. 49 and passim.

the stroke by which one becomes such can be given neither at university nor at ordination.

But even if we assume that along with the knowledge of God there is also this courage to speak about him in spite of everything, there is still the last and most serious question by what right we may really do so. If you are not already aware of it, then let me tell you that the quiet judgment of the world on us theologians is that our work is a tactless aggression, presumption, and usurpation. Who made us guardians and administrators of the sanctuary? Do we not have decisive reasons to maintain the respect-ful silence about ultimate things which most others think it their duty to do even though they are as knowledgeable and daring as we are? Do we really think we have the right to preach faith and repentance to others, to require it of them? Are we not unaccredited blusterers from whom people rightly hold aloof? Good for us if we have placed ourselves under this sword of Damocles, under this question of authority, before others do so. We will not try, of course, to appeal to our qualifications and credentials, to our Christian knowledge, and least of all, it is to be hoped, to the supposed experiences and illuminations that we think we have behind us. Insight into the incongruence between what we say and what we are, into the judgment under which we set ourselves when we keep on saying what is too high for us, will, it is to be hoped, cut off all excuses before they pass our lips. Where is the "You may" which must precede the "I must" in face of this task? But to what may we then appeal? Have we anything to appeal to? Will not the knowledge that qualifies us, but that is never our own, begin with a recognition that we are not in fact qualified? We do not really have the courage or the knowledge. We lack the presuppositions which must be present if there is to be any meaningful speaking about God. But if this is so, then we have obviously done badly in the Socratic examination in the very first quarter of an hour. And our only hope, I may add, is that we will at least fundamentally see this.

II. Permission and Command to Preach

We have now reached the point where we can see the principial breadth of the venture that Christian preaching entails and where we can discuss what might be the permission and command to engage in it. The position is this. We are not set in the calm after the storm, nor placed before the happy solution to every difficulty, when we turn to this permission and command. On the contrary, it is only now that we can understand the venture as such, and that the matter becomes mortally dangerous in principle. The exposed position of Christian preachers might seem to many people, even perhaps to many of you, much less great than I have depicted it. Why should we not accept the reasons for certainty that friendly philosophers of religion offer us on all sides? We need only take a little less strictly the question of the object and subject of the knowledge of God and we are rescued and can begin to talk about God. When it is a question of the courage that is needed to do so, why should we not find comfort in the consideration that happily the good Lord has provided us theologians as well as other creatures with a modest or less modest amount of vitality which will enable us, if we take a good run at it, to make the high jump with some measure of success? And as regards authority, among the many things that we have mentioned (qualifications, credentials, theological knowledge, and religious experience), does not something remain on the basis of which, if we are not over-fussy, we may feel justified and go to work? Against my whole depiction might not the question be raised on what ground I put the matter so radically? Does not the result, namely, that we are left hanging in the air, prove that the questioning is too tight, that it needs to be relaxed, that an agreeable, practicable solution needs to be found? Somehow theology has to go on. The church is there and must be good for something. You want to be pastors, and to this end it is impossible that we should say at the outset that no one can be a pastor.

To this objection I make the following reply. There is indeed a permission and command to speak about God and to become pastors. There is therefore, in answer to our first subsection, a knowledge of God, a courage to talk about him, a validation. But precisely this permission and command entail the characterizing of the venture of Christian preaching as an unheard-of and absolutely unique venture. They precisely force us to put the question of knowledge, courage, and authority so radically and exclusively that we are left in the air. They insist on being the *only* permission and command to talk about God, and we must have none other beside them [cf. Exod. 20:3]. Precisely when we look them sharply in the eye, precisely when we find comfort in them, all others crumble, and we can no longer find any comfort in not being over-fussy, in accepting apologetic arguments for theology, in thinking we can be pastors in other ways, in turning to mediating solutions. When the reference is to this permission and command, then we shall no longer expect an unavoidable appeasement but a material demonstration why there can be no appeasement, why the questioning is everywhere justified, and will always be so, why we can be pastors only as we recognize that we cannot be so, that is, "as dying and behold we live" [2 Cor. 6:9], allowing our situation to be lit up by a word which in the first instance cannot really be on our own lips. It *is* possible to speak about God, but the basis of this possibility does not cancel out in the least what has been said about the impossibility of finding any other basis for this venture.

To be sure, the church is there. This is what we must say first. The venture of Christian preaching is the venture of the Christian church. Christian preachers are not just individuals, as Kierkegaard depicted them.[14] They are that too — and woe to them if they are not — but they are not just that. In talking about God they place themselves in a series, on the ground of a certain piece of history, under an order. The Christian *church* dares to speak about God, and so we must broaden our statement before coming back to its narrower form. It dares to do this in the light of a historical datum that is the constitutive basis of its own existence. It dares to do it because it finds in this basis an imperative to the effect that no matter what the cost, it must do so. It has differentiated this datum from other data and facts and defined it as the canon. A canon is a rod, then a measure or ruler, then a rule or prescript or law, then a model or example, and finally an area,[15] a definite sphere of activity or responsibility. Cf. 2 Cor. 10:13-18; Gal. 6:16; (?)Phil. 3:16.[16] We cannot understand the terms "church" and "preaching" unless we note and understand the reference to this specific historical datum. The claim that such and such writings are the canon meant that the church found its marching orders and working directions in these writings. By the presence of these writings, and at the very first partly by the oral proclamation of their authors, it felt itself enlisted in their host. The monuments of the witness of departed prophets and apostles were for it a command not to leave their places empty, to pass on their witness, itself to talk about God, always in the light of what they said, but precisely through this light with the knowledge, courage, and authority to do so. Inevitably the term "canon" also denoted a limit and negation. From the flood of apocryphal, pseudoprophetic, pseudoapostolic, and heretical writings this literature alone emerged as

---

14. Cf. Kierkegaard's *Sickness unto Death* (Princeton, 1954), pp. 250ff.

15. C. L. W. Grimm, *Lexikon Graeco-Latinum*, 3rd ed. (Leipzig, 1888), p. 225.

16. The question mark before Phil. 3:16 indicates that the word *kanōn* is found in many variant readings but not in the main Nestle text.

canonical, as the witness of the real prophets and apostles, as the historical imperative to go and preach [cf. Mark 16:15]. The negative aspect does not concern us here. Primary in the concept of the canon is the positive thing, the imperative, the inescapable impression that in these writings we have to do with the command to speak about God.

We might illustrate this impression by an example that is very dear to me, namely, by the strange processes that led especially to the formation of the Reformed churches in the 16th century. I call them strange because the most positive impulse accompanying the many negative and from a Christian standpoint very dubious things that were also at work was to us the amazingly passionate rediscovery, acknowledgment, and assertion of the ancient canonical literature, because in a way that was acute, sudden, and revolutionary the Bible again became the marching orders and direction to preach, because it was understood as the canon not merely in the critical sense but also in the imperative sense. In this field the ancient book — and much more distinctly than in the Lutheran reformation, the book itself — the whole Bible and not just a specific truth in the Bible as in the case of Luther, commanded with an almost uncanny dynamic a new attention, respect, and obedience. To a degree and with an intensity that are almost intolerable to us today, people had to speak again about God in the light of this historical datum as though it could be done and had never been attempted before. Read some of the sermons of Calvin with this in mind. How this man is grasped and stilled and claimed — not too quickly must one suppose by his experience of conversion, or by the thought of predestination, or by Christ, or even, as is commonly said, by passion for God's glory — no, but in the first instance simply by the authority of the biblical books, which year by year he never tired of expounding systematically down to the very last verse! How this man, moving always along the uncrossable wall of this authority, copying down what he finds copied there, as if the living words of God were heard there (as he himself says in the *Institutes*),[17] becomes himself wholly voice and speech and persuasion, and can never exhaust or empty himself,[18] as though nothing were more self-evident than this torrential talk about God in spite of all the objections which might be urged against it, and which he himself knew well enough! Why was this? In the first instance we can find no other reason than this: Because he heard Moses, Jeremiah, and

---

17. *Inst.* I, 7, 1.
18. Cf. F. von Schiller, *Der Taucher* (1797), strophe 6, line 35.

Paul speak about God, because he heard there the trumpet that summoned him to battle. In something of the same way 1400 years earlier, in the historically obscure early period when the old book was not yet old, the oral and written witness of the same prophets and apostles affected the people of the second generation and brought about the rise of the early church, that is, the rise of Christian preaching.

It is significant that formally — but this formal factor is identical with a very material one — all real epochs of church history are characterized by a fresh attention to the initial historical datum which commands and provokes talk about God. It is also significant — even if it is not understood by those who most need to understand it, even if the practice often enough makes nonsense of the fact — that in all its confessions the church has related its proclamation even externally to this original datum of all talk about God, to a biblical text. In so doing it shows why it dares to speak about God even though from every angle this is an impossible venture. It shows that here we are not talking about God on our own, on the basis of our own knowledge, courage, or authority; that no independent knowledge is presented here, no philosophy, not even a philosophy of religion; that we are not speaking by inspiration or in ecstasy even though we cannot speak without the Spirit and without *ek-stasis* (going out of the self), but that because the canon speaks about God, and in the light of the canon, we are confessing that we are forbidden *not* to speak about God in spite of the serious danger that in so doing we are doing something impossible, and in spite of the severe objections, known best of all to ourselves, to which we expose (ourselves) thereby. The answer that the church gives to every objection is first and simply that it acknowledges them to be justified, that it raises them much more energetically than those who are outside and untested usually do, but that it then refers to the text, to the authority with which the prophets and apostles talked about God and which demands that we do likewise. It thus dares to dare what they dared. Or rather, it does *not* dare *not* to do so. Here is the historical sequence or order in which Christian preachers place themselves.

But this step from the church to the Bible has not yet reached its goal. The reference to the canon explains why the church talks about God, but we have not yet seen how far the canon causes and even forces it to do so. We have not seen what is the permission and the command. The answer that the church has always given to this question, and unavoidably has to give to it if it is to press on to that permission and command, is the well-known one that in the canon, in the words of the prophets and apostles, it recognizes God's Word. By its incomparably paradoxical form, which very crudely assaults the principle of noncontradiction, this answer makes it clear that the historical heteronomy in the relationship of authority between the Bible and the church, which is the initial issue, is only a reflection of the absolute heteronomy which gives it meaning, justification, and emphasis. The canon, the commanding rod which gives the church its marching orders and directions, and which the church obeys, is not just picked up off the street. It lies in a living, stretched-out hand, and it is this hand, not the rod itself, which by means of the rod gives direction, which commands, which gives the marching orders and points out the way. The authority that the church grants to the historical datum is real, constraining authority. But this means that the historical datum as such can be its historical proclamation but not its source. This source, to put it spatially, is to be sought further back, in a suprahistorical sphere, beyond the datum.

The impulse to proclaim, the *anankē* of which Paul speaks [1 Cor. 9:16], is absolute. It may be illustrated by Paul but it is not based upon Paul, nor does it proceed from him. The venture to which the church knows it is directed by scripture is not a venturesome imitation of heroic religious personalities, although it is by such that the direction comes to us. This venture is *obedience* in the strict sense, obedience to the law which has taken form in these personalities. The witness of the prophets and apostles, which to our joy or sorrow makes it necessary for us to talk about God, is not to the effect that they, the prophets and apostles, *could* talk about God, and that for this reason we too, perhaps appropriating their words or at least their thoughts, should also try to do so. The prophets and apostles could no more talk about God than we can. Their witness, then, is: *Deus dixit,* God has spoken. Scripture is the basis of preaching, but it, too, has a basis in a third thing even further back. It is the witness to revelation. But in this distinction between the historical witness and the revelation itself to which it bears witness, scripture itself as the words of the prophets and apostles is the Word of God, the permission and command to speak about God.

The older Protestantism was well aware of this distinction. It did not simply equate the *Deus dixit* with the *Paulus dixit,* although it recognized God's Word fully and unconditionally in the *Paulus dixit.* When it called God the author of holy scripture, it did not think that God dictated the words and stylistic features, nor did it make the words and stylistic features of scripture into Delphic oracles. The letters and words are flesh, writes Bullinger. They are holy because they speak about holy things, says Wolfgang Musculus. They are the expression of divine wisdom, says Peter Martyr, and Bartholomew Keckermann (d. 1669) can still call them a medium.[19] Over against them and distinct from them are what Bullinger calls the divine statements, Musculus the holy things, Peter Martyr the divine wisdom, and Keckermann God's own institutes. Most forceful of all is Calvin, who finds the supreme proof of scripture in the fact that God speaks in it personally.[20] Even in later Reformed and Lutheran dogmatics, though not so well understood and asserted, the distinction remained between the Word *agraphon* and the Word *egraphon,* between the inner Word *to* the apostles and the outer Word *of* the apostles, between the matter and form in scripture, between direct revelation and indirect revelation.[21] Insofar as it still knew and utilized this distinction, the older Protestantism still understood that the definition of scripture as God's Word, or of God as its author, is a strictly paradoxical one and must always remain so. Revelation gives rise to scripture and itself speaks in it. This is what makes scripture God's Word without ceasing to be historically no more than the words of the prophets and apostles, sharing the relativity, the ambiguity, and the distance that are proper to everything historical: the letters and words are flesh.

In distinction from scripture, however, revelation is God's Word itself, God's own speaking in which he alone is the subject, in which no flesh also speaks, but he and he alone. This is found in scripture, this pregnant *Deus dixit,* God speaking personally as the subject, God as the author, God not only giving authentic information about himself but himself speaking about himself. This is what makes scripture the Word of God. This is the living hand which imperiously waves the rod, the canon. This is the authority of the canon, the unconditional constraint which issues from it. This is what makes the historical heteronomy in the relationship between the church and the Bible into an absolute heteronomy. The fact that God himself is on the scene, speaking about himself, is an adequate reason to speak about him. It is the permission and command to do so. God in his revelation, God as speaking subject, is a possible object of human speech which at once becomes a necessary object. This is *how* scripture bears witness to him. This is *why* it does. This is *how* he

---

19. Schweizer, pp. 199-201.
20. *Inst.* I, 7, 4.
21. Heppe, p. 16; Heppe-Bizer, p. 17; ET p. 15; Hase, p. 66.

speaks through the medium of scripture. This is how the permission and command to speak about God come into history at the start of the series to which we ourselves belong. God's own speaking is the final authority, the summit of the mountain above which there is only heaven, the summit to which we are led when, directed by preaching to the church and by the church to the Bible, we come up against the direction that the Bible itself gives us. It directs us to God. But God can and will direct us only to himself.

III. The Meaning of *Deus Dixit*

We have now reached the point from which we can survey to some extent the situation of Christian preaching. But before we do this, we must make sure by a few small delimitations that we are not mistaken, that we have really reached this point together. What can this *Deus dixit* mean to which we have been driven? What must it mean?

1. Obviously, it is an address. The presupposition of the Bible is not that God is but that he spoke. We are directed, not to God in himself, but to God communicating himself. What makes scripture holy scripture is not the correctness of the prophetic and apostolic statements and thoughts about God but the I-Thou encounter, person to person, about which these thoughts and statements tell us. Only within this I-Thou relation, in which one speaks and another is spoken to, in which there is communication and reception, only in full *action* is revelation revelation. When we do not think of revelation as such, that is, one person speaking and another spoken to, God revealing himself to us and we to whom he reveals himself; when revelation is seen from the standpoint of the noninvolved spectator, then it amounts to nonrevelation. God is completely inconceivable, concealed, and absent for those whom he does not address and who are not addressed by him. To receive revelation is to be addressed by God.

2. Obviously, too, revelation means disclosure, *apokalypsis, phanerosis, revelatio.* Being revelation only in action, in the event of address, revelation is not a direct openness on God's part but a becoming open. God tears away the veil, the husk, the concealment when he reveals himself. He removes the incomprehensibility. He makes impossible the possibility of taking offense, of not believing. These things are essentially related to revelation. Later Protestant orthodoxy did incalculable damage with its doctrine of inspiration in which it did not accept the paradox that in

scripture God's Word is given to us in the concealment of true and authentic human words, when it removed the salutary barrier between scripture and revelation, when it adopted pagan ideas and made the authors of the Bible into the amanuenses, pens, or flutes of the Holy Spirit, and thus found in the Bible an open and directly given revelation, as though this were not a contradiction in terms.[22] Long before the Enlightenment this meant no more and no less than a pitiful historicizing of revelation, which then continued if in another form. To deny the hiddenness of revelation even in scripture is to deny revelation itself, and with it the Word of God. For God's Word is no longer God's Word when the truth that is new every morning [cf. Lam. 3:23] is made into a sacred reality, when the miracle of God that is encircled with the possibility of offense is made into a marvel to which one may quietly point. The same applies, of course, to modern theories of revelation which in place of the supposed sacred letter posit a supposed sacred history as the palpable reality. The holy that is obvious, the sacral, is never the true holy. The true holy is spirit, not thing. The *Deus dixit* is revelation, not revealedness.

3. Obviously, too, the *Deus dixit* means a here and now. Or rather a then and there, for it is better to say that there is no avoiding the offensive "*there* in Palestine" and "*then* in the years A.D. 1-30" if we are really to think the thought of Christian revelation. I have chosen the Latin *Deus dixit* not least because of the Latin perfect tense *(dixit)*, which expresses something that the translations do not. To be sure, we have here a remarkable and unique perfect. What is denoted is an eternal perfect. But in the first instance it takes the form of the usual perfect, and the meaning cannot be separated from this form. The contingent fact that the church finds the witness to revelation in these specific writings, and that in the witness it finds revelation, is no accident. The contingency lies in the nature of revelation. *Deus dixit* indicates a special, once-for-all, contingent event to which these specific writings rather than any possible writings bear witness.

I do not know what Schelling meant when he called the world the self-revelation of the absolute subject, or God.[23] I do not know either what Schleiermacher meant when he spoke of revelation wherever there en-

---

22. Cf. J. Cocceius (Heppe-Bizer, p. 17; ET p. 18); W. Bucanus (Schweizer, p. 202); J. Gerhard and J. A. Quenstedt (Schmid, p. 21; ET p. 43); J. A. Quenstedt (Luthardt, p. 259); J. H. Heidegger (Schweizer, p. 202).

23. For this basic thought of Schelling's cf. *Die Weltalter,* in *Sämmtliche Werke,* I, vol. 8 (Stuttgart/Augsburg, 1861), pp. 195ff., e.g., p. 305; also idem, *Philosophische Untersuchungen . . . ,* in ibid., vol. 7 (1860), p. 347.

counters people, in a particular view of the universum, something new which cannot be explained in terms of the causal nexus.[24] I am sure, however, that neither of them, nor many others like them, had in mind the *Deus dixit* to which we have become attentive. For the view that the whole world, or anything within it, is revelation, conflicts with this *Deus dixit*. Even the general truths of reason (e.g., mathematical axioms) are not what is meant by it, nor is their manifestation and perception, as though revelation were only the symbol of something that is latently and potentially present and given, even if in a higher sphere. If we were to call revelation a symbol, it would have to be the symbol of the truth which is nowhere and never the truth except in itself. The *Deus dixit* is the revelation of God, not the epitome of eruptions of the unconditioned. Even if we very naively say "God" and refrain from general concepts, in the first instance we are not confessing universal revelation but singular revelation, and the former only by way of the latter. The self-evidence of revelation is not that of the universal but that of the particular, the particular of *God*, but still the *particular* of God (Tillich!!).[25]

4. Obviously, too, the concealed and unique address that we call God's revelation is *qualified* history. What I mean by that is as follows. The *logia tou theou* [Rom. 3:2], that which is disclosed out of hiddenness, the here and now of revelation, are an event in time and space (otherwise there would be no here and now), but as revelation they are not in sequence with all else in time and space. Their relation to the whole of contingent reality (to which they belong) is similar (I glance aside to a philosophical correlation only by way of analogy) to that of the concept of limit or idea to the concept of reason. They do not negate it, but they bracket it — provisionally, we should not say more. They encounter it with principial superiority. This leads us to the Ritschlians, especially Kaftan,[26] Wendt, and Troeltsch, with their more or less all-embracing apotheosis of history, which supposedly reached in Jesus a peak which very probably will never be surpassed, at least not before the next ice age, as Troeltsch finally

---

24. Cf. *Reden über die Religion* (Berlin, 1799); repr. in PhB, 255 (Hamburg, 1958), p. 66; ET *On Religion: Speeches to its Cultured Despisers* (New York, 1950), p. 88.

25. Cf. the debate between Barth and Tillich about the concept of paradox in *TBl* 2 (1923) 287-99; repr. in J. Moltmann, *Die Anfänge der dialektischen Theologie*, TBü, 17/1, 4th ed. (Munich, 1977), pp. 165ff.; ET *The Beginnings of Dialectic Theology*, ed. J. Moltmann (Richmond, 1968), pp. 142ff.

26. Cf. Kaftan, pp. 43ff.; idem, *Die Wahrheit der christlichen Religion* (Basel, 1888), pp. 505-6; ET *The Truth of the Christian Religion* (Edinburgh, 1894), pp. 404-5.

perceived,[27] so that one might call this peak of history revelation, since it surpasses all else to such a degree that the distinction becomes principial (Haering),[28] Wendt obviously leaning toward the statement of Schelling that strictly and very generally the whole world is revelation.[29] I need only mention this view (the "inclusive supernaturalism" of Troeltsch)[30] to make clear to you that what is done here is something that must not be done to attain access to the *Deus dixit*. A ramp is built so that one may easily ("casually"!)[31] climb up from the general history of the spirit and religion to Jesus at the top, that is, to revelation. We must smash this ramp, or at least see that revelation is not there at the top. The history of *Deus dixit* has, as qualified history, no such links with the rest of history. It must either be understood in and for itself or not at all.

5. Obviously, too, *God* is always the subject, and God the *subject*, in this concealed and singular address which is not in continuity with other events. Only revelation in the strict sense overcomes the dilemma which haunts all religious philosophy, namely, that the object escapes or transcends the subject. Revelation means the knowledge of God through God and from God. It means that the object becomes the subject. It is not our own work if we receive God's address, if we know God in faith. It is God's work in us. Our own work either breaks down here or it succeeds and the result is — an idol. But revelation means that God's work is done in us whose own work would necessarily end either the one way or the other. The modern locating of revelation in feeling or experience or what is called inwardness is so terrible just because in relation to God it ascribes to us an organ, and the use of an organ, which is ours apart from God; just because it makes God an object *without* God, and in so doing it denies

---

27. Cf. E. Troeltsch, "Die Bedeutung der Geschichtlichkeit Jesu für den Glauben," in *Die XV. Christliche Studentenkonferenz* (Aarau, 1911), pp. 85ff., repr. in *Die Absolutheit des Christentums . . .* (Munich/Hamburg, 1969), pp. 132ff., esp. p. 141. Cf. also idem, *Gesammelte Schriften*, II (Tübingen, 1913), p. 487.

28. Cf. Haering, pp. 131-34; ET pp. 91ff., 178ff.

29. Wendt, p. 270.

30. E. Tröltsch [sic], "Religionsphilosophie," in *Die Philosophie im Beginn des zwanzigsten Jahrhunderts,* I, ed. W. Windelband (Heidelberg, 1904), p. 133, where Troeltsch argues that the criticism of miracle has destroyed *exclusive supernaturalism* but proposes instead an *inclusive supernaturalism* that finds revelation and miracle in every religion.

31. Barth uses here the word *schlanter,* which has not been found, but we do find a dialect form *schlanderig* or *schlanterig* for *nachlässig;* cf. *S. Rheinisches Wörterbuch,* 7 (Berlin, 1948-1958), s.v.

revelation, in which the *Deus dixit* never ceases to be *Deus dixit* even when we believe, even when we think we feel and experience it, even when we try to speak about God. *God* is the subject even when we hear his Word in the witness of the prophets and apostles. To honor heroes, even the man Jesus of Nazareth, is to deny revelation, for it forgets the *Deus dixit,* the divine nature in Christ, to which alone honor and worship belong. *God* is subject even in what we try to say about him. Only improperly and representatively, as it were, may we feel that we ourselves are the subjects of what is said if every word that we think we may and can say objectively about God is not to be again a denial of revelation. Nowhere and never is the *Deus dixit* a reality except in God's own most proper reality.

6. Obviously, too, the process of God's self-revealing is a *dicere,* its content is Word. It is indeed *God's* Word, which we may not take on our own lips or repeat. It differs radically from all the words that we speak. Yet it is not matter, thing, or nature. It is word, *logos,* intellectual communication, a revelation of reason, and our being addressed by God is in the most pregnant sense knowledge, appropriation of word, thinking the thoughts of God that are communicated to us and that demand our hearing and obedience. To be sure, these are God's thoughts and God's reason. We stand by what we said about the relation of subject and object in this regard. Strictly, as subjects that think the thoughts of God, we can only posit God. His thoughts are not our thoughts [cf. Isa. 55:8]. They never will be. At issue in faith, however, and precisely in faith, is the Word, and knowledge of the Word. No modern anti-intellectualism and anti-moralism should cause us to put life, the irrational, the holy, etc., in place of the Word, or to put experience, violent emotion, the sense of being overpowered, etc., in place of knowledge. With such concepts — Schleiermacher is a warning here rather than an example — we slip willy-nilly into the neutral sphere[32] where the I and Thou merge into one another, where revelation becomes an influencing or an evolution, and its content becomes something given. Its real content, however, is the truth, and it thus comes to us in a form that corresponds to the truth: not in the form of an ambivalent being, but in the form of the Word which seeks to be known as the bearer of the truth, which gives itself to be known, spirit speaking to spirit through the Spirit. This is why the witness of the prophets and apostles takes the form of words, and this is why the per-

---

32. N. p. 16 has *Nebel-Sphäre* ("hazy sphere") for Barth's *neutrale Sphäre.*

mission and command are to *speak* about God, not to babble or mime or make music. I remember Ps. 150 [vv. 3-5] with its orchestra praising the Lord when I say this. But it is not for nothing that these notes are sounded at the end of the Psalter. Before them we have, for example, Ps. 119 with its 176 verses stressing the laws, the testimonies, the ways, the statutes, the commands, the ordinances — that is, the Word of the Lord. When we pass through this narrow gate [cf. Matt. 7:13] of speaking and hearing, other things become possible and necessary as well as speaking and hearing — I do not dispute this — but not before. And we are speaking about the narrow gate where it all begins when we are speaking about revelation. Here we must insist on the *Deus dixit.* The Word, the Logos, is revelation.

IV. The Situation of Preachers

With these six delimitations we have reached the point where we can draw the inferences for the situation of Christian preachers at which we began. We have seen that there is in fact a permission and command to talk about God. What happens when preachers do this, as I put it in the thesis, is that they adopt "the witness of the prophets and apostles that underlies the church, the witness which is to the effect that God has spoken and that for this reason, and with this reference, they, too, must speak about God." One might say quite simply that this happens when they set themselves in the sphere of the Christian church. This church points us — there can be no doubt about this — to the basic historical datum, the canon, and the canon points us — there can be no doubt about this either — to revelation, to the *Deus dixit* as we have tried to describe it conceptually. Referred to this court, we can and may and should speak about God. Do you understand what I said at the beginning of the second subsection of this section, namely, that the permission and command that do exist do not in any way remove from the venture of speaking about God the truly serious difficulties and suspicions that confront it, that it is precisely this permission and this command that make the matter such a venture, that make it so mortally dangerous?

You can test this by an illustration. Do not set yourself in the sphere of the Christian church, do not bother about the church's reference to the Bible or the Bible's reference to the *Deus dixit,* as is always the privilege of even Christian theologians, and lo! it is easy to talk about God. The matter becomes feather-light once you are freed from the fatal *Deus dixit.* In the depths of our own soul, or the national soul, or the world soul, you can now find something that your heart can truly experience, that you can call your God, and that you can talk about because you know it really and surely and nonparadoxically. There is now a serious or joyful reason to take courage for this task. Vigorously ventured, why should it not be as possible as any other? Surely, too, you can now find somewhere a valid vocation, fulfilling an inner drive, or proclaiming an ideal truth, or offering kindly service to your neighbors, or simply serving as an official in charge of this matter. If there is some other permission and command for speaking about God apart from the Christian permission and command — and those who pass by the latter will have to say this and, it is to be hoped, prove it — then happy are those who find it, for they escape all the worries that we spoke about at the beginning of the section, and they can be quiet pastors who never bring disquiet to anyone. On their own responsibility they may go their way in peace. Regarding the Christian permission and command, however, we have to say to those who choose it, or who at least partially rely on it too (and who would not?), that when it is given to us it plunges us into the press of anxieties and questions, and never leads us out again.

We must not present these anxieties and questions, of which knowing God is the first, as dogmatic textbooks often present them, that is, as though they attacked poor Christian theologians from outside, from the wicked, unbelieving, ungodly world, while inwardly, as Christians, as believers, these theologians would very easily achieve security if the external atheism, which is also present in their own heads and hearts, did not make so many objections: as though it were the resistance of the obtuse world that weakened and shattered their own courage; as though it were the world with its criticism and lack of respect which put a question mark against theology and the church. The very opposite is the case. If we had to do only with the world, apart from the bit of bother that is bound up with any job, we should be mostly at peace, quickly assisted by a little apologetics, routine, and sense of duty. The world does not know what real doubts are, real collapse, really being at one's wits' end, real destructive criticism. But when we follow the Christian permission and command to talk about God, we have to do with God, or, more precisely, we have to do with the Word of God in his revelation, with the *Deus dixit*. It is the *Deus dixit* that puts us in that exposed position, and with us, of course, those who only ten percent or one percent rely on this permission and command. Faith only as big as a grain of mustard seed [cf. Matt. 17:20], the last and least relic of the *Deus dixit*, is enough in fact to put us in that position (glad though we would have been to escape it), to expose us to those questions and anxieties.

Must I prove this from the definitions of the concept of revelation that we have discovered? Is it not mortally dangerous if I know that I must speak — not speak in tongues, not make an impression, not speak well, but speak words on the basis of God's Word with the aim of awakening knowledge, this knowledge, the knowledge of God? I know that I have to speak and not keep silence, to speak consciously and responsibly, and if the significance of what I say is to be that not I but the subject who alone can bear witness to God because he is God is to speak his Word in my words? If I have to speak but will deceive my hearers and myself if I build for them ramps and access roads to what I really have to say, if I lead them to some human peak supposing that I can show them God there? Why can I not do this? Because revelation can be understood only in terms of itself. Is it not mortally dangerous, too, if I know that I have to speak but all that I might say very generally about truth, freedom, eternity, peace, heaven, earth, and humanity helps me not at all because I have to speak about the absolutely unique and particular thing, the "accidental truth of history"[33] that is Jesus Christ (whether I name the name or not), saying that this is the *Deus dixit?* If, finally, I know that I can never directly communicate that about which I speak, that I can never set it before my hearers as a given thing, that on pain of complete failure from a Christian standpoint, I can never even make the attempt to enforce direct communication, either by orthodox or biblicist pressures, or by dialectical surprises, or by emotion, enthusiasm, inwardness, or the like, because this is a denial of revelation, which is always the disclosing of something hidden by God himself, the direct communication from one person to another of something that is already disclosed, of a mystery that is no longer a mystery. These are the commands and prohibitions that surround the Christian permission and command to talk about God.

Is it not clear that those who receive this permission and command, who speak about God on these presuppositions, who must always, when they speak, remember the *Deus dixit* as the truth and the judgment, the grounding and the transcending, of all that they can say — that such people know what is meant by real doubt of God as an object of human thought and speech, by the real shattering and collapse of human courage

---

33. Echoing Lessing's famous phrase, *Über den Beweis,* p. 12; ET *Theological Writings,* p. 53.

for this undertaking, by real criticism of their own authority? What do others know about this? And because there are not many theologians who in what they say about God can constantly suppress the *Deus dixit* which stands in the background, there are not many who do not at least know something about these problems. Good for them that with this something they really have Christian permission and command for what they are doing. In this light we might simply laugh at what is said against the church and theology by the world's consciousness of itself both ancient and modern, by a rational ethics, or by various philosophies. We do not laugh because we know only too well where all their objections finally come from, how justified they are, perhaps not on the lips of those who make them, but objectively, as rocks which necessarily lie in the path of those who want to speak about God on the basis of revelation. But in this light we can understand the saying that we should not fear mere humans — even ourselves — but God, that we should not fear those who can kill the body but not the soul, but him who can destroy both body and soul in hell [Matt. 10:28]. I have expressed this line of thought in the thesis in the words: "This assumption . . . means that with fear and trembling they recognize God as the true subject of the biblical witness and their own proclamation."

A final and decisive thing has still to be said about the condition under which Christian preachers stand, the permission and command to speak that they are given, the cause of their greater or lesser problems in relation to other religious speakers. We can hardly do more than touch upon it, than show that when we raise a final question we come up against something that has no basis, or has a basis only in itself, that has its basis and must be given its basis only in God. Revelation means address. This was the first definition to which we drew attention. Without the correlation of address and being addressed, revelation is not revelation. Without this correlation there is also no Christian permission or command to talk about God. But who of us can say on our own that we stand in this correlation, that our eyes can see the eternal light, and have in fact seen it? Is it, then, only in this way, following the reference of the Christian church, the witness of the prophets and apostles, and by this medium coming to the *Deus dixit* and in fear and trembling pondering it, that we can receive the Christian permission and command to talk about God? What is there to receive if it is an inalienable condition of revelation that God must be the subject before he can be the object? Is it not clear that we have to be received before we can receive, so that the decisive condition of the existence of Christian preachers is that they must accept the divine address as directed to themselves too?

It is as well not to conclude too rashly that we hear and therefore receive, that we believe and therefore speak, just because we say what the prophets and apostles say. What they say can be thought and said by us only with a final circumspection. If we think otherwise, we probably do not know what it is all about. Whether we stand in the correlation of address and being addressed is always a radical question inasmuch as we are human. It was a question for the prophets and apostles as well. Over against "I believe and therefore I speak" stands "I am greatly afflicted" (Ps. 116:10).[34] The correlation of faith and question accompanies that of revelation and faith (see § 4 below). If there were no question, if the question were not a vital one, if there were a security in us, if we had answered and done away with the question, the correlate of faith would certainly not be revelation or the *Deus dixit*. The bad thing about the modern theology of experience is that it builds its certainty about God upon something that is given in the human subject when the only thing that is given in this subject, even in the believer, is the question. To be real, our certainty about God must always lie in God's hands. Those who wait upon God, not those who have found certainty in themselves, will get new strength and mount up with wings like eagles [Isa. 40:31]. To believe is to be content to wait, to know that assurance is hidden securely in God, which is infinitely better than having it in ourselves. *Deus dixit* is our confidence, not experience. We can *only* believe. We can only believe even that our faith is true faith.[35] The righteousness of faith is God's righteousness. Nevertheless, it was not bad advice when medieval theologians and pastors — for at this point theology merges into pastoral care — pointed those who faced this final question to the representative faith of the Christian church which sustains that of individuals. Those who see in the church God's church will not find in this thought, which the young Luther espoused,[36] anything objectionably "catholic" that they may and should reject. Modern theologians are also advised from time to time, instead of engaging in apologetics, to remember that when they were infants it was once said to them on the lips of the church: "I baptize thee

---

34. Barth follows the LXX here, like Paul in 2 Cor. 4:13.

35. Marginal note: "Unending dialectic? Unending *parable* of the eternal. God!"

36. Cf. Luther's sermon on proper preparation for receiving the eucharist (1518), in WA, 1, 333, 23-26.

in the name of the Father, the Son, and the Holy Ghost." This address and being addressed, at any rate, took place without any confusion with experience being able to slip in. We did not (fortunately) experience our baptism, yet we *are* baptized.

Such a "we are" without experience is what Calvin likes to recall and appeal to in this connection: the secret testimony of the Holy Spirit by which the witness of scripture becomes God's self-witness to us.[37] But can the *Deus dixit* to which scripture bears witness become visible and conceivable in all its distinctness without our being addressed? Could we put the question whether we are really addressed if we had not already heard the address, if we were not already addressed? Yet the very reference to the Holy Spirit, that is, to God himself in the present, in the church, and in us, is also a reminder that we have here something neither to be experienced nor to be thought nor — the third possibility — to be asserted, that God himself bears witness to himself. That he does so, not the "heart," is what makes a theologian.[38] Here is the knowledge, courage, and authority of the Christian preacher. Even for those of us who are not prophets, here is the coal from the altar which the seraph took with tongs and with which he touched the prophet's lips when he confessed that he was lost in the presence of the Lord of Hosts on account of the unclean lips of himself and his people [Isa. 6:5-7].

37. *Inst.* I, 7, 4.

38. Cf. C. Ullmann's Preface to A. Neander, *Allgemeine Geschichte der christlichen Religion und Kirche,* I, 4th ed. (Gotha, 1863), p. XXIII, for Neander's statement that we need not be ashamed to say that the heart makes a theologian, since it helps theology back from a dead scholasticism to the living divine word; ET *General History* (Boston, 1871), p. XXIII.

§ 4

Man* and His Question

God's revelation, which is the basis of Christian preaching, is the answer to our question how we can overcome the contradiction in our existence, which we have to view not as our destiny but as our responsible act, and which we know that we cannot overcome. But we know ourselves in this regard only as God makes himself known to us. We would not ask about God had not God already answered us. Because of this, we can neither evade the question about God nor settle it in any sense.

I. The Concept of Man

In the preceding section we achieved a very general concept of the final thing to which dogmatic reflection must relate, that is, God's Word in revelation, by starting with the question how we can ever dare to speak about God. But we must now perceive more than the very general concept if we are to attain to unshakable clarity about this point of reference. It is thus essential that we continue our scrutiny of this nail on which all dogmatics as well as Christian preaching hangs by means of further questions. In so doing we shall unavoidably touch as it were a priori on some of the burning questions of dogmatics proper in the light of revelation,

---

*In this translation we have for the most part avoided terms that have come to be regarded as sexist. In this section, however, we could have done this only with the help of clumsy circumlocutions and artificial constructions which are anachronistic in content. It should be understood that in retaining "man" we are using it in the primary generic sense (German: *Mensch*), which was generally recognized and accepted at the time when Barth delivered these lectures.

but you must not expect a thorough treatment of the complexes of questions that come to light here. This will follow a posteriori in the next semester when we deal with the content of Christian preaching.

The first burning issue, as you might gather from the thesis, is in my view the concept of man. If in the preceding section we asked where what is said in Christian preaching comes from, the next question, which will serve to elucidate this decisive "whence," is that of the "whither," that is, to whom is it directed? Today, of course, we need hardly stress that it is not a monologue, for modern preaching is only too heavily directed to people, only too emphatically aimed at the public. But the fact that preachers pay attention to the needs, interests, situation, and capacity of the public is no guarantee that they are really addressing man, for in no case[1] is the man who ought to be addressed and waits to be addressed the public. He is arcane, secret, hidden. Sermons which should stir and edify and move him will probably leave this man empty and cold and untouched. By the high-angle fire of heavy artillery directed above the head of the public to the more distant entrenched position, this man is perhaps better served in truth than by the all-too-zealous pounding of the forward trenches, which he has long since derisively evacuated.

To be sure, preaching is not a monologue. It is a kind of dialogue. And people are the partners in this dialogue — where would we find man except in people as they are and as they live? But what sermons aim at is the *human* in people: not their morality that needs confirming and strengthening, not their devotion that needs to be piously nurtured, not their culture that needs religious underpinnings, not their nationality and its peculiar values that need to be conserved, not the bourgeois element in them that longs for peace and order, and naturally not the proletarian element in them that seeks justification for its dissatisfaction and rebelliousness. People are all these things, but not the *human* in them. The distinction must be considered at least as exactly as the distinction between God and the gods. It is only a hair's breadth from this. If preaching does not press on through all those things — through them indeed, but still *through* them — to the fortress which is the seat of man, arrogantly and despairingly entrenched behind them; if it does not see their relativity even in human terms but remains stuck in them; if it does not begin with the presupposition that man wants to be taken more seriously by it than he takes himself, namely, with *total* seriousness, then it is setting its sights too low, and its effort is meaningless no matter how great its sound and fury.

I am not making up what I am saying. I think it is obvious to anybody

---

1. Barth uses here the dialect form *von wegen* for *auf keinen Fall*.

who realizes that style is not an external but an internal matter, not a matter of form but of content. The apparatus and staging and claim of Christian preaching have always made it very plain, and still do so today. The refutation of preaching that aims at the public rather than the arcane hearer lies in the following facts (and please accustom yourselves once again to weighing the force of such arguments). Prayer is offered before and after preaching, and this seems to indicate that we are pressing on to the frontiers of human existence between such acts. Certain hymns are sung, and if we are not honest enough to change them as some of the older rationalists did, these are an open protest against a preaching which does not deal with the wound which the older hymns more or less tastefully tell us about. Preaching takes place from the pulpit (a place which by its awesome but obviously intentional height differs from a rostrum), and on the pulpit, as a final warning to those who ascend it, there is a big Bible. Preachers also wear a robe — I am not embarrassed even to say this — and they should do so, for it is a salutary reminder that from those who wear this special garment the people expect a special word. A formidable and even demonic instrument, the organ, is also active, and in order that town and country alike should be aware of the preaching, bells are rung (about the philosophy of which you may find some discussion in Spengler).[2] Gothic arches and windows — even if unfortunately some of them do come from the 1890s — remind you at least from afar of the Gothic spirit, and hence remind you vigorously of the arcane rather than the public element. And if none of these things helps, will not the crosses in the churchyard which quietly look in through the windows tell you unambiguously what is relevant here and what is not? All human things, you might object. Yes indeed, I reply. But it is the human element in preaching that is our present concern.

Through all these human things — I do not regard them as more — does not the man who is to be addressed in preaching show us as what, in what sphere, and on what level he desires and expects to be addressed in it? Is not the very style which it seems this action must have — and even freethinking speakers and their auditoriums, we find, constantly come back to a kind of ecclesiastical style — is not this style a cogent indication of the fact that quite apart from its theological content, and even from the human angle, this action is meant to be and is regarded as a very singular action which touches and concerns a point on the frontier of humanity which nothing else touches? Understandably, modern Protestant preaching feels pressured by this style, and feels that it must attack it if possible for deeply religious reasons. As though we could not just as well

---

2. No such discussion has been found in Spengler's works.

walk on our hands as escape this style in face of what man (not men) basically and rightly expects from this action! As though it would not be much better to be corrected by the pressure that undoubtedly lies on us here, to be called back to the insight that the man to whom we turn in preaching is not public but hidden, so that on the basis of this better insight into the "whither" of preaching we may perhaps get a better conception of its "whence!"

II. What Is Man?

But who and what is the man to whom Christian preaching is and should be addressed if he is not to be confused with the public, if those human things that surround preaching are to point us to the fact that if this man turns to us theologians at all he feels that he is misunderstood if we address him in terms of what he usually seems to be at a first glance and on the surface? What is man — "that thou art mindful of him," as we go on to read very pertinently in Ps. 8 [v. 5]. We cannot proceed by consulting philosophy about the concept of man. We are asking about the man who is addressed, and is to be addressed, in Christian preaching, about the man who is presupposed by the revelation that is the basis of Christian preaching. At important points the picture of this man might coincide with man's own picture of himself, but we can establish this only later. We cannot begin with that self-portrait, even though in its own place it might have value and significance. It does not have this in basic dogmatics. "That thou art mindful of him" is what interests us about man, the reflection of man in revelation, in the *Deus dixit* which is the source of preaching, and it does so, not in order that we may understand man better, but that we may understand revelation better.

What must man be because revelation is? This is how I pose the question in all candor. Putting it this way has at least the advantage that later we will not have to make illegitimate leaps and introduce a Deus ex machina. The Deus ex machina is already on the stage. I will first develop what I think I perceive in general terms and then work out some detailed definitions.

God's revealing of himself to man, his making himself known out of his hiddenness, presupposes that man is separated from God but should not be so, revelation being a repairing of damage. Alone, away from God, man is in a far country. Older theologians (I first find the expression in

Bonaventura) said that holy scripture (they meant theology as a whole) is addressed to pilgrim man.[3] This man is not at home in the houses in and between which he comes and goes. His home is with God, but he is alone, not with God. Hence this pilgrim man presupposed by revelation cannot be identical with the man who is at home with God, who does not have to desire God because he already has him present in his heart or conscience, in his morals or works, in his relation to nature or in the ardor of his life's course, because he knows himself, is at peace with himself, and is thus at home with God. If there were really such a man, then the Word of God, the Word from the home country to a foreign land, the Word to the pilgrim who with Paul is wandering far from God [cf. 2 Cor. 5:6-9], would not apply to this man. What would there be to say to him? He would need no Word of God. He would not be able to hear it. Distance is needed to hear God's Word. But we do not see any such man any more than we see the Christian preacher (see § 3.IV above) who can really mention a permission and command to talk about God that is not Christian. We never meet up with either the one or the other. We can only construct people of this kind.

But how can we understand the alienation of solitary man that is proper to the real man to whom God's revelation comes? It obviously means that his being here or there, or this or that, or this way or that way, or this person or that person, which in all its manifold fluidity constitutes his existence, stands under the caveat that anything that he is, he also is not, so that he has no rest but is subject to change, like a traveler who can only stop but never settle down, who must always go on again when he arrives. If even a little or for a moment his existence, his being, were being without nonbeing, then he would be at home with God. But this is not so. Here is the contradiction of his being. This is what makes him a wanderer on the road and abroad. I illustrate. He lives and must die. He knows truths and goals and meaning, but as his knowledge grows, the more his knowledge of the total truth and goal and meaning recedes. He scatters as he gathers. He knows the good that he ought to do, but as he knows it, and the better he knows it, he also knows that he does not do it and never will. He thinks the conclusive thought of eternity, but as he thinks it, he has to see that he has only thought something temporal and material, an absolute which is a monstrous relative. He dreams the dream of his own divine likeness and knows that the dream is not a dream but truth, and then he opens his eyes

---

3. *Breviloquium,* Prol. 3.

and finds that in all honesty he stands at every point in an incontestable relationship to the beast. He wants to settle down, but he has to move on. Or, from another angle, he determines to be content with the knowledge, the admiration, and the enjoyment of the finite, but as such is not everything finite, even the smallest thing, the boundary of the infinite? Every desire wants eternity.[4] The enemy that changes satisfaction into dissatisfaction is already at the gate and is entering. He tries to reach a settlement with the profound syllogism that all persons must die, that Caius is a person, and hence that Caius must die too,[5] but what is the life with which he tries to reach a settlement by means of this syllogism? He resolves to choose action instead of reflection — who does not have to do this, who does not do it? — we act even when we reflect on the futility of our action — but how does the fact that we act, and the brisk courage with which we do it, alter the relentlessness of the crisis which comes upon our will as the demand for a good will, as the question from some unknown sphere beyond concerning the goodness of what we actually do? I want to say yes to myself. We think it is the climax of our lives when we manage to do that, when we live through the exciting hours of passion or knowledge or action, as though the stone guest were not already knocking at the door, if Don Juan is so mad and so sure of his I that he opens to the one who will destroy this I.[6] Man always wants to settle down, but he must always move on, with no rest, no dwelling, either among angels or animals, either in body or soul, either in nature or spirit, either in the finite or the infinite, either in being or thought, either in the empirical consciousness or the transcendental, either in the non-I or the I, either in himself or for himself. Why? Because he is by himself, and he himself is always both things, and twist and turn as he will, he is always the one under the almost crushing contradiction of the other, so that he cannot be glad about the one because of the other. "The flesh lusts against the Spirit and the Spirit against the flesh; these are opposed to one another" (Gal. 5:17). This opposition is our foreign land, our human existence.

Such is the man to whom revelation is directed. This is how we must see him and think of him because of revelation. He does not know himself, he cannot handle himself or be satisfied with himself. In spite of all the assurance that he assumes and with which he believes in the norms

---

4. Cf. F. Nietzsche, *Also sprach Zarathustra*, IV/10, in *Werke*, II (Darmstadt, 1963), p. 557.

5. The classical example of the syllogism.

6. W. A. Mozart, *Don Giovanni*, II, 1.

and values that he has set up, he cannot escape the rift that runs through himself as one who has been uprooted from his home, who has been thrown into the absolute tumult of the unleashed elements, who has long since attempted everything that can be done with the body without the soul, or with the spirit against nature, or in the finite apart from the infinite, or in life as though there were no death, or with a pious scorn for the world or a worldly despising of piety, as one who knows that we can accomplish absolutely nothing in any of these fields, that we move in a circle whether we begin right or left or above or below.

It is not that everything boils down to one thing; it would be meaningless to say that. The real trouble is that there are always two. Man has an incurable wound. He has a thorn in the flesh [cf. 2 Cor. 12:7] of which he cannot be rid because he cannot be rid of himself. He suffers from the fact that he is something that has to be overcome[7] and cannot be overcome. In his subjectivity he cannot be glad for a moment, because not for a moment is he secure, because notoriously he is constantly what he is not and is not what he is. This is the man to whom God's revelation comes. This is the man for whom God becomes subject.

We may quietly agree in passing that the general picture of this man is not unknown in philosophical reflection or deeper human self-reflection in general. I have expressly indicated this by means of various allusions. In the attempt to understand himself, if it is not undertaken in a trifling and bungling manner, man can understand the basic features of his whole structure only as he has to be understood as one who is addressed by God's Word. The contact that we make with philosophy at this point is welcome to us as a secondary confirmation that even from a human standpoint we have not been describing a phantom but the form that anyone might know. I think that with or without this support from philosophy we may quietly assume that as Christian preachers we are addressing real man, the man in men, the secret man and not the public man, when we accept this depiction of man, when we presuppose that this question is the true concern which wittingly or unwittingly has led him to us in the church, when we realize that we must speak to this contradiction, this riddle, these questions, and that the value of what we say will be measured by whether it means anything in this situation.

Nevertheless, with what we have said thus far, we have not yet

---

7. Cf. F. Nietzsche, *Also sprach Zarathustra*, p. 279: "Man is something that has to be overcome."

exhausted the content of the question how we are to think of man because of revelation. We must go further along this path. The Christian concept of man, like that of revelation, demands some detailed definitions. I will try to see what they are in what follows.

III. Man as Pilgrim

1. On the presupposition of revelation, the contradiction in man cannot in any circumstances or in any sense be viewed as a rule or order, let alone as a divinely willed order. It is an intervening disorder, disruption, curse. The ancient heretic Marcion chose the better part here in contrast to the oversynthetic thinking of the main church both past and present, little though we may applaud his demiurge. Let us recall the element in the concept of revelation that I have called contingency or singularity. Why cannot the Word of God be written very generally, spanning the whole harmoniously like a rainbow? Why the historical contingency of the *Deus dixit?* Again, why is not that which the Word of God is meant to restore something general and orderly and planned? Unlike speculative thinkers in every age, from Origen by way of Zwingli to Schleiermacher and Hegel,[8] we must not view man's alienation from God as[9] a stage in God's will that man necessarily had to go through, as a process that could not have been different. It is instead the very epitome of the particular that cannot be reduced to a system. It is an episode. Man is not understood, at least in a Christian sense, if his being is as it were sanctioned by theological or philosophical systematizing, even though the concept of God's glory stands at the head of the system, as in Zwingli.[10] God is not glorified by our using the concepts of creation and providence to sanctify that which from a Christian standpoint at least is unholy and has to be overcome. Even as the Creator and Ruler of all things God can be praised only by calling upon him in our need. And need means that the thesis and antithesis in the contradiction are not balanced like the arms of a scales. Otherwise it would not be a need and we would not have to call upon God. This leads us at once to the next point.

---

8. For examples cf. *ChD*, pp. 97-98, nn. 14, 16, 17, 18.

9. Barth had a *zu* here, which the editor has replaced by *als*.

10. Cf. Zwingli's sermon *On Providence*, ch. 5, Opera, IV, p. 109; ET (Durham, NC, 1983), p. 177.

2. From a Christian standpoint the definition of man as a pilgrim is a definition of existence, not merely of thought. There is no reason why it should not have also logical, epistemological, and dialectical significance. The whole history of philosophy shows this. But the decisive point for the Christian understanding of this feature is that what is understood thereby is first of all the real dialectic of life. Pilgrim man stands between Scylla and Charybdis, between two truths that make each other, and man as a third thing between them, impossible. Even in his family and nation and church and culture, man is truly uprooted, no matter how strongly or weakly this may be apparent. He may reflect upon his path, he may find pleasure in the tireless self-movement of the idea, he may erect a system of paradoxes, he may be very comfortable in his humanity. He can do these things, but he is not pilgrim man as he does so. We reach here a point at which Kierkegaard once thought that he should vindicate the interests of Christianity against Hegel. The relation of Hegel's dialectic to the real dialectic seemed to him to be like that of Leporello with his record to his master Don Juan, who in contrast *himself* drinks and seduces and enjoys life, and hence *himself* goes to hell.[11] The "himself" must be asserted. The Christian concept of man becomes unambivalent only when it ceases to denote a mere relation and begins to denote what happens in the relation, when man is not the subject of mere discussion or clarification but the participant in a battle report who has just emerged from the fray. We may compare this definition, the existentiality of the human contradiction, with that of revelation, which I have called address. God's address is to pilgrim man himself, not to his philosophical shadow.

3. With this is connected the third point. Man cannot view the disorder in which he is entangled as his fate. He must view it as his responsible act, his fault. The element of fate that all of us, parents and children, are human, and that we are thus implicated in the contradiction, in the alienation from God, is beyond dispute. But this consideration cannot be our final one. The rift goes through our existence because we cause it ourselves and are not just spectators of this tragedy. In defining revelation, we stressed the fact that God's address is a miracle, not a marvel. It is an act of God, not a manifest givenness of the divine. In the same

---

11. Barth has in mind the general tenor of Kierkegaard's criticism of Hegel and combines it with the reference in *Die Tagebücher,* I, 1834-1848, ed. T. Haecker (Innsbruck, 1923), p. 97.

way we are not to view in natural or material or static terms the situation of the man to whom this address relates, the hiddenness of God for us if he did not address us, our nonseeing and nonhearing of God were he not himself both eye and ear. Man must not meet God's grace — as we may best describe his action — with a mere insight into his own relativity, finitude, creatureliness, etc., with a mere assertion that he is merely a man, but with shame that he is *this* man. "Fools and slow of heart" [Luke 24:25] — this is what we are with our nonseeing and nonhearing. Sighing at the plight we are in, if we see things aright, must go deeper and become pain at our sin, without which we do not see that the alienation of pilgrim man is really alienation from God. The final point follows at once.

4. From a Christian standpoint, the human situation is seen to be a final one apart from the divine possibility. The contradiction cannot be overcome. This follows from the fact that man must always view it also and primarily as his own act. Overcoming it would mean removing the subject that causes it, the subject in which it continually has its origin. In keeping with this is the truth that in revelation we always have to do with the fact that God becomes the subject. God overcomes the contradiction by himself becoming man and by creating faith and obedience in us by his Spirit. But because this is exclusively *his* possibility, to say this is to say that *man* has no possibilities in this direction. In this final definition we tear up by the roots all the optimism to which people so readily yield in modern theology. It will not do to accept the contradiction and then to give the assurance that something which transcends it, a third and higher thing, a synthesis in which the antitheses can come to rest, presses upon us so ineluctably that we cannot avoid positing it as real and thereby overcoming the contradiction. It is we who (rather boldly) dare to do this. And it is we who still engage in the contradiction as we do so, for in so doing how are we in any position to do anything but posit a new contradiction? Nor will it do to accept the impossibility of overcoming the contradiction and then to make it all the object of a dialectical reversal, attaining in this way to the saving position of making a truly radical negation and then promptly altering the sign, and securing a happy ending, on the ground that because a contradiction that we cannot remove is one side of the equation, its overcoming is its conceptually necessary counterpart. Certainly we can and must *think* this, but we can *only* think it. Thinking the possibility that is the opposite of an impossibility does not alter the finality of the impossibility. On the contrary, it confirms it. The sign

that we have altered says no more and no less than everything that we do. What hands have built. . . .[12]

In my view, it also will not do that after perhaps renouncing the two above procedures, at the last moment, when all other lights have been put out, we try to retrieve the lost situation by bringing in a visible historical entity, Jesus of Nazareth, in which the contradiction is supposedly overcome. I am not contesting, of course, the material significance of this final attempt at a solution. It points to the divine possibility of a solution that announces itself in revelation. But we should not introduce this reference as a final human attempt, as obviously happens when an emphasis on the *historical* entity Jesus approvingly recalls its presence in our own sphere, and an emphasis on the visibility approvingly recalls our own ability to grasp it. As though this entity were not thereby brought into the dialectic of our contradiction! As though by being made an instrument of the human attempt at a solution it could be made to serve an apologetic purpose and be a solution, an overcoming, or an answer! As though it would not instead confirm the finality of the judgment that stands over all things human!

When I say that the contradiction is final, I mean that no word that man speaks as subject is the word of reconciliation, not even the word "Jesus Christ," which is not a magic formula. There is room for this word only when God as subject makes room for it, when he takes it up and speaks it. Only on this presupposition, to which we should not have resort only at the last when we can do nothing else, but at the very outset, only thus is the reference to Jesus Christ anything better than an evasion. In the place which God creates, as God's own Word, this Word can in fact be the Word of reconciliation, of overcoming, of homecoming. But if it is to be such a Word on our lips, we must first learn radically to renounce its compromising use as a Deus ex machina, as a final resort in a not quite hopeless situation.

I hope that you will at least agree with me to the extent of seeing that if we put the concept of revelation at the head, the concept of man necessarily demands with all strictness this final definition, the definitive nature of his being out on the street. It will not have escaped you that with what we have said in subsections II and III we have touched on the basic features of what will call for treatment in dogmatics proper as the doctrines of the fall, original sin, and the bondage of the will.

---

12. F. von Schiller, *Wilhelm Tell*, I, 3: "What hands have built, hands can throw down."

IV. Man in Relation to God

When we try to see man in the light of the concept of revelation, and in so doing arrive at this result, we are forced to say a final thing that we would otherwise (i.e., apart from this starting point and result) be forbidden to say. We are forced to say that we may not and cannot understand him except in relation to God. If we strongly endorse this view of man in contradiction according to the aforementioned Christian definitions, then we endorse equally strongly the view that this man stands before God. "We know ourselves only as God makes himself known to us." I do not know whether you wish to object that this is a circular argument, an attempt like others to do what was previously rejected as impossible, a piece of artifice, and not a very good one in view of its logical poverty, consisting as it does of an initial definition of man in terms of God's revelation, and then of the statement that man as thus defined can be understood only in terms of this revelation. To this my reply is as follows.

1. Let us understand one another. I naturally took this course intentionally and quite openly. I do not think at all that we can admire here a dialectical device or fabulous theological discovery, a novel trick whereby the good Lord may be brought in by the back door. You must understand the second part of the thesis in the strictest sense analytically. I said expressly that the presupposition of our consideration of man is that God is at work, that God is addressing him. The result of the inquiry was "pilgrim man" who himself stands responsibly and inescapably under the curse of his contradiction and who simply has at his command no devices or discoveries or escapes in the direction of God. What we are doing is nothing other, and is meant to be nothing other, than a recalling of this presupposition. Because God is at work, because he addresses man, man has to be seen and thought of thus, with this result. This is my general answer by way of clarifying the situation.

2. I realize fully that this line of thought has the same logical form of a begging of the question as does that of the modern theology that I believe I must reject. The difference is (a) that I see the matter to be necessary in advance and do not have to find it so later to my shame, (b) that what I am begging is directly opposite, and (c) that the circle thus moves in the opposite direction. As a second answer, then, I would put three questions for your consideration.

(a) What else is theology all about but—not just any begging of the question but the begging of the question par excellence? No matter how we define the task of theology in detail, whether we start with the consciousness of faith, or a church doctrine, or the Bible, or, as I have proposed, with the concept of preaching, we always have as the theme of this science an axiom, a final and nonderivable thing that is grounded in itself and is original in the absolute sense. From one or other of those starting points it is this that we are seeking, but how and where can it be sought if it is not already presupposed as the axiom behind the given factors with which we begin? Otherwise it would not be this principle, the principle of all principles. If we do not presuppose what we are seeking, we do not know what we are seeking and we will certainly find something other than *this* principle. Or else in the course of our search we will have to admit shamefacedly and blushingly that we really were seeking something other than what we at first made out, namely, this principle. Then (with dangerous maneuvers in which we might fall overboard) we shall have to alter our theme and method. But this is an undertaking which as a mixture of slyness and stupidity has brought theology into a discredit which, it seems to me, might have been avoided if we had resolved at the outset to make it clear to ourselves and to others what we were doing. If theology is ashamed of begging the question, of begging this question, then it is ashamed of the gospel [cf. Rom. 1:16], and this cannot have good results either in this world or the next.

(b) If we accept this general point, then the principle, the first datum which we have to accept because it is the first, cannot be derived from anything else. It can only be the point of derivation to which we must constantly return. It has not first to be discovered; it has simply to be rediscovered as something that has been forgotten, for we already know it. But can this principle, then, be anything other than God? Is it an insignificant matter that this whole discipline bears the name *theo*logy? Or do modern theologians really think that man and his religion are the first datum, self-grounded and ultimate, and that God simply relates to these as predicate to subject, a predicate that is posited later, and can only be posited later? They usually protect themselves against the idea that this is their real view, or that of the sainted Schleiermacher. They make strenuous efforts to move on in some way from man and his religion to the statement that "God is." They also give very sincere assurances that they want nothing whatever to do with the wicked Feuerbach. These efforts and assurances show that it is not in fact their real view. But why in the world, if their real view is that originally and prior to all other determinations man stands before God, is addressed by him, is to be understood in this light, and hence only in relation to God — why in the world do they not come right out with this real view of theirs, or why do they come out with it only when it might seem to be a way out of a difficulty?

(c) If this be granted, then we must ask whether the course of reflection, once we have found the principle (the divine address in revelation) can be any other than that of a movement from God (this principle or first datum) to his counterpart, to man, and then a movement back from this counterpart, now set in the light of the original principle, to the place from which we come. If it be presupposed that in theology we are dealing with the principle of all principles, which irrespective of secondary principles can be sought only when one starts with its original givenness, and if it also be presupposed that this principle is identical, not with man but with God, then is it not clear that we learn about man from God and his Word when it is a matter of man's supposed dealings with God, and that conversely our findings about this man are to be explained only in terms of his relation to God, his being known by God [cf. Gal. 4:9]? To what, then, may we compare the teaching about principles that we find in modern theology? Is it not like a clock which is constructed in such a way that the fingers move the other way round? What does this mean? It is an attempt to force a way to God from man considered without God, and then, when God is reached and understood in this way, to end very happily with man reconsidered through the prism of this man-god. Is it not clear that with boundless sentimentality and exaggeration this means, first, that we must ascribe to man a consciousness of God, experiences of transcendence, unavoidable feelings, and the like, which no man has ever really had; second, that on this basis we must then attempt a change of genus to the existence of God, to which our philosophical neighbors, whom we are trying to please, can respond only with a forgiving smile, and rightly so; third, that in this way we can only acquire a god which is an image and likeness, to which the second commandment expressly forbids us to pray or to offer service [Exod. 20:4-5]; and fourth, that after the detour of all these half-measures and incredibilities, returning to earth after this Icarus-flight, we probably have less to tell those who have remained on earth than they can tell themselves without such religious fireworks?

As regards the "circle," I would put three questions of my own. If theology understands itself seriously and is to be taken seriously, can it be anything other than a fundamental begging of this question, openly undertaken as such? Can the principle of theology be sought anywhere but in God himself and known in any way but from God himself, that is, from revelation? Can man know himself except as he is primarily known by God himself?

If we must answer no to all these questions, then you can hardly fail to see that the second part of our thesis is self-evident. At any rate, you must perceive that it has nothing whatever to do with the customary attempts to break the finality of the contradiction in human existence, to expunge the impossibility of transition to a higher third thing or to a dialectical opposite. On the contrary, the whole validity of the second part of our thesis depends on the inviolability of our fourth definition. Modern theology cannot press on with a good conscience to the statement of Pascal that we could not seek God if we had not already found him.[13] This is most likely because it does not take seriously the prohibition established by our fourth definition. Rushing past the insight that *we* can only *ask* after God, smuggling in answers and solutions to our questions, possessing and enjoying God in our being in contradiction, it cannot possibly have the backbone for the thesis that we could not ask after God if he had not already answered us, that we stand before God in a contradiction that we ourselves cannot overcome, that we are addressed by him who overcomes it — our Reconciler, Creator, and Redeemer. Once we acknowledge the prohibition, which might well stand in a not very distant relation to the prohibition of the fruit of a certain tree [Gen. 2:17], we may and must venture the thesis. It is not then a venture but something self-evident, not a synthetic statement but an analytic statement.

I can best illustrate this conclusion from the history of Reformed theology. The older Reformed catechisms begin their questions and answers, in contrast to what one might expect from current views of Reformed theology, with the theme of this section, with man and his question. They apparently begin from below, inductively, not from above, deductively. They ask by whom or to what end we were created (Leo Jud, Emden, Micronius),[14] or what is the end of human life (Calvin, Westminster),[15] or what is our only comfort in life and death (Heidelberg).[16]

---

13. B. Pascal, *Pensées* (1670), Fr. 553: "Console-toi, tu ne me chercherais pas, si tu ne m'avais trouvé."

14. *Der kurze Katechismus Leo Juds* (1941); *Emdener Katechismus* (1554), in *BSRK,* p. 666.23ff., qu. 1; *Der kleine Katechismus Microns* (1539).

15. Calvin's Geneva Catechism (1945), in *BSRK,* p. 117.7ff.; Westminster Shorter Catechism (1647), in Schaff, p. 676.

16. Heidelberg Catechism (1563), in *BSRK,* p. 682.20ff.; Schaff, p. 322.

Note the words "created," "end," and "comfort," which are all two-sided. "Created" expresses an awareness of human creatureliness, but already even before the answer is given it also expresses an awareness of the Creator and hence of the meaning of creation. "End" means both conclusion or limit and purpose or task. In the question about "comfort" lies both a knowledge of the need for it, of the total need for it (for there is only one comfort), and also of the fact that comfort exists. All these are questions, but as such, even though they are sharp and ruthless and final questions, they also document the answers that will be given. When the answers are given, they are simply analyses of the questions: God has created me to share his good things, to be his image, to learn to know and serve him, that he may be glorified in us (Calvin). With body and soul, in life and death, I am not my own, but belong to my faithful Savior, Jesus Christ (Heidelberg). Where would the questions come from if the answers were not already there? What are the questions but projections of the answers that follow them in time and logic? Those who ask the right question about God show that they already know God's answer. It is not as the prisoners of an ungodly world or their own ignorance that they ask in this way, precisely when they ask, and simply ask, and ask principially, about the meaning of their creatureliness, about the end of human life, about their only comfort, and, we might add, about the overcoming of the final rift that is impossible for us. Those who ask thus are prisoners of Zion (Ps. 126:1), God's prisoners. God has cut off every escape, bolted every door, made all accommodation impossible, so that they have to ask, and can only ask, but have to ask the question to which only God can give and be the answer, but to which he does give and is the answer. How else can we understand those who ask thus except in relation to God? In the question to which as such, from a human standpoint, there is no answer, their relation to God lies. It does not mean that they have now put a bridge across the abyss. It means that the bridge has already been put there, that they are addressed by God.

V. The Concrete Situation of Preachers

"For this reason we can neither evade the question about God nor settle it in any sense," runs the conclusion of our thesis. I want to come back to the concrete situation at which we started, namely, that of preachers and those whom they address. The way to the man in men is the well-considered theological begging of the question. Men are to be addressed because God addresses them and has already done so. Christian preachers must believe in God and accept the validity of the presupposition of revelation not only for their own sake but also for that of those to whom they turn. Then they speak to man and not just men, to the arcane man and not just the public man. Then their preaching is not a monologue but part of a dialogue. Then they will understand even when they are not understood. This means two things.

1. We must start with the presupposition that man knows, understands, and accepts God's Word. We must not start, then, with his ungodliness or ignorance or incomprehension or contradiction. These things are certainly present, but they are a presupposition which falls away the moment I proclaim God's Word to him, and must have fallen away already if he is to hear. But primarily they must have fallen away in me if this is to happen. I must count him to be God's with the same axiomatic certainty with which I place myself under the *Deus dixit*. I must stop all contrasting of myself with him, all complaining and judging, all trying to win him or persuade him or bring him over as though he were not already alongside me. This could rest only on a secret denial of revelation. Naturally, I do not do this on account of his piety, not at all, but on account of his wretched and naked humanity, on account of his sin and pain and helplessness and mortality, on account of the rift in which he finds himself, on account of the impossibility of his ever overcoming this rift. I do it because he is a prisoner of Zion who has to ask and can only ask but who asks as such, as one whom God has driven into a corner, as one to whom God has given himself to be known, whose whole being is one single question. Counting him to be God's means that in his very lostness I see him standing before God; that I know he is addressed by God; that I am confident I am not telling him anything new or remote but something familiar and close, something that is already his; that I am reminding both him and myself that God is on the stage.

I mean it concretely when I say that man's question about God, viewed as a reflection of the love with which he first loved us [1 John 4:19], cannot be treated as something avoidable or problematical, and certainly not as something that must be presupposed. It is instead the "give me a place to stand,"[17] the only possible place that there is between

---

17. The legendary saying of Archimedes (285-212 B.C.): "Give me a place to stand and I will move the earth."

preacher and hearer. For how can we say anything, for example, about the forgiveness of sin, unless we put ourselves on this basis? To see this, however, we should not deny revelation.

2. We should not try to suppress the question about man in order to help him or to settle it. I might support this by simply saying that we cannot do this, that we can never succeed. The rift, the imprisonment, the question of man, is still there even when we have finely answered and comforted and persuaded and assured. All the arts with which we try to do more than we should inevitably come to nought. But once again I prefer to say that in principle the question should not be suppressed. Instead, it should be wakened and kept awake. All the answers that we might give should aim to set man again and more truly in the question of his existence which possibly and very probably he has forgotten again. He should recall once again that on earth he has no continuing city [Heb. 13:14], that he is a sinner [Rom. 3:23], that he must die [Ps. 90:12]. He must be made afraid again of what it means to be a man. He must note how truly uprooted he is. Why? Because he reads this in Dostoyevski?[18] Because he takes pleasure in the problems and paradoxes of life? Those who talk this way do not know what they are talking about and would be better to stay silent. No, but because in any case only the man who knows himself is known by God, who stands there stands before God, who asks and is himself a single question, the true and radical question, receives an answer. Those who do not ask, who do not ask very radically what is their one and only comfort in life and death, must be told to their faces that they also do not believe. Believers are not secure people. They are those who first know what questioning means. To be rid of the question is to be rid of revelation and not to be addressed by God, or to be addressed by him no longer.

We are told of the prisoners of Zion that the Lord will redeem them [Ps. 126:1]. I need not say that in this regard, as preachers of the law that uncovers us, we cannot be servants of the divine Word unless we stand alongside people as those who question (and who are thus addressed by God), not setting ourselves a single inch above them. We cannot have the theological begging of the question as cheaply as spectators might imagine. It leads through the narrow gate where we understand atheists better than they understand themselves. But it is the way that leads to life [cf. Matt. 7:14].

---

18. Cf. E. Thurneysen, *Dostojewski* (1921; repr. Zurich/Stuttgart, 1963), esp. pp. 42ff.; ET *Dostoevsky* (Richmond, 1964), pp. 37ff.

§ 5

God: Father, Son, and Holy Spirit

The content of revelation is God alone, wholly God, God himself. But as God solely and wholly reveals himself, he makes himself known in the three persons of his one essence. He, the eternal Father, is the Lord at the beginning and end of the contradiction of our existence. He, the eternal Son of the Father, is the living Lord in the midst of our contradiction. He, the eternal Spirit of the Father and the Son, is and becomes our own Lord by proclaiming victory over the contradiction, addressing us as God's children and servants, and giving us faith and obedience.

I. God the Subject of Revelation

In § 3 we defined the place, the presuppositions, and the conditions under which alone the *Deus dixit* or revelation that is the basis of Christian preaching takes place, or, as we might say more cautiously, under which alone we can relevantly speak about it. In § 4 we then defined man as he must be thought of when addressed from this place in revelation. We now inquire into the subject of revelation. That this subject, God, is the subject par excellence, *the* subject, which is never and nowhere object, because it is grounded only in itself and may be known only by itself, we have already shown in § 3 to be a decisive factor in the concept of revelation. God is seen, believed, recognized, and known only in the act of his self-revelation. The human act of seeing, believing, recognizing, and knowing is primarily his work.

Building on this, we might say that the question: What is revealed?

may at once be traced back to the question: Who does the revealing?; that the question of content may be traced back to that of subject. What would God want to reveal but himself? What could he reveal but himself? *Deus dixit* means that God spoke about himself. Anything more in this case would obviously be less. What else can his essence be but the "I am that I am" [Exod. 3:14] in which Israel heard spoken the name of God that may not be spoken by human lips because only God can speak it, because God is God in and because of the fact that he says this about himself? God's attributes or predicates that we might try to enumerate would only be partial and imperfect descriptions of this unique subject, not saying anything even in their totality because they cancel out one another. They can all of them be only references back, not to the statement "God is," but to the statement "God spoke." For even the statement "God is" is obviously a reference back to God's self-knowledge in his Word. God's action in relation to the world and us, what does it consist of but simply his making himself known in this relation as the one who himself and alone acts? Thus "the content of revelation is God alone, wholly God, God himself." Christian preaching must be aware of this.

Here obviously is the basic decision — about its content too. It cannot want this or that. It cannot offer many things. It cannot assert a second and different thing alongside God, not even something ever so directly derived from God. It can give the glory only to God, speak only about God, assert God alone. More precisely, in all that it speaks about, and must speak about, in order to be human speech and therefore to serve God's Word, it must be no more than a reference back to the speaking of God who himself wills to speak about himself. It can only create space as it were, arouse the necessary attention, drive the sheep to the shepherd, so that God's work may be done. It must really be a human ministry of the divine Word. As such it is address to pilgrim man,[1] and itself the divine Word.

The first sentence of the thesis in which this is formulated needs delimitation on four sides.

1. "The content of revelation is *God.*" In saying this I take issue with the usual distinction between a formal and a material principle in the concept of revelation and dogmatics in general. I do not differentiate between a content-less speaking or self-revealing of God in itself (as though God's revelation could even for a single second be thought of as a blank sheet) and a specific, concrete content of this speaking which consists of

---

1. Cf. § 4 above, n. 3.

the communication of his love, his desire for fellowship with us, his forgiveness of sin and the like (as though God's Word could be filled out more concretely, materially, and with greater content than simply by the fact that it is God's Word). Those who think that the *Deus dixit* can be empty do not really know it; they have some other concept in mind. God cannot reveal anything more certain, more specific, more living than himself. Any emptiness or abstraction that we might first feel when hearing the term "God" is on our side.

Here, too, it might be as well for theology to begin with a great concession to our own hardness of heart when we argue that because we cannot think of anything concrete when we hear the term "God," we will ourselves give it content with one or many of the terms with which we describe God's being or qualities or acts, as though these terms could help us when the term "God" which denotes their subject is really supposed to be empty, abstract, and dead, as though the fulness of all divine truth and acts and gifts did not lie in the fact that they are his, God's truths and acts and gifts. Everything lies in the source of the truths, the doer of the acts, the giver of the gifts. If he is posited, they are all posited with him. If he is not posited, or if he is posited only as something abstract that we may rush on past to the real order of business, if the divine predicates are detached from the divine subject and given a being and glory of their own, then they are idols, nonentities even though they might be called love or forgiveness. All the divine predicates live and move and have their being in the *Deus dixit*. We say it all when we say that God is the content of revelation. In understanding the concept of revelation everything depends on our seeing this. No distrust or dissatisfaction or haste to press on must find a place in us vis-à-vis the form of the divine *autousia*, of God's subjectivity, which embraces and realizes and expresses the whole content. There is nothing more objective than this.

2. "The content of revelation is God *alone*." It is not an object of real or possible experience as such, even though in it we might have before us a mediator, bearer, instrument, or organ of revelation, and except in this form there is no revelation. But in this case the form is not the content. If I say that this or that is a revelation to me, I mean only that it brings, proclaims, or mediates revelation to me. It is here that I hear: *Deus dixit*. This is the situation, as we pointed out in § 3, with the equation: scripture is revelation.[2] As no thing, no contingent entity, no historical fact as such is the speaker, so none can be what is said, the content of revelation.

---

2. See pp. 56-57 above.

This is true — and I now touch for the first time on a critical point — even though the historical fact be Jesus of Nazareth, the historical personality, the human nature of Christ in itself and as such. We will be speaking about revelation in the incarnation in the next section. For the moment we are simply making the point that even in the humanity of Christ the content of revelation as well as the subject is God alone. According to the teaching of the older Protestant dogmaticians (including the Lutherans!), the historical phenomenon of Jesus as such is a creature of the triune God — a creature, so that the Reformed could emphasize and expressly state that the rule that the infinite is not capable of the finite applies to this creature too.[3] Both Lutherans and Reformed, so as to obviate any possible misunderstanding, even went so far as to deny to Christ's human nature any personality at all. The person of the God-man is exclusively the Word, the Logos of God.[4] No matter what we think of this paradoxical thesis, the so-called *anhypostasis* of Christ's human nature, it would certainly have been wiser to consider its content instead of getting worked up about it. But from the 18th century onward everybody began to focus more zealously on the man Jesus of Nazareth, on the hero, the religious personality, his inner life so far as we may know it, his view of God and the world and life, the "fairest Lord Jesus,"[5] revelation being now found in the teaching, loving, and suffering Jesus — the accents might vary — but at any rate in the living Jesus, not in the crucified and risen Jesus, as in Paul and the Reformers. Zinzendorf with his often repeated but in both form and content rather dubious cry: "I have only one passion and that is he and he alone,"[6] and Schleiermacher in his christology are at this point simply the proponents of one and the same erroneous development. For make no mistake: there is something more than suspicious about this apparently laudable movement in which an increasingly fervent christocentrism goes hand in hand with an increasingly defective understanding of the concept of revelation. In all its exaggeration, it simply means that because the Logos, the *Deus dixit*, which is the meaning and content of

---

3. Cf. L. van Riissen with reference to the gifts imparted to Christ's humanity, in Heppe-Bizer, p. 346; ET p. 437.

4. Cf. J. A. Quenstedt, in Schmid-Pöhlmann, p. 201; Schmid ET p. 300; and J. H. Heidegger, in Heppe-Bizer, p. 340; ET p. 340.

5. Barth had the well-known hymn in mind (Münster, 1677).

6. Cf. the 4th stanza of the hymn by C. R. von Zinzendorf: "Ach, was in meiner armen Seel," which is sometimes printed as the 3rd stanza of the hymn: "Mir ward Vergebung reich zuteil." As quoted by Barth the saying supposedly goes back to N. L. von Zinzendorf; cf. *RGG,* VI, 2nd ed., 1913.

the incarnation, was no longer on the throne, and because on the other side there was need of a contingent presence of God to give life and relationship to personal divine inwardness, it was thought that the desperate measure should be taken of making the empty throne, that is, the historical Jesus without the content of divine *autousia,* into an object of ever more ardent worship, but it was not realized that when a bad conscience produced such actions, the result could only be a confusion of above and below, a deifying of the creature, which older theologians had wisely avoided. Even the sincere piety with which all this was done could not improve things. We must see it for what it is, and totally abandon it. In my view both dogmatics and the preaching which follows it must dare to be less christocentric and therefore to be more objective and valiant by again giving God the significance that is his due precisely according to his revelation through the historical fact of Jesus of Nazareth, namely, that he *alone* is the content of revelation.

3. "The content of revelation is *wholly* God." The point here is simply that God is not just half revealed or partly revealed, so that another part of his being or attributes or acts will have to remain hidden or will have to be imparted in some other way than by revelation. As regards the second possibility, we have to think especially of the increasing role played in Protestant theology from the end of the 16th century by what is variously called natural theology or revelation or religion (as distinct from the supernatural or Christian revelation). Natural revelation includes not only the voice of God in nature, as the name indicates, but also such things as conscience, the moral light of nature, religious feelings or dispositions or tendencies in us, mathematical and philosophical axioms, what better pagans know about the existence and unity of God, and the creation and overruling of the world by him, and non-Christian analogies even to such central Christian mysteries as the Trinity and the incarnation. Theologians usually regarded and employed this natural revelation as a good and useful narthex or first stage on the way to the true Christian revelation. The older Reformed theology in particular attached high importance to this preliminary structure. According to A. Schweizer one might even see in it one of the most valuable features of Reformed theology.[7] It was given a place of honor in the 19th century both in the first part of Schleiermacher's *Christian Faith* and in Schweizer's own *Glaubenslehre.*[8] *Vestigia terrent!* For my part, although I am Reformed, I want no part of it. You will not be

---

7. Schweizer, p. 107 (§19).
8. *Cf.* §§ 32-61; A. Schweizer, *Christliche Glaubenslehre;* cf. vol. I, p. VI.

surprised at this in view of what I have said earlier. Either God speaks, or he does not. But he does not speak more or less, or partially, or in pieces, here a bit and there a bit. This is a contradiction in terms, an anthropomorphism, a basic naturalizing of revelation which fits Schleiermacher very well, but which ought not to have found any place among the older Reformed. Calvin at the end of the discussion in the first chapters of the *Institutes* was perspicacious enough to raise the whole question again, to oppose the Christian knowledge of God dialectically to natural knowledge, and to proceed as though there were only the former.[9] And even in Thomas Aquinas the insights one can gain into God's nature apart from revelation have the significance only of a possible and necessary ancillary construction that pays secondary honor to the truth of revelation.[10] If God *speaks,* then *God* speaks, and we have to do with the one Logos that the prophets and apostles received, the one revelation in the incarnation which the people of the Bible know and attest as either promised or manifested. Nothing prevents us, and much urgently inclines us to suppose that others, too, might have had a share, and might still have a share, in the same divine answer. We do well at this point to confess the free and broad outlook of Aquinas when he said that all truth, no matter who speaks it, is of the Holy Spirit, or of Zwingli when he said that whoever speaks truth speaks of God.[11] But the truth must then be understood as the one totality of truth, and the words "Holy Spirit" and "God" must be taken in a pregnant sense. Truth that really goes back to God cannot be a particle of truth. It is either the whole truth or it does not go back to God and is not revelation at all.

I would thus take the one part of the material that has been mentioned by what is called natural theology and include it at once in the true Christian theology that is called supernatural, that is, in revelation, as the older apologists did. If God does not speak, then it is not God that we hear in those supposed voices of God but a voice from this world, from this unredeemed world, from the contradiction of our existence. There might well be gods and animals and people that really do speak in what is called natural revelation. And insofar as the material in natural theology about which we have to say this is a completion of the picture of man and his question, we must set it on

---

9. *Inst.* I, 3-6.

10. *STh* I, q. 1, a ad 2.

11. *STh* Ia, IIae, q. 109, a ad 1; H. Zwingli, *On Providence,* ch. 3; cf. Opera, IV, p. 95; ET (Durham, NC, 1983), p. 154.

the side that stands over against revelation. Either God or man, either revelation or not; between these millstones the grain of what is called natural revelation must be ground. It has no independent existence.

The other question is whether God has finally concealed one part of his nature in revelation, or whether we are to view the totality in the light of Amos 3:7, namely, that God does nothing and is nothing and has nothing that he keeps secret from his servants the prophets. Humility seems at first to favor the first possibility. Even in revelation how can more be revealed to us than a mere drop in the ocean of God? But this humility is falsely adduced. It simply shows that we are falsely equating revelation with revealedness to us instead of thinking of it as revelation in act, in God's act. I do not know whether you are aware that the lines in Luther's hymn: "Ask ye who is this same? Christ Jesus is His name, The Lord Sabaoth's Son; He, and no other one,"[12] were originally meant as a polemic against the idea that there is a God who stands hidden behind revelation in this sense as a part that is held back.[13] Against this view one must also object that a God who reveals himself quantitatively is not God. Certainly our apprehension, comprehension, appropriation, and attestation of revelation is only a drop in relation to the ocean, a particle of truth. What is partial, very partial, is simply the human hearing and speaking of God's Word. In this regard even the prophets and apostles are no better than we are: "We know in part" (1 Cor. 13:9).

In contrast, God does not give his Spirit in part (John 3:34), and it is said of the same Spirit of God that he searches all the depths of God (1 Cor. 2:10), and of Christ that all the fulness of the Godhead dwells bodily in him (Col. 2:9). We should not ascribe our own lack to revelation. Revelation is either the whole revelation of God or it is not revelation. God's hiddenness, his incomprehensibility, is his hiddenness not alongside or behind revelation but in it. Who, then, knows the hidden God, the truly unknown God, his dwelling in light that none can approach [1 Tim. 6:16], the impenetrable mystery of his Godhead, grace, and judgment? Those who are naive and religiously brazen think they can lay bare the mystery, and in so doing they show that they know nothing. The revealed God and the hidden God are one and the same, and he is the total God, the Lord Sabaoth, beside whom there is no other.

---

12. "Ein feste Burg ist unser Gott" (A Mighty Fortress Is Our God). In the German the last line is "und ist kein andrer Gott."

13. Cf. Luther's Genesis Lectures, WA, 43, 463, 3-12, in which Luther equates Jesus Christ with the Lord Zebaoth and states that there is no other God (LW, 5, 50).

4. "The content of revelation is God *himself.*" What I mean is that it is not an enlightenment of reason or the actualization of a religious disposition. Both these take place where revelation takes place. In face of what God does we do something corresponding, parallel, and analogous in our own sphere of existence. More strongly or more weakly our rational activity receives a specific theoretical and practical orientation. Unmistakable religious phenomena come on the scene, gratifying or not. Perhaps they do so to an extraordinary degree in specially gifted or guided individuals. But all this can be only the shadow of revelation. It is not as though we as such thereby become in our own sphere the recipients, bearers, and owners of revelation. In the strictest sense revelation is God's own work lying in his own hands. First and last, with or without the new orientation, or the religious phenomena, our part is one of division and question. For reason is the epitome of those who stand not above the rift but in it, of those who question. Our more or less vital religion and piety — a very special function of reason — is the human (again the human) tendency to overcome the division.

We shall come back to both factors. For the moment I want to presuppose it as evident that reason and religion on the one side, and revelation and faith on the other, cannot be conjoined qualitatively, and are not therefore to be put on the same level and intertwined, but must be soberly kept apart dialectically as question and answer. Only then, as must also happen, of course, can they be strictly brought together and related to one another, in an iron hinge which moves up and down, not in glue that is meant to put them on a single surface. Then we shall no longer finish up with those barren quantitative distinctions and debates about reason and revelation, faith and knowledge, etc., which the modern age has made into the veritable passion story of theology. No, when God reveals himself, this means that God himself, known *and* making known, speaking *and* hearing,[14] is present on the stage, and no matter whether we call this revelation or faith, it is an event with which what we do in our own sphere may well be in analogy but cannot be in continuity, as though our thinking and feeling were a kind of outflow or continuation of revelation, not to speak of the arrogance with which the Middle Ages sometimes equated intellectual contemplation, as they called it, with revelation, and with which the modern age has naturally made a similar equation in

---

14. N. p. 31 adds: "as mouth and ear."

the case of religious experience. God himself, or the Holy Spirit (which is the same thing), is the content of revelation.

II. The Doctrine of the Trinity

In the first subsection of this section, expounding the formula that the content of revelation is God alone, wholly God, God himself, I have proposed and tried to defend the four theses (1) that in revelation as such we may not distinguish between form and content, that is, between the revealing subject and the revealed object; but (2) we may distinguish between revelation itself, which is identical in subject and object, and all the means of revelation; (3) that the revealed object, because it is one with the revealing subject, is not a greater or lesser quantity, so that one neither can nor should speak of different or partial revelations, but only of one revelation; and (4) that revelation as God's answer is never and nowhere coincident with the human question represented in the concepts of reason and religion.[15]

These discussions have necessarily led us to the point whose treatment will form the main content of the present section. If we say that the content of revelation is identical with God alone, wholly God, God himself, the word "God" can only denote what was called God in the doctrine whose presentation and understanding the early church, and with it the medieval period, the Reformation, and post-Reformation theology as well, have all viewed as the presupposition of all the doctrinal presuppositions of Christian preaching — a view which in thesis even most of the Protestant dogmaticians of the modern age have not disputed, but which many of them with more or less good arguments have expressly championed. I refer to the doctrine of the Trinity. It is *this* God who in his revelation is never revealed object except as revealing

---

15. This paragraph is not found in a first version of the MS. Instead we find an early draft in the margin: "In the first subsection of this section, expounding the formula that the content of revelation is God alone, wholly God, God himself, we have proposed and defended the theses (1) that there is no distinction between the form and content of revelation; (2) there is instead a distinction between revelation itself and the means of revelation; (3) revelation is not quantitatively more or less, so that there are no different or partial revelations; (4) revelation as God's answer is never and nowhere coincident with our question about God, i.e., with reason and religion."

subject: the God who reveals himself as Father, in the Father as the Son, and in the Father and the Son as the Spirit. It is *this* God who in his inexhaustible vitality, that is, in his indestructible subjectivity, makes superfluous and meaningless the question whether there is some special content of revelation alongside the fact that it is *his* revelation. *This* God, who as he reveals himself, always remains the same, is the jealous God [Exod. 20:5], the monocrator who cannot share his glory with anyone or anything else [Isa. 42:8; 48:11]. The revelation of this God is not quantitative or partial, because no matter in which person he reveals himself he is always the one God, and always reveals the whole, always reveals himself. The revelation of *this* God, as his answer to pilgrim man, cannot be confused or admixed with man's question, because no matter in which person he reveals himself, in virtue of the unity of his three persons he escapes every attempt of man to identify him with himself, and as a final Word that both attracts and repels he constantly tells man that he himself is God.

Before embarking on a development of the formula: God: Father, Son, and Holy Spirit, along with its more detailed definitions, I will formulate and establish three theses which should bring us closer to our theme.

1. Treatment of the doctrine of the Trinity belongs to dogmatic prolegomena. Its significance as the presupposition of the basic principles that must be set forth in dogmatics proper — and many have theoretically admitted this, as already said — does not come out well in the traditional position assigned to it (usually at the end of the specific doctrine of God). Again, it does not have any natural force, or at the most only decorative force, when after the manner of Schleiermacher it is put right at the end of dogmatics.[16] Is it not a remarkable thing that the doctrine of the Trinity was so basic for Calvin that he even had Servetus burned for obstinately deleting it, and yet one would never suspect his urgent interest in it from the position he gives it in his train of thought in the *Institutes*.[17] J. Gerhard writes concerning it that anyone who does not know the mystery of the Trinity does not know God as he has revealed himself in his Word, and already before him M. Chemnitz says that because we think of God as he has revealed himself we believe, know, confess, and invoke the three persons, while B. Keckermann states that God cannot be God unless he have three distinct

---

16. *CF,* §§ 170-72.
17. *Inst.* I, 13.

modes of existing or persons.[18] If they are all right, if the matter is so fundamental, why do the Lutheran and Reformed dogmaticians of those centuries simply list it with what they say about God's name and existence and nature and attributes as though — not really knowing why, or what light it would shed on what preceded — they suddenly found to their surprise that they had to teach something about God's triunity? Or listen to a modern theologian, to Bavinck, whose presentation of the Trinity is in itself one of the most careful and instructive that I know. He tells us that the whole of Christianity stands or falls with the doctrine of the Trinity, the whole of special revelation. It is the core of the Christian faith, the root of all dogmas, the substance of the new covenant.[19] But this high estimation does not come to expression in his arrangement.

On the other side there are dogmaticians like Haering[20] in whom the special part is constructed under the three heads of Father, Son, and Spirit.[21] This possibility demands serious consideration. But then the general part must be the obvious basis if it is not to seem that this arrangement follows the Apostles' Creed rather than any material necessity. Instead, it is only later, at a somewhat hidden place in his third part, that Haering has a special discussion of the question of the Trinity.[22] Troeltsch, too, calls the doctrine of the Trinity — and naturally so in the way he views it — "the enduring classical formula of Christianity."[23]

Now if this is so — and rather remarkably almost all dogmaticians talk along these lines — we may well ask whether it is not advisable to consider first whether we shall really be talking about this God when we come to define his nature, qualities, etc., for it will not do to have God as a general concept within which the Christian God as he is basically

---

18. J. Gerhard, in Schmid-Pöhlmann, p. 101; Schmid ET p. 137; M. Chemnitz, in ibid.; B. Keckermann, in Heppe-Bizer, p. 92; ET p. 106; cf. Schmid, pp. 96-97; Heppe, p. 86.

19. Bavinck, II, p. 346.

20. Marginal note: "Martensen, Rade." Martensen's *Die Christliche Dogmatik* (Berlin, 1856) has an Introduction, a first main section, "The Christian Concept of God," and then three sections: "The Doctrine of the Father," "The Doctrine of the Son," and "The Doctrine of the Spirit." Rade's three volumes of *Glaubenslehre* bear the three titles *God* (Gotha, 1924), *Christ* (1926), and *Spirit* (1927).

21. The special part of Haering's *Dogmatik* falls into three sections: "Belief in God the Father," "Belief in Jesus Christ, the Son of God," and "Belief in the Holy Spirit."

22. Haering, pp. 537-44, at the end of the section on "The Work of the Holy Spirit (Faith)."

23. Cf. § 1 above, n. 19; and Troeltsch, *Glaubenslehre*, p. 124, 4.

known in the doctrine of the Trinity is only a special instance. If there is an enduring classical formula for Christianity, then it will be worth our while to get to know it before beginning dogmatic work in the narrower sense. This will not stop us from returning to the matter at the proper place when the formula is just one doctrine among others. Schleiermacher said of the doctrine of the Trinity that it is not a direct expression of the Christian consciousness, and therefore that with Christ's resurrection and ascension it is not a true doctrine of the faith.[24] We like that, and add at once the remark of Heinrich Alsted (d. 1638) that the mystery of the Trinity is discovered neither by the light of nature nor by the light of grace, and even by the light of glory it cannot be understood by any creature.[25] Note that this mystery can be uncovered neither by natural insight nor by the insight based on grace nor by the insight that we have in eternal glory. It cannot be perceived, understood, or comprehended by any creature, even though we might be angels or the blessed and could do theology at that level. The Trinity would still be a mystery, this old Reformed theologian thought, and the Lutheran J. A. Quenstedt agreed when he declared that the mystery of the Trinity is beyond mind or speech or understanding.[26] Over against this, then, stands the admission with which Schleiermacher remarkably enough closes his *Christian Faith,* namely, that in face of this formula his method, which is oriented to the religious consciousness rather than to God and his Word, breaks down. In view of all this, the formula seems to be pointing us to something strangely outside or beyond as the a priori of all dogmas. Obviously its discussion is to be viewed as a *pro*legomenon par excellence.

2. The problem of the doctrine of the Trinity is the recognition of the inexhaustible vitality or the indestructible subjectivity of God in his revelation. This leads us first to the history of its development. As is well known, this history is in the first instance the history of the concept of the Logos.[27] At the juncture of two worlds, at the point to which Moses and the prophets look ahead and the apostles look back, a point denoted by the name Jesus of Nazareth, about whom historical information is very scanty and uncertain, primitive Christianity thought that it had perceived the *logos tou theou,* the divine address to itself, and through itself to all the

---

24. *CF,* § 170. On the resurrection and ascension cf. § 99.
25. Heppe, p. 86; Heppe-Bizer, p. 93; ET p. 108.
26. For the full quotation see Hase, p. 180.
27. O. Scheel, "Trinitätslehre," *RGG,* V, 1st ed., 1348.

world: *Deus dixit,* God alone, wholly God, God himself. In trying to take account of what this means, how we are to think about it, and above all how we are to speak about it (for the Word of God insists at once on becoming human words), in thus seeking to answer the question of the content of revelation, it works out the formula Father, Son, and Holy Spirit — we can hardly say when it first does this, but traces of the formula go back to the NT canon itself, and so we cannot put it too late. Obviously the second member of the formula, the Son, the Logos of God, whom the church believed it saw in Jesus, was the true center and point of crystallization. *He* constituted what was perceived at that juncture. *He* was the one about whom they wished to speak, and had to speak, in human words. *He* was the revelation whose content they wanted to grasp. "Jesus the Lord," or "Christ," seems to have been the oldest Christian confession, and in this name alone believers seem originally to have been baptized. The reflection that led to the triune formula began with what was perceived under this name, as did also, understandably and materially, all further reflection on what the formula was intended to denote. We can agree with Harnack when he says that the confession of Father, Son, and Holy Spirit is a development of the belief that Jesus is the Christ.[28]

But by way of an experiment let us try to develop with the early church that which needs to be developed here. It was to the question what we perceive in Jesus, what disclosure or communication, received through him, forces us to look at this point of history as if bewitched, forces us to make the unheard-of statement that this is the Kyrios, the Christ — it was to this question that they thought they should give the answer that what meets us here is not a something but a Someone, namely, God himself, the eternal Father. There is thus a reference back to a first subject of revelation. Again, when it is asked what is manifested to us in God the Father, what answer can be given but a second reference back to the point from which we came, not a something but a Someone, God the eternal Son, the very one who made us ask the first question that we only now understand aright, and understand ourselves also with our confession: the Kyrios, the Christ. Thus a second revealing subject is the content of the revelation of the first. This one, equal to the Father, is the revelation of the Father. If it is then asked what the two reveal, the Father and the Son, the answer — how could it be anything else? — is again for a third time,

---

28. A. von Harnack, *Lehrbuch der Dogmengeschichte,* I, 4th ed. (Tübingen, 1909), p. 90 n. 1; ET *History of Dogma,* I (New York, 1961), p. 80 n. 2.

not a something, but a Someone, God the eternal Spirit of the Father and the Son, a third revealing subject whose revealed object — the circle closes — is again no other than the Father and the Son. Three subjects of revelation then? Yes indeed, one cannot avoid working out and establishing this thought — the strange history of the details does not belong in this context — three subjects of revelation, three persons, *prosopa,* or *hypostases* of the one divine substance, *ousia,* or *essentia.*

But what was the source and nature of the necessity with which the early church thought it could and should take this step — a necessity that we observers find it almost impossible to understand? What is the logic in this foolhardy dialectic? What is the why and wherefore of this doctrinal construct, in face of which any fool who shows with his fingers that three cannot be one and one cannot be three may be a sage and hero? Whence springs this unheard-of challenge to human reason and also to human piety, which obviously does not want to hear about concepts and numbers but about love and life? Why the emphatic placing of this unheard-of doctrine at the very foundation of the whole dogmatic structure, the violent strife until this was done, and the solemn bitterness with which it was defended on every hand? Is there any other material answer but this one: Because the church wanted to build inescapably on the fact that in revelation we are dealing with the revelation of God and therefore — twist and turn as we might — with the divine subject which here and here and here is the one God himself? Why does the Son have to be more than the supreme and most glorious creature of the Father, the one God? objected Arius and his followers. Why may not the same be said at least of the third person? the Pneumatomachians then asked. Because, the answer read, the revelation in the Son would not be the revelation of *God* if the subject, the Son, were not of one substance with the Father, the one God. Because the Father, the one God, cannot be thought of as God in himself, but proves that he is himself subject in revelation in His Son who is of one substance with him. Because the Spirit would not be the *Holy* Spirit if he were only a power or potency, if he were not himself God. God must be the subject in revelation, and the subject in revelation must be God. This was the nerve of the arguments with which the church combated this heresy.

But why not at least subordination, a distinction of degrees in the relationship? the Subordinationists had asked even before the decrees of Nicea: the Father prior to and greater than the Son, and the Son prior to and greater than the Spirit, for the sake of the monotheism which otherwise seems to be threatened. But behind this is there really anything but the desire for a Father God in which God's subjectivity can come to rest without our having to think of the equal and no less eternal and divine subjectivity in the Son and the Spirit? Is it not precisely for the sake of a well-considered monotheism that we have to value the three subjects as equally great and eternal manifestations of the one living God? But only manifestations, a third group argued, Sabellius and his followers, with their error which Schleiermacher and other modern theologians have endorsed, namely, that the whole business of persons is simply a matter of arrangement, condescension, or economy, a mode of revelation for our sake, that the three divine persons, *hypostases,* or *prosopa* are not more than masks, or means of manifestation, or modes of subsistence, and that behind them God's essence is concealed as something different and higher, the one true substance. O man, how you try to flee and save yourself and secure your own safety, inventing a God in himself who is only an object, who in his peaceful unity will not beset us on all sides [Ps. 139:5], who will not scan us behind, before, and from above with his eyes, but who on the far side of his subjectivity will be enthroned by us at a safe distance. Monotheism may seem to be rescued in this safe haven of the hidden essence of God, but revelation is lost. As though God did not reveal himself as he is, his essence, when he reveals himself! as though for him manifestation and essence, economic being and immanent being, were not one in revelation rather than two! as though to all eternity and in the deepest depth of his deity he were not this God, the *one* in *three,* because he is *God:* the object that turns and becomes *subject,* wherever and however we may think it, when we think of this object.

What are we to say to all this? First, I want to say just one thing. In no circumstances and on no pretext should we fail either to see, or to learn to see, the real problem that arises with this construct. We should not be put off by recalling the similar triadic formulas of theological content which in every age and place have been advanced outside Christianity. That according to a certain universal law this happened also in the Christian church is part of the momentous fact that the church is wholly and totally a part of history,[29] and it should not stop us considering in what special sense it happened in this sphere. Again, we should not be put

---

29. Obviously alluding to Barth's famous statement that Christianity that is not wholly and totally eschatology has nothing whatever to do with Christ; see *Der Römerbrief,* 2nd ed. (Munich, 1922), p. 300; ET *The Epistle to the Romans* (London, 1933), p. 314.

off by recalling the humanly speaking unpleasant and suspicious and even wicked historical processes out of which the dogma developed. Perhaps we would understand many things better, especially the personal passion with which the battles were fought, if we really learned better to see these ancient conflicts from within, that is, as participants. This is not to excuse the ugly things. Especially the way in which orthodox and heterodox alike, with little confidence in the power of truth, knew how to get the emperor, highly placed women, and the mob active in their cause, will always constitute a disturbingly scandalous shadow under which the doctrine stands. But when, without losing sight of good and evil, we become so radically unsentimental that we really dare to see church history in the context of secular history, and not to expect to reap figs from thistles [cf. Matt. 7:16], then in spite of recalling such things our eyes will be open to what was really the moving factor in this great historical cloud of dust. Again, we should not finally be frightened off from taking the problem seriously as such by the assertion that the thought-forms in which the discussion took place were those of Neoplatonic and even at times Gnostic philosophy, that the people who helped to fashion the doctrine were for the most part Greeks who delighted in speculation, and that the simple *kyrios Iēsous* which formed the starting point eventually developed, in the Nicene and Athanasian Creeds, into a well-furnished arsenal of theological dialectic. Those who regard the *kyrios Iēsous* as simple and readily understandable, or who desire a different, less Greek, and less complicated development of its content than that which actually took place in the church's doctrine of the Trinity, will have to show: first, that they know what is at issue in this original formula with which it all seems to have begun; second, that they are at least as serious as the ancients were about the truth of what they are saying; third, that they have no less dialectical courage than the ancients to follow the matter through to the point where they have only heaven above them, where the formula in its defiant and conscious helplessness is really as good a formula for God as any formula can be; and fourth, that they really have something better to present than the church's dogma and not just a repristination of one of the heresies which have been exposed and dismissed for some 1500 years. If they can fulfil these four conditions, then let them come forth.

In sum, I would say that the issue in the doctrine of the Trinity is revelation, and that early Christianity — though rightly enough there may be different opinions on this — really believed that this was the issue for it. It is a matter of talking about revelation, of the problem of talking about it correctly, of talking appropriately about its content. The church could not stop at the first nonspeaking hearing, seeing, and tasting of "the word of life" (1 John 1:1), nor even at the mere *kyrios Iēsous,* nor, indeed, at the first and simple Father, Son, and Spirit without closer definition, for every real confession points backward and forward to knowledge, and witness as distinct from mere assertion rests on reflection and demands reflection. Theological thinking and theological formulating — no matter how abstract and alien to the world they finally become — are not a game nor are they a scandal, and there is nothing in them to provoke horror. They are praiseworthy and necessary and good (even though J. Müller[30] and other anti-intellectuals of the world might be angry at them or laugh at them). For they provide an orderly basis for what the church says. If one recognizes the need for such a basis, then one will adopt a new, more open, and more understanding attitude to the ancient doctrine of the Trinity than has been the custom for the past two hundred years. In face of what is, in spite of every appearance to the contrary, the practical and living relation of the developing church, which stood, of course, in the midst of history and was charged with the heavy burden of preaching, to that which constituted its basis, one will become a participant instead of a spectator, shirker, or referee. One might view the church's basis as a great X and take up only a hypothetical position, but one will still be inside and not alongside, and that is what counts. One might still remain open as concerns the formula itself and its development in the Eastern and Western churches. But one cannot remain closed to the necessity of the problem and its treatment. One will understand the statements of the older orthodoxy about the absolute mystery with which the formula deals. One will understand that Schleiermacher could have no understanding of it. I would say that everything, or almost everything, is gained in this matter if one does not stay with closed eyes outside but if one enters into the matter, if one sees that here the dogma of all dogmas is established, the doctrine of God's subjectivity in his revelation.

3. One should not try to understand, develop, or establish the doctrine of the Trinity except in terms of its specific origin. By its specific origin I mean the confession of revelation in Jesus, the confession *Iēsous*

---

30. Cf. J. Müller, *Von den Quellen des Lebens. Sieben Aufsätze,* 5th ed. (Munich, 1919), p. 83, where the author complains that if God is a superior reality, the picture that the church has made of him with philosophical concepts and human features is that of a man writ large, and that instead we should begin very reverently to worship the Incomprehensible.

Kyrios. The story of the doctrine of the Trinity shows that falling like a spring rain on plants and weeds alike, it led in an uncanny way to the discovery of every possible trinity and trinitarian doctrine. In these other trinities people saw either edifying analogies and similitudes of the Trinity or pleasing and helpful proofs for it, until finally they came to explain and prove it so brilliantly and profoundly by these auxiliary constructions that they reversed the relation and made the Trinity itself a mere likeness of the true and proper triunity that had only now been discovered, that is, that of the god of spirit, world, or nature that philosophy had independently established, or else they made the Trinity a special instance, a mere drop in a whole sea of religious, intellectual, and other trinities.

I cannot possibly present the relevant material with anything approaching completeness.[31] People were pleased to point to the three sons of Noah and the three decks of his ark,[32] to the three sections of the tabernacle, to the three favorite disciples of Jesus, and to the three crosses on Golgotha. They found the Trinity reflected in the three social orders of education, military, and economy; also within the family in husband, wife, and child; in the key-note, third, and fifth; in the basic colors yellow, red, and blue; in the solid, fluid, and gaseous states; in the active, passive, and middle tenses in grammar; in the logic, physics, and ethics of medieval learning;[33] in the triple hierarchy of Dionysius the Areopagite; in the heaven, hell, and purgatory of Dante's *Divine Comedy;* in the animal, plant, and mineral kingdoms in nature; and we must not forget the true, the beautiful, and the good. Classical significance was achieved by Augustine's attempt to construct the doctrine of the Trinity with the help of the three essential elements in the human spirit: *mens, notitia, amor,* and in the process of human consciousness: *memoria, intellegentia, voluntas.* This idea was current throughout the medieval period, and at the time of the Reformation it was adopted by Melanchthon and later, among the Reformed, by Keckermann. Then Hegel discovered the trinity of the subjective, objective, and absolute Spirit, in itself, for itself, and in and for itself. This was simply a variation on Augustine's ancient insight. Augustine himself had another solution, namely, the relation between loving, loved, and love, which in the Middle Ages was adopted and developed by the Victorines.

---

31. In what follows Barth seems to have used the list in Bavinck, II, pp. 289-95; cf. also *ChD,* pp. 184-90 nn. 44-81.

32. Marginal note: "The three who visited Abraham."

33. Marginal note: "grammatica, dialectica, rhetorica."

II. The Doctrine of the Trinity

When people thought mostly of the revelationary or economic side, it was tempting to rediscover the Father, Son, and Spirit in certain historical periods. Thus Gregory of Nazianzus related the old covenant to the Fathers, the new to the Son, and the Christian church to the Spirit. Hugh of St. Victor found in the age of the Father the kingdom of fear, the age of the Son the kingdom of truth in which we now stand, and the age of the Spirit the coming third kingdom of love. Schelling viewed the whole cosmic process as a self-development of God in three potencies, which when complete becomes the three persons. In the modern age all this material has been extended further by a consideration of the universal history of religion, in which scholars have been pleased to find the Brahman Trimurti: Brahma, Siva, Vishnu; the Buddhist trio: Buddha, Dharma, Sangha; the Germanic Odin, Thor, and Loki; and also Egyptian and Persian parallels to the Christian Trinity.

What are we to say to all this? Three attitudes are obviously possible. A fourth, which I myself recommend, stands outside the series inasmuch as it does not essentially bother about the history. First, we might take the whole material in the same sense as that in which it was originally advanced, namely, as a cloud of witnesses to the truth, which are at least edifying and perhaps instructive supports for the basic Christian doctrine, and which (who knows?) may even form real proofs. Augustine's epistemological solution, which he valued but did not overvalue, was meant as an indication, but it ended up in Hegel with the replacement of the Christian Trinity by a logical and metaphysical Trinity and by the relegation of the Christian Trinity to the sphere of naive, symbolical, and inadequate conceptions.[34] Second, we can view the matter in the light of this fatal result. The apologist who wants to prove or reconstruct what one should really believe makes common cause with unbelief in so doing. How easily in the course of the discussion a small reversal of roles takes place. The better a proof of the Christian doctrine of the Trinity on a different basis succeeds, the more the doctrine itself becomes superfluous. The Trinity becomes a general law of thought which willy-nilly the bold church fathers observe with their Logos-Christ along with the Indians and Egyptians and the mysterious rhythm of natural and intellectual life. Why, then, should the Christian Trinity be the primary thing, the archetype, and all the rest copies? Why not the other way round? The primary thing could be the

---

34. Cf. G. W. F. Hegel, *Vorlesungen über die Philosophie der Religion,* I: "Begriff der Religion," ed. G. Lasson, PhB, 59 (Hamburg, 1925), pp. 41-42.

educational, military, and economic trinity, or that of the beautiful, the true, and the good, or perhaps (not an unheard-of thought in the age of Artur Dinter)[35] Odin, Thor, and Loki. Or it might be that all these trinities at once, and the Christian Trinity with them, are expressions of an original and final and hidden triunity which is either investigated in detail in Hegel or which is ineffable and unqualified. The result in any case is the troubling one that the Christian Trinity submerges, and becomes interesting or uninteresting, in a sea of generality in which there are many trinities but in no demonstrable way is there any specific divine Triunity par excellence, in which the one drop of the Christian Trinity can make no special claim to be the sea itself, that is, the truth. Finally, in contrast to the first and second attitudes, one might counsel critical caution.

Thus it might be allowed on the one hand that the apologists and church philosophers attempted too much, that the material they assembled does not suffice to make possible a tenable construction of the Trinity in terms of pure thought, that in many cases, and perhaps most of them, the number three is the only thing that is demonstrated, and that the proof or even the analogy fails in relation to the persons and their significance or in relation to the essential equality in unity.[36] On the other hand, the same criticism might be brought against objections to the church's doctrine, against attempts to replace it by something philosophical or to relativize it with reference to other divine triads. If the result of such attempts is that all that is left by way of witness to the church's doctrine is an obscure general sense of a supreme Trinity, for this very reason the Christian doctrine cannot be reduced to a general law of thought, but at this or that point is to be distinguished from the Trimurti or the triads of Hegel and Schelling. In this remaining portion, which is quite large, a more general spiritual and religious life may then take root as in an Indian reservation. What is distinctive about the Christian teaching is recognizable at a specific point, emerging as something particular which is also the expression of something universal, just as the top of a mountain is the *top* but is also the top of the *mountain* and is something special and supreme only in this relation. A cautious critical view of this kind can certainly be

---

35. Artur Dinter (b. 6.27.1875 in Mülhausen, Alsace) wrote a novel *Die Sünde wider das Blut* (1918) in which he united anti-Semitic propaganda with an attempted restoration of pure Germanic religion.

36. Marginal note: "Gerh. 381." This is a reference to J. Gerhard, *Loci theologici* (1610), III, 30, ed. E. Preuss, 2nd ed. (Lipsiae, 1885), I, p. 381 (cf. Schmid ET p. 135); cf. *ChD*, p. 193.

well worked out and deserves commendation. Much that must be said along these lines is indeed simply self-evident. For other things there is a good deal of evidence.

Nevertheless, I want to invite you to treat this cautious view with caution. My first reason is that perhaps the development of the genuine Christian concept of the Trinity from other concepts — who really knows how it came about? — was not so simple or at least so certain as critical apologists argue. Thus they themselves at once surrender the number three to ambivalence because we meet different kinds of threes. It also seems to be a fact that in ancient Babylon there was invocation of a divine triad bearing the names of Father, Son, and Advocate (Paraclete),[37] so that there is nothing original about these names. It can hardly be contested that the auxiliary concepts of essence, person, etc., which are indispensable for the exposition of the doctrine, derive from the academic vocabulary of later Greek philosophy. And now comes Söderblom who shows that it must be regarded as a general law that at least in the so-called institutional religions the revealer, the revealed, and what is accomplished by revelation are thought of as related in triunity,[38] so that even the concept of revelation, which for many moderns is the shibboleth of the Christian Trinity, cannot enjoy uncontested honor as such.

I am unable to judge whether Söderblom is right. But supposing he is? Supposing then — and this brings me to my second decisive point — that the establishment of the Christian doctrine depends on proving that he is wrong, or if not on showing with philosophical or historical help that there is still a good deal that is distinctively Christian, even though the Indian reservation is now somewhat smaller? But who knows whether undiscovered analogies might not still await us in inland Tibet? And who knows whether tomorrow a philosopher might not rise up among us who can deduce the Christian Trinity for us a priori better than Hegel did? Who knows? I regard it as an intolerable situation if the establishment of the basic Christian doctrine is thought of for a moment as dependent on whether natural, spiritual, and religious analogies are right, on whether philosophical proofs and substitutes pass muster. It is intolerable, not because it is uncomfortable, for those who are sure of their critical norms

---

37. Cf. H. Zimmern, *Vater, Sohn und Fürsprecher in der babylonischen Gottesvorstellung* . . . (Leipzig, 1896).

38. N. Söderblom, *Vater, Sohn und Geist unter den heiligen Dreiheiten und vor der religiösen Denkweise der Gegenwart* (Tübingen, 1909). Barth knew this work from Nitzsch-Stephan, p. 478 n. 1.

can be comfortable enough with it, but because the doctrine of revelation is no longer the doctrine of *this* matter the moment its validity is sought elsewhere than in the matter itself. It automatically becomes the doctrine of something else. Augustine still realized this, for it was only as a kind of retrospective reference that he wanted people to understand the famous auxiliary construction which Hegel changed into its opposite. Similarly, the apologetics of early and medieval theology was chiefly meant as adornment for a house that had already been built to live in, not as scaffolding for building it. It was meant as the ballast that one throws out of a balloon at 10,000 feet up, not as an attempt to lift the ballast up 10,000 feet. Nevertheless, in spite of Augustine as I might say, because the confusion did at once take place, I could almost wish that the first Christian theologian who found help in such constructions had suffered the fate of Ananias and Sapphira [cf. Acts 5:5, 10], or at least that he had undergone a minor miracle of punishment with the drying up of his ink so that he could not proceed any further. It simply ought not to have happened — this is my verdict — that Christian theology, sometimes in its most brilliant representatives, exposed itself to the poor appearance that what it said about revelation, and then basically revelation itself, had to be based on other foundations. This appeared to be the case from the very first even though it was zealously explained that this was not what was meant.

Those who want to talk about revelation, those who want to explain what it means, those who confess *Iēsous Kyrios,* must not try to strengthen their work with analogies, proofs, and references of some other provenance. They should perhaps let themselves be strengthened as Elijah was on the way to Horeb, the Mount of God, that is, by an angel, so that in the strength of the food that he was given he could go for forty days and forty nights [cf. 1 Kgs. 19:7ff.]. As they seek first God's kingdom and righteousness, all other things will be added to them [Matt. 6:33]. For those who love God, all things must work for the best [Rom. 8:28], even that which philosophers and historians say. But to the extent that they think that they should strengthen themselves, that they themselves should and could work all things for the best, that everything depends on them, that they have to see to it instead of casting all their care on the Lord [1 Pet. 5:7], to the extent that even a little bit they are frightened to venture it all on his foundation, they simply show that they are not really or unequivocally based on *his* foundation, and they rush on ineluctably to the point where they will be caught in their own cunning traps. They will be casting pearls before swine and giving what is holy to the dogs, and these will turn upon them and rend them [Matt. 7:6], and rightly so. To talk about revelation means strictly and exclusively to talk on the basis of revelation. The ontic and noetic basis is one and the same in this matter. When any other position is adopted, people are not speaking about *this* matter. To believe in revelation and to talk about it, we cannot look about for other revelations, for proofs, or even for analogies or similitudes. Revelation, known and affirmed as such, has no analogy. Any supposed analogue to it is in reality identical with it. Revelation is not the peak of the particular on the mountain of the usual and the universal. It is the heaven above all that is distinctive or general. When we venture to say "God," then in all else that we say there must resound in our ears like the thunder on Sinai: "I am the Lord thy God, thou shalt have none other gods but me" [Exod. 19:16; 20:2-3]. This is what *Iēsous Kyrios* meant on the lips of the first Christians. If as theologians we cannot trust ourselves to keep to the theme that is set us thereby, and to abstain from integrating theology into nature, or ordinary spiritual life, or religious history which is so rich in analogies, then we are like those who put their hands to the plow and look back [Luke 9:62]. We must not do this.

I do not know whether, when theology has rediscovered this theme and learned to pursue it objectively again, it might not be possible and permissible in a kind of festal overflow, to the glory of God and in the style of Ps. 150, to do apologetics again without theology giving up its freedom, or rather God's freedom, and without fatal results for theology and the church. Today, especially after the experiences of four centuries of Protestantism, it is a dangerous luxury that we do best to avoid. In the state of siege in which we now are, it is more fitting that we should again take a firm grip of our real theme and practice the insight that the confession *Iēsous Kyrios* means renouncing all bases and analogies, that it has its basis in itself, that it is beyond dispute if we have made it, even if only hypothetically but with understanding, and this in spite of its defenselessness on every hand, of the irremovable relativity with which this confession stands among thousands like it, even though we naturally appeal to revelation in all the words with which we can explain it. Not the words that make up the formula of the Trinity in its simpler or more complicated form, nor the concept of revelation to which it refers back, but the grasping of revelation as such, the material, unconditional, inescapable wrestling with the *Deus dixit* — but what am I saying? The *Deus dixit* itself is the basis of the doctrine of the Trinity. Everything depends on our acquiring again a theology which will dare to proceed on the basis of this beginning.

III. Jesus the Kyrios

I think that with what has just been said I have done what had to be done and could be done by way of a preliminary explanation of the real content of this section. We now stand directly at the foot of the cliff and — enough words have been exchanged[39] — we must now venture on the climb. God the eternal Father, God the eternal Son, God the eternal Spirit — this is the goal that we have to reach. Three considerations must be taken into account.

1. *Deus dixit,* the Logos of God, the Kyrios, revelation — this is the confession with which we see the early church face the qualified historical point denoted by the name Jesus of Nazareth. That it finds in Jesus the Kyrios, and what that means, we shall have to deal with in the next section. We now presuppose it, and turn our attention to the "Kyrios." We can take this term to be predominantly a translation of the OT name for God, or predominantly an enthusiastic transcending in principle of what Hellenistic paganism meant when it honored gods, demigods, emperors, and demons as *Kyrioi* and *kyriotētes.* Either way it denotes a personal being before whom people bow. They may do so with reverence, gratitude, love, or trust, seeking help or ready for obedience, but at any rate they bow as before no other being. For in this being, with the overwhelming force of destiny, they encounter the epitome of qualitative superiority, dignity, and power. In it they experience this epitome. Yet there is more, for even this process does not differ from other processes that do not have the same significance. In it they recognize and acknowledge this superior thing as such even as they themselves — and this is one and the same thing — are known by the Lord. They are not merely seized and shaken and struck by it. They obey it. They hear its command as command. For — and this is again one and the same thing — they have already heard it.

Kyrios means God — there can be no real doubt about that. But how does Jesus come to be called God? The early church, too, knew that this was not self-evident, that there was an inequality here which to our understanding had first to become equality. Obviously at the outset there is only one who is the Lord. Only God is God. Jesus is a second alongside him and below him, his Messiah, his Word, his Logos, his revelation. In principle, then, the dignity or *kyriotēs* of Jesus is different. The Synoptists,

---

39. Cf. J. W. von Goethe, *Faust* V, 214.

or the authors of the fragments that the Synoptists follow, seem to have written predominantly from this standpoint. It seems almost inconsistent, or at least strikes us as mysterious, when Jesus is called *Kyrios* here, for what is Jesus here but one great reference to *the* Kyrios, to the heavenly Father, the reigning subject of revelation here, as whose accredited envoy Jesus proclaims the imminent kingdom, making it visible by words and acts. But Paul and John, too, never tire of pointing not only to Jesus but also, and in some sense past or above Jesus, to the Father, the Father of Jesus Christ, and through him to the fount of all fatherhood both in heaven and on earth [Eph. 3:15]. Think of Phil. 2:11, where Jesus is Lord to the glory of God the Father, or of 1 Cor. 15:24, where he finally hands over the kingdom to God the Father, or John 14:28, where the Father is greater than he, or the familiar passage in Heb. 1:3, where the Son is called the brightness of God's glory and the express image of his person.

This relation has a general significance. If we presuppose that the church is the place where revelation is known through Jesus, and the *Deus dixit* is perceived, then the first and most natural and basic meaning is obviously that by means of his voice the voice of the other is heard. Who is this other, the Father, the *Kyrios* Yahweh in the first instance, compared to whom the title *Kyrios* might at first seem to be used for Jesus his servant (Acts 3:13) only improperly and in a transferred sense? Let us recall that it is pilgrim man, man with his question, man in his contradiction, who has to give an answer. What can he think when he bows before a Lord before whom he also sees Jesus bowing, when the astonishing and alarming thing about Jesus, that which makes him call him Lord, perhaps consists precisely of the bowing, the unheard-of obedience, which he sees Jesus render to this very different Lord, the obedience even to death, even to the death of the cross [Phil. 2:8], that is rendered here? Who is this other Lord to whom the life of Jesus is brought as an offering that seems to make it one long dying, but who then gives him the name that is above every name, the name of *Kyrios* [Phil. 2:9, 11]? Who is this one who has such power over Jesus and gives him such power? One thing is sure. The one who here sees cause to cry "Abba, Father," if he understands himself aright, must have in mind first and especially one who stands somewhere else, who lives and moves differently, who is totally different from himself. The death of Jesus, his death on the cross, is the place where his lordship is recognized incomparably far above this final place.[40] It is from the frontiers of humanity that the word goes forth whose messenger Jesus is. Its

---

40. Marginal note: "Rom. 4:24; 8:11; 10:9; 1 Cor. 6:14; 2 Cor. 4:14; Phil. 2:9."

author cannot be one who is himself in contradiction or in question. *He* knows that which marks our being only as something transcended — the opposing second thing which conditions and limits. The Father to whom Jesus points is free where we are bound. The kingdom that is proclaimed here is worlds above the insuperable conflict in which we languish. To repent in Jesus' sense is to turn around, *metanoein*, to direct our thoughts to where the conflict in which, with our human existence, we constantly move in our human acts, is *not yet* or *no longer*. Words like "maker of heaven and earth," or "of all things visible and invisible," as the Nicene Creed adds, or "Creator, Upholder, and Ruler of all things," force themselves upon our lips to describe the Lord whom Jesus seems to serve. The name "Father," when it is ventured in Jesus' name as a term for what Jesus reveals, denotes in any case (not this alone, so I say "in any case") the one who is first and last, who dwells in light unapproachable [1 Tim. 6:16], who is beyond all our frontiers, who is transcendent because all things are from him and are his, because he is one above our insuperable duality, the truth above the enigmas that constantly become more complicated for us, the antecedent which refers back to no higher antecedent, the one who has no part in the antithesis of transcendence and immanence in which we have to think, who has his existence from no other and his origin from no other, who is *anarchos*, neither born nor begotten, as the older theologians put it.[41] We should perhaps recall the "God alone" with which at the beginning of the section we differentiated the content of revelation from every creature. We have to think here the thought of eternity, of the eternity which transcends time.[42]

He is all this, of course, primarily as the Father of Jesus Christ, as the Father who has begotten this one, as the Lord whose lordship is so powerful in this one that the cry "It is the Lord" can be applied to him [John 21:7], as the one whom Jesus taught us to invoke: "Our Father in heaven" [Matt. 6:9], as the one who chose Jesus and made him a sign on earth [Luke 2:34], as the one whose image may be seen in him [2 Cor. 4:4]. He is Father according to his relation to the person of the Son. Not *ousiōdōs* or essentially, but *hypostatikōs* or personally, as the older theologians said.[43] Not as though Jesus subsequently gave and affixed the name of

---

41. Cf. *STh* I, q. 33, a. 4 i.c.; Heppe-Bizer, p. 100; ET p. 119; Schmid-Pöhlmann, p. 108; Schmid ET p. 150.

42. The last two sentences were added to the MS later.

43. Cf. Polanus, in Heppe-Bizer, p. 100; ET p. 119; and Hollaz, in Schmid-Pöhlmann, p. 109; Schmid ET p. 151.

Father to the known Creator of all things, to the Unconditioned, to the limit and critical negation of everything given, to the origin, to him who is self-existent. No, Jesus reveals the Father for the first time. He shows the Father, and with him all that the Father is and does. No one comes to the Father except by him [John 14:6]. First — and I mean first in the most basic sense — there is knowledge of the eternal Father in the Son, and then and therein comes the knowledge of what that means: The Lord at the beginning and end of the contradiction of our existence, the Creator of heaven and earth, what older theologians called the Father's outward character.

In this regard we have to consider at once that if there are other persons in God as well as the Father, this second and derived meaning, the outward character, the Creator of heaven and earth, will have to apply to them too, so that it belongs to the Father peculiarly but not exclusively.[44] Again, if the Son and Spirit are there as well as the Father, then the name "Father" itself, the concept of God's outward fatherhood, in relation to us and the world, takes on a different sound and content. He not only stands above the contradiction at its beginning and end; he also stands victoriously within it. His eternity over time becomes an eternity *in* time. We, too, have a share in his victory and have eternal life. From the "Our Father" it thus follows that *we* are his *children*.

But let us not hurry on too fast. It is not self-evident that the Father of the Crucified is the Father of life, that the Creator is the Redeemer. He is so, but only because he is *God*. The so-called father-god in whom we think we can see combined everything that is good and true and helpful is sheer nonsense, one of the insolent and hollow discoveries of an age that does not understand that the God-relation is never a general truth but is there only in revelation. The Father is indeed all these things: Creator, Redeemer, Consummator. But we do not arrive at this insight by stringing together the various sayings of Jesus about him, and even less so by making logical deductions from the concept of fatherhood. He is these things because God is *God*. And that might mean at once: Because and inasmuch as he is not just the Father, because the Son glorifies the Father [John 17:1], because the Spirit is the Father's eternal presence.

But it might be more Christian to stop at the person of the Father and its distinctive outward character, not trying to know and say everything that is Christian all at once, but waiting until it is said to us. If we go

---

44. Cf. J. A. Quenstedt, in Schmid-Pöhlmann, p. 110; Schmid ET p. 151.

directly to the source of all truth, not to make our own observations and reflections there, but simply to drink, to hear what is said to us the moment Jesus shows us the Father, then to the extent that we call him who is shown us there God, we stand before *this* truth, this person of God, who is not, for example, to be confused with Jesus, for Jesus looks unconditionally at God — in him he finds his absolute whence and origin, before him he humbles himself in a way that perhaps for the first time makes us aware what humbling or bowing down really means. Nor do we confuse this person with the Spirit, who in us says Yes to this God, for if we know this Spirit we know that he says Yes to another and not to himself.

Is it not fitting and relevant to halt here with the confession that we stand before *one* person of God, before a subsistence in the divine essence which is related to the others but also distinguished by an incommunicable quality, as Calvin put it in his definition of person?[45] And no matter what may come after, do we not stand here before the first person in God, the *principium* (not to be confused with *causa*) in deity, the fount of deity,[46] the one who is our Lord as the eternal Father, although not as something other than the one living God, for now it is precisely as the eternal Father that he is the one living God, and also not as though a division or ranking or sequence were posited in the deity, for it is precisely as the eternal Father that he begets the eternal Son and is the source of the eternal Spirit?

2. We return to our starting point. *Iēsous Kyrios* was the confession of the first Christians. But *Kyrios* means God. There is no avoiding this. How can Jesus be called God? We have already asked this question and left it open. From the angle that we have pursued, presupposing the essential deity of the Father, the following alternatives seem to be inescapable. On the one side what is stated with the title *Kyrios,* the deity of Christ, might be seen as an improper way of speaking, a hyperbolical expression for the bearer of revelation, for the speaker of God's Word, for a human envoy of the Father to whom he bears witness, a pious metaphor which has first to be justified in dogmatics and then given its true and not so dangerous content. Or on the other side the expression might be taken to denote the mythologizing positing of a second God or divine being alongside or under God, which dogmatics must then characterize

---

45. *Inst.* I, 13, 6.
46. Cf. the statement of the 11th Council of Toledo (A.D. 675), in DS, 525: "On the Divine Trinity." Cf. also Augustine, *De Trinitate* IV, 20, 29.

as what it is and what it signifies. The NT witness, however, avoids these alternatives and affirms a third thing about Jesus. Similarly, the church's dogma concerning Christ is nothing other than a consciously critical rejection of these alternatives and the explication of the third thing that must be said about Jesus in truth. The line that the church's doctrine steers between Scylla and Charybdis is, of course, a very fine one, and we can discern it only when we see that it lies on a plane that *intersects* vertically from above the plane on which Scylla and Charybdis are found.

At a first glance the relevant thesis seems in fact to be truly puzzling and ambivalent. It seems to involve great inconsistency. It does not seem to fit. It seems to need explanation in face of the previously imparted content of revelation. The thesis is to the effect that the Word of God whose glory was supposedly seen incarnate in Jesus (John 1:14) was not just a Word of God or a Word about God, that it was not just *pros ton theon,* but that it was itself *theos* (John 1:1). Were we not right to sum up the knowledge of God the Father precisely as it was disclosed to us in Jesus under the formula "God alone," and was not the revelation or the Revealer himself *theos* as well as the one revealed by him, a *Kyrios* Yahweh of the second order, a Son begotten by the *Kyrios* Yahweh of the first order, in whom his image may be seen? What idealistic or even mythological view of man seems to have been presented here!

This thesis might have two implications according to whether we see it from below or from above. First, it might imply the apotheosis of a man, of the founder of this church and religion, of the initiator of the Christian belief in God the Father through the thankful love and adoration of his people; his apotheosis from a rabbi to a prophet, to a political and heavenly Messiah, until, as the intensity increases with historical distance, the equation is made that Christ is God, the idea being that at a certain moment, at his baptism or his resurrection, God exalted him to this dignity, a fitting symbol for what the church itself was obviously doing in the zeal of its enthusiasm for Christ. Second, it might imply the hypostatizing of the divine communication that people thought they had received in this man, the personification of what they perceived God to be in him, through him, and over him, a programmatic descent of the Son of Man of Daniel on the clouds of heaven [Dan. 7:13], or the incarnation of the preexistent Logos by which, according to Philo, God created the world,[47] or the making visible of an analogue of one of the manifestations of the

---

47. Philo, *De opificio mundi* 24.

divine essence as taught by the rabbis when they spoke about the *memra* (the Word), the *shekinah* (the glory), and the *metatron* (the supreme archangel of God),[48] or again in terms of equation, a theophany in the true sense: *God* is Christ. Who can doubt that in the main the primitive Christians followed these expanding lines of thought, as is perhaps most evident in John's Gospel?

Yet have we rightly understood the meaning of this process if we describe it in either of these ways? Is it not all very puzzling again the moment we stop trying to describe and assert, and ask instead: What is meant by the first step on the path at whose end a man is equated with God, or what is meant by the first step on the path at whose end God is a man? Can this be the end of a path if it was not already its beginning? Do we not have here too a begging of the question? Does not the decisive assertion have to be understood not as a result but as the presupposition? If we grant the first Christians one little thing, namely, that they understood the distinction between God and man qualitatively and thus posited it as infinite, then we have to concede that we do justice to their thinking only if we see that this first or last step of their christology, whether it moved from below to above (adoptionism) or from above to below (hypostatizing), this first or last step in which they equate unequal things, precisely in its enigmatic and severely paradoxical nature, is the point of the twofold movement of the thinking. It is the principle of these developments rather than the final member. It is the a priori of their conception rather than its boldly asserted or posited result.

How are we really to think of these people who simply because they contingently came across those ascending or descending habits of thought, that metaphysically mythological conceptual material, and simply because they contingently encountered Jesus, equally contingently came to this result by applying these concepts to Jesus? And how are we to think of the obvious zeal, or especially the ability, in the light of the supposed result, to obliterate all traces of those paths so carefully that we today can construct them only hypothetically, and in fact even at the supposed beginnings we already run up against the supposed result, the formulated or unformulated equation that Christ is God and God is Christ, the unmistakable *Iēsous Kyrios?* J. Weiss, when reflecting upon this question, once said that the conjunction of hitherto unconnected conceptual ele-

---

48. Cf. M. Kähler, "Christologie, Schriftlehre," *RE*, IV, 3rd ed., 7. For further examples cf. *ChD*, p. 248 n. 5.

ments around a solid center presupposes a power of attraction that we can never think of as too strong. How powerful must have been the direct and indirect effect of the personality of Jesus on the souls of his adherents that they could believe this about him and be ready to die for their belief.[49] Yes indeed! But what do we mean in this case by power of attraction, or by direct and indirect effect, when this is the effect? Materially, was not the church simply correct when it took its stand on the result or the presupposition of the whole process, eliminated all that might remind it of the paths of thought (by way of apotheosis or hypostatizing) along which it had achieved it, recognized that all this was nonessential, left it to Gnostics and heretics to shunt up and down in these sidings,[50] and unhesitatingly based its teaching on the thesis that because Jesus is the same *Kyrios* as the Father, because he bears the same name as the Father, because he is the eternal Son of the eternal Father, therefore and in this sense we receive and adopt the witness: *theos ēn ho logos* [John 1:1].

Now what does it mean, what can it mean, in distinction from the divinizing of a man or the humanizing of God, to say that Christ is God, God's Son? For the moment let us set aside the fact that it is specifically Christ (the dogma of the incarnation is always to be distinguished from that of the Trinity; it represents a different element in the concept of revelation). On the basis of our first consideration, we start with the point that Christ reveals the Father. But the Father is God. He who reveals the Father reveals God. But who can reveal God but God himself? He who does this (and it is our presupposition that Christ does it) must himself be God. Precisely not an elevated man! Precisely not an intermediate being descending from above! God himself, or, to emphasize our second formula, *wholly* God. Only God in totality, with no subtraction or diminution, with no "more or less," with no "almost," can reveal the Father. The finite is not capable of the infinite.[51] This established thesis eliminates at a stroke all trinitarian heresies. Those who confess a revealer confess — an either/or is valid here — one who is equal to the Father, equal in deity, not, of course, inasmuch as he is the Father's Son. One can also take the other approach and say that in Christ the Father reveals himself. But what does the Father reveal — the Father who is God? What God reveals must be

---

49. J. Weiss, "Christologie: I. des Urchristentums," *RGG*, I, 1st ed., 1713.
50. Barth uses *Stumpengeleisen* here for the usual *Abstellgeleisen*.
51. Cf. Heppe-Pöhlmann, p. 346; ET p. 437; and for the history of the phrase and its significance in the 1920s, see *ChD*, pp. 251-52 n. 12.

God himself, wholly God, equal to God. Would revelation be revelation if something smaller, intermediate, or partial were its content? Those who confess a revealer of the Father, if they know what they are doing — an either/or is valid here — confess one who is equal to the Father, equal in his deity, yet not the Father again, but the Son in the equality of deity.

We must now inquire into the meaning of the term "Son" in this context. Let us first consider again that revelation is directed to pilgrim man, to man in his contradiction. Only in this light can we understand who and what reveals itself. To know the Lord, not merely to know him as the source of revelation but to see and hear and touch him in revelation [1 John 1:1], obviously means to know him not merely *above* the contradiction of our existence but *in* it, where we are. Wonder of wonders, God is there too. He is so much the eternal Lord that the limit set for us does not exist for him. He who overcomes the contradiction is with us.[52] We are clear about our possibilities, and also about the impossibility that fences us in. We know the misery of our lack of limits, the unconditional nature of our being conditioned, the bondage of our wills, our lack of freedom to stand above antitheses, our inability even to think of the beginning and the end, let alone to be at the origin and the goal. Revelation does not mean only that we are told about the Father to whom all this does not apply, about the nature of *his* possibility, about the Creator of heaven and earth, about Jerusalem the free woman that is above [Gal. 4:26]. It does mean this too, and this is incommensurable; it contains the totality if we hear it totally. But because God in revelation is himself both Revealer and Revealed it also means expressly that this totality is here and now as well as there and then. The unlimited contradiction in which we live, the whole flux of two worlds into which we are thrust, is *non sine numine,*[53] not without the presence of the Logos of God. God is not just Lord and Victor over all things but *in* all things, not just as they were and will be but as they are in their sinfulness and corruptibility. Our whole existence from the highest to the lowest should be seen in the light of his revelation and then interpreted as a single vestige of the Trinity.[54] We do not have merely

---

52. Marginal note: "Reconciled the world, 2 Cor. 5:19; *apokatallaxai ta panta,* Col. 1:20; *egenēthēte engys,* Eph. 2:13; *eirēnē,* Eph. 2:14; *airōn tēn hamartian,* John 1:29; *mesitēs,* 1 Tim. 2:5; NB Heb. 9:15; 12:24."

53. For this phrase cf. esp. Zwingli, *On Providence,* Opera, IV (Turici, 1841), p. 108; ET p. 176.

54. "Vestiges of the Trinity" is the common phrase for the supposed analogies discussed above, pp. 103ff.

isolated rays of his power and wisdom. We have his Word in which he totally declares himself in his essence, in which he has given up his own Son to our existence here.

What does the word "Son" imply in this context? That God is not unfruitful, not *monadikos,* not solitary, not a dry fountain, not an ice-cold starry heaven? He would be this if we wanted to stop at the picture of the Father as the Lord *above* the contradiction of the world. But then we would not really have seen the picture of the Father, of the Father who reveals and communicates and makes manifest, and reveals, indeed, not merely something, not merely a reflection of himself, but in the reflection, in his image, his very self, his whole self, the one who is thus known in revelation to have a Son of his own, equal to himself. In the christological struggles of the 4th century it was constantly stressed that denial of the full deity of the Son infringes too directly on the Father, the *principium* of deity, the very concept of God. God would not be God were he not so truly God that without in any way emptying out his deity he could not and did not encounter himself as a second (and still in this second himself). Only as the Redeemer God, as the Father of the Son, is he truly known as the Creator God, the *principium* of deity, the true and living God.

On the other side the word "Son" implies that the world is not forsaken by God but that in all its unredeemed secularity, in its character as a foreign land, as the world of fallen, sinful, mortal humanity, it is sanctified and borne and ruled and set in the light of the most certain hope because it is set in the light of its origin. The God who in the generation of the Son, of the Redeemer God, encounters himself as a second (and in this second himself) has to be regarded as the Creator God at the beginning and end of our contradiction, for the generation of the Son is the great model of the creation of the world. Yet he is not to be regarded merely as one who stands over against the world, who views and moves it from outside. He is to be regarded as the one who, although he is distinct from it and remains distinct, upholds and preserves and directs it inwardly, as the one without whom nothing is, since nothing came to be without him [John 1:3], as the hidden wisdom in great unwisdom, as the forgotten and unknown but only true Word which has to be redis- covered and in which all things are one as they were and will be, as the revelation par excellence in which there is not only a summons and invitation home, but home comes to us, the kingdom of heaven is near, *ēngiken* [Mark 1:15], as the gospel expresses it with both urgency and restraint.

Yet we should also consider at this point that the kingdom of God which in the Son is set up amid our contradiction, the revelation of the Father in the world that takes place through him, the divine Yes to the world that is pronounced in him, is simply his outward work in which we know him as he actually gives himself to be known. He is not who he is, the Son, merely because he does this outward work. As he is Creator in exactly the same sense as the Father, so the Father is Redeemer in exactly the same sense as the Son, and we shall see that the same is to be said about the Spirit, and even more about the Father, Son, and Spirit. He is what he is as the Son of the Father who sends him into the world. But his sending into the world by the Father in time is to be distinguished from the eternal relationship between the two which underlies it. The Son is what he is because God in his revelation, in his Word, does not just posit something but posits himself. He is both subject and predicate, and truly subject only in the predicate. Only thus far and as such does he do his outward work and can all that is said about his lordship in the contradiction be meaningfully said.

In regard to the Son, too, there is no general truth. The Son is not the self-evidently present relation of God to the world, the divine cosmic principle, or even finally, in less cautious speculation, the world itself. The name "Son" is not just a Christian label attached to a fact that is known in some other way, namely, that God is not only beyond the world but also in it, that he is not unfruitful, that the world is not abandoned by God. All this is metaphysical chatter. It is an illegitimate and unsuccessful attempt to comfort ourselves once it breaks loose even for a moment from the context of the basic principle which is not a principle but the exclusive truth about God: that God is *God,* that he is God there and in that way, the one God in the person of the Son over against the Father. Also impermissible, however, is the apparently more Christian way, the so-called christocentric way, in which Jesus is directly and nondialectically made into an entity that is God[55] in itself with no reference or basis, as though everything did not depend on this reference and basis, on the fact that as the Son of the Father he is the *one* God.

The early church tried to work out this recollection of the primary context, which has life-and-death significance for all that follows, in the special definitions of its doctrine of the Son, in the doctrine of generation and sonship that we find summed up in the Nicene Creed. "I believe in

---

55. The MS has "is made God."

. . . the only-begotten Son." The only-begotten Son! This is how God reveals himself. This revealing of himself is something new, a second thing which is posited by God, not merely asserted or inferred by us. He is thus the Son, wholly God, a second in the same God; in the same God and thus "only-begotten." There is only one revelation, one Son. The revelation of the Son, of the Logos, is revelation. What is not the revelation of the Son is not revelation. It belongs to the side of humanity in its contradiction. Recall what was said in the first subsection about the formula "wholly God." He was "begotten of his Father." Later theologians rightly took this to mean that he did not come into being by a special act of the Father's will, although naturally not without this will. It is the nature of the Father and his will to beget the Son, this one Son.[56] It is his eternal will to do it. "Before all worlds," and not therefore by the incarnation, by the virgin birth, by his baptism in the Jordan, or by his resurrection and exaltation. These things belong to another context. The "before" is not to be taken chronologically. The begetting, like the will, is as eternal as God himself. There was no time when the Son was not, when he was not begotten, and there will be none when he will not be begotten. The "this day" in the much-quoted Psalm [2:7]: "Thou art my Son, this day have I begotten thee," is the day of immutable eternity.[57] It is yesterday, today, and tomorrow. Not as though the generation were incomplete, not as though the idea of development slips in here by the back door; no, the act is perfect as a work but it is also — a joyous protest against all theological objectivizing — perpetual in its operation.[58] What is true in God has to be, and it needs no supplementing, for it is true in God, as God's mercies are fresh each morning [Lam. 2:23]. The Son is "God of God, Light of Light, very God of very God," and therefore "begotten, not made," *gennētheis ou poiētheis.*

The church naturally took note of the inadequacy of this whole picture of the Father and the Son. Obviously these are only human words. Yet the church chooses them and insists on them, sharply differentiating generation and creation, because everything depends on the one decisive term of comparison in the picture. The Father does not bring forth the Son out of nothing or out of something else but out of his own essence, the essence of deity, which is not to be regarded, of course, as a special

---

56. Cf. A. Polanus, in Heppe-Bizer, p. 100; ET pp. 120-21.
57. Cf. J. A. Quenstedt, in Schmid-Pöhlmann, p. 110; Schmid ET pp. 152-53.
58. Schmid, p. 108; Schmid-Pöhlmann, p. 111; Schmid ET p. 153.

content alongside the person that begets and the person that is begotten, and naturally not as nothing, but as the negation of all matter, of all content outside the deity, the actuosity, the most pure and simple act of the divine being itself.[59] What is safeguarded by the image of generation is the direct continuity between the first and second persons, the direct "of God, of Light, of very God," and what is ruled out is all improper talk of an exalted man or a descending divine being. In revelation we have to do with nothing but God, with no work or emanation or part of God but — all similes are inadequate — with his only-begotten Son, with his express image, with God himself, but with God himself in a second person. The inconsistency of the comparison guards against a naturalistic interpretation, for it is always necessary to equate the Son with the Logos, the begetting of God with his speaking.

Finally, we have "of one substance with the Father," the famous *homoousios* of Athanasius. In this context I can say nothing more specific about this than that we are not to call it pedantry or a straining of language, that it was not a battle about a diphthong, about an *i* which would have made equality of substance into likeness of substance. On this *i*, or rather on its rejection, depended the understanding and securing of the truth that the substance of the Father is undividedly, unabbreviatedly, and unrestrictedly that of the Son as well. The Son (a second in God) shares that which makes the Father (the first) God, the actuosity that excludes all other content apart from the fulness of deity itself, with no deletion — for what could be deleted? We have here an either/or. The battle of Athanasius was at least as important as that of Luther for faith and justification. At issue was the presupposition without which one cannot understand the Reformation, without which, if we were to put it against another background, the "faith alone" would be unbearably one-sided, and would rightly call for correction by Pietism and the Enlightenment. Because faith relates to revelation, because the content of revelation is not a second thing alongside God, but a second *in* God, the fulness of God in the Son, for this reason we can and must say: "by faith alone." Without it, it would be better not to say that, and better still, perhaps, to say nothing about God at all.

Here, too, the doctrine of the Trinity poses a demand to stand still before the incomprehensible reality of God. It is not self-evident that God

---

59. A. Polanus, in Heppe, p. 94; Heppe-Bizer, pp. 101-2; ET p. 122; cf. also Polanus, in Heppe-Bizer, p. 43; ET p. 53.

reveals the Father or that the Father has a Revealer. We are too hasty if we rush past the problems that lie in these statements. If we do, we rush into incredibility. Today, as in the first centuries, they will be confirmed, or perhaps not confirmed, only with either sentimental exaggerations or dubious mythologies. The doctrine of the Trinity gives a *legitimate* answer by referring truly to God, to God in his totality, with no deletion or reservation. If we accept this reference, we stand clearly and unequivocally before the second person in God, the Son.

3. We now turn a third time to the situation of primitive Christianity, of its confession *Iēsous Kyrios. Kyrios* means God. How can people take this *Kyrios* on their lips? we now ask. It is assumed that they know what they are doing when they do it. They do not have in mind a superman or a demigod, but God. They are to be taken seriously with their confession. They believe, and therefore speak [2 Cor. 4:13]. We thus come up against a third problem which is no less great and severe than the question who it is that Jesus reveals, or who it is that reveals himself in Jesus. Do we not have here a third and specific riddle that arises directly in face of the people whom we see believing and confessing the *Iēsous Kyrios,* that is, the Father and the Son according to all that precedes? How does this content come into this vessel? Can the vessel hold it? Will it not burst it?[60] Does not this predicate: faith in God the Father and the Son, destroy this human subject? How can anyone have this faith [cf. 2 Thess. 3:2]?

Always and everywhere, of course, people have been able to believe in supermen and demigods, in leaders and heroes and great personalities, in powers and hypostases, in monstrous divinizations or humanizations. The finite is capable of the finite, as religious history testifies. No one either can or should prevent us from trying to understand the NT, too, in terms of religious history. It is a healthy and commendable exercise to do this, and in this way to come to see what we really have in the NT if we leave out the Holy Spirit. We can then say that the objects of the faith and confession of the first Christians are finite things. *Kyrios* is meant improperly by way of apotheosis or hypostasis. So too, then, are Father and Son. These are entities alongside which there are others — angels, demons, pagan deities, etc. — the former are great, the latter small. There are analogies for all this in Judaism or Hellenism. That people might have believed in God is a question that may interest historians in the quiet of

---

60. The MS mistakenly has the vessel bursting the content (*es ihn* instead of *er es*)!

their own rooms, but scholarship cannot take it into account and need not do so. Infinitesimal calculus is not its job. In this case, of course, our present question offers no serious difficulty. There is some astonishment, perhaps, at the faith of the disciples in the risen Lord directly after the crucifixion, or at the Lucan account of the miracle of Pentecost. Possibly psychologists are consulted for advice on what such things might mean, and happily they cannot indicate anything that stands outside analogy or discussion even if everything cannot be satisfactorily explained. Along these lines, in keeping with the theme, faith and the accompanying confession of the Word and of life become an understandable and possible action like other things with which[61] we see people occupy themselves in the present or past ages.

You will know that NT scholarship today, precisely on its most radical wing, is being seriously threatened by the demand that it should really learn infinitesimal calculus, that it should find a place for revelation and faith as incommensurable factors.[62] But we do not have the time to wait for the conversion of NT scholarship. We must be content to state that even without that, there is nothing to stop us from reading the NT properly instead of improperly, that is, from really thinking of God when we find *Kyrios,* and therefore from not banishing the riddle of these texts but insisting on its real severity: How could such faith and confession be possible? Are we really in any position to conceive of people who could act in this way, for example, of Paul? Assuming that they really do, are they not necessarily unhistorical in so doing? Have human beings an organ for God that we can assume to be well known, that we also have, so that we can understand those people by analogy? This is sometimes stated. It is said, for example, that there is a feeling of absolute dependence, that there are experiences of God. But this can be said only humorously, with tongue in cheek, and not strictly! *Can* we believe, believe in *God?* Is not this something that is conceptually impossible? If we could have such a faith, would it not burn us like contact with a high-voltage circuit, but

---

61. The MS has "in which."

62. Barth had in mind Bultmann's lecture "Die liberale Theologie und die jüngste theologische Bewegung," *TBl* 3 (1924) 73-86; repr. in *Glauben und Verstehen,* I (Tübingen, 1933), pp. 1-25; ET "Liberal Theology and the Latest Theological Movement," in *Faith and Understanding* (London, 1969), pp. 28-52. Barth attended the lecture in Marburg on Feb. 6, 1924; cf. Barth-Thurneysen correspondence in *Revolutionary Theology in the Making* (Richmond, 1964), p. 171, and Barth's letter to Bultmann in *Barth/Bultmann Letters* (Grand Rapids, 1981), pp. 12-13.

much more severely? The OT prophets, who knew something about the matter, plainly said so [cf. Deut. 4:24]. To believe in God, if we take each word categorically and seriously, means standing in relation to God, being in continuity with him, being able to hear him and even to answer him. Can we do this? Does the fact that we have religion prove that we can? But if the claim of what is called religion to be a relationship with God is true, then the riddle confronts us once more — how can there be such a thing as religion?

We agreed, however, to concede to the first Christians that they *did* believe in God and confess him with their *Iēsous Kyrios.* Let us allow these Christians themselves to tell us how they regarded this fact, the decisive fact in their lives. It really was for them an inexplicable fact. We are forcefully pointed to this by their answer: *oudeis dynatai eipein; Kyrios Iēsous, ei mē en pneumati hagiō* (1 Cor. 12:3). Note the *oudeis* and the *ei mē* [!] *en pneumati hagiō.* A new element comes in here which is not identical with their faith and confession but is obviously an a priori of their faith and confession. To know the *Kyrios* to whom Jesus points was one thing. To know the *Kyrios* in Jesus himself was a second. But what is the third thing on which the knowing itself, obviously on our part, must be grounded, but not *by* and *in* us, as the expression itself shows, so that it cannot be confused with religion and the like? What is the *pneuma hagion?*

If we first return to the situation of man as a wanderer between two worlds, the obvious reply must be that the third thing is that the Lord who is over and in the world makes himself known to me, the person I am, as *my* Lord, that he stands in *my* life, that he is seen by *me* as a factor with which I have to reckon. He is and becomes our own Lord. He places over us the sign of the victory which is his own being, and his lordship becomes the decisive determination of our existence. I said in the thesis that he proclaims victory over the contradiction, addresses us as God's children and servants, and gives us faith and obedience. By this means I wanted to stress as strongly as possible that the issue here is the most positive relation of God to us, to man. Those who in spite of every safeguard would have God's lordship over and in the contradiction understood as merely a metaphysical, logical, dialectical relation should at least finally waken to the fact that it concerns them,[63] that the contradiction is *theirs,* that the Lord over and in it is *their* Lord. The expressions "he is

---

63. Barth quotes Horace here, *Epistles* I, 18, 84: *tuares agitur.*

and becomes" our own Lord, "children and servants," and "faith and obedience" are meant to show us that this lordship of God over us, in which the concept of divine *kyriotēs* achieves material completeness, includes two things: first, a specific relation of God *to us,* namely, that he is our Lord and we are his children, that is, we are, just as we are, his offspring [cf. Acts 17:28], and that we acknowledge this in faith; and second, a specific relation of us *to God,* namely, that he becomes our Lord and we are his servants, not belonging to ourselves but to someone else, and that we acknowledge this in obedience. We shall return to all this later, but we must say it already at this point so that no false objectivism should creep into the doctrine of the Trinity, and so that a sign may be set up that this doctrine, and the whole problem of revelation here, where the last word concerns the Holy Spirit, is at all events acutely, existentially, and inescapably personal.

I would ask you to note that all these statements about the lordship of God tell us nothing about man in himself and as such, neither about his nature nor his spirit, neither about his heart nor his conscience, neither about his experience, feeling, knowledge, will nor his achievement. These things are written both before and after in another book, in the book of man and his ambiguity, this irremovable contradiction, the bondage of his will. *God* proclaims, *God* speaks, *God* gives. The words "being," "becoming," "child," "servant," "faith," and "obedience" say nothing about a quantitative or qualitative enrichment, enlargement, development, or outworking of man and his situation. He is man, and he remains man at every point and according to all the definitions, without exception, that we mentioned in § 4. It is to *this* man that God proclaims his victory over the contradiction, to *this* man that he speaks as to his child and servant, to *this* man that he gives faith and obedience, which are gifts of God in the strictest sense. And what does all this mean but that God reveals or communicates *himself* to *this* man.

We have again reached our third formula from subsection 1. God himself is the content of revelation even in our receiving of his Word, even in our being addressed, even in the reception of his gift. No one represents God but God himself, and no one represents us, least of all ourselves, but God himself. This is the epistemological theory of revelation in brief: God represents himself with us and us with himself. In his light we see light (Ps. 36:9). In a strange misunderstanding we cannot be content with this. In addition to the pledge, the *arrabōn,* of the Spirit [2 Cor. 1:22], we think there is needed a special qualitative or quantitative betterment, uplifting, deepening, interiorizing, or experience of man, his permeation by God or uniting with God, and in some way a better, more direct, more real, and more essential guarantee of the truth of revelation than that which God's own coming gives. Those who want more here are really asking less. They do not have God himself in mind if they are not content with God himself, if God himself is for them form and not content, something negative and not something supremely positive. They give up God if they seek another. God himself is not *one* spirit among others, something spiritually finite, as he obviously would be if there were intermingling or marriage or even identification between him and our spirits. If I may use Hegelian terms, God is the absolute Spirit, the pure act of the Spirit. Even in his most direct proximity as the Spirit of the Son, he is distant as the Spirit of the Father. Those who stand before God in the Spirit can only pray. They do not think they already are or have or do or possess anything. To pray is not to have. We must all seek. We can pray only like the publican in the temple, from a distance [Luke 18:13]. Precisely in the Spirit we know our own emptiness, nakedness, bad conscience, worldliness, contrite and broken heart (Ps. 51:17). We know that we can only pray for a clean heart, a new and confident human spirit, in the words of the same Psalm (v. 10). We know that what is born of flesh is flesh. We know that we can stand before God only in God and by God, that only what is born of the Spirit is spirit (John 3:6). We know that we cannot equate this new, regenerate person, this subject that can truly, indicatively, say of itself, "I believe, I obey," that we cannot equate this person with ourselves. We must stay with the petition: *Come, Creator Spirit.*[64] We cannot make it into an indicative or a perfect, as though the Spirit *had* come. Here again we have a perpetual operation.[65] This is how we stand before God, how we receive revelation, how we are the Lord's [Rom. 14:8], in this way and no other. Anything more is not man, his state, his given situation, but God himself, God the Spirit. We should not view this as a limitation of the work of the Spirit, as a truncation or depletion of the relation to God, or as a rendering uncertain of what is most certain about faith and obedience. No, everything depends on this, the true work and creativity of the Spirit, the richness and fulness of the relation to God, the strength of faith and obedience. All this depends on our seeking the basis, power, and truth of it all in God and nowhere else.

---

64. Cf. the Whitsun hymn ascribed to Rabanus Maurus (ca. 776-856).
65. Cf. Schmid, p. 108; Schmid-Pöhlmann, p. 111; Schmid ET p. 153.

Here too, however, we have spoken only of the outward action, of the work of the Spirit in virtue of which the church calls him the Holy Spirit, *pneuma hagiōsynēs* [Rom. 1:4]. Here again, then, we must remember that all that is said rests on the equation: *ho kyrios to pneuma* [2 Cor. 3:17], on the presupposition that the Spirit is really God himself, of one substance with the Father and the Son. Here too, then, we must differentiate this working, or, from God's standpoint, this outpouring, the Spirit's mission in time, from the eternal relation in God himself which simply finds expression in the work, the gift, the mission of the Spirit. As God is Father and Son from and in eternity, as the Father begets the Son and the Son is begotten by the Father, so from and in eternity God is the Spirit. "Who proceedeth from the Father and the Son, who with the Father and the Son together is worshipped and glorified," says the third article of the Nicene Creed in this regard.

God's relation to us is not accidental. It is necessarily contained and grounded in God's being. All that the Father does and the Son does, the Spirit does with them. The Spirit, God's express turning to us, is already Creator, Ruler, and Upholder of all things. He is already Redeemer and Mediator. We have stressed again and again that the outward works are not divided,[66] and here again, in the third article, this principle is important. The turning to us is not something subsequent, something episodic. God himself, the Creator and Redeemer, stands or falls with what takes place as the divine Yes to us in the outpouring and reception of the Holy Spirit in time. This is the very live and concrete thing in what seems to be the very abstract doctrine of the deity of the Spirit too. This doctrine does not rest on a theoretical need for completeness, on an attempt to fill out the number three. It rests on the deep insight that God would not be God if the relation to us were not intrinsic to him from the very first.

The eternal relation of the Spirit to the Father and the Son has been called *spiratio,* the divine breathing, the *processio spiritus sancti,* the procession of God from himself. When people ask how this process differs from the generation of the Son, they find themselves in some difficulty. The answer has been that there can be no doubling in God, that the Spirit is not the brother of the Son and naturally not the son of the Son and grandson of the Father,[67] and therefore the procession has to differ from

---

66. Cf. W. Bucanus, in Heppe-Bizer, p. 98; ET p. 116. For the history of the formula cf. *ChD,* p. 228 n. 94.

67. Cf. Bavinck, II, p. 288.

the generation. But what is it then? An ineffable communication of essence, it is said. Yet there is a touching readiness to admit quite simply that we cannot explain what the difference is, as Melchior Leydecker (d. 1673) says.[68] And long before Leydecker greater theologians like Augustine in the West and John of Damascus in the East declared that they could give no help.[69] As a reminder of the relativity of all doctrine, of all figurative language and dialectic as such, it is a good thing that our perspicacity really fails at some points.

As is well known, a debate which had far-reaching ecclesiastical consequences stands behind the formula "from the Father and the Son" *(filioque)*. The *filioque* was brought into the Nicene Creed in the West from A.D. 589, and because it rejected it the Eastern Church broke off relations with the Latin West. It is hard to discuss the matter. For us a certain obscurity lies over the conflict. I do not recall having heard or read anything very plausible about it. Our orthodox Protestant theologians obviously did not really know what the concern was. According to the Greeks the Spirit proceeds from the Father alone even if, as the Council of Florence (1439) was ready to concede, he does so through the Son *(per filium)*. In the West, however, this *per filium* was taken to mean that the Son has from the Father the power that means the Spirit proceeds from him as well as from the Father. They viewed the *spiratio* as the act of the Father and the Son united as one *principium* in this instance. In contrast, the Easterners would agree only that the Son was a cause or instrument in the hand of the Father.[70] They would not go beyond this at the Old Catholic Conference in Bonn in 1875.[71] Do we have in the Greek view an unsubjugated remnant of subordinationism, as though the Father were more and greater than the Son? Or is it a reflection of the very mystically oriented piety of the East which, bypassing the revelation in the Son, would relate man directly to the original Revealer, the *principium* or fount of deity,[72] as though one could and should do this?

The Easterners for their part base their position on the difficulty

---

68. Cf. Heppe-Bizer, p. 102; ET p. 123.

69. Cf. G. Sohnius, in Heppe-Bizer, p. 105; ET p. 130; cf. also *ChD,* pp. 284-85 nn. 35, 38.

70. Cf. the *Bulla unionis Graecorum "Laetentur caeli"* (Eugenius IV, 1439), *Decretum pro Graecis* (DS, 1300-1302).

71. *Bericht über die vom 10. bis 16. August 1875 zu Bonn gehaltenen Unions-Conferenzen,* ed. F. H. Reusch (Bonn, 1875), p. 92.

72. Cf. n. 46 above.

of maintaining one principle of the Spirit according to the Western view, an objection which is not very illuminating considering the orthodox view of the Father and the Son. I admit, however, that I do not understand the motives of the Eastern Church clearly enough to reach any definitive conclusion. Nevertheless, it seems to me that a threat to the unity of the concept of God lies in the denial of the *filioque*. Thus, although we can agree with some of the Reformed orthodox of the 17th century that we might understand the Greek teaching in better part,[73] we still have no reason to hold aloof from the Western form. It expresses much better the drift of the whole doctrine as we have thought we must understand it.

The main point here is acknowledgment of the deity and person-hood of the Spirit: of the deity, because only by God himself can God himself be known by us; the personhood, because this third thing, this knowing of God by us, this relation of God to us, is not self-evident, is no more a general truth than is God's fatherhood or his sonship, for it cannot simply be inferred from the concepts but is a new and third thing, the miracle of the same God which closes the circle and which is to be recognized as a distinct subsistence in the one divine substance. The unheard-of thing that we believe and obey, a fact which in its significance is unique and totally incalculable, is not really posited by our thinking of God as Revealer and Revealed. We have also to think of something special in addition. God is God in another way as well (which we might modestly call an ineffable communication). He is Lord not only *over* all things and *in* all things, but as we are special things among all other things, uniquely at the center of all things, God is *our* Lord, *mine* and *yours,* the God who stands related to us as I and Thou, as Thou and I, from eternity to eternity. If this special thing is clear, then it cannot fail to be clear that in the Holy Spirit we have to do with a third person in God.

---

73. Cf. L. van Riisen and the Leiden Synopsis, in Heppe-Bizer, p. 106; ET p. 131.

§ 6

The Incarnation of God

God's revealing of himself to man presupposes his encounter with man. All testimonies to God's revelation are hoping, knowing, and promising references to this encounter. When the time was fulfilled, the Word became flesh and dwelt among us. God was in Christ. In the irremovable mystery of his deity, encircled by every possibility of offense, he was the Crucified, he could be known only through himself in the resurrection of Christ from the dead, but in history, in time, he could be known truly, definitively, and sufficiently, encountering man.

I. The Possibility of Incarnation

To form the concept of revelation, the concept of the Word of God in its most principal sense, we must borrow again from the material of dogmatics proper. Like the nature of man (see § 4 above) and the divine Trinity (§ 5), Jesus Christ is naturally a theme of Christian preaching, and therefore also of dogma and its inquiry. But how can we speak about the principle in which Christian preaching has its final root, which has to count as the ultimate norm in dogmatic statements, without already speaking about Jesus Christ, even if with the proviso once again that we shall have to come back to the topic? I regard the doctrine of the Trinity as the true center of the concept of revelation. But I can also sympathize with the view of B. Keckermann when he preferred to see in the doctrine of the incarnation the nucleus of all theology,[1] and in view of the significant and

---

1. Heppe-Bizer, p. 329; ET p. 401.

in my opinion fateful role that christology plays in modern dogmatics, I would not think it right not to seek some clarity on the subject as we are now trying to lay the foundations, quite apart from the fact that we have been forcefully referred to the matter in the course of our deliberations.

If you perhaps think that this anticipatory process is surprising and dubious, then ask yourselves whether this is not possibly so because I openly and frankly confess what I am doing, whereas others do the same thing more surreptitiously when laying down their principles. I do not really see how any discussion of the preliminary questions of dogmatics is possible unless at certain points we explicitly or implicitly enter upon such questions and give specific answers in advance. Thus those who want to show and present religion, for example, as the regulative principle of their dogmatics anticipate therewith certain questions regarding the nature of God, of humanity, and of their relation, although these questions can be really decided only in dogmatics itself. With their psychological approach to principles, then, they already give very definite and momentous answers to all kinds of questions. Schleiermacher's *Christian Faith* is a brilliant example.[2] Again, those who set up apologetics as a pedestal for dogmatics make and demonstrate a presupposition which is significant in all kinds of ways, namely, that the contents of their dogmatics proper, in general if not in detail, both need and are capable of justification in terms of thinking that has its basis elsewhere. In so doing they cannot avoid mentioning and describing in advance some of these contents, probably with very definite conclusions as to their greater or lesser importance. Again, a Roman Catholic theology which will supposedly include some teaching on the church and its dogma in the prolegomena, or a Vilmarian theology which will give some teaching on ecclesiastical office,[3] will already in a very decisive way anticipate much more than one particular dogma.

Now I myself think it better to be aware of the circle in which

---

2. Schleiermacher, *Der christlichen Glaube* (1821, 1830); ET *CF.*

3. Speculation on the shape of prolegomena in a Vilmarian dogmatics perhaps goes back to Barth's reading of a manuscript by R. Schlunk on A. F. C. Vilmar (1800-1868) which circulated among the contributors to *Zwischen den Zeiten* in the spring of 1924 (cf. Barth/Thurneysen, *Briefwechsel,* II: 1921-1930 [Zurich, 1974], p. 249 n. 3; cf. ET *Revolutionary Theology in the Making* [Richmond, 1964], p. 180). In Vilmar's own *Dogmatik* (Gütersloh, 1874), which Barth did not yet know, this doctrine does not have a central place in the prolegomena, but for its central position in his theology cf. Barth's depiction in *Die protestantische Theologie im 19. Jahrhundert* (Zollikon/Zurich, 1947), pp. 576-77; ET *Protestant Theology in the Nineteenth Century* (Valley Forge, 1973), pp. 625ff.

dogmatics necessarily moves, and to admit that the principle above dogmas by which one will later judge what must be dogma and what not, can be known only in the mirror of examples very carefully selected from the plenitude of dogmas, that the norm can be known only by means of provisional but very stringently executed applications of it. In my view the decision that governs all individual decisions must not be taken in a Schleiermacherian or any other obscurity. If we cannot do dogmatics without some begging of the question, this decision must be taken in broad daylight with the help of demonstrations from individual decisions. Naturally this will mean some technical exposure. Along these lines we show that dogmatics can be proved only dogmatically, that all its theses can only support one another mutually except insofar as they are supported by their theme, which is not a thesis. Unavoidably, then, we give an impression of a certain caprice. It was not only for material reasons but for this technical reason as well that the ancients did not give their dogmatics any prolegomena, or only the most rudimentary. If we want to avoid the problem, then we had better follow this classical path.

But I have already said that for us poor moderns in our present state, for whom even the most obvious things about God are not yet or no longer obvious, I do think it is advisable to begin by considering in principle that which is principial in dogmatics, even if there is a danger that we will be shown to be begging the question and that we have to indulge in the apparently arbitrary anticipations in which we are now engaged. Let us hope that our children or grandchildren will no longer need the crutches of a special doctrine of principles and in this regard will be better off than we are because what is principial will again be self-evident. But we need these crutches, and hence we have to indulge intentionally in anticipations. We can do so, however, only if we openly tell ourselves and others what we are doing, namely, that we are really using the anticipations as exercises, but above all that we do so with the hope that the right answers will be given to the right questions, and that thus the anticipations will at least be made correctly.

Along the path that we have trodden thus far in clarification of the *Deus dixit,* at the point that we have now reached we have come up against the problem of the incarnation. We spoke about the nature of revelation in § 3, about its addressees in § 4, about its content or subject in § 5. Now that we have reached a climax with an equation between the content and the subject, we are obviously compelled to inquire into its *possibility.* To do so, however, we must first speak about its temporality or historicity, that is, about Jesus Christ. Then, in the next section, we must speak about human receptivity for it, that is, faith and obedience. [The final section of the chapter will then deal with the place or reality of revelation, i.e., the church.][4]

II. The Historicity of the Incarnation

The problem that confronts us is that of the *possibility* of revelation, I have just said. The development of the doctrine of the Trinity as the doctrine of the content, that is, the eternal subject of revelation, has forced upon us the question whether the final thing that one can say along these lines is not that three times God remains eternally in himself: in himself above the world as Father, in himself in the world as Son, and in himself turned toward us as Spirit, yet always in himself, always God, always wholly *he,* never and nowhere *we.* Point by point we have seen that we must accept this "he not we" if we are to talk seriously about revelation. God alone, wholly God, God himself must be the one whose revealing is worthy of the name of God. What is less or other is not God or God's revelation. God is *God.*[5] The limit that is thereby set for us has nothing whatever to do with a one-sided emphasis on God's transcendence, majesty, or negativity. We have seen that the picture would be the same if we started with God's immanence in the Son or his eternal turning to us in the Spirit. "Thou dost surround me on all sides and lay thy hand upon me. Such knowledge is too wonderful and too high for me, I cannot attain to it. Where shall I flee from thy Spirit, and where shall I flee from thy countenance?" (Ps. 139:5-6). From thy Spirit, which is never ours, and from thy countenance, whose gaze we cannot bear? we might add in the spirit of the Psalmist. We must always understand revelation as God's revelation. In revelation God is always, not quantitatively (for what is gigantic or infinite does not make God God), but qualitatively different from us, not spatially, but occupying a totally different place according to the mode of space. In his deity, for which no picture or likeness or symbol is appropriate

---

4. Barth later put this sentence in square brackets because he never carried out this plan in his lectures.

5. This saying, one of the slogans of Dialectical Theology, is found in the 1st ed. of *Römerbrief* (Bern, 1919), pp. 47, 79-97; cf. also *ChD,* p. 290 n. 2; the Preface to the 4th ed. of *Römerbrief* (Munich, 1933), p. XXIV; ET *Epistle to the Romans* (London, 1933), pp. 20-21; also A. Schlatter's criticism, *Die Furche* 12 (1922) 231-32.

(for, strictly, symbols apply only to gods and not to God), and in which he can never in any way be an object for us, all comprehension fails us, all such statements as "thou art" or "he is." "I am who I am" [Exod. 3:14]. God is only in the first person. And we are there, and what organ or capability do we have to grasp him, to penetrate this divine I which alone is God? Woe to us if we confuse our own I with this I! The most basic, the oldest, and yet always the newest of illusions! "You shall be as God" [Gen. 3:5]. We will never be as God is. We can never put ourselves in God's place. It is to our shame that we continually want and try to do so.

But if this is so, what does it mean that God himself is exclusively revealed, but that he is not revealed to us with our organs, abilities, and capacities? It is as well to stop for a moment, the more so as we have here a truth in our relation to God which we cannot overcome as a mere appearance but which we have to leave victorious — or, rather, the truth of God's appearance which is always the truth in all that we might perhaps say about it. Indeed, everything that we might perhaps say about it can be said only in face of this truth, only as we stand by it, namely, the truth that also and precisely in his revelation God is the hidden God. We might miss this insight. Those who do not know the revealed God, what do they know of the hidden God? Only God's dearest children know that he is a fearful God.[6] God is hidden then, not because of the relativity of all human knowledge, but because he is the living God who reveals himself as he is, the triune God, inexhaustibly living, immutably the subject, from himself and not from us. It is not a much too skeptical philosophy that makes him the hidden God. If we could learn something better from philosophy, moving on perhaps from critical idealism to critical realism, from Plato to Aristotle, from Kant to Hegel or back to Thomas, who would not gladly accept such instruction? But even the most basic epistemological teaching can give little or no help if God is the hidden God precisely because he is the living God, the self-revealing God, the God before whose Godhead we can neither flee from transcendence to immanence nor vice versa, the one who is never so distant as when he is near, the one who, because he is God, can never be an object. Is revelation itself, then, "nonrevelation"? If so, then the very fact that it is God who reveals himself is what prevents him from revealing himself to us![7]

But what are we talking about? We are still talking about revelation

---

6. N. p. 48 adds: "he is as dear to them as that."
7. N. p. 48 adds: "Does not the very obstacle also have to be the way?"

even as we make this dreadful equation. In its place we now have nonrevelation, God's concealment. We have to admit that we cannot see, hear, feel, touch, or either inwardly or outwardly perceive the one who reveals himself, not because he is invisible or pure spirit, but because he is God, because he is wholly himself, "I am who I am," the subject that escapes our grasp, our attempt to make him an object. What we see, hear, feel, touch, and inwardly or outwardly perceive is always something different, a counterpart, a second thing, an I that is not this I. Yet we are still talking about revelation. On what condition can we rightly say this? Can our concept of God really be the concept of his revelation that comes to us? On what condition, even though revelation be still "nonrevelation," do we have to reverse the equation and say that nonrevelation is revelation, that the hidden God is the revealed God? Obviously on the condition that God is a free Lord not only over the contradiction but also over his own deity. What if God be so much God that without ceasing to be God he can also be, and is willing to be, not God as well.[8] What if he were to come down from his unsearchable height and become something different. What if he, the immutable subject, were to make himself object. What if he who is indivisibly one were to take the form of a second. What if he who is unconditionally here were to be also there. What if he who is unchangeably who *he* is were also to meet me as a *thou*. This is the decisive point. He would have to be not merely an object but a recognizable I, a human being. If nonrevelation is to be revelation, everything hinges on God covering his inaccessible divine I-ness with a human I-ness as with a veil so that we can grasp him as a person, as one like ourselves.[9]

But why human? Might not God conceal his deity in some other being, in a star or stone or animal, so as to be objective to us, so as to be comprehensible to us, so as to enable him to encounter us, to reveal himself as the hidden God? He must become human because all the distinction,

---

8. Beside this statement Barth put a question mark in the margin.

9. In the margin Barth had the following summary as a lead into the next lecture: "Dialectic of the concept of revelation on the basis of the doctrine of the Trinity. If God is so immutably God (transcendence, immanence, turning to us), does he reveal himself? Is he not hidden precisely in his revelation? We accepted this — how could we not? — but then went on to consider the condition on which the reverse might be true, that the hidden God is as such the revealed God. We said that this will be so if God be so much God that he can conceal his deity by being another, his being as subject by a being as object, his indissoluble I-ness by a dissoluble I that meets us in an I-Thou relation, if God can become like us, a man."

objectivity, and nonrevelation comes into focus and becomes unambiguous only in the problem of man. It is in human beings that we meet the epitome of the I which is not here but there, which we cannot reverse, which I cannot penetrate and grasp from within as *I* become *he*. In all other objects it is not fully or unequivocally ruled out that I am their subject because I have them in my consciousness. This assumption founders on the problem of man. A human being is obviously his own subject. We can easily infer from the problem of man that the way to the inner core of nature is in fact closed to us.[10] If we were surrounded only by things or plants or animals, then we might fancy — and the greater the fulness of things (think of India) the more easily we might fancy — that we have in the cosmos only a positing or even a creation of our own consciousness, of our own I, or else we might at least dream of being God. The great disruption of this dream, noted or, to our shame, not noted, is the problem of man, the fact that we cannot penetrate the other, the fellow human being, who obviously wills also to be a subject without our being able to stop it. No other creature sets us so forcibly before the limit that God has set for us, whether we recognize it or not. No other creature can do what God in his pure deity cannot do, namely, really meet us, become objective, perceptible, and comprehensible to us as one of ourselves. From human to human, and only there, is there speech, understanding, communication, although naturally with the final proviso that man is not only the *greatest* riddle but *the* great riddle of man. Yet man can encounter man as one of his own. He can at least make known to him by analogies the riddle that he finally is for him. He can become objective to him in his puzzling character. All communication or fellowship between us human beings, the better it succeeds, consists of our mutually setting before ourselves this ultimately puzzling character as the epitome of the objective. Kierkegaard is only too right. No matter how we look at it, one of his most profound insights is that the subjective is the objective.[11] The whole greatness and the whole tragedy of human life together is enclosed in the fact that as we make ourselves known to one another we are unknown to one another. Woe to us if it is not the hiddenness of *God* that we then

---

10. Cf. J. W. von Goethe's poem *Allerdings* (1820), which begins with a quotation from Albrecht von Haller warning Philistines that no created spirit can penetrate the inner core of nature.

11. Cf. esp. his *Philosophical Fragments* (Princeton, repr. 1967) and *Concluding Unscientific Postscript* (Princeton, repr. 1968), pp. 267-322.

come up against! If God's concealment is really to be his revelation, if the barrier before which we stand is also to be a door that opens, if God is to make himself known, then this must take place by God's concealing his pure deity, by his emptying himself of the *morphē theou,* as Phil. 2:6 puts it, by his becoming human. Here and herewith the decision is and must be taken whether revelation is possible.

Let us spend some time on this condition. I think I discern four more detailed definitions which follow from this conditionally advanced main statement.

1. God will have to be wholly God in this concealment that makes him comprehensible. The concealment cannot mean that he is less in it than is his due according to the definitions of the doctrine of the Trinity. In this concealment the truth must still hold good: God alone, wholly God, God himself. No less impregnable, the divine subjectivity must still triumph as before in the human objectivity in which it has hidden itself. Otherwise it would not be God's revelation that becomes comprehensible here in lowliness through God's becoming human. The Lord who is *over* the world and *in* the world, who turns to us from all eternity, the Creator, the Redeemer, the Life-Giver, must be present in this concealment without restriction or deletion. Not a mere particle or emanation of deity must be present, not an angel or hero, but deity itself. It must really be God who encounters us if revelation is to be possible.

2. The human being through whom God conceals himself and makes himself comprehensible must be no less fully human. The concealment must be complete. The divine incognito must be total. He must not be a direct Revealer. He must not make God so perceptible that anyone can see and perceive at once that here is God. For if he were not wholly human, and only in his humanity the organ by which God makes himself perceptible, then he would not be the Revealer at all. A superman or spirit or angel that even in part revealed God directly would again withdraw him from our perception. God must really meet man, and that means that he himself must be truly and totally human and nothing else.

3. The real deity and the real humanity must be so united that neither can be changed into the other or mixed with it. The relation must be an open and loose one inasmuch as the deity does not pass into the humanity or the humanity become identical with the deity. Otherwise it would no longer be God that meets us, or he would cease to meet us truly. On no side, then, can the union become an equation. It must be a union in inequality, in differentiation. It must be a strictly dialectical union. The

deity and humanity must be distinguished in such a way that we cannot detach the one from the other or consider the one apart from the other. The relation must remain a closed one to the extent that we must not regard the deity as the true thing, the content of the humanity, separate from it and exalted above it, nor describe the humanity as a separate life sundered from the deity and standing under its own law. The inequality or distinction must in no case lead to a severing of the unity. Otherwise we would again be denying that God *meets* us or that *God* meets us. The differentiation must be strictly dialectical, a differentiation in union. Any depreciation of either the distinction or the union will imperil or jettison either one or the other of the two necessary things that are at issue here, and with the one it will do the same to the other.[12]

4. By its very nature this union of deity and humanity cannot be general or multiple but only once and for all. It cannot be general. The whole hubris of certain mystical trends, and in their wake the hubris of speculative idealism, was needed to transform the idea of divine humanity into a universal predicate of the human, that is, to make divine revelation a human attribute.[13] No plant can resist this pest except the most ruthless reflection on all that reminds us of the animal creatureliness of our humanity until the contradiction in which we find ourselves becomes a burning one again, until we realize again that we are human and no more, until we respect again the absolute singularity of this idea.

But again, the union of deity and humanity could not be multiple. It could not happen more than once that God should meet us as a human being. There could not have been several God-men. For this would mean the dissolution of the union between deity and humanity that we have seen to be an essential mark of the God-man. Only accidentally would the deity have then lighted upon the humanity. It could then have broken loose again and joined itself to a second and a third humanity as one changes clothes. No, to have assumed humanity, the deity must have united itself with it, with this humanity, in a way that allows of neither dissolution nor repetition, since there is only *one* God. It God really willed to reveal himself in the hiddenness of a human life, this had to be once and for all. This, then, would be the one encounter with us. There would be no second or third. For revelation

---

12. In this paragraph Barth has the Chalcedonian Definition in mind; cf. DS, 302.

13. N. p. 51 adds: "We should not make God's revelation into an anthropology."

is *one.* The characteristic of uniqueness cannot be thought away from the condition on which revelation is possible.

With this more precise definition of the condition we can validly reverse the fatal equation of revelation and nonrevelation, not by dialectical artifice, but in a legitimately achieved recognition of the content. The point is that God reveals himself in his nonrevelation inasmuch as he, no more and no less than he, wholly God, encounters us therein in his very concealment in a way that is human, visible, perceptible, and comprehensible. He shows himself to us, to our eyes, our ears, our feeling, our perception. He shows himself from behind, as he did to Moses in the cleft of the rock (Exod. 33:20ff.: "My face you cannot see, for no one can see me and live"), but he really shows himself. On this objective condition, then, revelation is possible. Note that I do not say more than "possible." Through the transparency of this concealment, because it is not just any concealment but God's, the light of God's revelation can be seen. We cannot take it for granted that it really is seen. This still rests with God, with God who is the light that must enlighten both his own hiddenness and the eye that sees only the hiddenness. In his light we see light [Ps. 36:9]. We see it both objectively and subjectively (cf. § 7 below) but *only* in *his* light. But if God meets this condition, God removes the impossibility. He can then be heard and seen in his revelation.

I think that at this point you may perhaps entertain a serious suspicion that the whole train of thought that I have just concluded is an attempt to construct a priori the objective possibility of revelation, and with it no more and no less than the incarnation of God, without ever mentioning Jesus Christ, deducing the God-man, as it were, from the dialectic of the concept of revelation and positing it as a necessary concept. I will close this second subsection with a brief explanation of the meaning of what we have just done. Please note the four points that follow.

(a) I am in good company in what I have done. It is the same thing, although not in the same specifically soteriological setting, as what Anselm did in Book II of his *Cur deus homo?,*[14] and after him the authors of the Heidelberg Catechism in Questions 12-17. In both places (and for this reason this section of the Heidelberg Catechism is not greatly loved by modern catechists),[15] we find a deduction of what the Redeemer must be like to be

---

14. Anselm of Canterbury, *Cur deus homo?,* II, chs. 6-9; ET LCC, X (Philadelphia, 1956), pp. 150ff.

15. Cf. E. C. Achelis, *Lehrbuch der praktischen Theologie,* II, 3rd ed. (Leipzig, 1911), p. 421; A. Lang, *Der kurze Katechismus Leo Juds,* p. LXXXIX.

the Redeemer, namely, very God and very man, which at first glance seems desperately similar to a construction of Christ a priori. I say this only to set your minds at rest. I am not surprising you with an unheard-of innovation, but plainly setting the burden of responsibility on other shoulders.

(b) I have, of course, done some construction. What I have constructed, however, is not the possibility of revelation but the *recognition* of this possibility, the condition on which we can speak of it, the *possibility* of the possibility, as we might say, the question which must be put and the answer which must be given on the presupposition that truly God has truly revealed himself to man. It was not for my own pleasure that I talked for nearly half an hour in subjunctives. I wanted to denote the empty space where the great truth of the incarnation belongs in the concept of revelation, namely, the space where, coming from the doctrine of the Trinity, we have to ask in all seriousness how God can reveal himself, and whether this is possible in any way but by his becoming human.

(c) But I have not constructed, and will advisedly refrain from constructing, the main thing without which the dialectical union of deity and humanity has no object, namely, the Logos, the Son of God, who in fact unites deity and humanity without confusion or separation, who is both God and man in one, not the formula of the God-man but the God-man himself.

(d) What I have constructed, namely, the empty space that denotes the problem before which we stand, was obviously a construction a posteriori. How could I have attained to the idea of incarnation, that unheard-of idea, except by abstraction from a fact that is even more unheard-of? I have not been talking hypothetically about a hypothetical entity but about the actually existent possibility of revelation, about Jesus Christ, about the way that God comes to us as it is known and confessed in the Christian church. I could not speak specifically about the condition without finally, as you have noted, adopting the terms of the Chalcedonian Definition, in which the church gave classical formulation, not to a deduction of Christ a priori, but to an account of the actual reality of Christ. I, too, have simply counted on the fact that truly God does truly reveal himself to man. I had no thought of trying to deduce the fact. I simply wanted to explain and elucidate the conditions on which it is a fact. To these conditions respecting the possibility belongs objectively the incarnation of God.[16]

---

16. In the margin Barth summarizes the above lecture as follows: "In the last but one hour before the break we came up against the serious question of the objective

III. The Reality of the Incarnation

We can at once link the second preparatory step that we must take to what we have just said. I could not seriously raise the problem of the possibility of revelation without knowing its reality, without starting with the fact that God does reveal himself, without implicitly talking about Jesus Christ (although without mentioning his name). Is this true only in my case, or do we have here a general rule? Is it chance or caprice that I could admittedly say all that I said (in the subjunctive) about the possibility of revelation only with reference to Jesus Christ? Or can we advance such considerations only because Jesus Christ is the God-man, only because God's encounter with us is a fact in him, so that this fact is actually the primary and fundamental thing, and all deliberations upon it are only abstractions from this concrete thing, or, as I say in the thesis, "hoping, knowing, promising references" to this concrete thing, rays of the sun, as it were, which stream out from this center and necessarily lead back to it again? If we take this fact into account, then there can be no doubt that we have to decide for the latter option. In the light of this fact all hypothetical talk about the possibility of revelation (and what human talk about this possibility is not hypothetical even though we may put it in the strongest indicatives) is to be regarded simply as one long Advent prophecy.

Let us consider the statements of the OT prophets first. From the

---

possibility of revelation. If God is as immutably himself as we have seen in discussing the doctrine of the Trinity, can his revelation be anything but his concealment? We accepted this, and in the last hour we believed that we had found the key to this paradoxical answer in the incarnation. God must become human so as to meet us as the epitome of hiddenness (which one person is to another) but also as the epitome of an I objectively encountering us (as again one person is to another). Even as the hidden God he can thus be revealed to us. We first tried to think through hypothetically the various aspects of this condition of revelation. True deity must assume true humanity, we saw. In a strict dialectic the deity and humanity must be both one and distinct. This unity and distinctness cannot be general or multiple. As there is only one God and one revelation, so it, too, must be thought of as unique, as God's incarnation in one man. As thus defined, the incarnation is the objective possibility of revelation. At the end of this line of thought we laid down our arms and openly confessed that this whole construction, like those in Anselm and the Heidelberg Catechism, is a construction a posteriori in which the actual presence of this possibility is totally and expressly presupposed, so that it does not have the significance of an attempt to prescribe for God what is possible or not possible for him, but only of an attempt to achieve a more precise understanding of the incarnation which is known to have taken place in the fact of Jesus Christ, of the revelation which objectively God himself has made possible."

central point of the NT, the Christian church understands these figures, distant though they are, as witnesses of revelation. What revelation? God's revelation, and thus the one and only real revelation. Who does not see that they all stand together before the mystery of the hidden God, from Moses to Ezekiel? If revelation were the direct communication of the divine,[17] then truly these figures could not be described as witnesses of revelation, nor could they have been this. Those who want direct revelation, those who would have it that revelation is the removal of God's hiddenness, those who cannot bear the thought that God himself, being God, reveals himself precisely in his hiddenness, will always show an inclination to abrogate the OT along with Marcion, Socinius, Schleiermacher, and Harnack,[18] and in so doing they will misinterpret the NT as well. But the church with its recognition of the OT has ascribed to its witness to the hidden God the full dignity of revelation by giving it a specific interpretation, that is, by viewing it as a prophecy of Christ. This is what they meant, to this they pointed, the whole series from Abraham to the last psalmist — they saw the day of Christ, the day of the crucified and risen Lord, and they were glad [John 8:56].

Their very strong witness to the God who dwells in inaccessible light [1 Tim. 6:16] was as such a witness to revelation, and what, then, was it but witness to the encounter of God with us as it really took place? Was it simply the unhistorical mind of the first Christians that worked out this interpretation, or is it a necessary interpretation presupposing that we seriously reckon with the fact of Jesus Christ and do not just toy with it? This presupposition is naturally decisive. If we do not make it, or if we do so only hesitantly and halfheartedly without considering what we must accept if we call Jesus Christ the revelation of God, if this is merely an edifying phrase with which we do not think we can link any essential, existential, categorical meaning, if we are startled by the courage with which we have just confessed our faith in the Lord Jesus Christ, if we do not see that with this confession we have said something definite, momentous, and irrevocable, then obviously every theological recruit who has heard something about "historical method" will be cleverer than Irenaeus or Calvin, to mention only these two with their astonishing doctrine of the identity of the two Testaments,[19] about which we must now speak.

---

17. The concept of direct or indirect communication, in a christological context, goes back to Kierkegaard, *Training in Christianity* (Princeton, repr. 1967), pp. 96ff.

18. For examples cf. *ChD*, p. 324 nn. 33-36.

19. Cf. Irenaeus, *Adversus haereses*, IV, SC, 100, pp. 382ff.; Calvin, *Inst.* II, 10-11.

We begin — and I have never concealed the fact that I never think of doing anything else — with the *Deus dixit* to which the Bible testifies as our first scientific datum. In the light of this testimony (first in its totality) we face the question of the objective possibility of this *Deus dixit*. We ask, then, how according to the biblical testimony God brings it about that he comes to us with his Word without ceasing to be God. We see that the biblical testimony in its totality consists of two members, one earlier and one later, one on that side and another on this side of the central point of which on this side, later, we can say that "The Word was made flesh" [John 1:14], that "God was in Christ" [2 Cor. 5:19], that this is how God managed to come to us without ceasing to be God. In this way we can give precision to the concept of revelation as we have carefully done already in relation to the theme in § 3.III.3. We have seen that the issue in revelation is not the manifestation of a general relation between the finite and the infinite, between time and eternity, but this concrete, contingent, historically accidental fact in which it becomes objectively possible and apart from which we would know nothing about it because apart from it it would not come to us but would remain an unknown movement in God.

We have finally accepted this Christian concept of revelation, believing in God's revelation in Christ. This being so — irrespective of the historical method, which does not come into the picture here and has not the slightest relevance — we cannot avoid thinking the following thoughts. By its very concept revelation can be only *one* revelation, namely, God's. What is attested and confessed as God's revelation, no matter by whom, is either this one revelation or it is not revelation at all. But according to our proof (our a posteriori proof, even though the presupposition is assumed), revelation is not objectively possible except by God's incarnation. Now God's revelation in any case means God's revelation in his concealment. It means the radical dedivinization of the world and nature and history, the complete divine incognito,[20] God's dealings with us exclusively by indirect communication, revelation by law and limit, by distance and judgment. We have seen in subsection II that all this could not be said more sharply than with the Word of God which consists of God becoming human. But in all this, of course, we have God's revelation, his covenant with the race: "I will be your God and you shall be my people" [Lev. 26:12], grace and truth. We have it in this way, in concealment, out of

---

20. For this concept cf. Kierkegaard, *Training in Christianity,* pp. 127-32.

the cloud on Sinai [Exod. 19:9], yet we have total grace and total truth, without diminution or need of supplementation.

And now the question arises: Is the OT a witness to this revelation or is it not? To some extent a very incomplete witness, of course, but to some extent this is true no less of the apostolic witness of the NT as well, and this is not our present question. Our question is this: Complete or incomplete, is it witness to this revelation or not? Does it make sense to insist that Christianity is one religion and Judaism another (as though one could not equally well distinguish different religions in Christianity itself and not usually speak — quite correctly — of only one Christian revelation in spite of the big distance between a Sicilian peasant woman and a Berlin professor)? Does it make sense to insist on the further fact that historically considered the religion of Israel is naturally one religion among many others and under the indisputable influence of many others (as though one could not say exactly the same of Christianity up to and including our own form of it, and yet still not hesitate — quite correctly — to trace it back to revelation in some special sense, even if perhaps in a rather muffled Schleiermacherian voice)? Or does it make more sense to go on to the even more remarkable fact on which the more perspicacious early church and its theology insisted, namely, that both here and there, in both the prophets and the apostles, we have to do with one and the same revelation, that here we see it negatively, on the side of promise, there we see it positively, on the side of fulfilment; and yet it is not as though the prophets lived only in promise and the apostles only in fulfilment, but both lived wholly in both (with no more or less), for both lived face to face with the object of both promise and fulfilment, the one indivisible revelation of the triune God, and therefore, since this revelation is objectively possible only by God's becoming human, the revelation in Christ? Naturally, it is not as though the people of the OT could see Jesus of Nazareth walking the fields of Galilee as if with telescopes hundreds of years ahead. No, the prophets live in their own historical sphere and the apostles in theirs. The OT is prophecy, not prophesying in the banal sense of predicting chronologically future events. Being face to face with the revelation in Christ, even for the people of the NT, is not the same as seeing Jesus of Nazareth walk the meadows. Many saw him and did not stand face to face with revelation. Paul was a witness to Jesus Christ and never saw Jesus. By the proof of prophecy, the *hina plērōthē,* the assertion of the contemporaneity or unity of Old and New Testament revelation which we find in the NT itself, in the early church, and very powerfully in the older Protestant theology, especially the Reformed, something much richer is meant than usually appears from critics and defenders. One can multiply supposed or real analogies between the OT and NT and still not see at all what is at issue. One can also have a very strict historical view down to the last detail, and perhaps accept none of the analogies that held sway at an earlier time, and still stand with closed eyes on the threshold of the real problem.

The issue is this. The witnesses of the old covenant confront the same God as those of the new, namely, the hidden God who is also the revealed God. I do not see why a cautious OT scholar should have any objection to this formula. But now I draw the deduction and say that this God, the almighty and unsearchable God of Moses, Jeremiah, Job, and Pss. 39 and 139, is also the God of Galilee, Gethsemane, and Golgotha, the God who meets us *en morphē doulou* (Phil. 2 [v. 7]), and who thus makes his revelation objectively possible. Because this possibility of his revelation is from God, is given by him, is created by him, how can earlier and later make a division here? What is the relevance here of the concept of time? This "because" gives us a principial, not a historical, basis. It is for this reason that the prophets believe and witness and cry.[21] They have faith in this God — whom else? They bear witness to this God. In a crooked and stubborn generation [Ezek. 2:3-4; Phil. 2:15], they cry to this God as the covenant God of their people, who is still the God of all peoples and the Lord of the world. In Christ, an Israelite without guile [John 1:47] would have to recognize at once not a new religion, but what is most proper to him, his own God. The name *Kyrios* Yahweh, with which the primitive community worshiped Jesus, was not an accidental hyperbole but the necessary expression of a recognition of this unity.

We should not attempt dogmatic correction or let the wind be taken out by bringing in the tiresome question of historical genesis which has nothing whatever to do with the question of what is true. Being correct and being true are two different things. The account given by Wellhausen or Gunkel[22] of a very interesting or uninteresting tribal religion in the Near East may perhaps be *correct* with a few revisions for which we may rely on what are called positive OT scholars.[23] But once we are *on* rather than *beside* the basis on which we have to stand as Christian theologians,

---

21. Cf. the last verse of P. F. Hiller's hymn "Jesus Christus herrscht als König" (1755): "Ich auch auf der tiefsten Stufen Ich will glauben, zeugen, rufen."

22. Cf. J. Wellhausen, *Grundrisse zum AT,* ed. R. Smend, TBü, 27 (Munich, 1965), pp. 65-105; H. Gunkel, commentaries on Genesis (1901) and Psalms (1926).

23. Cf. S. Oettli, *Geschichte Israel bis Alexander den Grossen* (Calwer/Stuttgart, 1905); R. Kittel, *Die Religion des Volkes Israel* (Leipzig, 1921); ET *Religion of the People of Israel* (London, 1925).

even the revised account is not *true*. What is true is the historical interpretation of Hebrews with its cloud of OT witnesses by whom the NT
witness sees himself surrounded in full and unbroken contemporaneity
[Heb. 12:1]. What is true and meaningful and to the point is the dictum
of Luther, which Loofs quotes with an expression of horror, that Adam
was a Christian long before Christ's birth, for he had the faith in Christ
that we have.[24] What is true, for all the reservations that we may think
necessary in detail, is what Calvin says about the matter in *Inst.* II, 10-11,[25]
which I simply ask you to read so that you will be persuaded that I am
not just presenting a private view here. I do not know whether you are
able to think these thoughts. But I cannot help either myself or you. If
revelation is revelation and faith is faith, then you have to think them,
and not by a finger's breadth should we let ourselves be jostled away from
them.

The NT apostles form the second great group of witnesses to God's
encounter with us. It seems easier to grasp that we are to call the apostles
witnesses of revelation. But this view does not rest on our own insight.
The gap between them and revelation is no less great than that between
Moses and revelation, nor is their closeness to it any greater than his. The
content of the years A.D. 1-30 certainly has the significance of the decision
concerning the objective possibility of revelation and therefore of faith.
But the question of earlier or later, of greater or smaller distance from this
period, has no decisive importance, no importance in principle, either for
revelation or for faith. Those who think that it has, those who think that
we have revelation in direct communication in this background, or at least
in the NT, in historical proximity to Jesus, in the radius of his historical
action, in the history that came under his influence, have removed in part
at least the hiddenness of God and changed it into a simple revealedness.
It is true that the apostles call themselves witnesses of the resurrection,[26]
as no prophet ever did. They look back upon the incarnation as an event.
The element of the divinely *given* comes to the forefront as compared to
the *divinely* given. Revelation is now seen as the time of fulfilment. Pre-

---

24. F. Loofs, *Leitfaden zum Studium der Dogmengeschichte,* 4th ed. (Halle, 1906),
pp. 772-73. The Luther quotation, which is from the sermons on Genesis in WA, 24,
99-100, may be found on p. 773 n. 1.

25. *Inst.* II, 10 deals with the similarity of the Old and New Testaments, II, 11
with the difference. In II, 11, 6 Calvin points out that almost no Christian can be compared
with Abraham in excellence of faith.

26. Cf. Acts 1:22; 2:32; 3:15; 10:40-41; etc.

dominant now is confession and preaching of the revealed God, of the Revealer in concealment.

And now that the people of God — a warning of incomparable urgency to the recipients of revelation in every age — has smitten the Fulfiller of its own promise on the cross, this promise is no longer restricted to any people. The only distinction is that of belief or unbelief that Christ has come in the flesh [cf. 1 John 4:2; 2 John 7]. But is not this the same distinction as that which separated the true Israel from the false? Was not the cross of Christ, the question of the Messiah, the crisis which came upon the old recipients of revelation? Read Calvin, who tells us that the distinction between earlier and later is a distinction in the historical administration of revelation, of the covenant between God and us, but not a distinction in its substance.[27] The nerve of the statement that Christ has come in the flesh does not lie in the little word "has," in the chronological perfect, but in the words "come in the flesh." This is the fulfilment for which the fathers waited,[28] but with the "has" the waiting did not stop; it truly began at that point.

To be sure, Christian revelation and Christian faith are historical. But they are not so in the way that is commonly depicted today. The stock phrases about a turning point in world history with Christ's birth, and his supposed historical effects and impact, may well be true, but they have nothing whatever to do with the revelation of God in the incarnation or with faith in it. To me a revelation that is a turning point in *world* history would be too tidy a revelation. Where would be the concealment? Where the need for faith in it, and for faith alone? Where its qualitative distinction from other turning points? No, revelation and faith are historical in the NT in exactly the same sense as in the OT. They belong to prehistory or primal history, that is, they are historical in such a way that here, where it is a matter of the present or the immediate past, what has happened in time escapes direct observation just as much as there, where the event is still future. Thus the way to it is just the same now as it was then. It is the way of revelation and faith alone. The contemporaneity is exclusively that of faith. There can be no question of direct communication in revelation, of an end of concealment, of God being revealed only in the NT.

---

27. *Inst.* II, 11, 1.

28. Barth seems have in mind here vv. 2 and 3 of C. F. Gellert's Christmas hymn "Dies ist der Tag, den Gott gemacht" (1757), which speak of the peoples waiting for Christ and the fathers seeing him in hope.

III. The Reality of the Incarnation

What is the direct communication that the first disciples have, according to the Synoptics? Obviously this, that after the brief shining of a new and strange and uncomprehended light in the one whom they followed, they experienced a swift and dreadful catastrophe, the end result being that they "all forsook him and fled" [Matt. 26:56]. Are they any different from Job or better than him? Between God's concealment and revelation in Christ there stands as powerfully as ever the cross and the resurrection, the possibility of and the miracle of faith. Faith in the promise is also faith in the fulfilment, for in the fulfilment, too, one can only have faith, just as faith in the promise is not without fulfilment. The OT does not end in the NT but continues in it, just as the NT is already present in the OT. There is transition here, too, from law to grace, from sin to righteousness, from Moses to Christ, and the consummation of the future resurrection.[29] The NT is not a second step above the OT, albeit at a higher stage of development. It is later witness alongside earlier witness. Only secular thinking which confuses the significance of God's incarnation with the impact of the rise of Christianity can ascribe to the OT, as the earlier witness, a lesser dignity than it does to the NT, can ascribe to the witness and baptism of John a lesser dignity than to the witness and baptism of the apostles. What made the NT a *holy* book in the eyes of the church, alongside the OT, was not its relation to the period A.D. 1-30 but its relation to the content of this period, to the reality of revelation, to God's encounter with us, to the concrete event of the incarnation at the center, not the relation to the historical Jesus as such but the relation to the crucified and risen Jesus.

The question arises whether there might not be a third group of witnesses to revelation, for example, prophets and apostles outside the canon, at a distance, but still true worshipers of the one God. The figure of Socrates has constantly been for the church a paradigm of this problem. Today many might be more inclined to think of Lao-Tse or Buddha. They recall the sayings that we have already quoted from Thomas and Zwingli about all who speak the truth speaking from God.[30] And you perhaps know that to Luther's strong disapproval, and with much shaking of the head from Calvin, Zwingli was ready to people the Christian heaven with

---

29. Luther, *Op. ex. lat.,* 14, 67; *Operationes in Psalmos* (1519-1521), WA, 5, 61, 19-23.

30. Cf. *STh* Ia, IIae, q. 109, a ad 1; H. Zwingli, *On Providence,* ch. 3; cf. Opera, IV, p. 395; ET p. 154.

a whole series of noble pagans, including Hercules and Theseus, since as he saw it these pagans, like Abraham and his people, all knew and believed the one revelation.[31] We need to treat this idea with caution on both sides. To shout "Impossible" might be a sign of culpable obduracy. The way in which the Bible itself speaks about so-called pagans (Melchizedek King of Salem, Ruth the Moabitess, the wise men from the East, the centurions of Capernaum and Caesarea)[32] should be a warning to us that pagans are not to be regarded only as an object of mission. According to Rom. 9–11 it seems that the relation between those inside and those outside can sometimes undergo an astounding reversal. Paul's Areopagus address [Acts 17:22-31] with its appeal to pagan knowledge of the unknown God sounds much more circumspect than a good deal that has been said later, with more or less conviction, about the exclusive possession of truth by the Christian church. We have properly no reason to maintain the absoluteness of Christianity. It is revelation that is absolute. Who is to say that it could not come as well to those whose voices we do not hear in the canon? The canon, the witness to revelation, cannot be thought of as closed in principle. Nevertheless, before we extend it even hypothetically, we must remember what we must find in such nonbiblical witnesses to revelation — if they are indeed genuine witnesses to *revelation* — the one revelation at all events, that is, indirect communication of the hidden God who is as such the revealed God, God's encounter with us, and hence the cross and the resurrection, offense and faith. This is the issue in the canon, in the OT and the NT. This is what the witness to revelation, to the incarnation, to Christ, is all about.

But is this really the issue in Hercules and Theseus, in Socrates, in Lao-Tse, or in Buddha? Perhaps, but also perhaps not. It makes no sense to shut the gates of the castle in this matter, for where might not this perhaps have been the issue, the *theos agnōstos* of Paul [Acts 17:23]? But it also makes no sense to tear down the gates as though this were always self-evidently the issue throughout religious history. That is the question. We cannot set up any criterion here. We can only say in principle that if and insofar as there might really have been other witnesses of revelation, then what we have, as in the OT and the NT, will have to be hoping, knowing, and promising references to the incarnation. The problem of the possibility of revelation, no matter in what place or at what time it

---

31. *The Exposition of the Faith*, LCC, XXIV (Philadelphia, 1953), pp. 275-76.
32. Gen. 14:18-20; Ruth; Matt. 2:1-12; 8:5-13; Acts 10.

supposedly occurred, can be seriously raised only with reference to this reality. And the seriousness of the inquiry and the reference to this reality must show themselves materially in the fact that the full paradox of God's encounter with us is seen and expressed and not in some way concealed, expunged, softened, or eliminated. Revelation in the Bible, and whatever might be identical with it elsewhere, differs radically from all else that might be called revelation in religious history by reason of the fact that it is indirect communication. And indirect communication means God's incarnation.

Why do I say all this in this context? To make it clear to you that human thought and speech, even that of direct witnesses of revelation, can do no more in face of revelation than what we tried to do in the second subsection above in analogy to what Anselm and the Heidelberg Catechism did. We can seriously raise and treat the problem of the possibility of revelation only when we know its reality. Fundamentally we can construct it only a posteriori. All reflection on how God *can* reveal himself is in truth only a "thinking after" of the fact that God *has* revealed himself. The fact of revelation, wholly unheard of as it is, is presupposed in the OT and NT and wherever there is serious inquiry into its possibility. With all that we can think and say at this point we can only put ourselves in the great sequence of Advent prophecy on the left side of the depiction of the incarnation on Grünewald's altarpiece, where according to a reliable interpretation[33] Mary herself, the direct recipient of grace, at the exit from this world of Advent but still within it, worships within the sanctuary of the old covenant, from which the curtain is drawn back in face of the Christmas miracle, and does so alongside and at the head of the world of human beings and angels and spirits, all of whom are turned toward this miracle. Worship (i.e., the seeking of what is already found), hope, knowledge, and promise — these are the signs under which a christology that is worthy of the name must stand. Christology must describe the reality of revelation, but for this very reason it must not try to posit it. It must stay at a distance from its object. It must know its limit, which is set for it by the fact that its object is God's indirect communication par excellence. The actual birth of the baby belongs all alone on the right side of the depiction. We see the baby, but we do not see directly what kind of baby it is. It might well be some other baby. Grünewald was clearly not afraid to remind us unmistakably of earth and of all other earthly babies. Only

---

33. O. Hagen, *Matthias Grünewald* (Munich, 1919), p. 128.

the Father in his unsearchable height sees the Son, and only the Son, not even Mary the God-bearer, sees the Father. We can see the light of God in the height, which lies over the birth. The church sees it, and hence it recognizes revelation in Christ. But it sees it only in this way, indirectly. It sees the Father only in the Son, and the Son only through the Father. The high, dark partition which separates the sanctuary of the old covenant from the possibility of perceiving directly that this little child is the Son of the Father does not fall down even in face of the miracle of Christmas, for otherwise this would not be the *miracle* of Christmas. Worshiping Mary on the left side is just another expression of the pointing hand of John the Baptist on the picture of the crucifixion — the hand that only points. All christology must be like this. Christ alone belongs on the right side. No christology does, no talk about Christ.

IV. Incarnation and Revelation

We must now move on to a positive development of the doctrine of the incarnation in the context of our concept of revelation. I hope that the preceding subsection will have protected us to some extent against the incipient, the only too incipient misunderstanding that such an undertaking might involve an arrogant and inquisitive attempt to pierce the divine secrets. In reply I have tried to show that the incarnation itself, the fact of Jesus Christ in indirect communication, stands alone on the right side over against all that one may think or say about it, even over against the personal witnesses, let alone the earlier witnesses, let alone all others who might bear witness to it, let alone all a priori constructions such as we attempted experimentally. Only God himself sees Jesus Christ directly, and we have every reason to refrain from trying to force ourselves into his place. The very last thing that we must seek to do in christology is to master this fact in some way, to perceive what only God the Father perceives. Instead, our real task is to see that this fact is one that we humans cannot master, so that on our part only the movements of faith and obedience are appropriate — movements which we shall have to discuss later.

Christology, set face to face with the fact of Jesus Christ, is an effort to understand that the objective possibility of God's revelation involves what our thesis calls the "irremovable mystery" of God in his indirect communication, but also the mystery of God which has entered time and history, which has become palpable and actual, in God's encounter with us by virtue of the incarnation. Not seeking at all to remove veils that human thought and speech cannot and should not remove, a serious christology (I mean by this one that is not historicized or psychologized), a christology like that which the early church enjoyed and we must try to recover, is a necessary and elementary theological measure which we must take in order to ensure the revelatory character of the final basis of Christian preaching, in order to safeguard the insight that not just God's deity in itself (the theme of the doctrine of the Trinity) but also what he extends to us without ceasing to be himself, in a factual encounter, is a mystery of God which we must worship as such and also contemplate and confess as such: *homologoumenōs mega . . . to tēs eusebeias mystērion* (1 Tim. 3:16). Only an age which increasingly lost all sense of God's mystery in revelation and lusted after direct communication could so fail to see the salutary intention of the early Christian doctrine that it accused it of the very thing of which it was itself guilty in a different and most monstrous way, that is, of trying to penetrate and master the divine, not perceiving how much more respect there was for the element of inaccessibility, for the hidden God, in the so-called theological intellectualism of the ancients than in its own sentimentalism, with which it thought it could smuggle itself into the world of God, not with the mind, but with the heart, conscience, and feelings.

Let us now return to the established starting point which we selected for our understanding of the doctrine of the Trinity, the confession of the primitive community, *Iēsous Kyrios*. In the preceding section we have dealt only with the meaning of this confession without stressing the very special circumstance that it related to a specific historical man who lived in the years A.D. 1-30. Let us consider the paradox of this circumstance itself. This *man, this* man (we must emphasize both), is God himself who reveals God himself, who by God himself is revealed as God himself. He is God who is not just there but also here, who is not just at the beginning and end but also in the middle, who is not just with himself but also with us in the world. He is living proof of the fact that God is not unfruitful and that the world is not forsaken by God. In the reality of this man the primitive church thought it saw provided the objective possibility of the revelation of God. This paradox, its radical outworking from every angle, its defense against every attempt to weaken it or dissolve it, became the theme of early Christian christology. Only in this paradox, in the doctrine of the *enanthrōpēsis* or incarnation, did the underlying doctrine of the Trinity itself become alive

153

and relevant and acute, one might say. Only this second basic dogma, with the irreconcilably contingent element at its core which resists all idealizing or generalizing, lifted the doctrine of the Trinity unequivocally, because fundamentally, out of the sphere of the Gnostic metaphysical system of God and the world. Only with this dogma did the distinctive scandal of the Christian concept of revelation become manifest, and faith as the presupposition of the acceptance of this revelation unavoidable. It was not that people mischievously wanted to pierce a secret. It was rather that they thought they stood before a secret, before the basis of the church and Christian preaching. They thought it essential that this secret should be recognized and perpetually acknowledged as such, and that they should thus establish it fundamentally against all caprice or pressure. This is why they fashioned the doctrine which culminated in the *atreptōs kai asynchytōs, adiairetōs kai achōristōs,* in the dialectical distinction and unity of the divine and the human in Christ as it was fixed at Chalcedon.[34] If we like, we can of course contest whether the early church was right when it thought it stood before this mystery, but we cannot argue about whether it was right to try to establish the doctrine as it did.

Let us now try to clarify in detail the main thoughts which had and have to be thought to this end, so far as they are accessible to us.

1. We have to do with God's Son, the second person of the Godhead, who becomes human. It is not simply that God becomes human. True, the whole Trinity is the subject of revelation, of the incarnation: the Father as the fount of action, the Son as the medium, the Spirit as the one by whom conception in the virgin takes place, as the "terminus." The result, however, is the incarnate Logos, not the incarnate Trinity.[35] The divine subject the Son, who becomes human, points back to the divine subject the Father, who does not. Again, the Holy Spirit, who opens our eyes to the manifest mystery [1 Tim. 3:16], does not become human. The basic definition shows already that the mystery remains a mystery in revelation. We have to remember that there are heights and depths in God *beyond* the incarnation. We have no cause to historicize revelation. But we must also remember the positive side that revelation means the overcoming of the antithesis between God and the world which through us is entangled in contradiction with him. On the one hand is the majesty of the Father *above* the contradiction, on the other we humans who are totally *in* it. Who intervenes at this point but the Logos who is

---

34. DS, 302.
35. Cf. the Leiden Synopsis, in Heppe-Bizer, p. 331; ET p. 403.

consubstantial with the Father, the model that God followed in the creation of all things, the principle of all being? He comes to his own [John 1:11]. He can and will do what no human or angel could do as the image of the Father [2 Cor. 4:4] which he also is — that is, come between, reconcile, make two one [Eph. 2:15], because in him they are already one. He who is the Mediator between God and the world is also called to be the Mediator of its redemption.

2. Revelation, or, more precisely, incarnation, as we said in § 4, is the divine answer to the human question concerning the overcoming of the contradiction of human existence. To anticipate an expression from dogmatics proper, it takes place because of the *fall*, to reverse the fall, to redeem us from evil, from guilt and its penalty. It is because of man and his contradiction that revelation must be made objectively possible instead of simply *being* possible and actual. It is because of man and his contradiction that God must leave his self-resting deity for a second time after creation and come into action. Man as God created him, paradisal man, needed no divine revelation or incarnation. Not, of course, as incarnate God, which is not what his creation means, but as man unconditionally related to God, with no reservation, no "Yes, but," he stood before the revelation that was always and everywhere given to him directly. He was what the Romantics would have liked to have been, that is, immediate to God,[36] without this involving impudence or disorder, in such a way that it was all right and proper. God was not a problem for man when man was not a problem for himself. The solving of the problem of God, the restoration of the original relation between God and man with no distance or alienation or antithesis, would be directly the solution to the problem of man. As God comes to man again, pilgrim man who is alone and without God comes back home. His home is to be both with himself and with God, not himself God but a human, a creature, yet still with God, seeing God face to face [1 Cor. 13:12], as it was in the beginning when God dealt with him in the garden as with one of his own [Gen. 3:8]. It is this homecoming that is announced in revelation, that is visible, audible, and palpable as a possibility in the chaos of contradictions. It is not yet consummated. Revelation does not bring heaven. Revelation only proclaims the resurrection of the dead. Nevertheless, it does proclaim it. The kingdom of heaven is at hand [Matt. 4:17]. This is the meaning of revelation.

The incarnation of the Son, then, is not an eternal relation like that of the Son to the Father, although it is enclosed by the wisdom of

---

36. Marginal note: "but with a need for eternal consummation."

God from all eternity. It is something new, an action like creation. Certainly we know the Son only through the Incarnate, in Jesus Christ, whom the fathers saw in hope.[37] But he is also the Logos of God beyond his union with humanity, just as the Trinity is more than the incarnation. As the Father is not just the Creator, so the Logos is what he is even apart from Jesus Christ. The kingdom of Christ has a specific limit as well as a specific meaning as the work of redemption. When the work is done, the Son hands over the kingdom to the Father [1 Cor. 15:28]. Not that he ceases to be the incarnate Son any more than we cease to be men and women, but in such a way that his humanity is no longer needed and revelation ends as it began.

3. The incarnation implies that the Son assumes human nature. This is how our homecoming, the removal of the rift, is proclaimed. This is how revelation is effected. Early writers called the act of union an assumption. It is not, then, a changing or alteration of the divine nature of the Son, but with his divine mode of existence the Son takes a human mode of existence, uniting it — the "grace of union" — to his person, just as the divine mode of existence is eternally united to his person, yet without in any way altering his divine mode of existence.[38] The kenosis of the Son in the incarnation is not that he wholly or partially ceases to be the eternal Son of the Father (otherwise the incarnation would not be revelation) but that as the Son of God he is also made the Son of Man.[39] The short description favored by the older Lutherans, namely, that the divine nature (or substance) becomes one with the human,[40] contains an inaccuracy. The older Reformed held a more dynamic view to the extent that for them the stress fell on the *person,* the divine *subject.* The incarnation is a personal, not a natural work.[41] They emphasized the fact that the Logos *(sermo),* not deity, was made flesh.[42] Not the deity as such, not the substance common to the Father, Son, and Spirit became human, but the Son, although naturally without ceasing to be who he is, and therein and with his entire deity. In contrast, the human nature that the Son assumes and unites to his person is the nature that is common to all human persons,

---

37. Cf. above, n. 28.

38. Cf. Calvin, Zanchius, van Mastricht, and Heidegger for this idea and the phrase "grace of union" (Heppe-Bizer, pp. 331, 340; ET pp. 414, 428).

39. *Inst.* II, 14, 1.

40. Cf. J. A. Quenstedt, in Schmid-Pöhlmann, p. 200; Schmid ET p. 298.

41. Cf. von Riissen, in Heppe-Bizer, pp. 332-33; ET p. 416.

42. J. H. Heidegger, in Heppe-Bizer, p. 332; ET p. 415.

the substance of man, his being as body and soul with all the limitation and frailty that this means, the servant form [Phil. 2:7] of this substance,[43] yet without sin, which is not part of this substance but an inalienable determination of the man we know, fallen man in contradiction. This human nature is now compressed into one individual, *natura en atomō* (Zanchius).[44]

Nevertheless — and this is where the emphasis falls — this individual that incorporates human nature has never existed anywhere as such. The humanity of Christ, although it is body and soul, and an individual, is nothing subsistent or real in itself. Thus it did not exist prior to its union with the Logos. It has no independent existence alongside or apart from him. Those who want to see revelation in the idea of humanity as such are grasping at something that in itself is not just meaningless but nonexistent. So are those who seek revelation in Jesus as a human individual. They are all necessarily groping in the void. This idea, the idea of humanity, and this individual who incorporates it, cannot for a single moment be abstracted from their assumption into the person of the Logos. The divine subject who unites himself with them makes them revelation. The human nature of Christ has no personhood of its own. It is *anhypostatos* — the formula in which the description culminates. Or, more positively, it is *enhypostatos*. It has personhood, subsistence, reality, only in its union with the Logos of God.[45] An inference from this definition is the description of Mary by the early church as the *mater Domini, theotokos, deipara,* the God-bearer.[46] The orthodox Lutherans and Reformed thoroughly approved of this description.[47] The one whom Mary bore was not an other or a second; he was nothing apart from being God's Son. He was in human nature, but this human nature was real only in the person of God's Son.

A further inference is that those who saw and heard and handled Jesus did not see and hear and handle a mere appearance or vesture or dwelling of the Logos but the Logos himself in the flesh of Christ. To be

---

43. N. p. 61 adds: "that which distinguishes man as the creature of God."

44. Zanchius, in Heppe-Bizer, p. 333; ET p. 417.

45. Cf. Schmid-Pöhlmann, pp. 201-2; Schmid ET pp. 300-301; Heppe-Bizer, p. 334; ET pp. 417-18.

46. Cf. the Council of Ephesus (A.D. 431), in DS, 251.

47. Cf. the Lutherans A. Calov, *Systema locorum theologicorum,* VII (Wittebergae, 1677), pp. 187-88; J. A. Quenstedt, *Theologia didactico-polemica,* Part III c, § 2, vol. III, 4th ed. (Wittebergae, 1701), p. 152. Among the Reformed cf. the Leiden Synopsis, in Heppe-Bizer, p. 334; ET p. 418; and J. Wolleb and L. van Riisen, in Heppe-Bizer, p. 352; ET p. 444.

sure, it was the servant form of the human nature — and this means here, too, the indirectness of revelation, the possibility of offense, the demand for faith — but it was still the Logos himself, not a second alongside him.

A third inference is that any cult of Jesus, any seeking of revelation in the flesh of Christ as such, no matter whether we think of the body or the soul, is not just a divinization of the creature but is also pointless. "Even though we knew Christ according to the flesh, we now know him thus no longer" (2 Cor. 5:16). Jesus exists only in and through Christ. He is the Son of God or his existence is negated. As Keckermann puts it, apart from the Logos he could not consist for a moment.[48]

4. The statement that the human nature has subsistence only by and in the Logos may not be reversed. We may not say that the Logos subsists only in the human nature of Christ. I have to advance here a special Reformed doctrine. The older Lutherans said that the flesh of Christ was so united to the Logos that wherever the Logos is, there it has the flesh most present with it.[49] With this statement they wanted to do justice to the concern that we stressed in § 5.I.1, that God totally reveals himself in his revelation and that a hidden portion of his essence does not remain unrevealed. The older Reformed recognized this concern. For this reason they did not contest the fact that the whole Logos dwells in the human nature of Christ. What they did contest was that he is enclosed in the human nature: "we do not imagine that he was confined therein."[50] The Lutherans for their part did want to enclose the Logos in the flesh of Christ, so that, for example, the Logos was only in Galilee or Jerusalem during the time of the incarnation. Not wanting to separate the Logos in any way from the flesh of Christ, they then had to move on logically to the position that in virtue of the union of the flesh of Christ with the Logos the divine freedom from limitation is just as proper to this flesh as to the Logos himself, so that simultaneously it could[51] be in Galilee, in other places, and in heaven, as Christ desired.[52] In this inevitable deduction the Reformed then perceived an evaporation and even an elimination of the concept of flesh or of human nature in the individual. If the human

---

48. Heppe-Bizer, p. 334; ET p. 444.

49. J. Gerhard, in Schmid, p. 230; Schmid-Pöhlmann, p. 205; Schmid ET p. 308.

50. Calvin, *Inst.* II, 13, 4, in LCC, XX, p. 481.

51. The *konnte* here should perhaps be *könnte* (might).

52. For the Lutheran doctrine of the communication of the attributes, and esp. the ubiquity of the flesh, cf. Schmid-Pöhlmann, pp. 219ff.; Schmid ET pp. 321ff.

nature is no longer finite, then it is no longer human nature, and how, then, can it be the organ of revelation? They thus advanced the thesis that the Logos, while dwelling wholly in the flesh, also remains wholly outside it. "Wonderfully God's Son descended from heaven, yet without leaving heaven. Wonderfully he willed to be born in the virgin's womb, to go about the earth . . . , yet he continuously filled the world even as he had done from the beginning."[53] The first part of these statements may be said of the Incarnate, the second of the Logos apart from the man Jesus. Reformed theology, then, knows only *one* ubiquity, that of the Logos.

In its humiliation as in its exaltation, the humanity of Christ, in contrast, is in a specific, prescribed place, for it remains finite, and the finite is not capable of the infinite. In the Lord's Supper, then, it can be present spiritually, and believers can be fed spiritually with the true body and can spiritually drink the true blood, but it cannot be bread and wine, nor can it be received really *(realiter)*, but bread and wine are and remain its signs or seals. We find the clearest summary of this Reformed doctrine of the relation between Logos and flesh in the statement of Maresius that the Logos so unites the human nature to himself that he totally indwells it and yet is totally transcendent and infinite outside it.[54] The doctrine is expressly presented, but in reverse order, in the Heidelberg Catechism, Qu. 48, which asks whether the fact that the two natures are not separated in Christ means that the humanity is everywhere where the deity is, but in the answer flatly denies this, for the deity is inconceivable and omnipresent. Thus it follows that it is outside the flesh that it has assumed, and yet is no less present in it, and remains personally united with it.[55]

The Lutherans, however, heard in all this only the word "outside" *(extra)*, and they thus termed this doctrine the Calvinistic *extra*. I have three reasons for fully accepting this Calvinistic *extra*. (a) It does not really damage the justifiable Lutheran concern that God is wholly in his revelation. The Logos in Christ's flesh and the Logos outside Christ's flesh are naturally not two different entities, the one a revealing part of the Logos and the other a part that remains hidden. In both cases — the double "totally" of Maresius is instructive in this regard — they are the same

---

53. Calvin, *Inst.* II, 13, 4. After "to go about the earth" Calvin has "and to hang upon the cross."

54. Heppe-Bizer, p. 335; ET p. 418. Barth follows the less correct Heppe, p. 305.

55. *BSRK*, p. 695.7-15; Schaff, p. 322. Marginal note: "A summary of the previous hour in the margin: 1. *Son* of God; 2. fall; 3. union of the Logos with human nature, which exists only in and by him; 4. no reversal: the Logos also wholly outside."

totality. No other God is maintained, but the same God who is in Christ on earth is seen at the same time in heaven. This is no weakening of the "wholly God" but an underlining of the fact that we are dealing wholly with *God* in the incarnation. (b) I do not see how the Lutheran counter-doctrine, which ties the Logos inseparably[56] to the flesh of Christ, can avoid deducing the ubiquity of the flesh, or how this deduction can escape evaporating the true humanity of the Redeemer and thereby eliminating the objective possibility of revelation. (c) I find in the dialectic of the "totally in and totally outside" a further valuable safeguard of the mystery, of the indirectness of revelation. Note the double *"mirabiliter"* in the quotation from Calvin and the first reason advanced in the Heidelberg Catechism, Qu. 48, namely, that the deity is inconceivable (Lat. *cum divinitas comprehendi non queat*).[57] At one and the same time God is wholly in his revelation and without subtraction a perceptible object, man, and also wholly not an object, a man, but the immutable divine subject, not merely as Father and Spirit but also in the medium of revelation itself, in the Mediator, the Son. The Son is both *logos ensarkos* and *logos asarkos*. Do we not have to say this afresh and for the first time truly the moment we speak about the union of God and man in revelation lest we forget that we stand here before the miracle of God? Can we ever have said it enough?

5. We now come to the definitions that constitute the doctrine of the incarnation in the strictest sense, namely, to all that must be said along the lines and in elucidation of the statement in the creed: "Conceived by the Holy Ghost, born of the Virgin Mary."[58]

Let us first consider the general significance of the dogma. I need hardly say that it expresses the absolutely miraculous character of revelation in an unequivocal way for which there is a later parallel only in the affirmation that "the third day he rose again from the dead,"[59] which stands in the strictest correlation with it. God is in the flesh, in time, in the world of contradiction, himself human, pilgrim man, a man like any other, yet God, so that the time is fulfilled,[60] and a limit is set for the contradiction. He is the man born from above [John 8:23], born like all

---

56. Cf. B. M. Hafenreffer, in Schmid-Pöhlmann, p. 205; Schmid ET p. 307.
57. For the Latin cf. Heppe-Bizer, p. 335; ET p. 418.
58. *BSLK*, p. 21.10-12.
59. *BSLK*, p. 21.14-15.
60. Cf. Gal. 4:4; Eph. 1:10.

others, yet born of the Virgin Mary and conceived by the Holy Spirit. He is human like all of us, yet as such the head of a new humanity. He is in history, yet in history as the end of the old history and the beginning of the new history. He is flesh of Adam's flesh, yet the second, heavenly Adam [1 Cor. 15:49], strong enough to draw to himself, along with the nature of the first Adam, the first Adam himself and all his offspring, to assume them to himself, to set them in his heavenly nature [Eph. 2:6], because he is God himself — God encountering us, and with this encounter restoring the original and authentic relation between God and us, bringing back our lost home, that we might be with ourselves and yet also with God. Indeed, who will understand this mystery?[61]

Concerning the miracle of the conception by the Spirit and the virgin birth, we must also say above all that no matter what stance we adopt we must accept it as a miracle. One can, of course, reject it, as one can reject miracles in general. This is in order. A miracle is an event that one can only reject, only declare to be impossible and absurd, or only believe. Anything that softens or removes this either/or disrupts the concept of miracle. Thus to make the conception by the Spirit plausible by referring to instances of parthogenesis in the lower plant and animal kingdoms makes no more sense than to defend the resurrection with the help of occultism and spiritism. These are nonclassical, second-rate, impure enterprises, as we should see even if we are resolved on rejection instead of belief. Why not come out plainly with rejection instead of engaging in apologetics? An explained miracle is obviously a miracle no longer. It is no longer exposed to rejection. It no longer has to be believed. Those who explain a miracle, even if they do so in a more sophisticated way than we usually find among rationalists, are simply showing thereby that they do not want to have to decide between rejection and belief. No less than everything depends on our seeing that on the height of the incarnation (as of every Christian doctrine) we have to declare that miracle cannot be set aside or toned down. If we did not have the "conceived by the Holy Ghost," we would have to have something different but no less pregnant and unheard of.

I myself do not see why we should not say what the creed says along with all the early church. All that we have to say about the reality of revelation (and therefore implicitly about its objective possibility); all that we have to say

---

61. Cf. v. 4 of G. Tersteegen's hymn "Jauchzet, ihr Himmel" (1731): "God is in the flesh; who can understand this mystery?" (Barth has *will* for *kann*).

about the reality of God (as distinct from all the reality of the world), not in order to exhaust it, to establish it, or to understand it, but in order to acknowledge it, to describe it reverently, to remain standing before it, and also to point to it — all this may be compressed on the one side into "conceived by the Holy Ghost" as it may be compressed on the other side into "the third day he rose again from the dead." The miraculous conception tells us that the God-man is the *objective possibility* of revelation, and the resurrection tells us that he is the objective possibility of *revelation.* The miraculous conception is revelation in *concealment,* the resurrection is *revelation* in concealment. The resurrection of Christ has its basis in his miraculous conception, and is thus inevitable. The miraculous conception discloses, shows itself, and makes itself known by his resurrection. Both play an exclusive role in this regard, the miracle at the beginning and the miracle at the end. Miracle is the basis of miracle, and miracle makes miracle known. There can thus be no escaping or misunderstanding or ambiguity in relation to the *Deus, deus dixit.* In his light we see light [Ps. 36:9].

6. Let us first consider the phrase "born of the Virgin Mary." The older dogmaticians gave two main reasons why Christ had to be born of a virgin. Negatively, he was not to share in the original sin of Adam, and positively, as a human he was to be God's image.[62] We take it that as a human he had to break the continuity of factual, historical, familiar humanity, restore the continuity of original paradisal humanity which the fall had broken, and therewith commence a new continuity of humanity. He had to do this if he was to be God's answer to the riddle of human life. But what does this breaking consist of, this restoring, this new commencing? What does "born of the virgin" mean as the supposed condition of all this happening? We are naturally tempted to think of the absence of the natural act of procreation by male participation. But what has this absence to do with the breaking of the sequence of sinful humanity, the restoration of the original humanity, and the initiation of a new sequence? Medieval theology, which thought it saw the essence of original sin in sexual concupiscence, still never went to the point of declaring sexuality itself, or its expression in carnal union, to be wicked or ungodly as such. Calvin formulated a general Scholastic insight when he said that the generation of man is not impure or vicious per se, but is accidentally so due to the fall.[63] If we agree, then it is hard to see why the breaking,

62. Barth is referring here to Heppe-Bizer, pp. 324-25; ET p. 421 (Olevian).
63. *Inst.* II, 13, 4.

restoring, and renewing of humanity in Christ should not have taken the form of a miraculous justification and sanctification of a natural act of sex which is sinful and unholy in itself due to the fall!

It is very tempting to imagine how simple everything would immediately become if the church, in view perhaps of the uncertain or at least the equivocal attestation of the virgin birth in the NT, had developed a doctrine not of the virgin birth but of the offspring of a chosen married couple enjoying the blessing of heaven. Nor can we ignore the helpful practical applications that such a doctrine would have enjoyed. The church decided, however, for the fatal "born of the Virgin." What did it intend if the discrediting of sexuality as such, as Marcion proclaimed it,[64] was not its purpose? Obviously the sex act is not in any sense the issue, although in part at least the miracle does involve its absence. The primary point of the miracle, however, is not the absence of the sex act but the absence of the male act. Why the *male* act? In subsection III above (the doctrine of the *anhypostasis* of the human nature of Christ) we saw that the constitution of the God-man does not involve the union of the Logos and a human person but the union of the Logos and human nature, since the Logos, the Son of God himself, wills to be the person of the God-man. Now the person (which is absent in this case) *is* the human being, and the person has name, historical place, status, and rights from the father, from the relation not to the mother but to the begetting *male.* World history is not for nothing male history. Economics, politics, art, and science, with some exceptions and exceptional circmstances such as we find today, are male affairs. The creative shaping of things, the personal fashioning of existence, so far as the eye can see, is a male privilege. This is how it is — the only thing that we can say, no matter how much it is open to criticism. The sequence that must be broken, restored, and renewed is from Adam. *He* was created in God's image, through *him* sin came into the world, *he* must be renewed in God's image. But this has to mean — and view it how we will, this is where a reversal takes place in favor of the female — that Adam has to be replaced if a new Adam is to be born. Adam is the bearer of original sin, and therefore he must go or stand aside. In this renewal, this ending of his own history and beginning of a better one, he cannot participate in the typically male position of a presiding father, lord, and ruler. If he did, it would mean a prolonging and continuing of the old

64. Cf. A. von Harnack, *Marcion: Das Evangelium vom fremden Gott* (Leipzig, 1921), pp. 101, 186-87.

history. No, at this point he can only be there, he can only be a spectator in the rather sorry role which the gospel story and church tradition and art ascribe to the good Joseph as the foster-father of the heavenly child. Nothing at all is missing if on the Grünewald depiction that we have mentioned, as on many others, he is not there at all. The removal of the person is the removal of original sin. But the removal of the person is the removal of the male, his ejection from that role as creator. Precisely his creativity does *not* come into account at all as an organ of revelation. He, the sinner, can beget only sinners. God must take his place. That is the point. The person of the Son must be conceived by the person of the Spirit in order that a new humanity may arise. What remains on man's side after the deletion of the person is human nature as such, man in himself, the impersonal substratum of history, man as creature, not creator. The bearer of human creatureliness is the female.

The creature, too, has undoubtedly fallen and needs redemption. The woman as a person has also sinned with Adam, is far from God, and has become alien to him no less than Adam. For revelation to be possible, however, the creature does not need to be replaced, only renewed and changed. Even though fallen, the creature is not incapable of being justified and sanctified by the miracle of God. For revelation to be possible, then, the woman, unlike the man, has to be there as a vessel that receives new content. The miracle of God, revelation in concealment, is that human nature as such becomes the dwelling of the Logos, the substratum of a new history. Precisely as revelation in concealment, the disclosure of the new being in the resurrection will be that this mortal and corruptible will put on immortality and incorruptibility [1 Cor. 15:54]. The woman Mary, the virgin who has no connection with a man, representing a humanity that is not creative, that does not fashion history or determine and shape things, although still entangled in sin, guilt, punishment, and the contradiction of existence just as much as the man, is the human possibility that stands over against the impossible possibility of God and can become an organ for God as God's miracle makes her this. This, then, is revelation. This is why we have "born of the Virgin Mary."

By way of a historical note on all this, one must say that there is naturally a connection between this christological dogma and the ideal of virginity, the Roman Catholic celibacy of priests, monks, and nuns, sexual asceticism in general, and the shadow which has always stood, and will always stand, and must inevitably stand over sex life in the Christian world. But we must understand this connection properly. The christological dogma comes first. We must not reverse this. Monasticism did not produce the concept of revelation. It was from a certain not incorrect, but in the Roman Catholic church only partly correct, understanding of the event of revelation that monasticism developed, and that there also developed that shadow — ethics is the place to speak about it — which lies over the sphere of sex and which no real Christianity may ever seek to dispel.

7. Why "by the Holy Ghost"? we must now ask. We have given the answer in the doctrine of the Trinity. The Holy Ghost has a place in the revelation of God inasmuch as God is not only *over* the world but also *in* it, God also as the Spirit of the Father and the Son who turns to us, who makes us able to receive him, who brings about his own reception in us. Note that the Creed says "by," not "from," the Holy Ghost. Matt. 1:18 says expressly: *ek pneumatos hagiou*. This *ek*, the older dogmaticians said, is to be construed after the analogy of Rom. 11:36 (all things *ex autou*) and 1 John 3:9 (Christians born *ek tou theou*). In both these cases the "by" does not denote the material cause, the direct, substantial relation of the world or the Christian to God, but the efficient cause. Hence the *ek* of Matt. 1 is to be taken in the sense of *apo*.[65] The Spirit, the power of the Most High, who according to Luke 1:35 comes on the virgin and over-shadows her *(epeleusetai . . . episkiasei)*, must be viewed, then, as the efficient, not the material, cause. The Holy Spirit takes the place of the male, yet he does not do what the male does, but what only God can do as the Creator (not the progenitor) of the creature. The virgin becomes pregnant, not of his substance, but by his power. What takes place is not so much a conception but (as at creation) a "God said," a word, a command, a blessing. Yet the substratum upon which the action takes place is not nothing, as at creation. It is human nature in the virgin. To regard the Holy Spirit as the Father of the God-man would be almost a bad joke. It is certainly an inappropriate, impermissible, and mistaken inference from the "conceived by the Holy Ghost." As a divine *person* (and Christ is *only a divine* person) Christ has only one Father, for whom the Holy Spirit cannot be a substitute. As Christ the divine person is absolutely *amētōr* (Heb. 7:3), so according to his human nature he is absolutely *apatōr*.[66] If we respect the distinction, strictly developed by the older theologians, that the Spirit's work is not a generating but a commanding or blessing,[67] then we shall refrain from relating the dogma to the familiar

---

65. Cf. L. van Riissen, in Heppe-Bizer, p. 338; ET p. 424.
66. Cf. A. Polanus, in Heppe-Bizer, p. 337; ET pp. 421-22.
67. Cf. J. Wollebius, in Heppe-Bizer, p. 339; ET p. 424.

and piquant myths about Jupiter and other gods lusting after the daughters of the sons of earth. The Spirit through whom the virgin conceives is really Spirit, *pneuma,* not apotheosized man. His work is strictly spiritual, not physical, and is not to set in analogy to any physical operation. Those who become confused in this regard and mix things up, engaging in speculative natural philosophy, have no understanding of the matter at all.

8. But what is this qualified and exclusive work of the Spirit in the incarnation? At this point where we threaten to lose our breath the older theologians engaged in discussions which are so meaningful that it is worth our while to follow them. They distinguished in the true "conceived by the Holy Ghost" three (simultaneous) acts: (a) formation, that is, the preformation of a particle of the blood and semen of the virgin Mary as human.[68] One part of the miracle — although the least important — is that this took place without the participation of male seed. (b) The second and greater side of the miracle is sanctification. This particle of human nature, of the nature of Adam, is separated from the mass of flesh by the power of the Spirit *(hagiasmos),* and by divine pronouncement, forensically, the sin of Adam is not imputed to it. As the Zurich theologian Heidegger boldly concluded, Christ, although preexisting according to his human nature in the loins of Adam, did not sin as Adam sinned.[69] At any rate, this particle of human nature, preformed to become real man, is also preformed to be the dwelling of the Logos. A distinctive if slight deviation may be found in the confessions at this point. The Lutherans thought it necessary to stress that the sanctification means that Christ's human nature will have a supreme elegance and beauty of form[70] — the Lutheran Christ is a handsome man — whereas the Reformed set no store by that and regarded the human nature as equivalent to a servant form.[71] (c) Assumption, as we heard last time, is the decisive act of incarnation. At the very moment when this particle of human nature and creatureliness becomes a man by the Spirit, the third and true miracle occurs, for again by the Spirit the Logos takes possession of this particle, becomes the subject of this predicate, gives it substance in his own person, and makes it his organ, temple, or medium.[72] *Ho logos sarx egeneto* (John 1:14). God the Son has

---

68. Cf. J. H. Heidegger, in Heppe-Bizer, p. 325; ET p. 426.
69. Heppe-Bizer, p. 340; ET p. 427.
70. Cf. Schmid-Pöhlmann, p. 202; Schmid ET p. 302.
71. Cf. the Leiden Synopsis, in Heppe-Bizer, p. 336; ET p. 420.
72. For "organ" cf. J. H. Heidegger, in Heppe-Bizer, p. 341; ET pp. 428-29; for

become human, a temporal, bodily, finite, visible, mortal creature, limited in ability and knowledge. The objective possibility of revelation has been provided. God can meet man as man without ceasing to be God.

In this fourth subsection, as in the third, I have followed closely, in a way that you may perhaps have found strange, the ancient dogma and even the older orthodox dogmatics. If you ask me why I have done this, I reply with the counterquestion whether you know any better way of working it out so as to achieve a positive presentation of the concept of the incarnation. If we want classical, solid, circumspect, and yet also comprehensive definitions of the basic concepts that are in keeping with the dignity of the theme, then whether we like it or not we shall have to tread the paths that were taken by the early church doctrine. There are more modern ways that are perhaps more accessible and easier to tread, but they cannot serve us as we need because, to put it mildly, they rest upon a much less profound and serious knowledge of the matter. If you sigh that we surely do not have to use this language to speak scientifically about the subject, then I sigh with you, but I have to tell you that in my view we have to do so. It is unavoidable. At the very point in dogmatics where we have to make decisive statements, we have no option (if we are not to talk rubbish) but to follow the sense of the early definitions. For some 200 years (i.e., since a knowledge of the matter was increasingly lost), the scientific tradition of Protestant dogmatics has been broken off, as I see it. To take it up again is not so easy. Before we can do so, and then perhaps work out more contemporary formulations, we must first see what is at issue. The best way to do this, it seems to me, is to study carefully the statements made by older theologians who did know what is at issue. We can rightly bring many criticisms against the older orthodox. But they did at least know what they were talking about. This is what we have to learn again in some way or other.

"temple," J. Cocceius, in Heppe-Bizer, p. 341; ET p. 429; for "medium," see Heppe-Bizer, p. 326; ET p. 428.

§ 7

Faith and Obedience

That God truly reveals himself truly to humanity also presupposes that humanity stands before God. The existence of so-called religion as a determination of humanity's feeling or direct self-consciousness does not in itself[1] mean that this presupposition is present. To stand before God means rather to move toward God's answer and to set oneself under the question which it addresses to humanity. It thus means recognizing God and accepting his authority. As the miracle of faith and obedience, this knowledge and action are both effected by the Holy Spirit, whom no one and nothing can replace as the subjective possibility of revelation.[2]

I. The Subjective Possibility of Revelation

We must now discuss the subjective possibility of revelation, that is, human receptivity for it, which is obviously indispensable to complete the concept. What we have in view is the element in the concept which as attention or openness to it confronts directly our constitutional inability to grasp God's incarnation. It is the element which means that revelation is not a light that shines among the blind but real revelation, God's encounter with us, God's address to us, an address that is heard. Let us begin this time with some small delimitations regarding the title of the section.

---

1. N. p. 68: "In the lecture Barth dictated: 'in and for itself.'"
2. Marginal note: "Heppe 381! 384-85." See Heppe-Bizer, pp. 417-18, 421-22; ET pp. 513, 517.

1. If I were lecturing to you on Roman Catholic theology, then the title would undoubtedly read: "Participation in the Holy Sacraments." To stand before God with eyes open to the incarnation, and thus to partake of its grace, to receive God's address, to be "in Christ" [2 Cor. 5:17], is to participate in the grace of the sacraments within the Roman Catholic Church. In that body, participation in the grace of the sacraments is incorporation into the fruit of the incarnation, into the mystical body of Christ. For by instituting the sacraments Christ established a channel by which revelation becomes effective revelation to us, a fence by which we may be known as his, a means by which the Creator and Comforter Spirit not only assures us of his blessed presence but effects it. By the sacraments Christ takes the step into reality with, on, and in us, making us a dwelling place for the triune God. To receive the sacraments means directly that this step is taken. Everything else comes after. It follows or accompanies this grace. It is its expression, confession, affirmation, acceptance, and appropriation. It makes it fruitful. To things of this second rank, according to Roman Catholics, belong, for example, the faith and obedience that we have set at the head.

Here is the parting of the ways. To acknowledge at this point and in this context the precedence of sacramental reception over faith and obedience is tantamount to retreating from Protestant theology back to Roman Catholic theology. It is worth our while to be clear historically that at this point where the issue must be the subjective possibility of revelation, its accessibility, Roman Catholicism speaks about receiving the sacraments. This helps us to understand the situation better, to see what has to be said at this point. In dogmatics we must not toy with the idea that sacramental reception comes in at this point, as in Roman Catholicism, unless what we want is what we actually achieve thereby, namely, the liquidation of Protestantism. For undoubtedly the Protestant heresy, the Reformation, was fundamentally an attack on this primacy of sacramental reception. Not on the sacraments themselves — we understand Calvin, for example, very badly if we do not see what a wholly co-decisive role the sacraments played in his theology, especially the Lord's Supper. With equal emphasis the Lutherans and Reformed correlated Word and sacrament, but in this order, which includes an irreversible super- and sub-ordination — not sacrament and Word. The Word undergirds and sustains and fills the sacrament — not the sacrament the Word. Faith is the condition of worthy and effective sacramental reception. Sacramental reception is not the condition of true faith, little as a true faith will neglect it. Even Lutheran sacramental teaching,[3] in which sign and matter finally merge, is only a special case within the general Reformation view that the sacrament is a visible and palpable word which is represented materially, and has even become matter according to Luther, but which in itself, apart from the Word of promise with which it is united and which constitutes it a sacrament, is only a sign or seal, so that sacramental reception is empty and neutral, as though it had never been, as though it were to the judgment of the recipient, a work which is not done by its mere performance, unless it be related to the Word and therefore to faith.[4]

Here in Protestantism, however, the vacated primacy in the question of the subjective possibility of revelation is taken over by what I have called faith in the last few sentences, using the abbreviated Lutheran description. Protestants, if they understand themselves aright, do not think that they stand directly before God's revelation. They know this revelation only in the form of the Word and therefore (for the sacrament is also Word) the sacrament. Correlative to the Word, however, is faith, not the *opus operatum* of sacramental reception, though faith has no wish to dispense with this reception. From the Roman Catholic standpoint, we must undoubtedly say that Protestant sacramental reception, Protestant incorporation into the mystical body of Christ, is faith, and we must then deplore the replacement of the true sacrament by something that is secondary, ambiguous, and uncertain. This reversal or substitution is the great venture of Protestantism. We have to see that it is indeed a venture which was undertaken because the Reformers thought, conversely, that Roman Catholic sacramentalism either is or had itself become an intolerable ambiguity and quid pro quo, and they therefore let the pendulum swing powerfully the other way. Protestantism went through some bad experiences in making this venture. We may seriously question today whether the recognition that is finally at issue, the recognition that the subjective possibility of revelation is wholly and exclusively the possibility of *God*, is not relatively better upheld in Roman Catholic sacramentalism than in

---

3. Cf. Barth's essay "Ansatz und Absicht in Luthers Abendmahlslehre" (1923), in *Die Theologie und die Kirche* (Munich, 1928), pp. 26-75; ET "Luther's Doctrine of the Eucharist: Its Basis and Purpose," in *Theology and Church* (New York, 1962), pp. 74-111.

4. Barth refers here to the doctrine *ex opere operato* — a term first found in the 13th century — according to which the correct administration (rather than worthy reception — *opus operantis*) guarantees grace. Cf. the Council of Trent, 7th Session (1547), in DS, 1608.

I. The Subjective Possibility of Revelation

Protestant fideism, where we can now see what an ugly brew of emotion, experience, feeling, etc., has developed out of that which in the form of faith has for 400 years been put in the place of sacramental reception in proud superiority, isolation, and dignity. Those who are not mistaken about this incontestable situation in Protestantism, and who are thus less frightened by the ambiguity of Roman Catholic sacramentalism, will have to concede the point.

I can obviously give no short answer to the question why I do not agree with them, why I do not want to make this concession. I can only point out that *meta phobou kai tromou* [Phil. 2:12], with no fervor or triumph, with no cultural or evangelical overtones, yet also with no fear, in spite of everything I decide for the Protestant, not the Roman Catholic possibility, and therefore at every point I do Protestant dogmatics. Only the course as a whole can answer the question. It may well be that Roman Catholic sacramentalism and Protestant fideism are both one-sided, that we have to go beyond both, and that we can do so by truly and unequivocally associating Word and sacrament. For the time being the balance is disturbed on both sides, and I would regard it as hubris to build my dogmatics on such a future possibility. For us heretics sacramental reception can only be an annex, a manifestation or confirmation. Being Reformed, I would indeed put it plainly and say that it is a symbol of faith. So long as we have no reason to go to Canossa, we cannot accord it basic significance for the concept of revelation. I ask you, then, to take the title of the section for what it really is in this context — an unemphatic yet definite confession of Protestantism.

2. The title would have to be different if I were lecturing on Lutheran dogmatics. It would then be simply "Faith." Luther and Lutheranism view revelation as a cone with a point which consists of a single communication of God to us: Your sins are forgiven you [Mark 2:5]. At this point revelation coincides with the gospel, the declaration of grace. This, at least, is how Luther and Lutheranism have had an impact historically. Revelation is to be regarded as the gospel, and only when the gospel has been heard is right use to be made of it, so that it is also seen as law. Thus faith and faith alone is our true and direct relation to it, faith being the Yes of a startled conscience which grasps confidently (*fiducialiter*) the divine answer to the human question.

According to the Reformed view, however, revelation has no such point, and thus there can be no such one-sided counterpart on our side. That God reveals himself means here, apparently formally, not this or that, but primarily that he reveals *himself*— his will and power and glory. He thus gives us, of course, the consoling and reconciling answer to our question, but in so doing he sharpens it and makes it for the first time a true question. Alongside the gospel, without in the least suspending its character as gospel, there stands with equal dignity the law, alongside the proclamation of grace the demand for repentance, in this order and not the reverse as in Lutheranism, where repentance is only preparation and good works are only the result of faith. Thus I say "Faith and Obedience," not just "Faith." In his 1545 Catechism Calvin could even distinguish four categories for what must take place on our part (naturally as the work of the Holy Spirit): faith, obedience, prayer, and thanksgiving.[5] Yet only two persist: faith and obedience. This pair is so universal and distinctive that Reformed dogmatics cannot possibly fail to assert them.

Note that the proud sacramental isolation of faith as such is broken by them. Faith is no longer the only possibility. Another possibility stands alongside it. The relation to God is both established and shattered. A deep disquietening of conscience accompanies its quietening. God's gracious answer never stands alone. With it, and not before or behind it, there comes the question which is thrust into our lives by this answer. God does not only justify sinners, but in a parallel and simultaneous and not a dependent action he also sanctifies them. Otherwise it is not with God that they have to do. Never for a moment does the gospel stand alone to be only believed, though justification is undoubtedly by faith. We have to do very radically with *God,* with *his* will and *his* honor. Thus it cannot be merely a matter of being justified and believing. With the need for faith there arises the need for repentance, for obedience, for the Christian life.[6] We cannot accept God's answer without placing ourselves under the question that is put to us.[7] We cannot recognize God without accepting his authority. We cannot have knowledge in relation to God without action.

According to the Reformed view revelation is like a ball which we must balance alternately with one hand and the other. Its subjective possibility is similar. It is dialectical like the objective possibility, like Reformed christology with its *extra*. Because we are thinking of God, we have always to think of the other side, the opposite. The danger of fideism,

---

5. *BSRK,* p. 117.23-28.

6. Cf. the title of *Inst.* III, 6: "The Life of the Christian Man."

7. N. p. 71 adds: "All rest, all certainty, must lie in God, and we must be content to go through the world as pilgrims, and to know that God cares for us."

of hypostatizing faith, is less serious here. There can hardly be any question of quietism, of an illegitimate resting in the divine answer without bothering about the question. That in faith we are dealing with God and not man can be less easily forgotten here, precisely because faith is relativized. But I will try to show why I am deciding for the Reformed possibility in the rest of my lectures — that it is not just because of my position. The title indicates the choice. There is enough Lutheranism in Calvinism, and for good or ill Lutheranism has had to take enough Calvinism into its system, to prevent us from talking about a fork in the road at this point. We may refer, however, to an instructive distinction which cannot be sufficiently taken into account on both sides.

3. If my dogmatics were a modern dogmatics, the title of the section would have to be "Religion." I want to point out to you as earnestly as I can that this is not what I mean when I say "Faith and Obedience." The reason for this distinction will be a major part of the section. Hence I cannot anticipate it. I may simply say in advance that if we mean it seriously that according to the Protestant view faith and therefore faith and obedience form the subjective possibility of revelation, then the event that these terms describe must occupy the place which sacramental reception occupies according to the Roman Catholic view. This event must stand in contrast to all purely psychological happenings with just the same reality and superiority. We must be permitted to say just as strictly and definitely about it that as a work of the Holy Spirit it is the organ by which we grasp and comprehend God and enter into true fellowship with him. But can we really, with a good conscience, say about what is called religion that it is commensurable in dignity with sacramental reception? Is it such an unambiguous entity that it can carry this weight? In a fateful way will we not say less than Roman Catholics think that they should say at this point if now, in face of the miracle of the incarnation, where we have to mention the organ by which we grasp this miracle, we want to talk about religion? If with me you simply have enough sense of style to perceive that this will not do, that in this context and at this point faith and obedience denote something that is on an entirely different plane from religion, then you can see, thirdly, that my title is a rejection of modern dogmatics with its religionism. It is meant to be this.

II. Conditions of the Subjective Possibility

It will be worth our while to ask abstractly, and just as strictly as in the preceding section, about the conditions of the subjective possibility of revelation. How can God come to us without ceasing to be God? The doctrine of the incarnation has given us an answer. But how can we humans stand before God without ceasing to be human? This is clearly a second question apart, no less difficult and urgent than the first. We must now go back to our definitions of man in § 4.III, especially the fourth, where we saw that from a Christian standpoint our alienation from God must be regarded as invincible and definitive because overcoming the contradiction in which we find ourselves would mean deleting the human subject. For we do not merely suffer from this contradiction. We constantly produce it by the free responsible act of our existence. And it is not as though we might not do so. We have to do so, yet without being able to blame compulsion or natural necessity or fate — no, but to our shame, and exposed to justifiable complaint, simply as the people we are.

This means, as we stated in § 5.I.4, that we have no organ by which to receive God's revelation. For God himself is the content as well as the subject of revelation. What element in human self-consciousness can come into consideration as an organ by which to grasp this reality, as a way to this goal, as a carrier for the movement that has to be executed here? If we know no answer to this question, then we confront a repetition of the paradoxical situation in which we found ourselves in the previous section, when on the basis of the doctrine of the Trinity we tried to clarify the meaning of the statement that God reveals himself on its objective side. We humans who stand before God, we now have to say, are precisely those who *cannot* stand before God (just as we saw earlier that precisely the God who reveals himself is the God who conceals himself). We have no quality, capacity, or possibility whereby to stand before God, we must now say. We would no longer be human if any such could be ascribed to us. A human relation to God (no matter how we think of it) — this predicate eludes us. We really have to handle this predicate very cautiously in theology.

Admittedly, this is so when seen precisely from the Christian standpoint. We have not arrived at this definition apart from revelation but in the light of the concept of revelation. "What is man that thou art mindful of him?" [Ps. 8:4]. What must man be because revelation exists, from the standpoint that he is addressed by God? This is how we put the question which we answered in § 4.II. There is no escaping it here either. It would be fine if we might be able to escape it with a little conversion from critical philosophy to a more friendly philosophy. Who would not be ready to do so if the situation could be eased? But we have made the presupposition that man stands before *God,* and precisely on the basis of this presupposition we must now say rather oddly that man cannot stand before God but can only "vanish" before him,[8] to recall Isa. 6 [v. 5] once again.

Thus we again stand inescapably before a shocking equation similar to the one that occupied us so long in the previous section; shocking not merely because it confronts us so unambiguously with the contradiction but also because of its content, which tells us that the within is also a without, that the Yes itself means a No, that in the very closeness of God our distance from him is disclosed. Again we have to give precision, then, to the question of the possibility of revelation by asking about the condition on which the fatal equation can perhaps be reversed, so that we might say that we humans who cannot stand before God are the very ones who do stand before God. Obviously the condition that would make the reversal possible and legitimate is that in the relation, as God can step out of his deity, so we can step out of our humanity, although without surrendering but rather activating it; that we can step out of ourselves, out of our being and our awareness of being caught in the contradiction, and be with God and even in God, learning from God to know God in his revelation with eyes[9] that God has opened. In other words, there will have to be an activation of the humanity that is entangled, definitively entangled, in the contradiction. God will have to bear and fill and make good our human incapacity by the capacity, the sufficiency, the adequacy which can be present only in God himself for God himself. There will have to be an activation in which we ourselves will and do and achieve but God does what we ourselves cannot do, positing himself as the beginning, middle, and end of this human activity, granting us his good pleasure of his own free grace, that is, granting us meaning, truth, power, and success, being himself the organ and way and movement in this human activity, so that it is no longer without an object but has God himself as its object.

If, then, there is a being in God in the very activation of our humanity, or, in other words, if there is an activation of our humanity

---

8. N. p. 73 adds: "like snow before the sun."
9. N. p. 74 adds: "and ears."

which is from God and in God, then obviously (for how can God fail to know and find himself?) we will stand before God and over against God, in the contradiction to be sure, yet still before and over against God. We will then be vessels (earthen vessels [2 Cor. 4:7], but still vessels) for the content of revelation, for God himself. There will then be revelation, that is, the establishment of fellowship between God and us by God's communication to us. Revelation will then be subjectively possible, that is, from the standpoint of the recipients. The human activity on which God's good pleasure rests, for all its fallibility, will be identical (not in itself, but in virtue of the divine good pleasure) with the effective reception, perception, and acceptance of revelation. On this condition we may reverse the fatal equation: Those who do not stand before God do stand before God. They do so not only because God stands before them as an object but also because, for all their impotence, God is with them and indeed in them as the subject, so that God makes the connection, building the bridge that they cannot build. They stand before God because God's revelation is a here as well as a there, something subjective as well as something objective, because God not only reveals himself in the *Son* but reveals himself in the Son by the *Spirit.*

With this last statement I have betrayed the fact that in this section, as distinct from the previous one, I anticipate the solution to the puzzle. My account of the condition is naturally not an a priori construction but the subsequent description of an unheard-of reality, just as unheard-of as the incarnation of God in which we learned to know the objective possibility of revelation. With what I have tried to formulate here I have had in mind the miracle of the Holy Spirit who creates faith and obedience in us and thus places us before God. He "creates" them. That is to say, as he creates the world out of nothing, and as he makes a particle of human nature in the body of the virgin the dwelling of the Logos, so he makes a piece of broken humanity into human knowing and doing, with himself in his revelation as the object. As in creation and the incarnation, so here, too, we have a *miracle,* an event which has its only ontic and noetic basis in the freedom and majesty of God. That this is so should be plain from the paradoxical equation in which the problem culminates and the even more paradoxical reversal of the equation with which we have to denote the reality. No more and no less is needed than God himself, *his* reality, to solve the puzzle, to fill the vacuum denoted by the paradox. The reality of God at *this* point, in *us,* the possibility that we are in God and hence from God to God, is the wholly specific thing which does not result merely from the essence of God and which is not exhausted by the divine Father-hood or the divine Sonship. It is God in the third person, the Holy Spirit. *His* work is the activation of our humanity that is caught in contradiction to the extent that this work of his enables us to see and hear and receive and accept, that it makes us receptive to God, that it places us before God incarnate in Christ, that it sets us in fellowship with God. Apart from this reality of the Holy Spirit, the construction of the subjective possibility of revelation is a bridge that ends in the void. How could we ever imagine this event in which we remain ourselves but move out of ourselves, this activation of our humanity which is essentially done by God, of which we are not the essential subjects even though it is our own? We have abstracted it from the reality. We could never imagine it were it not true and had it not happened. In thinking and saying what we do, we are putting ourselves, as in the previous section, on the ground of the church (in the broadest sense — the church to which Abraham also belonged), which perceives both the objective and the subjective possibility of revelation, in which they are a reality, in which faith and obedience are the counterpart of revelation, directly and inseparably linked with it.

But having anticipated thus, with the proviso that is indicated, let us think further for a moment along the lines of *possibility*. To have solid ground under our feet in what follows, we must define more narrowly the condition on which the subjective possibility is present. How can we think in these terms, we ask, if it is true that we precisely who cannot stand before God do stand before God? I think I perceive the four vital points that follow.

1. In this relation we have to be viewed soberly, totally, and pitilessly for what we really are: poor, miserable, naked, and empty with reference to God, people in a contradiction from which we cannot break free. God's being in us and our being in God take place in the relation, but they can in no way serve as a pretext for smuggling away anything that belongs to our human character as it is seen in the light of revelation, or for smuggling in anything that does not belong to it. No one can deny, of course, that in the relation we may experience lofty sentiments, moral aspirations, religious feelings, enthusiasms, and even perhaps ecstatic and mystical trances. These are unfortunate mishaps, I almost said, that none of us can escape. But it must still be obvious that they cannot denote any qualitative alteration of our human position and role in the relation. If there is to be a real subjective possibility of revelation in the relation, the point at issue is not that such happenings on our side put us in a position to stand before

God on our own, that is, apart from the third person of the Trinity. This cannot be because it would mean the end of any possibility of our really coming to stand before God. This possibility (which we have abstracted from the reality of the matter, we just said) relates only to those who even in their most lofty experiences cannot stand before God on their own. This possibility (the possibility in which we count on the third person of the Trinity) consists of the reversal of the fatal equation. If it is no longer fatal, if a means has been found to expunge its fatal character, if it has become the analytical statement that those who can appeal to this or that Godward experience of the inner life stand before God, very well then, no reversal is needed. Such people have their reward [Matt. 6:2]. Let them rejoice in their experience if they can. For the possibility at issue consists of the reversal of the equation, not its rendering innocuous. It is a dubious matter if we have to admit that the Holy Spirit has become superfluous because we already have him, or that we no longer need faith and obedience because we have something better. Not the Son of God alone goes incognito on the earth.[10] The same is true of that which makes his own people really his people: Your life is hid with Christ in God (Col. 3:3). And the incognito of this life may not be broken, the indirect relation may not be changed into a direct relation. Otherwise it is no longer *this* relation.

2. Just as unequivocally, God has to be really God in this relation, God himself, Spirit, not just any spirit but the Holy Spirit, and indeed the Creator Spirit.[11] Not, then, a somehow that lies in us or that we find ourselves in, not a something, a thing, or a cause, especially not a cause, nor a stream of life or grace in which we may bathe, as Goethe once said in a poem,[12] for none of these things is God.

Yet I must be more specific. Certainty is needed that those who are far from God, who are alien to him, who have turned away from him, do in fact move from God to God. If we are to say this seriously, it cannot be a matter of something inferred or felt or conjectured, of an obscure source for our own states, for example, for our religious emotions,[13] which

---

10. Cf. Kierkegaard, *Training in Christianity,* pp. 127-32.

11. Cf. the Whitsun hymn ascribed to Rabanus Maurus (ca. 776-856).

12. Cf. J. W. von Goethe's "Gott, Gemüt und Welt" (1812-1814), in which he speaks of walking the broad and colorful meadow of primal nature, and of the beautiful fount of tradition and grace in which he bathes.

13. Cf. *CF,* § 4.4, which equates the source of the feeling of absolute dependence with God.

certainly have to come from somewhere (as though they could not come from somewhere else). We need to recognize him to whom we go above us, and who comes to us, with the same definiteness as we do ourselves, with the *autopistia* of revelation. God must not be in any sense a problem in this relation but the air in which we breathe. Again, we must be able at any moment to distinguish God from ourselves and our states and activity, and we must be ready to do so. Being with God has to mean being with another, with one who is inalienably other. A God who is merely the extension of our own life impulse or the incommensurable background of our own élan vital[14] is in no case God. The truth and power of the relation at issue depend on its really being a relation; indeed, a relation in which God confronts us in qualitative and not just quantitative superiority. We have to understand and assert this qualitative distinction so radically that there can be no question of any erasure of the boundary. Finally, in this relation God must confront us in a relation of Creator and creature, that is, as person and not merely basis or cause, as Spirit who as in the virgin birth does not need to generate but only to command and bless, only to create. His work, the new qualification of our human frailty that is called faith and obedience and is pleasing to God, can have nothing in common with an event of nature. Relevant here is neither a mechanical relation of cause and effect, of pressure and impress, of a great and small quantity, nor the organic one of growth in its various stages or of life in its various forms. If what we call God is not safeguarded in the sense of not being an "it" but a "he," Spirit, person, then there can be no question of that reversal, that is, of conversion. We can be converted to God only if God himself is really on the scene.

3. The place in the life of us mortal sinners in which our activity leads to an encounter with God because God is the Creator must really be an activation. In this relation we cannot be mere objects. We must be just as much self-conscious subjects as God himself is. As our existence in contradiction — we must constantly stress this — is not just something we suffer from but our own *act,* so our encounter with God must be not merely something that comes upon us like fate or a roaring hailstorm. If this encounter means question and answer, speaking and hearing, giving and receiving between us and God, then we must be actors in the relation. We must not be mere leaves growing on the divine tree or floating in the divine breeze, nor must we be drops in the divine ocean, nor stones rolled

---

14. A basic concept in the philosophy of Henri Bergson (1859-1941).

down by the divine avalanche, nor wheels driven round by the divine motor. On such views the relation is much too continuous, much too much on the same level. And standing before God is taken with far too little seriousness. If fellowship between God and us is to mean anything, then it must mean that we in our sphere turn no less to God than God turns to us in his sphere. Revelation is really present only in action, we laid down already in § 3.III.2. We must apply this on the subjective side too. There has to be a recognition, an acceptance, an acknowledgment, a respecting, a bowing down. This is why there has to be faith and obedience. This is why expressly there has to be knowledge and action, not just sinking and vanishing, not just stillness and passivity, not just a "feeling of absolute dependence."[15]

4. The relation between God and us in which, as Ps. 119:18 puts it, God opens our eyes so that we see wonderful things in his law, in which revelation becomes manifest to us, has to be something that is a free and not a natural event on both sides. It must not set up anything constant or given, any natural necessity. It must not involve the immutability of a mathematical relation. It must be fully flexible. It must be a relation which, in order to remain true, must be renewed every moment both by God's work and word and in our own knowing and doing. Is not this unavoidable if God's free good pleasure on the one side, and faith and obedience as our own free acts on the other, are really the deciding factors? The relation has to be a conversation, a drama, a struggle, in which there are dangers and turning points, surprises and discoveries, repulses and advances, victories and defeats, standings and fallings. It has to be a wrestling like that of Jacob in which we must risk being lamed so long as we insist that we will not let God go unless he blesses us [Gen. 32:25ff.]. Each moment must be unique and nonrepeatable, for our other partner is God and he demands that we hazard our whole existence. How can things be any different if this relation is really the subjective possibility of revelation, our opening up to the light in the darkness of our being, to the triumph over the contradiction, to the end of our alienation?

If God is so much God that he does these things too, that he is not just himself the light, but also himself the light in which we see light [Ps. 36:9], and if we know that for us the only issue is that we should know God in this fellowship with God, then how can our worship in spirit and in truth [John 4:24], how can our watching and praying and beseech-

---

15. *Cf.* § 4.3.

ing[16] ever cease or change themselves into possessing and enjoying? No, it is on a knife-edge, that is, in the midst of existential decision, that this relation — I will not say, stands — but *takes place* (for if it does not continuously take place, it is not *this* relation). On the one side we have God's unsearchable good pleasure, his free and majestic choosing, calling, and blessing, and on the other side we have our own knowing and doing, which must be constantly established afresh. The calm and facticity and impregnability of the relation, which Roman Catholicism denotes by the concept *opus operatum,* must be sought and found in the fact that the relation is enduring and indestructible, that the decision is inescapable, and that the vitality of the encounter between God and us is constant. Roman Catholicism cannot finally mean anything else by its *opus operatum.* There can be no subjective possibility of revelation but this one.

Thus the condition of this possibility, formally distinguished under four heads, may be summed up as follows: (a) Unequivocal humanity as one side of the relation; (b) the sure, distinguishable, personal presence of God himself on the other side; (c) human activity or action in its own sphere; (d) indestructible flexibility in the realization of the relation.

III. The Concept of Religion

With the help of these definitions we may now move on to a critical discussion of the concept which in a modern theology of revelation would be the theme of the first section, or which at the very latest would have to come up here in a consideration of the subjective possibility of revelation — the concept of religion. To anticipate, this concept will appear in my own train of thought only at once to disappear again. You have probably never heard me use the words "religion," "religiosity," and "religious" except when quoting the thoughts of others; then they are apposite. Similarly, in my vocabulary the words "religious knowledge," "religious history," "religious philosophy," and "religious psychology" denote something which, if it is not entirely mistaken, still has no place in theology as I see it.

In what follows, then, I do not propose to advance my own view of religion. I have no interest in this concept, not even enough to participate in

---

16. Cf. the first and last verses of J. B. Freystein's hymn "Machen dich, mein Geist, bereit" (1695).

efforts to give it a new significance or content.[17] This would not be impossible. In the rendering that philologists usually give the word *religio* today,[18] that is, awe, regard, respect, or reverence, I might with the help of a little dialectical accommodation claim it as a master concept for what I call faith and obedience, and in my view with more right than Schleiermacher had for what he understood by it. But for me the term is too freighted and stained with all the nonsense that has been made of it during the last two hundred years, and above all, the apologetic nonsense. I can no longer hear or pronounce the word "religion" without the adverse recollection that in modern intellectual history it has in fact been a flag denoting the place of refuge to which Protestant and a good deal of Roman Catholic theology began a more or less headlong retreat when it no longer had the courage to think in terms of its object, that is, the Word of God, but was glad to find at the place where the little banner of religion waved a small field of historical and psychological reality to which, renouncing all else, it could devote itself as a true "as though" theology, at peace with the modern understanding of science. Behind the alien word "religion" and all that it entails, and also behind the word "piety," which some prefer, there lies concealed either shamefully or shamelessly a confession that as moderns we no longer dare in principle, primarily, and with uplifted voice to speak about God. Even with the best dialectical accommodation, I cannot today detach this historical background from even the better sense of the word *religio*. Perhaps a time will come when we can again speak about religion, as Zwingli and Calvin did,[19] innocuously and uninhibitedly, and without having to blush.

But today is another day. I thus refrain from giving a positive account of the concept of religion and stick with what Schleiermacher understood by it at the climax of the modern development, for without going into details we may assume that the modern concept of religion derives from Schleiermacher, and the question that I have to put to this understanding is whether it can serve as the subjective possibility of revelation according to the conditions we have stated. Obviously in a systematic treatment we cannot evaluate Schleiermacher in the setting of his age or present his thoughts in their own context. I assume that you have already

---

17. Marginal note: "Lagarde, Deutsche Schr. p. 46." In *ChD*, p. 398, and *CD*, I/2, p. 284, Barth gives the quotation, which is from P. de Lagarde, *Über das Verhältnis des deutsch-Staates zu Theologie, Kirche und Religion* (1873), in *Deutsche Schriften*, 4th ed. (Göttingen, 1892), p. 46.

18. Cf. F. Kluge, *Etymologisches Wörterbuch der deutschen Sprache*, 11th ed. (Berlin/Leipzig, 1934), pp. 478ff.

19. Cf. Zwingli's *Commentary on True and False Religion* and Calvin's *Institutes*.

dealt with this man along such lines, or that you will do so in the future, and I will accept him as "the greatest Evangelical theologian" or as "the church father of the 19th century,"[20] as he has often enough been.

1. Unequivocal humanity, we postulated first. But we run at once into confusion if we open Schleiermacher's *Speeches* with this presupposition. For there man is not poor and miserable and naked and empty. Instead, we are led to the pinnacles of the temple of humanity.[21] And without ambiguity we read immediately that religion is a human disposition, that it is part of human nature, that it proceeds of itself from within every better nature, that it has its own province in the soul, that it is a continuum in the human soul, that it has entered the human heart (1 Cor. 2 v. 9!) as a distinctive movement of the soul, namely, as a taste and feeling for the infinite, that there is a part of the soul in which deity prefers to dwell, in which it manifests and contemplates itself in its direct workings.[22] Certainly there are relatively few people who can be called the virtuosi, mediators, priests, or heroes of religion,[23] but there are such people, and for them as for the rest the actualizing of the religious disposition is only a matter of the experiences that they need to have, of the understanding that they must acquire for their own innermost being, and of the correct development that they must enjoy.[24] If a proper view joins forces with the proper feeling, then the moment of the experience of the eternal comes (Schleiermacher calls it a kind of wedding),[25] and it is the highest but attainable blossoming of these highest functions of life that is known at least to the author of these speeches.

---

20. Cf. C. Lülmann, *Schleiermacher, der Kirchenvater des 19. Jahrhunderts* (Tübingen, 1907).

21. F. Schleiermacher, *Reden über die Religion*, p. 11 (20) (the page numbers in parentheses are those of the original edition); ET *On Religion: Speeches to its Cultured Despisers*, p. 12. (Despite the title of the English translation, we will refer to the book by its traditional title, *Speeches*.)

22. Ibid.; cf. p. 13 (23), ET p. 13; p. 20 (37), ET p. 23; p. 78 (139), ET p. 122; cf. p. 165 (298), ET p. 245; p. 27 (47), ET p. 33; p. 14 (26), ET p. 14; p. 30 (53), ET p. 39; p. 150 (269), ET p. 229.

23. Ibid., pp. 5-6 (10), ET p. 6; p. 7 (12), ET p. 8; p. 16 (29), ET p. 17; p. 36 (63), ET p. 40; p. 54 (97), ET p. 79; p. 67 (121), ET p. 86; p. 88 (158), ET p. 136; p. 90 (162); cf. ET pp. 175ff.

24. Ibid., p. 55 (98); ET p. 65; and cf. K. Barth, *Die Theologie Schleiermachers*, ed. D. Ritschl (Zurich, 1978), p. 445; ET *The Theology of Schleiermacher* (Grand Rapids, 1982), p. 249.

25. *Reden*, p. 149 (267); ET *Speeches*, p. 228; cf. *Reden*, p. 41 (74); ET *Speeches*, p. 43.

In *Christian Faith* Schleiermacher expresses the same thoughts just as clearly, although more cautiously. Thus we are told in § 3.3-4 that beyond thought and volition, sometimes pushing them on, sometimes quietly accompanying them, there is a third element in the consciousness, direct self-consciousness or feeling. This element, which is regarded as pure receptivity in contrast to the other two, and which is distinctively determined (by a special "view" according to the *Speeches*), is piety. We then read in § 5.5 that it is a continuous consciousness even though its powers may wax and wane, and then again in § 6.1 that it is an essential and universal element in human nature. The obscurity which Schleiermacher has to some extent spread around the concept of religion by defining it as the feeling of absolute dependence should not mislead us into thinking that we have here a purely transcendental factor somewhat like a Kantian a priori. No, according to Schleiermacher's own explanations (especially in §§ 29 and 32) it is a given factor in us, in us ourselves, in our self-consciousness, as the union of our own human being with the divine being in the self-consciousness. In relation to this universal religion within us (which is not just possible but actual, though it is never present abstractly but always in particular instances, in specific religions), Christianity, being based on a particular view, that of Jesus of Nazareth,[26] is simply one specimen of the genus. Nature is the totality. We read this not only in the *Speeches* but also in *Christian Faith,* where this presupposition was so important for Schleiermacher that in § 33 he could believe that it replaces all proofs of God's existence and could make it the principle according to which the whole work is arranged.

It should be quite clear that this universal religion that is a given, existent factor has nothing whatever to do with the unequivocal humanity that is far from God, estranged from him, and in need of the intervention of the third person of the Trinity. A fatal equation does not have to be reversed in Schleiermacher, nor an incurable hurt made good. No incognito of the divine forms a threat here. Everything is immediate. There is only a quantitative distinction between man and the divine. All this might be called religion, but it belongs to a completely different world from revelation. It cannot be the subjective possibility of revelation. It certainly cannot be confused with faith and obedience.

2. We thought that we should advance as the second part of the condition of a subjective possibility of revelation the sure and unambigu-

---

26. *CF,* § 11; etc.; cf. *Reden,* pp. 166-69 (300-305); ET *Speeches,* pp. 246ff.

ously distinguishable, personal presence of God with us and in us. When we come to Schleiermacher we cannot fail to see that there can be no question of this, for everything possible is done to weaken and indeed to set aside the idea that there can be a clear and evident knowledge of God, that we have to do with another, with a counterpart, when we take the word "God" on our lips, that God can be person, Spirit, subject. Here instead the subjective possibility of revelation is that we grasp the divine subjectivity and ascribe it to ourselves. For how else can we construe it when in the *Speeches* Schleiermacher describes as follows the decisive moment of the wedding of man with the universum in religious experience: "I lie on the bosom of the infinite world; at this moment I am its soul, it is at this moment my body, for I feel all its powers and muscles and members as my own, and its innermost nerves move according to my mind and feeling as my own."[27] We grossly misunderstand Schleiermacher if we try to see in what he called "view" or "feeling" the way or step to another, to a truly *new* world. No, religion is a product of human nature, grounded in one of its essential modes of action or impulses or whatever we wish to call it.[28] Those who make a distinction between this world and the next deceive themselves — all those at least who have religion believe in only one world.[29] Naturally! Far from denoting a step from here to there, Schleiermacher's religion is a peaceful vegetating in a here and there which not only cannot be separated but are also completely undistinguished and indistinguishable. It lives its life in the infinite nature of the whole, the one in all.[30] It is the revelation of universal life in our own breasts and the world around us.[31] Whether we call this totality, this life, by the name of God and think of this God *personally* depends on the drift of our imagination.[32] Schleiermacher never hid the fact that his own imagination did not work along these lines. Neither matter has for him any importance in principle. A religion without God can be better than one with God.[33] God is not everything in religion but only one thing (a religious concept like any other), and the universum is *more*.[34]

---

27. *Reden,* pp. 41-42 (74); ET *Speeches,* p. 43.
28. Ibid., p. 12 (22); ET pp. 11-12.
29. Ibid., p. 19 (34); ET p. 20. (Barth has *betrügt* for *betört.*)
30. Ibid., p. 29 (51); ET p. 36.
31. Ibid., p. 82 (147); ET p. 135.
32. Ibid., p. 71 (128-29); ET pp. 97-98.
33. Ibid., p. 70 (126); ET p. 97. (Barth here reverses a dependent clause.)
34. Ibid., pp. 73-74 (132-33); ET pp. 98ff.

We learn something more cautious but materially the same when we turn to *Christian Faith,* especially the well-known § 4. Here at any rate we are told that piety, that is, the sense of absolute dependence, is the same as the sense of our relation to God.[35] But what does this mean? The remarkable way in which Schleiermacher comes to assert this feeling of absolute dependence is a separate question. Let us stay with the result in § 4.4. This is to the effect that in direct self-consciousness, which is per se a feeling of absolute dependence, that is, of total conditioning and even positing by another, there is posited, given, included, and revealed the source of our whole being and of all finite being, to which we push back our existence and nature and which, when we reflect on it, we call *God.* Note that not merely the sense of the source but the source itself, the final source of all being, which is called God when feeling expresses itself in speech — that this source is posited *in* the self-consciousness. And we should remember that this feeling does not have the source (God) as an object (otherwise it would not be a feeling of *absolute* dependence!) but that in a primal way God is given in the feeling itself. Any other way in which God might be given is completely ruled out, we are told expressly. All that we have is symbolizing when the term God is referred to an object, when its content is not just put back within the feeling but taken out of it and juxtaposed with the feeling person.

The description "of absolute dependence" which Schleiermacher adds to "feeling" in order to smuggle in a relative transcendence for God is one that I regard as totally untenable. Even the transcendental elements that survive in *Christian Faith* (e.g., all the christology) do so only within feeling, which is not just a single aspect but the whole of Schleiermacher's world of faith. §§ 11-14 document in a remarkable way the consistency with which Schleiermacher knew how to render the Christian concept of revelation harmless even before he began his account of the faith, how to entangle the whole of Christianity as a spider does a fly, so that apart from the inward impact no real inkling of it may be detected at all. Quite naturally, then, "Christian doctrines are accounts of the Christian religious affections set forth in speech" (the thesis of § 15). They are nothing else at all. In *no* way are they truth, or the expression of a truth that meets these inner states of ours in a manner that is new and strange and superior. No, only their expression meets us, and in this regard Schleiermacher thinks that the most original expression of religious feeling is mime, and

---

35. *CF,* § 4 (thesis) and §4.4.

that the most adequate expression is music, not word.[36] If in *Christian Faith* we have not only a direct description of pious states of soul but also statements about the fashioning of the world and the attributes of God (although only in very close connection with the former), this was a concession according to the opinion plainly expressed by Schleiermacher in his *Second Open Letter to Lücke.* The ideal of dogmatics that hovered before him would have been a presentation of the reflections of the pious soul about itself. He refrained from this course only because he wanted his work to adopt a historical approach and to have a churchly character.[37]

From this brief survey it should be plain that the God of Schleiermacher, who is inescapably enclosed in human feeling and posited with it, has absolutely nothing whatever to do with the *autopistia,* the supremacy, and the unequivocal spirituality of what we have had to know as God in the context of our doctrine of revelation. This God is a something, a neuter, not a He. He is a cause, a whence, like the source of a river, not the Creator. He is simply a relative counterpart in a steady series of given factors of which we, too, are members, belonging to the same circle to which all things belong, including ourselves, not an object, or only symbolically and improperly so, and therefore obviously not a true subject. Who can deny that this concept of God does in fact describe a reality? But let us consider what this reality is. We can very definitely say that it is not the reality of the Holy Spirit who sets us before God. Schleiermacher could only ridicule or bewail as a Judaism that must be speedily overcome the whole concept of standing before God that I advance here as the subjective possibility of revelation. We cannot relevantly equate with *religio* in the sense of reverence Schleiermacher's relation of love to the universum or his feeling of absolute dependence. Reverence needs an object. Schleiermacher's religion has no object. Its fervor rests on its lack of object. For it there is no one and nothing outside to which respect and fear are due. Everything is within. Even less can it mention faith and obedience together.

3. We demanded action on our part in the broadest sense of the word. Revelation can be subjective only in full action. In contrast, we find in

---

36. Ibid., § 15.1.

37. *Schleiermachers Sendschreiben über seine Glaubenslehre an Lücke,* ed. H. Mulert (Giessen, 1908), pp. 47-48. He here described the sections on the fashioning of the world and the attributes of God as subsidiary and inessential. Yet he granted that a structure which omitted them would not show a proper historical approach or have a purely churchly character.

Schleiermacher's *Speeches* the famous passionate complaint against a confusion of religion with metaphysics and morality. Religion should neither have a tendency to state eternal truths nor use the universum for the inferring of duties.[38] The idea of religious action or thought is something secondary, derived, and inauthentic, if not a pollution of the true essence of religion. Practice is art, knowledge science, religion a feeling and taste for the infinite.[39] This is what we are told in the decisive passage, and there then follows the transition to the great depiction of contemplation of the universum and feeling for it, both of which are the direct opposite of action. We should learn to see that everything finite is an impress or representation of the infinite.[40] We should look at the world spirit and perceive and observe his working.[41] The universum alone is tirelessly active[42] and fashions for itself — what? — its own spectators and admirers, and even as that happens we must simply look on to the extent that it lets us do so.[43]

In an exact parallel in *Christian Faith*, §§ 3-6, the doctrine of the feeling of absolute dependence concretely links this to knowledge and action, yet it is piety, not in this combination, but in its purity as a wholly passive and inward matter on the part of the subject. I will leave aside the difficulties which beset the development of this thesis at every point. Suffice it to say that Schleiermacher did try to develop it. The relation to God in its truest and deepest content lies beyond the thinking and willing self-consciousness with which it enters into a kind of symbiosis. It is a pure, inward, nonqualitative being and resting that is determined by itself alone and remains itself. It is a kind of pedal-note that persists through every variation. The declaration in § 9, for which there is neither preparation nor basis, and which is to the effect that Christianity is distinctively a teleological religion relating all activity to the kingdom of God, offers illumination here, as does the disproportionate emphasis on the work of culture in the sermons.[44] They both shed light on the fact that what Schleiermacher calls religion is from the very first and in itself — he never fails to come back to this — neither knowledge nor action (how can it be

---

38. *Reden*, pp. 24-25 (43); ET *Speeches*, pp. 31ff.
39. Ibid., p. 30 (52-53); ET p. 39.
40. Ibid., p. 29 (51); ET p. 37.
41. Ibid., p. 45 (80); ET p. 48.
42. Ibid., pp. 31-32 (55-56); ET pp. 41-42.
43. Ibid., p. 79 (143); ET pp. 122-23.
44. K. Barth, *Die Theologie Schleiermachers*, pp. 63-78; ET *Theology of Schleiermacher*, pp. 31ff.

since it has no object?) but rather something that stands in at any rate a close relation to the quietism of mysticism — "peace" is the distinctive catchword in the later sermons.[45] Obviously, since God and man are seen on the same level and in the same context, there can be no real turning of man to God, no receiving of his Word, no obedience proffered to him. Here in a forceful and fatal way God, or what is called God, crushes man at the very point where there ought to be spiritual fellowship, speaking and hearing, commanding and obedience. In this regard Schleiermacher ought to serve as a warning example to show what happens when God and man are brought as close as they are here. There can then be no understanding of faith as a venture or of obedience as a duty.

4. This leads us at once to the fourth point, to our postulate that the relation to God on our side must always be a wrestling like Jacob's [Gen. 32:25ff.] in which constancy is sought only in God and not in us. Schleiermacher, however, has no time for what we have called the flexibility of the relation to God. With the greatest assurance he tells us that we live and move and have our being in God — although not in the same sense as Paul [Acts 17:18]. In the *Speeches* he says that the universum is in unbroken activity and that it reveals itself to us every moment.[46] To view every event in the world as an act of the one God is religion.[47] Miracle is the religious name for an event . . . "for me everything is miracle."[48] The whole world is a gallery of religious portraits.[49] The church is a republic where each in turn is leader and people, each follows in others the same force that he feels in himself and by which he also rules others.[50] As regards the different religions, the insight is simply that they are all one, that the whole religious world is an indivisible totality into which they all merge.[51] In every way the universum is contemplated and worshiped. Innumerable forms of religion are possible.[52] Paul's view [Rom. 9:21] that God fashioned some vessels to honor and some to dishonor is bluntly branded as irreligious. No, we should all rejoice at the place where we stand.[53] Every-

---

45. Ibid., pp. 14-17, 26-29, 31-32, 78-82, 92; ET pp. 4ff., 11ff., 39ff.
46. *Reden,* p. 32 (56); ET *Speeches,* p. 48.
47. Ibid., p. 32 (57); ET p. 49.
48. Ibid., pp. 65-66 (118); ET p. 88.
49. Ibid., p. 78 (141); ET p. 132.
50. Ibid., p. 102 (184-85); ET p. 153.
51. Ibid., pp. 103-4 (185, 187); ET p. 154.
52. Ibid., p. 172 (310); ET p. 252.
53. Ibid., p. 51 (91-92); ET p. 73.

one and everything is a work of the universum, and only thus can religion view people.[54]

Thus revelation, truth, God — whatever one wants to call it — moves like a monstrous roller over everything that creeps and crawls. To be sure, Schleiermacher built up the second part of *Christian Faith* on the antithesis of sin and grace, and presented Christianity in this schema as the religion of redemption. But now the presupposed passivity avenges itself in the central systematic concept. According to § 5 pious feeling as such does not participate in this antithesis which touches the objective self-consciousness only tangentially. Thus even here the antithesis is only relative and quantitative. It is the emergence of the intrinsically continuous self-consciousness in the individual moments of the objective consciousness. This is more or less easy or hard, free or hampered. But nowhere and never is there any full, exclusive, irreconcilable antithesis in principle. No one dies of sin and no one is judged by grace. There is merely a fleeting differentiation or oscillation of the same feeling (which is never itself called in question) between two extreme limits that are never actually reached, let alone crossed.[55] We find a similar relativism in the account of the relation between Christianity and religious history,[56] which begins with an attempt to prove the supreme validity of Christianity as a monotheistic religion with the help of the concept of development, and ends — for revelation is always present when religion is present — with the conclusion that the only distinctiveness of the Christian religion in principle is that it is the religion of redemption founded by Jesus of Nazareth. Perfect truth would mean God's disclosing himself as he is in and for himself. But such a disclosure could not come externally from any fact, even though such a fact could reach the human soul in some inconceivable way; it could not itself be comprehended or established as a thought; and if it could not be in any way perceived or established, it could not be effective.[57]

This line of thought shows exactly what the ditch is that Schleiermacher cannot jump across, or does not want to jump across. This is the point where we have to enter into the existential warfare of faith and obedience. That is to say, it is the point where we have to reckon with the Holy Spirit. From this moment on there ought to be real conflict in

---

54. Ibid., p. 80 (143); ET p. 124.
55. Cf. *CF*, §§ 5, 11, 62-64.
56. Ibid., §§ 7-10.
57. Ibid., § 10, Postscript.

theology with regard to sin and grace, revelation and nonrevelation, truth and error. We are not set in a state but thrust into the middle of a decision, a life-and-death either/or. The subjective possibility of revelation stands and consists in this either/or, not in its resolution, but in the either/or itself. Here is the parting of the ways. I need hardly say that the way of Schleiermacher, from which we now totally diverge, is not the way of Schleiermacher alone.[58]

IV. Faith and Obedience in the Doctrine of Revelation

Let us now attempt a brief development of the doctrine of faith and obedience insofar as this is necessary and possible within a general doctrine of revelation.

1. The problem in this doctrine is the coming of God's Word to us, its perception and reception by us, our own participation in revelation. It need hardly be said that the doctrine of revelation is not only not complete but is not the doctrine of revelation at all if this final element is missing. As revelation would not be revelation if *God* did not reveal himself, if God did not reveal *himself,* if God did not reveal himself to *man,* so it would not be revelation if as God reveals himself to man he were not manifest to him, did not not come to him, did not enter into him. Calvin formulated the problem when he said "as long as Christ remains outside of us, and we are separated from him, all that he has suffered and done for the salvation of the human race remains useless and of no value for us. Therefore, to share with us what he had received from the Father, he had to become ours and to dwell within us."[59] Or again: "The Word of God is like the sun, shining on all those to whom it is proclaimed, but with no effect among the blind. Now, all of us are blind by nature in this respect. Accordingly, it cannot penetrate into our minds unless the Spirit, as the inner teacher, through his illumination makes entry for it."[60] The Spirit the inner teacher! If by a reminder of Schleiermacher we are definitively warned against the temptation of a religious anthro-

---

58. Marginal note: "Thus rel. is not standing before God (if it were it would have to be something different). Rel. does not exclude standing before God, but it does not include it per se."

59. *Inst.* III, 1, 1: Barth has *nobis est inutile* for Calvin's *nobis esse inutile.*

60. Ibid., III, 2, 34.

pology, we cannot in any sense regard the overcoming of this "outside of us" — this human blindness to God — as something that is given in us or achieved by us; if on this last, concluding side revelation must be viewed exclusively as the act and work of God, then it is clear that the true object of a doctrine of faith and obedience can only be the teacher Spirit, the Holy Spirit. It is a miracle no less than that of the incarnation, but corresponding to it exactly, if the subjective possibility does actually take the form of faith and obedience. As the miracle of the incarnation cannot be perceived historically, but only by the Holy Spirit who as he performs it opens eyes and ears to perceive it, so the miracle of faith and obedience cannot be seen psychologically but only through the Son who as he himself assumes human nature gives us a share in his fellowship with the Father. At this point, at the eleventh hour, there can be no question of a sudden change, of our being either able or permitted to leave the self-enclosed circle of the *Deus dixit.* Any effort in this direction will at once avenge itself as we lose our birthright [Gen. 25:29ff.] — theological objectivity — for the sake of a mess of pottage — a clear conceptuality. No, our only option is to fix the point within the self-enclosed circle, the side of the reality of revelation, to which Christian preaching relates and to which testimony is given in holy scripture. Our only option is to describe the point where God's Word is not only *God's* speech, God's address to us, but also God's address to us that is *heard* by us.

2. Following a basic intention of Reformed thinking, I have divided this point into the two elements of faith and obedience. But first of all let us view it as a unity. What does it mean to stand before *God,* to believe in him and to obey him? If we have been right about the objective revelation of God in the incarnation of God, then obviously there can be no question of an immediate or direct relation to God in this subjective possibility either. The incarnation means that God becomes objective and concrete. Coming into history, into the circle of human comprehension, God's Word becomes complex instead of simple. It is adopted and transmitted by the proclamation of the Christian community in distinct communications and demands.

Faith and obedience vis-à-vis revelation stand face to face first of all with this historical, self-explicating revelation, or else they do not stand before revelation. It would be a comfortable conjuring away of the offense, but no more and no less than the conjuring away of revelation itself, if we were to say that we will cling to God himself but will have nothing whatever to do with all the astonishing things that are linked to our being able to cling to God himself. Faith means not only believing in God but also believing in this and that. To put it with all the offense that it involves, it means believing in the Trinity, or in the NT miracles, or in the virgin birth. And obedience means not only uniting our own wills with God's[61] but, for example, keeping the ten commandments. It is not a matter of the number of explications in which revelation comes to us but fundamentally of the offense that meets us in the explications, namely, that revelation comes to us in this form, and that in this form it demands our faith and obedience. But now we must also say on the other side that as little as we may evade the explications, the concrete communications and demands, the dogmas, as little as we may take refuge in something general, mystical, and immediate, so little are the explications themselves revelation, so little do we stand before God by standing before even a very complete sum of truths of revelation. Naturally these truths, and the faith and obedience that we must bring to them, refer to God, and to God *alone*. The inalienable subjectivity of God conceals itself in the hard objectivity of revelation. Thus the miracle of the Holy Spirit is first of all that at the very point where the humanity of revelation cannot be evaded but is experienced in all its offensiveness, its divinity speaks imperiously to us and is willingly heard by us.

3. Once again from the standpoint of the unity of faith and obedience, we ask: What does it mean for *man* to stand before God, to believe in him and to obey him? In subsections II and III of this section we have sharply stressed the element of human activity. I do not mean subconscious or superconscious activity. Very simply — I must again put it rather brutally so as to be understood — I mean, for example, regarding it as true that Jesus Christ rose from the dead, resolving to pray and to love my neighbor as myself, and trusting that I am in the hands of God. Now all this sounds very naive to me too. Objections at once arise against the idea that such dubious and ambivalent knowing and doing can be real knowing and doing relative to God. My knowing and doing are indeed dubious and ambivalent down to the very roots, even to the very point where in my heart and conscience I think I am one with God, which, it is to be hoped, I will not think too quickly or talk about too quickly. Yet I cannot suppress this knowing and doing, any more than I can suppress those fatal explications; otherwise with my supposedly profound restraint I shall be

---

61. Cf. K. Holl, "Der Neubau der Sittlichkeit" (1919), in *Gesammelte Aufsätze zur Kirchengeschichte*, I: *Luther*, 2nd-3rd ed. (Tübingen, 1923), p. 207.

like the slothful servant who took his money and buried it because he knew that his master was a hard master [Matt. 25:18, 24]. It is only in the form of this knowing and doing, dubious and ambivalent though it is, that I can stand before God and that there can be any question of a meeting between God and man. But now on the other side, of course, even the most zealous faith and obedience helps us not at all, just as the most perfect dogmatics helps us not all, without the origin and goal in God himself that these relations have to have. For in themselves, apart from God, they are empty husks and human marvels, just as the mere humanity of revelation is. God himself must himself come to us, we said earlier.

As I see it, then, the second miracle of the Holy Spirit is that cheek by jowl we again have the human side, that of man with his religion, with his watching and praying [Mark 14:38], and we also have the divine side, God hearing and seeing his own voice and deed in this human stammering and stumbling (which is certainly never worse than when in addition to all else it is also devout), God recognizing his own work in these human marvels and weaknesses, so that it can be true, although without any Christ mysticism: "I live, yet not I, but Christ lives in me" [Gal. 2:20], and we all have a share in what is said to the one: "Thou art my beloved Son, in whom I am well pleased" [Matt. 3:17].

4. Starting on both sides with what is concrete and human, I infer that the point where God's address is heard by man must divide into two elements: faith and obedience. We need only recall that objective revelation in the incarnation is not direct revelation but revelation in concealment, and also that God in revelation does not merely give an answer to the human question but in and with the answer truly puts the question for the first time, and we shall see at once that at least from God's standpoint we always have two things at the same time. We can mention the grace that comes to us when God enters into fellowship with us, but then at once we have to remember that this fellowship is a judgment for us, because it is only by God's encountering us in grace that we can realize what it means to be human. Or we can talk about the promise that comes to us with the incarnate Logos and the imminent kingdom of heaven, but then undoubtedly we must at once speak also about a demand which this Word and kingdom direct to us. We might also sum up the antithesis in the familiar formula of gospel and law. And if this is so, if we cannot resolve either to suppress one of these elements or to play down one in favor of the other, if we embrace both in the higher unity of the Word of God,

and take them both with equal seriousness, as on the specifically Reformed view, then in some way we must do the same on the subjective side as well.

Here, too, we may distinguish between a response and a willing appropriation and affirmation, a recognition and an acknowledgment and acceptance, a knowing and a doing. Both take place in the same person, and we never have the one without the other. Yet there are still two things in the unity, and the vitality of the relation to God depends on there being two: that I put myself under grace but also under judgment, under the promise but also under the demand, under the gospel but also under the law, in faith but also in penitence and obedience; that I receive God's answer but also bow under his question. Naturally, they cannot be present only in degree, with the relativity that obtains in Schleiermacher's Christian understanding and that kills off all true seriousness. Both have to be present totally at all times as though there were nothing else: total grace, yet for that very reason total guilt; total gospel, yet for that very reason total law. Each must be pushed to the extreme where from the human standpoint it reigns alone and exclusively. There must be no purely fleeting difference from the opposite but a deep valley must separate it from the opposite. The relation must always be one of either/or to which only God has the key, the solution.

A third aspect of the miracle of the Holy Spirit, then, is that we are not torn asunder by the Word that leads us to the heights and to the depths, that we are not plunged into despair by it, that we are upheld and carried and led in both cases because it is the Word of God, because God does not deceive us but also will not let himself be mocked [Gal. 6:7], either by a belief that is not ready to be obedience or by a zeal for God's kingdom that wants to be without faith. I believe it will be worth our while to give to Luther's *sola fide* this extended interpretation. The concern that lies behind it could not be better brought out than by setting it in the light of Calvin's *soli Deo gloria.*

5. Let us now turn in detail to the concept of faith. All the Reformers thought it important to define this concept more narrowly as *fiducia* (trust),[62] and all of them, including Calvin, stressed that it was *fiducia cordis* (the heart's trust). They stressed the emotion, the inner experience, even the feeling with which God's word must be grasped if it is to be really grasped. We have advanced sufficient counterbalances to

---

62. For examples see *ChD*, p. 248 n. 9.

enjoy the freedom to admit that they were right in this regard. Those who like Luther could say that they did not imagine that there was anything like a quality called faith or love in the heart, but set Jesus Christ in place of everything of that kind,[63] might allow themselves to say occasionally that the location of faith is on the left side of the breast,[64] and might even argue that the human heart is deified in faith,[65] notwithstanding all the dangerous modern nonsense that usually appeals to these and similar sayings of Luther.

What does all this mean? In faith we have to do with revelation in concealment, with Christ the risen Lord, with the divine once-for-all pronounced in the incarnation, with reception into the fellowship of the new man from above, with participation in his triumph over the contradiction, with the statement that even though human we are God's children, with the completed atonement. This is the peace of God that passes all understanding [cf. Phil. 4:7], the Reformers wanted to say. It is just as inaccessible to the understanding as to thought. It is accessible only because it is revealed. The antithesis between the heart and the head can imply this; why not? The irrational element in us is a salutary reminder that in face of revelation the point is not to grasp but to be grasped. If we are careful to avoid the confusion that the irrational element is for this reason revelation itself, then it is true that the heart grasps the distinction better and more quickly than the head, though undoubtedly the heart has to repent just as radically as the head if we are to be able to say this. For the Reformers, at least, the decisive point is not the psychological advantage of emotion over the intellect, but its[66] significance for the claiming of our existence, of our innermost being, of what is most real in us, of that which is claimed by faith in revelation. The relation of reality to reality, of God to us, of the unconditioned to the unconditioned — that is experience in the context of the Reformers' thinking. And we have only to recall that for all of them the correlate of faith is the promise, that *fiducia* (see § 1 above) means agreement in the light of a pledge, to see clearly that faith, no matter how it is located or described psychologically, no matter what

---

63. Cf. Luther's postscript to a letter of Melanchthon to Johannes Brenz, May 1531, WA, B 6, 100-101, quoted from F. Loofs, *Leitfaden*, § 6, p. 765 n. 21.

64. Cf. Luther's sermon on Dec. 27, 1533, WA, 37, 148, 18-19.

65. Cf. Luther, *Das XIV und XV Kapitel Johannis* (1538), WA, 45, 540, 13-15, on John 14:13-14; LW, 24, 87.

66. The editor changed Barth's *ihre* to *seine* here, since *ihre* could refer only to the Reformers.

great things may and must be said about it as the reception and possession of divine things, can never be a direct influencing of life, an experience in this sense, but is always the trust and venture of the heart. For faith links the soul to God's invisible, ineffable, unnameable, eternal, and incomprehensible Word, and at the same times severs it from all things visible.[67] Just because revelation is given contingently in Jesus Christ, but given therefore in concealment, the faith that grasps and affirms it is a leap in the dark and never ceases to be so. It is a psychological impossibility, just as revelation is a historical impossibility. It may be conceived — no, it may be asserted and described only as a miracle of the Holy Spirit (the same thing again seen from the other side) that forces us to do what we cannot do, that is, to believe in God, not because we have access to God but because he, the Holy Spirit, is himself God and creates access where there is none.

6. The Spirit forces us, I have just said. He does not do this mechanically or naturalistically, of course, but after the manner of the Spirit. But he does force us. This gives us a glimpse already of the other side of the relation. Divine forcing means demand, law, judgment. Faith is not self-evident. When we believe, a miracle takes place, On this side of the miracle we confront God in all our impossibility. God asks us: "Adam, where art thou?" [cf. Gen. 3:9]. But the question no less than the answer links us to God as God's servants who cannot escape but can only obey, letting our minds be taken captive to the obedience of Christ [cf. 2 Cor. 10:5]. Reason comes into play, not the reason beyond whose limit we are carried as in faith, but the reason whose limit is definitively set for us: revelation in concealment, the crucified Christ, the strange work of God,[68] the possibility of offense and despair, but in all these things *God,* who upholds us, who places himself in our path, who becomes our limit, who demands the keeping of his commands, who demands that we let ourselves be disturbed in our acts, that we learn to consider that we are human and not God, that we are put under a Thou shalt and a Thou shalt not, so that our eyes may be opened and we may give God the glory.

I need hardly say that from this point derive fear and trembling in

---

67. Luther, *E. Op. lat.,* XIV, 81, WA, 5, 69, 29-31. Marginal note: "Calvin, *Inst.* II, 9, 3: Quamvis. . . ." [The passage is to the effect that although Christ offers us a wealth of spiritual blessings, we enjoy them only in hope as the Spirit bids us rely on the promises in which Christ is clad, so that Christ dwells in us but we still walk by faith.]

68. For this familiar expression, which goes back to the Vulgate of Isa. 28:21b, cf. Luther, WA, 1, 112, 24ff.; 6, 63, 36ff.

our relation to God, brokenness and questioning. Trust is possible only if and when there is this assent, this acceptance of God's demand. It is a fearful thing to come up against God's will in revelation. It is not self-evident that this will is gracious, that with the terror that keeps us at a distance from God — genuinely *with* it, for we have here a paradoxical juxtaposition — a childlike faith in the revelation of this God is possible, even if it is only as a prisoner sees the sun through the bars of his window.[69] Nothing is obvious here except that the Holy Spirit who forces us must also make us free, free to believe penitently, as it is only penitently that we can believe.

After these six points I need not discuss in detail the final statement of the thesis. I will simply repeat that no one and nothing can replace the Holy Spirit as the subjective possibility of revelation.[70]

---

69. *Inst.* III, 2, 19.
70. At the bottom of the MS page Barth has the notation: "2 Cor. 10:5."

CHAPTER 2

THE WORD OF GOD AS
HOLY SCRIPTURE

§ 8

The Scripture Principle

Christian preachers dare to talk about God. If this is possible on the basis of the perceived address of God in his revelation, a second presupposition of the venture is that on the basis of a second address of God there is a contemporaneity between people of every age and revelation. The Word of God in this second form, as the communication of God in history, is scripture, naturally not as a record of ancient religions but as holy scripture, that is, as the witness of the prophets and apostles to Jesus Christ in which, and over against which, God the Holy Spirit bears witness to himself.

I. Direct Witness to Revelation

Christian preachers dare to talk about God. With this statement I reach back to the beginning of the first chapter. To avoid the repetition which is needed I would ask you to read again what was said in § 3.I-II about the meaning of the fact denoted by the statement. Much that is pertinent to our present theme was unavoidably dealt with there already. I will sum it up as follows. Starting with the concrete situation of preachers mounting the pulpit steps, in the introductory discussion we came up against the question of the possibility of the venture, and we were finally thrust back against the granite wall of revelation, of the *Deus dixit,* whose central presuppositions and implications we then considered. We next asked to whom the *Deus dixit* is addressed, what is revealed thereby, and how revelation is possible first on God's side, then on ours. The circle that this presupposition of all presuppositions must draw is undoubtedly indicated, if not fully outlined, with the answers that we discovered.

But now we recall the beginning again. We found the most tenable basis of the venture of preaching in the fact that preachers are not private entrepreneurs, that they are not alone, they they belong to a series or order or history, that they have an office. The Christian church dares to talk about God, we said. But if we inquire further along these lines, we do not come up against revelation first, but against something else. The church dares to talk about God on the basis of a historical fact in which it sees its marching orders and working instructions, that is, the biblical canon. We could not stop there, of course, for we wanted to begin at the beginning. Scripture does indeed bear witness to revelation, but it is not revelation itself. The historical heteronomy points us on to an absolute heteronomy. The supreme proof of scripture is always that God speaks in it in person.[1] Thus we again come up against a *Deus dixit,* against revelation behind, above, and beyond the Bible, with its center in the fact of Jesus Christ.

With this in view, we now go back and take up again the question of the canon. Not first of all the church. We can certainly speak about the church already in the context of the concept of revelation. If time had permitted, in a last section of the first chapter I would have discussed the communion of saints as the place where both the objective and the subjective possibilities of revelation are given, the mystical body of Christ,[2] in which the incarnate Son of God and the faith and obedience of his people meet. We must now leave this great truth for dogmatics proper. But in the present context of the question of the Word of God which makes preaching possible, scripture would still stand above the church, as in the same context it must self-evidently stand also above faith and obedience.

It is advisable at this point, if we are not to short-circuit a problem, to start with the direct witness to revelation. For the church, there is always something between it and revelation which makes its relation to revelation either impossible or possible. To put it very bluntly, first of all there is time, the fatal disjunction and succession of history, the ugly ditch about

---

1. See Calvin, *Inst.* I, 7, 4.

2. This expression is common in dogmatic texts from the end of the 12th century; cf. M. Schmaus, *Katholische Dogmatik,* III/1, 3rd-5th ed. (Munich, 1958), pp. 46-47. In a papal pronouncement it is first found in the bull of Boniface VIII, *Unam sanctam* (1302), in DS, 870.

which Lessing had so much to say[3] and that caused so much trouble to the earliest fathers, the incontestable fact that neither they nor we have seen the risen Christ, that he did not appear to us. All this obviously means no more and no less than the impossibility of the relation. Whence then do we have our marching orders and working instructions? How is the present-day church constituted by revelation? With what right does it think it can perceive and proclaim God's Word just as well as the primitive church? If we are not to overturn once again all that we stated concerning the climax of the concept of revelation in the doctrine of the incarnation, in the there and then of Jesus Christ, how can we appeal to the address of God in his revelation for the venture of preaching? Have we really received this address? And how did it come about if we believe we did? Do we not have to assume the existence of a bridge that will lead us from there to here, or will lead revelation from there to here, over the abyss of a shorter or longer time? Do we not need something that will make possible the relation between the church and revelation?

Roman Catholicism and Protestantism part company at this point. Materially the point is, of course, the same one as that which we reached at the beginning of the last section when we had to decide whether receiving the sacraments is the basis of true faith or faith is the basis of true receiving of the sacraments. According to Roman Catholic teaching no bridge is needed over the abyss of the time between revelation and the church. The church is itself the bridge, or rather it is the straight road that leads from revelation to revelation. The church is immediate to revelation. The faith and obedience of individuals may have to be constantly renewed and reestablished, but the church as such, which makes it possible to meet this need, is solidly grounded, beyond question, nondialectical, and direct. From Pius XI and even the humblest village priest to the apostle Peter there is a direct and ultimately only a gradually ascending line, as there is also from the decisions of popes and councils to the Bible, no matter how highly the special dignity of the latter is valued and taught. Roman Catholicism receives and venerates with equal piety and reverence the traditions that have been continually preserved in the church.[4] It is the church that

---

3. Cf. G. E. Lessing, *Über den Beweis des Geistes und der Kraft* (1877), in *Werke,* VIII, ed. G. Göpfert (Munich, 1979), p. 13; ET *Theological Writings,* ed. H. Chadwick (Stanford, 1956), p. 53.

4. *Decretum de libris sacris et de traditionibus recipiendis,* Trent Session, IV (4.8.1546), in DS, 1501.

has given force to scripture, not scripture to the church. Time, the great obstacle of history, plays no part as a problem. The church itself has filled the ditch. The church has the keys of the kingdom once and for all, and the gates of hell shall not prevail against it [Matt. 16:18-19]. Roman Catholics can only laugh at the distinction made in the thesis between a first and a second address of God, and even more so, of course, at that of a third, to which we shall come later. As there is only one Word of God, so for them there is only one address of God to us. As Protestants, however, we have three questions to put to this Roman Catholic solution to the problem.

1. What is the meaning of the opposing Protestant solution which between revelation and the church does in fact see not a second Word of God but a second address of God, the Word of God as scripture, by which the church is first established as the church, and in which the church must always seek its basis? At all events it denotes a differentiation, a break, a disruption of the relation. It means the assertion of a special mediation of revelation alongside the church itself, and even before the church, as the organ by means of which revelation communicates itself. This bridge obviously sets the church itself radically in question. The church no longer has its back unconditionally free. One day the bridge might be blocked, or at worst it might collapse. Remember that scripture is a historical entity. It is the historical beginning which as such has at any rate far-reaching significance for the continuation of the relation between revelation and the church. It certainly cannot be detached from the obvious connection between the two, but in this context it serves in principle as a question mark and an exclamation mark.

Here, in the relation of the church to scripture, the decision is made again, and must always be made afresh, whether the church's relation to revelation is genuine and legitimate or not. Or not? Does not this introduce ambiguity into the contemporaneity of the church and revelation which the church plainly ought to be able to believe and teach as unambiguous? Thus the question "whether or not" is an open one, and if the church by its very existence is not itself a positive decision, then who is to decide? It is not a good sign for Protestants, or for the depth of their view, if they do not feel the difficulties that afflict the scripture principle as compared to the church principle of Roman Catholics. It is not a good sign if they cannot present or hear the Roman Catholic doctrine without a certain homesickness for its unheard-of soberness and certainty. It is not a good sign if they have an immediate desire for polemics at this point.

2. What, then, can we always learn from the Roman Catholic doctrine? As in the case of the sacraments, we can certainly learn that in the question of what establishes the church, when Roman Catholics simply say the church again with redoubled force, we are not to propose something insignificant and indecisive; that where Roman Catholics make a loud and joyful confession we are not to mutter and mumble; that the introduction of the scripture principle must not mean at once a second ambiguity. A *question,* a threat, a shaking of the church indeed; Protestantism stands or falls with this. But a question of the same caliber must be introduced at the point where Roman Catholicism gives its very loud and sure answer by equating Christ and the church. Only the question of Christ, put for the sake of the genuineness and vitality of the answer, can be a match for the specific force of the Roman Catholic teaching. This, then, is what the scripture principle of Protestantism must mean — not that we halfheartedly abandon the unconditional contemporaneity of the church with revelation, but that we are seeking it in order to find it, wooing it in order to have it, receiving it in order to possess it. We must outbid rather than underbid the Roman Catholic doctrine in order that the decision "whether or not" may not be anticipated but referred to a real historical entity — scripture. It must be clear that in this regard we are not doing the same as when Pilate is brought into the creed, but remembering that God is the living God whom we have learned to know in the doctrine of the Trinity, and that his is an immutable subjectivity, so that we are again leaving it in his hands whether there is revelation across the times and in the history of all times, whether there is a church. Only when by the scripture that we interpose between revelation and the church we do not simply mean the historical entity, but we unequivocally mean God's Word, *God's* Word, which sets revelation in the church in question because it is a recollection of revelation itself — only then, to put it modestly and cautiously, does the Protestant scripture principle stand on the same level as the Roman Catholic church principle.

In my view we should not evade the older Protestant paradox that is so often ridiculed, namely, that in sum scripture is for us what the pope is for them.[5] In making such a transposition, we cannot view scripture

---

5. Cf. E. Troeltsch, "Protestantisches Christentum und Kirche in der Neuzeit," in *Die Kultur der Gegenwart*, I, IV, 1, ed. P. Hinneberg (Berlin/Leipzig, 1906), p. 265. Troeltsch seems to have been alluding to J. Gerhard, *Loci theologici . . .* (Tübingen, 1762), I, p. 56, whom he quotes in full in *Vernunft und Offenbarung bei Johann Gerhard und Melanchthon* (Göttingen, 1891), p. 28.

merely as a religious record, as the earliest and hence the normative account of the historical origins of Christianity. As though a record of this kind, no matter what it records, could be normative for what is or is not revelation for those who live on their own responsibility today! As though a bridge of this kind could bear the weight of revelation in its passage from the past to the present, or could carry us from a revelation-less present back to the past! As though we could talk seriously of what is first and normative when we simply have something that is historically different — the religion of insignificant people in the ancient Near East! This would be just like putting Pilate in the creed. No Herder-like enthusiasm for the originality and value and beauty of the Bible in this sense[6] should blind us to the fact that this means a surrender of the scripture principle, that with such an apotheosis of history we are entering on a way which by a broad detour, of course, might lead us straight back to the Roman Catholic doctrine, and that in this case it would be more perspicacious, honest, and sensible to take the more direct path. If, then, we are to espouse the Protestant doctrine we must understand the historical entity of scripture in a true and radical dialectic as the Word of God. If we do not, Roman Catholicism may justly ask us how we can measure the greater by the smaller. It may rightly protest that the Protestant scripture principle disrupts and even destroys the indispensable contemporaneity with revelation. To measure the great by a greater, to point with a new credibility to the affirmed contemporaneity, must be the basic concern of the Protestant doctrine of scripture.

3. In this light we may then ask: Why and to what extent must we reject the Roman Catholic doctrine? If it is to be worth our while to make it, our objection must be aware how perilous our own Protestant position is. It must be made from a point which is at least on a level with the Roman Catholic doctrine. It must also concern what is central and not what is external or accidental. Finally, it must be clear and definite and confident. Thus we too maintain, or rather we believe, the contemporaneity of the church with revelation, the presence of God's Word in the church of today. We have to say this or else we are attacking not Roman Catholicism but the Christian church.

But the question — and this is where our protest begins — is whether this presence may be assumed to be given by the historical sequence of the church as a whole, or whether by its very nature (for it is

---

6. Cf. Herder's *Spirit of Hebrew Poetry* (1782/83).

the presence of *God's* Word) it does not have to be established and sought and found and given afresh for each member of the series, and I do not just mean for each individual Christian, though that is also true, but for each age in the church. The question is whether we do well to establish contemporaneity by ignoring or setting aside the problem of time, the ugly ditch, or whether the temporality of revelation does not work itself out and reflect itself in the recognition of a temporally conditioned form of the communication of revelation too. The question is whether in the form of a sure and self-established and triumphant church we can make revelation in concealment into open, direct, and unequivocal revelation, or whether there is not a connection between the inalienable concealment of revelation and a time-related, historical form of its historical propagation and communication to later generations, an unforgettable and unavoidable connection between the cross of Christ and the necessary distance that the church of Christ must keep from the normative historical principle that gives it birth.

The most incisive argument of the Reformers in their polemic against the Roman Catholic view of the church is plainly their association of it with the enthusiasts, their statement that in the medieval church and the spiritualizing forerunners of modern Christianity we have an illegitimate immediacy of revelation that both sought to achieve by leaping past the written Word, that in both we have an apotheosis of history or of every present as the quintessence, or the normative, divinely willed evolutionary result, of a temporal sequence that is per se filled with revelation — an apotheosis which infringes on the honor of God, who reserves it for himself to reveal himself or to be revealed individually and specifically to every age, and even to every age in the church. We may meaningfully continue this polemic today by pointing out that there is unmistakable kinship between the Roman Catholic concept of the church and the modern concept of history as it is found especially in Herder and the Romantics, and that at least up to our own day there have always been those who with remarkable ease and swiftness have found their way from the latter to the former. The church is obviously secure against the confusion of the church and history only when it places itself under a criterion in which it unambiguously seeks (if not finds), and knows to be unambiguously given, the distinction between what belongs to history and what belongs truly and validly to the church, that is, that which in its existence is the communication of revelation and not just human development. If the church is really to know its nature not merely as the Christian world (i.e., as the religious counterpart of the usual world) but as the place where God's Word is proclaimed and received, then it must know a place from which it may expect God's decision concerning its worth or worthlessness; a place where for the sake of the authority that it claims for itself, it sets itself as the communion of saints under God's authority; a place where, knowing itself to be the body of Christ, it invokes the judgment and mercy of God; a place in which it perceives not merely the source but the absolutely superior *ratio* by which it is what it is and for this reason must continually become what it is (since it is what it is in time). It is not enough if Roman Catholic apologetics simply names Christ himself, or the Spirit who was promised to the church and poured out upon it at Pentecost, as this higher place which stands above the church and the authority of its offices, traditions, and decisions. We will refrain from disputing this, but if Christ and the Spirit are really to denote a criterion or place above the church, then we have to be referring to the crucified Christ whose life is revealed in the church only to the extent that it is revealed to it and against it, and to the Holy Spirit for whom even after Pentecost the church (not just the individual believer but the church of Christ as such) has to pray as an essential function of its existence: "Come, Creator Spirit," and to pray this with the same earnestness as one does when praying for what one does not have. Thus the asserted presence of Christ and the Spirit necessarily includes tension between the first coming of Christ as promise and the second coming at his return as consummation.

At any rate we may and must seriously ask whether the church principle of Roman Catholicism, its appeal to Christ and the Spirit, does not suspiciously obscure and erase and weaken these points if it does not deny them outright. How else can we understand the direct step to revelation which the Roman Catholic church thinks it can take at any moment, the triumphant evading or ignoring of the problem of time which it believes it can achieve, except as a basically non-eschatological if not totally anti-eschatological view? In this light we can appreciate that the younger Luther thought he could reduce his protest against the medieval church to the formula "theology of the cross" as distinct from "theology of glory,"[7] and that later in the Schmalcaldic Articles he wanted to make the thesis that the pope is Antichrist an article of faith.[8] It is along these

---

7. Cf. *Disputatio Heidelbergae habita* (1518), Thesis 21, WA, 1, 354, 21-22, and the development of the thesis, WA, 1, 362, 20-34; LW, 31, 40 and 53.

8. *BSLK*, p. 430.30-32; p. 432.33; Tappert, pp. 300-301.

lines that Protestantism must understand itself. This is the drift of its protest. This is its suspicion and objection when it comes up against the church principle of Roman Catholicism. Whether we moderns are capable of making the objection is another question, but we must make it if we are to have a good conscience. Under the guise of a very real theocracy does not this principle involve a most subtle glorification of history and humanity? Under appeal to union with Christ and the presence of the Spirit does it not involve an actual denial of both? Does not its brilliant establishment of contemporaneity with revelation involve a fatal threat to it?

The basis of the objection, then, is that the place where Roman Catholic teaching finds the criterion, where the distinction is made and the divine decision falls, even though this place may be called Christ or the Spirit, really lies just as much within the church itself — the analogy is unmistakable — as does Schleiermacher's God within religious feeling. The church is simply affirming itself when it affirms Christ, and it is simply talking to itself when it pretends to be listening to the Spirit or speaking in Christ's name. The place outside and above the church whose evident presence would destroy this suspicion, establish the analogy to the hiddenness of revelation, to the crucified Christ, and maintain rather than set aside the paradox of the temporality, uniqueness, and contingency of the primary Word of God in this secondary form of historical mediation; the place where the relation between the church and revelation is really set up and is therefore sought and continually sought afresh not merely by individuals but by the church as such — this place must lie in history no less than the church itself, confronting the church as something just as contingent, temporally accidental, repellent, and offensive, carrying with it in a divinely mysterious way both promise and threat, and proclaiming them to the world no less than the church itself does.

Only when it stands under a *real* crisis can the church itself be a real crisis for the world. The Roman Catholic church, we go on to say, does indeed set the world under its own judgment executed in God's name, but it does so without legitimacy, not having placed itself in the same sense under the judgment of the same God. It knows no historical place, superior in principle in this historicity, from which the judgment of God passes upon it, and precisely in so doing equips it for its divine vocation to the rest of history. It knows no criterion that is not set up in and with its own existence, but under which it stands from century to century and indeed from hour to hour. In the last analysis it knows only itself. Even though it feels that it is a maid, it cannot forget for a moment that it is the queen. It may reform itself, but it cannot repent in head and members and let itself be reformed. For who or what is the counterpart which might do this reforming? It knows Christ and the Spirit, but not in a distinction in principle from itself. It will not have it that its contemporaneity with revelation, to be real and authentic, must be questioned and established by a Word of God which is not at all contemporary but historical and time-bound. It does not know and will not know the antithesis, tension, or friction between a divine moment and a human moment from which the presence of revelation springs out like a spark and has to spring out again and again. Everything depends on that divine moment being a real, historical, conditioned moment, but also on its being this divine moment, and as such supreme, normative, critical, and fruitful in principle, even though it belongs to the same series as other human moments. This is how it must be if revelation is to enter history and history is to have a part in revelation. There has to be antithesis, but antithesis between equals, between history and history, between moment and moment. Roman Catholic teaching denies this. It knows only the sequence of the church's moments, all in a directly given relation to revelation, so that this relation, in contrast to all these moments, has to be realized and to come into effect in a divine moment within the same sequence. It knows no relative heteronomy, only the absolute heteronomy that derives from its own *nomos*. We doubt whether there can be any absolute heteronomy for those who will not bow to a relative one. Its temporality is permanently filled with eternity. We doubt whether this can be true eternity. Nothing *takes place* in matters of this relation. Everything is already there. We do not believe that this is how things are in the realm of truth. Our conclusion, to put it radically, is that it knows no holy scripture (in infinite qualitative distinction from other writings). We regard this as wrong.

A Protestant polemic that knows what it wants must move along these lines. It must do so, at least, if we regard it as advisable to engage in polemics against Roman Catholicism. But perhaps there are reasons to leave the matter for the time being. For such arguments will have force and weight again only when they are presented with the older, raging, and fearful anger of the Reformers, only when we dare to go on to say with Luther, for example, that the pope is Antichrist. But we need all our breath to do this, for it is something very different from the usual Protestant grumbling at Rome, whose fervor normally derives most inappropriately from popular national, rationalistic, and Christian elements. This means that there is something which must be said against the papal church solely in terms of Christian principle, but it must be said by an inner necessity, that is, by a material necessity which is clearly based on our own position. To have the breath to do this, and to say something adequate against Roman Catholicism, we need a good conscience. But modern Protestantism does not have a good conscience. At root it does all the same things (but very ineptly) that it might accuse Roman Catholicism of doing. We find in it the forbidden immediacy, the direct manipulation of Christ and the Spirit, the underhand and hence not genuinely achieved contemporaneity, the abrogation of scripture as the independent Word of God in history, the conjuring away of the historical offense by the historicizing of revelation, the forgetting of a criterion that stands above the church. It has long since raised all these things to the level of a principle, but in a nonclassical, disreputable, hole-in-a-corner way, whereas Roman Catholicism has done it in a classical, noble, magnificent, and imposing way. It is heir not so much to the Reformers (for details see Troeltsch)[9] as to the left-wing opposition that the Reformers had to fight against. Unbroken threads undoubtedly lead us from the Anabaptists to Pietism, Zinzendorf, and Schleiermacher, and from the Radicals to the Socinians, the Remonstrants, the Rationalists, and Schleiermacher again, and then from Schleiermacher to ourselves. I would hazard the statement, therefore, that Roman Catholicism with its church principle and modern Protestantism are counterbalancing heresies, and if I had to choose between them I am not sure whether I would not have to prefer the classical heresy to the nonclassical one. At all events we have to realize that the Reformers' protest against the church principle applies above all to ourselves and leaves us in the air. For this reason I think it advisable to stop all inveighing against Rome, or to do it with tongue in cheek if the concrete situation so demands. For a long time we shall have our hands full putting our own house in order. Much later, perhaps, we can again think of protesting against what goes on elsewhere.

II. The Scripture Principle of Protestantism

We shall now try to give a positive account of the scripture principle of Protestantism, and then consider its basis in a third subsection. Please

---

9. Cf. E. Troeltsch, *Protestantisches Christentum und Kirche in der Neuzeit,* pp. 304-5.

remember in what follows that this principle is not my own invention, and that you must ascribe the difficulties and knotty points that come to light not to me but to the material nexus of Christian teaching into which we now place ourselves if we do not regard the Roman Catholic or the modern Protestant view as tenable. As we wrestle with these difficulties and knotty points, not trying to avoid them but seeking to understand them as necessary, let us remember that we are wrestling implicitly for an understanding of Luther and the whole Reformation, and not merely for an understanding but for the right to be called their legitimate heirs. The Reformation stands or falls with its scripture principle. If we really draw back here, I do not see why tomorrow we should not become Roman Catholics again.

1. At this point on our path, let us recall once more where we first came up against scripture. We saw that the church traces back its essential work of preaching to the historical datum of the canon, of a collection of literature in which it recognizes a ruler or plumb line or rule, an imperative: "Go and preach" [cf. Mark 16:15], preach *this,* preach *in this way.* The question of the meaning of the canon, of the basis of its constraint, of the authority of this authority, of the absolute heteronomy that is reflected in this relative heteronomy, then led us to revelation, to the author of scripture.

Let us now stop at scripture as such. In no way can it be self-evident that there should be a body of literature which, without itself being revelation, sets us before revelation, points us to it, and bears witness to it. If there really is such a thing, if scripture is related in this way to revelation, then something special has to be said about it. In this regard it is different from all other writings. How does it come to be even the reflection or echo or historical mediation of revelation? If we remain strictly faithful to our concept of revelation, we shall now recall again that God can be known only by God. God can make himself known only by God. We thus come to the center of the concept of revelation, to the fact of Jesus Christ. If, then, God gives himself to be known by scripture, even if only relatively in the form of an indication or historical mediation, we can hardly avoid seeing in this mediation God's own Word, the *logos,* even if in a special form which is distinct from the incarnation and stands over against it, not now in the form of God's direct speaking, but only indirectly in the form of human speaking about God in the face of God's own speaking, in the form of a "Thus saith the Lord" whose content will then be human, earthly, historical words. This participation of human words in God's Word is the principial element in the scripture principle.

2. These human words are the words of the prophets and apostles as the witnesses of Jesus Christ. I have tried to show in § 6.III that in this context we must put the OT and the NT together. Here, with reference to the distinction between witnesses of the Christ who is expected and witnesses of the Christ who has come, I would speak of a "fluid" distinction, a distinction of more or less. The prophets are the former witnesses, the apostles the latter. But the prophets are also apostles and the apostles are also prophets. Their seeing and hearing and therefore their speaking differ. But incomparably more important than this difference is the unity in their theme, in the revelation that they see and hear and believe and obey and speak about. In contrast, they all differ in principle from all the others to whom revelation is mediated by their witness, even though the success of their mediation is that through them revelation is visible and audible and credible and authoritative for these others in exactly the same way as it is for them, and even though among these others there might be those who can be called witnesses of Jesus Christ just as much as they can, and who, historically considered, might have been much more active and powerful and illuminating witnesses of Jesus Christ than these first witnesses.

In terms of experience there are few among us who do not have to confess in all honesty that we have been placed before the reality of revelation much more impressively and clearly by some such later witness, for example, Luther, or it may be a little, unknown witness, than by Paul or John, not to speak of Jude or the Apocalyptist, or one of the in some ways very odd witnesses of the OT. A professor of theology once told me that he had learned much more from his devout mother than from the whole Bible. To this our reply must be that recognition of the special dignity of the biblical witnesses is not a matter of one experience among others. It is all very well to realize, perhaps, that one may learn more from all kinds of greater or lesser prophets or apostles of a later period, or even of our own time, than from reading the Bible. Yet the issue is not where we learn most, but where we learn the one thing, the truth. It is not a matter of arguing that the Bible is the finest book, but that it is the standard of all fine books. Our learning or experience is in any case indirect, and so are the sources on which we draw. Let us presuppose that it really is Jesus Christ or revelation that is mediated to us; the question then arises how we know this, how we are to recognize it. The question is that of a norm or rule which is indubitably above me but also above my closest authorities. The real question is not the question of what impresses me most sharply but the question of what is the truth, what is revelation, in that which impresses me. It is thus the question of the canon, and this is the question to which the Christian answer is given. All our lives we may perhaps get more from other witnesses who are more directly accessible[10] to us and better understood by us, and yet (perhaps for this very reason) we may still recognize that there have to be witnesses in a different sense whose witness must vouch for the credibility and authority of the first witnesses and by whose witness they must be measured[11] if they are to have credibility and authority.

Nevertheless, are not these other, firsthand witnesses human too? Is not their witness a relative historical entity? Would it not be better to go back from our own experience, from the most impressive sources of experience that we know, immediately and directly to revelation itself, to Christ and the Spirit? As we saw last time, this is the way of the Roman Catholic church, and in a rather nonclassical way of modern Protestantism as well. We have seen why this way is impossible. If we are not to pursue a theology of glory, then a real, authenticated, and incontestably superior mediation of revelation which finally answers the question of truth must stand so much above history that in keeping with the concealment of revelation and the cross of Christ, as the mediation of revelation and full of the divine mystery, it stands in history itself. What is demanded at this point is precisely a relative historical entity, that is, human beings and their human words. To eliminate this contingent entity which gives such urgency to the question of faith or offense would be equivalent to eliminating the concealment of revelation and therefore revelation itself. The recognition that revelation is not a part of human history as such, that we have it only as we are given it, that our experience, even though we learn from a devout mother or a Luther or an Augustine, stands under a final *caveat,* under the crisis of the question of truth — this recognition, if it is to be authentic, must take the form of a recognition not merely of revelation itself, which might be the forbidden leap into immediacy, but also of a canon in the realm of mediacy, in a halting of the movement back to the sources on this side of revelation. Faith that Jesus Christ is the Son of God must derive strength from an admission that the communication that brings us this truth, if it is to be able to do so, if it is to be strong enough as a bridge for this movement, must share in what Jesus Christ himself is

---

10. The editor has here corrected the "more directly more accessible" of the MS.
11. The editor has here corrected the "it must be measured" of the MS.

(i.e., God's Word), and must therefore share also in his uniqueness, historicity, and contingency. Like through like in both cases.

If we see this, then we see the distinction in principle between the prophets and apostles on the one side, and the church fathers, Reformers, religious geniuses, and devout mothers on the other. The latter may in fact give us a hundred times more, but if they are to give us not merely reality but the truth of revelation, if what is given us is in truth to be divinely given, then a beginning of all this giving and receiving has to be presupposed which is a beginning not merely in time but also in principle, yet not merely in principle but also in time. This beginning is the credibility and authority of the apostles and prophets: the Word of God not merely as revelation but also as holy scripture.

3. It would be fruitless to try to close our eyes to a paradox that can only be perceived and not resolved, namely, that of the thesis that scripture is God's Word. We may now simply add the necessary negation. To say that scripture is God's Word is to say that we do not know Christ outside or alongside scripture but only in scripture. We also know nothing about the Holy Spirit apart from scripture. We know nothing about a church where there is no scripture. But scripture does not mean the personal life and experience of the authors beyond the text, nor some kind of history, for example, that of the people of Israel, the life of Jesus, or the history of the primitive church, nor anything at all beyond the thoughts that are presented in words and sentences. There can be no denying, of course, that this "beyond," that is, the religion and piety and inner life of a Paul or a Jeremiah, or that threefold history, is present and even to some extent recognizable. But what would give us the courage to call *that* the Word of God? There *is* a "beyond" in scripture. This is the Word of God, namely, revelation. But we must insist that revelation meets us only indirectly, only in scripture — there is no escaping this — and this means in biblical texts, in words and sentences. The prophets and apostles and their witness exist for us only in this way. Those who construct other realities by means of the text, whether in the form of their own spiritual history or the life of Jesus, may perhaps find wonderful things, but they no longer find the prophets and apostles and their witness. If we want to hear the prophets and apostles and their witness, we must listen to what they were trying to say and did say, not to things that we might perhaps hear in them and that for various reasons may perhaps interest us more than what they did say, for example, the processes of their inner lives, or certain purely historical relations, or this

or that antiquarian reference.[12] The texts bear *witness,* and *the texts* are the witness that we are to perceive. We cannot leap out of this circle. The reality of revelation is indirectly identical with the reality of scripture. Indirectly, for the Bible is not the same as revelation. The tension remains. The Bible is one thing and revelation another. Nevertheless, we have revelation not in itself but in the Bible. For we have the witnesses of revelation, those upon whom its reflection rests, the prophets and apostles, only as they presented themselves, that is, in the Bible, in the texts of the Bible.

In this very specific sense, then, the Bible is the first mediation and norm, the standard or principle of all communication, the historical basis of all experience, the salutary caveat that must be set over against all experience. As we have said, there can be no undermining the paradox of this thesis. It will simply be by way of elucidation if I say that precisely at the point where in Platonic and Kantian thinking the regulative idea has to stand, here we find the codex of the Old and New Testaments; that precisely at the point where philosophy speaks about the relation of the human consciousness to the infinite or, more religiously, about the divine likeness and fellowship which humanity cannot forfeit, here what is at issue is God's new and once-for-all message to us, his making of his thoughts both finite and human. God gives his revelation a suitable, relevant, and historical form, that is, an absolutely factual form, that of the word of the prophets and apostles. He makes this human word his own Word for all ages by his Spirit, who made the prophets prophets and the apostles apostles, who opened their eyes and ears and then their lips, who made them the witnesses of his revelation. The record of this unique witness — unique because revelation itself is unique — is the Bible.

4. In conclusion we may perhaps relax the tension and ease the burden by recalling that in all this we do not have to withdraw the Bible from purely historical consideration. Naturally, like any other literature, the Bible has its place in the history of literature, culture, and religion. Naturally this applies without restriction to all parts of the Bible and in every direction in which these disciplines might push out their feelers.[13] Naturally they have to work with the methods which they use in dealing

---

12. N. p. 105 adds: "The moment we inquire into the background of scripture, theology ends and philosophy begins."

13. N. p. 106 adds: "These disciplines are all legitimate so long as they do not call themselves theology."

with other subjects. If we were to contest this, even in part, we would be cutting the ground from under our own feet, the ground of the historical, unique, and contingent, which is ambivalent as such. For the sake of the concealment of revelation, its communication must always be a human affair. For this reason, precisely on a theological view, the 17th-century doctrine of verbal inspiration, the idea that the biblical authors did not think and write on their own but simply took down heavenly dictation, is so deplorable. This view changes revelation into direct revelation. It thus sets it aside. It does not just put scripture in the pope's place but makes it a pope, a paper pope, from which we are to get oracles as we get shoes from a shoemaker.

This view is obviously a sign that believers no longer understood the statement that scripture is God's Word. They could no longer bear the paradox of it.[14] They could no longer bear to stand on the knife-edge between faith and unbelief in face of this purely historical entity. They could no longer bear to read the Bible as a human word, to read the texts exactly as they are with all that they imply when read historically. They could no longer face up to the great and unavoidable temptation to see in them absolutely nothing but the record of a Near Eastern tribal religion and a Hellenistic cult religion (one of a dozen); the great temptation to find the Bible interesting or not in the same way as everything human is interesting or not; the great temptation to treat the Bible objectively as though it did not mean much or anything for them, or to run wild subjectively and to take from it all kinds of things that have nothing whatever to do with revelation. They could no longer bear to see that they might indeed in some way yield to these temptations very honestly, seriously, and earnestly, then laugh in the face of the whole seriousness of this approach that seems, and more than seems, to be the only possible one, and still hear as God's Word these texts that are defenselessly tossed to the winds, hearing them as the witness to revelation, to Jesus Christ, as records of prophecy and fulfilment rather than religious history, as the work of prophets and apostles rather than religious geniuses, not as texts like others, but as texts in which contingently — very contingently — the Spirit speaks God's Word, so that it is well worthwhile to ponder them word for word — the doctrine of verbal inspiration has truth in it in this regard.

The theologians of the 17th century no longer had the courage to

---

14. The editor has here changed the *ihre Paradoxie* of the MS to *seine Paradoxie* to show that the reference is to "the statement" rather than "scripture."

face this paradox. They did not have too much faith but too little. They did not see in the growing seriousness of the historical approach a challenge to balance the scales the other way, to undertake the venture of faith and obedience more boldly. They thought that they should restrict the historical approach by a mechanization and stabilization of the Word of God that reaches back to the most primitive elements in religion. As though God's Word, because of the unbelief of theologians in particular, would want to be made proof against doubt by being committed to paper like canon law!

I need not describe the disaster which then followed on the other side. Marching, not without cause, under the banner of truth and credibility, historicism would never have taken on the openly anti-Christian significance that it did had Christianity itself, and especially Christian theology, ventured to insist on its own truth and credibility, and to maintain the *indirect* identity of the Bible with revelation. This is what we today have to learn again — and it will be a very painful process. We will have a harder job than Luther in this regard. We will have to accept all that has taken place in the intervening period as an inescapable factor in European thinking. The wrathful judgment of historicism, with its claim to sole validity which crushes all faith and promotes all kinds of religious nonsense, hangs over us like an endlessly pouring thundercloud. For this reason no one can be angry at us if we do not find it so easy to be joyful theologians in the way that Luther so often was. We must be glad at least to know again that there is a sun above the clouds and to realize that the flood might have an end. This will not mean that we should close our eyes again to the historical reality of the Bible but that with the same eyes we should see again how precisely in this reality the Bible is *indirectly* revelation *for us*.

III. The Historical Reality of Revelation

We must now discuss how it is that the Bible in its historical reality comes to be the communication of revelation for us, and as such God's Word. If we study the painful history of the Protestant scripture principle in the last three centuries, and perceive even something of the sense and nonsense in it, then we shall first consider that the great perspicacity that is needed to answer this question, and the great simplicity that has already answered it before it is asked, must come together and indeed be one and the same if we do not want to fall into one of the big historical pits that threaten us on both the right side of our path and the left. The plight in which we still find ourselves began when cleverness and simplicity parted company, and subtlety on the one side, limitation on the other, carefully concealed unbelief here and equally carefully concealed superstition there, came to mark the situation. This is what we must avoid. Simplicity is necessary if we are to put all our cards on the table, cleverness also if we are to play them well.

Let us begin at once with the unavoidable insight that the Bible cannot come to be God's Word if it is not this already. In principle all that we might say in establishment of the scripture principle can be only a very clever paraphrase of this childishly simple statement. In the Reformation period and later, Protestant and Roman Catholic theologians debated the question whether the authenticity and authority that we ascribe to holy scripture are established and guaranteed by scripture itself or by the authority of the church. Roman Catholic theology naturally took the latter view. The saying of Augustine that he would not have believed the gospel if the authority of the church had not compelled him to do so[15] was a commonly adduced proof text which Protestants not too convincingly took to mean that while scripture does indeed become God's authoritative Word in the church, it does not do so by the church but by itself. Thus the Dutch theologian Riissen argued that we cannot distinguish between an authority of scripture in itself and an authority for us. Either scripture has no authority or the two are identical. Arguments for the former ought to persuade us to accept the latter.[16] And Cocceius thought that to assume that what God has spoken may be doubted or has to be proved does injury to scripture, as though there were no radiance of divinity in it.[17] If only these theologians had had the perception to cling to this simplicity *not merely* in opposition to the church principle of Roman Catholicism!

Insofar as they did so, the idea has remained a sound one right up to our own time. Thus we do best to begin here. As the introduction to the Second Helvetic Confession puts it, we believe and confess that the canonical scriptures have sufficient authority from themselves and not from humans. God himself spoke to the patriarchs, prophets, and apostles,

---

15. Cf. Augustine, *Contra epistulam Manichaeorum*, 5, 6, CSEL, 25/I, 197, 22-23.
16. Heppe, p. 19; Heppe-Bizer, p. 20; ET p. 21.
17. Heppe, p. 18; Heppe-Bizer, p. 19; ET p. 18.

and he speaks to us through the holy scriptures.[18] What Zwingli said about grace must obviously apply without restriction to the revelation of grace and hence also to its communication across the abyss of the centuries: "Nothing can make us certain of the grace of God but God himself."[19] Unfortunately, however, the virile straightforwardness of the reply that scripture *is* God's Word because it is *God's* Word did not persist except in the polemic against Roman Catholicism. The basic statements of the Reformation itself — the confessional writings are normative in this regard — betray a remarkable tendency to develop this one argument into an apparent multiplicity of arguments. The appeal to scripture finds support in the declaration that it is the oldest and most perfect philosophy.[20] Or its perspicuity, sufficiency, and perfection are praised[21] (in matters of salvation, the English prudently added, thus leaving themselves a free hand in practical life).[22] All this was harmless only to the degree that all these superlative generalities could admittedly amount to no more than an analysis of the concept of divine, final, and absolute authority, or paraphrases of the statement that scripture is the Word of God.

It was a more serious matter when people began to be noticeably more specific and to stress miracles, the fulfilment of OT prophecies, and the like. Although making little use of them later, even Calvin, so as not to omit anything, did not hesitate to refer expressly to such things, though not for eternity, one should say.[23] The Westminster Confession in 1647 can adduce the following proofs: the witness of the church, the heavenly contents of the Bible, the force of its teaching, the majesty of its style, the agreement of all its parts, its aim to glorify God, its usefulness in showing the way of salvation.[24]

I need hardly say that this line of argument brings us into a sphere in which the pros and cons are secretly or openly set alongside one another, in which we cannot do more than advance probabilities, and in which it

---

18. *BSRK,* p. 170.26-30; Schaff, p. 831.

19. *Fidei ratio,* in *BSRK,* p. 81.47 (Barth has *nihil hominem certum* for the original *nihil enim illum certum*); ET (Durham, NC, 1983), p. 39.

20. Barth quotes the Latin translation (1581) of the First Helvetic Confession; cf. J. C. G. Augusti, *Corpus Librorum Symbolicorum . . . ,* 2nd ed. (Lipsiae, 1846), p. 94 (Art. 1); cf. Schaff, p. 211.

21. Cf. *BSRK,* p. 257.39; p. 411.8; p. 506.33-34; p. 527.1ff.; p. 872.16ff.; p. 913.1ff.

22. Cf. the Westminster Confession (1647), I, 7, in Schaff, p. 604.

23. *Inst.* I, 8.

24. See *BSRK,* p. 544.30(-39).

is not impossible that one day the opposite might be stated and proved. How, then, if we rely on such arguments? That day has obviously come. At all events, such things can be said only in brackets and were not meant as the real proof even in the 17th century and on into the 18th. The heading of Calvin's chapter tells us that the reliability of scripture does not rest on such arguments as are open to human reason, and the final statement calls into question everything that precedes when it says that it is foolish to try to prove to unbelievers that scripture is God's Word, for this can be known only by faith.[25] In its conclusion the Westminster Confession resigns itself to a similar statement.[26]

In all these ancient documents the *one* reason or proof for the authority of the Bible is not to be confused with other arguments or proofs that might be adduced. It stands in splendid isolation in Calvin.[27] One can only say that in that early Protestant period the right foot stood on good and solid ground, but the left foot, though always ready to retreat, touched lightly on marshy ground which might easily give way. So long as the right foot was firmly planted on the soil of the one and only argument, and it was realized that the weight should never fall on the left,[28] on the other arguments, apologetics was a game that a Calvin might play to the glory of God. But when these presuppositions are not present, the ineluctable movement is into a dead end in which we see rationalists and supernaturalists, believers and unbelievers, fighting about something whose true significance escapes both. For if the thesis that scripture is God's Word is seriously doubted or seriously proved, it may be all kinds of things but it is not any longer the Protestant scripture principle. That thesis is the Protestant scripture principle only to the extent that it stands firm, that it can be neither seriously doubted nor seriously proved, that the decision about recognizing and acknowledging it is not a question that we can answer but that God himself has answered, answers, and will answer, in and by scripture.

We must reaccustom ourselves to this thought in order to learn to appreciate and use again the only solid ground on which we can stand. We would do well, then, to hasten past that dead end with a quick nod even though we find Calvin himself at the entrance to it. *We* can no longer

---

25. Cf. the heading of *Inst.* I, 8; and the final statement in I, 8, 13.

26. Cf. Schaff, pp. 602-3. (The reference is to the full conviction and certainty of the infallibility of scripture that come only by the inner work of the Spirit.)

27. *Inst.* I, 7.

28. N. p. 109 adds "foot."

play the apologetic game to God's glory. Let us then stick to the oldest and simplest version of the Reformation concept: Only the Word of God himself can bear witness to the Word of God in scripture. As Calvin says in a statement that is often quoted and often censured, scripture cannot achieve full authority among believers until they recognize that it comes from heaven as if the living voice of God were heard in it.[29] How do we know this if we are not to believe it on the authority of the church? In exactly the same way as when we ask how to distinguish light and darkness, black and white, sweet and bitter, Calvin continues.[30] Recognition of the authority of the Bible coincides with recognition of God as its author. We do not praise the prophets and apostles for their acumen. They claim no credibility for themselves. They offer no reasons in proof. They advance the holy name of the Lord whereby to compel the whole world to obey. God alone can be a competent witness on his own behalf. Scripture is *autopistos,* and we are forbidden to submit it to any argument or proof.[31]

But what does this self-evidence of holy scripture mean? In formal logic the statement undoubtedly has the form of a philosophical or mathematical axiom, and when Calvin refers to the difference between light and darkness, etc., he seems materially to bring it into very close proximity to such axioms. But the resemblance is only formal, and the passage finally does no more than refer to the analogy of axiomatic statements. The statement itself is not an axiom because it relates to a contingent entity, holy scripture. We would have to call it an axiom of a totally contingent kind, and that would destroy the whole concept of an axiom. Thus philosophy and mathematics give us no help. The certainty in question has to be a very different one.

The time has now come to recall a concept that we have left aside for a while, namely, that of the Spirit. As we saw in the doctrine of revelation, the Spirit is God as he turns to us, addresses us, discloses himself to us, opens our eyes and ears, gives us faith and obedience, and intercedes with us. Scripture, corresponding to the incarnation, is itself *logos* as the objective possibility of historical communication. Similarly, its subjective communication, its self-evidence, that in it which enforces authority, corresponding to the basis of faith and obedience, is itself spirit. By the Spirit scripture bears witness that it is God's Word. It needs no other

---

29. *Inst.* I, 7, 1.
30. Ibid., I, 7, 2.
31. Ibid., I, 7, 5.

arguments, and there is no possibility of doubting it, because *in* it as the witness of the prophets and apostles, and also *over against* it (and therefore in us), God the Spirit bears witness to himself. The only competent witness in this matter has spoken, speaks, and will speak — the inner testimony of the Spirit.[32] But how are we to define more closely the significance of this absolutely decisive factor in the present context?

Two ways suggest themselves. At the end of the one stands the 17th-century theory of inspiration, at the end of the other the modern theology of experience. To work out this idea of the witness of the Spirit a distinction seems almost unavoidable. The Spirit of truth speaks to us from the words of the prophets and apostles as their own true author. They spoke and wrote by the Spirit as they came to share in the Spirit of revelation. We thus have to obey *the Spirit in words*. The Spirit of truth also bears witness to us that the prophets and apostles did not speak and write of themselves, just as revelation was not from them but from God. The Spirit in us gives us a share in the revelation to which they bear witness. Hence we have to obey *the Spirit in us*. We cannot handle this distinction too carefully. When we think through the first thought, namely, that God himself speaks out of the patriarchs, prophets, and apostles,[33] we arrive at the remarkable idea of a sacred text of great antiquity, of human voices in which very remarkably, in distinction from other human voices, we may all at once hear God's voice. How far? What does inspiration in this sense imply? The divine origin of the inner life and experience of those people? Or even of their words? Even to the Hebrew pointing, as some would have it at the end of the 18th century?[34]

But even if we could accept this rather strained idea, would we have revelation? God's Word? How do they apply to me, these distant people and their lives and intricate thoughts and strange words? Even assuming that this ancient book is God's Word, what does it have to do with me? This is by no means obvious. The older doctrine of inspiration does not come to grief on historical criticism but on the inner incredibility of God's speaking, of God's Word, in a book that confronts us with this wooden objectivity, this inauthentic revealedness. We must not try to develop the thought of the self-evidence of scripture in this direction if we are not to

---

32. Ibid., I, 7, 4.

33. Cf. Second Helvetic Confession, in *BSRK*, p. 170.26-30; Schaff, p. 831.

34. A slip for the 17th century; cf. the Formula Consensus Helvetic of 1675, Canones, II, in *BSRK*, p. 862.42-46.

get stuck in the worst form of mythology. A historical datum as such cannot be autopistic. Two things are necessary for this. *Something* has to be credible, and it has to be credible to *someone.*

Similar problems arise with the second idea, that of God's speaking to us.[35] The witness of the Spirit is in this case understood solely as his witness in our own hearts and consciences. We enjoy a remarkable illumination or experience whereby the scales suddenly fall from our eyes and we see scripture as God's Word. One might call this "inspiration," but how far such a shock or experience or illumination differs from what fanatics in every age have claimed to experience, how far *I myself* with an appeal to *my* experience can claim validity for my thesis that the Bible is God's Word and for my special understanding of the Bible, how far this experience is truly of divine rather than demonic origin and sets me in touch with God's revelation — all this is not so easily seen. Is it not refreshing to read the Göttingen professor Michaelis (at the end of the 18th century) when he says in his dogmatics that he must candidly admit that although he is firmly persuaded of the truth of revelation, in his own life he never had any such experience of the Holy Spirit.[36] With its clarity of perception, his generation was indeed inclined to view this aspect of the matter as so much enthusiastic nonsense. But this second part of the doctrine came to grief not on rationalistic soberness but on an inner, material impossibility. Revealedness *in* us is a false subjectivism just as revealedness *confronting* us is a false objectivism. Pietistic and romantic importunities do not alter the fact that an inner experience as such can be no more autopistic than a historical datum as such. Two things are necessary for this. It has to be certain to *someone,* but *something* has also to be certain.

We have thus to see how provisional and relative is the separation between the Spirit in scripture and the Spirit in us, between the outer and the inner aspects, the then and now, the there and here. Once we isolate either aspect, we pervert things. Nor is it as though we could link them with a "not only . . . but also." Two perversions do not make a truth. We have to remember, however, that primarily the reference on both sides is to the Holy Spirit. But the Holy Spirit is neither a magical quality of some ancient text nor an inner sentiment. The Holy Spirit is God speaking to

---

35. Cf. Second Helvetic Confession, in *BSRK,* p. 170.26-30; Schaff, p. 831.

36. J. D. Michaelis, *Dogmatik,* 2nd ed. (Göttingen, 1784), p. 92. Barth is quoting from Luthardt, p. 268.

us, making us his children and servants, giving us mouths and ears and eyes for God's revelation. For he himself is God.

In relation to the Holy Spirit, then, we have to say that we must view inspiration as a single, timeless — or rather, contemporary — act of God (its communication, too, is really an act) in *both* the biblical authors *and* ourselves. It is an act in which the Spirit speaks to spirit, and spirit receives the Spirit. With reference to the holiness of scripture we are not to distinguish between the ontic basis (then, there, outside) and the noetic basis (here, today, inside). We are not to distinguish between the fact that there are canonical books and the fact that we know them to be such. We are not to distinguish between the light that the Bible sheds and the eye that perceives this light. We can distinguish these things only in the form of questions when we think in human terms, and face to face with the notorious lack of arguments for the thesis that scripture is God's Word. When we see that this lack of arguments is the real argument by reason of the reality of the Spirit and the address of God, then we must associate together as with an iron clamp the fact that God has spoken and the fact that he speaks to us. Even if we then have to go on to differentiate these facts, we must remember the mysterious unity in which inspiration, that is, the holiness of scripture, is one with our recognition that it is holy.

Calvin brilliantly states what I have in mind when he says that the same Spirit who has spoken through the mouths of the prophets must find entry into our hearts and persuade us that they rendered faithfully what they had been told to say by God.[37] I also find a very good summary in the later and less classical Zurich theologian Heidegger, who says that the witness of the Holy Spirit is neither a mere persuasion of the mind, which might leave a suspicion of deception (objectivism), nor an irrational movement of the heart such as enthusiasts peddle as divine (subjectivism), but a glowing and shining of the Spirit in our dark hearts which gives us the light of the knowledge of the glory of God in the face of Jesus Christ [2 Cor. 4:6], so that, all obstacles being removed, we are put in a position to see the whole superiority and wealth of the divine Word.[38] H. Alsted called the doctrine of the testimony of the Spirit, which is the foundation of truth, the basis of all theology.[39] In contrast, D. F. Strauss described it

---

37. *Inst.* I, 7, 4.
38. Heppe, p. 22; Heppe-Bizer, p. 23; ET p. 25.
39. Heppe-Bizer, p. 24; ET p. 26.

as the Achilles heel of the Protestant system.[40] Whether it is the one or the other, or more the one than the other, will not be decided in the lecture hall or on paper but on the battlefield of actuality on which alone we find full truth. For how can truth be truth except in act? In God's act! We can find no other argument for the Protestant scripture principle, for the thesis that scripture is God's Word. We can desire no other argument, whether axiomatic, historical, or psychological. The only basis is the one act of lordship which is grounded in God, which proceeds from God, and by [which] revelation is ours and we share in revelation.

Do we accept this? Or dare we say that we do not? One might perhaps say what Michaelis did of the pietistically weakened testimony of the Spirit. But we should think twice before saying that we do not know the Holy Spirit. In any case, the last mysterious obstacle that we all come across as we are all ready at any moment to deny the Holy Spirit is not a reason for resorting to apologetics for the Bible. Instead, it is a good reason for turning to another doctrine that is closely related to inspiration. I mean the doctrine of double predestination, of the decision about us which is hidden in God. At any rate those who reflect on what this denotes will not let themselves be swept into revolts against the constantly new incomprehensiblity of the scripture principle.

---

40. D. F. Strauss, *Die christliche Glaubenslehre . . .* , I (Tübingen/Stuttgart 1840), p. 136.

§ 9

Authority

That God's Word speaks to us in scripture is first conditioned historically by the authority of the church. The scope and form in which the witness of the prophets and apostles comes to us, the interpretation which it is given by individual teachers and the church's universal doctrinal church definitions, and finally the outer and inner situation of each historical moment — all these things are factors which necessarily determine our hearing of the Word. Nevertheless, this authority is historical, relative, and formal. It is reserved exclusively for scripture as God's Word to secure for itself direct, absolute, material authority.

I. Conditions of the Objective Possibility

I will first summarize briefly what I said in the preceding section. The church does not make revelation contemporary with us who come later, nor does it make us contemporary with revelation. Scripture itself does this as the witness of the prophets and apostles to revelation inasmuch as in it and over against it the Spirit speaks to spirit. Scripture does it as God's Word. This is the scripture principle of Protestantism.

It is really the scripture *principle.* It is the basic and universal and unconditional element in the question of the communication of revelation that here concerns us. We had first to restate it free from confusion with secondary problems. In what remains of this second chapter two sections will now follow in which I will relate this basic and unconditional answer to the problems that I have called secondary. They really are secondary inasmuch as the answer to them depends totally on the great either/or which we have just been considering. One could, of course, call them primary too insofar as they deal with matters that we at once come across, on the threshold as it were, when reflecting on our main problem. And if we do not see that they are still only secondary, we might become bogged down in them. We have to realize that we can speak about them at all only if our hearts are first resolved to close in on that great either/or, and to do so with the sword of Alexander the Great, with which alone we can achieve anything here. We have to do so, however, as we plunge down sharply from the heights of the doctrines of the Trinity, of the incarnation, and of faith into these lower regions. If we have acquitted ourselves well there, but only so, we can hardly fail to find the truth here.

But if we are to speak meaningfully about these secondary matters in the doctrine of scripture, about the questions which in practice lie closest to us and are also the most urgent, then we must keep in mind not only the basic lines of the preceding section but also the whole doctrine of revelation from which the lines have been drawn. The section on the scripture principle (§ 8) corresponds to that on the Trinity (§ 5). It says what has to be said about the reality of the communication of revelation, namely, that this is itself God's Word. But to think of this reality not merely conceptually but as reality, we must obviously come to some understanding of its possibility. How can it happen that scripture speaks to us as God's Word? How can it be God's Word if it does not do so? But how does it do so — how does it speak to *us?* In §8.III we spoke about *autopistia* as the inner principle of the reality of this happening. But this reality must also have an *outer* principle, and this is its possibility. The meaning and power of the self-achieved credibility of scripture are a single, timeless, contemporary, divine act of lordship, we said. But insofar as they are visible and effective, two things belong to the *autopistia: something* which is credible of itself, and *someone* to whom it is credible of itself, an objective factor and a subjective factor. These two together form the outer principle of the reality of the communication of revelation, or, then, its possibility.

In the present section I will sum up the first side of the matter, the condition of the objective possibility, under the concept of authority (with the church in view). This section (§ 9), then, will correspond logically to § 6. In § 10 I will then sum up the condition of the subjective possibility under the concept of freedom (with the individual in view). This final section will correspond to that on faith and obedience (§ 7).

I will make another preliminary observation only to be on the safe side. It is really self-evident and purely analytic. In speaking here about the possibility or the conditions of the event that God's Word addresses us, we naturally have in view only the *historical* possibility or the *genetic* side of the matter. If the reality of the event really is as we have stated, then obviously its fundamental possibility coincides with its reality. The conditions that we enumerate can only be descriptions of how it comes about that God's Word addresses us. Why this happens belongs to another book, or to our own section § 8. I hope, then, that none of you will be misled by the first statement of the present thesis as though it involved some retreat from what was said in § 8.I. The word "historically" in the thesis should protect us against any such misunderstanding. At the climax of the two sections, as the final statement in the thesis shows, we shall return in each case to the why or wherefore. But for the sake of complete unambiguity it will perhaps be as well if I sum up at once the conclusion of the two sections: Not the church, but scripture as God's Word, has true and definitive authority. Not the individual, but again scripture as God's Word, has true and definitive freedom. What we are now to speak about is simply historical, improper, propaedeutic authority and freedom.

II. Historical Authority

If scripture comes to us, or we to it, across the abyss of the centuries, this rests on a series of objective facts that are wholly independent of our own views or attitudes and that we simply have to state as such. What is it that comes to us? A complex of words. Its most original constituent is a collection of Hebrew and Greek words that have been transmitted from generation to generation as the Bible of the Old and New Testaments. But scripture has not come to anyone merely in these words. A second constituent of the complex (though individuals, of course, may not be completely aware of it) is the collection of further words with which nineteen centuries have expounded those ancient texts, the ideas and concepts which they have associated with the original words of the prophets and apostles.[1] No one reads the Bible directly. We all read it through spectacles, whether we like it or not, and even if it be only in the necessary translation into our own language, though in fact infinitely more is in-

---

1. N. p. 113 adds: "All these ring and wing along when I read the Bible."

volved. How much the words of the one man Luther, for example, have meant for the way in which scripture has come to millions of people, and still comes! Nor is that all. For in addition to nineteen centuries, the present in a pregnant sense also speaks decisively — the historical situation of the present moment, the words and special and unique concerns which unavoidably press in on me at the very time when I read or hear the biblical words and that which accompanies them in the form of tradition.

In pure receptivity I also confront the *logos* of the situation, the word of the hour which necessarily rings out in this age and in my circumstances, the provisional balance of my existence thus far, the cross section of the historical moment which more or less strongly or weakly affects it. I read or hear this *logos,* too, when I hear or read scripture. I need only open my mouth to say what I have heard or read, and this comes to light. And we must consider this threefold collection of words not only from the standpoint that they come to us, perhaps, under the same conditions as do the *Iliad* or the *Odyssey,* but also from the standpoint that they claim to be God's Word to us. What does this claim mean in reference to this question? Three things are clear.

1. All along the line in that with which we have to do here, from the text to the words which speak in me from my own situation when I read it, we have words, human words, human words as God's Word. This means that I come up against a barrier. I do not hear God himself speak. I only hear from God and about God. His own Word comes to me only in this broken form. The ancients had more to say than is usually thought about this brokenness of all theology, of all speaking and hearing about God. In the introductions to older dogmatics we find apparently odd distinctions such as this: There is a *theologia archetypos,* God's own wisdom, and a *theologia ektypos,* its earthly reflection, and then within the latter there is a *theologia comprehensorum* or *patriae,* which we shall have in the next world, and a *theologia viatorum* or *viae,* which is possible in this life, and then again in the latter there is a theology prior to the fall, or *theologia paradisiaca* (Adam) and a theology after the fall, or *post lapsum.*[2] Obviously what we as theologians know of speaking and hearing about God is only *theologia ektypos, viatorum, post lapsum.*[3] This is the barrier that confronts us. We believe we find it in the fact that *the* Word comes to us only in

---

2. For examples cf. Schmid-Pöhlmann, p. 28; Schmid ET p. 16; Heppe-Bizer, p. 6; ET p. 16.

3. N. p. 114 adds: "What we have can be only a reflection of God's thinking."

words, in human words. We must halt at this barrier and acknowledge it. This is obviously the first implication of the claim that scripture is God's Word. It comes to us as an authority in history, and only thus. If there were for us a *theologia archetypos, comprehensorum,* or *paradisiaca,* then we would be without authority, because without words. But there is no such thing for us.

2. The fact that they are human words, that they are a confusion of strange voices pressing in upon me, and desiring to be received and acknowledged by me as God's Word, means that I am not alone in my relation to God and his revelation. I am in a fellowship. *History* is what presses in upon me and speaks to me and with me. Obviously, then, I am pulled out of my proud isolation. Precisely in relation to the last and deepest things I cannot be my own free lord; instead I am the servant of all [cf. 1 Cor. 9:19]. I must respect not merely the prophets and apostles as witnesses but also, perhaps unwittingly, a long series and nexus of witnesses, the witnesses who put their own word in the balances. I must also respect the *kairos,* the significance of the situation, which will not let me hear and accept what suits myself as though I lived around A.D. 1500 or 1000, but only what I must hear and accept today as one who is alive here and now. I have to put myself in this chain as one of its links. This is what the barrier means when I understand that the words are human words. The Word of God in scripture comes to me in the form of the authority of the fellowship, not as my own law, but as a *heteros nomos.*

3. Though their number is incalculable, we are still dealing with specific words and not just any human words. These ancient words have come down to us as the Bible, not as the *Iliad* or the *Odyssey* but as Isaiah and John. What concerns me is the canon that was selected by a distant Christian generation. Again, the interpretative tradition that speaks with it is not at all identical with the totality of what has been spoken and written about Christianity and the Bible. Specific thoughts have determined and ruled this tradition, others less so, others again not at all, while others still have been deliberately restricted and suppressed. What Athanasius thought and said is valid. What Luther said still speaks, at least where we stand, whereas voices like those of Marcion, Arius, and Servetus are silent, or *ought* to be so. The claim that scripture is God's Word implies a selection from among all the words that are spoken around us. Only relatively few come into serious consideration in this regard. Even the *logos* of the situation which seeks to speak with scripture, and is able to do so, is a very definite *logos* which differs from other things that might come

into my head. As I see it, then, the fellowship of which I have to count myself a member if I am to do justice to the claim of scripture is not the totality of the race but the totality of those who were and are in like case to myself. This fellowship with its words reminds me of my human limitation — that my theology can be only *ektypos, viatorum, post lapsum.* This fellowship demands respect for God but also for itself, for its by no means accidental history, for the ordinances and norms that obtain in it, for the names that it honors, for that which here and now seems great and precious to it. In *its* sequence I must place myself, in the light of *its* witness I must receive God's Word in that of the prophets and apostles, to *its* interpretation I must adhere, with *it* together I must let scripture be God's Word in the sense of the moment. The authority of the church is what really encounters me as scripture comes to me, as it comes to me with the claim to be God's Word. If scripture comes to me at all, this is how it comes to me.

III. Authority and Freedom

An authority is a limitation in which the human fellowship meets me in a very specific form, directs me out of immediacy into mediacy, and demands obedience from me. There are different kinds of authorities, more definite and less definite, more categorical and more restrained, lower and higher. Finally, in contrast to the whole series of conditioned and hierarchically related authorities, there is the unconditioned authority which is self-grounded. The concept itself is clear. It stands dialectically over against the concept of freedom, under which I understand myself as my own counterpart, again with various possible definitions and distinctions. Over against all my freedoms there is again my unconditional freedom, which, correctly understood, necessarily coincides with the unconditional authority.

If I perceive God's Word in scripture, this means per se that I set myself under the authority of the church. I do not determine myself. I am determined, primarily by God, but secondarily (with no possible outer separation between the secondary and the primary aspects) by historical and human factors.

1. In the thesis I mentioned as the first determinative and authoritative factor "the scope and form in which the witness of the prophets and apostles comes to us." I naturally had in mind the canon and text of the

Old and New Testaments. Holy scripture is a specifically defined body of writings, not assembled privately by individuals but collected by the church as such, by the historical fellowship of all those who receive God's Word in this literature. Even the Reformers did not view the agreement of the early church on what is and is not the canon as merely a practical technical measure but as a fundamental act of faith and obedience. The Holy Spirit tells believers what holy scripture is. This is our basic principle, and Calvin, for example, applies it expressly to the formation of the canon.[4]

According to the Protestant view this act of faith on the part of the church cannot in principle be repeated or brought to completion. A whole series of especially Reformed confessional writings thought it valuable formally to renew the establishment of the canon, sometimes by enumerating the books,[5] in some cases with the express exclusion of the Apocrypha.[6] The possible extension or restriction of the canon cannot be ruled out in principle, but it would have to be an act of the church as such, an act of faith. The church simply took over the OT as it was from the synagogue. This is a strong proof of the sense of the unity of the Testaments which was still felt in the early church. It was recognized that the synagogue had been God's church and had thus been able to distinguish the sacred writings from all others. The mark of canonicity for the NT works was obviously the concept of apostolicity. It was not that of antiquity, of historical credibility, or of the closest proximity to Jesus. The name of Paul, which governs much of the NT, makes the latter qualifications of apostolicity quite impossible, not to speak of such disciples of the apostles as Mark and Luke. A person is an apostle, and can qualify for the canon, as a witness of the risen Lord, not as a historical eyewitness. Hence the church needs the Spirit and faith, not historical research, to decide what is canonical and what is not.

This means that the result of this act of faith, the canon, is in the first

---

4. Gallican Confession (1559), Art. 4, in *BSRK*, p. 222.26-30; Schaff, pp. 361-62.

5. Cf. the Gallican Confession, 1559 (*BSRK*, p. 222.5-24), the Belgic, 1561 (pp. 233.31-234.13), the Irish, 1615 (p. 526.16-21), the Westminster, 1647 (pp. 543.10-544.9), the Waldensian, 1655 (pp. 500.35-501.12), the Calvinist Methodist, 1823 (p. 872.1-13), the Cumberland Presbyterian, 1883 (p. 912.6-32); cf. also Schaff, pp. 360-61, 601-2.

6. Cf. the Zurich Confession, 1545 (*BSRK*, p. 155.10-15) and Anglican Articles, 1552 (p. 507.4-30); cf. also Schaff, p. 490. Confessions that note the noncanonical rank of the Apocrypha include the Belgic, 1561 (p. 234.24-33), the Irish, 1615 (p. 526.22-27), and the Westminster, 1647 (p. 544.11-18); cf. also Schaff, pp. 387-88, 526-27, 602-3.

instance simply there as such. The church that baptized us pronounced over us the associated promise on the basis of this Word. We are referred to this Word, and we must have this Word in view when we believe that we have knowledge of a Word of God, unless we deliberately want to put ourselves outside the church, the historical fellowship of the faith, or unless the church itself wants to revise its decision.[7] This is the authority of the canon. It is not fundamentally an unconditional or absolute authority. It stands or falls with the church's act of faith, with the witness of the Spirit who leads into all truth [John 16:13]. But it is an authority with all the weight which accrues historically to such a unanimous and universal act of faith on the church's part, with all the weight of that which preceded our own faith and that of those who were before us. In calling us to faith, the church sets the canon before us as a reflection of the loneliness and isolation of God himself: This is holy scripture, not all kinds of things, but this in particular.

We may have doubts and qualms about the contingent "this," just as we have about all the contingent things with which the question of faith is put to us. We may regret it that the *Didache* or Luther's *Freedom of a Christian Man* or various other good works that the church may profitably read are *not* holy scripture. We need not regard the verdict that pronounces Yes and No in this matter as God's verdict. We may even have divergent private opinions and prefer them to this verdict. Nevertheless, we have to realize that all divergent opinions in this matter are in fact private opinions and do not have authority as such. The Word of God comes to us with historical authority within the confines of the canon, *this* canon.

I would also like to say something about the idea of an authoritative biblical text, absurd though it might seem to be to think of such a thing in the present age. As we all know, the Roman Catholic church has such a text in the Vulgate, at least so far as Latin, the language of the cultus, is concerned. The thought that there might be such a thing was not strange to older Protestantism either, as is shown by the tenacity with which the text of Luther's translation has been able to hold its own. Not merely a limited conservatism, or a half-devotional, half-esthetic pleasure in Luther's vigorous language, lies behind the resistance to revisions of this text, or to its replacement by the renderings of a Weizsäcker or a Stage,[8] but the obscure, yet not incorrect, awareness that scripture as God's Word must

---

7. Barth here uses *zurückkommen auf* in the sense of "reconsider" or "revise."

8. C. H. von Weizsäcker's translation of the NT came out in 1875, that of C. Stage in 1896.

be handed down to us not merely in specific confines but also in a specific form which is determined by the Spirit for faith.

On the Reformed side there was an even more striking push in this direction when in Switzerland toward the end of the 17th century a very obscure urge led people to take up the cudgels against an increasing uncertainty regarding the original text, especially of the OT. In what has become the notorious Helvetic Formula of Consensus of 1675, the theses were championed that the Word which God entrusted to Moses and the prophets and apostles, and which he has thus far defended against all the cunning of Satan, must have been preserved in the church without the loss of a single letter or vowel point. At a time when OT criticism was first beginning, this was seen to apply especially to the Hebrew codex of the OT which we have received by tradition from the Jewish church, to which the *logia tou theou* were entrusted according to Rom. 3:2, and it applies to both the consonants and the vowels, no matter whether we think of vowel points that were really inserted or only of their possibility *(potestas).* The official *lectio Hebraica* does not rest on mere caprice, nor should we try to emend it in accordance with the Septuagint or other Greek translations, the Samaritan text, the Targums, early church exposition, or mere reason. The restoration of a supposedly authentic text by critical means is totally forbidden. We must keep to the official text of the synagogue.[9] An exhibit from the darkest corner of the orthodox chamber of horrors!

Yet if we consider the matter quietly, we have to say that this wholly fruitless attempt to kick against the pricks is unfortunate only because it did not succeed, and because its authors themselves (Heidegger)[10] were not really sure what they were after. They confused the question of an authoritative text for the church with that of verbal inspiration and declared the *lectio Hebraica* to be unalterable because it was inspired. I need hardly return to that. What was really in their minds — and the best Orientalists like the two Buxtorfs[11] were thinking along these lines — was the perfectly correct thought that the question of the oldest text and the question of the authentic text, the historical question and the theological

---

9. *BSRK,* pp. 862.42-863.17. Cf. above, § 8 n. 34.

10. The Zurich theologian J. H. Heidegger (1633-1698) drew up the Formula, assisted by F. Turrettini (1623-1687) of Geneva and L. Gernler (1625-1675) of Basel.

11. Johann Buxtorf (1564-1629) was Professor of Hebrew at Basel; his son Johann (1599-1664) succeeded him in 1630 and became Professor of OT in 1654.

question, were two separate things that ought not to be confused, that only the judgment of the church and not disinterested philological scholarship can decide the wording of a sacred text, and therefore that the official findings of the synagogue as the church's predecessor are more interesting and binding for Christians than even the most probable findings of critical research into the OT.

One must at least say that a problem arises here which very wrongly is not even considered today. Dogmatically the question of a *textus receptus* is not so simple as a one-sidedly historical theology imagines. What are the Protestant churches really thinking of when they regard it as obvious to leave the establishment of a correct text to a scholarship which perhaps has no inkling of what is really meant by "correct" in this context? If the Protestant church really knew what it was doing when it called scripture God's Word, would it not assume the authority for saying, e.g., that in Rom. 5:1, for reasons that historians may not appreciate but that we see very clearly, Paul the apostle of Jesus Christ could not possibly have written *eirēnēn echōmen* (with *ō*, a long *o*), but that the official text has to be *echomen* (with a short *o*) no matter what the manuscripts or textual research may say?[12]

It is in terms of an inner relation to the prophetic and apostolic witness — such as a church must have — that certain guidelines, which are totally independent of historical problems, must necessarily be fixed whereby to establish an authoritative church form both of the original text and of translations,[13] authoritative, of course, not in the sense of inspired but once again, as in the case of the canon, in terms of its recognition by an act of faith on the church's part, relatively and historically authoritative until the church is better instructed, but still authoritative. Here, too, people are quite free to have divergent private opinions that may be academically very interesting and even perhaps right. But they are still private opinions, and the church has to be clear about its own competence and responsibility, not in matters of the earliest and so-called genuine text, but in matters of the sacred and authoritative text.[14] Perhaps it could then with a better conscience demand respect for the Bible again. I could not

---

12. N. p. 120 adds: "does a long or a short *o* in Rom. 5 depend on some professor or on the church?"

13. In a marginal note Barth has a quotation from Heidegger (taken from Schweizer, I, 220) to the effect that even in translation the Bible is still God's Word.

14. N. p. 120 adds: "We have to be bold enough to think in such categories as that of the sacred text."

speak to this issue without at least drawing your attention to this strange gap in Protestant dogmatics.

2. I referred in the thesis to "the interpretation which it [revelation] is given by individual church teachers and the church's universal doctrinal definitions." This is the second authoritative factor that governs our hearing of the Word. It does so in fact whether we like it or not. To laypeople at least, when they read the Bible, Luther constantly speaks, or the modern translators with their theology. But apart from that, we cannot possibly read the Bible without a whole tradition being incessantly associated with the relevant texts, interpreting, expounding, and applying them, and perhaps also concealing and estranging them. At this point a historically oriented theology will naturally break in and say that if we are to understand scripture we must jettison this whole ballast of tradition and stick to its first and oldest and unadorned meaning. But this makes no sense at all if we are really to understand scripture as God's Word. God's Word in scripture is not at all identical with its oldest sense. It is *through* this that the Spirit speaks to spirit.

In faith the human wording must indeed be heard as God's own Word, as the echo of revelation. If this is so, with what right can we bypass what the Spirit said to spirit before us? With what right can we bypass the series of acts of faith in which those who were before us received the Word? Only if we think we are merely dealing with history, with past events, may we do this. But in these interpretations that also speak and seek to be heard we are dealing with the church, with the church that baptized us and that has set us under the Word of promise in a very specific sense. The act of faith that so dramatically precedes me cannot possibly be of indifference to me, is not of indifference to me, even though I may think that I should adopt so directly a historical posture. Here, too, the saying is true that we are blessed if we know what we are doing.[15] We have to realize that we always live by authorities. What we have to see is by what authorities, and with what right.

And here we come up against an even greater gap in Protestant dogmatics which I do not have the confidence to fill but which I do at least want to bring to your notice. Beyond all question Protestant theology both in the pulpit and on the rostrum does not really live by scripture alone — and perhaps only to a fairly small extent if we bring the truth to

---

15. The reference is to the saying which follows Luke 6:14 in Codex D; cf. J. Jeremias, *Unbekannte Jesusworte* (Gütersloh, 1980), pp. 61ff.

light. Thus we constantly hear Luther quoted, certainly no less so than Thomas is in Roman Catholic theology. When we hear the formula: "Luther said somewhere," then we know that the speaker is doing something that is at least penultimate, that really hits the nail on the head. If Luther said it, it must be really true! But in what modern Protestant dogmatics do we find anything said in principle about this by no means self-evident procedure? How does it relate to the Protestant scripture principle? Are there, then, Protestant fathers? Authorities that are normative for our understanding of scripture as God's Word? Obviously! But if so, we should say so. Early Lutheran dogmatics recognized the problem and included an article on Luther's vocation.[16] This was clear and consistent. Something similar should be done again. We should also consider whether it is really in order and legitimate to appeal to Augustine in Protestant theology. The Reformers did so freely, but it has been impressed more forcibly on us than on them how Catholic Augustine already was. Is it still true that he is one of those to whom we should turn and with whom we might agree? And how about Thomas? The older orthodox, especially among the Reformed, sometimes used Thomas very ardently ("Thomas Aquinas the defender of evangelical truth").[17] Should we do the same? Since then Thomas has very definitely become the normative theologian of modern Roman Catholicism.[18]

We must also consider fundamentally by what right or method we may really expound the Bible in terms of Fichte or Goethe, or whether we are right in our own century to perpetuate the description of Schleiermacher as the church father of the 19th century.[19] What is really happening when someone suddenly comes along with Blumhardt or Kierkegaard or Dostoyevski on his banner? By what right? Are these men fathers, and if so, in what sense? Do any of us Protestants have the freedom to proclaim fathers as we fancy at the risk that one day we might suddenly proclaim

---

16. Cf. J. Gerhard, *Loci theologici* (1610-1622), Locus 23, § 8; A. Calov, *Systema locorum theologicorum* (1655-1677), VIII, art. 3, ch. 2, q. 2; J. A. Quenstedt, *Theologia didactico-polemica sive systema theologicum* (1685), Part IV, ch. 12, § 2, q. 3; D. Hollaz, *Examen theologicum acroamaticum* (1707), ch. 2, q. 10.

17. Barth is alluding to a book by J. G. Dorsche, *Thomas Aquinas exhibitus Confessor Veritatis Evangelicae . . .* (Frankfurt, 1656); cf. F. Loofs, *Leitfaden*, 4th ed. (Halle, 1906), p. 690 n. 3.

18. The rank of Thomas as a normative theologian was officially sanctioned by Leo XIII, Pius X, and Pius XI; see DS, 3139, 3601ff., 3665.

19. Cf. C. Lülmann, *Schleiermacher, der Kirchenvater des 19. Jahrhunderts* (Tübingen, 1907).

St. Catherine of Siena or St. Theresa of Jesus to be a mother of the church? Calvinism has to consider in principle whether it may follow the example of the Lutherans and Zwinglians and call Calvin a master in Israel [cf. John 3:10]. Fundamentally, the Reformed did not do this at first. I am only asking questions. My only contention is that individual teachers of the church like this (including Fichte and Goethe) do in fact speak very vigorously in the church too. The church must have the courage openly to confess this and to achieve dogmatic clarity about the presence and the relative validity of such authorities. In Roman Catholic theology the concept of a *doctor ecclesiae* is clearly defined.[20] We undoubtedly have the thing itself, but we are hazy about it and do not really know whether to take it seriously. This is bad. I need hardly say that this one apparently subsidiary question of fathers provides a good illustration of the hopeless confusion of our Protestant situation.

A word must also be said here about the authority of church confessions, of dogma that has achieved symbolical or official status. How can we hear God's Word in scripture today without also hearing what the church of God, the fellowship of believers, has in different centuries deposited in these official documents as the clear result of their hearing? Again we can ignore this factor only if we regard the time between the prophetic and apostolic testimony and the present period simply as history and not as church history in the pregnant sense of the term, that is, as the history of the church of God which may at times be hidden but is never wholly missing. Belief in the present activity of the Holy Spirit today cannot possibly go hand in hand with a radical denial of his past activity, nor, then, with a lack of attention to the testimonies in which the past solemnly confessed its faith on the basis of scripture and the Spirit, the more so as individuals in their own historical place have to see in such confessions the faith of a very special past, that is, that of the church which has baptized them.

What is at issue is attentiveness to them. We are not simply to think and speak in detachment from them, as though the church began only today with us — not even if we use the Bible. At every point we must at least take note of the way in which the church thought it should understand the witness to revelation at the great crises in its history. Those

---

20. "Church doctor" is an honorary title that has been conferred on sacred scholars, including some who are not fathers, from ca. 1300 (Boniface VIII). Some 25 are listed by Bartmann, p. 31.

who radically scorn to do this, or are not too particular about it, show thereby that they are sectarians and possibly heretics. We cannot believe in the unity of the Spirit, that is, of God, and be indifferent to the universal or partial unity of the church.

Yet more is demanded than attentiveness, than taking note historically. Respect is also demanded. From the very first, in face of the confessions, regardless of their content, we must be ready to take direction from them, to find in them a norm, to let ourselves be bound, not unconditionally, only relatively, yet truly by them. It is the same as when we hear Luther speaking. Indeed, we must have some sense that a church confession as such, as the record of a universal and official act of faith, has a higher and different kind of authority and claim than even the most profound and powerful saying of Luther or any other church teacher. For example, Lutherans cannot ignore the fact that the record of the consolidation of the Lutheran church is not Luther's *Commentary on Galatians,* and even less so the 1516 *Commentary on Romans,* but Melanchthon's Augsburg Confession, in relation to which Luther's Catechisms are only commentaries according to the basic idea of the Book of Concord.[21] It would also be very forward and arbitrary for Reformed theologians, out of a liking for Zwingli, to ignore the fact that the confessions that the different Reformed churches finally adopted are more oriented to Calvin than to Zwingli.

That which is historically original, or which speaks better to us personally, may not be the same as what confronts us with a claim to authority. How far we are to accept this claim is still a question, but we must not overlook the fact that it is there in all its distinctiveness and that it has to be taken into account. It is there as dogma in the strict and pregnant sense, not as an individual opinion but as the confession of the church that has baptized us. We are guilty of an inappropriate arbitrariness if we say that for us (Lipsius, Kaftan)[22] the only authority at issue is, of course, that of the Reformation confessions. As though the Reformation churches, no less than the Roman Catholics, did not base their claim to be the Christian church on the fact that they formally presupposed an acknowledgment and confession of the symbols of the first five centuries,

---

21. Cf. the Preface (1580), in *BSLK,* p. 8.9-20; p. 14.48-56; Tappert, pp. 7-8, 13-14.

22. Cf. R. A. Lipsius, *Lehrbuch der evangelisch-protestantische Dogmatik,* § 210; Kaftan, pp. 85, 89-91.

and as though for an understanding of Protestant dogmas we could set aside even for a single moment the Nicene doctrine of the Trinity and Chalcedonian christology. No, if in its own specific and relative sphere there is a category of dogma just as there is a category of doctors of the church, then we cannot possible think that church history began in 1517, and even as Protestants we have to think in Catholic terms, and we must never lose sight of the "always, everywhere, and by all."[23]

In this respect, too, we must be aware of what we are doing. As a result of the Roman Catholic concept of the church, dogma in the Roman Catholic sense merges into revelation. According to the Lutheran church, dogma occupies a distinctive middle position between church teachers and scripture. The Augsburg Confession derives from God's Word[24] to a higher qualitative degree than can be said of the private writings of Luther or Melanchthon. For later Lutheran dogmatics, indeed, the whole Book of Concord ranks as inspired. It came into being under a special concursus of the Holy Spirit, though naturally in a lesser sense than holy scripture.[25] In contrast, the Reformed church plainly views its confessions as human confessions of faith, and with few exceptions does not use the term "symbol" for them but works out very clearly the relativity and variability of dogma and the basic subordination of even the most solemn confession to scripture.[26] Precisely when Reformed theologians recognize church authority, they hold fast to this view of authority which unavoidably brings out its dialectic, and they avoid any possible flirting with the Roman Catholic concept even though they think they see what its meaning is. In any case, however, we have to say that the concept of church authority, whether old or new, whether Roman Catholic, Lutheran, or Reformed, implies a church that claims this authority for itself and places itself behind its dogma in the narrower or broader sense, so that those within and those without all know that its concern is not with anything and everything (or perhaps nothing), but with these specific things.

But now we come up against the real difficulty in this matter. I have already touched on it earlier. It is the fact that the present-day Protestant church leaves its theologians in the lurch, as it were, when it comes to defining what the dogma is that has such authority. It leaves the field so wide open that

---

23. Cf. Vincent of Lerins, *Commonitorium primum,* ch. 2 (MPL, 50, 640).
24. Cf. *BSLK,* p. 6.45-48 (Tappert, p. 6); p. 3.22-25 (Tappert, p. 3); p. 5.27-29 (Tappert, p. 5).
25. Cf. D. Hollaz, in Schmid-Pöhlmann, p. 79; Schmid ET p. 101.
26. Cf. *BSRK,* p. 2.17-18; p. 100.14-18.

theology needs to remind the church again of the need for dogma and dogmatic authority. At this point again I can only put a big question mark. Where scripture is heard as God's Word, there undoubtedly has to be some kind of church authority too, a devout agreement regarding the understanding of scripture in a more or less precise form, a dogma in the sense of a symbol. But the church's act of faith in virtue of which this comes into being cannot be a mere historical reality. It has to be a present and ongoing act of faith, whether in the form of a definite declaration what parts of the dogma of the early church it wants to claim as its own confession (not merely as an old flag that is piously preserved), or in the form of the composition of a new confession, something which is not outside the realm of possibility if we are to some extent confident about our faith and the special concursus of the Holy Spirit, or finally in the form of the proclamation of an interim state in which the church as such will renounce dogmatic authority, leave the quest for the necessary norms to clergy fellowships, and be content, as things now are, to play the part of a special society. This, too, might be an act of faith, if rather a desperate one. It might be an honest recognition that today we see that the link between the Holy Spirit and the church is a broken one, so that we have to find comfort in the thought that the church and its authority might still be present in individuals. What the church is in fact doing today, however, is not an act of faith. It is simply dithering uncertainly between conservatism, modernism, and independency, without giving to any of the three the honor that is their due. It honors neither the connection of our faith with what has been believed always, everywhere, and by all, nor the indubitably valid desire for new words for the faith of a new age, nor the command that we should be truthful in relation to the situation as it now is. This dithering makes it seem that the solution of independency is the most obvious in spite of all the objections that one might have against it.

Finally, then, in relation to the problem of fathers and dogma, I can only indicate the problem and the gap that opens up here in the Protestant teaching on first principles. Perhaps it will seem to you that it is more in keeping with the matter if I simply leave it at that and do not try to fill the gap with any construction of my own. Any authority that I might claim from this rostrum would be intrinsically ridiculous and no authority at all. The only thing that I can do is to show you by my approach in all these lectures that without being covered by any church I exercise my freedom to reckon with authorities, with fathers and dogmas, and that in so doing I tacitly challenge you to do the same.

3. As a third authoritative factor I mentioned in the thesis "the outer

and inner situation of each historical moment." Naturally I mean a moment in which there is some significance and which can thus be claimed as an authority in the church of God. Here, then, I do not mean the moment as the result of historical sequence. Historical doings as such are not the doing of God's will, and inner and outer necessities that crowd in upon me today are not as such the command of God directed to me.[27] If, however, you think that what I am saying is dark and obscure, remember that I am speaking for the most part of a reality whose specific meaning in its own specific place we Protestants have still to learn once again. We must not think of the historical moment as empty, so that it is left to our individual caprice to understand it as we like and to see this or that command in it; so that it is left to the individual conscience to decide how we are to receive scripture as God's Word here and now in this very concrete present-day situation. Nor at this point should we yet discern the possibility of prophecy, about which we shall have to speak in the next section. We are dealing with a reality that must be understood not in the category of freedom but exclusively in that of authority. It may be very closely related to prophecy, then, but it stands in contrast to it, for prophecy belongs to the category of freedom. Even less should we fall back upon the scandalous idea that since the time of Christ, history has acquired a Christian impregnation or inoculation or coloring, and historical forces and trends and aspirations have come into history to which we have only to attach ourselves to achieve true faith and obedience. As though the Christian things that we have to believe and obey, although they are certainly in time, did not even in time have to come down to us directly from above,[28] from eternity! As though the Christian naturalism which views salvation history as merely a stream or nexus of life were not the worst of all naturalisms!

In contrast to all such things, I want to offer something that corresponds to what Roman Catholic theology calls the teaching office. Ordinarily, of course, we immediately raise an objection against the restriction of this concept to the ecclesiastical hierarchy, as though the church's teaching office were not in principle a function of the church of God as a whole, and as though its authority, although it might be discharged by certain persons, could be arbitrarily limited to the circle of those who hold specific offices. This does not alter the fact, however, that

---

27. N. pp. 124-25 adds: "The command of God directed to me may force me to be disobedient to the history that confronts me."

28. For this expression see K. Barth, *The Word of God and the Word of Man* (Grand Rapids, 1935), e.g., p. 93; and *The Epistle to the Romans* (London, 1933), pp. 30, 102.

in a way that the church of God which is the fellowship of believers may perceive, there has to be a command of the hour, a Word which sums up comprehensively the meaning of each individual moment, and which brings to a climax the series of relative determinations under which we are to receive God's Word in scripture. It is not enough that we have the canon and text of scripture, the fathers as teachers, and dogma as a standard. If the category of authority is to be taken seriously (in the relative sense that is our present concern), then there has to be an authority in each immediate present, concealed in the mystery of its outer and inner historical aspect, yet manifest to those who really perceive God's Word in scripture, so that the perception of the Word is not at the last moment an arbitrary matter but stands under an order and has to take place with some kind of necessity.

The fellowship of believers cannot possibly let itself be pushed and pulled around by history, by life, as only too often happens, and even less so by the occasional whims or illuminations of individuals. If it is, then scripture is a purely historical authority and not a vital and actual authority. The fellowship of believers in its receiving of the Word must not run behind history, remembering only later, when some disaster has happened, that it need not have happened if faith and obedience had been there on time. A tardy word of this kind (at least 30 years too late) is, for example, the well-intentioned social message of the Bethel Conference in 1924.[29] But where were the German churches in 1890 at the time of the law against the Socialists?[30] It was then, or much earlier, that this, or perhaps something rather different, ought to have been said in order to be an authority and to have authority. I need hardly say that this office of the church as watchman and leader, which it should discharge every historical moment as an organ of the truth which is truth here and now today, and which has to be proclaimed as such, should naturally be absolutely free from all national, social, and cultural ties, and is an authority only in such freedom, like the Word to which the prophets of Israel listened; free also from regard for the church as an external institution, basically nondiplomatic, not opportunistic, not asking what respectable people want or say, not asking at all but knowing, knowing the Word as it is to be received today. I refer to remote and apparently impossible things. But nothing is

---

29. Cf. K. Kupisch, *Quellen zur Geschichte des deutschen Protestantismus* (1871-1945) (Göttingen/Berlin/Frankfurt, 1960), pp. 155-60.

30. Barth's reference is to Bismarck's measure against the Social Democrats (10.21.1878), which lapsed in 1890.

impossible to those who believe [Mark 9:23]. The church must believe again. Then it will have authority again, real authority.

IV. Relative and Absolute Authority

Our thesis closes with the words: "Nevertheless, this authority is historical, relative, and formal. It is reserved exclusively for scripture as God's Word to secure for itself direct, absolute, material authority." These two statements bracket all that precedes. But they must not erase or remove or negate it. Doing so I would regard as totally illegitimate. It would be a violent, wrong, and meaningless application of the Protestant scripture principle to use this principle to set aside the authority of the church. As scripture comes to us as God's Word, the problem of the church's authority is everywhere an urgent one. Indeed, as we have already seen, it is actually confirmed. Scripture cannot come to us as God's Word without there being an authoritative canon and text, fathers, dogma, and a teaching office. To be sure, there is also the possibility, reality, and necessity of evolutions and revolutions, of the passing or permanent suspensions, alterations, or reconstructions of certain things that fall under this concept. There has also to be caution in face of all reconstructions. But the concept itself remains, along with all its most important forms. There *is* an authority of the church. The only question is whether the church itself knows and claims and uses it because it believes, because it is really grounded in scripture. Insofar as this is so, its authority is a real one in all the areas mentioned under III.

But it is a real one, we now conclude, in *brackets,* and these brackets must not be excised. There is undoubtedly a great and notable difference in height between Lüneberg Heath and Mont Blanc, but the presuppposition of both is space. The difference is great or small in space. It is defined or becomes an infinite one in space. It has its origin in space. The space of the church's authority is scripture as God's Word. Measured by this, it is historical, relative, and formal. "Historical" means temporal, limited, variable, and finally temporary. "Relative" means only as a reference or indication, an *epideixis* of something else. "Formal" means denoting only the form, the mode of coming, the channel through which the Word comes to us. I have refrained from putting an "only" before these three words. The "nevertheless" with which the sentence begins says enough, says it all. Why should not the three words be positive ones behind this "nevertheless"? Taken positively, these three words sum up the whole reality of our lives apart from the reality of God himself.

Naturally, however, the "nevertheless" contains an unexpressed but unmistakable "only." It puts the church's authority under a higher authority. It limits the limit that is set for us by the church. It is a crisis of the crisis, a norm by which all norms are measured and must let themselves be measured. It is important to discern where this "nevertheless" with its secret "only" comes from. There is an ungodly, merely intellectual, "enlightenment" view of things as historical, relative, and formal to which the historical, relative, and formal authority of the church need not submit if it comes from faith, if the church can have the good conscience of knowing what it is doing. When church authority is grounded in faith and asserted in faith, it can always be stronger than all mere liberalism or skepticism in spite of the "nevertheless" under which it stands. Even a church whose own faith is really weak, in virtue of the impact of the faith of the fathers, is ten times a match for any mass attack from this quarter, although we should not tarry too long in a church of this kind, for judgment by the Assyrians and Babylonians can overtake a Jerusalem which itself is serving idols. Yet only a Jeremiah is in such circumstances permitted to give the advice to open the gates to the enemy [cf. Jer. 38:17-18]. Those who are not prophets may let themselves be told that the world's attempt to suspend, alter, or replace the church's authority for rational, liberal, anti-clerical, or enlightened reasons can never succeed. An attack on the church's authority may be necessary, but it can succeed only when mounted from the source of that authority. The "nevertheless" which really brackets church authorities and gives rise to true revolutions is the "nevertheless" of faith which derives from the Word and makes the church strong against every other "nevertheless."

To work through our definitions once again, a criticism of the canon, an angry call to reduce or increase what we now call holy scripture, is by no means an inconceivable possibility. The canon did not fall from heaven. The church and the church alone fixed it. But the church is not a final court. Above it stands scripture as the Word of God by which the church is established. If the protest comes from this angle, then we cannot rule it out theoretically that one day the principle that scripture is its own interpreter[31] would have to mean that it is its own judge, and that James, for example (this is not my own view), would have to be removed from the NT — Luther had leanings in this direction, as we all know[32] — and

---

31. Cf. Luther, WA, 7, 97, 23.
32. Cf. WA, Deutsche Bibel, 6, 10, 33-34; 7, 387, 15-17.

either replaced by another witness or not replaced at all. But this would have to take place in faith, in sure agreement with the Holy Spirit. The canon will stand for long enough yet against the "it seems to me"[33] of some agitators. Again, it is conceivable that an authoritative biblical text as I have postulated it might have to be emended or that the customary translation might have to be quietly replaced by a new one. Naturally not even the most well-considered text, not even the Luther Bible, is untouchable. Wisdom might bring new insights from the same source, or a new Luther might arise. Purely philological criticism, however, cannot prevail at this point against the authority of the church.

Similarly, we might have to put a big question mark against the authority of certain acknowledged fathers, adducing and honoring some other light that has not thus far been recognized. This must not be a matter of mere antipathy or sympathy, nor of purely historical erudition. It must be by scripture, and finally by scripture alone, that we decide to whom among our predecessors we should accord the dignity and confidence that befit a teacher in the church. If a final verdict can be given on the question whether the distinctive relation of the Lutheran church to Luther is a valid one or not, or whether the attitude of the 19th century to Schleiermacher is right or wrong, we must seek this final word in scripture, and those who know what this means will not come out too quickly with their positive or negative answers.

We must also stand fast radically and relentlessly by the principle that even the most central and universal dogmas can be corrected or transcended. The decisions of Nicea and Chalcedon, the Formula of Concord and the canons of Dort, arose on earth and not in heaven, and it is remarkable that they almost all did so in not the happiest of human circumstances. Appeal to a higher court in face of which the decisions were supposedly reached, control of the decisions by the source from which they supposedly derived, has to be permitted. This is not, of course, a matter of some freewheeling modern caprice which chafes at an orthodoxy that it usually does not know and which thinks it can feel free before it has made any attempt to let itself be bound. Instead, it is a matter of discussion which takes dogma seriously in its relativity, which is obedient to its intention, to its reference to that to which it is relative, and which thus engages in criticism of dogma and asks for new dogma. Such criticism of the confession, however, must come from within, from the matter itself, from scripture. I need hardly assure you that I do not find this quality, at

---

33. Cf. Zinzendorf in Barth, *Das christliche Leben* (Zurich, 1976), pp. 304-5 n. 75; ET *The Christian Life* (Grand Rapids, 1981), p. 180.

least in the criticism that has come down to us from the radicals and Socinians of the 16th century by way of the Enlightenment. The Erasmian spirit of these centuries has not really been a match for the Athanasian spirit of the early church, even though this, too, was only a human spirit.

It is also clear that the authority with which the church discharges its office as watchman and leader in the light of the present moment, speaking the right word at the right time, if this authority is to be real authority, must be inwardly broken by the authority of the Word which is spoken for all times. This is a recognition which must act as a brake to retard the church when it wants to speak too hastily and too eagerly to the situation. It might well be that the synods and commissions of the church and pastors in their pulpits would have carefully suppressed many things which they have now proclaimed to the world if they had reflected even a little on what actually stands in the Bible, and that their silence would then have been much more authoritative than their speech. Here again, however, final word must be that the world must not close the mouth of the church. The church must not let anyone or anything do this except the Word of the Lord before which all our human words are only sound and fury.

We have thus come back to our starting point. This is how things stand with the objective possibility of communicating revelation. If we now try at least to indicate the final word that must be said in this regard, we have to go back to what we described as its reality in the previous section. You will perhaps have noted how I phrased the final statement in the thesis. Everything hangs on the word "exclusively." The authority of scripture has the significance that we have presupposed throughout this section only if we ascribe to it this uniqueness or exclusiveness compared to all other authorities. Only in its isolation can we seriously think of it as *the* authority to which all the other authorities refer and are relative, namely, as *the* historical communication of revelation. If we put it in the same series as the fathers, dogma, and the present situation, even as the first link in the series, then we come back to the position that God's Word is not to be found in it but in the whole series, whether in the church as such, as in Roman Catholicism, or in history as such, as in modern Protestantism.

We have already stated our objections to this position in § 8.I. Both forms of it involve a surreptitious immediacy of revelation. The scripture principle of Protestantism, with its sharp isolation of the prophetic and apostolic witness from both church and history, maintains the mediacy of revelation, but therewith also the source and limit of all authorities. The *source,* for revelation is an authority, barrier, norm, and crisis as it comes into the hiddenness or mediacy of this historical datum. There can be historical and ecclesiastical authorities only in relation to this datum. They are authorities only insofar as they are scriptural. They are witnesses only insofar as they follow this primary witness, not wanting to do or to be anything apart from witnessing to what is witnessed here. But this authority is also the *limit* of all authorities. Other authorities can only place themselves under this primary witness as their original principle. They can try only to repeat and vary and apply what takes place there. They can only orient themselves to this point of reference. If we were to take this point away, they would be pointless. They *are* pointless to the extent that they do not orient themselves to it. All authority above or outside scripture can imply only a relapse into pseudo-immediacy. Everything depends on hearing God's Word *in* scripture. Here is revelation, concealed in history as the Son of Man himself was, yet revelation in this way and in this way alone.

The thesis that scripture is God's Word and has direct authority as such even though it is obviously indirect, that it has absolute authority even though it is obviously supremely relative and "only" relative, deriving from the absolute, that it has material authority even though we usually regard the scripture principle as only a formal principle — this thesis is an insoluble paradox even in this context. Intentionally, then, I have not repeated it expressly because I could not give it any further basis in this context. But it is present all the same, even if not explicitly. No triumphant proof can be at this point the keystone of the arch. The keystone is that scripture itself imposes this authority. It does not receive it from dogmatics along with its basis. It imposes it. Let us remember that we are dealing with revelation: with revelation in mediacy, in history, yet still with revelation. Revelation is real only in the act, only as it takes place. God himself is its sole subject. The event that God speaks and we hear, that the Spirit is the truth both there in the prophets and apostles and here in us, both then and now, so that we find — no, have found — the direct *in* the historical, the absolute *in* the relative, the material *in* the formal — this timeless, contemporary act of God's lordship in virtue of which there is an *autopistia* of scripture and an inner witness of the Spirit is itself the point of reference to which all church authorities relate, in which they are grounded, and by which they are superseded. This event between heaven and earth is what sets authorities up and casts them down, what casts them down and sets them up.

§ 10

Freedom

The fact that God's Word speaks to us in scripture is conditioned secondly by the freedom of individuals. The historical picture that I make for myself of the witness of the prophets and apostles, the way in which I try to grasp it in accordance with the ineluctabilities of my thinking, the light in which it appears to me at a given moment — all these are factors which make the hearing of the Word my independent and responsible act in which I cannot finally let others also have a say. Nevertheless, this freedom, too, is historical, relative, and formal. Direct, absolute, and material freedom can again be ascribed only to scripture as God's Word.

I. Subjectivity

Obviously we do not fully describe the possibility of the communication of revelation in history if we stop at the concept of authority which represents the objective side. The church whose reality rests on this mediation, on God's act of lordship by which the prophetic and apostolic witness speaks and is heard, is not just a fellowship but is a fellowship of believers, the communion of saints. We must always remember that two things belong to that act of divine lordship. God, of course, is there on both sides, both here as light and there as eye, here as Word and there as Spirit, here speaking and there hearing. When we try to think of this reality as possibility, we may not overlook the second or subjective side. When presented in the form of authority, the communication of revelation is a natural or material happening.

I. Subjectivity

Unavoidably, then, even though we stress ever so strongly that God's authority is finally at issue, the idea of a rigid causality arises. But this may not be. We are dealing with God's address to people. But people as such cannot be regarded as the effects of causes. When they are on their own and conscious of themselves they set themselves apart from and over against the nexus of cause and effect. They are not merely conditioned. They also condition. They think and will. What might come to them as mere authority and make them effects does not really come to them. It does not touch their humanity. We are saying that God's Word speaks to us. Here is an event that cannot take an automatic form. It has the form of a constraint that is possible and actual only in the sphere of freedom. The same is true when we say that someone believes and obeys. The compulsion here is obviously different from that of a rolling ball. It either takes place in freedom or not at all. We ultimately understand the concept of authority itself very poorly if we think of it only as a superior force and do not see that we have here the power of a command which can be heard and obeyed only in the sphere of freedom. But to avoid such a misunderstanding we must expressly discuss this second side of the matter too.

It is obvious that here we come across the specifically Protestant aspect of the whole problem. But I would regard it as suspicious if we identified Roman Catholicism with the principle of authority and Protestantism with that of freedom, far too freely celebrating it as the great achievement of the Reformers to have upheld the rights of the subject over against the object or the individual over against the church. The Reformers themselves at least were of another view. Undoubtedly, they championed the freedom of Christians in face of a materialistic, naturalistic, and mechanical authority. But they did so only in the form of a battle for real authority, for the real authority of the church. Those who see the Reformers as typical freedom fighters, who confuse them with the humanists and radicals, make of the whole of the Reformation no more than a reaction, a swing of the pendulum to the other side. We can do no better service to Roman Catholic polemics than to view the matter thus.

Roman Catholics will reply by pointing out that the Roman Catholic Church stands above this conflict inasmuch as it sees that over against the strongly asserted authority of the church there is free room for individual willing and thinking in everything that is not covered by this authority, whereas Protestantism in its heretical one-sidedness has obviously abandoned authority in favor of simple freedom. Protestants are foolish if they let themselves be pressed into this dead end, the more so as we have to concede to Roman Catholics that their reproach concerning our loss of authority is not unfounded.

Our reply ought to be that this harm that Israel has indeed suffered is due to the fact that modern Protestantism has fallen into the Roman Catholic habit of thought according to which there is neither total authority nor total freedom but only a little of both, each in its own sphere; the only difference is that modern Protestantism has put freedom in the center just as one-sidedly as Roman Catholicism has put authority. In contrast, the original Reformation had an idea of authority and freedom according to which the two do not confront one another partially, quantitatively, and competitively but are conjoined in a dialectical unity as the objective and subjective possibility of the same thing. "A Christian is a free lord of all things and subject to none, a Christian is a servant of all things and subject to all."[1] In Calvin, if not in Luther, it is quite clear that on one side the Reformation is just as definitely a battle *for* God's order and the church's authority against caprice, autonomy, and riot, as it is a battle on the other side for the immediacy of conscience and the freedom and responsibility of the individual against the tyranny of a priestly church. If we do not confuse Protestantism with the Enlightenment or mysticism, we can as little admit that the principle of freedom is in isolation and nondialectically the essence of Protestantism as prudent Roman Catholics can stake everything on the principle of authority.

There is some truth, of course, in each of these theses. It is no accident that the work of Luther that I quoted is entitled *The* Freedom *of a Christian Man*. The historical drift of Protestantism, the starting point of its protest, is the matter of freedom, just as the contrary concern of Roman Catholicism is that of authority. Because we regard the Protestant concern as justifiable and necessary, we must uphold it. But there can be no question on that account of setting aside the principle of authority or even subordinating it to that of freedom, even though Protestant theology has often made this inference from its historical beginnings. Mature Protestant thinking on this issue will certainly try to uphold the concept of freedom that in our view is stunted in Roman Catholicism — the only way to do full justice to the concept of authority as well — but in this attempt it will see that the two series of historical authorities and historical freedoms are equally valuable, significant, and important.

I need hardly repeat expressly what I said at the end of § 9.I, namely,

---

1. Cf. Luther's *Freedom of a Christian Man* (1520), WA, 7, 21, 1ff.; LW, 35, 362, 395-96.

that the freedom of the individual of which we must speak in antithesis to the authority of the church is, like the latter, a *historical* determination of the possibility of the communication of revelation. The freedom of the individual is the second necessary answer to the question *how* scripture speaks to us as God's Word. To the question *whether* and *why* this takes place there is only one answer — the reference to the act of divine lordship in which the Spirit speaks to spirit. With this reference we shall have to close the present section too.

II. The Meaning of Scripture as the Word of God

Let us again begin with the facts. Scripture comes to me like any object as I become aware of it. No recollection of the means that promote this and play their own part alters the banal fact that the last and obviously the true recipient of the prophetic and apostolic witness is the human consciousness — the church, of course, but the church as a fellowship of people. These people read and hear. Certain ideas are awakened in them. Certain thoughts, however well or badly, have to be thought, or thought *after*. But this involves something else that is unavoidable. The formation of ideas is a spontaneous act in which my other ideas play a very lively part. And thinking *after* means thinking *with*. We can follow the thoughts of others only when, however slightly, we can think something with our own thoughts as well. "We are with you," we say, and we mean that we are able with our own thoughts to accompany the thoughts of others along a particular path. Scripture, too, comes to me only as there is in my own ideas at least some place or possibility of contact for its ideas, and I am with it only as I can accompany, however modestly, the thoughts that may be seen in these ideas. But that is not all. In this way it can only draw near to me. To come to me in the pregnant sense of coming into my consciousness, the accompanying has to become what may again be a very primitive thinking of the thoughts of scripture for myself, an appropriating of the witness of the prophets and apostles, my own necessary witness to that to which they bear witness, even when the Bible is closed. These are the unqualified facts which do not differ from the facts in similar spheres. Homer or Goethe could and can come to me in the same way.

But now let us presuppose that scripture comes to us as the Word of God. Here is a claim that goes beyond the mere facts. We have to see what this claim is.

1. It obviously means that I have not merely to think the thoughts of scripture after it, to think with these thoughts, to think them for myself, but that I have also to think them as truth. The formula that the subjective possibility of receiving revelation is primarily an acceptance of it as true has clearly been scorned in modern theology. Yet I do not see how we can avoid it. We are not dealing merely with ideas and narratives and concepts and images. These are simply the means by which the prophets and apostles gave their witness. We are dealing with the thoughts of the witness itself that I am invited to think after, to think with, to think for myself. Perhaps I can do no better than think with the help of the ideas, even though they are remote and strange to me as such. We best think certain things by saying Yes and Amen to what is there. This will be the rule at the climax of the biblical witness. But it is not fundamentally a question of saying Yes and Amen to what is there. What is there is simply a reference to what is behind it, i.e., to revelation. The biblical thoughts constitute this reference or references.

But in any case, even less than a matter of ideas, it is not a matter of kindling certain feelings, impressions, or experiences. A retreat to feelings means a retreat to esthetics and a renunciation of truth. What is at issue — and the logico-ethical sphere is the proper place for this — is the acknowledgment of truth. The fact the scripture comes to us as God's Word means that we regard its thoughts as true, that is, that we accept its reference to revelation. No matter what our attitude to the words and the historical aspect of the witness may be, we have to regard them as transparencies through which a light shines. It shines with varying degrees of brightness and clarity — no one need argue that Jude is as powerful a witness as Romans — yet it is always a light, *the* light. Everything relates to this light, everything that we might view as a transparent medium pointing us in this direction. Even Jude is in its own way a witness to Jesus Christ and not to someone or something else. In this sense — and again the understanding of the historical element is a secondary concern — everything is truth. There is no possibility of regarding scripture as merely historical. There is no possibility of folding our arms and adopting the stance of onlookers or spectators. The only possibility is that of seriousness, of decision, of being taken captive, of faithfulness, of an act of supreme spontaneity.

2. If scripture comes to us as the Word of God, this means that as the Word of (God's) truth it comes to people. It means judgment and blessing for these people, law and gospel, God's fellowship with them. This

is what it refers to, and its reference to this is truth, the Word of God. Thinking the thoughts of scripture, thinking with them, thinking them for oneself, is very definitely a thinking of these thoughts. It is our thinking about ourselves, a self-scrutiny in the light of what God says to us. We not only cannot detach ourselves from ourselves and our situation; we ought not to do so. We have to come to ourselves — with God and from God. We have to be there. For this concerns us.

3. It is not a matter of people in general but of *myself*, this person. We remember what we said earlier about the connection between revelation and existence. Where God's Word is present, there is address. It is not a matter of human knowledge in general in its relation to God. It is something very different — my own knowledge in an I-Thou relation. The claim does not come collectively to humanity or even to Christendom but to the individual. The individual is judged and blessed. The individual is responsible for what has to be received and for what is made of it. The burden falls on the individual. The individual has to be helped. All acknowledgment of the truth, all self-scrutiny in the light of God, is true only in the act of this sharp turning in which it all becomes my own story.

To sum up, it is a matter of knowing the truth, the truth about people, the truth about me. This is what is meant by hearing scripture as God's Word. This is what is entailed by the insight that the hearing is conditioned, as on the one side by the authority of the church, so on the other side by the freedom of the individual. What happens to me really happens to *me*. If scripture comes to me at all as God's Word, it comes to me.

III. Various Freedoms in Relation to Scripture

Freedom means independence. It involves an individual act of spontaneity. It implies my own determining of the data. It is a negation of dependence, mediacy, and bondage. It entails a possibility of beginning directly at the beginning. As there are different kinds and degrees of authority, so it is with freedom. In contrast, there is also an unconditional and self-grounded freedom that is one and the same as self-grounded authority. We must now take a look at the various freedoms in relation to scripture. We may as little deny or expunge them as their equivalents on the side of authority.

1. As the first subjectively spontaneous factor I mentioned in the thesis "the historical picture that I make for myself of the witness of the

prophets and apostles." The witness of the prophets and apostles is a collection of records of concrete historical situations. As I study these, I unavoidably try to reconstruct these situations. On the basis of what is in the text I try to establish how things were then, what the authors had in mind when they said this or that, and apart from the authors and the texts how the events took place which they record. I combine these findings with other things that the same authors might have said about the same subjects or others. When the text is silent, I try to supplement its thoughts with cautious conjectures so as to form them into a whole. I try to understand them on the basis of what earlier or contemporary authors say on whom they might be dependent or with whom they might share a common legacy. I will especially use this procedure in relation to historical reports, and with the aid of further sources I will try to construct a picture of the events that the authors record. As I have either earlier or at the same time, by a similar procedure, formed some picture of the whole period, its events, relationships, and movements, its external and internal makeup, I fit the pictures that I have taken from the texts into this larger picture, and when I adduce similarly achieved pictures of the times that precede and follow, set these pictures in the framework of historical development, and look at them in this way, then I have carried through what might be called the act of historical investigation.

Naturally, this act, which begins with the attempt to relate the different words and word groups of a text, is an absolutely necessary act if I am to have any knowledge of scripture at all. The degree of skill and method and competence will vary, as will also the apparatus used and the various motions. There is a wide gap between the refined research of a Harnack or a Holl and the simple investigation of an old peasant sitting down with a Luther Bible. But the degree of skill and the wealth of aids do not decide whether the historical investigation that takes place is true and useful or not. Yet this is not our present point. Our present point is that no one can evade the act of historical inquiry, and that the result of this act, the historical picture that I form, is never an authority that confronts me but always a work of my freedom. *I* have made this picture. Instead of claiming that that is how it is or was, I have to admit freely that I did not photograph it but sketched it with my own greater or lesser degree of skill.

We can speak of the objectivity of this picture only with the reservation that we must make in relation to all scholarly depictions. We certainly cannot speak of an authority. Its objectivity is disputable to the degree that I depart from the sources and from lexicographical findings and resort to combinations and conjectures and constructions. The canon has authority, and so does the text that the church has received, but not a construct that is defended, perhaps very plausibly, even though it goes beyond the text and canon. It is not as though the making of such pictures is illegitimate or unnecessary. The act of historical observation is essential. It is the basis of a knowledge of scripture. This is why the Reformers demanded the grammatical investigation of scripture.

Yet we must be aware that this act is subjectively conditioned. We may respect its findings, but there is no reason to make an idol of them, as though the speaking of God's Word in scripture took place in the mere contemplation of such a historical picture (e.g., to mention the most important, the historical Jesus). Perhaps it does, but if so something else has to happen. And perhaps it does not. The freedom — and we hope it will be a Christian freedom and not some other — in which the act of investigation takes place, and the other freedoms — which we also hope will be Christian — that will call for mention later, are all conditioned freedoms, and are not to be confused with the unconditioned and self-grounded freedom in which the hearing of God's Word is absolutely an event.

We can say only one thing positively, namely, that regard for the authority of the canon and the text should not lead to[2] a prohibition of (completely) free biblical research along the lines of such historical investigation, but that this free research ought to be demanded on the basis of that authority. So long as more is not claimed for it than it can deliver, so long as it is radically aware of its relativity, it is an indispensable instrument in shaping the raw material. Questions may arise about the method, or individual abilities, or the historical position and task of individual teachers or scholars, but all of them make use of the same freedom, and all of them ought to do so.

2. I mention as the second spontaneously subjective factor "the way in which I try to grasp it [the prophetic and apostolic witness] in accordance with the ineluctabilities of my thinking." This brings us to the "thinking after" and the "thinking with" that are essential to a knowledge of scripture. It is obvious that this process cannot be separated in practice from the act of historical investigation. Historians usually take pride in the fact that they only want to observe, to reproduce alien strains of

---

2. The MS has "be."

thought exactly as they occur, to describe events and figures exactly as they are. We have seen what this involves.

But now a second subjective condition enters in. In reality none of us can study scripture without accompanying with our own thoughts that which we establish more or less without prejudice, without doing so even in the very process of establishing it.[3] After the manner of a double rainbow a second picture — that of thought — arises above the first picture — that of observation. This second picture is made up of presuppositions — you can see them even in a commentary like that of Lietzmann, not to speak of J. Weiss, in whom they are palpable — with which supposedly pure historians approach their material.[4] They cannot make the sacrifice of renouncing their own thinking and simply letting the text speak. In letting the text speak, they cannot avoid betraying the fact that they have a specific epistemology, a specific logic and ethics, specific ideas about the relations of God and the world and humanity, specific ideals — in short, a specific philosophy. This is what I mean when I refer to "the ineluctabilities of my thinking." Naturally, I am not negating a general necessity of thinking, a true philosophy, but like everything general and true this appears only in the form of philosophies, of individual efforts to order human thinking.[5] Naturally, few readers of the Bible or biblical scholars are philosophers by profession. But there are simple, popular, dilettante philosophies as well as academic philosophies. Even the old peasant has some philosophy — and perhaps not the worst. Even the so-called common sense of empiricists and pragmatists who abstain from speculation is naturally a philosophy. There are also bad philosophies.

This factor, at any rate, plays a part. None of us has any right to boast that *we* do not intermingle the NT with our own worldview but simply let the thoughts of scripture speak for themselves. Even as we do this, we betray clearly, even though we be, for example, a J. T. Beck, that we are younger contemporaries of Schelling or Baader, and that we may well have read even J. Böhme with some profit or impact.[6] By the cosily pragmatic and unreflecting way in which we work we may show that we

---

3. N. p. 141 adds: "without peopling the existing material with our own constructs."

4. *Handbuch zum NT,* ed. H. Lietzmann (Tübingen, 1906ff.); *Die Schriften des NT neu übersetzt und für die Gegenwart erklärt,* ed. J. Weiss (Göttingen, 1906-1907).

5. N. p. 141: "This is one such attempt."

6. Cf. J. T. Beck, *Über die wissenschaftliche Behandlung der christlichen Lehre . . .* (Heilbronn, 1878), p. 13.

are naive followers of Aristotle, or by the manner in which we stay aloof from the content of the text and merely study it we may give evidence that we are modern agnostics, or by the dialectical movement in which alone the texts gain vitality for us we may show that we are disciples of the thought of Plato and Kant.

I set myself wholly in the same group. I do not pretend to be any better than the rest. I only contest the right of the rest, whether they be biblicists on the one hand or historians on the other, to take themselves out of the group. None of us can do this. Of none of us is it true that we do not mix the gospel with philosophy.[7] Luther and Calvin had their philosophy. So far as I can see they were both Platonists, although of different schools. And to none of us in our understanding of scripture is it a matter of indifference where we come from in this sense or what presuppositions we bring with us. In one sense this is decisive, namely, for our fixing of the thoughts of scripture, of what is meant, or supposed to be said, with what is said in the text. Some people think that mystical feelings are the true content of the Bible, others think they find a semi-idealistic and semi-pietistic pragmatism, others a cosmic drama embracing heaven and earth, while others again have the impression — and this, too, rests on a philosophy — that the Bible does not mean anything or want to say anything at all. In this sense the much-quoted verse of the old Basel theologian Werenfels is true, namely, that we all seek our dogmas in the Bible and find them as seems best to ourselves.[8] In this sense we all engage in allegorical exegesis, that is, we impose a second meaning on what is there — a meaning which is not there but which we have to impose on it in order to understand it.

I am not of the view that we must scorn all this if only for the reason that we can make no practical use of such scorn. But we should at least honestly admit what we are doing. We should be kind enough to give the child its right name and not boast of an objectivity that is as little in place here as in the act of investigation, not confusing with authority

---

7. N. p. 142 adds: "Here it must be said that this is part of the questionability of our existence."

8. Barth quotes this verse in the form in which we find it in K. R. Hagenbach, *Die theologische Schule Basels . . .* (Basel, 1860), p. 39: "Hic liber est in quo quisque sua dogmata quaerit, invenit atque iterum dogmata quisque sua." The original in W. Werenfels, *Opuscula theologica . . .* (Basel, 1792), p. 362, under the heading "S. Scripturae abusus," is as follows: "Hic liber est, in quo sua quaerit dogmata quisque, Invenit et pariter dogmata quisque sua."

the court from which all our thinking after and thinking with derive, not wrapping ourselves in the virtuous mantle of historicism, but calling freedom freedom. Then we may cold-bloodedly tell ourselves that our philosophy, whether good or bad, whether academic or dilettante, is a factor which can and should help to determine my hearing of the Word inasmuch as the Word comes to me, a human being, a thinking person, a person who thinks in this particular way.

In this light, however, we can also see that there has to be an authority in the church, fathers and dogmas, to hold in check the caprice that threatens us here, to show to each new generation the way which the church has followed thus far in this understanding of scripture, to prevent us from thinking that anything and everything is possible. Historicism will not protect us against capricious exposition, for only too often it is itself a new form of caprice. What will protect us is a bit of the Apostles' Creed, a bit of Luther or Calvin, viewed not as thinkers or heroes but as authorities by which to orient ourselves. Free thinking with the help of authorities — this is the way. I am aware of the relativity of this formula, but we are now talking only about relative conditions. Freedom and authority are not mutually exclusive once one considers that both are totalities operating on different levels. When it is thus understood, with this counterbalance, freedom of thought — Christian freedom, we hope — is a demand that must be made unconditionally. True hearing of the Word in scripture depends upon my thinking something in relation to what I hear. I cannot maintain that what I think is Christian philosophy. It bears too plainly the marks of human and profane philosophy. But I can and should *hope* that it is. And that is perhaps enough.

3. As a third factor in the thesis I have distinguished from the above "the light in which it [the prophetic and apostolic witness] appears to me at a given moment." You will see how closely freedom and authority belong together when you compare this statement with the corresponding one in the previous section: "the inner and outer situation of each historical moment." I elucidated this condition — that of authority here, today, and now, in terms of the concept of the church's teaching office.

I might set over against this authority, on the side of freedom, the concept of prophecy. I mean by this what secularists might call congeniality with the witnesses of revelation and what yesterday I described as thinking the thoughts of scripture for oneself. In the second edition of my *Romans* I caused some offense by saying that in exposition a point is reached when I almost forget that I am not the author, since I almost understand him so well that I can have him speak in my name or can even speak in his.[9] This is what I have in mind here. The sharpest historical observation and the most intensive thinking after and thinking with do not help me at all if first and last there does not enter in something of this identification between me and the author, the author and me. I number this among the relative conditions of hearing. Over against this congeniality the absolute freedom with which the Spirit gives witness that the Spirit speaks the truth is something different. But in the relative sphere this congeniality should not be overlooked as the last and concluding definition of the concept of freedom. With it the whole process of hearing finally moves out of the empirical sphere and the reflective sphere into the existential sphere. I do not merely investigate or think. No, the witness to revelation now appears to me in this very special light. Historical distance and conceptual abstraction are overcome. The witness becomes for me a Word, a Word for the hour. Even as I do this, Romans, which I investigate and reflect on, becomes a letter to me and a letter which I must write to the people of Göttingen and to anyone who will listen.

You must remember that this is not at all a personal aspiration which someone might have, nor is it, of course, something for which one has to be specifically a theologian. We have here a category that applies wherever there is real hearing of the Word. The author here crosses my threshold, or I cross his. The *nyni de* [Rom. 3:21; 7:6; etc.] comes into force here. Without our raising the ridiculous claim to be prophets, what we do comes under the concept of prophecy. We have heard the witness in such a way that we have to accept it and pass it on. But we have to do so without authority, in freedom. I will really guard carefully against confusing myself with the apostle Paul and putting my witness on a level with his. The only thing is that the Word is not heard if hearing does not reach a climax in this moment in relation to which all observation and reflection can be no more than preparation.

Again it is essential that over against this last and supreme freedom there should stand directly as a corrective the last and supreme authority of the church in its office as present-day watchman and teacher. If we are clear about this, about the relativity of this last and supreme freedom, not erasing the boundary but realizing and considering that I am saying this, not the Lord [cf. 1 Cor. 7:12], even at the moment when I seem to stand on the same level as scripture in my understanding and reception and

---

9. K. Barth, *Römerbrief,* 2nd ed. (Munich, 1922), p. XI; ET *Romans,* p. 8.

further witness; if I keep in mind the distance which unconditionally separates even this moment of congenial freedom — Christian freedom, we hope — from the absolute freedom of the Word itself, then there can be no talk of enthusiasm or the like without doing harm to the living character of the Word. Instead, we may then see that even in this final matter we do not merely have a permission but an unconditional demand.

IV. Individual and Scriptural Freedom

The final point in the thesis is exactly parallel to the corresponding one in § 9: "Nevertheless, this freedom, too, is historical, relative, and formal. Direct, absolute, and material freedom can again be ascribed only to scripture as God's Word." I will deal with this briefly. In the light of what has gone before you can think it out for yourselves. The "nevertheless" again denotes a bracket which does not negate what is said in subsection III but which must not be removed. We must again consider that the "nevertheless" or limitation which has to be set over against the freedom of the individual as well as the authority of the church is valid and efficacious only if it does not come from the world, from outside, in this case from a human authority, but from the source or origin of freedom, so that freedom is held in check by freedom. Human authority can act as a corrective. But the arrogance of historians and philosophers and minor prophets (and all of us are all these things) can be broken only by the freedom of God.

Finally, then, we again go back to our starting point. With the mediacy of revelation the scripture principle of Protestantism also proclaims its immediacy. It speaks about scripture and the Spirit, about the Spirit in scripture. Where the Spirit is, there is freedom [2 Cor. 3:17]. All freedoms have their source here. They also have their limit here. Freed from the freedom of God, all our freedoms become irrelevant and meaningless liberalism, subjectivism, or spiritualism. Christian freedom, we hope — I have said this more than once. The immediacy to God in which the Word sets us ends all false immediacies. This is what is at issue in scripture. Truly? Yes, truly. But that belongs to another book. It is not a capstone that we dare to put in place as dogmaticians. It is really true only in act, in the act of the *autopistia* of scripture or the inner testimony of the Spirit, in the event whose subject is God himself, and regarding which we can say only that in it all our freedoms, like all our authorities, are both set up and cast down, both cast down and set up.

CHAPTER 3

THE WORD OF GOD AS
CHRISTIAN PREACHING

§ 11

Pure Doctrine

Christian preachers dare to talk about God. Even on the presupposition of the mediation of revelation by holy scripture this venture would always be impossible without the third presupposition that God acknowledges it and will himself speak as we speak, just as he spoke to the prophets and apostles and still speaks through them. The Word of God in this third form, as the present-day communication of revelation, is Christian preaching. It is pure doctrine if the word of the preacher gives free play to God's own Word. Insofar as it does this, and should do it, the word of the preacher is the subject matter of dogmatic work.

I. The Riddle of Christian Preaching

Let us recall the difficulty we ran into when at the beginning of § 3 we looked for comfort regarding the possibility of the venture of Christian preaching. Take as much or as little as you like of what I am here presenting to you, but believe me — *credite experto*[1] — that this venture and its difficulty are no joke. You will perhaps be having a quiet laugh at the sentence which recurs so monotonously: "Christian preachers dare to talk about God." But in a few years your own path will lead into this impasse. I know what I am about when I keep repeating this statement. *Ta auta graphein hymin emoi men ouk oknēron, hymin de asphales* (Phil. 3:1). It is better in my view that you should laugh a little now rather than that you

---

1. Cf. Vergil, *Aeneid* XI, 283: "Experto credite."

should bewail the fact later that at university no one prepared you for the existential question that awaits you.[2]

Let us recall, then, that in that impasse we finally proposed a way that led from the church to the canon and from the canon to revelation. Carefully looking around on all sides, we have now descended again this mountain path and we find ourselves once more at our starting point. Are we, then, more cheerful-hearted? I think not. We have seen that the only possible way out of the difficulty leads us into another difficulty. If the essential questions *there* — hard enough in themselves — were those of authenticity, courage, and legitimacy — questions that finally everyone tries to answer with some kind of compromise — *here* in the doctrines of revelation and scripture, in which we had to see our way out with teeth tightly clenched, the questions both on the right hand and the left are those of faith and obedience, of God, Christ, and Spirit — absolute questions to which there can be none but absolute answers. We have also seen that in this high mountain country of absolute questions and answers there can be no possibilities of settling down, of digging in and spending the winter. Those who want fixed positions will not find them here. Here there is only the most vigorous war of movement. Our way through the doctrines of revelation and scripture was like the course of a rolling ball. It touched only for a moment on any given point. It had to keep changing. One might also think of a streambed that one can cross only by leaping from one stone to another if one is not to fall in (Thurneysen).[3]

If this does not please you — and why should we disguise the fact that it does not please any of us, including myself? — I would put three questions to you. (a) In view of the situation depicted at the beginning of § 3, for this is the decisive point, do you know of any other way that will lead neither into a morass nor on to this mountain trail? (b) Is it clear to you that not merely we theologians but Christians in general, if they want to get out of this impasse but not fall into a morass, have no option but to exchange the smaller difficulty for the greater, the little burden for the big one, or, as we might say, sin for judgment, suffering for the cross?[4] (c) Do you not think that if we really have to do with the reality of God,

---

2. Marginal note: "The most relevant in theology."

3. Cf. E. Thurneysen, "Schrift und Offenbarung" (1924), in *Das Wort Gottes und die Kirche*, TBü, 44 (Munich, 1971), p. 61.

4. N. p. 148 adds: "the battle of life for the battle of faith. If we theologians have to sigh, there is nothing unusual about this; it is the lot of all Christian. Because the waves go over us, we are not to think that this is something unheard-of; it is all as it should be."

even if only in the harmless academic way in which we are now proceeding, then for us there is no other situation than that of the flexibility with which we have surveyed it, so that, in view of this reason for our unrest, in the last resort and at the final depth we have good cause to be at rest?

We thus come back to our starting point, to which, before we move on in the winter to the real work that has to be done,[5] we must orient ourselves more fundamentally now that we are enriched by the questions, insights, and viewpoints that we have achieved in the meantime. In what has preceded we have ascertained two things regarding the venture of Christian preaching. The first has to do with the enacted and received address of God in his revelation, the second with the establishment of contemporaneity between revelation and us. Can we talk about God on the basis of this twofold presupposition?

Consider first something that we came across at the climax of each of the preceding sections. In § 9 we met a last and supreme authority in the church (the teaching office) which consists of grasping divine necessity in the inner and outer situation of a given moment and hence proclaiming what scripture (and through scripture revelation, and through revelation God) is saying to us today. And in § 10 we met a last and supreme freedom of the individual (prophecy) which consists of an independent thinking and stating today of the thoughts of scripture (and therewith of the truth of revelation, and therewith of the truth of God). The venture of Christian preaching lies precisely between these two points, and if we think of these points as an ideal unity, then we have to say that the venture of Christian preaching is the act which is at one and the same time an act of the last and supreme authority of the church and an act of the last and supreme freedom of the individual. But then we have also to recall that we had to see and say of both these acts that they are the last and supreme acts only within a bracket, for being human and historical they are to be differentiated from the true authority and freedom that are divine. This authority and freedom, we have seen, are reserved for scripture, that is, for the Spirit, for revelation, that is, for God. Thus the venture of Christian preaching is also made within the bracket. Even now we cannot talk about God. To talk about God is to talk with divine authority and freedom, so that our object is also our subject. But God has reserved this for himself. In the way that he spoke to the prophets and apostles and still speaks

---

5. Barth continued his Dogmatics in the winter semester of 1924/25 and then again in the summer semester of 1925.

through them, *we* cannot speak about him. We cannot speak about God as we would about some other object. We know that when God is not the subject he is also not the object. We are really talking about something else.

We come up here against the painful and tragic riddle of Christian preaching. In a thousand tongues it speaks about God, and truly not without quoting a last and supreme authority and claiming last and supreme freedoms. Why, then, do people not hear that we are talking about God? Why does everything remain so dumb, gray, dull, and dead around us as though we were talking about something else? God has spoken to the prophets and apostles and still speaks through them. His revelation is real and possible, its contemporaneity is real and possible, but we are always talking about something other than God. It is as though there were God the Father and the Logos, but no Holy Spirit, no God *for* us and *with* us and *in* us. Everything here cries out for a solution if Christian preaching on our lips is not to be folly, talk about an object that as a mere object is certainly not God but something else. Was it a mere pious postulate or desperate hyperbole that our fathers had in view, we must ask, or were they talking about a reality that is just as real as revelation or scripture, when they ventured a bold equation and handed down to us even today at least as an ecclesiastical formula — namely, the belief that the word proclaimed even by preachers alive today is not just their own word (their own talk about God, though it is this too) but that it is the Word of God that is inseparably bound up with their own word, the same Word of God that speaks in scripture, the same Word of God that the prophets and apostles themselves heard?

"The preaching of the Word of God is the Word of God."[6] One has to make a choice here. Either this is an arrogant exaggeration, postulate, or hyperbole, one of the piously shameless acts that religion is always perpetrating, one of the ecclesiastical formulas that we repeat because they are first told to us, or else it is reality, the wholly new reality of the Spirit, of God, which we can only await afresh, understand afresh, and need to seek and find and thankfully receive afresh. There is no other option.

What does it mean if preaching is God's Word? It obviously does not mean that pastors in the pulpit cease to be pastors and become instead the flutes of the Holy Spirit.[7] They are this just as little as Isaiah or Paul.

---

6. Second Helvetic Confession, Art. 1, 2, in *BSRK*, p. 171.10; Schaff, p. 382.
7. Barth has in view a comparison often used in the discussion of inspiration.

No, if pastors are not wholly pastors there can be no talk of the Holy Spirit or of inspiration, as in the case of the biblical authors. What they say does not suddenly cease to be human talk about God and therefore to be in itself talk about something else and not God. No, they are now really aware what it means to stand within that bracket with the last and highest that they can bring by way of authority or freedom. Nor is it as though they stop taking pains about what they should say because it will be in any case God's Word. No, if it is to be that, they must now truly begin to meditate on the law of God day and night [Ps. 1:2], even if they were doing so already. Thus there is no palpable alteration of the situation, no miracle unless it be that pastors suddenly perceive what they really ought to be. Yet it is nonetheless a miracle, a reality of the Spirit, of God, no less incomprehensible, unfathomable, and nonderivable than revelation itself or its communication through the prophetic and apostolic Word. No less than there we have here a presupposition, a hypothesis, which we can only believe, which only God makes real and understandable.

We can never be too bashful or restrained or modest in thinking and speaking about this third presupposition. Little is gained by simply putting preaching alongside revelation and scripture and then making deductions as though we had to make this presupposition. It is not for nothing that such a laborious, unsatisfying, and difficult thing as dogmatics finds its necessary source here. All the trouble that is caused us theologians by this unavoidable enterprise is obviously a big warning finger. Not for a moment is it self-evident that this third presupposition is correct. It is a great thing to presuppose that Jesus Christ is the Logos. It is an even greater and more daring thing to presuppose that the same Logos still speaks today through the Word of his witnesses. But from our standpoint it is indubitably the most dangerous and ambivalent and burdensome thing to presuppose that the same Logos speaks again and will constantly speak as Christian preaching, especially when we are not just spectators of the process but participants in it, when we are affected by it, when we either are or will be Christian preachers ourselves. We can make this third presupposition only with fear and trembling. By a sound and sober doctrine of the spiritual office, we can only clarify and sharpen and intensify it, not expunge or inoculate it. Precisely when, as we desire, theology is not detached from the Bible or its witness but strictly related to it, we cannot do it without existential anxiety, without unceasing reflection, without work in the sweat of our faces.

Let us remember and continually remember the sequence here.

Jesus Christ speaks, then the prophets and apostles speak, and then we come with our bit of speaking about God, and it is all a Word of God himself. The fact that it is so follows from the concept of revelation if we understand it aright, and especially from the doctrine of the Holy Spirit. The Son of the Father is not without the Spirit of the Father and the Son. God would not be God if we were not also there, if his Word were not put in our hearts and on our lips. The fact that it is so follows also from the concept of scripture if we understand it aright, and especially from the doctrine of its *autopistia* and the inner testimony of the Spirit. Scripture would not be scripture if the spirit in us were not set in dialogue with the Spirit in it. But what help are any of these doctrines as such in face of the inconceivability, the unheard-of character, the burning and shining of the reality about which they speak and which, if we will dare to make this third presupposition, will attack us so mysteriously?

The question with which all our deliberations of the semester began — the question whether and how we can speak about God — finds its third and decisive answer in this third presupposition. Christian preaching is God's Word in and for the present just as holy scripture is God's Word in time and revelation is God's eternal Word. Let us see what this implies. It cannot imply that we may now appropriate revelation, change places with Jesus Christ, and equate our speaking with the *Deus dixit,* regarding ourselves as eternal in the moment that is ours.[8] *Mē genoito.* It cannot imply that we may view ourselves as prophets and apostles, equate our own spirit with the Spirit of the first witnesses,[9] and regard our own words as a historical development of the coming of revelation into history, of the testimony to it. Again, *mē genoito.* No, revelation remains revelation, scripture scripture, and preaching preaching. We must not separate the three, but we must also distinguish them and not confuse them. Only the one Word that speaks three times is the true Word of God, just as only the triune God is the living God.

Thus there can be no question of our forgetting that even the last and supreme authority that we know in history, the teaching office of the church, and even the last and supreme freedom that we know in history, the prophecy of individuals, stand always in brackets, lest we secretly draw back the bolt that is placed for us in history by holy scripture as the witness to revelation, or with a bold leap set ourselves on the throne of God. No,

8. *Reden*, p. 74; ET *Speeches*, p. 101.
9. K. H. Bogatzky's hymn "Wach auf du Geist der ersten Zeugen."

even and precisely of Christian preachers it is true that all of us are liars [Ps. 116:11]. It must be solely the truth and miracle of God if his Logos, as he does not regard the lowliness of his handmaiden [Luke 1:48] or view the unclean lips of Isaiah as an obstacle [Isa. 6:5-7], does not think it impossible to pitch his tent in what is at best our poor and insignificant and stammering talk about God, to acknowledge this talk even though it remains our own, to speak himself when we speak, to fill with himself the completely empty vessel of Christian preaching. As the human nature of Christ has to be human nature still in the revelation of the Logos, and as the historical datum of holy scripture has to be historical datum still, so our talk about God, precisely as the communication of revelation, has still to be human talk with no mystical fusion or change. Here too — and the weakness of our speaking sees to it that we recognize it — we have the indirectness and hiddenness of revelation to which we have often referred. If revelation is really revelation in concealment, if God acknowledges our Word, if he speaks when we speak, then here as everywhere that God speaks the glory and the power and the wisdom are *his* and not ours. God is always the subject. This is the possibility or the condition under which we can talk about God.

Here, then, is the situation at the starting point of our deliberations which is also their goal. You understand me aright if you make the inference that the whole difficulty remains into which we are plunged by the question whether we can speak about God. It does indeed remain. All that might be said against it from an epistemological, ethical, or purely practical standpoint can still be said against it. We have in no sense tried to replace the unsuccessful apologetics in which help is sought at this point with a better one. We have not made a possibility out of the venture of talking about God. We have not built a bridge over the abyss. We have simply described three presuppositions, or rather the one Word of God which might give us cause to make the venture. Thus the difficulty has become greater rather than less. For if the Word of God gives us cause to make the venture of talking about God, this presupposes faith and obedience.

There meets us then the further question whether we will believe and obey. We might also put it this way: If we do believe and obey, there has met us the Holy Spirit who makes our speaking the vessel of the divine Word, and even more, makes it one with this Word. The Holy Spirit, God himself, who comes to us and gives himself to us without ceasing to be God, *he* is the one who gives us the ability and the right and the perception and the courage to speak about God. Without him and apart from him we have none of these things. We need only for a single moment look away from the Holy Spirit and think about ourselves, and it is as clear as daylight that we cannot talk about God but only about something else. Only God can talk about God. To this extent, in appropriate application of a christological formulation, we might say of preaching as the Word of God that it is "conceived by the Holy Ghost."[10]

II. Preaching as a Human Task

I have given this section the title "Pure Doctrine." If you have grasped the strictly dialectical relation between Christian preaching and God's Word, you will not be surprised if I now continue rather drily: Christian preaching is a human task like any other. It may be done profoundly or superficially, carefully or sloppily, well or badly. Precisely because Christian preaching is God's Word it becomes a human *task*. That is to say, the human activity denoted thereby acquires its necessity, meaning, norm, and goal. It comes under the question and the requirement under which all human activity stands. The Word of God is the basis of ethics. What I mean is that as the simple being and performing of this or that human action is set in relation to God's Word, to his address to us, it comes up against a demand, a law, a command, an ideal, and what is given becomes a task, chaos becomes cosmos. We have related the specific activity of Christian preaching as closely as possible to the Word of God in a relationship of indirect identity. This activity, if any, is thus set under the question and requirement. We have understood this relationship poorly if we can draw from it any other deduction than that Christian preaching must be done as profoundly, carefully, and well as possible, that we must do all that can be done to make it pure doctrine.

Naturally, if Christian preaching is something other than God's Word, precisely then it cannot be a human *task*. It is wholly on a level with what takes place in nature. It is an act of caprice, a product of the imagination, something that one may either do or not do. The particular quality of this activity means that we cannot give it a rational place among other human activities. It is everywhere without a home. For what is

---

10. Barth here quotes the Latin of the Apostles' Creed: *conceptus est de spiritu sancto.*

preaching? Where does it belong? Is it a function of public order? Or of moral instruction? Or of intellectual development? Or does it finally belong fundamentally to the sphere of the beautiful, to esthetics? In the school of Schleiermacher we almost inevitably arrive at this last opinion. But have not all these places been taken long ago? Popular education, the cultivation of morality and patriotism, the nurture of the emotions — none of these really needs us theologians. Others can do these and similar things much better than we can. The world knows this and acts accordingly. We are examined and rejected, and rightly so, before we become apprentices in such dilettante occupations. Our activity really becomes necessary and significant again before God and the world only when it rediscovers its own authentic relationship. It again has its place in society, a truly remarkable place, only when it stands under a norm. It is a possible task once more only when we see that the only way out is that as human talk about God it stands in that relationship of indirect identity to God's Word.

At a stroke, then, it becomes an activity which is necessary, grounded, and regulated. What the world says and thinks about it is another matter, as with any activity, but it is no longer without a home, it no longer lives in lodgings, it is no longer on the street (I use this ambiguous expression intentionally), it is no longer a parasite, it has its own roots. If the theologians of the 19th century had shown only a tenth of their concern for human autonomy when it was a matter of the autonomy of their own heritage — I will not go further back — then we would not be where we are today. They did not, and hence we are compelled today to engage again in all kinds of paradoxical movements of thought that really ought to be self-evident.

If it is true that talk about God, theology, or preaching means that God himself speaks, then the task of defining the activity and making individual provisos is clear in principle. Human speech must do everything it can do to leave room for God's own speech. I call this task the task of pure doctrine. If I had wanted to provoke you more, I would have called it orthodoxy instead. But orthodoxy means "right opinion," and here it is a matter of talk, not opinion. Christian preaching is not an idea or a thought but an event, an action, an act. Do not be afraid of the stiff and much despised word "doctrine." It expresses very well what is at issue here, namely, that one person should tell another or others what they do not know. Christian preaching is a synthetic act. Anti-intellectualistic fear of the word "doctrine" rests on a secret or — from the time of Schleiermacher

— open naturalism. Nothing new must come to us. But God's Word does bring something very new. If preaching is God's Word, it cannot feel awkward about being doctrine.

As regards the word "pure," it is better than "right" or "correct" because it better denotes what is meant, that is, it brings out its specific content better. When I say that doctrine must be pure (and to that extent "right" or "correct," *orthē*), I mean that it should be clear and transparent like polished glass. It is not there for its own sake but so that we may see through the human word to the present, living Word of God. The less it puts a third thing between God's Word and us; the more it removes every third thing and displaces everything that is falsely divine or overarrogantly human; the more positively it is merely a reference or a pointing of the finger compelling us to look at the other thing with which it is indirectly identical; the more clearly the hidden Word of God can shine through the concealing human word, the more it is *pure* doctrine. It was not for nothing that in the Middle Ages a crystal-clear and polished glass vessel was one of the most familiar symbols for Mary. The Logos seeks vessels such as this. To make our talk about God into one such vessel is a task. This is not to say that even where the doctrine is purest, God will really confess it, speaking when we speak. It is not to say that he cannot speak even through the medium of very impure doctrine. But God's freedom does not alter the fact that we are set a task. When we have done everything that we are required to do, we should still say that we are unprofitable servants [Luke 17:10]. But those who infer from this that we may be indolent servants show thereby that they do not understand the matter at all.

III. Dogmatics and Preaching

Dogmatic work serves this required search for pure doctrine. It does not follow automatically that the human word of preachers leaves free room for God's Word, so that there is an equation between God's Word and Christian preaching in accordance with our third presupposition. If and when this happens, it is not a state but an event, a human action corresponding to the simultaneously occurring divine action. The same is naturally true of the concept of pure doctrine in which we have finally summed up the preacher's task. Pure doctrine is not a formula or system of formulas. This was the fatal error into which the older Protestantism fell when it also came to regard holy scripture as an inspired letter. The very fact that people thought they had still to write new and better dogmatics was itself a remarkable refutation of the view that they already had pure doctrine. It was an express acknowledgment that they still had to seek it and develop it and produce it afresh. As revelation in Jesus Christ is present only in act as God's act, and is revelation only on the presupposition of its objective and subjective possibility and not in itself, and as holy scripture is *holy* scripture only in the divine act of lordship above the middle point between last and supreme human authority and freedom, and not in itself, so Christian preaching is not in itself God's Word but is so only in act as God's address, and this is the same concrete sense which it is absolutely decisive that we grasp in the doctrines of revelation and scripture.

Thus the concept of pure doctrine under which we have summed up the activity of the Christian preacher must not be made static so that it no longer denotes an action but something that has been done and thought and said and written, a letter which has only to be repeated as a letter for pure doctrine to be present. No, we must not ossify or freeze anything here. We must not make anything into a block or stock. If we have to call the identity between Christian preaching and God's Word a gift *(Gabe),* by the concept of pure doctrine we denote a human task *(Aufgabe)* which is written not on paper but on the conscience of the church and its individual members, which we cannot make a matter of mere repetition but which we have to work at, which arises always in the fiery pressure between authority and freedom that repeats itself on this level, which — as we may say quite plainly — has always to be done afresh.

Here, then, we have the task of dogmatics. But let us be cautious and modest. In the thesis, in harmony with what I said under § 2.I, I stated that the word of the preacher is the subject matter of dogmatic work. This says relatively little. But we should not say too much at this point. We should not say that dogmatics fashions pure doctrine. It would be strange if this vital function of the church were put in the hands of professors of systematic theology and a few experts in the field. The hurt done to Israel would then be much greater than it is today. We should not say either that individual Christian preachers in their secondary office as greater or lesser systematicians are the subjects of pure doctrine. No, pure doctrine, the human word that leaves room for God's Word, is not a product of the study, although it probably would not come into being without the study. It arises in the narrow defile between the Bible with its witness to revelation and the people of the present with their question. The church and its pastors act and suffer in this defile. The pulpit is the place where there is either pure doctrine or not, where there is either room for God's Word or not. Dogmatics stands at a distance from this place of decision and what happens there. Dogmatics and preaching are related in the same way as service at headquarters and at the front. Headquarters has to be there if anything essential is to be done at the front. Dogmatics has to serve the church. It has to help to purify doctrine.

When I say dogmatics I naturally have in mind not only what goes on at the university and in books — though I mean that too — but also everything that individual theologians do all their lives as also official systematicians, everything that goes on always and everywhere behind the front of proclamation, everything that I called reflection in § 5. The only thing is that we must not confuse dogmatics and preaching. You should not go out and for a few years overpower your poor congregations with the contents of your notebooks, with the objective and subjective possibilities of revelation, with exercises in the ancient and modern theologies of the schools that we have to study here, with the dialectical corners into which I have to lead you here. You must draw the content of your sermons from the well which stands precisely between the Bible, your own concrete situation, and that of your hearers. Homiletics and practical theology as a whole will deal with it. In no case, however, must you draw on my own or any other dogmatics, and please, not from the dogmatics that probably each of you will work out for private use.[11] Everything in its own time and place. Dogmatics is an exercise, an academic exercise, a necessary and useful exercise when it is done properly, but still an exercise, a preparatory act behind the scenes. If other people are interested in it, then we must not forbid this, but as a whole I would say to you that there is hardly anything that we theologians should keep as much to ourselves as dogmatics.[12]

At any rate we must not think that we can do anything out in the world with what we have to say here. The considerations that we have to take into account here are much too secondary and indirect and deliberative. We have to concern ourselves with much that is too historical to be perspicuous to those who are at a distance. Yet in this inner workshop of

---

11. Parenthetical note: "Student sermons! C. F. Meyer, *Der Schuss von der Kanzel.*"
12. Barth put this sentence in the margin of the MS with a wavy line and a question mark.

ours we also must not let ourselves be influenced by the wishes of the public, e.g., of philosophers and historians. Those who accept no responsibility for the venture of Christian preaching will offer counsel that we will prudently take note of, but they cannot be normative critics of the work that we must do there. They may not like what we have to do but we cannot do it differently for their sake. Only when we keep ourselves and our work in the background with the necessary modesty can we tackle it with the necessary composure and assurance.

The main point to be made, however, is that in dogmatics it is not a matter of advancing or establishing or proving anything. God's Word as Christian preaching is already there long before dogmatics, and also, we hope, something of pure doctrine. First, then, dogmatics has to listen, to receive, to record. Ideally, though this will not happen before the millennium, it would have to do no more, simply stating how things are when human words are a clear and unsullied mirror for God's Word. Dogmatics could then declare bankruptcy, as it has often been advised to do. In this ideal situation the task of Christian preaching would already be done, the act would be pure act, pure doctrine would be an event. If there were no task, there would be no need of this help. But things are not like this. To be sure, there is hardly a single feeble proclamation of the gospel that is totally defective as regards pure doctrine, that does not leave room somewhere and somehow for God's own speaking. At the same time — and I am thinking now not merely of feeble preachers but of those who are called good — there is also much darkness, much deplorable human vanity, limitation, confusion, indecision, and superficiality, much too much of the human, temporal, and secular element that bars free course in the Word. I said earlier that to every age the church's preaching has been sick.

At any rate, questions upon questions abound. Was that God's Word? If no, why not? Was it God's fault? How could it be? Was it not simply because something fundamental was not well done before the preacher mounted the pulpit and delivered the sermon or even thought of doing so? What? The preacher ought to have realized, or come to realize, that pure doctrine would not be a matter of chance but that every effort should be directed one-sidedly to allowing the human word to leave room not for itself but for God's Word. Clarity on this point, however, is not such a matter of simple reflection as it might seem to be at a first glance. It is not a matter of doing nothing but of doing something. It is not a matter of keeping silence (how simple it would all be if this were so) but of speaking. But how can I speak in such a way that God speaks through me? This is the issue. In this difficulty dogmatics, which has previously had to listen, must now begin to say something, not prescribing a panacea for the sickness, but at least offering some sober and well-considered advice like a good physician.

What can dogmatics do? It can lead to reflection on what the church is preaching. It can pick out a number of key terms that constantly recur in what Christian preachers say, for example, God, his love, wisdom, power, and similar attributes, creation, providence, sin, guilt, Christ, reconciliation, faith, etc. These key words were called *loci* at the time of the Reformation. The term *communes* was added. Literally — do not be alarmed — what the full description denotes is commonplaces, Christian commonplaces, concepts which either explicitly or implicitly will always occur in what pastors say. With the help of these commonplaces dogmatics will then try to show in detail in what sense and context, with what presuppositions and consequences, with what relations and delimitations such words must be used in order that no block or brake should stand in the way of God's Word but the human word should be a pure mirror for God's glory. In this work statements and formulas and summaries will obviously find a place. As we have seen earlier, these are dogmas in the most general sense of the word, the primarily nonbinding purifications which some great or small dogmatician has proposed in relation to the key words, *loci,* or commonplaces. They have no place in the pulpit, but pastors in the pulpit should give evidence that they know them by their silent adherence to them. They should preach nondogmatically but with a solid dogmatics behind them. If this is a good dogmatics, then even though some presuppositions may not be present the sermon will be pure doctrine, or not too impure. Thus dogmatics does not make pure doctrine, but with its *loci* it contributes to it, to what goes on in the pulpit.

We naturally ask how dogmatics with the help of these concepts can bring it about that when people speak about God they do not get in the way — we will be content to put it in this negative form. To be able to do this it must obviously be in a position to test all these words, to work on them critically, to track their meaning insofar as they have a meaning in this direction, to the honor of God and his Word. Clearly, then, it needs a standard, and it must know how to handle it, how to measure. We thus come up against what we were talking about in the previous two sections. As we said in § 5, dogmatics has to go back to scripture and revelation, which are the basis of preaching. These two things, which I will call the dogmatic norm, are the law by which dogmatics judges, the light in which the dogmatician sets the adopted *loci*. As a going back, a seeking of the meaning of the *loci*, the act is what I would call dogmatic thinking. You will see without difficulty that we are again dealing with an objective and a subjective possibility — this time of pure doctrine — and that I thus perceive a correspondence between the problems that occupy us here and that which occupied us in Chapter 1 as the relation between incarnation and faith and obedience, and then again in Chapter 2 as the relation between authority and freedom. Everywhere the situation is the same. The possibility does not create the reality. The reality on the top step is *Deus dixit,* on the second step scripture, and on the third step pure doctrine. But to grasp the reality as such we have to grasp the possibility too. This applies here as well, where the reality, in contrast to Chapters 1 and 2, is so close to us that it is our own task. If by means of these objective and subjective factors we succeed in fixing the admittedly limited but still significant place and aim of dogmatics as the science of the norms of Christian proclamation, we shall have reached the goal of these prolegomena.

§ 12

The Dogmatic Norm

Dogmatic work consists first of the fact that over against the pious words of Christian preachers it magnifies the authority of Word of God as this is spoken in revelation and as witness is borne to it by scripture. The heteronomy under which the statements of dogmatics thus arise means that it must show a biblical attitude and respect for the confessional theological school and the will of the church. But it must not mean seeking to be traditional or sinking to the level of a mere historical reference. It means primarily that we have to think and speak here with constant regard for the original Deus dixit.

I. Pious Words of Preachers

The pious words of Christian preachers are the fact with which dogmatics always begins and to which it must always return. With intentional ambivalence I say "pious words." Obviously this might mean very different things for us. But the fact itself is ambivalent; this is what makes dogmatics necessary. That these words may be pure doctrine — something unambivalent — is the work of dogmatics. The ideal result of dogmatics is that we should not be able to think very different things in relation to what pastors say in all their piety, but only one thing, namely, the thoughts of God triumphantly appearing above and behind and in what they are saying. If it were to achieve this result, it could pack up, its task done, like medicine if there were only healthy people or law if all self-seeking, disorder, and wickedness were to vanish from the earth. It could then be merely a fine and merry game. In the works of high scholasticism (cf.

Bonaventura) one has the impression that this latter view was already normative. Since the church already has and proclaims the truth, theological scholarship is simply its artistically refined mirror and almost an end in itself. I would never deny that there may have been times that were nearer the millennium than our own, and that in many respects the Christian Middle Ages formed one such time, and such a dogmatics was possible at that period. But perhaps they were already wrong about the distances. In every age theologians are so easily wrong in this regard. However that may be, we do not live in such a period. The fact to which dogmatics relates today is ambivalent. We do not really do dogmatics as an end in itself, nor for the joy of scholarship, but because it is bitterly necessary.

To describe the fact to which I refer I can again turn to the modern theological standpoint and say that it consists of Christians communicating God and divine things to others on the basis of their deepest and sincerest inner personal life and experience, of their giving direction and counsel with reference to their own relationship to God and divine things. The word "pious" in the thesis is not one that you need put in quotation marks. The ambivalence to which I referred is not simply that there might be an insincere and hypocritical piety as well as one that is sincere and genuine, but also that there might be a sincere and genuine *pagan* piety. Our deepest piety is no guarantee that our words will really be the ministry of God's Word, pure doctrine. On the contrary, for who of us knows whether our only too profound piety might not be an obstacle. The prophets and apostles at least do not seem to have been recruited as a whole from among the most pious circles.

But I also ask you not to put the word "Christian" in quotation marks. It is the same with this as with the word "pious." Even the most serious and accredited Christians, whose Christianity it would be foolish arrogance to deny, can have no certainty that their words will be pure doctrine. From the very beginning church history has known very zealous Christians — they were often better than their opponents — who in their proclamation undoubtedly obscured and corrupted the proclamation of the Word of God and were thus not unjustly combatted by their less worthy opponents. One can undoubtedly set aside or ignore or kindly overlook the ambivalence of the fact to which dogmatics relates. One can simply cling to the concept of piety as the essence of religion, or, more precisely, of Christianity, and make it the dogmatic norm. This is what Schleiermacher did, and his whole school with him. But if we do this we are refusing to face the problem that piety is a psychological determination and Christianity a historical determination. We are also taking the view that this determination essentially suffices as a norm or criterion for what we say about God, that it is really a measure by which this can be measured, tested, and corrected. Why should we not make these presuppositions and erect a dogmatics on the basis of them? Dozens and even hundreds of clever people and books teach us that it can be done, and we have every reason respectfully to tip our hats to the theological achievement of the last century which rested on these presuppositions.

But not surprisingly, in detail, these presuppositions have not led to an incisive crisis and testing of pious words, to a serious differentiation between true and false talk about God, to a ruthless contesting of impure, untrue, and corrupt doctrine such as we find in past centuries. For when there is mutual confidence in each other's piety and Christianity, and no doubt is cast on the absoluteness and normative character of this piety and Christianity, no one can be really critical of others. The various pious words, being relative, are in secret (or in Schleiermacher open) juxtaposition, none of them measured, tested, or proved — for the measure by which they were and are measured in this dogmatics is itself relative. If we once accept these presuppositions, then the human is measured by the human, our pious words by experience, what we say about God by our own psychological and historical inclination, even if this be made a transcendental concept, and there is an obvious catch in this as regards the historical aspect.

The question may be permitted whether dogmatics on these presuppositions can be anything other than a description of the fact — always an ambivalent fact — of the pious words of Christian preachers. So long and so far as we are content with this, not feeling disquieted by the thought that this fact ought to be indirectly identical with God's Word, and that this identity might demand a tumultuous drive for nonambivalence, so long and so far we may acquiesce in a dogmatics of the Christian self-consciousness in which dogmaticians see their own face as in a mirror. But we for our part are in fact disquieted by that thought, and in face of that identity we find little comfort if dogmatics does no more than help people, pious Christian people, to an understanding of themselves in relation to what God says, and even to union with themselves, even though it be at the deepest level of their being. It makes no difference that this might not rule out a consultation of the Bible and a subsequent attempt to move on from there to God. Is it not unsettling that according to our third presupposition the intrinsically harmless fact of the pious words of Christian preachers has a reverse side where in connection with the divine address we find Jesus Christ, the prophets and apostles?

What does it mean for Christian preachers, their self-consciousness and their personal life and experience, no matter how deep and serious, suddenly to find themselves in this company? Can they still be pleased to try to be their own judges? How can they answer when they themselves and all their answers are put in question? Can they still be content to posit and understand themselves as a fact? Does it not make them uneasy that this fact as such stands in an incomparably close relation to God's speaking? Is there not already present a very different norm and crisis for what they are saying? Does not their monologue ineluctably become a dialogue and therefore genuine reflection? If these questions really are questions, if we feel startled out of the beautiful peace of a theology of consciousness, then above all things we must reestablish the insight that that fact is ambivalent. Piety and Christianity, even at their best and purest and deepest, are human determinations. The pious words of Christian preachers are always human words. As such they *can* serve the Word of God which seeks to speak through them in incomparable fashion (they can leave it space to do so).

Yet at the same time they *cannot* do it. They do the very opposite. Because of their pious Christian content they seem to be pointing to the fact that God has said something. As an answer to what God has said, or as a new question put to it, they seem to be an echo of the divine voice and therefore to be pure doctrine. But it might well be that none of this happens, that people are simply talking among themselves, and that with their loud noise they prevent others from hearing the divine voice. Whether the one thing happens or the other is not decided by the piety and Christianity which simply characterize the words as human, no matter how distinctively. It is decided by their relation to what God says. This means putting them under a norm and crisis, setting them in this relation, directing to them the question of their relation to what God says. This is the question that dogmatics brings to the pious words of Christian preachers. It does not do so with distrust, but with a willing and attentive ear for what is really pure doctrine in these words, yet not with an initial readiness to say Yes and Amen simply because they are psychologically pious and historically Christian, but critically, that is, on the basis of an a priori knowledge of the *Deus dixit* to which witness is given by holy scripture, and of the accompanying recognition that this norm will decide whether and how far the human word is or is not a pure vessel for the divine Word. In the question of the divine Word in the human word, what can our criterion be but the divine Word itself?

From one angle dogmatic work simply means validating the divine Word over against the human word. The latter is simply there. It is the given factor with which dogmatics works. The temptation is an enticing one — we have already seen it — to stop at this factor, to try to understand it in terms of its own nature and law, and to accept it. The temptation is all the stronger because this factor is something of our own, of our best and deepest. Dogmatics must not give way to this temptation. It must consider why it is itself necessary, what is meant by the task of assessing pious words, what difficulty and what promise it thereby introduces. If we remember this, and the presuppositions on which alone talk about God is possible, we will not be so soft, or perhaps so hard, as to leave pious orators to themselves and their own devices. We will recall the glory of the divine Word, of this divine Word — since the divine Word in preaching is the problem — as it is spoken in revelation and witness is given to it in scripture. Here at any rate we ourselves are not speaking but are spoken to. Here questions are put and answers are given which are not our own. Here things are brought to our attention which belong to a different plane from that of our own consciousness. Here we are set before God, not a God in himself, but the God who enters into fellowship with us. God's speaking is now to proceed and be true as a wholly new address in what we ourselves say about God. *We* do not say something about God but God speaks for himself as he did in Jesus Christ and the prophets and apostles. This is what pious words are meant to be. What else can self-reflection be but reflection on these things?

But for this to happen we have to establish this as the norm and crisis. Dogmatic deliberation that is worthy of the name may not begin with the question what I want to say, or may or can say, if I dare to speak about God. Nor can it begin with the question how I may so speak. Its first question must be this: Of what or whom will I speak? We then have to realize that already an answer has been and will be given to this question of the what or whom. We stand before scripture and revelation — *before* it, not *in* it. We are still human. We are not Jesus Christ or prophets or apostles. Yet we do stand before it and not somewhere else. There before it, facing the *Deus dixit* and the "It is written," there has to take place the exercise that consists of dogmatic formulation, that is, of the attempt, as we listen to what is said to people, to be clear about what we may say to them. Naturally, the decisive and salutary act is not the formulation itself but the place where it happens — the fact that we do not think and speak on our own, or especially about ourselves, but that we let ourselves be addressed, and thus let our own speaking be simply an echo of this being addressed. That this superior place is seen, that there is such a being and standing before it, a clarifying and illuminating of our own words by it — that is the possibility of pure doctrine which must be the first concern of dogmatics.

II. Heteronomy

From what has been said it will at least be generally clear to you if I say in the thesis that the formation of dogmatic statements takes place under a heteronomy. The basic task of dogmatics is to confront the pious words of Christian preachers with the Word of God which is spoken in revelation and to which scripture gives witness. It is to lead human religious experience and thinking to the point where we can get no further with experience and thinking, where they come up against their limit because they come up against the life and thoughts of God. This being so, dogmatic trains of thought, and the statements to which they give rise, obviously cannot be autonomous nor can they derive merely from religious experience or from some critically epistemological or speculative thinking abstracted from religious experience.

I say *not merely* from these. I refer with some reserve to a heteronomy under which dogmatics stands. I admit that one can also speak of an autonomy in this connection. Experience and thinking also have their say in dogmatics no less than preaching. This is part of the fact that dogmatics and preaching are human activities or functions. Dogmatic statements are just as little the statements of a *theologia archetypos*,[1] of God's own knowledge of himself, as the letters and words of scripture are the letters and words of God himself, or the lips of preachers are the lips of God himself. We cannot expect even the best dogmaticians to speak to the church's instruction and edification as though the Holy Spirit dictated to them.[2] Only in heaven, when according to the signif-

---

1. Cf. Schmid-Pöhlmann, p. 28; Schmid ET p. 16; Heppe-Bizer, p. 6; ET p.16.
2. Perhaps an allusion to the doctrine of biblical inspiration in Protestant orthodoxy; cf. G. Voetius, in Heppe-Bizer, p. 19 n.; ET p. 19; and J. A. Quenstedt, in Schmid-Pöhlmann, p. 43; Schmid ET p. 45.

icant teaching of older dogmaticians we have moved on from a *theologia viatorum* to a *theologia comprehensorum,* can this be expected. I would imagine that this will be a theology which will no longer have any need of dialectic. But since God will still be distinct from us even in heaven, this, too, can still be only a *theologia ektypos.* In my view there is no theonomous theology. Hence there is none that is only heteronomous, that is, none in which human speech can reproduce God's truth without the cooperation of experience and thinking. Nor is there any that is only autonomous, that is, none in which experience and thinking alone produce God's truth in human speech. Neither of these exists. "God is in heaven and you upon earth" [Eccl. 5:2]. There is, then, both a heteronomy and an autonomy, a relative heteronomy and a relative autonomy, and both are limited by theonomy, by the absolute heteronomy or autonomy which gives them their title, to which they refer back but which they cannot claim for themselves.

We have to speak about the heteronomy first. The function of dogmatics is to measure the human word of preaching by the Word of God which is supposed to be spoken in it. If there is to be real measuring here, a real crisis, it cannot simply go by the Word of God which it actually receives or thinks it receives in preaching. It cannot be a mere asseveration that this or that is the ideal, profound, academically formulated content of the preaching of, for example, the Evangelical Church. This would simply lead us back to the concept of dogmatics which we find in Schleiermacher's *Kurze Darstellung*[3] and which is close to the Roman Catholic concept of the church. No, in relation to what we are saying we have to be summoned to reflect on what God is possibly speaking through us today. But to make this possible dogmatics must reach back methodically to the Word of God which confronts us unequivocally and by which we can measure our own word objectively, that is, to God's first address in revelation and his second address in scripture. Here is the *heteros nomos* that dogmatics opposes to experience and thinking like a regulating weir. It is this for the experience and thinking of dogmaticians as well as preachers. Dogmaticians, the church's doctors, are not like popes in their relation to preachers, the church's pastors. Fundamentally, they are in just the same situation. As trusted and commissioned office-bearers they exercise a conscious critical function, but they stand under the same norm no

---

3. F. Schleiermacher, *Kurze Darstellung des theologisches Studiums* . . . (1830); cf. the ed. of H. Scholz (Leipzig, 1910), §§ 97-101 and §§ 195-232.

less than the church as a whole. Hence the trains of thought and the statements in which they exercise their critical function stand under the *heteros nomos* which they themselves have to advance. Dogmatic thinking and speaking is not preaching but it is a paradigm of the way that preaching ought to think and speak. If in preaching the decisive point is the confrontation of the human word with the Word of God that unequivocally stands over against it, then in its paradigm, in dogmatics, there cannot fundamentally be anything other than a series of such confrontations. Every dogmatic train of thought, by working on a specific concept, must try to bring that regulating weir to light, to repeat that confrontation with the *heteros nomos*. Materially, of course, it rests on our religious experience and the corresponding thinking. But we have to qualify this material factor. Everything depends on this qualifying, that is, on the relating of the human side to the Word of God. If we neglect this qualifying, if we stop at the fact of experience and the thinking that has it in view, our work may be very erudite and methodical, but we are not doing dogmatic work. As dogmaticians, even if to an enhanced and improved degree, we would simply be unqualified religious people who might just as well be pagans or heretics or false teachers. The "Doctrine of the Faith" that we might then produce could be very comprehensive and basic and perspicacious, but in fact we would not be discharging the commission that the church has laid upon us.

Dogmatic thinking, then, may not simply be humanly autonomous or humanly productive. It may be this only materially. In dogmatics no more than preaching can there be a material reproduction of the divine Word. By its form, then, dogmatics has to be a demonstration or signal or intimation, within the sphere of human experience and thinking, of the presence and validity of the *heteros nomos,* the Word of God. Indirectly, then, it has to be the crisis or measuring of the human word by God's Word. It is not the case that in dogmatics, even the best dogmatics, as distinct from preaching, the Word of God is present literally, directly, translated into human speech. If this is not so in holy scripture, or in preaching that is directly related to scripture and revelation, how much less is it so in dogmatics, which ultimately has only the function of an aid to preaching. No, the *heteros nomos* remains behind the scenes. That which makes scripture and preaching the Word of God, that is, the *Deus dixit,* revelation, may be seen only indirectly in its effects. We cannot see the light, only its reflection, or, to put it another way, created light, not uncreated light. Not a material quantity of the *Deus dixit,* but the formal determination of human experience and thinking by the *Deus dixit* in the witness of scripture is what distinguishes dogmatic or dogmatically instructed speaking about God from that which is unrelated and unqualified. Here again we remain human, and God is always God. The fellowship lies only in the relation. Fellowship! The barrier is also a *door*. Here, too, the highly critical but also the highly positive business of dogmatics is to see this door, to guard it, to keep out what is unfit and to admit what is fit, to use its simple proclamation as a reminder to all whom it may concern of the decision which has always to be made at this door.

But what is the formal determination under which dogmatic thinking and speaking places itself as well as preaching? If we were right to find the formal principle in the biblical witness to revelation — and since we have here something active we must stress the formal aspect rather than the determinative — then obviously at this point, if we are to be specific, we must return to the doctrine of the three authorities that we worked out in § 9. The objective possibilities of the communication of revelation which (with the caveat of relativity) we found there must now clearly lead us (with the same caveat) to the objective possibilities of the proclamation of revelation and of pure doctrine. We found there (a) the canon and text, (b) the fathers and dogma, and (c) the church's teaching office. Along similar lines I will sum up the three formal determinations of dogmatics in three catchwords. (I trust your understanding in so doing. Caution! We might finally smash a good deal of crockery with these catchwords. Before naming them, I would remind you again that they all stand under the caveat of relativity. They are not the *heteros nomos*. They merely reflect it. They are only the *formal* determinations of human thinking. Do not quote me without remembering this caveat and the elucidations that I will at once append.) The three concepts that necessarily spring to mind, then, are (1) Bible, (2) School, and (3) Church. Let us discuss them in sequence, but under the rather clearer titles that I proposed in the thesis.

1. Dogmatic statements need to show a biblical attitude. I do not mean primarily or fundamentally that at every point they must be formulated only in face of the revelation mediated through the Bible. In this principial sense I would not group the Bible with the school and the church. What I mean is a second-degree biblicism, one of the formal determinations by which dogmatic statements display their character as such, bearing witness to the formative principle. The biblical attitude, that of the prophets and apostles, is the attitude of witnesses, the attitude that put the scriptures in the canon and called their text holy, the attitude not

of spectators or reporters or thinkers, but of people who come down from an absolute presupposition, the *Deus dixit*, with all the irresistible momentum of a boulder rolling down a mountainside. Naturally, this attitude reflects a thousandfold in detail the problems of human existence that are there for all of us, yet it is *this* attitude. *Deus dixit* is not a problem. This attitude is normative for dogmatics. It is the first formal principle that we must always remember and at every point apply.

In detail, of course, dogmatic thinking will everywhere be made up of partly historical, partly psychological, and partly philosophical elements. But if things are to be done aright we must never for a moment let these elements, the *stocheia tou kosmou* [Col. 2:8], become independent or a presupposition.[4] In dogmatics we cannot for a moment think seriously in historical, psychological, or philosophical terms. We cannot fail to make *Deus dixit* the presupposition, or do so only questioningly or partially, trying to think our way up to God by means of history or experience or a concept, as though God had not spoken, as though God were a problem and not the ground of all problems and also, whether we have eyes to see it or not, the solution to all problems. From the roots up dogmatic thinking is either *kata ton Christon* [Col. 2:8] or it is not dogmatic, theological thinking. Let us be on guard not against criticism or doubt or skepticism — these are not the enemies — but instead against apologetics, against trying to get at the matter by detours, as though God could be known without God, as though he could be the second thing, as though he were not already quite unambiguously the first.

We are not trying to anticipate specific answers to specific questions. Everything is open to question. Every moment the problem behind every group of problems might be opened up and become acute. No answers stand here at the crux of the question. A biblical attitude involves no comfortable dogmatism. It is the common denominator of every question and answer. It is the bracket that is around them all, the ground on which we must stand with our questions and answers, as logicians do with their principle of contradiction. Again, we do not have here a certainty that must be experienced and enjoyed and known but a category that we must learn to think in as dogmaticians. Again, we do not have here a category that we can learn to study and think in apart from the witness of the prophets and apostles. I admit, for example, that I take no pleasure in the doctrine that I find in K. Heim in this regard: the irreversibility of

---

4. N. p. 161: "The building plans decide where the stones go."

time, the inexchangeability of the ego, the inexplicability of the so-called primal constellation and laws of world occurrence, the problem of action.[5] These things are all very interesting and they are certainly not to be despised as analogies, but they cannot be confused with the biblical attitude and lie on a very different plane from the *ananke* with which Paul preaches the gospel [1 Cor. 9:16].

The biblical attitude is the most simple and naive and direct: "I believe, Lord, help thou mine unbelief" [Mark 9:24]. This is the first article of the constitution which embraces and conditions and permeates everything else. If you ask me how I arrive at this first article, I can give no answer but this. Biblicism, a biblical attitude, comes from the Bible itself. Read in the Bible so long that you have it, that with the help of Old and New Testament texts you become used to it as a rule of thought like any other. In this way, with this formal determination, we think and speak when we speak about revelation. Otherwise we are definitely speaking about something else. Everything else will follow if we grasp this rule of thought, simply grasp it, without enthusiasm, experiences, or surprises.

It is plain that one cannot do dogmatics without a constant feel for exegesis. This is the first and decisive thing that we have to learn. With it dogmatics can begin. No matter what path it may take, no matter whether it be more historically, psychologically, or philosophically oriented, no matter what may be the content of its statements — these are all secondary concerns — it cannot forget this one thing, this biblical forgetting of all else, this regarding of all else as *skybala* [Phil. 3:8], the holding to this one thing unconditionally, the doubting of all else but never for a moment of this one thing: the divine address. This at any rate will be the form which willingly or unwillingly unqualified religious experience and thinking will have to accept in dogmatics.

I call this biblicism. I need to tell you what I do not understand by biblicism and why I cannot go along with it. I do not understand by it what J. T. Beck did when he thought he could take his dogmatics directly from the Bible.[6] Nor do I understand by it what Calvin and the older Protestantism did, namely, the obligation to produce biblical proofs and references for every statement and even for every turn of thought in dogmatics. Nor do I have in mind the procedure that is followed, for

---

5. K. Heim, *Leitfaden der Dogmatik . . .* , Part II, 2nd ed. (Halle, 1921), pp. 5-6.
6. Cf. J. T. Beck, *Die christliche Lehr-Wissenschaft nach den biblischen Urkunden. Ein Versuch* (Stuttgart, 1841), p. 8.

example, in the dogmatics of Kaftan, that is, the presenting of all the loci in three stages: (a) the biblical teaching; (b) the teaching of the church; and (c) his own development.7 I reject this material biblicism because it rests, on the one hand, on a confusion of dogmatics and exegesis. I repeat that exegesis is the indispensable presupposition of dogmatics. But it is not for that reason a part of dogmatics or identical with it. At the climax of biblical exposition what happens (cf. §§ 9, 10 above) is that the church and individuals have to think and proclaim the thoughts of scripture as their own and on their own responsibility. This is the birth of Christian preaching. But the norm and criterion of Christian preaching, that which distinguishes it from unqualified religious experience and thinking, cannot again be biblical exposition. We must now seek a form into which religious experience and thinking must be poured if all is to be well with the birth of Christian preaching. We must seek the normativity of scripture, not its content. We must seek what Paul in 2 Cor. 10:5 calls taking every *noēma* captive to the *hypokoēn tou Christou,* that is, the biblical attitude. The result of material biblicism has often been that no criterion may be seen, that under the banner of scripture the experience and thinking are extremely subjective, that they do not have form or obedience, that the constraint of the *Deus dixit* is not the binding standard. Conversely, where material biblicism proves useful, for example, among the Reformers, the whole weight of the biblical references adduced amounts finally to nothing other than the establishing of a formal principle of Christian thinking.

Another misunderstanding in material biblicism is the idea that in dogmatics we can think God's thoughts after him, these thoughts being identical with those of scripture. But according to scripture itself God's thoughts are much higher above our thoughts than heaven is above the earth (Isa. 55:8-9). A *theologia archetypos* cannot be our business. The biblical canon and text are a relative authority, not an absolute. Scripture gives us the *Word* of God, not his *words.* It gives us the Word of God in the shell of human words. The criterion whether our own human words are God's Word cannot be whether they repeat those human words. It can be only whether they stand with those words under a formal law. Always remember that biblicism can be only a relative principle. It is a human attitude which we can learn and exercise and study, which we can grow accustomed to, in which the more or less of any human attitude will always play a part. Biblicism is not identical with faith and obedience. It is a rule

7. Cf. Kaftan, § 12.

of thought resulting from them. The Word of God in the present, identical with the Word in scripture and the Word in revelation itself, is the presupposition to which the biblical attitude of dogmatics relates and which it must reflect, proclaim, and establish. But it will definitely not try to do this by making bold to master it or to posit it itself. Naturally, even in dogmatics we will not refrain from quoting the Bible. In innumerable cases we cannot convey the formed character of our own thinking any better than by recalling some biblical passage. Biblicism, however, is not biblical quotation. It is the formulation in which human thinking and speaking yields to the *Deus dixit* and hence recognizes the authority of the biblical canon and texts, not in words but in deeds.

2. Dogmatics must show respect to the confessional theological school. Fathers and dogma were the corresponding authority in § 9. If we were right there, if the speaking of God's Word to us has been historically conditioned by the interpretation of the individual teachers and the universal doctrinal decisions of the church, then in our present discussion of the speaking of the Word of God through us we have to do with the outworking of this as previously we had to do with the presence of the relative authority of the biblical canon and text. In this regard, too, dogmatic thinking must stand under a norm. It must display a formal determination which distinguishes it from unqualified and undisciplined religious experience and thinking. We spoke about a place that stands over against the revelation to which scripture bears witness — the place to which dogmatics has to lead Christian preachers. In this respect, too, that place has to be a very specific one. That is to say, both dogmaticians and preachers have to have a home within a church which is divided confessionally and theologically. I do not mean by this that they have to have a *historical* consciousness or piety. It is not a matter of the idol "History." It is a matter of seriously acknowledging a fact which may be regrettable or may be necessary but which is at least a given fact, namely, that within the *una sancta* not merely silent listeners but also preachers of the Word and dogmaticians have to belong to parts of the church. Certainly dogmatics must have a bias toward what is ecumenically Christian. This is obligatory in view of the revelation in Christ to which scripture bears witness and by which preaching and dogmatics measure themselves. Dogmatics must also make in principle a claim to universal validity. We cannot think or speak dogmatically if we also believe that we might just as well think and speak in some other way — even though we will certainly put our work at once under the proviso that we might in the future be better

instructed. Thus there can be no Roman Catholic, Lutheran, or Reformed dogmatics, but properly understood, in principle, content, and intention there can be only Christian dogmatics.

Nevertheless, this does not alter the fact that on account of its direct relation to preaching a dogmatics has to be in each case a formally determined dogmatics, that is, one which is determined in the sense of confessional theology. If the relative authority of fathers and dogma is[8] in fact an authority — we have seen, of course, that we cannot be wholly clear about what this means today — then we cannot do dogmatics in a vacuum but only as we are influenced by a group of authorities which for inner or outer reasons holds good for the dogmatician concerned. If we may compare the biblical attitude with the backbone that differentiates humans from animals, we may compare the confessional theological school with the features by which humans may be known as individuals. If blurred, ambivalent, characterless features do not become people, we may perhaps say that it is unbecoming for a dogmatics not to give evidence of a school. The idea of a union-dogmatics, that is, a dogmatics that seeks to respect two schools at the same time, is one that the experts have all resisted for centuries.

But the objection that we have to raise is not just esthetic. Far from promoting peace in the *una sancta,* the lack of a school would mean the constant uncertainty, subjectivity, and divisiveness of dogmatic work and hence unavoidably of preaching as well. Those who at one and the same time can think along both Lutheran and Reformed lines will probably not do either with any seriousness but eclectically fashion a third or fourth or fifth thing in a mixture of some kind. The formation of academic theological schools is a poor way to make good the lack of confessional theological schools in view of the very uncertain continuity of such constructs, which have neither church nor authority behind them. Those who are wise will with their dogmatics adhere to a school in the confessional sense.

If the formal determination of dogmatic thinking that I have called a biblical attitude denotes the "whence," the second determination that I call School denotes the "how," that is, the distinctive shape that religious experience and thinking must accept, the specific order, emphasis, color, orientation, and practical goal in the handling of more or less every individual concept. We will scorn and hate this specific formal determination as a straitjacket only if we do not see that the particular church-form

---

8. Correcting the "are" of the MS.

offers protection, even if only relative, against Christian caprice and riot, against the pious eclecticism of Protestants who, misunderstanding and misusing the scripture principle, want to leap over every barrier and move on directly to revelation.

Under a few headings I will give you what I think I recognize as the decisive marks of the Reformed school, which I myself follow in my dogmatics: (a) Formalism in the teaching on principles; the Word vouches for the content, not vice versa; (b) in the understanding of the relation to God, emphasis on the thought of God; our salvation is enclosed in the glorifying of God, not vice versa; (c) in the thought of God, stress on God's subjectivity, freedom, and majesty; (d) in the concept of the objective possibility of revelation, a strictly dialectical christology; (e) in the concept of the subjective possibility of revelation, an equal presence of both the religious and the ethical elements, of both faith and obedience. I hope that you will bear me witness that in some degree even here in the Prolegomena I have respected what I regard as the valid rules of my own school. By studying the symbols or the Reformed confessions or Calvin's *Institutes* you may make sure for yourselves that these do in fact have to be the main rules of a Christian, Reformed dogmatics.

I must now say what I do not mean by confessionalism. I do not mean a repristination of the older Christian or Reformed dogmatics, any more than by biblicism I mean a reproduction of the thoughts of scripture. Confessionalism denotes a rule of thought, not its content. Naturally, dogmatics cannot ignore earlier dogma or earlier dogmatics. Naturally, in these mines of dogmatic insight it will always seek and find points of contact, and at certain climaxes it will itself become a presentation of dogma. But it does not have to do so. It does not aim to do so. As regards content, it is a free and not a captive science. As I say in the thesis, where I have this point particularly in view, it does not seek to be traditional or sink to the level of a mere reference.

A word about the latter point. Historical allusions and recollections and quotations in a dogmatics are not historical references. That would indeed be sinking to another level. It is one thing to quote a document like the Nicene Creed as a contemporary source and quite another to read and understand it as an authority. Dogmaticians do the latter. They have a right and even a duty to so so. Do not expect that I will here present and expound Calvin. When I let Calvin speak, I let him do so in my own train of thought, certainly with as much regard as possible for the historical meaning of his words, but only in order to achieve the elucidation of a matter which a quotation from Calvin can give at this particular moment. In my view this historical, ecclesiastical, confessional respect with which we go our way as dogmaticians, whether quoting or not quoting, whether expressly attaching ourselves to a school or continuing its tradition in our own words, consists, like biblicism, in deeds rather than words, that is, in the formulation of words, in their determination in this regard, too, by the church's past and its past teaching, and thus by demonstrating and proclaiming authority in accordance with the purpose of dogmatics. The wind blows where it wills, and you hear the sound of it but do not know where it comes from or where it goes [John 3:8]. This saying is true in this area too. Here again the absolute authority on behalf of which the demonstration has to be made remains behind the scenes. One can be confessional only *kata pneuma;* one cannot be so *kata sarka.*

3. I mentioned the church as my third formal principle. This corresponds to the third authority mentioned in § 9, namely, the actual teaching office of the church. At each moment, in each historical situation, the church has a word to speak. Whether it knows and says this is another matter. It has to speak a word of truth absolutely to the situation, as we put it. Its own word today is the peak of its authority, and it has to be there, alongside the text and canon, the fathers and dogma, if its authority is to be real authority. This is what I mean by "Church" at the present point. Dogmatics must not ignore the present, the moment. Dogmaticians must not think and speak timelessly as though they were people of the 4th or 16th century, even though they may be convinced that in this way they could do so much better and more perfectly and accurately and completely. Dogmatics must not be romantic in any sense. Naturally, what it has to relate to is not just the political, intellectual, or economic situation but the word which is hidden beneath this surface — the word which the church speaks or ought to speak. Dogmatics must not turn aside from this present reality (even though it may be only a task or a problem). As dogmaticians we must not be in any sense scholastics. We must not treat our work as a private affair, as a private intellectual game, no matter how gifted we are academically. Naturally, we do not have to be directly edifying, practical, or hortatory. Dogmatics is not preaching any more than preaching is dogmatics. But as dogmaticians no less than preachers we must sympathetically bear the burdens of all our contemporaries.[9]

---

9. Cf. the fifth stanza of S. Preiswerk's "Zerstreut und mannigfach geschieden" in *Evangelischer Liederkranz aus älterer und neuerer Zeit* (Basel, 1844), no. 124.

We must remember that what is at issue is the Word of God which must be addressed to people today. This will not bring dogmatics into connivance with the spirit of the age. On the contrary, in every age it will undoubtedly bring it into conflict with the spirit of the age, which from a Christian standpoint is an enemy of contemporaries, but which is still a brake or restraint on the tendency toward profound archaisms or philosophical speculations which stand in no relation to the hidden, actual word of the church but only to my private preferences or, better, my private needs. Everything that the NT has to say about the relation of the strong to the weak[10] is pertinent here, for in their relation to the church's preachers dogmaticians are the strong, the superior, the free, the critics, those who control the norms. They might well at any moment evade and ignore and escape from the church, from its need, from its struggle for the Word which alone will give it real authority. But they must not. They must want the church. Dogmatic thinking and speaking must have a secret relevance. They must relate to what ought to be said from the pulpit now. Every dogmatic statement must be an arrow which points this way even if perhaps from a great distance. This is the third formal determination of dogmatics.

The most obvious thing which I do not mean when I refer to the church has been noted already. I may simply add that I naturally do not mean adjustment to the church spirit of the age. This would be the worst service that dogmatics could render the church even in the form of regularizing the Christianity of certain advanced and impressive leaders, as, for example, in the theology of Troeltsch, which is unmistakably patterned on the work of Naumann,[11] or in the form of summing up certain concrete ethical demands of the day. Dogmatics must establish pure doctrine, and with such things it would hamper God's Word instead of giving it free course. No, the point here is a rule of thought and not its content, a norm, a discipline under which we must set ourselves irrespective of the content.

I have already made the necessary observations on the three formal determinations: Bible, School, and Church. I recall once more that they are all relative. They are human dispositions that we can adopt, learn, and more or less consistently practice. What we have here is not theonomy but relative heteronomy. Yet we cannot for this reason ignore it. We cannot with much liberal ado cast it off as a human trifle. We have no reason to

---

10. Rom. 14–15; 1 Cor. 8ff.
11. Cf. *ChD*, p. 567 n. 21.

complete the Reformation by setting aside these last restraints as though we were not setting aside the very beginning along with these last restraints. These restraints are meaningful as demonstrations, signals, and intimations. Today, indeed, they are often simply shouts for help. Yet in any case they are always pointers to the Word of God which is revealed according to the witness of scripture and which is in fact the *nomos theou*.

III. Conclusion

We have learned to know the heteronomy under which dogmatic thoughts are thought and dogmatic statements are fashioned. The ambivalent fact of the pious words of Christian preachers (subsection I) is no longer on its own when this heteronomy is in force. If it is *really* in force, that is, if the formal determinations are not just present but are doing their work as pointers to the absolute form of the Word of God whose earthly reflections they are and to which they owe their origin, then religious experience and thinking are no longer unqualified. They stand before a criterion which is not in any sense taken from them but which at every point stands over against them: the criterion which is normative above all in virtue of its content. The objective possibility of pure doctrine is then present.

§ 13

Dogmatic Thinking

Dogmatic work consists secondly of strictly and clearly relating the words of Christian preachers to the Word of God as it is spoken in revelation and as scripture bears witness to it. The autonomy of dogmatic thinking means that it is the thinking of faith and obedience, human thinking which at all costs has to orient itself to its theme, and finally the thinking of individuals who see themselves set before this theme. It does not mean that of ourselves we can or will think the truth of God. It means primarily the autonomy of the Holy Spirit.

I. Relating Preaching to God's Word

When I say that "dogmatic work consists secondly . . . ," you must bear in mind that "secondly" does not denote a second and different part of this work but a second and different and complementary understanding of the same work. In § 11 we spoke about the presupposed reality of pure doctrine, of Christian preaching through which God's Word speaks purely, authoritatively, and directly. Pure doctrine, we said, is possible insofar as Christian preaching is measured, that is, critically purified, by the measure of scripture and revelation. To measure by this measure, to press back from preaching to scripture and revelation, is the work of dogmatics. If we begin with the idea of measuring by a *measure,* then as the objective possibility of pure doctrine we arrive at the concept of the dogmatic norm, the relative heteronomy of dogmatic statements. We spoke about this in § 12. But if we take the reverse course — our second procedure — and begin with *measuring* by a measure, then as the subjective possibility of pure doctrine

298

we arrive at the concept of dogmatic thinking, of a relative autonomy in which dogmatic statements are formed. Instead of talking, as in § 12, about the validity of God's Word over against the pious words of Christian preachers, we now talk about *relating* the pious words of Christian preachers to God's Word. Materially, the process is the same. In each case we press back from preaching to scripture and revelation, and in this act we think we see the essence of dogmatic work.

But we are now looking at the process from the other side, the human side. Our first concern was for the norm of thinking that makes it dogmatic thinking. We discussed the formal determinations that it receives from this norm. But now obviously the thinking itself comes to the forefront, not so much the results, the statements that at the last it will provisionally adopt in relation to its theme, but the process itself, the movement, the way, the distinctive quality of a thinking that is engaged in measuring both itself and the thinking of preachers by that measure. Obviously, before going about our business as dogmaticians we must attain as much clarity in principle as we can about this matter. If it is true not only that revelation in scripture stands up against those pious words as a wall does against overflowing waters, but also that the words relate to revelation like waters that flow toward that wall, so that they have to dash and break against it, then we have to say something now about this subjective side, not merely about the determinations of dogmatic thinking which it necessarily acquires (being what it is) but also about those which it must necessarily give itself, not merely about what we must let ourselves be told as dogmaticians or preachers but also about what we say ourselves and must say to ourselves (even as we are told it and are ready to be told it). To this extent — in apparent contradiction — we have to speak about an autonomy of dogmatic thinking.

In this connection, as under the titles "Faith and Obedience" and "Freedom" in our first two chapters, we have to speak about the human subject before God. The concept of pure doctrine is not complete without this human subject, that is, the person who thinks dogmatically, the person who tries to set his or her pious words in relation to the revelation in scripture. This is obviously something different from the person who thinks philosophically, who purifies the concepts used by relating them to the idea of the unconditioned, the presupposed, the primal, or, in logic, the principle of contradiction. For the latter person it would be natural to equate the autonomy of thinking with the theonomy of truth. But for the former the autonomy is from the very first relative. If the heteronomy to which there is subjection is from the very first only relative, vicarious, and representative, and all the formal determinations of thinking are simply pointers to the absolute heteronomy of the Word of God, then the person who thinks autonomously is merely a vicar or substitute for a very different autonomous Thinker with whom there can be no confusion of the self and with whose knowledge of the truth there is no confusion of the self's own knowledge of the truth.

I used the term "*formal* determinations" for the distinctives of dogmatic thinking that are fashioned by the norm that confronts this thinking: Bible, School, and Church. In contrast, we must now obviously speak about *material* determinations. At this point once again the Lutheran and Reformed churches part company, and this time in a dubious and fateful way. For Lutheran dogmatics it is self-evident that dogmatics is constituted by a combination of the formal principle (what we called the "norm" in § 12) with a so-called material principle. Thinking that subjects itself to that norm will from the very first be thinking which is filled with a qualified and supremely Christian content. On the basis of this content, which in the prolegomena to Lutheran dogmatics is at once stated and established as a so-called basic principle, dogmatics proper will then be analytically developed with the help of the formal principle, usually in the form of what is called a system. The system is simply the logical unfolding of the basic principle and its individual parts. As I see it, Lutheran dogmatics already knows in advance what will arise when it works out the relation to scripture and revelation. It does at least know what the center is, the thesis on which all the dogmatic statements that it has to formulate will center. It knows all this even before what it knows has come into even the slightest contact with the formal principle which confronts it.

In older Lutheran dogmatics one such basic principle, which rests on Luther's saying about the standing or falling church,[1] is that of justification by faith alone, or forgiveness on account of the merits of Christ. According to Luthardt the material principle is fellowship with God in Christ which finds its reality in the righteousness of faith and on this basis comes to fulfilment as righteousness of life.[2] A. Ritschl finds the whole content of

---

1. This saying seems to have come only from the post-Reformation period; cf. F. Loofs, "Der articulus stantis et cadentis ecclesiae," *TSK* 90 (1917) 323-420, esp. 334; K. Barth, *CD*, IV/1, p. 525; but cf. M. Luther, WA, 40/III, 352, 3; *BSLK*, p. 415.39-40; Tappert, p. 292; *CD*, IV/1, pp. 521ff.

2. Luthardt, p. 18.

Christianity in the fact that its distinctive concept of God is always linked to recognition of the bearer of a special revelation and the valuing of the Christian community.[3] Kaftan offers the definition that in the kingdom of God that Jesus Christ proclaimed Christians recognize their eternal goal which lies above the world in God but to which the way leads only by moral development in the world. In virtue of the reconciliation with God that Jesus Christ has effected they know that in spite of their sin they are called to this kingdom. In both these things, which mutually define and determine one another, the Christian religion finds its vitality.[4] Since the Union the original and specifically Lutheran idea of the basic principle has found a following in nonconfessional dogmatics. Thus Nitzsch tells us that by actualizing the kingdom of God in humanity Jesus Christ has become the permanent Mediator of its salvation.[5] Troeltsch says that Christianity represents the decisive and principial turn to a religion of personality.[6] Its religious idea is that of redeeming and sanctifying human souls from the sin and suffering of the world, of lifting them up to God, of making them personalities of infinite worth by anchoring them in the divine life, of elevating them to the kingdom of God, that is, to a kingdom of personalities that are grounded in God and derive their actions from him. This exaltation comes about through a correct practical knowledge of God, by ethical self-sanctification for God, by a convinced surrender of the will to God. It receives its central impulse and its guaranteeing certainty from contemplation of the personality of Jesus. All further stimulations and empowerments group around this center.[7]

In these and similar versions, according to the Lutheran method, we fix a priori what the content of later dogmatic discussion will be. In the light of the references that I have given, and rejoicing in my own Reformed heritage, I need hardly say what my objection to this method of Lutheran dogmatics is. It begins easily with the doctrine of justification, though this comes only from Luther's very personal experience and from nothing else, and it ends with ethical self-sanctification for God and a

---

3. A. Ritschl, *Unterricht in der christlichen Religion* (1875), ed. G. Ruhbach (Gütersloh, 1966), p. 13.

4. Kaftan, p. 8.

5. Nitzsch-Stephan, p. 64.

6. Dogmatik I lectures (1908), p. 108.

7. For the same definition in a much altered form cf. the posthumous work by Troeltsch: *Glaubenslehre, Nach Heidelberger Vorlesungen aus den Jahren 1911 und 1912* (Munich/Leipzig, 1925), pp. 71-72.

sincere surrender of the will to him. Who can then arrest the process when it is possible and permissible to know some things in advance even before reference is made to the formal principle? Were the older Lutherans right when they were content with the righteousness of faith, or are the new ones right when they cautiously add righteousness of life? Is Nitzsch right when he makes the kingdom of God the central idea, or is Kaftan right when he wants to add reconciliation? Who is to decide which of these decisions is right when they are all taken at the threshold? And who is to stop Troeltsch from displaying his unlimited naivete, if this is academically possible?

Bear in mind the importance of the decision that must be made here. The whole of dogmatics follows from the analysis of the basic principle, or at least as this principle is laid down. One must also put the following question. Assuming that we can handle the subjectivism that gnaws at the roots here, how do these dogmaticians really know what they claim in advance to know? From history? But who decides what is a right understanding of history? From their own personal experience, like Luther himself? But what personal experience says, dogmatics is supposed to put on the scales and test. Again, why and in what sense is religious thinking to be later related to a second, formal norm which in principle stands over against it, when it already carries the material principle more or less concretely within it? Is God's Word in revelation and scripture perhaps no more than merely the regulating principle of a knowledge that we already possess? And if the answer is that we have naturally received it from revelation and scripture, why should we go to all the trouble of dogmatics when it is possible and permissible, prior to all dogmatics, to be certain either easily or more violently about that which will later be developed in dogmatics as the content of scripture?

These objections to the method of Lutheran dogmatics compel me to say that strictly there is no material dogmatic principle or fundamental thesis. In dogmatics we can speak about content in two ways. We might think of the contents of the religious consciousness and thinking which are unqualified according to our approach: God, holiness, creation, redemption, grace, love, faith, community, etc., as preachers say in the pulpit. These things might all be pure doctrine, but they might also be idolatry or heresy. Because of this ambivalence we need dogmatics. Whether and how far pure doctrine is proclaimed in these words will be brought to light in the dogmatic catharsis. Hence we cannot begin with these contents. No calling or experience offers any protection here. They are our material, but they cannot be a material principle. The other content that calls for consideration is that of revelation or scripture itself. We recall what we said about this in § 5.I. The content of revelation is God. God speaks — that is enough. If we do not think of God as the fulness of the whole content, we are thinking of something other than God.

Let us bear in mind that in the phrase "God speaks" both words are pregnant. The whole Trinity is expressed. The relation to this "God speaks," the formal principle, is itself the material principle. To this extent I can thus make a small concession to the Lutheran method. The older Reformed did so. Their teaching on principles contained a locus on the foundation of holy scripture.[8] For that which eventuates from God's speaking, if we assume that he is speaking to us, they used the concept of the *foedus,* the covenant, which in revelation, that is, in Christ, is made between God and us. Putting it the other way round (cf. especially Olevian), they referred to the personal, direct address of God to us in revelation. "In each and all of the articles of faith I remember the promise of God, that to thee is promised and given by God what stands in the article, if thou hast trust in thy heart and confessest it with thy mouth. . . . that his body and soul were formed for the Son of God, in order that all that had contributed to them might happen in the name and for the sake of believers one and all."[9] In this material statement we obviously anticipate nothing and know nothing in advance. It speaks about nothing but faith and obedience. Yet it implies revelation as the subject and object of its possibility. It analyzes the *Deus dixit.* If the Lutherans for their part had been content not to force their special experiences in advance into the *foedus* but simply to wait without presuppositions for what happens when religious thinking is related to this content, then we might agree (this is why I said "strictly speaking" earlier) and say that the formal principle is also a material principle. It is intolerable, however, to assume that there is a second material principle that is distinct from the formal principle and stands over against it.

If, then, we seek the opposite of our formal determinations in § 12, we will not find it in material determinations. Such determinations would be the dogmatic statements, the loci themselves, to the extent that these are all descriptions of the highly material *Deus dixit* in human thinking (or, to put it objectively, determinations of human thinking by

---

8. The title of Locus III in Heppe-Bizer.
9. Heppe, pp. 33-34; Heppe-Bizer, pp. 36-37; ET pp. 45-46.

the highly material *Deus dixit*). The only thing that is material about human thinking itself, however, is the ambivalent pious material that it brings with it for testing. If we look for the determinations of this thinking from the standpoint of its relative autonomy, from this angle, too, we must clearly stop at the middle point which is inaccessible to this thinking as such, which we have previously called a norm from the standpoint of heteronomy, and which now, when our starting point is thinking as a movement, we must call the scope or goal or theme. Dogmatic thinking, seen in terms of autonomy, is objectively determined. From the very first it deliberately renounces its own content in favor of its object. Because it is related to this very definite object as its scope, because it is oriented to it, it has to have certain specific features. We shall have to discuss the objective determinations of dogmatic thinking in the second subsection below.

But first we must do something else. I say in the thesis that the relation of the pious words of Christian preachers to the Word of God, in which dogmatic work takes place subjectively, has to be strict and clear. These words stand exactly at the point where in § 12 we said that we must endorse the authority of the Word of God over against the pious words of preachers. I hope that you will not view these expressions merely as so much rhetorical embellishment. I am laying stress upon them. On the two sides of the difficult ridge up which we are toiling they both tell us the same thing. Although the expressions are strong, what they tell us is, of course, relative. In the confrontation and relation the call is to cry aloud and spare not.[10] One cannot think dogmatically without a certain ruthlessness. Good care is taken that the trees will not reach to heaven, that the ruthlessness will not be absolute or theonomous. The force which human thinking is achieving or seeking is that of which we read in Jer. 23:29 that it is like a fire, or like a hammer that smashes rocks. If that does not happen, if the pious words can slip through the sieve of dogmatics without being salted and sharpened and freighted, then something is wrong. It is wrong when in this work people have time to make a system out of the component theses. If a system emerges, this is perhaps a sign of the art and skill of the builder concerned, but it is also perhaps a sign that thinking has come to a halt, which is not the aim of the dogmatic

---

10. Barth is quoting from an anonymous hymn (no. 803) in A. Knapp, *Lieder-schatz für Kirche, Schule und Haus,* 2nd ed. (Stuttgart/Tübingen, 1820), p. 376, the first strophe of which is based on Isa. 58:1.

exercise. At any rate, a system is not the goal. All that we need are a few carefully chosen standpoints from which to survey the material and then the loci. The decisions are always individual. The boldest and most illuminating general schemes are worthless if there is not authority on the one side, strictness and clarity on the other. Nor can dogmatics attempt a complete presentation of Christian truth. Christian preaching from that of Abraham at Bethel (Gen. 12:8) to the end of time is but a small drop in the total presentation of Christian truth. How, then, can one small dogmatician exhaust this ocean? No, dogmaticians should be modest. The usefulness of their work depends on its quality, not its quantity. And the quality depends on the courage and humility with which, according to human possibilities, they do what those two expressions state.

II. Freedom and Autonomy in Dogmatics

The object of the relation in which dogmatic thinking is done is the Word of God in revelation through scripture. It is autonomous thinking insofar as it makes this object or *nomos* its goal. From this angle, too, the work of dogmaticians is the same in principle as that of preachers — its paradigm, as it were. Their more or less wildly developed thoughts and words, whether deriving from experience, tradition, history, or the Bible itself, are now brought to the object to which they must be related if they are really to be media or agents for the Word of God. I ought to talk about God. I want to do so. I have dared to do so. If this is not to be an illusion, then I myself must see — no one else, no angel, can see it for me — that all my talk can be only a hastening and striving and aiming toward an object which naturally — in our poverty-stricken speech — is not an object: the *Deus dixit*. But we cannot understand this *Deus dixit* as a general possibility. How could it be? If it were, it would undoubtedly be merely an inversion of the fact that *I* speak. This "God speaks" comes to us as a reality through scripture. Scripture bears witness that it is real in revelation. With this insight dogmatics constitutes its object.

We must take the word "object" — inadequate though it is in this context — in a very concrete way as that which stands over against us. If this does not stand over against our thinking, if this thinking ceases to be a relation, if the object is viewed in the same way as, for example, the principle of contradiction is viewed, then the thinking is no longer dogmatic thinking and the object is no longer *this* object. The situation is exactly the same as that of Paul in Phil. 3:12: *Ouch hoti ēdē elabon ē ēdē teteleiōmai, diōkō de ei kai katalabō, eph hō kai katalēmphthēn hypo Christou Iēsou.* There can be no question of reaching the goal. The goal in dogmatics too is *anō klēsiōs tou theou en Christō Iēsou* [v. 14]. We do not reach this goal. It reaches us and then we chase after it. A preaching or dogmatics which finally reached it and no longer had an object or was no longer a relation (Schleiermacher was mercifully preserved, in a 3rd edition of his *Christian Faith,* from reaching this goal which he described as his ideal in his Open Letters to Lücke)[11] — such preaching or dogmatics would certainly be of the devil. If would be a supreme Luciferian revolt. The *nomos,* God's Word, does not come on the scene from this angle either. It is not our task to spread light from uncreated light.[12] Our thinking and speaking need to be determined by their object and hence to strive toward their goal. Yet the determination is only a relative one. The thinking and speaking can never be absolute. This arises out of what we have said. For the thinking is always our human thinking. In its relativity, however, it is the arrow, the longing, the outstretched arm of the signpost which directs our thinking to the Word that we can never think or speak. The relation is achieved in this very relativity. No way leads past it even in its relativity.

We must now obviously draw a parallel to the three determinations of the freedom in which there is knowledge of scripture as God's Word according to § 5. From the problem of freedom, of the appropriation of the biblical witness, there naturally arises mutatis mutandis the problem of the autonomy of dogmatic thinking which is determined by this witness (or the content of it) as its object. In that section we discussed the historical investigation of the witness, then the apprehension of its thoughts, and then a prophetic thinking of those thoughts for oneself. I will again draw the parallels in three catchwords which I ask you to take with the same caution as at the corresponding point in § 12. The catchwords are these: (1) Thinking in Faith and Obedience; (2) Dialectical Thinking; (3) Responsible Thinking. You can try to think through for yourselves the analogy in which these three points stand with a backward reference to § 10.III and a sideways reference to § 12.II. If you put together

---

11. Cf. *Schleiermachers Sendschreiben über seine Glaubenslehre an Lücke,* ed. H. Mulert (Giessen, 1908).

12. Cf. the hymn of C. Knorr von Rosenroth (1684) in *Gesangbuch für die evangelisch-reformierte Kirche der deutschen Schweiz* (1891), no. 43, with an allusion to the "light of light" of the Nicene Creed.

§ 9.III, § 10.III, § 12.II, and § 13.II, you will have a table of 4 × 3 categories by means of which you can perhaps see the relations between scripture and preaching from both sides.[13] I do not put the relations between revelation and scripture and revelation and preaching in the table because by their very nature these escape our notice. They are not relative but absolute. They can be seen only indirectly in the system of twelve relativities. But now to the point.

1. As determined by its object, dogmatic thinking is thinking in faith and obedience. In this quality the Word of God in scripture and revelation becomes its object. To note and establish that there is some such thing as a Word of God means believing and obeying. At this point I must presuppose, of course, that in some sense you have before you the content of § 7, which was devoted to these two concepts. I would urgently draw your attention to § 7. Precisely because it deals with what concerns us most closely, ourselves in relation to revelation, it is, in practice at least, the most decisive part of my doctrine of revelation, and decisive also for an understanding of chapters 2 and 3 above. If light dawns for you there, then in spite of every other obscurity in detail, you will understand what I am saying both before and after. If you are not with me there, then according to my judgment you cannot possibly understand my presentation either before or after. I tell you this because it might perhaps be a useful hint for you when you read through your notes later.

We have referred to faith and obedience as a work of the Holy Spirit, but just as sharply as a perceptible human knowing and doing which are the substratum of that work. We have done so in both cases in opposition to Schleiermacher and in analogy to the christological definitions which ineluctably encountered us in our inquiry into the objective possibility of revelation. As regards the second and perceptible part, human knowing and doing, we naturally do not abstract it away from the miracle of the Holy Spirit but set *this* aspect in *this* context. Dogmatic thinking must be the thinking of human beings who stand before God. It must be their thinking as it is determined and defined by the fact that they stand before God and are addressed by him. When we say this we have already said the decisive thing. It is a thinking of that which is inaccessible to

---

13. The categories are as follows: canon, doctrinal definitions, present moment (§ 9.III); historical picture, necessity of thought, appearance of the moment (§ 10.III); Bible, school, church (§ 12.II); thinking in faith and obedience, dialectical thinking, responsible thinking (§ 13.II).

thought. Thinking means thinking about objects or predicates. God, however, is pure subject. He is subject in his Word too. He himself is the content of his Word. Even in his predicates, even when he makes himself an object as he does in revelation, he is still himself, still subject. "I am who I am" [Exod. 3:14]. He cannot be accessible to thought. Or, as happens in revelation, he can be accessible only in his inaccessibility as the Word speaks by the Spirit to spirit.

Thinking, then, is always the thinking of objects. But it is not so in the case of God, who always stands outside *at* the door. Only in the Spirit, *en pneumati,* and indeed *en pneumati hagio,* is he inside. We can think about God as an object only in God. This is the miracle of the Holy Spirit — not anything that we can reach or achieve or possess or name our own, but the reality of God *for* us and *to* us and *in* us in his revelation. The thinking which stands outside, knocking, waiting, expecting, persisting in face of what is inaccessible, persisting because it is the secret of *God,* the open secret of God, not persisting in its own religious strength or in the power of human thought, but because inside the justifying, sanctifying, and saving miracle of the Holy Spirit is a reality — this is the thinking of faith and obedience. It is the thinking of faith because it is the trust and venture of the heart, which, not knowing what it is doing, presses on to the throne of God himself: "Lift up your hearts, that they may be with the Lord."[14] The kingdom of heaven is taken by storm, and those who storm it snatch it to themselves [Matt. 11:12]. This takes place in the Spirit, in the Holy Spirit, and no words are too bold for what takes place.

The thinking is also that of obedience because there is no choice in this matter, because the thinking is tied to God and taken captive in obedience to Christ [2 Cor. 10:5], because an answer to the human question has been given. The demand is there, the law is in force, judgment has been passed, and the servant is a servant. This is so in the Spirit, in the Holy Spirit. But even the thinking which believes and obeys inside is outside. It stands outside only before its limit, before the secret, before God whom it cannot think, completely unable to justify itself to itself, for example, to philosophical thinking, because of its sin against the principle of contradiction in really positing that which by its own concept cannot be posited, in binding itself in faith, in tying itself in obedience to the Word in which that which we can never posit posits itself. For when we speak by the Word or Spirit, when we are taken up by the Spirit, we stand

---

14. Barth is alluding to the *Sursum corda* of the Roman Missal.

before God and think before God. If we note and assert that there is such a thing as the Word of God, this can mean only that we assert that this Word has addressed us. Asserting this — asserting that we are *outside*, but outside, mark you, *before* this door — is thinking in faith and obedience. This is the basic objective determination of dogmatic thinking.

2. As it is determined by its object, dogmatic thinking is dialectical thinking. As I have put it in the thesis, what I mean is that it is human thinking which, cost what it will, has to orient itself to its object. Cost what it will! This is where the famous dialectic comes in. Do not let yourselves be bedazzled by the word. Above all do not use it too often. Learn to be relaxed when you come across it, for it is absolutely unavoidable. You will see from the context in which I refer to it that for me it is in fact only one of my tools, number 11 of the twelve relativities that I regard as indispensable for an understanding of the relation between scripture and preaching, among which, for good or ill, there is also number 11. There can be no question of the dialectic being itself revelation or the Spirit or the good Lord himself. But since we have to bear in mind most emphatically the earthly character of our dogmatics as distinct from that of the blessed in heaven or of God himself, there can also be no question of not needing to take it seriously, of imagining that we can think nondialectically.[15] This will not work, it is completely forbidden, not because we can and should delight in this disruptive factor, but because of the object of dogmatic thinking.

What does dialectic mean? To put it innocuously and in a way that should awaken confidence, *dialektein* means to converse with others, to deal with them, to discuss with them. Dialectic means, then, thinking in such a way that there is dialogue. Two are needed for this.[16] There must

---

15. The MS has here the marginal jottings: "speech reply explanation pastors why? We are human. This object! Be brave then."

16. At this point a sheet is imposed and one page of the original is struck out. Since at some points in the new text only headings are given, it may be conjectured that Barth decided on the change just before class on Aug. 1, 1924. The original, which helps to elucidate the new version, is as follows:

> I myself am the one, and I adopt the other into my thinking as a kind of alien body, speaking to myself in the name of this other. True dialectical thinking, then, means that the dialogue is really carried on by myself in my own thinking. But I have to let this other, who is not myself, really speak, with all that the distinction implies: I cannot break off halfway if what is said is unpleasant. The result when we do this will only be tensions, i.e., unreal, bearable, and secretly already tran-

be two incompatible but inseparable partners in my thinking: a word and a counter-word, for example, faith and obedience, authority and freedom, God and man, grace and sin, inside and outside, etc. How does the counter-word, and therefore the dialogue, come to have a place in my thinking? First I think pious words before God that are nondialectically neutral, as ought to happen in the thinking of faith and obedience. I even try to think about God himself with these words of mine. But I cannot

---

scended antitheses, harmless antinomies which are proposed but for which the solution is already at hand, the thinking which is just a matter of maneuvers with no shooting. Many people will call this dialectic, but it is not really so. It is like a party meeting at which we are sure from the very first that the president will have the last word. True dialectic means letting the other really speak. At times, of course, the dialogue will break off, but only at times. A victory is not on the agenda, and there will be no peace, only a significant silence when both sides have had their say. One side advances a solution to the problem but the other then poses it in a new way and more work is demanded. The true and invincible partner who finds a home in my thinking keeps on speaking. I cannot escape this other. I cannot stop his mouth. I do not want to be alone. I want him to speak. I want him to speak to me as a true and invincible other.

And now I ask whether there can be any other dogmatic thinking than this dialectical thinking. We have said that dogmatic thinking means thinking in faith and obedience, thinking that is determined by the fact that God's Word has addressed us. We thus have this other, this alien body, who has found a home even if only on the border of my thinking. This other whom I allow to speak must be in my own thinking. But I, too, must speak. Good care is taken that I do so. Dogmatic dialectic is nothing other than genuine, open, honest dialogue, with no confusion between me and the other, between this side and that, between object and subject. The aim is a purification of what I think and speak about God by what God thinks and speaks. In this process situations will arise like the one above in which we have to speak about that which is inaccessible as such becoming accessible, or about our thinking being wholly within with God and his being wholly without in relation to us. We will come across such antitheses as faith and obedience, the divine and human natures in Christ, authority and freedom, autonomy and heteronomy. We have found dozens of them in the Prolegomena and will meet with more as we move from one locus to another in dogmatics proper. Obviously all these things continually shatter and break our thinking. They continually lead us to points where we have the will but not the ability. What are we to say in face of them? Pitiably wringing our hands will be no help. The partner is there, and no partner so forces our thinking into dialectics in principle as does the one who belongs to the very concept of dogmatic thinking, the Word of God, that two-edged sword [Heb. 4:12] which will never let us be content with mere tensions, or let us constantly agree or range ourselves with it or make it like ourselves, at the risk, the sure and certain risk, of real shattering and breaking. Here, if anywhere in dogmatic thinking, there is need of a true *dialogein* that cannot be suppressed; the word of two parties is needed.

succeed. For every time, on the one side, when I believe that I have thought about God, I must remember that God is subject, not object. I have to turn around, then, and think radically, on the other side, whence I came in order to be able to do this. When this situation is seen again at any point there arises the dialectical relation of two concepts. Dialogue takes place in this relation, and to that extent, like all dogmatic thinking, it is a dialectical dialogue. Thinking nondialectically would mean in principle not thinking before God. Before God human thoughts *become* dialectical.

Everything depends, then, on the dialogue being conducted honestly and bravely. It must not be like maneuvers or party gatherings (mere tensions of unreal opposites, victory assured), or, as in Schleiermacher, a matter of feeling. Only the object is transcendent. For the sake of this object we do not want to be transcendent. We take every antithesis seriously even at the danger of contradiction. In the movement of our thinking we point to the object. We break off the dialogue and speak a nondialectical last word [?] only when new problems come to light.

In the passage of Israel through the Red Sea [Exod. 14:19-30] the Red Sea reminds us of words without knowledge that are not God's Word. The staff of Moses is dogmatic thinking, the thinking of faith and obedience. The waves on the right hand and the left are words and counter-words which inexplicably become still. The people of Israel suggests the knowledge of God, the Word of God which is spoken. Pharaoh is the kind of thinking that tries to achieve the same result without this object.

No one can think completely nondialectically, not Luther, Schleiermacher, or even Althaus.[17] The only question is whether we have more or less dialectical courage, whether we are more or less ready for the true dialectic that is demanded here. The ultimate issue is very simple. To think dialectically is to acknowledge that we are in contradiction, that we are sinful and fallen, that we are people who, not on our own inquisitive initiative, but because of the Word of God that is spoken to us, cannot escape giving God the glory and confessing that we are only human with our questions, but also — and here already is the dialectic — confessing God and God alone with his answer even as we confess ourselves. The dialogue with which this twofold confession begins in our thinking; the unheard-of movement, not between two poles — God is not the one pole

---

17. P. Althaus had criticized Barth's dialectic in *ZST* 1 (1923/24) 314-34, 741-86. Barth had discussed the debate with his students; cf. K. Barth/E. Thurneysen, *Briefwechsel,* 2: 1921-1930 (Zurich, 1974), pp. 266-67.

and we the other — but between us in our totality and God in his; the dynamic which grips every word because in this dialectic it is either the divine norm or the human relation to this norm; the world of doubtful but promising, of promising but doubtful relativities that open up here, encircled both above and below by the sole deity of God — this is dogmatic dialectic. It will no longer be needed in heaven. With the angels and the blessed we will have at least a share in God's central view of things.[18] But we need it on earth, and we will be thankful that we have it like any good gift of God. Let us see to it that we use it to God's glory, not as a game, but as the serious work of the catharsis of our pious words. How are these words to be purified for the purpose that they should serve if we do not think them together with the Word of God that is to be proclaimed through them, if we do not think dialectically?

3. As determined by its object, dogmatic thinking is responsible thinking. This is what I mean when in the thesis I say that it is the thinking of specific individuals who see themselves set before this object. "Thou art the man" [cf. 2 Sam. 12:7]. Think of what I said about prophecy in regard to freedom (§ 10.III above). God's Word comes to us in scripture as we ourselves think the thoughts of scripture as our own thoughts. Dogmatics is an office or function, whether we discharge it on the rostrum or in the quiet of the study. In it we take responsibility for the Word of God which speaks in revelation and scripture and which seeks to speak on in preaching. The responsibility, then, relates directly to preaching. Dogmatics can be a science when viewed technically as academic instruction and research. It can also be in effect a work of art. In essence, however, it is neither the one nor the other. It is a ministry of the church, the ministry of the Word of God at the second level. We cannot do dogmatics as spectators, nor because it is interesting, nor because it is there and has to be done. We can do it only because we know that we, too, have a duty and an obligation in the matter of Christian preaching, because we cannot be rid of the thought that something has to happen here. I do not intend this as ethical exhortation. I am simply asserting that this is one of the determinations of dogmatic thinking that is posited by its object. We do not come to dogmatic work out of our own pleasure in it, nor can we do it as we please. No matter who we are, we serve a cause in this matter.

---

18. Cf. F. C. Oetinger, "Anmerkungen 1. von der Central-Schau oder Erkenntnis, wie die Engel erkennen . . . ," *Sämmtliche Schriften,* ed. K. C. E. Ehmann, 2, V (Stuttgart, 1863), pp. 285-98.

III. The Autonomy of the Holy Spirit

I need hardly say anything specific in exposition of the last sentences of the thesis. The autonomy of dogmatic thinking does not mean that we can or should think the truth of God on our own. It means primarily the autonomy of the Holy Spirit. These two sentences mutually explain one another. *We* do the thinking. We have to do so. But when we think the truth, we think the thought that we can think the truth of God only in the Holy Spirit. The Spirit is himself God. But we are dust. The greatest courage *(Mut)* in dogmatics is the greatest humility *(Demut)*. The greatest joy in doing it is the greatest reverence for him who alone can do anything here. Do not take it as an edifying conclusion but as a material summing up of the relation of dogmaticians to their theme if I finally quote the verse in the Psalms: "Praise the Lord, O my soul, and all that is within me praise his holy name" [Ps. 103:1]. With that let us dismiss for this session.

CHAPTER 4

THE DOCTRINE OF GOD

§ 14

Introduction:
The Material and the Task of Dogmatics

Dogmatics is the science of the principles of Christian proclamation. It states that the church's preaching ventures to speak about God and about human beings in their relation to God, about what God is to them and what they have in God — and all this on the premise that it is speaking not only about God but also about God's Word. Dogmatics has to set forth this premise by asking step-by-step about the unity of what it says with God's Word, which the church thinks it has to see first in the revelation to which scripture bears witness.

I. Retrospect

Let us begin by recalling the most important insights and concepts with which we started work on dogmatics proper.

1. As the material of dogmatics, the fact to which this science relates, with which its questions start and to which its answers point, we referred to Christian preaching, the proclamation of the Christian church which takes place among us and in which we have a part insofar as we are theologians.[1] Dogmatics is not the science of God.[2] If there is such a science, it is a matter for philosophical metaphysics. Again, dogmatics is

---

1. See above, § 2.
2. See above, pp. 10-11.

not the science of religion or faith.[3] This would be a matter for the philosophy, history, or psychology of religion. Dogmatics is the science of preaching, not of its practical execution like homiletics, but of its principles, of its norm as this is grounded in the subject matter.

Four reasons have caused us to diverge from those two most common definitions, especially the second, which is almost everywhere the usual one today.[4] (a) Historically, dogma and dogmatics have never been in fact free presentations of God or of faith, but have always been either criticism of what is actually preached or norms for what ought to be preached. (b) At the outset of our study we need to find something that is unquestionably given. God and religion are neither unquestionable facts nor are they unquestionably given. But the preaching of the Christian church is, whether in the form of the stereotyped slogans that it offers (properly understood or not), or in the form of the general presuppositions on which it does so and to which dogmatics must subject it (whether it likes it or not). (c) We are seeking a recognizable aim for dogmatics, a relation between this center of theological science and the center of theological calling, a dogmatic work which in relation to the theme every theologian must do, not incidentally, but by his or her calling. If it is correct that this work must be found in the basic reflection to which theologians must submit their official proclamation, then the search is at an end. (d) We must deal with the misunderstanding that dogmatics has to set up a system of the epitome of what we must believe as Christians. Christian preaching as truth, that is, as God's Word, cannot be put in a system. Hence there is no such thing as the epitome of what we must believe as Christians, for believing faith is a knowledge, a believed faith, only in the act, from case to case. But there is, of course, reflection on true Christian teaching or proclamation, and the act of such reflection is dogmatics.

By dogmas we mean the principles of Christian preaching which have been reached by way of such reflection, whether or not they bear a symbolical character in the church.[5] In principle the relation of such dogmas to dogma, to the necessary idea of an inviolable and definitive law of Christian proclamation, is only that of approximations. They are thus fluid, and dogmatics must constantly generate and establish them

---

3. See above, pp. 9ff.
4. See above, pp. 27ff.
5. See above, pp. 17-18, 39ff.

afresh. The true meaning and result of dogmatic work lies then not in the fundamental principles that are achieved but in the fundamental nature of the work itself.

On this view dogmatics is, as it were, an esoteric science, an in-house dialogue on the part of theologians. Those who feel no responsibility for the fact of Christian proclamation can feel no interest. Dogmatics does not revive or edify, nor should it try to do so. At times it might seem not to be able to steer clear of artificial and farfetched discussions and ideas. In its statements it is not trying to offer a compendium, but truly, if in some detail, only a sketch, only first principles. Preaching, not dogmatics, must bring out the wealth of what is said. Finally, dogmatics is not an attempt to defend or establish Christian theses before the forum of other sciences, whether it be that of philosophy or of the exact sciences. It measures them by its own measure. However necessary or possible the task of apologetics might be, before we think of it we must first work out the principles of Christian proclamation according to their own criterion, doing so with much greater clarity than is usually done today, focusing on what it is that we must say to those outside. Apologetics is a later concern. At any rate, it is not in the light of apologetics that dogmatics must do its work of correction.

2. I have just referred to preaching's own criterion. When we looked critically at the transcendental basis of Christian preaching, we were led to the concept of the Word of God.[6] Because the church believes it knows an authentically attested revelation, it makes sense to speak about God. The Word that God spoke and that the prophets and apostles received, and we through them, wants to be spoken and received again. The problem of Christian preaching, its judgment and its only possible justification, is this: How can it be God's Word as a human word? We have tried to clarify the concept of God's Word in three stages. The point of the Bible is a *Deus dixit,* revelation, which draws the boundary of time and eternity. It is this that makes possible our question about God, awakening it, establishing it, and sustaining it. For, as we saw in the doctrine of the Trinity, God meets us in it and sets us before him, but before him in all the unsearchable mystery of his deity. Yet — the second stage[7] — the revelation that draws the boundary of time and eternity is not as such a past event. The revealed Word becomes contemporaneous with those who come

---

6. See above, ch. 1.
7. See above, ch. 2.

later. The record of this event becomes holy scripture. The Spirit who spoke to the first witnesses, by means of their word, traverses the centuries and continually makes their word his Word. Then — the third stage[8] — the same God will not keep silent today. His Word is not buried in a book. The old witnesses speak in order that new witnesses may arise. We thus come up against living Christian preaching. This must be pure doctrine, that is, doctrine which is God's Word and sets up a relation between God and us, in the same way as holy scripture or revelation itself. This is a promise but also a demand for constant self-testing. The measure by which preaching must measure itself is scripture and revelation. In this sense God's Word is its criterion. It is this precisely because preaching itself *is* God's Word, and — a human task — ought to be so.

3. We have tried to elucidate the concept of God's Word, and to show how the criterion applies, by considering the reality at the three stages under the category of possibility, of its conditions. We have come across two different sets,[9] the subjective and the objective possibilities, relating to the divine and human sides of the problem. Naturally we refer to the grounds of both *possibilities,* the conditions resulting from the reality of God's Word as it comes under these conditions, the ways in which this reality expresses and manifests itself as reality on these two sides, and not vice versa. We do not refer to the *grounds* of this reality, for it has no ground, it is self-grounded, the ground of all grounds.

Thus objectively (a) the incarnation of the Word is the condition under which revelation takes place. We tried to think this out in terms of the ancient doctrine of the incarnation with all its paradoxes. Then the authority of the church is the condition under which the Bible is holy scripture, the relative form in which the absolute authority of God's Word maintains and asserts itself in history. Finally, the presence of a dogmatic norm, of a specific form of Christian doctrine shaped by the divine Word that constantly stands over against the human word, is the condition under which pure doctrine arises. Then subjectively (b) revelation is not without human faith and obedience, holy scripture is not without the free act of individual knowledge, and pure doctrine is not without the relative autonomy of dogmatic thinking that knows it is determined by its object. Note (c) that all the coupled elements that stand over against one another and are dialectically connected are related to the Word of God like the lines of a Gothic arch that culminate

---

8. See above, ch. 3.
9. See above, §§6, 9, 12, and §§ 7, 10, 13.

at the center, except that in this case — the parallel is not wholly congruent — the center is open. The cornerstone, the center that gives point to the whole, upholding it and supporting it, the absolute to which all these relations are relative, the Word of God, is not itself a stone, a concept, a final thought that brings all the others to completion. It is heaven looking down from above on the human work. It is God himself, the Holy Spirit, in all the actuality with which he speaks the Word and human beings hear it. Only under this condition of all the conditions is the criterion authentic and its application, which makes all the elements fruitful, legitimate. Those who can think only of an idol where the living God—is not to be thought of, but actually stands and works and speaks, had best leave both dogmatics and Christian preaching alone. So much as a very brief summary of the way that we have taken thus far.

I know of no other way to address the tasks of dogmatics. I do not think that by laying this foundation I have overcome or set aside the difficulty, indeed, the mortal danger, of the task. On the contrary, I have brought it to light and given it centrality. Now that we plunge into the primeval forest of the matter itself, it will beset us again, becoming greater rather than smaller. This is unavoidable. If the apathy of Christian preaching follows the ridge between heaven and earth, the way of the science of its principles cannot be a comfortable highway. Along these lines, looking back to the Prolegomena, and ahead to what is to come, I would thus issue a warning to the inquisitive, or, in the classical expression: *Mēdeis bebēlos eisitō*.[10] I myself take courage to press on only because the task is a sacred task, and one that is unavoidably set for me by the facts of the situation: the plight of the church and the plight of the race.

II. Prospect

Regarding the course of the above treatment, one may note first that there has been no question of an integration or analysis on the basis of an admittedly presupposed definition of the essence and content of Christianity (a fundamental principle, as the older dogmatics would say)[11] resting on our

---

10. The source of the imperative form of this expression is unknown. The indicative form occurs in Chrysostom, *In Epistolam ad Hebraeos, Homilia XIX* (see MPG, 63, 140, on Heb. 10:22). Thanks to Prof. Michael Wolter of Beirut for this reference.

11. Cf. above, pp. 300ff.

own presuppositions, which are in conformity with the traditions of the specifically Reformed school. In the primary sense the essence and content of Christianity is God's own Word which was spoken in Christ and which speaks again and again. In a secondary sense the essence and content of Christianity is pure doctrine, the human word which is a true forerunner, herald, and bearer of this Word of God. The task of dogmatics is to work out the basic structure of this human word both in detail and in context. To assume that this is done, to presuppose specific connections and relations between the individual elements of Christian preaching, for example, to refer them to a particular point, which might be the doctrine of justification or the idea of the kingdom of God, and then to develop the system that is thus present *in nuce,* is to enter into a vicious circle in which, as the history of modern theology in particular shows, even with the best of intentions one cannot avoid all kinds of evil arbitrariness and a general Babylonian dispersion of dogmatic effort. We have already had an anthropocentric, a theocentric, a christocentric, and a staurocentric (cross-centered) theology.[12] I believe I could promise to build up a similar kind of theology on the basis of baptism or eschatology, but I want no part in this Protestant proliferation. We are thus presupposing nothing but the fact that the Christian church preaches and that this takes place in the belief that it is speaking not merely about God but about his Word. If the fact gives us our material, the belief, which in all naivete we take seriously and to which we bind the church, gives us our measure.

As regards a center, a material principle of dogmatics, of the basic theses to which we have to trace back the material, we are not aiming at any such if it is clear to us that as we apply the measure from case to case, the vital thing is that the true center lies always in God's Word itself, not in the words of preaching nor in the principles to which we relate them; that the formal principle is itself the real material principle; that the point of dogmatic work lies in its being done fundamentally and not in its establishing or elucidating or honoring of the formal principle. It belongs to the very nature of human thought that the resultant principles will probably lead finally to a kind of system, to a more or less enclosed nexus. In the Prolegomena last summer we found that our discussion of the

---

12. Barth has in view Schleiermacher and his school for anthropocentric theology, E. Schaeder (*Theozentrische Theologie* [Leipzig, 1909]) for theocentric, G. Thomasius (*Christi Person und Werk,* ed. F. J. Winter [Erlangen, 1886-88]) for christocentric, and H. Cremer for staurocentric.

presuppositions of dogmatics forced us ineluctably into a little system, and we must be prepared for the same thing happening again. But we are not aiming at this. This cannot be the goal of our work. At best it is only a by-product that we view with some distrust. We must certainly not begin with it. Because the center, the essence and content in the strict sense, one might also say the system, lies in principle outside every human word, even the human word that has been dogmatically purified and perhaps systematized, being found only in God's Word, the unavoidable bent toward a system can be only a matter of the sequence with which we move on from one aspect of the material, or of preaching, to another (from one locus, as older Protestantism would say, to another). Without too much mental effort, without any systematic genius or originality, we can let this sequence be prescribed for us by the logical content of Christian preaching.

We can agree that Christian preaching, described in the crassest of religious generalizations, deals with God, with human beings in their relation to God, or more specifically with what God is to and for human beings, and what they for their part have in God. Whether these elements are inwardly connected and all say the same thing is another question. Logically, at any rate, we may separate them, and in so doing specify the poles between which all Christian speaking usually moves. If we direct our own course accordingly, we are simply following the classical line that dogmatics has taken from Origen to Wegscheider, with Schleiermacher as the first exception: (a) God, (b) Anthropology, (c) Reconciliation, and (d) Salvation. I hope to deal with the first two this winter and the last two next summer. As usual, what is called eschatology will form the conclusion. However, according to its content and significance it is such a unique entity that I would like to deal with it, as with the prolegomena at the beginning, outside the order [of material loci] as a kind of great exclamation point to the whole.[13]

Similarly, in the disposition of the detailed parts I will keep to the logical content of ordinary Christian proclamation in its most general form. With more or less clarity and emphasis we shall find everywhere the elements or principles that we have to presuppose in setting forth the basic principles. No matter in what form they will be present, we can and must work them out scientifically. The material itself is always in some sense a matter of indifference. We can thus deal with it innocuously and uncritically. Everything depends on our succeeding in putting it in the light in

---

13. As it turned out Barth dealt with eschatology in the winter semester 1925/26 at Münster; see vol. II.

which it is more than material, the light in which the church's human word becomes transparent, in which its transcendental meaning finds voice and utterance: God's Word.

At the conclusion[14] of this introductory section I must not fail to bring to your notice the recent upsurge in works in this area. I can list no fewer than five dogmatics that have just been published: Reinhold Seeberg, Part I (Basis, Doctrine of God and Man); Hermann Lüdemann, Part I (Basis); Martin Rade, Part I (Doctrine of God); Karl Girgensohn, Outline; Werner Elert, Outline of Lutheran Doctrine.[15] I would also recommend that along with the lectures you read Heppe and Schmid as sources.[16]

---

14. This paragraph was added to the MS in the margin.

15. R. Seeberg, *Christliche Dogmatik,* I (Erlangen/Leipzig, 1924); H. Lüdemann, *Christliche Dogmatik,* I (Bern/Leipzig, 1924); M. Rade, *Glaubenslehre,* I (Gotha/Stuttgart, 1924); K. Girgensohn, *Grundriss der Dogmatik* (Leipzig/Erlangen, 1924); W. Elert, *Die Lehre des Luthertums im Abriss* (Munich, 1924).

16. Heppe, *Reformed Dogmatics* (London, 1950); Schmid ET *The Doctrinal Theology of the Evangelical Lutheran Church* (Philadelphia, 1899).

§ 15

The Knowability of God

The knowability of God has been put in question and posited by his revelation. God reveals himself to us as the irremovable subject: I am who I am. The objective knowledge of God which comes through his incarnation in faith and obedience, the knowledge of his being and existence which is effected by the Holy Spirit, is thus a knowledge of his mystery, of the limit that is set for our knowledge by him, of the necessity of asking after him. We find indications of God where we come up against this mystery. We form meaningful concepts of God when they elucidate this incomprehensibility of his. But it is always true only in the act of his revelation that the mystery is his mystery and the incomprehensibility his incomprehensibility.

I. God Is Knowable by Us

The fact of preaching, of talking about God, rests on the presupposition that God is knowable to us, that he is an object. But we must immediately question this presupposition and test its character as a true given. We do not put the question of God's knowability as philosophers. Not that we scorn participating in philosophical work, at least as vitally interested dilettantes. Not as though we could promise no good from a dialogue of philosophy with theology. But what we hear philosophers asking about is the knowability of the thing in itself, the absolute, the unconditioned, the origin of things. Before we can sit down to talk, we need to agree first whether this is the same as our own theological question as to the knowability of God. On our side such an agreement might come only on the basis of the completion of our own work and not before. But even when agreement is reached on the fact that the same thing is meant, or on the extent to which it is, the way in which the question of the knowability of this is handled will have to be different in the two disciplines if philosophy is not to become theology or theology philosophy.

The difficulty in the theological question of the knowability of God is a very special one. As preachers talk about God, they declare that they know God, that they are in a position to name him, to affirm his being, his existence, to ascribe certain attributes to him. For theology the real problem in all this does not lie on the side of the human capacity for knowledge. The question that dogmatics has to put to preaching would be there even if philosophy could without contradiction accept or proclaim God as an object of possible intellectual or intuitive experience. The doubt that dogmatics would have to raise even were there no critique of pure reason[1] rests on the recollection that, according to the definition of preaching, what ministers say about God is supposed to be God's Word. It is what God himself says. But God does not speak about anything other or secondary or inferior which as such can then be an object of human knowledge and speech, a knowable, definable, and describable object. God's Word to us is his covenant with us, his turning to us who have turned away from him. This is the whole content of what he says. The content of God's Word is God alone, wholly God, God himself, as we said in our discussion of the concept of revelation.[2] The new thing that the term "word" adds to the term "God" is that he is God in relation. But the term "word" is simply an analysis and development of the term "God" to make it more precise. Its content is that God is never without relation to us. He always turns to us. The covenant as the decree of his will is always in him. In relation he does not cease to be fully God.

It is precisely here in the concept of revelation that the problem of God's knowability arises. When we took with categorical seriousness the thesis on which the possibility of Christian preaching is finally based, namely, that Christ reveals God to us, it led us irresistibly to the ancient doctrine of the Trinity. We broke up the concept of revelation into its component parts and saw that when we asked about the what of revelation, or its whence in Christ, or its whither in us, the way to God as an object

---

1. See Immanuel Kant, *Kritik der reinen Vernunft* (1781); ET *Critique of Pure Reason* (New York, 1915).
2. See above, pp. 87, 89ff.

was always barred, for God's deity or person is never a mere object, an It or a He, but always an I. In his revelation, and precisely in his revelation, God is an irremovable subject that can never be confused with an object. God's being or *essentia,* as the ancients put it, is a separate problem.[3] We shall have to deal with it in the next section.

But in any case, as Father, Son, or Spirit, he is God. It makes no sense to add a restrictive "for us," to talk about a purely economic Trinity, as though we could objectify his Word, in which he is Father, Son, and Spirit, as a fourth thing apart from his essence. I was summarizing this point of the doctrine of the Trinity in my thesis when I recalled the answer that God gave Moses when he asked God for his name: "I am who I am" (Exod. 3:14). This does not mean: "I am *ho ōn,*" as the LXX translated it (i.e., "he who truly is"), in an over-rash abstraction. No matter how we construe the verb, the paradoxical repetition of the first person carries the sense: "Who I am, I will be." This subject is not giving an objective definition of himself but positing himself again as subject. In this remarkable biblical incident at a decisive point the refusal of the name is its revelation. This presents us *in nuce* with the problem of the knowability of God. The ancient Jews were right, though rather bureaucratically so, when they refrained from uttering this name, the name that does not point to an It or a He, but points to the one who wills exclusively to name himself, to be himself an object, whose qualities, words, and deeds are present only in act, and are his qualities, words, and deeds only as they stand behind the great I in which God alone is God. It made sense for the ancient OT prophets to begin their addresses with "Thus says the Lord," and to believe in a very pregnant sense that what they then went on to say was said in the name of this Lord, in the first person. In his revelation in which he distinguishes himself from all gods and idols, God is and exists only as subject. His revelation consists precisely of his refusal to be a He or an It, an object. Hallowed be thy name! To put it positively, his revelation consists of the fact that he himself encounters us, that we see ourselves set before God himself. This self is indissoluble; it cannot be reduced to a thing. It is irreversible; the I cannot become an It or a He; it cannot be objectified. Only thus, in this actuality, is God God in his Word.

Christian preaching talks about this God. It does so in human words, that is, it talks about him objectively. What else can it do if it is

---

3. Marginal note: "Essence and person are two different things but inseparable."

to talk about him at all? We who are not prophets cannot speak subjectively like the prophets. Very special necessity and revelation are needed for that. But our objective talk about God, though unavoidable, is subject to inevitable suspicion. We have to consider this. In many sermons we see that the preachers have never reflected on what they are doing at the very first step. They do not have the fear, the daring, the authorization, and the sense of responsibility that this step requires. We are undoubtedly putting something different and improper in the place of God when we talk about him objectively. Do we know with what right we may do this? Do we know the caveat that is bound up with this right? Do we know that objective talk about God might mean the erection of an idol? That it can only signify and be the office of a herald in place of God's own Word about himself? That when we engage in it we must have in view safeguards and emendations and corrections to relieve the human word of some of its peril, to divest it of its deceptive *autousia,* to restore to the divine I, which we cannot take on our lips but can only encapsulate in our It or He, in what is perhaps our justifiable objectivizing, its proper freedom, the *autousia* that is appropriate to it alone? We must not evade this suspicion, disruptive and restrictive though we may find it, whether at the first step or at any that follow.

What does this insight mean for the question of God's knowability? It would be over-hasty to infer from it that God is unknowable. Not at all! We have won this insight from revelation. As God reveals himself, he is knowable, or it would not be revelation. The result of our first discussion has to be positive. There is a name of God, the name that he gives himself. There is a knowability of God, in the knowledge with which he knows himself. These are not speculative statements. God has revealed himself by this name and in this knowability. We must bear in mind that God and God alone is the subject of this knowledge with which we have to reckon on the basis of revelation (Matt. 11:27; John 1:18). But we must also bear in mind that on the basis of revelation we do have to reckon with this knowledge, that where revelation is, there this knowledge takes place, for us, to us, and in us (we can say all that, but not that we are the subject and God the object).

In three little-noticed passages Paul called this revealed and imparted knowledge of God, which is always God's own knowledge, our being known by God (Gal. 4:9; 1 Cor. 8:3; 13:12). In Gal. 4:9 Christians are *gnontes theon, mallon de gnōsthentes hypo theou.* In 1 Cor. 8:3, *ei de tis agapa ton theon, houtos egnōstai hyp' autou,* and note should be taken of the preceding text, which tells us that if we think we have known, we have not known as we ought to know: *kathōs dei gnōnai* means being known by God. In 1 Cor. 13:12: *epignōsomai* (i.e., in the resurrection) *kathōs kai epegnōsthēn* (i.e., here and now, where our knowing is a *ginōskō ek merous*). I know of no better formulation of the relation achieved in God's Word between God's naming and knowing of himself on the one side, and our naming and knowing on the other, than Paul's highly paradoxical passive use of *gignōskein*. I had this relation in mind when in the thesis I said that the knowability of God is both given to and put in question by revelation; what is put in question is a knowledge of God of which we are the subject. We must let ourselves be told that God is not an object, and hence that our knowledge of God can relate only to his knowledge of himself. In revelation this knowledge is given, given to us. For the Spirit is given in revelation. "The Spirit searches everything, even the depths of God" [1 Cor. 2:10]. The Spirit is God, God for us and to us and in us and even through us, for at times, according to 2 Cor. 2:14, we can even impart an aroma of the knowledge of God to others, though the Spirit is not on that account our spirit or identical with us. Thus, in conclusion, we may not say that we know God, but that we know insofar as God knows himself. To quote Paul again, "in Christ are hid [*apokryphoi*] all the treasures of wisdom and knowledge" (Col. 2:3)!

II. The Adequacy of Our Indirect Knowledge of God

We can and must define more closely the knowability of God as thus described. We have said that as God reveals himself to us, he is knowable by us. We have been taught that he is knowable indirectly in his knowledge of himself, and we must always remember this when we talk about him as though we knew him directly, as though he were an object. But he is still knowable, and this is what we must now stress. Objective talk about God does not mean only human weakness, the impotence or indolence of our knowing, the erection of idols. It may be such things inasmuch as it is our talk. But the boundary between adequate and inadequate knowledge of God is not the same as the boundary between God's own direct knowledge and our indirect knowledge. Our indirect knowledge can be adequate, that is, appropriate to the relation between God and us that is set up by the Word. There is objective talk about God that is well-founded, justifiable, even commanded and not merely permitted. The indirect, objective knowledge of God that is ours can also be true knowledge, that *ginōskein ek merous,* our knowledge of the divine self-knowledge (as we put it), in which we grasp as it were from without the irreversible divine I in his action. It is so when it is knowledge in relation to revelation, knowledge by the Spirit. We would deny revelation as revelation if we contested this.

Let us recall the conditions under which revelation is factual. When God truly reveals himself truly to us, this presupposes (see §§ 6 and 7 above) (a) that God meets us and (b) that we stand before God. For our problem this means that God is an object of knowledge and we the subject. God becomes an object of knowledge by becoming man in Christ. We become the subject of knowledge by faith and obedience. Concretely and objectively something is there and takes place in human space and time — the humanity of Jesus Christ. Just as concretely and objectively we on the other side know and do something — our faith and obedience. The one thing in this twofold event is revelation. This twofold event is the condition under which God's Word is spoken and his covenant is concluded with us. Under this condition, in this simple subject-object relation, God is knowable by us. To deny that God accepts this condition and enters into this relation in which he is knowable would again be to deny revelation. This *is* revelation — what else could it be? God does not set aside or reverse his irremovable and irreversible I. He does not cease to be God in his revelation. But he conceals his I in a relation in which we can share in his self-knowledge, in which he can meet us, in which we can stand before him. He conceals his I in a human It or He. He conceals himself in a human seeing, hearing, touching, and tasting of this objective reality.

Let there be no mistake — it is he who thus conceals himself in this relation. *He* is its truth. *He* is the Word that is here spoken and heard. *He* concludes the covenant. But we are stammering when we say "he." We mean the I that the true God alone is from eternity to eternity. By him, the Spirit, the man Jesus of Nazareth is the God-Logos, the speaking God, and by him, the Spirit, he is the God who is perceived in our faith and obedience. But it is he who conceals himself in this relation and who is knowable in this concealment, because this concealment alone makes him knowable, even adequately knowable. He is so indirectly in the relation of revelation and under the limitation that is proper to this relation that points beyond itself, *ek merous,* as Paul said. Nevertheless, in this relation he is knowable in a way that is appropriate to his reality, truly, fully, and adequately. This is the second and positive insight that we have to achieve in discussing our question. As I said in the thesis, there is an "objective knowledge of God which comes through the incarnation in faith and obedience," "a knowledge of his being and existence which is effected by the Holy Spirit."

The next observation that we have to make about Christian preaching is that there can be no shaking or staining or explaining away the knowability of God in this sense, or its certainty or adequacy. Here in this sense, if objective talk about God is passing on knowledge of the relation of revelation, suspicion is just as little in place as the lack of it was earlier. True seriousness means lack of suspicion. In the concealment in which God meets us, in the indirectness of our knowledge, we now have to see quite simply the reality of his Word spoken and heard, and we must not be ashamed of the gospel. No relativism, no skepticism, no personal timidity should prevent us from talking about God very naively, very definitively, and in the same matter-of-fact way as we talk about any other data. God *is* a datum in revelation by the Spirit. Happy are we, then, if we can speak about him with this certainty, *en pneumati*. And woe to us if we do not.[4]

III. The Mystery and Limit of God's Knowability

The conditional nature of God's knowability leads on necessarily to a third question which we have described in the thesis in the terms "mystery" and "limit." The conditional nature of the knowability of God, and hence of the related talk about God, lies in the fact that God takes on concealment in his revelation. To know God is to know him indirectly. We have now to think out all aspects of this statement. God is known to us through his concealment, through his entry into the subject-object relation, which is his Word to us. Without a veil we cannot see him. Moses was to see God's

---

4. Marginal note: "Summary of previous subsection. We have seen (1) that the problem of God's knowability is posed by the fact that God's revelation is the revelation of his inalienable subjectivity. God knows himself. But by revelation *en pneumati* we come to share in this divine self-knowledge. Following Paul, we described this as being known by God. Then we said (2) that this sharing in the divine knowledge as it takes place in revelation encloses a knowability of God in the subject-object relation. In Christ God encounters us. Believing and obeying, we stand before God. Except under this condition revelation would not be revelation. True and adequate knowledge of God takes place under this condition insofar as the Spirit is thus given to us."

glory, but God had to hide him in a cleft of the rock and hold his hand over him until he had passed by. Moses could see him from behind, "but my face shall not be seen" (Exod. 33:21ff.). I must emphasize that the concern that I want to denote and represent by the words "mystery" and "limit" is not that of skepticism but precisely that of God's knowability. To deny the concealment in which God is knowable by us, the indirectness of the knowledge of God, is to deny revelation. If he is not knowable to us indirectly, he has not revealed himself to us at all. The reality of the relation of revelation in which Jesus Christ stands on the one side and our faith and obedience on the other — the divine Word being spoken by the Spirit there and received by the Spirit here — is equivalent to the fact that our knowledge of God in this relation is the knowledge of his mystery, of the limit that he has set for our knowledge, of the need to ask concerning him. All three expressions mean the same thing. They are attempts to describe the nature of our human knowledge precisely in the relation of revelation, precisely on the presupposition of a real knowability of God, which pitilessly carries with it God's concealment and hiddenness. Our knowledge runs up against God's mystery and recognizes it as such. It runs up against the objectivity in which God himself remains hidden in his subjectivity. It finds its own limit in this hidden subjectivity of God. Naturally, in relation to this hidden subjectivity of God there can fundamentally be only a question concerning it. But there has to be this question. In spite of the indirectness, or because of it, there can be true and adequate knowledge of God. This is because God can reveal himself only in this way, in the concealment of the subject-object relation. He cannot reveal himself in any other way without ceasing to be God. The indirectness of our knowledge is the correlate of the concealment in which God gives himself to be known. The reality of revelation stands or falls with it. At this point we should not violently try to grasp more than is proper for us. We will only finish up with less.

Paul called Christian knowledge, knowledge in the relation of revelation, a *gignōskein ek merous* (Cor. 13:9) and then a *gignōskein esoptrou en ainigmati* (v. 12). He was saying what has to be said. Directly, plainly, and in itself (in a way that is dialectically unreflecting), our knowledge has to do with a medium. This medium can impart the knowledge of God to us. But this already means indirect impartation.[5] The medium in itself

---

5. For this phrase and its derivation from Kierkegaard, see *Training in Christianity*, pp. 96ff.

does not impart the knowledge. It is a puzzle and not the solution to the puzzle. It is a part that expresses something else. It is a pointer to the truth, not the truth itself. The medium can become transparent, the puzzle can be solved, the pointer to the truth can be successful. But then a new and third thing comes in. The illuminating light of revelation makes the medium transparent. In itself it remains a medium. The puzzle remains a puzzle and the part a part. Our knowledge has to do with this puzzle or part. It receives from it its true nature even in the relation of revelation. It is always indirect knowledge. The medium to which we refer is naturally the condition of revelation as we expounded it in subsection II, its reality being objective in the incarnation and subjective in faith and obedience. The coupling is itself a confirmation of the *ek merous* with which Paul characterizes the knowledge that is oriented to this medium. Certainly in this medium, in Christ and the obedience of faith, God can be known only by the Holy Spirit by whom we participate in the knowledge that God has of himself.

The medium fulfils its purpose, it becomes luminous, it unveils even as it veils, it causes to shine, it bears witness, it imparts. For Christ is God's Son and the obedience of faith is his work. Because of this great possibility, which can be a reality at any time by the Holy Spirit, we must not say that the conditional nature of revelation through Christ and the obedience of faith is the same as the unknowability of God, as the impossibility and unreality of a true and adequate and satisfactory knowledge of God. But one also must not say — and this is much more common — that this twofold medium is itself unveiling, attestation, light, or impartation, as though the condition of revelation were identical with God's knowability. Far be it from us to say anything of the kind! If we did, we would be forgetting that the objective thing, the medium, which under the condition of revelation we know in Christ by the obedience of faith, is only the veil, the incognito,[6] in which the divine subjective, I am who I am, the living God, conceals himself and wills to be known, in this way giving himself to be known. We would be making the objective thing serve an idol rather than the living God if we omitted at this point the necessary dialectical reflection, that is, if we did not leave it to God himself, in relation to the object which is given to us in revelation and which marks the limit of our knowledge, to lift his own incognito and make himself known. In this regard Thomas Aquinas cautiously writes: Per revelationem

---

6. For this term, taken from Kierkegaard, see ibid., pp. 127-32.

gratiae in hoc vita non cognoscimus de Deo quid est, et sic ei quasi ignoto coniungimur,[7] and we must accept this!

We must press it indeed on two sides. In Elert's *Lehre des Luthertums* I find a § 23 headed: "The Features of God in the Face of Christ." From the face of Christ, Elert thinks, the people of the Bible, and we with them, can read off directly what he calls God's motivations, that is, his purpose of retribution, and especially alongside and beyond it his purpose of forgiveness. Insofar as he bears and makes known these divine features, Christ is to be called the Son of God according to the usage of the Bible and Christianity.[8] Similarly, Paul Althaus claims that the life of Jesus has the direct and positive significance of revelation, and he appeals in support to Luther's description of Christ as the mirror of the fatherly heart of God.[9] If these modern Lutherans are right, then there is no longer any mystery on this objective side. In the life of Jesus, or in some aspects of it, the divine subject may be read off directly by us. But this is to make the divine subject, the I am who I am, who reveals his name by refusing it, into an object. In the features of retribution and forgiveness found in the face of Christ (or holiness and love according to Althaus),[10] God may be seen in himself without the intervention of revelation as an act, without the Holy Spirit. Yet if Elert and Althaus undoubtedly did not mean this, do we not really have to say that revelation in a mirror is not in any case direct revelation? Alongside the *di' esoptrou* (1 Cor. 13:12) there stands expressly the *en ainigmati,* "in a dark saying," as Luther renders it. Can a dark saying really be read off directly? No, we say. The life of Jesus does not in itself impart the knowledge of God (John 14:8-9). In itself it is instead a riddle, a mystery, a veiling. Face-to-face with it there could and can be a failure to know God. All the contemporaries of Jesus, including his most intimate disciples, finally took offense at him. The word of the cross which sums up his life is *mōria,* foolishness, to those who are lost (1 Cor. 1:18-19).

Between the offense, the foolishness that the world sees, and what Paul calls the wisdom of God in 1 Cor. 1, or the *phōtismos tēs gnōseōs tēs doxēs tou theou* in the face of Christ in 2 Cor. 4:6, there stands according to the NT his cross and resurrection, in principle the end of his life in

---

7. Thomas Aquinas, *STh* I, q. 12, a. 13 ad 1.
8. W. Elert, *Lehre des Luthertums,* p. 19.
9. P. Althaus, "Theologie und Geschichte," *ZST* 1 (1923-24) 771.
10. Ibid., p. 776.

itself and the beginning of his life as the Son of God. Flesh and blood do not reveal this transformation, the revelation in the mystery, to Peter, but "my Father in heaven" (Matt. 16:17). The God who caused light to shine out of darkness has caused that *phōtismos* to shine in our hearts (2 Cor. 4:6). But the *gignōskein kata sarka Christon* comes up here against its natural limit and breaks off. We no longer know him thus, *ouketi.* To be in Christ and to know in Christ is to be a new creature (2 Cor. 5:16-17). But Paul does not call the knowledge of the new creature our own knowledge. It is our being known. Our own knowledge, even and precisely our knowledge of Christ, is knowledge in a mystery, not direct knowledge. God's hiddenness, his alien work, meets us[11] in Christ, and finally and supremely in the crucified Christ, for where is God so hidden as here, and where is the possibility of offense so great as here? The fact that the hiddenness is *God's,* and that he *reveals* himself in this hiddenness, is another matter. God himself, the Spirit, makes this known to us because and wherever this is *his* good pleasure — not ours. The wisdom of God *en mystēriō tēn apokekrymmenēn* (1 Cor. 2:7) is what we speak when we speak about it. And all that we say can only point to this mystery and make known our own limit. It can be only a stormy inquiry into the limit and the mystery!

But we have to establish this on the subjective side as well. I open Stephan's *Glaubenslehre* and read in § 5.3 that we have to thank Luther for overcoming the Catholic and older Protestant curtailment of the concept of faith. Faith for us, he argues, is not an expectancy of future bliss but a mighty present experience of God. More precisely it is the immediacy, the union with God, which takes place on the inner side of the consciousness that lies behind the psychologically apprehensible web of spiritual processes where the rational and empirical becomes the irrational and supraempirical.[12] As the appeal to Luther and the presence of the catchword "immediacy" show, we have here a fairly exact liberal parallel to the transgression of the limit by positive theologians about which we spoke a moment ago. If Stephan were right, then again, but this time on the subjective side, the mystery would be no mystery. On that remarkably irrational inner side of the consciousness faith there would be a breach of the subject-object relation, the divine subject would cease to be an object confronting us, and the knowledge with which

---

11. The original seems to have been *Ihnen,* or possibly *Ihm,* though with no obvious plural or singular antecedent (unless Paul is meant).
12. H. Stephan, *Glaubenslehre* (Giessen, 1921), p. 36.

God knows himself, as Hegel understood already, would be identical with our own knowledge.[13] What we have here is a modern and weaker form of the late Lutheran doctrine of the mystical union.[14] This doctrine led by way of Pietism directly to Schleiermacher! It then came to Stephan along with many others.

In opposition to it I confess what Stephan calls the Catholic and older Protestant curtailment of the concept of faith. Paul himself, so far as I can see, was guilty of it too. It makes faith an expectancy, a *hypostasis elpizomenōn,* an *elenchos pragmatōn ou blepomenōn* (Heb. 11:1). Or, to use our own terms, it makes faith a medium, a puzzle, a transparency, a concealment, a condition of revelation which in itself is not even subjectively the same as the knowability of God. The knowledge of faith, which materially is identical to the knowledge of Christ, is (like this) knowledge in a mystery, indirect and not direct knowledge, knowledge in a mirror, *gignōskein ek merous.* The certainty and truth of faith are not grounded in faith itself but in the act of revelation to which it relates, in God himself, the Holy Spirit, who creates it. Faith in itself might always be unbelief, false faith, or superstition *(Unglaube, Irrglaube, Aberglaube).* Between it and God's knowability stand the cross and resurrection, God's own Word by which we become new creatures. The faith with which we bracket this reality on the outside is always the faith or *fiducia* whose correlate is promise, as the Reformers put it.[15] It is thus expectancy, a knocking on the outside rather than a triumphant entering inside, a blind faith in which we are in no case or sense one with God, not even on the irrational inner side of the consciousness, in which instead (according to Heb. 11:13) we confess that we are guests and strangers on earth. That we do not believe for nothing, that God himself is the correlate of our *fiducia,* is a matter for God alone, and has to be a matter for God alone. Everything that we can say about it is at root no more than a touching of his mystery and our limit, a question, an inquiry about God, no matter how indicative and assertive the form of our thinking and speaking may be. It is indirect knowledge. In this way, only in this way on both sides, yet truly in this way, under this caveat, which has its basis in the matter itself, there is in the relation of revelation a knowability of God which can be calmly asserted over

---

13. Cf. G. W. F. Hegel, *Vorlesungen über die Philosophie der Religion,* II, in *Sämtliche Werke,* XVI (Stuttgart, 1928), p. 191.

14. Cf. Schmid-Pöhlmann, pp. 306ff.; Schmid ET pp. 480ff. *Unio mystica* comes here (§ 47) after *vocatio* (§ 44), *illuminatio* (§ 45), and *regeneratio* (§ 46) and before *renovatio* (§ 48).

15. See above, p. 11.

against all historically or psychologically grounded skepticism because it is self-established.

To clarify things, by way of an appendix or excursus attached to this third subsection, I will touch briefly on a problem which, so far as I can see, only Roman Catholic theology usually deals with expressly, namely, the problem of the so-called essential vision of God, seeing God face-to-face, *prosōpon pros prosōpon,* as Paul so aptly puts it in 1 Cor. 13:12. Thus far we have made the following equations. The knowability of God is knowledge in the relation of revelation, which is indirect knowledge. If we regard these equations as a closed circle that we cannot break out of, there arises at once a question that we cannot dismiss as such, namely, whether and how far there is something outside this circle, whether "in some way," as we might say for once, there is another circle of divine knowability. Roman Catholic theology affirms this in principle. It teaches that alongside the light of grace, or knowledge in the relation of revelation, there is also a light of glory, and in this light an immediate knowledge, or one that is mediated only by the light of glory, that is, the essential vision of God noted in Matt. 5:8.[16]

In principle we cannot possibly negate this idea, or one similar to it. The relation of revelation, with all the dialectical tensions with which I have tried consciously to reckon in my dogmatics, points beyond itself. The Word addressed to pilgrims[17] — *kat' anthrōpous legō* — once it has been spoken, has done its work. When its goal is reached the kingdom of the Son will be at an end (1 Cor. 15:24ff.). With it, with the relation of revelation, so too will be the knowledge in a mystery which we have defended so strongly in what precedes and to which for good reasons we shall have to come back at once. Expectancy does indeed point to entry upon the inheritance, promise to fulfilment, and faith to sight (2 Cor. 5:7). God does not speak his Word in order to make perpetual fools of us but to do what he promises.

As regards the problem of knowability, we may say once more with Paul in 1 Cor. 13:12 that *now* we see *di' esoptrou en ainigmati, tote de* — but *then* face-to-face. Now I know in part, but then I shall know as I am known. The human subject will know the divine subject directly and not just in hidden form as an object. As 1 John 3:2 says, we shall see Christ as he is. Then we shall indeed attain to essential vision, to an intuitive

---

16. Cf. Bartmann, pp. 35-36; and DS, 1000; also Aquinas, *STh* I, q. 12, a. 1-11.
17. Cf. above, p. 73.

knowledge of God, to that second circle or whatever else we want to call it.[18] The equation will then be: The knowability of God is the endowment of the creaturely spirit with the light of grace, which is an intuitive knowledge of God.

But how can we deal with this second knowability of God and its different methodology? We have seen already what Protestant theologians have made of it with a mistaken appeal to Luther. It is clear that that violent invoking of the features of God that may be read off directly from the face of Christ on the positive side, and of immediate experience of God on the liberal side, is nothing other than a poorly understood reminiscence of the great limiting truth of the vision of God. Impatiently and disruptively there is thrust into the relation of revelation, the knowledge of Christ and of faith, that which as the fulfilment of all things and the limit and end of dogmatics belongs to eschatology. In contrast I wish I could show you in some detail how soberly and cautiously Thomas handles the matter. For lack of time I must keep to the main passages. The essential vision of God is basically only for the blessed in heaven[19] and no one else, not even for the angels[20] or the prophets on earth.[21] Thomas finds one notable exception to this rule in the doctrine of rapture developed in II[2], 175. He has in mind the rapture of Paul in 2 Cor. 12:2. In the light of Num. 12:8 Moses might also be numbered among those who in their lifetime were supernaturally and extraordinarily taken out of the senses[22] and lifted up to essential vision. But note that this exception proves the rule, namely, that there is *no* such vision on earth. It is reserved for those who, being even higher than the angels, are at home with the Lord. With neither image nor similitude they will see, not with their earthly eyes (in spite of the bodily resurrection) but with the glorified eye of the mind.[23] In virtue of the supernatural perfecting of the intellect,[24] insofar as they are still distinct from the Creator as creatures, they will see that God is not comprehensible even to them.[25] All this, however, means that they have been separated from this mortal life.

---

18. Cf. Bartmann, p. 34.
19. *STh* I, q. 12, a. 1 i.c.
20. *STh* I, q. 56, a. 3 i.c.
21. *STh* IIa, IIae, q. 173, a. 1 i.c.
22. *STh* I, q. 12, a. 11 ad 2; IIa, IIae, q. 175, a. 4 i.c.
23. *STh* I, q. 12, a. 3 ad 1 and ad 2.
24. *STh* I, q. 12, a. 5 i.c.
25. *STh* I, q. 12, a. 7 i.c.

In the present context I will refrain from asking how the knowledge of angels, and the categorically akin knowledge of mystics,[26] stands related to this essential vision. According to Thomas at least the knowledge of angels is not a seeing face-to-face.[27] That the immediacy with which modern Protestant theology has not kept from toying[28] really belongs to eschatology was clearly perceived by the angelic doctor, as one may see from his discussion, and we should learn from his example to see this too. Christian preaching is directed not to the blessed in heaven but to pilgrims on earth, and dogmatics is the science of the principles of this preaching. We may thus allow Roman Catholic theology, which sees more clearly at this point, to confirm our thesis that in the here and now in which we have to reckon with the Word and its conditionality, knowability in the relation of revelation whose limits we come up against only in eschatology means knowledge in a mystery, or indirect knowledge. We walk in faith and *not* sight. The theology of the cross is the possibility with which we have to speak apart from a stammering word on the outer margin: *not* the theology of glory.[29]

IV. Judgment of Human Knowledge

We have developed the statement that God is knowable along three lines. (1) Human knowledge acquires by the Spirit a share in God's self-knowledge. (2) It is knowledge in the relation of revelation. (3) It is indirect knowledge. Analytically the statement leads necessarily, then, to a certain judgment about human knowledge in regard to God, or human knowledge as such. This judgment is as follows. Human knowledge as such has the ability to become knowledge of God under those three conditions. This ability remains even if the conditions are not met and no actual knowledge ensues. We are to be told and held to the fact that we can know God — "can" in the very general sense that God knows what he is doing when he turns to us with his Word, that the relation to him that God sets up under those three conditions is possible — obviously not

---

26. E. Peterson, "Zur Theologie der Mystik," *ZST* 2 (1924-25) 164.
27. *STh* I, q. 56, a.3.
28. Cf. Stephan, *Glaubenslehre*, p. 36; also pp. 25-26 above; and H. Kutter, *Das Unmittelbare. Eine Menschheitsfrage* (Berlin, 1902).
29. M. Luther, *Heidelberg Disputation* (1518), WA, 1, 353-374, esp. thesis 21, p. 362.

without God, or even partially so — but entirely through God, yet through God possible on our side too.

I am not thinking now of the obedience of faith, which would be actual knowledge of God in the relation of revelation, but simply of human knowledge and action. We are not unable but able to become obedient in faith, not in our own strength but in that of the Holy Spirit, since from the very outset we are not without God. If we compare the placing of human knowledge in the relation of revelation to the raising of the dead — as we must — then we might say that by its very nature the raising of the dead presupposes the presence of a corpse. Even if in some inscrutable way it had pleased God to address stones or oxen instead of us, or along with us, as he had addressed us with his Word, then we would still have to say that God knows what he is doing. He can obviously enter into relation with these strange partners. There is an ability or possibility on the side of these strange partners. The substratum, the corpse that is to be raised, is present. This ability or possibility to be the subject of real knowledge of God is an attribute of human knowledge, whether it ever comes to anything or not.

1. We must be clear that only because it does come to something can we say that there is such an ability. This is a strictly theological judgment. We do not achieve it from a consideration of human nature or an examination of the transcendental presuppositions of human knowledge. We are not advancing a religious a priori[30] or anything of that sort. All that we are saying is simply (a) that God speaks to us, (b) that God does nothing in vain, and (c) that therefore we are possible hearers of his Word. The first step here, divine revelation, the mighty presence of the Holy Spirit, is an act that does not take place everywhere, that is not self-evident, that is a matter of God's good pleasure. But the third step, which rests on the first two, expresses a conclusion which is always valid once it is drawn. If the reality of revelation is presupposed, then we must tell people, and hold them to it, that God has them in view, that he is seeking and finding them in his revelation, that it is possible for them to stand before God.

2. We must be clear also that we can say that there is such an ability, not merely on the *basis* of the knowledge of God in revelation, but also in *connection* with it. To be capable of this knowledge is to be capable of

---

30. E. Troeltsch introduced this expression; cf. esp. *Psychologie und Erkenntnistheorie in der Religionswissenschaft* (Tübingen, 1905), pp. 43ff.

participation in God's self-knowledge, of standing in the relation of revelation, of indirect knowledge of God. Philosophy must still decide about our ability or inability for metaphysical knowledge. Ours is a strictly theological judgment. If, especially at certain negative points, it seems to agree with philosophical epistemology, we accept this relative confirmation of its content, but we go on at once to say that the content itself, the positive point that it expresses, the Augustinian *ad te nos creasti*,[31] the possibility of our being related to the actuality of the revelation of the living God, cannot in any sense be identical with any epistemology. If it is presupposed that the content of possible knowledge to which we must refer here, God in his revelation, is not another God — and theology must very impatiently add that there is no other God — if this is presupposed, then we have to say that this knowledge is possible for us, and that this is true whether we attain to it or not. Once the reality of revelation is presupposed, we have to be taken seriously as those whose blind eyes and deaf ears are still eyes and ears that can be opened for revelation.

3. We must reach an understanding on what the possibility actually is. If we were right in viewing it as the possibility of the knowledge of revelation, and if we were right in subsection III to define it concretely as indirect knowledge, as the knowledge of God in a mystery, then we must add at once that for us the ability or possibility of knowledge of God consists of our being able to come up against the mystery, the object in which the divine subject conceals himself precisely in order to be known in this way. It consists of our being aware of the limit of our knowledge in regard to God, of our being able to ask after God, to ask after him necessarily. If the mystery is not just any mystery, if it is not the sphinx of human folly and wickedness, if it is really God's mystery, this is true only in the act of revelation, which is God's possibility and not ours. Nevertheless, in the act of revelation which is God's act we *can* run up against the mystery of God, the mystery of the object, the mystery of our own limit, the mystery of our own necessary asking. The fact that we can do this can be for us a pointer to God. Once our great presupposition is made, here is something that is possible for us. To deny this is to make a farce of revelation, of the fact that it has pleased God to turn to us with his Word.

You know the famous passage in Rom. 1:19-20 about the *gnōston*

---

31. *Confessions* I, 1: *fecisti nos ad te et inquietum est cor nostrum, donec requiescat in te.*

tou theou, about what may be known of God, about what is manifest to all people because God has made it manifest. What is this? Paradoxically enough, but very aptly, Paul calls it *aorata autou,* the ineffable things of God that one may perceive in his *poiēmata,* his eternal power and deity. People are *anapologētoi,* inexcusable, if they do not see what is shown to them and what they can see. Look also at Paul's Areopagus address in Acts 17:22ff. He found much fear of demons, *deisidaemonia,* in Athens, and finally and supremely an altar to the "unknown God." People are here on earth to seek God in the hope that they might in some way feel after him and find him, nor is he far from any one of us. For in him *zōmen kai kinoumetha kai esmen,* and we are his offspring. All the same, the "unknown God?" The answer — but now we have to move on to something other than human ability: God overlooks the present situation and proclaims to all people that they should repent in view of approaching judgment by the man through whom he has given them all the chance to believe by raising him from the dead. I proclaim this God to you, the unknown God who is now known.

4. Let us now move on from the possibility to the reality. Let us assume that the possibility becomes a reality, that the ability is put into practice, that we stand before the mystery, and that the mystery becomes a pointer to God. No matter how or where or when this might happen, we must then say that we stand in the relation of revelation, that God's Word is spoken to us and received by us, that the Holy Spirit is doing his work in us. No matter how or where or when, I say. The most obvious assertion will naturally be that the Christian church with its proclamation of the gospel and the law of Jesus Christ is the place where this possibility becomes a reality, and in practice we can accept this. But it will help to clarify the problem if we press the matter. Let us suppose that against all probability the possibility becomes a reality somewhere outside the Christian church, in pagan antiquity or the Orient. Let us suppose that this is a true work and not a deception of the devil. What can we conclude except that God's Word to us, one and the same Word, comes to people by other paths as well as that of Christian proclamation? There are good reasons to reject this conclusion. Yet we have to ask whether we are bold enough to state that the human possibility for knowledge of God can become a reality only by the path of Christian proclamation. If we are not bold enough to say this, if even hypothetically we think that the step from possibility to reality might be taken on paths that God alone knows, then we must be serious and say that if this is revelation, then it is the one revelation; if

this is real knowledge of God, then it is full knowledge of God — for neither real revelation nor real knowledge of God can be quantified — and we have to agree with Zwingli's view that Socrates, Cato, Seneca, and other enlightened pagans saw the day of Christ from afar like Abraham and the prophets, and in faith partake of full salvation.[32]

Let it be understood, *I* am not proclaiming this doctrine, nor indeed the opposite that there is no salvation outside the church.[33] I am simply saying that we come up against this problem when we try to move on from possibility to reality. What I will say is that this transition, no matter how narrowly or broadly we draw the circle, always means no less than entry into the kingdom of Christ. An either-or obtains here: either mere possibility, the corpse remaining a corpse, or full and true reality: Lazarus, come forth! [John 11:43]. Either the unknown God or the Father of Jesus Christ. To be ruled out are the various theories about only apparent death, or quantities or stages in the relation between God and us. These theories are possible only because we constantly think of revelation materially and objectively, as though there were several revelations that can be divided up or graded, instead of viewing revelation as the pure act of God himself which means for us and our knowing the crisis of possibility and reality, the crisis and not a mixture of the two. To be sure, there is a mixture in history; that is the place for it. But Christian doctrine has to present; not the truth of history but the truth of God's Word. Hence it has to proclaim not a mixture, not stages or transitions, but the crisis, the step from here to there, with no third thing between. *Ad te nos creasti,* we said at the outset. We now continue: *cor nostrum inquietum est.* If this is no mere phrase, it means that we are now standing before the mystery. And if God is gracious, then it is his mystery. *Donec requiescat in te.*[34] If this is true, then it means full and true Christian knowledge of God. The possibility has become a reality.

So much by way of basis. We are speaking here of things that the older theology used to deal with under the heading of the so-called natural knowledge of God. It regarded this locus as important up to the beginning of the 19th century. Roman Catholic theology still does so. Vatican I in 1870 expressly made it an article of faith that by the light of natural human reason God has made it possible for us to know him from the things that

---

32. H. Zwingli, *Exposition of the Faith,* LCC, XXIV, p. 275.
33. Cyprian *Ep.* 37, 21, in CSEL, 3/II, 795: *quia salus extra ecclesiam non est.*
34. See above, n. 31.

are made. A natural knowability of God is the beginning and end of all things.[35] This is not an absolutely necessary revelation, but it is a proof of the goodness of God with which he leads all people to their supernatural goal.[36] The Antimodernist Oath of 1910 added to the certain knowledge a possibility of proof, that is, a demonstrability of God,[37] with which we should compare the "not absolutely necessary."[38]

Our older Protestant predecessors took no offense at such statements. Quite the contrary. Nor need we do so, even if I say so with tongue in cheek. The decisive point is that on the Roman Catholic view the claiming of reason for the knowledge of God is an article of faith, an assertion of the church that thinks in terms of revelation. The older Orthodox were thinking along the same lines, as we see from a statement of Maresius (d. 1673): Revelation does not exclude but includes natural religion, as a major includes a minor.[39] Important, too, is the fact that a distinction is made in both Roman Catholic and the older Protestant dogmatics. The triune God, the God of real revelation, is not the object of this natural or rational religion, but the one God, the Creator of heaven and earth. Whether this distinction is tenable is another matter. The fact that the distinction was made shows an awareness of the problem.

So, too, does the fact that the older Protestant dogmatics (and Roman Catholic dogmatics does not disagree) very temperamentally declared that the value of natural knowledge for salvation is doubtful *(languida)*, imperfect, and even nil, since it mediates no knowledge of forgiveness.[40] It does not know *to ti* in relation to God, only *to hoti,* which is misused and in fact leads only to idolatry.[41] It finally results in terrible superstition.[42] Its only usefulness is that it makes us inexcusable according to Rom. 1:20, that it kindles a longing for revelation, and that by way of regress, as it were, it strengthens believers in faith.[43] In various serious and

---

35. DS, 3004, 3026.

36. DS, 3005; Barth crossed out the last sentence, perhaps because he realized that he had mistakenly related the council statement to natural revelation.

37. DS, 3538.

38. C. Mirbt, *Quellen zur Geschichte des Papsttums*, 4th ed. (Tübingen, 1924), pp. 457, 460, 516. The texts are the same as those in nn. 35-37 above.

39. Schweizer, p. 187.

40. Chemnitz, in Schmid-Pöhlmann, p. 83; Schmid ET p. 109.

41. Quenstedt, in Schmid, p. 72.

42. Maresius, in Schweizer, p. 77.

43. Heidegger, in Heppe, pp. 5-6; Heppe-Bizer, p. 6; ET p. 4.

severe temptations, we are all of us to some extent Epicureans and Stoics, admitted Chemnitz[44] with something of a sigh, and hence we need the corresponding arguments. All this is no evidence of the hopeless philosophical naivete with which our forefathers are often charged today. Even without Kant they knew something of the distance that we must keep here, of the dialectic that is at work here. The same might be said of the Aristotelianism of Roman Catholic dogmatics, naive though at first sight it may seem to be to us.

Nevertheless, one has to admit that among our predecessors a certain sharpness in posing the problem is regrettably absent. They far too readily put next to one another the book of nature and the book of scripture, as they called these two modes of revelation, adopting a medieval metaphor.[45] They far too readily contrasted natural revelation, religion, knowledge, or theology on the one side with supernatural revelation on the other,[46] as though in fact there were two forms of the knowledge of God, or two revelations, as though one could speak about revelation in general in a material or quantitative way. The unavoidable result was that what were thought to be the two forms of knowledge became involved in a conflict which in the 18th century, as we know, ended to the detriment of revealed knowledge. When a single knowledge was happily brought back, it was so broad that people thought they could see in revelation the crown of reason, or of nature, or, as one would now say, of history. We today have the task of distinguishing the two forms once again, or doing so better than was done or could be done then, that is, critically. We must engage in the dialectical reflection that is needed here. We must do so in such a way that, if possible, there will not be conflict again and then that dreadful peace.

Another mistake of the older doctrine was that it expressed itself very ambivalently on the question whether the natural knowledge of God is a habit, a true knowledge, or a mere faculty. On this point the Lutherans were stronger and more confident, usually taking the first view.[47] Among the Reformed, Riissen decided that the idea of God is merely a faculty of

---

44. Schmid, p. 75, quotes J. Gerhard, who in turn quotes M. Chemnitz; see Schmid-Pöhlmann, p. 85; Schmid ET p. 112.

45. Cf. Bonaventura *Breviloquium*, II, ch. 5, Opera omnia, V (1891), p. 222; the term "book of nature" occurs in Augustine, *De Genesis ad litteram* (see MPL, 32, 219ff.). Cf. Schmid-Pöhlmann, p. 80; Schmid ET p. 106.

46. Cf. Schmid-Pöhlmann, pp. 80ff.; Heppe-Bizer, pp. 1ff.; ET pp. 106ff.; 1ff.

47. Schmid-Pöhlmann, p. 82; Schmid ET p. 107.

knowledge.[48] Vatican I also spoke of *being able* to know or demonstrate.[49] If I had to swear the Antimodernist Oath,[50] I would have to stress this "being able" three times, though I could probably interpret it very freely. I showed at the outset that for us what is at issue is naturally only a faculty, a possible ability rather than a real one. There can be a real ability only in the relation of revelation.

The third point at which I part company with the older dogmaticians relates to their lack of clarity on what the ability that we assign to human knowledge really is. I will assemble the arguments that constitute the core of natural theology for two of the older Reformed, Ursinus and Polanus.[51] (1) Order in nature; (2) the rationality of the human spirit; (3) innate moral and theoretical ideas; (4) an innate sense of God; (5) the voice of conscience (which according to Polanus in particular is to be heard in thunderstorms, earthquakes, and the like); (6) the fact that evil is usually punished already on earth; (7) the presence of what is called political society; (8) biblical prophecies; (9) teleology in nature; (10) the law of causality; (11) the existence of outstanding people; (12) the fact of pagan and Christian worship; (13) general consent regarding God; (14) the immortality of the soul; (15) the occurrence of extraordinary and unexpected events. This varied list shows that they did not know what they really wanted. If they wanted to speak about the knowledge of God, even the natural knowledge, they should not have acted as if by this knowledge they meant any and every feeling, hope, fear, or wonder with no definable basis or object.

This seems to me to be also the most fatal defect in the so-called proofs of God which this natural theology evolved into in the Middle Ages. You can learn about them in any handbook of philosophy or dogmatic history. I will not discuss them in detail. In Thomas you will find them in his *Summa philosophica*,[52] not his *Summa theologica*.[53] You should notice just a few general points. We misunderstand the purpose of this remarkable theologoumenon if we think the older theologians were really establishing the existence of God in this way and therefore finding an intellectual basis for their belief in revelation. They realized that the exis-

---

48. Heppe-Bizer, pp. 4-5; ET pp. 1-2.

49. DS, 3004, 3026.

50. DS, 3538.

51. For Ursinus, see Heppe-Bizer, pp. 39-40; for Polanus, see Heppe-Bizer, p. 41; ET pp. 49-50.

52. *Summa contra gentiles* I, 13.

53. Barth added these words, but cf. *STh* I, q. 2, a. 3.

tence of God does not depend on any proof of it, and that it could thus be committed to human hands without ceasing to be the existence of *God.* The existence of God was not so tragically important for them as a presupposition as it has become for modern thought with its orientation to natural science. Standing with both feet in revelation, as a work of supererogation they went on to ask about God's existence, thinking proofs were worthwhile as a pointer to the problem and necessity of the *concept* of God.[54] One great Scholastic school, the Scotist, followed by the Reformed[55] (at least up to the 18th century), never took this route.[56]

As regards the anxious intellectualism with which the older dogmaticians supposedly clung to proofs so as to be able to believe, there is good evidence for this only from the 18th century. Superstitious faith in the proofs (Rade)[57] arose only when there was no longer any idea what revelation is. Nor do I think it any reproach against the proofs that on other presuppositions of thought they have obviously been refuted by Kant.[58] Their true concern, namely, that God be a necessary element in human thought, is still valid today even though we may no longer want to talk about a proof of existence. This concern has been underlined rather than overthrown by Kant's critique of reason with its regulative rational ideas that seriously threaten and bracket the consciously immanent operations of the understanding. If with many modern thinkers we say and recognize that the religious phenomenon ineluctably poses certain limiting problems for thought as such, I would assume that the real concern of the proofs of God has as such been upheld in the way that is possible after Kant. Again, the reproach that Seeberg brings against the proofs of God does not seem to me to be justified, namely, that they involve a fraudulent claim that a knowledge of God that is achieved by the path of religious knowledge is a necessary product of activity on the path of logical and theoretical knowledge.[59] Naturally, the sequence is as follows: Revelation

---

54. Marginal note: "Thomas in I, 2, 2 says that it is not here a matter of the articles of faith but of preambles to them. In 2, 1 he says that in the statement 'God is' the predicate is identical with the subject. But because we do not know God's essence we must demonstrate his existence." (See *STh* I, q. 2, a. 2 ad 1; I, q. 2, a. 1 i.c.)

55. The MS has *ihnen* for *ihr.*

56. Cf. K. R. Hagenbach, *Lehrbuch der Dogmengeschichte,* 6th ed. (Leipzig, 1888), p. 327; Heppe-Bizer, p. 41.

57. M. Rade, *Glaubenslehre,* I, p. 91.

58. I. Kant, *Critique of Pure Reason* (London, 1884), pp. 359ff.

59. R. Seeberg, *Christliche Dogmatik,* I, 305-7.

comes first, and provability, the proofs, and the insight and certainty that the proofs give, come second. "I believe in order to understand."[60] But when this is done so openly there can be no question of fraud. The medieval and older Protestant dogmaticians never disguised in principle the fact that we cannot bring people to faith by proving the existence of God but that the proofs at best can lead only to the place where faith comes on a very different presupposition, namely, that of grace.

If I am suspicious of the proofs, and would not for the time being help to bring them back into dogmatics, this is because in the whole process, as in natural theology generally, it is remarkably unclear how far the aim is really to give a proof, a necessary, cogent, and convincing pointer to God. What is meant by "God," by him who is to be proved? Is God the entity that can satisfactorily set aside some yawning gap or problem in human thought, the answer to some human question that is unfortunately open, the cornerstone in the arch of a total view of things that is set up to the best of human knowledge and in all good conscience? Is "God" the one who brings rest and peace and harmony? Is the nerve of the proof the fact that we want this harmony, this total view, this arch, and only the final word "God" is lacking, so that this last word is a necessity of thought, and we are therefore justified in saying it? The same applies to Schleiermacher's proof of God from the necessity of the feeling of absolute dependence as a universal element in life,[61] or to Ritschl's proof from the unavoidable data of the life of the spirit and especially the common nature of moral ends, which either cannot be explained at all or can be explained only by the scientific hypothesis of the idea of God.[62]

Over against all this I believe that if theology wants to engage in proofs, then it must see to it that the proof or proofs actually lead to the place where, presupposing the reality of revelation, the presence of the Holy Spirit, there can be talk of him whom it calls and has to call God. The proofs must lead human knowledge to the actuality of revelation, or at least seek to do so. But this place cannot be a refuge where all outstanding questions and riddles are solved, nor can the proof mean that their solution is not possible without the hypothesis of the idea of God.

The possibility or ability of human knowledge of God, of natural

---

60. Anselm, *Proslogion* 1: *Neque enim quaero intelligere ut credam, sed credo ut intelligam.*

61. *CF,* § 33.

62. A. Ritschl, *Die christliche lehre von der Rechtfertigung und Versöhnung,* III, 2nd ed. (Bonn, 1883), p. 209.

knowledge of God, consists, as we have seen, of the faculty of coming up against the mystery, of being limited by unanswered questions, of learning the finitude of such knowledge. Thus proof of the existence of God, a persuasion that we are referred to him with strict necessity and cannot escape him, must not mean the opening up of a refuge but must mean instead that in the possibility of knowledge we are shown that pitiless limitation, that immovable and unanswerable question. It must mean the plain demonstration, not of the satisfactory completion of that total view of things, but of its unsatisfactory presupposition. We are led to the reality of God, not as we say that we too may believe in God to the full appeasing of our disquiet, but as we are truly and definitively disquieted in all that concerning which our disquiet has been appeased. To know God, when we look at the human possibility of the process, does not mean finally reaching port and dropping anchor now that we have recognized that in the economy of the human consciousness or the universe, the religious element or the good God is an indispensable and welcome factor. Even as theologians, how can we think that we can make such a fool of God?

Over against the human possibility in question there still stands the mystery of revelation, the Yes concealed in the No, the Son of God on the cross, dying according to Mark [15:35] with the words: "My God, my God, why hast thou forsaken me?" The task of a proof of God is to find the analogy to this — only the analogy, of course — on the human side. Paul's real proof of God, to which the much-cited passages in Rom. 1 and 2 and Acts 17 are only preludes, is in Rom. 7, which concludes (v. 24): "Wretched man that I am! Who will deliver me from this body of death?" When we take this path — and we shall take it in the second part of our dogmatics, the anthropology — we reach the place which sets in direct juxtaposition the cry: "Thanks be to God through Jesus Christ our Lord!" [7:25].

The fifteen arguments that we considered (a clever Jesuit in the 17th century is supposed to have increased their number to 6,561!),[63] and the four or five classical arguments,[64] do not lead us to this place where God says: "Let light shine out of darkness" [2 Cor. 4:6], but to all kinds of other places. For this reason they leave us cold, having so little actuality

---

63. M. Rade, *Glaubenslehre*, I, p. 94: "The Jesuit Athanasius Kircher (d. 1680) counted 6,561 proofs of God."

64. The ontological, moral, cosmological, and teleological arguments, and the argument from consensus (Hase, pp. 132-34).

and cogency, resembling so many noughts before which there is no one, even though their concern is justifiable and important enough. More accurately, they are of value only to the extent that they unwittingly give evidence of the human analogy to the mystery of revelation. You will perhaps understand me if I say that Kant's critique of pure reason with its refutation of all the arguments for God, with the truly apocalyptic light that it sheds on human knowledge by proclaiming its autonomy, is incomparably better as a proof of God than the so-called moral argument[65] which Fichte[66] and others popularized, and which can only dim again the clarity that is attained in Kant's main work.

What Kant said about astronomy might be said of his own basic insight. The observations and calculations of astronomers have taught us many things that earn our admiration, but the most important thing is that they have discovered the depth of ignorance which human reason could never have imagined to be so great without such findings, and reflection upon which must surely bring about a great change in determining the final purpose of the use of reason.[67] And do not regard it merely as a literary flourish if I say that Dostoyevski, by confronting the unteachable atheist Ivan Karamazov with the pure fool Aliosha, who has no arguments against his revolt,[68] has perhaps done more for a real proof of God than Anselm and Thomas, Schleiermacher and Ritschl. If in the book of Job it is the questioning Job who is in the right and not his friends [Job 42:7], this probably means that if there is any pointer to God or proof of God for us at all, it will be found where we come up against the mystery of God.

---

65. I. Kant, *Kritik der Urteilskraft*, §§ 87-89.
66. J. G. Fichte, *Versuch einer Kritik aller Offenbarung* (1792), § 2.
67. I. Kant, *Critique of Pure Reason* (London, 1884), p. 354 n.
68. F. M. Dostoyevski, *The Brothers Karamazov* (New York, 1970), Book 5, chs. 3-5, pp. 273-319; cf. E. Thurneysen, *Dostojewski* (Munich, 1921), pp. 45-61; ET *Dostoevsky* (Richmond, 1964), pp. 51-68.

§ 16

The Nature of God

We know God's nature in his own Word to us. Hence our terms can denote and describe and expound him, but not comprehend him. He speaks to us as the Lord, but as the Lord who has none above or alongside him, and none of his own kind beneath him. In all that we say about him, then, we must regard his personality and aseity as the necessary determinations of his nature. The one word in which both are expressed neither will nor should pass over our lips.

I. Concept and Conceivability

Let us begin with a nexus of problems that we sketched in the thesis of the last section but must now discuss more fully. They concern the terms "concept," "conceiving," "conceivability," and "inconceivability." The medieval and older Protestant dogmaticians distinguished between knowing God and conceiving of him or comprehending him. With various reservations they accepted God's knowability. For them knowing God was humanity's most central matter. We recall the introduction to the Geneva Catechism of 1545: The chief end of human life is that we should know God, by whom we were created.[1] Similarly, the Lutheran J. Gerhard says that in creation and by his Word God came forth from the secret seat of his majesty in order that humans may truly know him and preserve the true doctrine of God pure from all the leaven of errors.[2] We cannot dismiss

---

1. J. Calvin, *Tracts and Treatises,* II, p. 37.
2. Schmid, p. 69; Schmid-Pöhlmann, p. 81; Schmid ET p. 104.

this with an anti-intellectualistic shrug of the shoulders. The knowledge of God, expressed in the ideal concept of pure doctrine, is for them, and for us too according to § 11 of the Prolegomena, the present-day actuality of the revelation to which scripture bears witness. Hence the knowledge of God from his Word can be called "perfect."[3] Along the same lines I have permitted myself in the preceding section to describe the knowledge of God that comes in the relation of revelation as adequate.

But one cannot say the same of God's conceivability or comprehensibility (which the older theologians called *katalēpsis,* as distinct from *gnōsis*). J. Gerhard said that we know God but we do not comprehend him.[4] I referred earlier to the view of Thomas that even to the blessed in heaven, who know God essentially, he is still not comprehensible.[5] Often comprehension is equated with perfect knowledge.[6] But the distinction is not quantitative. It is a distinction of principle. To comprehend is to define.[7] It is to reach the end of knowledge. It is to *have* known. We can indeed know God as act, as movement (for this is being known by him). But we cannot *have* known God in the perfect tense, as a state or completed act (cf. 1 Cor. 8:2-3). It is of the nature of the created spirit that such finality is basically denied to it. It was created to know God. And it will remain created spirit even in its consummation, even in the kingdom of glory, even in the vision of God face-to-face. God refuses to be defined.[8]

Nevertheless, human knowledge, even the act of knowing God, undoubtedly involves a series of acts of conceiving or comprehending, or of trying to do so. Knowledge without concepts would be the intuitive vision of the blessed. But our knowledge involves concepts. We determine the nature of objects by trying to establish as clearly and conclusively as possible their order and category and their distinction from others that come in the same group. It is easy to say that God is not an object, that he does not come under any order that includes other objects, and that he cannot, then, be distinguished from them. Hence God is inconceivable. Hence we must not fashion any concepts of his nature. If we accept and acknowledge this prohibition, we espouse mystical thinking. The basic

---

3. Schmid, p. 76; Schmid-Pöhlmann, p. 86; Schmid ET p. 113.
4. Schmid, p. 76.
5. See above, § 15, p. 338 n. 25.
6. See Schmid-Pöhlmann, p. 86; Schmid ET p. 113.
7. Schmid-Pöhlmann, pp. 86-87; Schmid ET p. 113.
8. Ursinus, in Heppe, p. 39 n.; ET p. 52 (here the statement is attributed to Polanus).

methodological principle of mystical thinking is that it draws from the incomprehensibility of God the practical conclusion that there must be no definition of God's nature. How far this thinking tries to range itself positively with the blessed in heaven and their essential vision is another matter. The desire to move in this direction, but also the obstacles that are felt in the process, may be seen very clearly in Eckhart, Suso, and Tauler. The negative point is plain enough. It is a protest against any concept of God as such. Mysticism and mystical thinking may well be one possibility even in the Christian church. Protestantism may have to stress the opposite side, but it was perhaps an exaggeration that is out of place even in Protestantism when Ritschl could find in this phenomenon only a sick phenomenon.[9] Since for me the "perhaps" is a probability, I could wish that Gogarten and Brunner would also sometimes express themselves with more restraint in this regard.[10]

But no matter what may be our fundamental evaluation of mysticism, we undoubtedly need to know what we are doing if we venture to think mystically. The protest against the definition of God's nature is a fateful one which we need to ponder in good time. Excluding the concept and trying to think only[11] purely and directly means excluding revelation, as Martensen has rightly pointed out.[12] As we laid down in § 15, the fact that God speaks, that he reveals himself, means that he reveals himself indirectly, that is, in the relation of revelation, in time and space as we ought perhaps to say more plainly to the mystic, and therefore in the sphere of concepts and objects. Knowledge of God in the relation of revelation is akin to the secular knowledge of "other" objects. It is thus consciously and fundamentally conceptual knowledge. It thus rejects the mystical conclusion even though it does not contest the correctness of its premises (namely, that God is not an object, that he belongs to no genus, that he cannot be distinguished from others of the same kind), even though it, too, says that God defies definition or that God is incomprehensible. It does not draw this conclusion because it has pleased God himself not to do so by becoming man and awakening the obedience of faith. It thus defines God and dares to say things about his nature. It also knows, of course, what it is doing, and hence it will not be slow to do justice at the

---

9. Cf. A. Ritschl, *Geschichte des Pietismus*, I (Bonn, 1880), p. 28.
10. Cf. F. Gogarten, *Von Glauben und Offenbarung* (Jena, 1923), p. 79.
11. The MS had here *nur noch und nur noch*, perhaps dittography.
12. H. Martensen, *Die christliche Dogmatik* (Berlin, 1856), p. 81.

right place to the truth that God defies definition. But it will do this at the right place, not in such a way that God's incomprehensibility closes the door to the house of human conceptuality, but by stating that with his revelation God has already entered this house and that we cannot ignore or reverse the fact, but have to deal with it and orient ourselves to it, come what may.

The way of mystical thinking is illuminating with its consistency and radicalism and apparent relevance. But does it not perhaps fail to illuminate specifically because, even though it does not deny — no prudent mystic has really done this — the birth of Christ and faith, that is, the relation of revelation, nevertheless it does seek to evade these, to replace an indirect relation by a direct one, and hence to escape perhaps the foolishness and offense of the cross? [cf. 1 Cor. 1:23]. As I have said, I do not want to say anything bad about mysticism. But it must be said that in no case can the way of dogmatics be this way, the way of evasion. Dogmatics is the science of preaching. Preaching bases itself on the Bible, and the Bible on revelation. Always, then, the knowledge of God in dogmatics is knowledge in the relation of revelation. It is thus indirect knowledge, and consequently conceptual knowledge. Hence, despite or because of all its knowledge of God's incomprehensibility, it cannot avoid saying things about the nature of God.

I should perhaps add a word on the reason why I used a restrained "perhaps" about mysticism, from which our path diverges at this point. I am now more impressed than I used to be by the fact that 1 Cor. 12:4ff. and Rom. 12:6ff. speak of the great variety of gifts and services and powers which have been provided in the Christian church. If we may recognize what we call preaching in *prophēteia* and *didaskalia,* we have to say that alongside this charism — and we have to call it such — there are others which in their own way are also *en Christō.* If only we knew more clearly what is meant by all the possibilities listed! But if appearances do not deceive, it is fairly certain that the list includes some things that we Protestants do not like at all. Paul approved of all of them and regarded them as gifts of the Holy Spirit (be it noted). Now among them there might well be what we call mysticism. If so, we cannot refuse to do justice to mystical gnosis in its own place, not under the banner of a skeptical relativism, but for the sake of Christ's body, under the sign: *to auto pneuma, ho autos kyrios, ho autos theos* (1 Cor. 12:4ff.). This possibility does not affect in any way the result of our deliberations. I simply mention it in order to advise caution and prudence. The ground on which we stand, though it may perhaps be in the same Christian church, is not that of mysticism. The direct, nonconceptual, noncompromising thinking of mysticism would be alien, inappropriate, and unobjective if applied here.

I now return to our older Protestant fathers with whose doctrine of knowing and conceiving we started. We agree with the premises of the mystical thesis in stating that what God is absolutely, what is his nature and substance, we know that no one can state, imagine, or declare by an essential definition, either by any dialectic reasoning or by keenness of human intellect.[13] For where will you find a genus more lofty or extensive than God himself? Where will you look for a proper or genuine differentiation?[14] Or, from a human standpoint, what is finite cannot comprehend what is infinite.[15] This is the typical Reformed statement of the problem. We will try to supplement this logical basis with one that is more material, standing as it does in a positive connection with what we have to say about the nature of God. But the basic insight that we are expressing, and that Thomas stated already with sober seriousness, must not be lost sight of for a moment, and we shall come back to it at the end of the section, as you will see from the thesis. It would be a fatal mistake to end a section on the nature of God with anything but the humble recognition that God defies definition. But to be able to come back to God's incomprehensibility, to give living and actual meaning to what seems to be so negative a formula, it must itself be something definite, and we cannot just stop at it. Our fathers did not do so. Several of the Reformed rightly consoled themselves with a saying of St. Bernard: God alone can never be sought in vain, even when he cannot be found.[16] Or they stated the negative in such a way that something positive could stand alongside it: No one can explain what God is, save God in his Word.[17] Or even more positively: We know as much as he himself reveals of himself to us of his infinite mercy.[18] Or they said that what we can comprehend of God, and ought to do so to his glory, is very simply his name as the name of the Lord.[19] Hence revelation, or the Word, or the name of God balances the scales against the divine incomprehensibility.

The freedom of God with which, without ceasing to be who he is, he

---

13. Selnekker, in Schmid, p. 75; Schmid-Pöhlmann, p. 86; Schmid ET p. 113.
14. Hyperius, in Heppe, p. 39; Heppe-Bizer, p. 42; ET p. 52.
15. Musculus, in Heppe, p. 39; Heppe-Bizer, p. 42; ET p. 52.
16. Alsted, in Heppe, p. 39; Danäus, in Heppe, p. 40; Heppe-Bizer, p. 42; ET p. 52.
17. Bullinger, in Heppe, p. 42; Heppe-Bizer, p. 45; ET p. 56.
18. Ursinus, in Heppe, p. 41; Heppe-Bizer, p. 44; ET p. 55.
19. Cocceius, in Heppe, p. 41; Heppe-Bizer, p. 45; ET p. 54.

can leave his mere incomprehensibility for our comprehensibility and even our conceptuality makes room — for what? For a definition *ousiōdēs?* No. God remains who he is even in his revelation. We rather say: For a definition *onomatōdēs,*[20] a subjective notion of God,[21] a sort of description of God as he is revealed to us.[22] One might sum up the position of these older theologians in the statement of M. Chemnitz: There is, therefore, a name of God occult and hidden, which is not to be searched out. There is, however, also a name of God made known that he wishes to be recognized, spoken about, praised, and worshiped.[23] In terms of this insight, and with the enclosed reservation, they thus ventured to say that we do not seek after God in vain even if we do not find him, and with humble head, knowing the relativity and dangerous nature of what we are doing but still with a certain defiance, we venture to give a definition of the nature of God. At this decisive point we may justly call this position neither intellectualistic, uncritical, nor disrespectful. We cannot do better than make it our own.

II. God's Incomprehensibility

In the thesis I formulated the relation between God's knowability and his conceivability more sharply than the older theologians. I did not say that God is inconceivable and yet that in his Word he gives himself to be known. I put it the other way round and said that in his Word God gives himself to be known and for that reason we cannot conceive of him, all our concepts being fundamentally no more than attempts to do so, denoting, describing, and expounding. I did not mean by this to change the intentions of the school but to pursue them along the same lines and with inner necessity. We must not get the wrong impression that the statement that God is incomprehensible is merely the broken confession of the human spirit as it becomes aware of the abyss of its own ignorance and despairs of itself, that it is merely the sum of Kant's critique of reason. Naturally it is this too. We have looked at it from this standpoint in § 15.IV. We have done so theologically, viewing it as the epitome of the possibility that we are given to know God, and finally even as the one

---

20. J. Gerhard, in Schmid, p. 76; Schmid-Pöhlmann, p. 87; Schmid ET p. 114.
21. Hutterus, in Hase, p. 129.
22. Polanus, in Heppe, p. 39; Heppe-Bizer, p. 43; ET p. 53.
23. Schmid, p. 76; Schmid-Pöhlmann, p. 86; Schmid ET p. 114.

objectively possible proof of God. But whether the proof proves, that is, whether it demonstrates not merely the mystery, question, or limit, but God in all these things, that stands with God, we had then to say. It does so only when and insofar as the revelation of God, the Word of God, meets this human knowledge of the mystery. A critique of reason is not in itself an analogue of the cross of Christ. The abysses of our ignorance are not in themselves the depths of God. The self-despair of the human spirit is not in itself the presence of the Holy Spirit.

Hence we must go on to say that the statement that God is incomprehensible is not in itself a statement that is really made by God or that rests on a true knowledge of God. In itself it may merely say that we know nothing about God, that we can only dream in metaphysical matters.[24] It may be simply an expression of resignation, skepticism, or relativism. It can be possible and meaningful even on the lips of a proud and shameless human self-assurance and complacency. "The view above is blocked. O fool, to turn your eyes there, blinking" — this is what God's refusal to be defined means for a Faust.[25] The thesis that God is incomprehensible, the confession of instructed ignorance,[26] can at any rate stand very ambivalently between human self-rejection and human self-exaltation, as was undoubtedly the case in the 18th century. (Either way, then, it can be very plainly meaningless in a Christian sense.) Indeed, things can be even worse when the weight that the older dogmaticians put on the other side of the scales, the Word, revelation, is viewed only perhaps as human self-illumination, for then we will not despair or drown when the ship of metaphysical comprehensibility sinks beneath us, but with an appeal perhaps to authority, or with an attempt at justification through some theory of postulates or experience, we will grasp after the plank of supernatural and irrational certainty which we might call the Word of God or revelation, and which seems for a while to serve as a counterpoise to the skepticism to which it owes its rise, namely, so long as this service is needed and desired, so long as skepticism on the other side does not become self-evident, so long as the swing from despair to arrogance does not take place, so long as the Faustian with his "God *in us*" is not yet born.[27] Who can

---

24. Cf. H. Cohen, *System der Philosophie,* II (Berlin, 1904), p. 418.

25. J. W. von Goethe, *Faust* II, vv. 11442ff. (Act 5).

26. The phrase *docta ignorantia* goes back to Augustine and was basic to the epistemology of Nicholas of Cusa: *De docta ignorantia,* 1440.

27. Cf. K. Bornhausen, "Est Deus in nobis?" *CW* 37 (1923) 734-43; and Ovid, *Fasti* 6, 3-6.

protect supposed revelation against the suspicion that it is simply a *fata morgana,* a mirage produced by the human embarrassment that makes a virtue of necessity? The older school with its naive dialectic that God is inconceivable but that he has revealed himself and may be known in his revelation could not really ward off the suspicion against either side of the antithesis. It was equivocal and compromising that they gave the divine incomprehensibility only a logical, human basis. As though it were not primarily *God's* incomprehensibility! It was undoubtedly meant to be this, yet apparently both the incomprehensibility and the fact that it is a matter of God in revelation could be dropped or viewed as supplementary definitions of our own nature. Our fathers certainly meant all this, and thought it through in detail, very objectively, critically, and respectfully. Yet they left far too much room for the interpretation of Feuerbach in which the shattering of modern Christian thought has reached and passed its high point.

We must learn today from the two centuries that lie behind us, from the disaster that they brought to Christian dogmatics. We must take sharper measures to clarify what the Christian church is wanting to say here. These measures are as follows. (a) We must reverse the dialectical relation of the two members. (b) We must strike out the "certainly" and bring in a "therefore." Revelation, therefore incomprehensibility, and therefore inadequate concepts. In other words, it is because and to the extent that we know God that we know his incomprehensibility.

The best clarification of these statements, since we are not mystics, will be to make the necessary dogmatic venture of a conceptual definition of God's nature on the basis of the knowledge of God in the relation of revelation. As I have already made clear, this is only an attempt. The concepts we achieve will be inadequate, for precisely in the relation of revelation God is known as the incomprehensible God.

Let us begin with some principial observations on that reversal and "therefore." The question of a concept of God's nature in its indissoluble connection with God's inconceivability is not merely a question for the theological teacher or student. Christian preaching works constantly with a concept of God's nature — how else could it speak about God? No matter whether it tries to develop it completely or incompletely; no matter whether it merely touches on it occasionally; no matter whether, without further exploration, it simply presupposes it in both speaker and hearers as the invisible but well-known focus, it names and acknowledges and affirms and proclaims God expressly or less directly as this or that, as an object that one can characterize and distinguish from other objects, not merely being able to do so but unfortunately having to do so as well. Nevertheless, God's incomprehensibility stands explicitly or implicitly behind Christian preaching as a decisive factor. As concerns the proclaimed or presupposed nature of God, this preaching must keep silence as well as speak; it must conceal as well as define; it must negate as well as affirm; it must draw back as well as venture forward. We shall speak later about the question of a correct concept. Already as regards the relation between conceivability and inconceivability Christian preachers need certain principial insights.

(a) We look first at conceivability. As theologians we must again become accustomed to the thought that we are not merely permitted but commanded to talk about God, and to do so definitely. For theologians who know what they are about, the concept of God is not something shameful or contemptible or even laughable. The idea that it is better to keep silence about God's nature than to speak about it, that it is better to represent it in music or song or poetry, leads finally to mystical knowledge and to its juggling away of the relation of revelation. God is indeed incomprehensible — God! But it is arrogance and disobedience to anticipate this incomprehensibility, to make it our own. Revelation is God's entry into the world of conceptuality. It caused the prophets and apostles to speak about God. This is always a venture. But in all soberness we have to say that the venture has to be made. For theologians to believe means having to make this venture. No, it means obeying. There is a hesitant, asthmatic, affected way of talking abut God, a mere whispering, which at best would rather not pronounce his name, yet which does not rest on respect for his mystery but on rebellion against revelation. In faith we should speak about God and his nature very definitely, thinking and saying and willing and doing this or that. Because of our lack of faith all this is *only* figurative or conceptual. In faith we should also denote and describe the mystery of God's nature, the negations that belong indispensably to the concept. Because of our lack of faith these, too, are *only* abstractions and the like.

For theologians faith means seeing in the "only" that would forbid us concepts a temptation of the devil, who wants to suppress God's Word. Hence they should not evade the appropriate defining, describing, and thinking. Let it be understood, they must do these things in faith in revelation, or, shall we say here, in obedience to revelation, with the courage *(Mut)* of the humility *(Demut)* which ventures to do what we

359

cannot do, what we can only fail as we try to do, attempting to define and describe and think out what only God himself can say, to construct and propound a concept of God. Only thus can justice be done, too, to God's inconceivability, which none of those who are in earnest will forget. By silence, by indefinite, weak, and generalized talk about God, by religious poetry, we neither come ourselves to the place where God himself gives us his Word, nor do we lead others there. We do this by obedient wrestling with the task that is assigned to us. This task has to be an impossible one for us because its point is not that our work should succeed. Its point is that by our failure, in the inadequacy of our speech that this brings to light, in the splintering of human thought that takes place where there is obedient wrestling for a true concept of God — God himself should speak his own Word. To this extent God's inconceivability is the meaning and basis of our conceptuality.

(b) As regards God's inconceivability, it is a matter of the inconceivability of *God*, of God in his *revelation*. The inconceivable God has come into the world of human conceptuality. What can all concepts of God be but elucidations of his inconceivability? But *his* inconceivability, we must stress again. Christian preaching, then, does not have to engage in the business of human skepticism and relativism, or of philosophical criticism. It has never to begin with us humans apart from revelation, with our nonconceiving, our weaknesses, doubts, uncertainties, limits, and mysteries, so that then, as often happens, it can mount up to God and therefore to the positive side with a weak and sapless "And yet!" Certainly we must be addressed in terms of our nonconceiving, but always in the light of revelation, of God; always from the standpoint of the Word which is inconceivably directed to nonconceiving humanity. Only as we believe for people and do not doubt with them can we set them before God's inconceivability. Only as we speak God's *Yes* to them can we make them hear the divine No that they must also hear.

The devil's temptation on this side is that we should explain our own and the general human hardness instead of God's gracious mystery. We must be careful that we do not let the negations that are part of the concept of God because of his inconceivability lead us to speak more of our impenitence than our faith. Revelation and revelation alone can produce truly fruitful and illuminating negations and veilings in Christian speech. The true force and significance of the inconceivability of God in Christian preaching will be achieved not directly but indirectly, in the quiet knowledge that accompanies all concepts, both negative and positive too; in the knowledge that God himself will speak; in restraint and modesty for all the definiteness that is given; in sober refusal to attempt any direct impartation, persuasion, influencing, or surprising; in an awareness that all Christian speech has the character of witness. It is thus again that we derive the strength and courage to speak as we are bidden. Without the restraint we cannot have the courage. To this degree it is precisely God's inconceivability that is the strength in the weakness of our conceptuality. A basic methodological principle is that we should always give material priority to revelation and make it the starting point of our thinking. From it derives the necessity of our conceiving as well as its inadequacy. If theology would again set itself on this basis it would no longer present a poor Feuerbach-type appearance.

III. Can We Define God's Nature?

At the very first step the attempt to define God's nature comes up concretely against the difficulty that has occupied us thus far in the form of God's general incomprehensibility. Our first step, then, must be to consider whether and how far a definable nature of God can be even thinkable for us.

Let us recall that God reveals himself as subject. Very generally, then, we have first to seek his nature in his divine subjectivity. But precisely as subject, precisely in revelation, God is concealed from us. Precisely in his revelation our knowledge of God is indirect. The I-Thou relation in which we are set to him there, *en pneumati,* is indirect. Insofar as God is revealed and knowable in this relation, he meets us objectively. What is directly knowable about him, the true immediacy in which he meets us, is his mystery. We must always stay with this, with what is directly knowable, in defining the nature of God. According to the insights we have gained thus far, there can be no leaping over this wall or evading it.

But now another distinction must come into force that we made in the previous section. We constantly emphasized there that it is *his* mystery, *God's* mystery, the *objective* form in which it has pleased him to meet us directly, and in this directness truly, to be revealed and knowable on an I and Thou level in his hidden nature, that is, to be knowable indirectly. The mystery is *his* mystery, and therefore and to that extent a blessed and revealing mystery, only in the act of his revelation. Hence the mystery to which we must keep if we are to define God's nature has to be this mystery, the mystery that meets us in the act of divine revelation. Otherwise we are not defining *God's* nature.

We must say even more: Otherwise we could not even think of any definable nature of God. There is a possibility — and we must speak about this first — of looking away from the act of revelation, of regarding revelation as a self-enclosed fact, of no more putting the question whether the mystery is really *God's* mystery. In this view God *has* revealed himself, and now the mystery before which we stand is our limit, the unavoidable and unanswerable question to which our knowledge leads. In itself and per se it is *God's* mystery. The lightning which has torn the darkness at a specific point has become a uniform sea of light which the eye of faith sees or at least senses and perceives equally behind the whole darkness before which we first stand. In place of an event between God and us, which has to be an event each morning with fresh actuality if it is to be truly an event between God and us, we have a finished event, a relation in which the hidden God and we who worship the God that dwells in darkness [cf. 1 Kgs. 8:12] confront one another in a rest that is the same in principle. In principle there is no longer a knowing and a being known. This is replaced by God's secret universal being on the one side and our own secret universal knowledge of him on the other.

This possibility is naturally none other than the mystical knowledge of God that we mentioned in another connection. According to it, what becomes of the defining of God's nature? We already know the answer: It comes to nothing. Incomprehensibility is the mystic's first word, and no second word follows in virtue of which the last word becomes the first. This word is there, and beside it there is no other. There is no definable nature of God unless we are to call God's incomprehensibility his nature. But let us look in greater detail at the way in which the mystic reaches this point. It will help us to understand the other and more objective way that we ourselves must take. Mystics, too, seek God's nature in the divine subjectivity. They, too, know (only too well) that our knowledge of God can be only indirect knowledge. They, too, stand before God's mystery. But the fact that the mystery is *God's* mystery is not for them a special question. A general and definitive answer has been given to it. If they, too, speak about revelation, they mean therewith the world of the objective in its totality, the limit of human knowledge to its full extent. Every point on this boundary is the place where we stand before God. All darkness has the sea of light behind it. Any limitation of this totality is only a contingent weakness. In terms of the principial approach it is a mistake in thought. In particular, a definition of God's nature would be such a mistake according to this approach. What is the divine nature? Obviously, a defining of the being of that divine subjectivity in contrast to all that it is not, in contrast also, however, to its own predicates, to the whole way in which it is. But on the presupposition of a consistent execution of the mystical view, how can there ever be any such definition? What can we say about that being except that, enthroned in general mystery, it is nonbeing as opposed to all being on this side the boundary of mystery, or, because even this dualism might be a weakness or limitation, as all profounder mystics have taught, from a more considered dialectical stand-point it is the being, the *arrēton*, that lies beyond the antagonism of being and nonbeing. This means, however, that defining God's nature consists of recognizing that he cannot be defined, that his nature is his incomprehensibility. For obviously we cannot distinguish between the way he is and the being of his subjectivity, or between his nature and his attributes.[28] Obviously, we can list the attributes of God seriously, as distinctions in his nature, only if[29] the knowledge of God in which we engage in such definition is an act in which there are distinctions, two things, a before and an after, the flash of the lightning and its disappearance. On this presupposition we can logically say something about the subject in whom we see these predicates, about the nature of God. But we cannot do so on the presupposition that the epistemological relation to this subject is static or habitual, that there is nothing new in God once we have come to know him. In that case to say that God is unconditioned[30] is to say the one thing and all the other things that can be said about him. All the other things are per se the one thing, the one thing is that which cannot be defined, and that which cannot be defined is the nature of God.

As we are better instructed, mystical theology is again the theology with which we must part company. But I might just as well say speculative theology, that is, all the theology that views revelation as a general relation and not a specific event. In this connection D. F. Strauss subjected the doctrine of God's nature and attributes to a searching criticism that could not be fully answered on the mystical-speculative presupposition.[31] A truly

---

28. K. R. Hagenbach, *Dogmengeschichte,* pp. 332-33, quoting Suso.

29. The German reads "on the presupposition that," substituting *dass* for Barth's *wenn.*

30. On this term see above, § 3.I.

31. D. F. Strauss, *Die christliche Glaubenslehre,* I (Tübingen/Stuttgart, 1840), pp. 363-614.

believing mysticism will hardly feel troubled by the discovery of a Strauss that all talk about God is futile, or by the irrefutability of this discovery. Did it not make the same discovery long before the critic? Does it not itself speak about God only to say that to have the known God in a mystery is better than speaking about him? Can it not just as well keep silence before God as speak about him?

Things are different for dogmatics. This is the science of Christian preaching, which cannot just as well remain dumb but has to proclaim God. "Woe to me if I do not preach the gospel!" (1 Cor. 9:16). For this reason there must be no failure to attempt to define God's nature, no fall into the abyss of divine incomprehensibility. The possibility of becoming believing mystics would be poor consolation for such a fall, for it would then be all up with the charism with which we have to do here, with *didaskalia.* If we want to avoid the plunge, then we cannot accept its presupposition, the mystical approach, which like all genuine approaches carries with it consequences that will come just as ineluctably as avalanches in spring.[32]

But let us not think it is as easy as all that not to take that approach. It is a natural one. It runs through modern Protestant thinking like a cleft. One finds strong traces of it also in the Reformers, the schoolmen, and Augustine. That even in revelation we know God's nature only in act; that the presupposition of a static revealedness of God and a static knowledge of it, if pressed, will make the defining of God's nature and Christian preaching impossible and therefore something to be avoided — this is an insight to which we must accustom ourselves and in which we must exercise ourselves until there develops the corresponding mental attitude that is lacking in most theologians, and gradually we can automatically think in no other way, or at least we will infallibly get a warning signal if we are slipping back into the old groove. The mystical way of knowledge with its plunge into incomprehensibility is tempting even to those who are not mystically endowed because it bears a strange but unmistakable affinity to what we have called the natural knowledge of God. To many it will not incorrectly seem that there is only a small step from Kant's critique of reason to Schleiermacher's theology of immediacy, or conversely from Meister Eckhart to Hegel. Can the limits of humanity that philosophers establish be different from God's revelation, and can God's revelation be other than a confirmation of the mystery of humanity? Are not both right, the rationalists who become mystics and the mystics who become rationalists? On the presupposition of a static relation of revelation that mystics may

---

32. In the MS Barth put in brackets the paragraph that is here put in fine print.

perhaps be allowed, and that seems to be the only possible one for natural knowledge, the step is in fact even smaller. We have found in the natural knowledge of God a serious dogmatic problem and thus incorporated critical rationalism into Christian thinking at least as a positive question mark. We have also, theoretically at least, seen in mysticism a remarkable possibility within the Christian church. With all the greater right, therefore, we take steps against allowing an illegitimate combination of the two (what Roman Catholic dogmatics calls the other side of mysticism)[33] to rot Christian proclamation at its root. Dogmatics must be on guard — no matter what others may do who think this is good — lest it take even the smallest step that would have such serious consequences. Instead, it must go its own way through all such things.

We thus come back to the fork where we saw the dead end of mystical speculation and in the light of our earlier deliberations maintained emphatically that it is not self-evident, and never will be, that the mystery we run up against is God's mystery, that what we may know, the object in which we find our limit, is what may be known of God, the *gnōston tou theou* (Rom. 1:19). It must be asked whether it pleases God here and now, in this thing or that, to conceal himself in order to reveal himself. God and humanity, God and nature, God and history — all very good, but softly please, for the question is — a real question — whether we can say all this. It is not self-evident that the cosmos with all its phenomena[34] is identical with the whole creation that reverently sings a song of praise to its Creator. This can never be taken for granted. Too much is at stake for us to be able to say this even in faith. Revelation is not a leveling roller that sets everything, even everything conditional, in relation to the unconditional, as even an eminent theological thinker like P. Tillich seems to think,[35] let alone the usual theological idealists. It is not so even when we have truly understood that there is only indirect knowledge of God, even when we know that the supposed general revelation is really revelation in a mystery, even when we realize better than the older Protestant friends of natural theology whom we have consulted that God does not reveal himself in the positive things of the objective world but, according to Job

---

33. Cf. Ritschl, *Geschichte des Pietismus,* p. 558.
34. Cf. J. W. von Goethe, *Faust* I, vv. 520-21.
35. Cf. esp. P. Tillich, *Die Überwindung des Religionsbegriffs in der Religions philosophie* (1922); idem, *Kritisches und positives Paradox . . .* (1923); and cf. Barth's reply: *Von der Paradoxie des "positiven Paradoxes"* (1923). See Tillich's *Gesammelte Werke,* I, 367ff.; VII, 196ff.

[Job 38:1], in its puzzles and terrors, in the whirlwind, in the things that bring into question both our consciousness and the universe. It is not so even when we are aware that knowledge of God by means of the object can be real knowledge of God only insofar as we find in this object an analogue of the cross of Christ. There is not even a negative revelation roller. There is no revealedness.

I must now recapitulate the result of our prolegomena in a statement that sounds harsh and limited: The preaching of the Christian church as the Word of God rests on the witness of holy scripture to revelation in Jesus Christ, and only of this object or mystery can it dare to say that here is revelation, here is God's Word. God's Word, not a state, not an opening through which any Tom, Dick, and Harry may look into heaven, but an event. There is mystery here, and here precisely. Moses and Jeremiah stand here and warn us that there is no direct access.[36] Paul refers here to what no eye has seen nor ear heard [1 Cor. 2:9]. The cross of Christ stands in the mist here. To you it is given to know the mystery of the kingdom of heaven, but to those outside everything is given in parables so that they may not understand (Mark 4:11-12). There is an event here by which the mystery is disclosed, and an event even in recognition of the event. In the power of the Holy Spirit the Word is made flesh [John 1:14] and finds faith and obedience, and not for a moment can we dissolve the event, not for a moment can it cease to be an event. Heaven and earth and all creation are called upon to be witnesses to the event,[37] to be an echo of God's Word, also to proclaim this Word, to participate in the one revelation as pointers and reflections. To be sure, they are not the revelation itself. Neither nature in itself nor history in itself is revelation in any sense. Creation in itself bears witness to the fall of angels and humans, not to their Creator, whether in its positive aspect or its negative aspect. It can become revelation insofar as it participates in that event, insofar as it is known to have been created by the Word (this one Word), insofar as through the Word (this one Word) it comes back to its origin. But here again truth lies only in the act, the event, the Holy Spirit and not just any Spirit, the Holy Spirit of God, the particular Spirit through whom Christ rose from the dead [Rom. 1:4] and gathers his community from among the nations. This event is God's address to us in the rift of our existence. The content of the address is: I am the Lord over the rift and in the rift,

---

36. Cf. Exod. 3:5; 33:22-23; Jer. 23:18, 28-29.
37. Ps. 66:1-4; 69:34; 148.

the Lord, God the Father, Son, and Spirit. The meaning of this content is a fellowship between God and us that is real because God has set it up and it rests wholly in him.

This then, and not anything and everything, is the object, what may be known of God, on which Christian preaching is founded. It has this God in view when it talks about God. It knows nothing other than this event. Dogmatics ranges itself alongside preaching and places itself under the same limitation because it knows no more than preaching and realizes more fundamentally that preaching may know only that all bypassing of this event misses the point. Here is where it asks about God and forms its concept of God. Its concept of God is not a general concept but a concept of the subject of this specific event. For here a subject becomes visible even though we have to admit that from the standpoint for our own vision God dwells in light that no one can approach [1 Tim. 6:16].

But what about the incomprehensibility of God and his refusal to be defined? If there is anywhere that we cannot forget this, if there is anywhere that it must be understood, then it is precisely here where it is understood concretely in the act, in the event of an I and Thou address at a specific point. The dogmatic concept of God's nature can only paraphrase the divine inconceivability, but it does so, and it does so joyfully and festively. When dogmatics, aware of its inadequacy, describes the nature of God, this has to be a song of praise, for it may do it only in relation to the Lord and therefore with confidence that it really is describing his nature, or, as we may quietly say, his inconceivability. Not any other darkness; not our human darkness. It is a weakness and mistake in dogmatics, not to say something limited about God, but to have a bad conscience in so doing, to distrust the Word, as though we were not permitted and indeed commanded by the Word to say who God is, as though concern about God's inconceivability had to be a concern for faith and obedience.

As regards the definition that we must now give, I can only repeat and explain what I said in the thesis. The question that we face cannot be: What is God? but has to be: Who is God? And the answer cannot be the definition of an It but has to be the definition of a He. This is the first and decisive description of the nature of God that arises out of the fact that God is knowable to us through his Word. Address cannot be for me a neutral thing. It involves a person. We must take seriously the insight that what Christian preaching calls God's revelation is a speaking, a *loqui*,[38]

---

38. Cf. above, § 3.

lightning that rends the darkness (still a lame comparison!), not a natural event or cause of which the knowledge of God is the effect, but Logos, the free divine Spirit who makes himself known to the creaturely human spirit as Spirit to spirit. We deal, of course, with *his* Word, God's Word, which he alone speaks, which cannot be repeated on human lips. The miracle or paradox of revelation is that he can speak to us this Word that we can receive. But the miracle of revelation is this address. Address is person to person. If God speaks to us in this way, he is a person, a thinking, willing, feeling I with all the marks of individuality, of absolute uniqueness, of specific distinction from every other I. God is not a something. God is someone, a person, an I, no matter whether, in thinking about the knowledge of revelation, we are reflecting upon the whence of the Word that is spoken, on its being spoken, or on its being spoken to us; God is Father, Son, and Spirit, subject, and never as such God objectively in himself. Christian revelation is trinitarian revelation, and this very firmly rules out any possibility of seeing God behind or above in his deity apart from his personality. To try to grasp his nature apart from his personality unavoidably means trying to get away from the knowledge of revelation understood as an act. We have seen that we must never try to do this. The church's doctrine of the three persons in God's essence (for details of which I must refer you back to § 5 of the Prolegomena) does not upset but underlines our present thesis. God is not a something but a someone in each of the possible relations in which he meets us in revelation. Precisely the strict form of the doctrine of the Trinity that rules out Sabellianism nails down fast the knowledge of God, or, better, keeps it alive, for it forbids us to seek its subject matter anywhere but in the divine subjectivity — and for this reason it is one of the axioms of Christian proclamation that we must never surrender. All that God is, he is as a person. He exists as a person. He is Father, Son, and Spirit from eternity to eternity. Once we abstract away, even for a moment, from the speaking person that *addresses* us, that addresses *us;* once we dissolve the deity in a general truth or idea that is no longer a person, we are no longer thinking about God.

We must be careful not to reverse the statement and say that the one who addresses us is God. This apparent predicate is no predicate, just as in the statement that God is one the apparent predicate is no predicate, but the subject a second time: I am who I am! [Exod. 3:14]. God is God. The second member adds nothing to the first when God names his own name. It is rather different when *we* speak about God. We cannot repeat God's revelation or take his own Word on our lips. We can only bear witness to him, and then God can speak his own Word through our witness. We cannot say "God is God" in such a way that this subject himself speaks and posits himself through our speaking. On our lips the statement can only be a tautology, perhaps significant, perhaps empty. To make it mean something to human ears, to proclaim the "I am who I am" as we are meant to do, in place of the second "I am" we have to put a paraphrase, a predicate, something apparently new. The indirectness of our knowledge of God means that our concept of God breaks in two. Our definition can consist only of two pieces which are both meant to say both things and both the one thing, but which can say only something partial. Nor can we combine the two things. This makes no sense, if we realize that the second thing is meant to be said with the first and vice versa, that only one thing is meant to be said with both. But this one thing is God's Word through which he himself says *who* — or, as we perceive it, *what* he is. We can put no surrogates here for God's own Word. We must bear witness to God's Word with our human words so that God himself may speak for himself. Thus attempts to join the two things together make no sense. We can say only the first thing and the second thing alongside one another as pointers to the one thing that God himself says. This is the most complete concept of God's nature that is available to us.

To speak about God, then, we have to add a second thing to the first — that he is He, a person. We now take up again the definition that was normative already in § 5 of the Prolegomena, and following a very common usage in both the OT and the NT as we try to paraphrase the second "I am," we say: "I am — the Lord."[39] This is the nature of God. In necessarily putting this biblical predicate here (and not a philosophical "Absolute" or the like, nor an edificatory "Love"), we are attempting at least an indication of the one thing which stands behind both human concepts, a recollection of the fact that strictly it can be only a matter of positing the subject a second time. For "Lord" is also the term for a person, an I. The term "Lord" fits our starting point, that is, the fact that we know God through his Word by which he addresses us.

But if we are not to stop with the tautology, or rather the hymn: "God is God," then we have to elucidate the second term "Lord" by a definition that is not intrinsically contained in the first point that God is a person. The I that addresses us in revelation is free. This is how we must first explain the term "Lord." This I differs from every other I by being

---

39. Cf. above, § 5.III.

free in the most unrestricted sense. Here is the Lord *kat' exochēn,* the Lord of all lords, the King of all kings (1 Tim. 6:15). We, too, feel that we are each an I, a lord, and free. But this is not true. Our individuality also denotes a limit. Our thinking, willing, and feeling break up once they cross this limit. We constantly have other lords alongside us and over us and under us. We are I in antithesis to not-I, and only thus. But God says: "I am the Lord." He is God inasmuch as he can say that he is free. In this regard, of course, he not only transcends but bursts apart every concept of personality known to us. If even for a moment we were to look aside from his Word, let alone from the fact that in his revelation he addresses us in I and Thou terms, we would have to abandon our first point and deny the personality of God, not saying that God is personally the Lord, but speaking of God impersonally as lordship, as supreme power, as free-dom, as the Absolute. But we have sworn not to abandon the actuality of the knowledge of revelation. We thus affirm that our concepts of personal-ity, of the I, break down when we apply them to God.[40] But we let ourselves be told by God's Word: "I am — the Lord," this is the nature of God.

In further elucidation or sharpening of this definition I must now recall that in the section on the Trinity we found that this second element in the concept of God relates to all three persons. God is the Lord. This means that he is the Lord at the beginning and end of the contradiction of our existence, the first and the last (Rev. 1:17), the eternal Father. He is also the living Lord *in* our contradiction, the eternal Son. He is also our own Lord, who not only addresses us as the children of God but gives us the ears needed to be addressed thus, that is, the eternal Spirit.[41] We have now to think of the lordship of God in all these relations, naturally remembering all the time that it is (divinely) personal if the formula "Lord" is really to be a term for God. Thus "Lord" would not denote God the Lord if it referred only to his so-called transcendence, his supraterrestriality, his standing above the antithesis. The word "absoluteness" points in this direction, and therefore I prefer not to use it to describe God as the Lord, though we might be able to give it a good sense, as we have to say in opposition to Ritschl.[42] Again, the Lord would not be God the Lord if

---

40. The editor substituted a plural here ("them") for a singular in the MS.
41. See above, pp. 112ff.
42. A. Ritschl, *Theologie und Metaphysik,* 3rd ed. (Göttingen, 1902), pp. 43-44. Barth had already taken issue with Ritschl on this point in his essay "Der Glaube an der persönlichen Gott," *ZTK* 24 (1914) 71-72.

the term denoted merely his so-called immanence, his paradoxical presence in this world that is so unlike the Father. Hence I prefer not to use 1 John 4:16 as a basis for defining God as love, though this can also be given a good sense. Finally, the Lord would not be God the Lord if his lordship were found one-sidedly in the fact that he is *our* Lord, the Lord of our life, so that I will not adduce here the *pneuma ho theos* of John 4:24 or use it to define God, true though it undoubtedly is to say that God is Spirit. The general biblical statement that God is the Lord is perhaps the best because it comprehends and encloses all these relations within itself in a relatively simple and illuminating way.

In the thesis I have summed up this second element in the nature of God, his lordship, in the foreign term "aseity," which commonly occurs at this point in the older Protestant dogmatics and which still does so today in Roman Catholic dogmatics.[43] God subsists, or exists, or is a cause, *a se.*[44] Many people use "independence" for "aseity."[45] But if we venture to seek an unequivocal essential predicate, to answer the question Who is God? not with a He but with an explanatory This — as we have done unavoidably even with the formula "Lord" — then it is best to say that God is *a se.* What we are told about, what is made known and imparted to us when we are addressed by God's Word, is the thinking, willing, and feeling of him who in his being and acts is conditioned by no one and nothing above, alongside, or below him, but purely and totally by himself as one who is absolutely free. "Unsearchable are his judgments and inscrutable his ways. For who has known the mind of the Lord, or who has been his counselor, or who has given something to him that he would have to be repaid? from him and through him and to him are all things. To him be glory for ever" (Rom. 11:33-36). It is this God and no other who addresses us through his Word, who through His Word establishes fellowship between him and us. But let us not forget that in itself the thought of aseity is not the thought of God. In itself what can it be but the mystery of our limit, the negation of human imperfection? Apart from the speaking I or person in the "I am the Lord," here too, along with a thousand paganisms, we have the thought of an idol, a non-god.

Let it also be understood that we ourselves cannot combine aseity

---

43. Marginal note: "Lipsius 223!" (R. A. Lipsius, *Lehrbuch der evangelisch-protestantischen Dogmatik* [Braunschweig, 1876], p. 223.)

44. Cf. Heppe-Bizer, p. 43; ET p. 53; Schmid-Pöhlmann, p. 88; Schmid ET p. 115; Bartmann, pp. 39-40.

45. Marginal note: "Reinhard, *Dogm.,* p. 106." Reinhard quotes Schleiermacher, *Christliche Glaube,* I, p. 290 n. 1; ET *CF,* I, § 54, Postscript, pp. 218-19.

and personality. If we try to give the Lord the predicate of personality, seeing the two as one concept from this angle, aseity dissolves and the lordship of God is limited, compromised, overthrown, and made improper. For personality means individuality, and individuality means limitation. As we said earlier, when we relate the concept of freedom to the concept of personality, it shatters it. So then, if even for a moment we were to look aside from God's Word, by which he calls himself the Lord, we would have to let go of this second thing, that is, freedom, the unconditional kingly rule of him who speaks to us. We could call him only one Lord along with others, and we would have ceased to think the thought of God.

If we are to be true to our starting point and not to turn aside from the act of the knowledge of revelation, we must say then that our concept of aseity breaks down when it is applied to God, so that with our word we cannot speak *the* Word. We can only speak two words if we are to describe the nature of God as it is. We can only say "I am" and "the Lord" — personality and aseity. These two words are one word as God's Word. Their only legitimacy is that they derive from God's Word. We could not say them if they did not. Theological thought and speech must venture to let itself be led by its object and to live in the strength of the truth of its object. In this disclosed weakness our words must be witnesses. Thought and speech about God must be ventured. But the final outcome must be left to God's own Word. This must come to expression in the theses of dogmatics too. Our final word to mystical thinkers, however, must be that we think we know better what the incomprehensibility of God implies than if we had refused to tread the path to the place where only adoration is possible; that we know what we are saying when we call this incomprehensibility a positive, *the* great positive, factor.

To confirm the insight thus achieved it will help us if here again we do not neglect to glance briefly in conclusion at the theological tradition. I will adduce first the definition of Polanus which I found very attractive for a moment: God is the most pure or simple act, essential actuosity.[46] God is event or act in him as whom he is knowable to us. Is this act, indeed, anything other than God himself, and is it not the simplest definition of his nature to reverse the statement and to say that God is this act? Yes, we say, if this amounts to anything more than the tautology that God is God. But the statement of Polanus does not even amount to

---

46. Heppe, p. 40; Heppe-Bizer, p. 43; ET p. 53. Heppe does not quote Polanus but summarizes Reformed teaching.

the tautology itself. The actuosity or most pure act is certainly God, but God is not for this reason the actuosity. God is not a thing, not even this thing. Nor can we hypostatize the event in which he makes himself known and put it in the place of God. This is not really the point of it. The same objection arises against all the older Protestant definitions of God. They show remarkably little concern for the first element, that of personality. God is eternal mind for Melanchthon,[47] infinite spiritual essence for Calov, Quenstedt, and König,[48] self-subsistent spiritual being or independent spirit for Hollaz and Baier,[49] independent essence for the Reformed Alsted[50] (a surprisingly bare definition). We have to seek the personal element here in terms like "mind" and "spirit." It was overlooked — unwittingly of course — that a term like "spirit" does not necessarily carry with it the concept of personality. And this avenged itself. In the 19th century, speculative criticism of the church's concept of God could rush into the gap, for example, in the dogmatics of Biedermann. Biedermann took the older dogmatics literally, assuming that they were speaking only of God's spiritual nature and absoluteness. He thus concluded that in his absolute being as spirit God does not need to subsist in the form of personality, which is a mark of finite spirit. The absolute process of thinking, willing, and feeling in which we have to know God's nature is impersonal. Only in our thinking, in the interplay of absolute spirit with finite spirit, is God personality.[51] This solves the problem of the incompatibility of personality and aseity, but at the cost of personality. All that is left in the concept of God is the aseity of spirit, and we have stated that this alone does not denote God, the God who reveals himself. I need not say that this solution is totally unacceptable to us because when we look away from the knowledge of revelation in act, the "I am" of the divine essence can become a matter of religious psychology, as in Biedermann. But the older Protestant concept of God was defenseless against this criticism and reinterpretation. We must take stronger measures here to protect the concept with which Christian proclamation speaks about God from being rendered innocuous in this way, and to safeguard the paradox of this concept against such dissolution.

---

47. Hase, p. 130.
48. Schmid-Pöhlmann, p. 85; Schmid ET pp. 112-13.
49. Schmid-Pöhlmann, p. 87; Schmid ET p. 115.
50. Heppe-Bizer, p. 43; ET p. 52.
51. A. E. Biedermann, *Christliche Dogmatik* (Zurich, 1869), pp. 630-47. In criticism cf. Barth's essay "Der Glaube an den persönlichen Gott," *ZTK* 24 (1914) 27-28, 65ff.

In another sense we must be grateful to Biedermann, and to D. F. Strauss before him,[52] for presenting the problem of the two elements so sharply and thus for trying to arouse Protestant dogmatics from its uncritical slumbers.[53] If only the answer had been a better one, namely, a defiant establishment and assertion of the paradox that is present here. Instead, they resorted to mediations, to remarkable attempts to show that the so-called absolute personality of God that we encounter here in many dogmatics is conceivable in spite of everything. For the most celebrated contribution to the debate theology is indebted to the philosopher R. H. Lotze, who thought that we can conceive of an I which does not confront a non-I, a personal stream of thoughts, volitions, and feelings which wells up eternally from itself, an absolute personal spirit, and who identified this with the divine essence.[54] I can only advise against such artifices. Strauss and Biedermann saw what is at issue, what can and cannot be done when we think rigorously, much better than Lotze and the many theologians (Max Reischle is a notable exception)[55] who applauded him. I would rather not speak about God's "absolute personality" because this term veils the fact that we must use two words in dealing with God's nature, and that it is not in our power to make the two one. Christian dogmatics can speak the truth only when it finds concepts that are carefully adjusted to the knowable God, and with them knocks at the gates of the truth of God. We should not try to disguise this. If in some respects our dogmatics must be more refined that that of our predecessors, this refinement can consist only in a better recognition of the foolishness of the gospel.

---

52. D. F. Strauss, *Die christliche Glaubenslehre*, I, pp. 502-24.

53. Cf. Barth, *ZTK* 24 (1914) 80-81.

54. R. H. Lotze, *Mikrokosmos. Ideen für Naturgeschichte und Geschichte der Menschheit*, III (Leipzig, 1880), p. 177; in criticism cf. Barth, *ZTK* 24 (1914) 81-82.

55. M. Reischle, "Erkennen wir die Tiefen Gottes?" *ZTK* 1 (1891) 287-366. Cf. Barth, *ZTK* 24 (1914) 82.

§ 17

The Attributes of God

God's attributes are the conditions under which his nature makes itself known to us by the Word. It does not reveal itself to us as an undifferentiated unit but as the fulness of its communicable and incommunicable perfections. We cannot know it without a conception of its attributes. But each attribute of God is necessarily his whole nature. Thus their manifoldness reminds us of the limitation of our concepts and of their relation to the fact that our conceiving can be only an attempt at understanding. In line with our discussions of God's knowability and his nature we distinguish (1) the attributes of personality or of the God who discloses himself, the communicable attributes, God's life and God's power, God's wisdom and God's holy, righteous, and merciful will, God's love and God's blessedness; and (2) the attributes of aseity or of the hidden God, the incommunicable attributes, namely, God's unity, God's eternity, God's omnipresence, God's constancy, and God's glory. But the communicable attributes have their power precisely in their participation in the mystery of the incommunicable attributes, and the truth of the incommunicable attributes lies precisely in their participation in the disclosure of the communicable attributes. Only as the perfection of the one divine nature are both what they are. The word for both would also be the word for the one divine nature. But this can be spoken only by the mouth of God, the basis and limit of our concepts.

I. Comunicable Attributes

The doctrine of the divine attributes relates to that of the nature of God as the doctrine of the incarnation does to belief in the doctrine of the

375

Trinity. We saw in that connection (§ 5 of the Prolegomena) that logically considered the doctrine of the incarnation and that of faith and obedience are strictly no more than explications of the basic datum of revelation. Materially, they are posited with this, with the Word of the Lord, Father, Son, and Spirit. They are the conditions under which this reality is possible, God meeting us and we standing before God. Analytically, things are the same with the doctrine of God's attributes. It is not as though we were really setting forth predicates of God, not as though we were adding anything to the nature of God, not as though we were putting content in this empty form, flesh on these bones, the green tree of life alongside gray theory.[1] God himself must be what is proper to him, his "Property." Something accidental or alien or nondivine in God would conflict with his deity, with his "I am the Lord," with his aseity. To know his qualities is to know his nature, the "I am," the "I am the Lord," the personality of God and the aseity of God in their puzzling unity.

But when we ask how we arrive at this knowledge of the divine nature, what it implies to know it, or under what conditions and in what modality we can do so, we come up against the concept of attributes in distinction from that of the nature. The object that we know is exactly the same but we are now looking at this same object from the standpoint that it is knowable. We are analyzing the fact that this object reveals itself (indirectly, see § 15 above) to us, and how (aware of its inconceivability, § 16) we come to form that twofold concept of it: "I am the Lord." God has spoken in revelation the Word by which he becomes knowable if not comprehensible. We must now go on to elucidate in concepts what the fact of knowability means when put in human thoughts and words. These further concepts that explain the basic datum as datum are the qualities, attributes, properties, affections, or perfections of God. As the older theologians put it, in a rather banal comparison, they are the ripples by which we see that a big stone has really fallen into our pond.

This is what we must say first in order to set the matter at once in its right place. In fact, of course, things are usually done the other way round. The datum that has to be explained is not the reality, the revealed nature of God, but possibilities, divine possibilities, with the vague sound that the word has when it is not read off a posteriori from the reality but stands abstractly on its own. With the doctrine of the divine attributes we are already deep into the arsenal of Christian preaching. God's life and

---

1. Cf. J. W. von Goethe, *Faust* I, vv. 2038-39.

love and glory, in relation to the determinations of the divine nature, either are or appear to be very concrete concepts of God, things that we can say about him with a sense of understanding and being understood. If this is true, then a good possibility is present. God's Word is proclaimed when these concepts of God are understood and come to be understood. But there is also the threat and perhaps the reality of the opposite possibility that this will not be so, that life, love, and glory, along with other divine predicates, no matter how we formulate them, will float in the air like withered leaves separated from the branch that nourishes them, melancholy religious possibilities. What are we saying when we speak about them? What do they say to us? Where do they belong? To what alphabet do these strange letters belong? I need not fill out for you the sorry situation when the divine attributes are only the related words, mere possibilities; when what they convey is only something pathetic, touching, pious, or traditional; when the reality is not there to which the possibility belongs; when the reality is not there as its a priori; when God's Word is *not* proclaimed but only human words. When and where is the situation not at least critical in this regard?

Dogmatics, then, must above all things bring clarity here by reminding us how things are, by showing how critical the situation is, by insisting that God's attributes are attributes of God's nature. Only as such are they *God's* attributes. Only to the extent that they express the nature of God, giving nearness, form, color, and tone to the strangely remote "I am" and "the Lord," do they carry any weight. As conditions under which he is known, they have none. As merely a human impression, a secretly erected idol, an idea, a power, they are also nothing, or only something subordinate, impotent, half-true, or quarter-true. Everything depends on good salt replacing salt that has lost its savor, on our understanding them again as conditions under which the nature of God is known by the Word, the revealed nature of God which is not to be confused with any other. This reality must be sought and meant, and when it is, then the possibilities are not just possibilities but channels of reality. Then there will be no more pious, hypocritical, garrulous religious phrases, but the same words can still today be bearers of God's Word. Then we can have the same relation from the other side.

First, then, I call the divine attributes "conditions," conditions under which we know God's Word to us. "I am" and "the Lord" are not knowable in themselves. They are a pure expression of God's nature. How do they become knowable? How are they knowable? Life, power, knowledge, will . . . unity, eternity, omnipresence . . . these tell us something about this "I" and this "Lord." As we hear them, the nature is knowable. The "I" is knowable in the fulness of relations whose epitome is the concept of personality, and the "Lord" in the fulness of his freedoms, in his aseity. The attributes are as it were the letters of the divine Word without which it would be no Word. But the letters make sense only as they are joined to the Word, the divine attributes only as the knowability of the nature. One might perhaps compare the nature to the soul understood as an entelechy, and the attributes to the body. Where God speaks his own Word, he is known, and where he is known, his attributes are known. The nature is known in and through the attributes. God's attributes are the eyes with which he sees us, says Bartmann.[2] I could not put it more clearly.

II. The Debate about Objectivity and Subjectivity

The story of the doctrine of the attributes of God is shot through with a great debate which we must try to understand and in some sense settle after this introduction. It is a question of the specificity, distinction, and juxtaposition of the attributes, whether all this takes place in God himself or only in our knowledge of God, whether it is objective or merely subjective, real or unreal. This is no hairsplitting, no purely academic question, but a vital matter. The emotion is very appropriate with which modern dogmaticians like Martensen and Haering have attacked the nominalistic view of the undifferentiated character of the divine nature, which does violence to revelation, and indeed denies it, leading ultimately to the unknowability of God.[3] In fact, if everything is only one in God, he is unknowable. Where we can see only one color, we can see nothing. Where we can hear only one sound, it is as if we were deaf.

The thesis that the differentiation, multiplicity, and juxtaposition of the attributes is only a matter of our knowing, the mystical proposition — for we are again dealing with mystical knowledge here — that God in his nature is a circle whose center is everywhere and periphery nowhere,[4] describes at root a situation that we must regard as the negation of

---

2. Bartmann, I, p. 42: "Thus God's attributes become eyes with which he sees us, and our mental attributes become eyes with which we see God."

3. H. Martensen, *Christliche Dogmatik,* pp. 84-85; Haering, p. 318.

4. Cf. Suso, quoted in Hagenbach, *Lehrbuch der Dogmengeschichte,* p. 333.

revelation. On the one hand is God's nature, which as God's cannot give itself to be known by us, and on the other hand is our knowing, which as ours cannot press on to the nature of God. We may see something of this already in Augustine's doctrine of God, then in that of William of Occam and Gabriel Biel (every distinction is only nominal),[5] and not least in Schleiermacher, who believes that the qualities that we attribute to God do not denote specific things in God but only different moments in the pious self-consciousness, that is, specific forms of the feeling of absolute dependence on God.[6]

Yet those who reject this thesis must consider how to answer the three questions that follow. (a) Are the attributes of God something other in him than his nature, and if so, does not this mean that in part he is not God? (b) Does not the multiplicity of his attributes negate his unity or simplicity? (c) Is not God hereby subsumed under higher general concepts such as infinity, truth, and righteousness?[7] In a word, is not the idea of attributes in God an attack on the essential element of aseity, of unconditional lordship, of freedom and supremacy in God, in virtue of which he himself is all that he is, the one God who cannot be subsumed, but who is original?

If we are not to come under the judgment of this question, we must take care not to oppose to the unequivocal nominalistic thesis a no less unequivocal realistic one to the effect that in God's nature there is in fact a quantitative or qualitative division and distinction of attributes. For this reason our older Protestant fathers (with the sureness of instinct that always surprises us in the theologoumena of earlier centuries, no matter how baroque their garb) refused to be drawn into this apparently inescapable alternative of "in God or in us," and stated that the divine attributes are distinguished from God's nature and from one another, not nominally or really but formally, namely, according to our mode of conceiving, but not without a sure basis of distinction.[8] The distinction takes place not merely by ratiocinating reason but by ratiocinated reason[9] (by known knowing).[10] Thus our conceiving,[11] which the determination,

---

5. D. F. Strauss, *Christliche Glaubenslehre,* I, p. 529 n. 43.

6. *CF,* I, § 50, pp. 194-95.

7. Nitzsch-Stephan, pp. 446-47.

8. Hollaz, in ibid., p. 448.

9. Ibid.

10. Barth's interpretive rendering can hardly be correct. According to Quenstedt the difference is in objects, not in ways of knowing.

11. Heppe-Bizer, p. 55; ET pp. 60-61.

distinction, or juxtaposition of the attributes is in fact, is necessary and objective, being grounded in itself, not insofar as we see the thing (i.e., God) in and for itself,[12] but in respect of God's various acts or of the different objects in which he puts forth his powers.[13] Naturally, all the determinations of the attributes of God are nothing other than determinations of his nature. Each is itself identical with the divine nature. Yet their disposition, distinction, and juxtaposition is no mere appearance. They are an objective description of the nature of God entering into relation to the world and us, and known in this relation, just as a single ray of the sun, according to the difference in the objects on which it falls, both illumines and warms, bleaches and darkens, softens and hardens.[14]

This view, then, includes rather than excludes the positive content of the opposing mystical, nominalistic view. It, too, says all that has been said since Augustine about the identity of nature and attributes. It excludes only the exclusiveness of the nominalistic view, which makes the identity static and nondialectical, drawing from it the inference that the wealth of the one God manifested in the fulness of divine attributes denotes only the limitation of our knowledge, the imbecility of our mind,[15] and overlooking the fact that the knowledge of a phenomenon as a phenomenon ought not to prevent us from regarding it as the manifestation of a fact, of reckoning with a sure basis for our mode of conceiving.[16] Quenstedt could thus say on the one hand that strictly God has no properties and yet on the other hand they are truly his.[17] This view of the later Protestant orthodoxy goes back to Thomas Aquinas, who compared the multiple grasping of the one simple God to the mental grasping of physical things. In neither case is the grasping wrong because it is our grasping and not the thing itself.[18]

The presupposition with which the antinominalist or supranominalist view that we adopt here either stands or falls is that there is a kind of divine ratiocination of our reason,[19] an objective knowability of God

---

12. Schmid-Pöhlmann, pp. 91-92; Schmid ET p. 122 (Gerhard).

13. Braun, in Heppe, p. 53; Heppe-Bizer, p. 53; ET p. 59.

14. Quenstedt, in Strauss, *Christliche Glaubenslehre*, I, 54.

15. J. A. L. Wegscheider, *Institutiones theologiae christianae dogmaticae* (1817), p. 139.

16. See Nitzsch-Stephan, p. 448.

17. See Thomasius, *Christi Person und Werke*, I, 36-37.

18. *STh* I, q. 13, a. 12 ad 3.

19. See above, n. 10.

determined by the divine act. We have laid down this presupposition, and established it so far as is possible (see § 15 above). We cannot accept that either-or, clear though it seems to be, because it overlooks the decisive category with which we must work.

Strauss could easily scoff at the church doctrine for putting itself in the "unhappy middle" between the reality and nonreality of its concepts of the attributes.[20] It did not do this, but it put itself in the place where such concepts have to be formed and can be formed so long as we recognize that they are and always will be *our* concepts. This is the place where we reflect not on the relevant subject and object as such but on the act of the knowledge of revelation, on ratiocinated reason, so that the relation between subjectivity and objectivity, between reality and nonreality, is strictly dialectical. By viewing the divine qualities as marks or conditions or modalities of the knowledge of God's nature, we do not expound them as merely subjective and nonreal. To know God is to know God's self-revealing nature. Nevertheless, we are not importing into God's nature something objective and real that is distinct from this nature. We have knowledge of God in his revelation with the caveat of inconceivability, and therefore we can have concepts of his nature (the plurality, limitation, and reciprocal relation of our concepts of the attributes in salutary fashion remind us of this) only and in all circumstances as attempts at interpretation. Engendered by the act of divine revelation, and grounded in it, they arise and are formed in the act of the knowledge of revelation. They are an expression of revelation and a description of the knowledge of revelation. They are subjectively nonreal as our formulas, and objectively real as that in the act which our formulas denote.

We may thus reply as follows to the three nominalistic objections. (a) With the attributes, are we not positing something nonessential, that is, nondivine in God? Answer: Not at all. There is nothing accidental in God.[21] God's infinitude is not a quality, his goodness is not a quality, his action is not a movement, his pity is not an emotion. He is nonspatially everywhere, first and last outside time and beyond time, the Lord of all things without habit or addition.[22] God is all things essentially. Those who posit nonessential predicates in God, those who in all that they say about God do not remember that they are always talking about God himself,

---

20. Strauss, *Christliche Glaubenslehre,* I, 541.
21. Schmid-Pöhlmann, p. 91; Schmid ET p. 121 (Chemnitz).
22. Polanus, in Heppe, p. 52; Heppe-Bizer, p. 55; ET p. 57.

those who do not know what they are doing when they take the name of God on their lips, might be legitimate targets of this objection. But they have not really said anything about God. To turn the tables, however, nominalists and mystics should also remember that the attributes are necessary and essential things that divinely redeemed reason cannot deny.[23] Without essential attributes God cannot exist, unless he exist without himself.[24] Without such attributes God would cease to be the true and living God, says Frank.[25] I would put it this way: Those who in their interest in God, but their neglect of revelation, are too grand to attribute predicates to God, believing that in all they say about God they are naming God himself and his nature; those who refuse to take the revealed name of God (his predicates) on their lips, are also not speaking about God, for how can they speak about him except by naming his attributes?

(b) Does not the multiplicity of the attributes negate the unity of God's nature? Answer: In no way. The attributes are really God's nature, and differ neither from it nor among themselves. We are certainly not to think, as Wegscheider does, that the attributes are parts of the total perfection connected by a very short link.[26] Each attribute is the total essence of God. In one and the same act he is simple, infinite, and immutable. In one and the same act he lives, knows, wills, and loves. In God, being means knowing, and being good, omnipotent, and merciful is one and the same thing.[27] To this extent, in this positive point, nominalists are right and their objection is a necessary challenge to us to talk about God not in linear terms but dialectically, that is, not to draw parallels but to draw radii which precisely because they are not parallel, in their very multiplicity, point to the one center. Those who do not remember the unity in the multiplicity, those who speak about the multiplicity without reflecting on the unity, are not speaking about God.

Nevertheless, we must insist against the nominalists that this dialectical multiplicity of what we must say about God must not be eliminated for the sake of the purity of the idea of God and replaced by one great solemn unit. This applies also to what Gregory of Nazianzus (a forerunner of the

---

23. Hutterus, in Hase, pp. 137-38.

24. Polanus, in Heppe, p. 52; Heppe-Bizer, p. 55; ET p. 59.

25. Thomasius, *Christi Person und Werke,* I, 38; F. H. R. Frank, *System der christlichen Wahrheit,* I, 2nd ed. (Erlangen, 1885), p. 222, quoted in Thomasius, *Christi Person und Werke.*

26. Wegscheider, *Institutiones,* p. 139.

27. Polanus, in Heppe, pp. 51-52; Heppe-Bizer, pp. 54-55; ET p. 58. Heppe-Bizer has *animat,* Heppe *amat.*

nominalist view) had in mind when he said that God rejoices especially in the names that denote his perfect agreement with himself and other beings, namely, peace and love,[28] as though what we know as peace and love were adequate concepts for the unity of the divine nature; as though these concepts, like all others, did not need dialectical reflection and double reflection if they are really to denote the divine nature. No, in the light of the one we must venture the movement and juxtaposition of the many. For the many are an expression of the revelation of the one, a description of knowledge of it. Those who want to arrive at the goal must take the path. We cannot speak about God without speaking about the many even as we remember the one.

(c) Does not talk about the divine attributes mean subsuming God in general concepts? On the contrary, we answer, for nothing is not subsistent per se in God.[29] We do not know God in his infinitude, righteousness, and blessedness after first learning elsewhere what infinitude, righteousness, and blessedness are, and then being in a position to conceive of God under these categories, so that the categories are set above the divine, above God's nature. Again, the nominalist objection is a good corrective against an over-easy tendency to make God in our own image. The categories that we use to form a conception of God can in fact serve as such only if we think of them as subordinate to the category of the divine; only if we view God as the source and origin of all ideas, perfections, and general concepts; only if God does not stand under our laws but is regarded as the lawgiver, no, as the despot who is his own law and as such the guardian of all truth.[30]

But now we look at the other side. If God has revealed himself, then precisely our ideas and perfections and general concepts and laws are set in relation to God and in absolute dependence upon him. In the relation of revelation our limits becomes sites for divine communication. Again it means denying revelation if, in order not to do violence to God because we know that no limit as such is divine communication, we ignore the presence of such sites and fail to move on from the ideas to the idea of all ideas, from the attributes, and in them, to the nature of God. The place where we conceive of the absolute is the relative. This is the result of revelation. Even and precisely in revelation we must not confuse the relative with the absolute. But even less must we overlook the fact that we

---

28. Hagenbach, *Lehrbuch der Dogmengeschichte*, p. 250, quoting Gregory, *Orat.*, VI, 12.

29. Polanus, in Heppe, p. 52; Heppe-Bizer, p. 54; ET p. 58.

30. Cf. Heppe-Bizer, pp. 79-80; ET pp. 84-85.

may now say that revelation does not permit us not to take seriously the conceptuality with which we define our limits. Those who are ashamed of this cannot talk about God. And whether they even mean God with their spiritualism is the real question.

In sum, it is not true that stating the divine attributes is in itself an attack on the essential element of aseity, of divine freedom and supremacy. We take this objection very seriously. We have done justice to the element of aseity in positing the concept of attributes. We will do so again in the question of their division and in dealing with each of them separately. How could we speak about God and even for a moment not think about his aseity? But we cannot on this account accept a prohibition against speaking seriously about the attributes. On the contrary, where some try to impose this prohibition on us, we wonder whether the aseity that is so threateningly alleged against us for this purpose (Strauss)[31] is really an element in the divine nature and not perhaps an idol of the same name fabricated out of abstraction. The aseity of the divine nature cannot be abstracted away from God's personality. Where we know it as such, where we know it in the paradox of revelation, is it possible to use it to set aside the paradox of the knowledge of revelation (which is at issue in the doctrine of the attributes), to reduce this knowledge of revelation to the banality that God is ineffably and indivisibly one *thing*? Our partners in debate should surely know that they ought to say one *person!* If God is really one person for them, and if we assure them that even though this means many things for us, in everything we, too, have to do with this one person, then they will perhaps see that they have every reason to repent a little and withdraw their much too consistent protest.

III. Deducing and Dividing God's Attributes

We now turn to the question how to deduce and divide God's attributes. When you hear this, you will perhaps have to suppress some amusement. How can we not only assert God's attributes but also deduce and divide them? But be patient.[32] Where do we really stand?[33] Are we merely trying

---

31. Cf. D. F. Strauss, *Christliche Glaubenslehre*, p. 541.
32. Barth here quotes Horace, *Ars poetica* V, 5.
33. This phrase of Adolf Preiswerk had become a common one in Barth's circle (Swiss German: *Wo stömer aigedlig?*).

to satisfy our need or urge for logical and aesthetic completeness or our aesthetic sense? What can such deliberations have to do with the gift and task of Christian preaching? I reply to the last question first by reminding you that the statements we make here in dogmatics are not adapted or meant to be the stuff of preaching and teaching. They are academic exercises that we must have done before we can preach and teach. At school we do many things in preparation for life that later in life we have to know but that we will repeat, not as we need to do in school but in a more popular way. This applies to the whole apparatus of dogmatics, not merely to parts like this where we find it especially obvious and alien. I repeat, dogmatics is an esoteric and typically specialized science. We have always to realize this if we are not to balk at the work and lose the needed objectivity through objecting how strange and artificial and abstract the discussions are that we have to engage in here. If it achieves its purpose of making our thinking sharp and alert and mobile at every point in the particular way that is needed for proclamation of God's Word according to human judgment, then the objection will fall away in all its forms.

Why then, and for what purpose, must we deduce and divide the divine attributes? Certainly not for our own satisfaction or as a work of supererogation, but because to be able to speak about God we cannot fail to assert that his one unsearchable nature gives itself to be known by us under specific conditions, and therefore we have to have a picture — not of God, for the Bible expressly and rightly forbids this [Exod. 20:4], but — of these conditions of his knowability, of these possibilities that represent the reality of his own Word in human words. To speak is to speak about something, about an object.

As regards the objectivity of God in his revelation, we have to take this seriously. We could spend a year and more on building up a doctrine of God's attributes and we would only have begun to gain a picture of what may be known of God. The number of the radii of a circle is infinite. Hence there can be no question of giving here an exhaustive description. But no matter how scanty or sketchy the picture may be, it will be a real picture to the extent that it is on a surface on which there is an up and a down, a right and a left, with specific contours at each point. The circle with its infinite number of radii — perhaps we should stick to this rather imaginative but clear comparison, at least in the classroom — can be imagined only if we draw some of the radii from the top and the bottom, the right or the left.

The first question is that of the possibility of orientation. To deduce and divide God's attributes is simply to fix the point from which and to which the lines ought to run, and in so doing to fix at the same time what is up and down or right and left. To speak plainly, we must find out how far we can in fact speak about God's attributes, and this will show us in what order and sequence we must do so, in what mutual relationship the statements ought to stand to one another. But we cannot examine these two questions separately. We cannot deduce without dividing nor divide apart from a certain deducing. The basis of division is the principle of deduction and vice versa. If, as 1 Cor. 14:33 tells us, God in his revelation is not a God of disorder but of peace, and if Christian preaching (and after it dogmatics), based on this revelation, is not to engage in religious fascism or bolshevism, it will perhaps be clear that an academic inquiry such as ours cannot be as empty and futile as it might seem to be at a first glance. If only we had the same remarkable objectivity and perspicacity with which the masters of the old theological school attacked such questions.

Let us first recall an odd academic phenomenon that we come across at the outset. In almost all dogmatics, when the authors consider how to speak about God's attributes and from what standpoint to do so, they first state with some discomfort (or with a certain superior smile) that many whom they know and many more whom they do not know have attempted the same task, and like sand on the seashore have all given their own constructions of the nature of God. They thus express or suggest astonishment at the differences among their predecessors. They then explain that it is impossible to enumerate them all, let alone discuss them. Finally, turning aside to their own masterpiece,[34] rather gruffly from this wealth of presentations that is viewed so skeptically, they all the more resolutely put out their own new, thousandth construction of the nature of God. Indeed, nowhere perhaps does the personal conditioning of dogmatic efforts come out so strongly as at this cardinal point. Nor does it seem to help any of them that they see this. As though under some mysterious compulsion we find all of them here, whether in the age of orthodoxy or the modern period, unfailingly putting the lamp of their own originality on the candlestick in this regard. In some way this Caudine yoke seems to be waiting for all of us, and in some way we have to put it on. It is as well if we do not try to be better than our predecessors [cf. 1 Kgs. 19:4]. Let us admit at once that we, too, are in fact astonished at the variety of what has already been attempted here and that finally we

---

34. Barth has a quotation here from an unknown source.

cannot do more than venture our own attempt at a little originality. Perhaps we can try to achieve some clarity on what we are really doing, and avoid to some extent the mistakes and dangers with which we are obviously surrounded. But we will do this incidentally by turning at once to the matter in hand.

Above all we must say that the chaos of views that meets us when we survey earlier dogmatic work is certainly bad, but not so bad as is sometimes stated. If it is hard to deal with it critically, it is not impossible. Strictly, among the various principles of deduction and division, only four types stand out plainly and call for consideration.

The first is the psychological. This begins with the nature of God as the absolute personality and posits in God either his being, knowing, and willing,[35] his feeling, willing, and objective consciousness,[36] or his willing, thinking, and feeling.[37] The element of absoluteness, which seems to be less prominent here, is the bracket that encloses all these categories and characterizes them, in Biedermann even to the extent that it actually absorbs them, and the psychological form of the concept of God becomes the purely nonreal form of the impersonal process of absolute spirit. I do not believe that we can express the element of absoluteness (or aseity) in God's nature within the framework of a psychological schema and escape the loss of personality that results in Biedermann. The element of personality and the psychological schema must have their place as a principle of deduction and division, just as aseity is undoubtedly an element in the divine nature, yet not as a master concept, for, as we saw in § 16, we cannot bring personality and aseity together in a single concept, and consequently personality has to be an independent source of knowledge alongside aseity. I see an acute danger that in the psychological schema aseity will either not retain its independent dignity as it should, or will take away that of personality, and I believe that this danger is a decisive reason for rejecting the schema.

The second type is the religious, or rather the religious-genetic, represented by Schleiermacher and his perhaps most congenial and almost completely loyal disciple Alexander Schweizer. We have seen already that in Schleiermacher the qualities are viewed almost nominalistically as mere objectivizings of detailed elements in the pious consciousness.[38] As he sees

---

35. Hutterus, in Hase, pp. 139-40; W. Schmidt, *Christliche Dogmatik*, Part 2 (Bonn, 1898), §§ 17-18, 19-20, 21, 22ff.

36. Biedermann, *Christliche Dogmatik*, pp. 635ff.

37. Seeberg, *Christliche Dogmatik*, I, p. 405.

38. See *CF,* I, § 50, pp. 194-95.

it, the pious consciousness itself, apart from the antithesis of grace and sin, gives rise to God's eternity, omnipresence, omnipotence, and omniscience.[39] Under the antithesis, as a consciousness of sin, it gives rise to God's holiness and righteousness.[40] In the overcoming of the antithesis, as the consciousness of grace, it gives rise to God's love and wisdom.[41] In Schweizer pious feeling finds God in the world of nature as omnipotence omniscience, eternity, and omnipresence,[42] in the moral world as goodness, holiness, wisdom, and righteousness,[43] and in the specifically Christian life of salvation it finds him as love and grace, as fatherly wisdom and mercy.[44] I need hardly say that we cannot accept his schema on account of its nominalistic starting point. Furthermore, especially in Schweizer, it almost inevitably leaves the bad impression that God's nature is torn apart into a series of qualities that exist and may be known for themselves — something our predecessors consistently sought to avoid.

At the lower level, is there really a knowledge of God's eternity apart from his holiness or love? Conversely, at the highest stage, is there a knowledge of God's mercy compared to which that of his holiness and that of his omnipresence are only stations on the road that have now been left behind? Is this the mercy of *God?* Does not the norm that decides whether we really have a divine attribute before us depend on all the attributes being present and posited together, so that we know God's nature in them only in their totality, or only as we see each one in the light of their totality? Does not this norm inevitably become ambiguous if we introduce the genetic principle and an odd interest in the various stages of religious experience? If we do not want to dissolve the unity of the divine nature in this way; if we concede that it is either known totally or not at all at each possible stage; if, as expressly in the case of Schleiermacher, we view the stages as strata of one and the same religious consciousness that are present and posited together, why is there this interest in them, and why do they rate as sources of knowledge? Should we not see that the genetic approach cannot be used with the knowledge of revelation, and even less so with its content?

---

39. Ibid., §§ 50-55.
40. Ibid., §§ 79-84.
41. Ibid., II, §§ 164-69.
42. A. Schweizer, *Die christliche Glaubenslehre nach protestantischen Grundsätzen*, I, 2nd ed. (Leipzig, 1877), §§ 63-69.
43. Ibid., §§ 82-86.
44. Ibid., §§ 104-6.

Schleiermacher's concept of the attributes, and that of nominalism in general, which seeks precisely to safeguard the unity of God, is in my view nowhere more seriously compromised than in the deducing and dividing of the attributes that logically results from it. If we take seriously its genetic character — Schleiermacher was clever enough to conceal this to some extent but it is obvious in Schweizer — this leads not to attributes of the one nature of God but to a hierarchy of upper and lower attributes, and essentially to divine or religious ideas and hypostases that are left hanging in the air. One finds what one is looking for — gigantic reflections or projections of the religious consciousness. "This separation, whereby for followers of Schleiermacher God the Creator does not have such attributes as righteousness, wisdom, and mercy, is a very natural result of the attempt to construct the idea of God out of the human understanding and consciousness, so that things are said about God which have in themselves no warrant or reality, but only formal validity."[45]

The third type one might best describe as the intuitive. It is the one which in my view merits the strongest disapproval and rejection even though, or precisely because, H. Stephan proclaims it to be that of modern dogmatics and commends it because of its great simplicity and religious depth.[46] We can best see what it involves from the dogmatics of Julius Kaftan.[47] Its first point is that what we have called the essential divine element of aseity (the absolute) resulted only from the intrusion of the otherworldly form of early church piety and the philosophical traditions of antiquity into Christian theology and their retention in Protestant orthodoxy, which was unfortunately dependent on Scholasticism, and regrettably even in Luther in his *Bondage of the Will*.[48] In opposition to it we must now return, we are told, to the revelation of God which, attested in scripture and received in faith, is rooted and expressed supremely in the inner core of the personal life of Jesus.[49] When it has been argued that the absolute is no more than the schema of the knowledge of God in intellectual religion,[50] from the known source it is directly and unbrokenly gathered — though we do not know exactly how — (a) that God is a

---

45. J. Wichelhaus, *Die Lehre der heiligen Schrift vom Worte Gottes* . . . , ed. A. Zahn, 3rd ed. (Stuttgart, 1892), p. 333.
46. Nitzsch-Stephan, pp. 451-52.
47. Kaftan, §§ 13-18, pp. 121-85.
48. Ibid., pp. 137-43.
49. Ibid., p. 136.
50. Ibid., p. 166; cf. p. 169.

transcendent personal Spirit (though transcendent has only the negative sense that his being and life are not entangled with the world),[51] and (b) that his attributes are love, holiness, and omnipotence.[52] The light-heartedness with which this theology ignores the very serious problems with which the early theologians wrestled here, as though all this were merely a slight confusion of Christianity and Neoplatonism; the audacity with which the essential element of aseity is robbed of its significance for the concept of God (Kaftan stands at the opposite pole from Biedermann in this regard, but if I had to choose I would opt for Biedermann); the assurance with which faith and revelation are manipulated to gain a purely personalist picture of God, as though precisely the knowledge of faith and revelation did not block the kind of one-sidedness that we find in Kaftan; the total arbitrariness and fortuitousness with which love and holiness and omnipotence are finally hit upon as though one could not just as well posit other concepts of personal life than those laid down by Kaftan; and finally, the dead point at which one stands at the last with these concepts in hand, taught nondialectically that this is the Christian knowledge of faith, without need of further reflection on what has been received, without any reference back to what has not been received with these concepts, without Christian thought being set and kept in motion — all these things make this type of doctrine of the attributes (Kaftan is only one example!) even more unacceptable than those that precede.

The fourth type, which is clearly distinguishable from the first three, is the dialectical, represented by the serried ranks of the older orthodoxy and by a few moderns who have not bowed the knee to Baal [cf. 1 Kgs. 19:18]; I may respectfully mention here the three names — far apart from one another — of Martensen, Lipsius, and Wichelhaus.[53] Since we ourselves are basically following the main highway of the past, we are at least to some extent pursuing the originality that is so much feared. Yet you need not be afraid that I for my part am inviting you to form a fifth group. No, at this point we breathe native air in the fourth group, for here the confusing number three, which is suspicious in this connection, disappears from the structure, being replaced by the honest number two, which in the light of our previous deliberations kindles more confidence and holds out more promise. In this fourth group, of course, we come up

---

51. Ibid., pp. 172, 179.
52. Ibid., pp. 184-95.
53. Marginal note: "Wegscheider."

against the wealth of possibilities which has so often been bewailed and scorned. But precisely here, on a closer inspection, we have to say that objectively this wealth is not such a bad thing.

To help you to make up your own minds, I will give you a list of the distinctions current in the 16th and 17th centuries. Theologians then distinguished between negative and positive attributes, quiescent and operative, internal and external, absolute and relative, immanent and transient, eternal and temporal, primitive and derived.[54] Wegscheider also distinguishes between attributes of God's infinite substance and attributes of his spiritual substance.[55] Among the moderns Martensen also distinguishes according to the relation of unity and antithesis in which God finds himself regarding the world,[56] Lipsius sees metaphysical and psychological attributes,[57] and Wichelhaus divides according to the divine names Elohim and Yahweh, *theos* and *kyrios*.[58] Indeed, even into the ranks of the Ritschlians, with the different motifs that then became normative, we find traces of this schema, as when Kirn distinguishes between the formal attributes of the divine preeminence and the material attributes of the execution of the divine will,[59] or Häring between the attributes of absolute personality and those of God's holy love,[60] or finally even Stephan between God's holiness and his nearness.[61]

The nomenclature of the divisions may vary, the allocation of individual attributes to one or the other side of the distinction may differ at times even among the fathers, and the distinction may sometimes be obscure, yet the standpoint from which the deduction and division are made is fundamentally the same among the fathers and also among the moderns that we have just named. To put you in the picture I will give you the division in the Lutheran Baier.[62] For him the negative attributes are unity, simplicity, immutability, infinity, immensity, and eternity, while

---

54. Cf. Schmid-Pöhlmann, pp. 89, 93; Schmid ET pp. 118ff.; Heppe-Bizer, p. 46; ET p. 60; Hase, p. 139.

55. Wegscheider, *Institutiones,* § 62.

56. Martensen, *Christliche Dogmatik,* p. 85.

57. Lipsius, *Lehrbuch der evangelisch-protestantischen Dogmatik,* §§ 296, 302-11, 312-36.

58. Wichelhaus, *Die Lehre der heiligen Schrift,* p. 333. Marginal note: "He fails to follow through."

59. O. Kirn, *Grundriss der Evangelischen Dogmatik* (Leipzig, 1905), p. 45.

60. Haering, p. 320.

61. Stephan, *Glaubenslehre,* §§ 11-12.

62. Schmid, p. 80; Schmid-Pöhlmann, pp. 89-91; Schmid ET pp. 118ff.

the positive attributes are life, knowledge, wisdom, holiness, justice, veracity, power, goodness, and perfection. What is the principle behind this division? It does not start with a uniform concept of the nature of God, with an absolute personality (Group 1). The concern is not with the sequence in which awareness of God's attributes comes (Group 2). No attempt is made to read off God's attributes from the life of Jesus as from a table (Group 3). It is realized that God is inconceivable in his nature, and that as we may conceive of it, he is always twofold (personality and aseity are our names for the two elements), so that the knowledge of his attributes (in which alone we may know his nature) is also twofold.

If the concept of revelation as act contains the paradoxical simultaneity on the one hand of the "Lord," of the second "I am" in Exod. 3 in which God conceals his name, of the face that no one can see [Exod. 33:20], of his secret, direct deity, and on the other hand of the first and revealing "I am" of Exod. 3 in which God makes himself known, objectifies himself, makes himself indirect, and turns to us, then obviously a description of God in his revelation, a doctrine of God's attributes, must take pains to retain this simultaneity, making it clear that as we know God we both conceive of him and also do not conceive of him. We conceive of him as he reveals himself and do not conceive of him as he conceals himself. We conceive of him in his objectivity and do not conceive of him in his subjectivity. We conceive of him in his Word, that is, in his being for us, and do not conceive of him in his being in himself. We conceive of him indirectly and do not conceive of him directly. We conceive of him in everything in which there is relation between him and us in virtue of his revelation, and we do not conceive of him outside this relation, in the outside that we also become aware of through the relation. We conceive of him in his personality — let us now say — and we do not conceive of him in his aseity. A doctrine of the attributes that is meant to represent the knowledge of God must take this duality into account — both the conceiving and the nonconceiving.

It must take both aspects into account. The concepts of what we do not comprehend are to be regarded as just as important and independent as those of what we do. If we were to favor the former over the latter, crowding out the positive attributes by the negative, we would be relapsing into mysticism. I need hardly say that this must not happen. Nor must the opposite. Suppressing the negative attributes by the positive, trying to describe only the supposedly conceivable God, expounding only the positive attributes (see Kaftan) — this Ritschlian one-sidedness is just as much a departure from the knowledge of revelation as its mystical counterpart. Indeed, because this is the great theological mistake of the present century, we have the historical though not the systematic right to reject it a little more vigorously than the other one. The classical, dialectical doctrine of the attributes avoids both forms of one-sidedness. It rightly, solemnly, and objectively lays equal emphasis on both sides: on what may be said about God himself insofar as the limits of conceivability, like the rays of the moon on the side that is eternally turned away from the earth, point us to his mystery; and on what may be said about God in relation insofar as that boundary encloses a territory of the conceivable.

For the simple reason that it conforms so closely to its object, we adopt the classical form of the doctrine. Naturally, we cannot understand and apply this division naively and mechanically. Whether we are speaking about the first group of qualities or the second, we are speaking about the divine nature that cannot be divided. The conceivable stands under the shadow of the inconceivable and the inconceivable in the light of the conceivable. We may not speak about the negative attributes as mystics do nor about the positive attributes as Ritschlians do. In both cases we are speaking about the *divine* perfections only if we speak with our gaze fixed on the one divine nature, and hence in practice on the attributes of the other group. God's eternity must elucidate what God's love is, and God's will must tell us what is meant by God's omnipresence. I have brought this out in the sentences at the end of the thesis, I keep it always before me, and I will come back to it expressly at the end. The division that is our present concern must also be taken with a pinch of salt, or, better, understood *en pneumati*.

After making this distinction in principle, I must not proceed without being open with you and indicating expressly at what points the total view stated in the thesis diverges from the fourth type or represents a special form within it. (a) I have made the antithesis between the classes of attributes stronger than usual and brought it into close and explicit connection with revelation. The older Lutherans, whom I have thus far followed in the main, mostly spoke directly in logical dialectical categories (absolute and relative, negative and positive, immanent and transcendent, etc.). I could do this with a good conscience (in spite of Althaus),[63] but I prefer to keep closer to the act on which everything turns here, and my

---

63. The reference is to the polemic against Barth in P. Althaus, "Theologie und Geschichte," *ZST* 1 (1923-24), esp. pp. 752-63.

emphasis thus falls on the self-revealing God on the one side, the hidden God on the other. Closest to my own distinctions are the attributes that are ascribed to God from eternity and in time.[64] (b) I have related the antithesis to that between personality and aseity. I told you in § 16 that the failure to work out the element of personality in the concept of the nature was a serious weakness of the older school. To avoid the ambiguity that led to the Straussian criticism of the Christian doctrine of God,[65] I regard it as imperative to bring out into the open the paradox in the concept of the nature, and to state pointedly that God becomes conceivable in his address to us, in the knowledge of the attributes of his personality. (c) I have reversed the sequence of the two classes, and this is perhaps the most important change. I suspect that in the usual arrangement — negative-positive qualities, God in himself-God in relation to the world — formal logic plays an understandable but impermissible role. Since we realize that what is at issue here is the dialectic of revelation and not just any dialectic, we put the older negative qualities, those of aseity, in the second place. We do not do this because we value them less, like Ritschl. On the contrary, we do so because this is in keeping with the actual course of our knowledge. We move on from the Yes to the No, from the first "I am" to the second, which is a corrective, a warning, but which is also full of promise. It seems that some of the older Reformed took the same path.[66] After what I have said, you can form your own judgment on whether I am falling into an illusion if I do not view my presentation as another innovation but as a reformulation of the older doctrine of the schools which time has made necessary.

Another distinctive point in the thesis is not primarily a fad of my own but something peculiar to the older Reformed dogmatics tradition which I am adopting. I mean that as a critical concept I have chosen in the third place that of communicability: communicable and incommunicable attributes instead of positive and negative. Already in the 16th century, in distinction from the colorful variety of formulas that we find among the Lutherans, Reformed theological schools were resolutely and harmoniously opting for this differentiation,[67] and it is insightful and important enough to be worth restoring, especially in view of the fact that

---

64. Cf. Schmid-Pöhlmann, p. 93; Schmid ET p. 123.
65. Cf. Strauss, *Christliche Glaubenslehre*, I, p. 541.
66. Cf. Braun, in Heppe-Bizer, p. 56; ET pp. 60-61; also Schweizer, p. 275.
67. Heppe-Bizer, pp. 56-58; ET pp. 60ff.

like many distinctive Reformed features it has vanished from theological discussion during the last 100 to 150 years, at least in Germany. There is here no objective difference in the division. The Reformed and Lutherans are putting the same attributes in the first and second classes. The difference lies in the characterizing of the standpoint from which the division is made. The Reformed were obviously trying to get beyond that purely logical, dialectical mode of distinction that we have found in the Lutherans and not regarded as wholly satisfactory. They were trying to get at the objective element in the dialectic of the positive and negative in God, and they found it in the concept of communicability, namely, the communicability of the attributes of God to the creature. Certain attributes are incommunicable. They belong to God alone and to no one and nothing outside him. Others are communicable in a limited sense. The first are naturally the attributes that are negative, absolute, immanent, and quiescent, as the Lutherans put it. The second are those that are positive, relative, transient, and operative.

Listen to some of the details. The definition of incommunicable attributes is comparatively simple. According to Cocceius they are those which separate God from creatures not only in *ousia* but also in name.[68] According to Maresius they are those whose opposite or absence marks the creature.[69] According to Bucanus there is no vestige of them in things created.[70] That God has put eternity in human hearts, as Oetinger translates the obscure verse Eccl. 3:11,[71] is something we cannot say according to Reformed orthodoxy, and if in a book of sermons you find a sermon that adopts Oetinger's translation, and that is closely associated with my name,[72] I bid you note that there the term "eternity" is with a good Reformed instinct interpreted as waiting for eternity.

In this definition of the incommunicable attributes you will perhaps sense that we have come up here, at a point where we would not expect to do so, against a question about which the Lutherans and Reformed felt it necessary to hold more than one conversation. You will perhaps have

---

68. Heppe, p. 54; Heppe-Bizer, p. 57; ET p. 61.

69. Schweizer, p. 277.

70. Schweizer, p. 275. Bucanus: *ut nullum eius vestigium in rebus creatis appareat.*

71. F. C. Oetinger, *Die Wahrheit des sensus communis . . . ,* Sämtliche Schriften (Stuttgart, 1861), Part 2, vol. 4, pp. 218-19.

72. Cf. E. Thurneysen's "Die neue Zeit" on Eccl. 3:11 in K. Barth and E. Thurneysen, *Komm Schöpfer Geist* (Munich, 1924), pp. 36ff.; ET "The New Time," in *Come Holy Spirit* (Grand Rapids, repr. 1978), pp. 36-45.

some inkling, too, why the Lutherans found this whole distinction offensive and unacceptable in spite of its advantages.[73] In your thoughts draw the line from here to christology, especially to the communication of the attributes and then to the doctrine of the Lord's Supper. According to the common teaching, created things include the human nature of Christ. But if in the creature there was no vestige but only the absence or even the opposite of these qualities, for example, of eternity and omnipresence, and if, as we have seen, a certain incommunicability is still to be found even in the communicable attributes, so that the communicability is only a matter of vestiges and analogies, then there can be no question of the creature sharing the attributes of God even in this case. The Reformed distinction was not formed with christology and eucharistic teaching in view, but confessional distinctiveness first became clear in these doctrines, and plainly it had to lead to serious differences in the whole doctrine of redemption. We can understand why the older Lutherans turned away with some horror from this distinction,[74] and you too, if your instinct is the Lutheran one that has to protest here, will have to consider whether and how far you are ready to adopt it.

In support I would simply ask whether we can dispense with the concept of incommunicability when we want to characterize the attributes of divine aseity or of the hidden God, and in this way establish the total concept of God. Is God truly *a se,* is his hiddenness serious and real, if we reject this sharpening of the concept of negative attributes? Can we give to the concept of revelation as divine act unequivocal clarity if we do not definitively safeguard this seriousness of the divine hiddenness, the second "I am"? If we say no here, as I think we must, then — as you will have noted before we came to this crossroads — the whole of dogmatics acquires a strictness in its emphasis on the contrast within the community of God and humanity that I realize is not for everyone. But there has to be this strictness somewhere in Protestant theology. For this reason, and not just because I happen to be Reformed, I must earnestly commend this incommunicability of the older Reformed to you for profound consideration.

The definition of the communicable attributes is more difficult. Are there any qualities that God shares with the creature? Does not the concept of aseity imply that all his qualities have to be incommunicable? In fact, if communicating means direct communicating, participation in

---

73. Cf. Heppe-Bizer, pp. 57-58; ET p. 62 (Van Mastricht).
74. Cf. Schweizer, pp. 276-77.

the divine substance, the removal of the antithesis of subjects, and hence a confusion of identity between Creator and creature, then there are no such attributes. Strictly speaking, writes Braun, there are no communicable attributes insofar as these are properties,[75] and Maresius says that nothing is common to God and creatures, so that no matter what the Lutherans say, all the properties are incommunicable to subjects of different species and nature.[76] But we cannot stop there. To do so would be a nondialectical relapse into mystical agnosticism. On this view, with what right could we venture to form human concepts of God's positive and negative attributes? What is the point of stressing the incommunicability so strongly if not to clarify unambiguously the true fellowship between God and the creature? Thus we must go on at once to state that there are other qualities of God of which we may see obscure vestiges,[77] analogies, and similar effects[78] in the creature,[79] for example, God's life, wisdom, will, power, and goodness. This analogy, which is purely formal but not on that account any the less significant, forms the point at which God and the creature meet, the means by which they reach agreement, the basis of their dealings with one another.

In order to understand this, let us think about what we said in §
15 about the problem of the natural knowledge of God. Remarkably, it is historically unmistakable that the true interest of the authors of the older Reformed doctrine is not in the first and more striking negative side but in the second and positive side, in the relation of certain creaturely attributes to God as we know and assert it by analogy. Polanus formulates it as follows: There is no perfection of creaturely things that does not have its most perfect idea or reason in God.[80] He worked out the parallelism between God and the creature in this way: What God is and has essentially, the creature is and has accidentally, God by nature and the creature by participation, God infinitely and the creature finitely, God perfectly and the creature imperfectly, God simply and the creature in distinction, God as original and the creature as copy, God primarily and the creature secondarily, God properly and the creature analogically, God unchangeably and the creature changeably.[81] This provides a basis in principle for us to

---

75. Heppe, p. 53; Heppe-Bizer, p. 56; ET p. 61.
76. Schweizer, pp. 276-77.
77. Ibid., p. 276.
78. Heppe-Bizer, p. 57; ET p. 61.
79. Marginal note: "Thom. I, 4, 3." (*STh* I, q. 4, a. 3 ad 3.)
80. Heppe, p. 43; Heppe-Bizer, pp. 46-47; ET pp. 49-50.
81. Heppe, p. 54; Heppe-Bizer, p. 57; ET pp. 61-62.

speak about positive predicates in God and negative predicates as their limit. We have a share in God and we also do not.

More can obviously be said about this. The value and significance of the second and positive part of the Reformed doctrine lies in demonstrating it. Regarding the way of doing this (Polanus), we have to say, however, that it is Platonism, for which we Reformed have always had a liking and aptitude. If we are to grasp the whole of the teaching we will have to do it from this angle. There is little fault to find with the negative side, but precisely here, on the positive side, we have to object that it impermissibly fills out a Christian concept that is related to revelation, as that of communicability was originally meant to be, with contents that are unmistakably philosophical and rationalistic, perhaps even trying to support it with the help of these.

In reply it might be asked whether it does not perhaps lie in the nature of the case that precisely here, where we have to clarify in principle the relation of God to that which is not God, theological and philosophical interests come together, and for a moment these neighbors exchange friendly greetings through the window, being able in good faith to speak at this point in each other's language. We have to consider whether we can forbid the use of philosophical terms and thought processes precisely at this point. Yet the problem remains.

The same suspicion that we have to raise against the Lutherans applies to the Reformed as well. It is still open to doubt whether the dialectic here is that of revelation or perhaps some other dialectic. We must try to find categories that have more content and are closer to the subject than those that we saw in the Lutherans, and the problem of communicability which is central here gives us a good push in this direction, helping to provide a much desired sharpening and clarifying of the question. Nevertheless, we can as little adopt the Reformed formula as we can the various Lutheran formulas. From a historical standpoint, then, I must reinterpret and develop the tradition. To understand the statement in the thesis you must not isolate the older Reformed formulas but set them in the context of what stands alongside them, viewing them as an amplification.

A final word of introduction is necessary in order to fit in a group of concepts that are usually mentioned with respect at this point in medieval and older Protestant theology but with less respect in most modern theology. I refer to what is called the threefold way of forming concepts in the knowledge of God: the way of causality, the way of eminence, and the way of negation.[82] A first point is that we must not expect anything materially new here, anything that will take us beyond the point reached with the main decisions that lie behind us. As regards the general possibility of the knowledge of God and the principle of dividing the attributes our position is related to this early methodology. Hence we can only show how we are to judge it, or interpret it, or reinterpret it in the light of our conclusions. We say, then, that what we have here is a method of forming concepts, not a proof of God nor a substitute for revelation. Even the worst Scholastics did not really think that we can climb up to God by the way of eminence or negation apart from revelation. Presupposing that there is real knowledge of God,[83] they believe that it comes about by the way of negation, etc. Many bad things that have been said about the threefold way would have been left unsaid had the methodological nature of the matter been kept clearly in view. Let us stipulate, then, that there is no human way to a knowledge of God in himself, that God himself and God alone is here the only way and goal. We may then calmly admit and even maintain that there are, and have to be, ways of conceiving of God in the inadequate form of human thoughts and words. To deny this would again be a relapse into mysticism. As God reveals himself he conceals himself and becomes an object, we have said, and yet he remains the subject even in the concealment. "I am who I am" [Exod. 3:14].

Personality and aseity: To this duality, two ways of forming concepts have to correspond. It is clearly by the way of eminence that we form concepts of God's personality, of the God who turns to us. God enters our conceptuality. Thus we may and must apply our conceptuality to him. Not directly, not in such a way as to make a god in our own image, but by the way of eminence as we allow our concept of personality to be determined, permeated, and transcended by the thought that God is the Lord, by the thought of the divine aseity. I need not waste words on the danger that is present here. But it is unjust of Wichelhaus to say scathingly that similarly Phidias shaped Jupiter by the way of eminence, giving him majesty, a commanding presence, greatness, and beauty to a supreme degree.[84] This is an ungodly possibility that lurks on the way of eminence, in a doctrine of the positive attributes. Naturally, Feuerbach is again

---

82. Cf. Schmid-Pöhlmann, pp. 89, 92-93; Schmid ET pp. 122ff.; Schweizer, pp. 273ff.; Hase, p. 138. Stephan, *Glaubenslehre*, p. 76, and Rade, *Glaubenslehre*, pp. 76-77, are in opposition.

83. Barth originally wrote "that knowledge of God is possible" but corrected this in the margin.

84. Wichelhaus, *Die Lehre der heiligen Schrift*, p. 332.

peeping through the window here. It is good for us to be constantly aware of the possibility of this view of the matter. Yet it is not the only possible one. Ideally, the way of eminence is simply the other side of the Reformed doctrine of the communicable attributes. We recognize that we participate in God, and according to the measure of this participation we try to conceive of God, remembering that we have to do with *God.* If this participation is strictly understood on the basis that God addresses us, that in every aspect of our humanity he summons us to respond, and that we for our part have to give an account of this, then the way of eminence is right and necessary.

Nevertheless, to form concepts one-sidedly in this positive direction is impossible. We do not tell the whole story when we say that we conceive of God. We must also grasp and state the point that we do not conceive of him. This leads us to the way of negation, to concepts of the aseity of God, of the hidden God, that is, the God who is hidden from us. Here, too, we apply *our* conceptuality to God, but we now begin where we previously stopped off, or at the point to which we were moving, with "the Lord," the one who is not communicated or limited or conditioned or dependent—not any of the things that we denoted with our positive concepts! Here, then, is a most profound and basic intellectual repentance, a renunciation of all that we think we can know and say, a minus before the bracket with the many pluses. It is in fact all the same whether we make things infinitely bigger or infinitely smaller, whether we posit or negate. The way of negation can be just as empty as the way of eminence.

Here again Feuerbach can make merry with us. But again it does not have to be so. There is the other possibility that the great and solemn No of the eternity of God which we are here thinking and pronouncing can be the confession that we have fully heard the Yes and therefore know that we are dust and ashes, that we do not stand before the empty space of our own nothingness but in awestruck adoration before the great truth of the incommunicability of God, that we truly recognize it in the fact that we do not at all participate, and that we can thus enjoy to the full this great negative gift of the equally serious and joyful reality of God. We can then talk legitimately about eternity. So much regarding these two ways, which are essentially identical with what Dionysius the Areopagite called *kataphatic* and *apophatic* theology.[85]

---

85. Cf. F. Loofs, *Leitfaden zum Studium der Dogmengeschichte,* 4th ed. (Halle, 1906), p. 320.

As regards the third way, the way of causality, I follow Schleiermacher and Alexander Schweizer[86] in not regarding this as a method coordinated with the other two but as the epitome of the two. According to the ancient formula, it simply means that the effect bears witness to the cause and its perfection,[87] but starting with the same effect we can describe this perfection of the cause either positively or negatively. Schleiermacher found in the way of causality nothing other than the actual feeling of absolute dependence.[88] We will not hide the fact that we do not like the terms "cause" and "effect" in this connection. We are dealing with God's hidden nature and the objectivity of his revelation. Staying close to revelation, we are seeking — this is the process — to conceive of God's nature, by the way of eminence on the right hand and that of negation on the left, in a way that corresponds to this nature. Perhaps it would be advisable to drop the expression "way of causality," and in paradoxical antithesis to the other two rename it the "way of revelation." For here where the two ways both begin and must also end, we have ratiocinated reason.[89]

IV. Attributes of Personality

Let us turn now to the attributes of personality, of the God who reveals himself, the positive or communicable attributes.[90] We know God, he speaks to us, he names his inconceivable name, as he is the *living* God. Only knowledge of the living God is knowledge of *God*. Only the voice of the living God is *God's* voice. Only worship of the living God is worship of *God*. We constantly read about the living God in the OT and NT. They contrast him with the gods and idols that have no life (Jer. 10:14; Acts 14:15). Life according to Thomas Aquinas is present where there is independent movement or activity.[91] Obviously following this definition, the Protestant orthodox defined God's life as the actuosity of the divine essence.[92] God's life is his knowing, willing, and loving as an act, indeed,

---

86. *CF,* I, § 50.3; Schweizer, pp. 274-75.
87. Schmid-Pöhlmann, p. 93; Schmid ET p. 123.
88. *CF,* I, p. 197.
89. See above, nn. 10, 11.
90. Marginal note: "Thom. I, 18." (*STh* I, q. 18: De vita Dei.)
91. *STh* I, q. 18, a. 1 i.c.
92. Van Til, in Heppe, p. 58; Heppe-Bizer, p. 62; ET p. 69.

as a pure act,[93] that is, one that is independent, not conditioned from outside but from inside by the nature of the one who acts. This definition is important, and as thus defined this attribute is primary and basic. God is the one — and all the other attributes hang on this as on a nail — whom we know only as we know his independent and unconditioned act which is possible and actual only through himself; only as we know him as the living God. Whatever may be outside this; whatever may be known apart or in abstraction from the living quality of his knowing and willing and loving, may well be called God and decked out with all the divine attributes, but it is only a dead idol, one of the nonentities[94] before which the world bows the knee, not knowing what revelation is. But once again, where the living God speaks and is heard, there *eo ipso* is the true God. In antithesis to the life of God we must think not only of the dead but also of what is not moved or independently moved in nature, of all static truth even in the life of the spirit. The nature and reality of God are not to be found on this level. Proper to him are the freedom, incomprehensibility, mobility, and inexhaustibility that belong to life in distinction from all such. If God is ever to be understood by us, it will have to be as we cast off all analogies from that level of viewing and conceiving and know him as the living God.

But now a word of caution and discretion. Like all the statements that we must now make, the statement that God is life is irreversible. It is formed by the way of eminence, and that means that the added predicate simply develops the subject a little and then it must be set aside and burst through as no more than an analogy for all its importance and the necessity of its contribution. We have to have in mind a different life from that known to us if we really have God in mind. Our result has thus to be set in the right light by the way of negation. You recall the statement in the thesis to the effect that the communicable attributes have their power precisely by participation in the mystery of the incommunicable attributes. We must now look at this.

God speaks to us and the first and decisive concept that we form and have to form of this one who meets us — and we take the material for it from a field where we ourselves are along with all other creatures — is the concept of life. But the one who meets us is the Lord. He is *a se.*

---

93. See Heppe, p. 40; Heppe-Bizer, p. 43; ET p. 53.
94. Cf. Lev. 19:4; 26:1; 1 Chr. 16:26; Ps. 96:5; 97:7; Jer. 2:8, 18, 20; 19:1, 3; 31:7; Hab. 2:18.

Thus the mark of independence, of purity of act in the concept of life, has to be taken in all strictness if this concept is correctly to describe God. The life of God cannot consist of participation in the reality of life in general. It must itself be the reality of the life in which all that lives apart from God merely participates. Life cannot for a moment be something that we abstract away from the living God. He must himself *be* life. This life must be truly unconditioned. It must not be conditioned by any cause, not even by the existence of the living God in time. It must have no beginning or end in time. It must not be tied to the temporal sequence or to what we perceive as change, movement, or activity in this sequence. In a word, it has to be the principle, the origin, the creator of life, eternal life, true life in contrast to all else that we call life, to what has simply come into being, no, to what has been created, to what is dependent upon and conditioned and limited by this life, to what receives its life from it. The act of God with which we have to do in his Word to us has to be the act of all acts. The distinction between the life of God and what we know as life is so much a matter of principle that Polanus can rightly say that strictly God alone can be said to live.[95] In no way does God share in our life, but we share totally in his. If this were not so, we would not be thinking of the life of him who is the Lord and *a se*. This living person who addresses us is alive in this way. There can be no confusing of his life with the life of nature or life in nature or in us, even in its highest form. All *this* life may and must show us — as we say in opposition to mystical agnosticism — in what direction to look in order to know God. But if and as we do know God, there breaks upon our vision his concealing incommunicable nature, his eternity, omnipresence, and immutability, forcing us to look not only *far* beyond this life but *totally* beyond it. The concept of life is burst through, I said. I might be more positive and say that it must burst open as a shell does to yield its sweet fruit. We must begin with it.

The first and powerful word to speak about God is that he is the living God. But we cannot think through this word to the end. It is a human word. It is inadequate. It is a mere attempt to grasp. It slides off finally into God's incomprehensibility. We have no way of viewing the life of which we are to think here. We have no concept for it. We know only of acts, supremely and finally of religious acts, but not of the act of all acts, the purest act. The God who reveals himself is the hidden God. Is it

---

95. Heppe, p. 44; Heppe-Bizer, p. 48; ET p. 53.

thus futile to try to comprehend him as the living God? No, precisely as we accept our inability, we do not comprehend him but we do know him as the living God. We have to realize that thus and precisely thus he is the living God in distinction from all gods and deities. This act is his, the act of his knowing and willing in which he reveals himself to us. If we know this, if we grasp that the life act is a transitory parable but that this transitory parable is also the life of which we have to speak here, then it may be that what we say will be full of the knowledge of God.

We now take a further step. God's address to us means directly the knowledge that God is almighty.[96] Address here means claiming, commandeering, binding to faith and obedience. When addressed by God we know that in our totality we are no longer our own. The act of the living God is *eo ipso* an act of lordship. The power that meets us is (first spatially) boundless and universal; it is omnipotence. Like the life of God this is a quality of God's person, of the God who reveals himself. Revelation that is not *eo ipso* a revelation of power, and indeed of omnipotence, is not revelation. Rightly Kaftan calls this God's attribute par excellence.[97] It is no accident that the earliest Christian creeds were content to name this one attribute: "I believe in God the Father Almighty."[98] This is an unavoidable concept when the "I am" makes itself heard, when this act takes place. The point of this moment is that we bow down before the living God: "'I am God Almighty, walk before me and be blameless. . . .' Then Abraham fell on his face" (Gen. 17:1-3). This bowing down, no, this *proskynēsis*, is a confession of God's omnipotence. This quality, too, is communicable, certainly not as omnipotence, for all God's attributes have an incommunicable point, but as power in general.

Here, too, we first take the way of eminence. From our own existence in the world we know and think we know what power is. It is to dispose of various possibilities, to be able to do what we will, not to be restricted by conditions outside our own will. If God is the living God, pure act, then he is also powerful. "With God nothing will be impossible" (Luke 1:37; Matt. 19:26). He can do what he wills, and he does it. We can hardly avoid this formula as an echo of the voice of the divine Word. Any restriction or reservation along these lines would mean that what we

---

96. Marginal note: "Thom. I, 25; Bartm. I, 161." (*STh* I, q. 25: De divina potentia; Bartmann, I, § 39, p. 161.)

97. Kaftan, p. 193.

98. DS, 30; cf. 10-29.

say is no longer an echo of this voice but in some way a refusal of faith and obedience. An Abraham can only trust that nothing is in fact impossible for the one who addresses him.

But now we take a sharp turn. If we compare the statements of the older dogmaticians about this matter with those of the moderns since Schleiermacher, we are struck at once how careful the former are to avoid doing anything apart from elucidating the statement that all things are possible for God and protecting it from misunderstanding, whereas the latter under the leadership of Schleiermacher proceed to set alongside this statement another one to the effect that because all things are possible for God all things are willed by him, and then a third to the effect that the will of God is perfectly realized in these real things. In Schleiermacher's *Christian Faith,* § 54 consists of a series of bold equations: possibility with reality, ability with volition with action, freedom with necessity, etc.[99] In Lipsius God's omnipotence is the same as his omnicausality,[100] and this again is the same as the natural order, the moral order of the world, and the order of salvation. Haering writes that what is real is so because God wills it.[101] And what God wills is all real. Seeberg says that God in pure actuality wills all that is and will be.[102] Stephan permits himself to blame older writers because their piety was not accustomed to experiencing God in reality. It was the piety of monks, academicians, or fantasizers who could not comprehend that there is nothing in the world that escapes the fulness of divine power.[103]

Although these and similar statements might appeal to Zwingli's *On Providence,*[104] in my view they are not good because they overlook the fact that the statement "God is power," like the statement "God is life," is not reversible; that here too the predicate carries only a little way the burden of this subject; that we have to recognize its analogical or figurative character; that we cannot endow it with purely logical or material consistency; that we must not press it to the point of absurdity. God is the Lord, God is *a se.* If the first truth is to have any force, and not to be merely a bit of formal logic, then we must take into account this second

---

99. *CF,* I, § 54.2-4.
100. Lipsius, *Lehrbuch der evangelisch-protestantischen Dogmatik,* pp. 235-36.
101. Haering, p. 327.
102. *Christliche Dogmatik,* I, p. 406.
103. Stephan, *Glaubenslehre,* pp. 83-84.
104. H. Zwingli, *Sermonis de providentia anamnema* (1530), Opera, ed. Schuler-Schulthess, IV (1844), pp. 79-144.

truth that intersects it. God is the Lord. He is not the prisoner of an intrinsically correct concept of his personality.

At this point, it seems to me that the aseity of the divine glory must come into play as a necessary corrective. God wills himself. He wills all else in this and for this. What he wills in this way, and only in this way, he can also do and also does. This is the confession of his omnipotence when it is made *in actu* and before the living God. This almighty person who addresses us here is not almighty in a random way but to this end. We must not abstract away from the fact that we have this almighty God in view when we talk about God's power. In this confession, if it is to mean anything, we must never forget for a moment that we are dealing with the God who has this goal. Power is in every sense a right concept for God, but we have to realize that it is a very different power from any known to us — a power that serves his glory. We forget that if we begin to manipulate the concept of reality, meaning by it known reality, actual occurrence in the world; if we make omnipotence into omnicausality. The latter concept belongs to eschatology, to the great future anticipation of the consummation to which we have not yet come. That God is all in all [cf. 1 Cor. 15:28] here and now is something that we cannot possibly say in the act of knowing God. The faith and obedience that accept God's Word say that he will be, and they are content to have dealings with the God for whom all things are possible. They must not be censured if they also see God's power at work in such and such things here and now — the act of knowing God is always a specific Yes to God's will as it is known in a specific situation. But we must flatly reject any but an eschatological omnicausality of God, since this is an intolerable, surreptitious term in face of our great difficulty in wrestling with reality to the very last. The logic of not merely recognizing God's power over all things but positing it unseen in every reality of power is bought only at the price of material incompatibility with the facts. The concept of omnipotence ascribes all power to God but does not ascribe divine reality to all power. We have here two different things. The former means knowledge of God, the latter an apotheosis of nature, history, destiny, and humanity. Zwingli, Schleiermacher, and the moderns crossed the boundary here, and this is impermissible. We must remember this when we come back to these questions in the doctrine of providence.

The other thesis that God's power is fully displayed and exhausted in reality, that is, in the orders known to us, so that the real is the measure of what is possible for God, is also wrong. We can say this only if we abstractly understand God's power as a general truth that we have reached by way of religion. If we then compare this truth with other general truths reached in other ways, and if we then run up against the probability that there is nothing new under the sun [cf. Eccl. 1:9], we shall naturally be able to venture the statement that God wills and can do more than we actually see him doing in the world. If we refrain from this abstraction; if in forming our concepts we stick to the knowledge of God *in actu;* if we remember that the power at issue here is the power of the Lord, then we shall not work things out as smoothly as, for example, Schleiermacher does in § 54. If God establishes fellowship between himself and us, if he speaks to us through his Word, then he certainly tells us that he is the hidden power in all reality and its orders, but he does so by opening up for us in principle the prospect of a new, different, transfigured reality. He does not simply confirm the world that is. He has not exhausted himself as Creator.[105] He relates the world that is to a coming world that he is creating anew. The power that he reveals to us is at the same time the promise of a very different power on which our concept of power is necessarily broken and which is not enclosed in any natural or moral law. In this regard, too, a recollection of God's aseity must keep the concept of omnipotence alive and fluid as it were, relating it to the mystery of God and restoring to it the dynamic which it has, for example, in Paul, but which is simply taken from it when it is left up in the air as an all too logical general truth, when it says everything and nothing as an unrestrictedly accepted omnicausality in all reality.

We will avoid, then, both modern extensions of the doctrine of God's power and be content to stress and underline with our predecessors the fact that we must understand God's *power* as *God's.* All things are possible for him. In God we have to do with him in face of whom no reality is reality except on the basis of the possibility that resides in him. Things are real in the strict sense only insofar as they actualize divine possibility. But this actualization, God's omnicausality, the absolute identity of what is with what he wills, is the end or consummation of all things. Hence we cannot simply read off the divine possibility of all things, God's power over them, from the reality that we perceive, or even from its regularity. What is possible for God might not be possible for us, and vice versa. Fundamentally we have to say with Heidegger that what is possible for God is not to be sought outside God himself. He himself is the basis

---

105. Martensen, *Christliche Dogmatik,* p. 89.

and root of all possibility. Outside him there is no life, possibility, or power.[106] The older dogmaticians maintained this at both the points where moderns have incautiously pushed ahead. They remembered that God's will has a specific content, and its purpose is the divine glory. God's power must not be distinguished from this purposeful will or regarded as neutral. In this sense it is not absolute power. Certain possibilities that we see realized, or think might be realized, are not possibilities for God, and therefore they are not possibilities at all.[107]

There are, then, things that are not possible for God. Does this imply a restriction of his power? Yes if we view the term power abstractly, but no if we remember that the glory of his power consists precisely of his not being able to do certain things. This is not a defect but the fulness and perfection of his power. We say that God cannot do certain things, but he cannot do them omnipotently. That is, he cannot do what is repugnant to his own nature. If he could, this would be impotence, weakness, defect. We could not predicate such things without destroying the subject. We refer to things like lying, sinning, dying, ceasing to be God, unmaking what is made, creating a creature as perfect as himself so that it is no longer a creature but itself God.[108] God cannot deny himself [2 Tim. 2:13] (Martensen).[109] This is the glory of his power. In the case of a conflict between the subject and the predicate, between God and power, it is the predicate power that fundamentally has to yield, or rather, we have to see the inadequacy of all our views and concepts of power. It is not a general concept of unlimited power, but God himself who decides what lies in his power, what ought to be possible. It is he also, and not a general concept of the limits of the possible, who decides what can be possible for him. He is the basis and root of all possibility in the sense also that no limit of the possible that is set for us can limit him. Every limit, rule, or law in terms of which we have to think of what is possible or impossible is grounded in him, not vice versa. What is true is true, what is good is good, two and two are four, because this is God's will, by divine decree and not *ipsa re*.[110] There is no self-grounded necessity that

---

106. Heppe, p. 77; Heppe-Bizer, p. 83; ET pp. 100-101.

107. Heppe-Bizer, pp. 83-84; ET p. 101 (Heidegger).

108. Heppe-Bizer, pp. 84-85; ET pp. 101-2 (Heidegger). Marginal note: "Thom. I, 25, 3." (*STh* I, q. 25, a. 3 i.c.)

109. Martensen, *Christliche Dogmatik*, pp. 88-89.

110. F. Burmann, *Synopsis theologicae*, I, 2nd ed. (Geneva, 1678), p. 145; cf. Heppe-Bizer, p. 84; ET pp. 100-101 (Heidegger).

does not have its *prius* in God, no reality that is contingent for God, no nature of rational creatures that is there before God's decree to create then, as Leibniz thought.[111] God is the free Lord of all reality and all truth. He alone is their possibility and basis. Does this mean caprice, uncertainty, fatalism? Yes, we may say again if we abstractly think of this free power of God over all things as just any power, the *X* of a capriciously posited possibility, as in William of Occam at the end of the Middle Ages, or Calvin, or Luther in his *Bondage of the Will,* but no, if even in face of existing rules and laws we remember by whose power they are in force so far as the eye extends, and conversely if we remember finally that it is for his own glory that God has assigned us our limits. In this glory, however, God himself is above the limits. Hence we have to differentiate between the ordered power that is known to us and his absolute power, his possibilities that are not known to us.[112] We have thus to accept in principle the possibility of miracles. In this regard we neither can nor should regard God as his own prisoner. As we cannot assign his power to him, saying what *must* be possible for him, so we cannot say what *might* be possible for him. If with Abraham we fall on our faces before him [cf. Gen. 17:3], we will do neither of these things, and it is only in this attitude that we can and should speak of his power. As in the case of life, we can only begin here, and we have to do so, but we can never come to an end. God meets us in person in his Word. We try to comprehend him. We stammer: "Thou art mighty." But woe to us, it is the Lord. The Lord's power is not only greater than all powers; it transcends them. We can only stammer. But precisely when we take this path, we have not spoken in vain.

Let us now try to advance further. God's power as it met us in his Word and cast us down is not mechanical power. It is also not a natural force. We made sure on both counts when we spoke of God as the living God. God is Spirit [John 4:24]. But for this very reason we must just as forcefully oppose any attempt to generalize or neutralize the concept of divine power. God's power is that of his knowing and willing. Mentioning these qualities, or groups of qualities, we definitively establish the concept of personality. God's Word is an expression of his thought or purpose. Here if anywhere we must be clear that in God we are not dealing with

---

111. Cf. G. W. Leibniz, *Théodicée,* II, 181, quoted in Strauss, *Christliche Glaubenslehre,* I, p. 589 n. 25.

112. Cf. Heppe-Bizer, p. 85; ET p. 103 (van Mastricht); also Schmid-Pöhlmann, p. 96; ET pp. 119-20 (Quenstedt).

an It but with a He. To the supreme clarity with which God meets us as a person there corresponds, of course, the supreme incomprehensibility that surrounds this person as the Lord.

Let us stipulate the most important reason for the great "But" that has to be uttered here. If at this center we wanted to speak in a way that is adequate to the concept of divine personality or appropriate to the object, we would not now be able to distinguish between God's knowing and his willing, but would have to describe both as a single personal act. This is naturally true of all the divine attributes, but it is worth pointing out how much it applies here, and precisely here. If God is the Lord, then obviously his knowing can have no object that has its possibility anywhere but in his willing, and conversely he can will nothing but what is already actual in his knowing. There can be between his knowing and willing only a harmony that is not to be distinguished from identity. Any distinction between them would mean a defect in one or the other. But this type of knowing and willing is far above anything that we can perceive or comprehend. Our knowing relates only to objects that are produced elsewhere, and our willing relates only to objects that we do not yet know as real. Knowing and willing are differentiated in us. We have no conception of the knowing and willing of God the Lord, and we have no word for this unique personal actuality of his. I point this out expressly because we are told that God's hiddenness ceases when we focus on Jesus Christ and on these very personal features of God.[113] As though the riddle or paradox of the "I am — the Lord" were not all the greater precisely where on any view, and not just mine, we deal especially with the revealed God. Again, we will not let ourselves be frightened into mysticism. We will go on at once, first to describe and delineate God's knowing, then as though it were a second thing, his willing, thinking them out as far as we are able. But from the very first we will remember the reservation under which alone we can do this, and we will not be surprised if this reservation at once shows itself to be the true goal of what we are doing.

We will begin with God's knowing.[114] As God addresses us, so incomparably alive and so shatteringly mighty that we have to believe and obey, we are understood and perceived and comprehended and known.

---

113. Cf. W. Elert, *Lehre der Luthertums,* p. 19; P. Althaus, "Theologie und Geschichte," *ZST* 1 (1923-24) 771.

114. Marginal note: "Thom. I, 14; Bartm. I, 142." (*STh* I, 14: De scientia Dei; Bartmann, I, §§ 33-35, pp. 142-53.)

In revelation God is not merely manifest to us; we are manifest to God. The central significance of God's knowing is not just an intellectualistic fad of the Scholastics. As God knows us, we acquire a share in his knowledge of himself, as we said in § 15.[115] In his knowing, then, we see also his holy, righteous, and merciful will. Our fellowship with God rests on the fact that he regards us, remembers us, knows what we are as his handiwork [Ps. 103:14]. To stand in this fellowship means *eo ipso* and fundamentally to know that there is no corner in us that this partner does not know, that he knows us infinitely better than we know ourselves. Hence we are his, his prisoners, for grace or perdition, for life or death. Those whom God knows can no longer escape him. You know how God is symbolically portrayed in older depictions: a triangle representing the Trinity, and in the middle of it an eye.[116] This is God, God in his revelation. God does not just have one eye; he is all eye.[117] He knows. For the strongest biblical statement of this fact, read Ps. 139: "O Lord, thou hast searched me and known me! I sit down or rise up, thou knowest it; thou understandest my thoughts from afar. I go or lie down, thou art about me and seest all my ways. Even before a word is on my tongue, lo, O Lord, thou knowest all about it. On all sides thou doest beset me, and layest thy hand upon me" [vv. 1-5].

The human response to this divine fact is the confession of God's omniscience. Listen to the way in which the Utrecht theologian Burmann describes what God is and does as the omniscient God. It is by a single, simple, constant, present act that God knows all things and observes and measures them as by one glance and regard, always as it were keeping to the same steadfast gaze. For there is one simple idea in God—the idea of himself, and to that extent the essence of God in which he sees and contemplates all things.[118] Thus God knows himself, and in himself he knows all things at a single glance. Quenstedt[119] expands this as follows: All the things that were and are and will be or can be, and then Heidegger: By genesis and not by analysis all things have their *prius* in his mind and not in themselves. God's knowledge is indeed the original of all things,

---

115. See above, pp. 328ff.

116. Known only from the 18th century; cf. G. Stuhlfauth, "Auge Gottes," *Reallexikon zur deutschen Kunstgeschichte*, I (Stuttgart, 1937), pp. 1243-48.

117. Martensen, *Christliche Dogmatik*, p. 87.

118. Burmann, *Synopsis theologicae*, I, p. 113.

119. By mistake the MS has König. Cf. Schmid, p. 81; Schmid-Pöhlmann, p. 90; Schmid ET p. 119.

the things themselves being simply its reflection or likeness.[120] We detect especially in the Reformed dogmaticians that we have mentioned the magnetic pull or pressure of the insight that God's knowledge is not different from his power, from that basis and root of all possibility,[121] nor from his will by which all reality is. Neither Lutherans nor Reformed ever thought of abandoning the truth that God's knowing is a special attribute alongside his willing. The fact that God knows us and all things, how we were, are, and will be, must never have the significance of a determination or fate, even though it cannot be separated from God's power over all things.

To avoid this conclusion the dogmaticians made a distinction between natural knowledge, the simple power of knowing by which God knows the world of the possible apart from what he wills as real, and free knowledge, the knowledge of vision by which as he who wills God also knows what has become real.[122] The first concept obviously leaves room for a real knowing of real objects, while the second leads us back to a knowing that can be differentiated only formally from willing. This whole effort, like that of the Jesuit Molina and the Lutheran school that followed him for a time, to set up a middle knowledge, a divine knowing of what is conditionally possible, a conditioned future[123] — all such efforts, and the Reformed expressly viewed them only as such,[124] indicate that there is a stone on the path at this point. What God knows he also wills, and this type of knowing is inconceivable for us. Knowledge that is also power — this is what we may say, and have to say, if we are to do justice to the facts posited in revelation. But we can neither conceive of this nor think it. Nevertheless, it makes sense to say it, for even if in doing so we come up against facts on which our concepts break, as they are broken they still tell us things about the facts that break them.[125] Notice in conclusion that the force of this attribute is to be sought precisely at the point where it

---

120. Heppe, p. 58; Heppe-Bizer, p. 63; ET p. 70. Marginal note: "Aug. in Thom. 14, 8." (*STh* I, q. 14, a. 8 s.c.)

121. Heppe-Bizer, p. 83; ET pp. 100-101.

122. Cf. Heppe-Bizer, pp. 48-49; ET pp. 73-74; Schmid-Pöhlmann, p. 94; Schmid ET pp. 126-27.

123. Cf. Heppe-Bizer, pp. 67-70; ET pp. 77ff. Cf. Schmid-Pöhlmann, p. 94; Schmid ET pp. 126-27; Hase, p. 143.

124. Cf. Heppe-Bizer, p. 66; ET pp. 76-77.

125. Marginal note: "Does God know evil? Yes, as such. Th. 10, 14, 16." (*STh* I, q. 14, a. 10 i.c.; a. 16 i.c.)

seems to vanish into incomprehensibility. The fact that the knowing at issue here is willing, active, creative knowing, as indicated by the ambiguous Hebrew term, is the very thing that makes it divine knowing. In the very breaking of our ideas and concepts here we can take comfort that we have not come up against an inert stone but against the reality of the living God.

The further point that God's knowing is wise can serve as a transition to the attributes of his willing. The knowledge with which God addresses us and knows us is one that contemplates perfectly and also plans perfectly. The psalmist in Ps. 139 says not only: "Search me, O God, and know my heart" [v. 23] but also — and really this comes first: "See if there be any wicked way in me, and lead me in the way everlasting!" [v. 24]. This guiding element in God's thinking that purposefully leads from the wicked to the good is his wisdom. Heidegger defines it as follows: It is the quality in God by which he knows how far the things created by him can illumine his glory, so that he can will them and call them into being in agreement with his nature, his perfection, and his glory.[126] Very rightly, then, one can agree with Lipsius that God's wisdom as a determination of his will means that God knows what he wills,[127] that is, why he wills it. All that has its possibility in him stands under the determination of being a means for his purpose, for his glory. This is God's wisdom.

Of course — and this brings us at once to the caveat under which we make mention of this attribute too — the goal toward which God directs all things lies in himself, so that there also lies in him the standard by which one may state how far all things stand under this direction and are a means or a way to this goal. No concept of the purpose of the world or of our own destiny can coincide with this purpose of God, and therefore no teleology that we discern in the world or our own lives can coincide with the divine wisdom or teleology. On the contrary, the wisdom of God known to us in his Word always seems at first to be foolishness to our wisdom with its very different standards (1 Cor. 1:18-19; 2:14). The reality that we confront conceals rather than reveals the divine possibility in all things in virtue of which they are instruments of his glory. As so often in Schleiermacher, it is the anticipation of an eschatological insight, or the changing of an indirect into a direct insight, when he describes the world as an absolute revelation of the supreme being or a perfectly harmonious

126. Heppe, p. 46; Heppe-Bizer, pp. 49-50; ET p. 76.
127. Lipsius, *Lehrbuch der evangelisch-protestantischen Dogmatik*, p. 252.

work of art in which everything is both means and end.[128] This is not how it is with the world. This is how it will be in the consummation, in the *futurum resurrectionis* (future of resurrection)[129] when all things are made new [cf. Rev. 21:5]. The wisdom of God is a wisdom concealed in reality. "Who has known the mind of the Lord?" (Rom. 11:34). We do not see how far all things serve his glory, how far all things, the world and we ourselves, either share or will share in his glory as a means to this end. To know the wisdom of God is to know him as the all-wise, to give glory to the *monos sophos* (Rom. 16:27; 1 Tim. 1:17). This is not the indestructible optimism of the Christian view of the world.[130] It is to confess with Job (42:3) in regard to both means and end: "I have uttered what I did not understand, things which are too high for me, and which I did not know." Knowledge of the wisdom of God comes with the overthrow of the rebellion of our own wisdom and in reverent adoration of God's wisdom, of his goal and way in all things. God reveals himself as the answer to every question, but the answer is: Because he is God. Consideration of this attribute ends here.

Let us now turn to God's will,[131] and first of all very generally. At this point we meet the life of the living God as the life of Spirit in distinction from all natural life. At this point we find the power of the Almighty as the power of Spirit in distinction from all natural power. At this point we come up against the creativity of the divine intelligence, the wisdom that addresses us in his Word, in the fact that a will meets us here, commanding and determining as only a spiritual will can do in distinction from a destiny that stands ineluctably before us, inexorably sweeping us along with it. God reveals himself because he wills something from us and with us, and this something, the content of his will, is the content of his revelation. We can understand and find very attractive the attempt that has constantly been made from Duns Scotus to Seeberg to give God's will a kind of preferential position or primacy among the divine attributes.[132] According to my whole understanding of the divine attributes and the

---

128. *CF,* II, §§ 168-69, pp. 732-37.

129. On this expression cf. Barth, *Epistle to the Romans,* e.g., p. 416.

130. Lipsius, *Lehrbuch der evangelisch-protestantischen Dogmatik,* p. 255.

131. Marginal note: "Thom. I, 19; Bartm. I, 153." (See *STh* I, q. 19: De voluntate Dei; Bartmann, I, §§ 36-43, pp. 153-78.)

132. On Scotus cf. Loofs, *Leitfaden zum Studium der Dogmengeschichte,* I, pp. 193-94; Seeberg, *Christliche Dogmatik,* I, pp. 336-40, 405-20. On Seeberg himself, *Christliche Dogmatik,* I, pp. 265-66.

divine nature, this is impossible. We have thought that we must view the attributes as the radii of a circle pointing to an imperceptible center.[133] The point is that they expound and describe the nature of God, his personality and aseity. Each of them must describe the nature of God as each of them is grounded in it. But none of them exhausts the divine nature, and even less can our description of the divine nature be exhausted or dominated by the describing of any one of them. We oppose giving a central position to infinitude (unconditionality)[134] as a quality of aseity. We must also oppose giving a central position to the will and its attributes as a quality of personality. From preferences or prejudices of this kind come many truncations and rigidities in Christian preaching in virtue of which this or that is powerfully proclaimed under the name of God, but the name of God that ought to shine forth in and above this or that is obscured. The will of God is, of course, one and all in the concept of God. Everything relates to it and is to be understood in the light of it. But is this not true of every divine attribute if it is meant in a Christian sense, if it is to have meaning and not be an idol, if it is to point beyond itself to the God who cannot be exhausted in any concept, not even in this one?

Here again we will begin with the definition of one of our older theologians, this time that of the Dutchman Peter van Mastricht, which ties in well with the definition of God's wisdom that we formed on the basis of Heidegger. Mastricht states that God's will is his most wise inclination to himself as supreme end, and to creatures for his own sake as means thereto.[135] The methodology in all these definitions is now gradually coming to light. God lives, we said. He lives his own life, and in it, as alone the living one, he lives the life of all creatures. God is almighty, and in his almightiness is the basis and root of all possibility.[136] God knows. He knows himself as the supreme idea, and in it all things that he himself is not. In his wisdom God posits himself as end, and for the sake of this end, in orientation to himself, all things as means thereto. And so God wills. He wills himself, and for his own sake, creation.

What is the new thing, or the new stress, that this definition brings to our concept of God? Obviously the element of freedom that we noted especially already in our discussion of the concept of omnipotence. God

---

133. See above, pp. 378ff.
134. See above, p. 387 n. 35.
135. Heppe, p. 47; Heppe-Bizer, p. 50; ET p. 81.
136. See Heppe-Bizer, p. 83; ET pp. 100-101.

does not have to live, or be almighty, or be wise, or whatever else we may have to say of him, whether in himself or for us. He is all that he is, and does all that he does, because he so wills, by inclination and not by whim or caprice, by most wise inclination, yet in freedom. Because God reveals himself as the one who commands and determines, because in his almightiness he meets us spiritually as the one who wills and not just as the one who acts, not merely in an event but in speech, in a Word that is both imperative and powerful, we cannot reverse the statements that God is life or that God is might; we cannot understand him unrestrictedly by the way of eminence; we cannot put him under a law or an idea. This would be to overlook his personality, his spiritual force. Will is something unique that cannot be subordinated or explained by something else. Will is freedom. Hence God is free. He is not under any alien law. He is *sui iuris*.[137] He wills, and he wills in this way. We have to accept this. The question whether he might have willed otherwise is irreverent and presumptuous. We cannot ask it in relation to *God's* will.

The answer to the foolish question whether God might not have willed himself lies in recollection of the attribute of divine blessedness. Not by compulsion but in joy God cannot will anything other than himself. The answer to the equally foolish question whether he might not have willed creation lies in recollection of God's love in virtue of which, again not by compulsion but in goodness, he cannot will anything other than the world. The fact that he cannot do anything other, then, does not overthrow his will or his freedom. It simply reminds us that we are speaking about *his* will and *his* freedom, and therefore about a reality which our concept cannot encompass, for[138] what we call "will" might always do something other. This concept, applied logically to God, leads to those foolish questions, and we thus have to see its inadequacy.

The innumerable distinctions that the older dogmaticians tried to make at this point are an expression of this insight. To elucidate the problem of freedom that we have touched on they distinguish between a natural will, which wills what it is not able not to will (himself), and a free will, which wills what it is able not to will (creation).[139] As I have said, I think it would be more in keeping with the situation to set aside the latter possibility in view

---

137. Hutterus, in Hase, p. 145.
138. MS has "because."
139. Schmid-Pöhlmann, p. 91; Schmid ET p. 127 (Baier); cf. Heppe-Bizer, p. 73; ET p. 84 (van Riissen).

of the love of God. Similarly, it is inadmissible to follow the older Lutherans, especially with regard to the will and freedom of creation, and to distinguish between an antecedent will, the will of God in itself, and a consequent will,[140] the will of God as it shapes itself on the basis of foreknowledge of certain conditions inherent in creation, or between an efficacious will by which God wills and does something, and an inefficacious will[141] by which he refrains from doing what he wills.

A will that is conditioned or inoperative is obviously not God's will, we must reply with the older Reformed,[142] though we acknowledge at this point, too, the inadequacy of the concept of a truly free and therefore an unconditioned and operative will of God in relation to creaturely freedom. The inadequacy, however, does not give us the right to abandon the concept in this way. Better are the distinctions that are made between the will of God that simply commands and the will that also determines, decides, and acts. The first is called the will of sign or precept. God gives us a sign of his will, he commands or forbids, he permits or counsels this or that with reference to our own action. The second is called the will of God's good pleasure or decree. He accomplishes his will, perhaps through human disobedience to his will of sign.[143] Within the latter distinction there is a further distinction in the will of decree between efficacious will and permissive will, naturally with a view to the occurrence of evil in the world that cannot be caused but only permitted by God.[144] In making this distinction we must not forget that the will of God is only one will, so that while the distinction is not inappropriate, it brings to light the further difficulty that a will which both commands and acts, which demands decision and brings about decision, sometimes in such a way that they do not coincide — that such a will is inconceivable to us, so that without being able to complete the concept we have to accept the insight that in both cases we actually have the one will of God.

The best way of summing up all these difficulties — and this is finally at issue in all the distinctions — is to differentiate between the revealed will and the secret will.[145] We know one will of God as he reveals

---

140. Schmid-Pöhlmann, p. 95; Schmid ET pp. 127-28.

141. Ibid.

142. Cf. Heppe-Bizer, p. 78; ET p. 90; Schweizer, pp. 365-66.

143. Heppe-Bizer, pp. 50-51, 73ff.; ET pp. 85ff.; Schmid-Pöhlmann, p. 95; Schmid ET pp. 127-28.

144. Heppe-Bizer, p. 77; ET pp. 89-90.

145. Bartmann, I, § 40.

himself to us. We stand under an intelligible command and a visible determination to which *in actu* we may submit in faith and obedience. This is the revealed will. But we have not thereby comprehended the will of God. The reality that we come up against bursts through our concept of it and conceals itself from us. It becomes the secret will for which we have no formula or conception, before which we can only bow, which reminds us that even in our knowledge of the divine will we must cling to God himself, not to his will no matter how we conceive of it, but to the one who wills. In other words, we must cling to the will of God which we know but cannot conceive of, with which our will is never congruent any more than our wisdom is congruent with his wisdom, concerning which we can only pray: Thy will be done! [Matt. 6:10]. This brings us to the vital point.

We can now continue at once and say that this will of God is a holy will.[146] The biblical concept of the Holy is, as we all know, the concept of that which is distinct or that which is supremely positive in God, though it seems that we can describe it only negatively as that wherein he is completely different from the gods and the world and humanity. It is in virtue of his holiness that God, making his will known to us, brings about in us that change, that leading, that conversion from the bad to the good that we had to speak of already in connection with the wisdom of God. In the first instance, however, the good is simply God himself. It is around this thought of the isolated and isolating factor in God's will that the definitions of the older dogmaticians circle, and they are remarkably varied at this point. Some stress the clarity and purity of God's will.[147] Hutterus simply says that holiness is the attribute in which God is the supreme good.[148] Polanus finds the holiness of God in the fact that he is a law to himself, so that what he wills is *eo ipso* right.[149] In a way that is particularly worth noting, Buddeus finds God's holiness in the love with which he loves himself.[150] Are we right if we sum up all the definitions in the thesis that God's will is holy insofar as it is his own will and cannot be exchanged or confused with any other, being self-grounded, jealous, and wrathful, and going its own way? We cannot expunge the more detailed OT defi-

---

146. Marginal note: "Bartm. I, 164." (Bartmann, I, § 40.)
147. Schmid, p. 81; Schmid-Pöhlmann, p. 90; ET p. 120.
148. Hase, p. 147.
149. Heppe, p. 73; Heppe-Bizer, p. 79; ET p. 95.
150. Hutterus, in Hase, p. 147 n. 7.

nitions at this point. In proof that older theologians knew already what Otto has been able to tell us so impressively about the Holy,[151] listen to what Wichelhaus says about God's holiness: It will not enlighten us that precisely because God is good he is also holy, and that precisely because he loves he is wrathful and chides and wounds and casts in the oven. The holiness of God is dreadful to us. In his holiness God has the appearance of a Moloch, a Saturn, a consuming fire. Precisely as such, if we are to be brought back to him, he must be loved and praised as the Most High.[152] That is to say, he must be claimed for himself in the jealous distinction or separation which brings to light this quality of his will.

We now proceed — and all the reservations and suspicions and explanations that are needed here must be adduced only in order that we may be led from knowledge to knowledge — and say at once that this holy will is righteous.[153] Righteousness is the more detailed definition of the divine will which distinguishes it, as we have already pointed out, from mere whim or caprice, from accident or *heimarmenē*, which justifies the self-love, the sacred egoism,[154] with which God wills his own glory, not, of course, before some other law but before the law of God's own nature. The will with which God turns to us, demanding on the one side as legislative righteousness, and disposing on the other side as distributive righteousness, is a definite will.[155] It rests on an order and reveals to us an order. This order is God's righteousness. We thus accept the definition of Polanus: Righteousness is the quality "by which God immutably and ineffably wills and approves, Himself does and effects in others, such things as He has laid down in His law; and all the things at variance with this order He neither wills nor approves nor works nor effects nor helps, but hates and detests."[156] What God wills of us and with us is the establishment and revelation of his order. Not as though it were above him! The good is good because God wills it, not vice versa.[157] But he wills the

---

151. R. Otto, *Das Heilige,* 2nd ed. (Breslau, 1918); ET *The Idea of the Holy* (London, 1958).

152. Wichelhaus, *Die Lehre der heiligen Schrift,* p. 343.

153. Marginal note: "Bartm. I, 167." (Bartmann, I, § 41.)

154. Introduced by Antonio Salandra of Italy in a speech on 10.17.1914, this expression was used by A. Jülicher in his review of Barth's *Römerbrief* (1st ed.) and cf. F. Gogarten in *CW* 34 (1920) 453-57.

155. Cf. Heppe-Bizer, p. 81; ET p. 96; and Schweizer, p. 434.

156. Heppe, pp. 49-50; Heppe-Bizer, p. 52; ET p. 96.

157. Heppe-Bizer, pp. 79-80; ET pp. 93-94.

good and hates evil. His will — and we see here that he is personal and spiritual — is an ordered and ordering will, a critical power, a power that says Yes and No according to a definite standard, that turns from and to, that punishes and rewards, that judges. When we know God *in actu* there can be no question of eliminating or giving less prominence to this attribute. As little as his holiness can God's righteousness merge into his mercy, of which we shall have to speak next. Nor would we do well to subordinate it to his love. Modern dogmatics, especially since Ritschl, has a strong tendency to do this.[158] We must not distinguish the revelation of Sinai from that of Golgotha. According to Rom. 3:21 the latter is indeed a revelation of righteousness. Far from being outdated, all that the OT says about God's right and righteousness and judgment is simply a foreshadowing of the judge par excellence, Jesus Christ, who satisfies the divine righteousness and brings unambiguously to light the divine crisis that lies over all that lives. We cannot take the standard of judgment into our own hands. This is the boundary that we come up against in regard to this quality. Precisely as and because the righteousness of God has been revealed in Jesus Christ over all flesh as the universal judgment or absolute crisis, we have to say that no human law is identical with the law of God's will, no human judgment can be the fulfilment of the divine crisis, no human theodicy can be a vindication of the righteous divine rule. We cannot sit on the judgment seat of Christ [2 Cor. 5:10], and world history is *not* world judgment.[159] God's righteousness is knowable but not conceivable. Here again recollection of God's aseity must make us put the stroke through the calculation which alone makes it correct.

We do this best if we turn at once to the third insight, namely, that God's will is merciful.[160] Like righteousness, we must understand mercy as a closer definition of the holiness of the divine will. The "holy" needs this closer definition. If we negate it or call it secondary — as seems to be Otto's view[161] — then we have indeed (Wichelhaus)[162] the image of a Moloch or Saturn, or at any rate an idol. Nor is the concept of righteousness, of the ordered that creates order, enough. The pagan goddess

---

158. A. Ritschl, *Die christliche Lehre von der Rechtfertigung und Versöhnung,* II, 4th ed. (Bonn, 1800), pp. 98-119; cf. also Kaftan, p. 163; Haering, pp. 320ff.; Nitzsch-Stephan, pp. 468-69.

159. Cf. F. von Schiller's poem *Resignation.*

160. Marginal note: "Bartm. I, 169." (Bartmann, I, § 42.)

161. See Otto, *The Idea of the Holy.*

162. See Wichelhaus, *Die Lehre der heiligen Schrift.*

Iustitia can be depicted with scales in her hand, eyes bound, impartially confirming what the scales and not she herself will decide. Of her, it may be said: "Let justice be done and the world perish."[163] Very good! This is an ideal concept of order. It is with this pitilessness and objectivity that we have to conceive of righteousness, even of God's righteousness.

But when we know God, then we have to see that this concept of order, true and necessary though it is, has its limits. What God's holiness has to say to us amounts to more than what we can comprehend as righteousness. God is so holy, so unique in his willing, that in this willing, as his Word reveals to us, within his turning from and to, within his rewarding and punishing, within the judgment and through the crisis there is revealed a quality of his will that we cannot understand as order, as legislative or distributive justice, as anything regulated, ordered, or order-ing, but only as something which, although it derives of course from his nature, is as such totally unexpected and free and superabundant, not the remainder in the sum of righteousness, but a subjective element in God in virtue of which, far from being just blindfolded, he is Lord of the scales with which he weighs as the righteous one, and as his command goes out and judgment falls he has pity on the object of his command and judg-ment, accepting solidarity with it and helping it.

We have to put all this anthropopathically at this point. This is God's mercy. We might have spoken here about his grace, or goodness, or patience. Does it all come into collision with his righteousness? It certainly does. We cannot think of it except in collision with God's righteousness, except as a breaking through this righteousness, God's triumph in it, the synthesis of its Yes and No. But for this very reason we must not separate the two, assigning righteousness to the OT and mercy to the NT, hiding ourselves under the shadow of the latter as though the righteousness of God no longer applied to us, or did so less. If we do this, how we deceive ourselves about the revelation of God also and precisely in the OT, which on almost every page is attested to us there as a revelation of the merciful God. How feebly we see God's mercy if we find it isolated as it were in the NT, as though it could still be mercy if it were abstracted away from righteousness. How we encroach upon the Holy One whose own unique will wills to triumph precisely in this step from righteousness to mercy (in this *step,* not in an achievement of the state of mercy). As the necessary boundary of the quality of mercy, the correction of the way of negation

---

163. A saying of Emperor Ferdinand I (1556-64).

which we must make here too, lest here too an idol arises by the way of eminence, mercy can be present only as we do not forget for a moment the righteousness of God in and on which mercy shines, the judicial office of the Father whose countenance shows us mercy; only as we do not rest in mercy without being caused unrest by God's righteousness. *Then* we truly see the Father; *then* we truly rest in his mercy. Righteousness achieves nothing and mercy achieves nothing unless the Holy One achieves it. And the Holy One does not achieve it unless God does. But they are all true and real — holiness, righteousness, and mercy — all of them are summed up in a word if and so far as we say that God achieves it, and it is in order to define God's action that we lisp these individual words. Happy are we if we realize why we have to lisp them, and if we realize that we really are lisping.

We conclude our consideration of the communicable attributes with a reference to God's love and blessedness. Like life and omnipotence at the beginning, and in some sense in correspondence with these basic attributes, I would view them as qualities of the divine personality in itself, and therefore not specifically as qualities of the divine knowing and willing. Love also comes within God's knowledge, for he knows all things in himself, and blessedness is also within his willing, for he wills what he wills for his own sake. The fact that God knows and God wills, along with what is knowable in more detail in this knowing and willing, does not exhaust the nature of God, precisely because we are so close in it to the perceptible nature of humanity. For this reason love and blessedness have also been called qualities of divine feeling.[164] It is probably better to agree here that to psychologize God in this way is a last resort and probably transgresses the limit of the permissible. But however that may be, in relation to what was said first about God's life and power, then about his knowing and willing, we lacked the necessary amplifications and concentrations that are to be found in the two words "love" and "blessedness." Both of them in a very concentrated way relate to what has encountered us as the problem of all the attributes, that is, God's relation to what he is not, to the world, creation, humanity. God's address is God's Word that gives us occasion to talk about him. In the fact of this address there is posited a relation of God to the other. How could we have spoken about any attribute of God if we had not been able to abstract it from this?

---

164. Biedermann, *Christliche Dogmatik,* p. 635; Frank, *System der christlichen Wahrheit,* I, p. 279.

But are there not special attributes of God in terms of which we must finally understand and describe that relation as such? Attributes, I say, and I name two: love and blessedness. What God's love[165] really is, what is meant when 1 John 4:8 says that God is love, has been defined in many different ways. A well-known definition is that of Ritschl, who says that love is the steadfast will which helps a spiritual person like oneself to the attainment of his or her own destiny in such a way that in so loving one also pursues one's own end therewith.[166] Perhaps as a definition of God's love this is too sparsely businesslike, and above all too narrow. When we read that God so loved the world [John 3:16], this surely has more in view than the relation of one spiritual person to another. Haering calls love a seeking of fellowship out of liking and goodwill for the achievement of common goals.[167] But is it not too much to talk about common goals between God and us? Kähler defines love as the choice of a mutual relation in which each posits the other as an end.[168] But like the other formulas, does not this suffer from the fact that it can be applied too easily to our love for God or for one another, and ought this to be so if we are describing the love of God? Could we not press on to God's real love by the way of eminence? In spite of its clumsy garb, the definition of Biedermann seems to be much better; he calls love a self-determination for the self-positing of the world process and for the immanence of the absolute God as its basis.[169] Yet it might be as well not to go the way of such speculative Gnosticism and therefore simply to say with Hutterus that God's love is the attribute whereby God as the supreme good willed from all eternity to have fellowship with all things.[170] God as the supreme good — did not have but willed to have — from all eternity — fellowship — all things; here we have an exhaustive description of the paradox, the nature, the uniqueness of this love. God does not will to be without the world. This is God's love, the miracle of God's love, we must say. It is not self-evident that God should so will. Any declaration about an end that he seeks therewith weakens the miracle. God's love seeks no end. Like all that God is, it is pure love. Hence it is free love. We remember our discussion of

---

165. Marginal note: "Thom. I, 20." (*STh* I, q. 20: De amore Dei.)
166. Ritschl, *Unterricht in der christlichen Religion,* 7th ed. (Gütersloh, 1960), § 12, p. 20.
167. Haering, p. 215.
168. In Nitzsch-Stephan, p. 471 n. 1.
169. Biedermann, *Christliche Dogmatik,* p. 636 (= 2nd ed., II, p. 534).
170. Hase, p. 147.

God's will. We may not say that he might have done differently, that he might have refrained from fellowship with the world. When we think about the Trinity, about the Son of God in whom he has turned to the world from all eternity, we have to say that the very idea of another use of his freedom is a denial of God, that there is in God no depth in which this willing of fellowship does not obtain. You will perhaps know, at least in part, the verses of Angelus Silesius:

> I know that without me God cannot live for an instant
> If I perish, then he will necessarily give up the ghost [I 8].
>
> God is as much dependent on me as I on him.
> I help his being as he upholds mine [I 100].
>
> What God can wish and desire in eternity
> He sees in me as his image [I 272].
>
> God is truly nothing, and if he is something,
> He is it only in me as he chooses me for himself [I 200].
>
> Nothing is but I and Thou, and if we two are not,
> God is no longer God and heaven collapses [II 178].[171]

The *Cherubinic Wanderer* in which we find this pious insolence was published in its day with the imprimatur of the Roman Catholic church.[172] At a pinch one might in fact justify it dogmatically in the light of that eternal will for fellowship. Yet it is still pious insolence, from which it is only a step, if that, to Feuerbach.[173] I quote it in order to impress upon you that the concept of the love of God can be pressed to the point of absurdity and has its limits. And I want to draw your attention to this because in more than one modern dogmatics you will find an attempt to make love the divine attribute par excellence, the definition of God's nature.[174] This will not do. If we carry the concept of love too far, we

---

171. *Des Angelus Silesius Cherubinischer Wandersmann,* ed. W. Bölsche (Jena/Leipzig, 1905), pp. 2, 14, 37, 65. Martensen also quotes three of these stanzas in the same context, *Christliche Dogmatik,* p. 93.

172. Bölsche prints the imprimatur of Vicar-General Sebastianus à Rostock (7.6.1617) and the approbation of the Dean of Vienna Theological Faculty, Nicolaus Avancinus, S.J. (4.2.1657).

173. See H. Martensen, *Christliche Dogmatik,* p. 93.

174. Cf. Kaftan, p. 163; Haering, p. 219.

arrive at a coordination of God and creature which obviously does not correspond to the relation that arises in this love. Usually we then seek help in the confession that God's love is not a weak and sentimental love, but a holy love, the term "holy" denoting a boundary of reverence that must be kept intact on our side of the relation.[175] But the possible deduction that God needs us, that he is tied to the world and a prisoner of his love, cannot be evaded in this way. Like all these concepts, that of love has a logical dynamism that one cannot check merely by appending an adjective. Those who supremely and finally want unequivocally to stick to love alone in describing God go the way of Angelus Silesius and Feuerbach. I think it advisable here too not to stick to one attribute, to be clear that the concept of love cannot be a last word since it is an inadequate word, that when it is rightly understood it points beyond itself, not to another last word but to God himself, who even in his pure and free love, without which he would not be God, is still God the Lord, *a se,* and not in any sense referred to us nor tied to the world.

If we take this seriously, then alongside love we must set another quality which brings this to expression and with which alone the love of God is God's love. I mean blessedness. With the Leiden Synopsis I define this as the beatitude in virtue of which God needs none else but enjoys himself and rests in himself as the fulness of all goods.[176] What can he miss or lack or be without who as the Father eternally possesses and contemplates himself in the Son through the Spirit? It has to be something more and new and not self-evident, but a miracle, if he, God, from all eternity is also not content with his own blessedness, if from all eternity he is love. Can we properly evaluate his love as love so long as we stand in the shadow of necessity, of what is self-evident, so long as we do not admit that he is blessed in himself? We said earlier that *God's* mercy means that the righteous one is merciful, and now we say that God's love means that the one who is eternally blessed in himself so loved the world that he gave his only begotten Son [John 3:16].

I need not show that it would be easy to press the concept of blessedness, too, to the point of absurdity. I repeat expressly that this again is not a last word. There can be no last words on our lips. *God* speaks the last word. Knowledge of God's personality lays all these words on our lips. Recollection of God's aseity characterizes them as next-to-the-last words,

---

175. Haering, p. 220.
176. Heppe, p. 79; Heppe-Bizer, p. 86; ET p. 104.

and commands that we correct and supplement them by one another. We say what we have to say, knowing about whom we are speaking and therefore what we cannot say and ought not to try to say with any other word. When we do this, then we do what is humanly possible, not preventing God from speaking his own last word, and perhaps even securing a hearing for what he himself wants to say.

V. The Hidden God

We now turn to the attributes of aseity or of the hidden God, the negative or incommunicable attributes. We recall that God's revelation takes place in a unity and simultaneity of unveiling and veiling, and that the knowledge of revelation thus takes place in a unity and simultaneity of conceiving and nonconceiving, because at one and the same time we both share in it and do not share in it. We posit and conceive of God (as in subsection IV above) in his objectivity, his unveiling, in the first "I am" in which he meets us, in relation, in his personality. Yet as we tried to comprehend him, at every point we had to admit that if this was really the knowledge of God in his revelation we could only *try* to conceive of him, that even as we did so we did not conceive of him, that even as by the way of eminence we formed words on the basis of our share in God and called him this or that from what we know of our own nature, always presupposing that we were sticking close to the knowledge of revelation, then by the way of negation we had also to question our share in him and admit that by using these words in this way we were saying something which, even though they seemed to be so clear and well known and familiar, made them unclear and unfamiliar and alien to us. If we firmly and unconditionally keep to the fact that with these words we want in all circumstances to speak about God in his revelation — "I will not let you go, unless you bless me" [Gen. 32:27] — then like Jacob we shall go away limping as the sun rises [v. 32]. Otherwise Jacob does not become Israel [v. 29]. Everywhere — there is no disguising this — we come up against the hidden God in the revealed God, the second divine I in the first, the divine subjectivity, aseity, or direct Godhead. But the fact that we come up against the hiddenness of God in his revelation, his aseity in his personality, the inconceivable in the conceiving, is the reason why at this point we do not merely lisp but can clearly see the limits of the communicable attributes at certain points. The concepts which mark these limits are God's incommunicable, negative, or absolute attributes, the attributes of his aseity, about which we now have to speak.

We now as it were change our theme or direction. Previously we were trying to state what we may comprehend by the way of eminence in the act of the knowledge of revelation. Now we must state the incomprehensible things that meet us by the way of negation. Naturally, we do so with the caution that we had to exercise in dealing with the attributes of personality. Abstractions are as little in place here as in relation to what we tried to say about God's life, knowledge, will, love, and so forth. The abstractions that come dangerously into view are those about which Luther and Calvin[177] constantly warned. Luther liked to tell us that instead of plunging into the depths of the hiddenness of God we should stop at the child in the crib.[178] If only all the modern theologians who repeat this ad nauseam had kept to the point of this advice in their discussion of the attributes of personality, holding strictly to revelation in act, and not going off into anthropomorphic statements that really have nothing whatever to do with the child in the crib. But vexation at the impermissible personalism or moralism of the Ritschlians, which today the so-called positives have for long enough been joyfully sharing,[179] ought not to cause us in reaction to make the opposite mistake which the Reformers rightly opposed. As we pass over this remarkable bridge, let us listen to the statements in which Melanchthon issued this warning: Christ leads us to the revelation of God. When Philip asked him to show them the Father, he gravely rebuked him, called him back from speculation, and said (John 14:9), "He that hath seen me hath seen the Father." He does not want us to ask about God in random speculations, but to fix our eyes on this revealed Son and to direct our invocation to this eternal Father, who revealed himself by sending this Son and giving the gospel.[180]

Taking this warning to heart, in the previous subsection, when personality was dangerously our theme, we constantly kept in mind God's aseity, and now, when aseity is equally dangerously our theme, we will constantly keep in mind God's personality, demonstrating by the resultant restraint that neither personality nor aseity is our theme, but the revealed God, unveiled and veiled, God himself, to whom here again we must give

---

177. J. Calvin, *Commentary on the Psalms,* CR, 60, on Ps. 103:8.
178. WA, 4, 649, 6-7; 391, 77, 28-29; 42, 295, 31ff.; WA TR, 1, 108, 25ff.
179. Cf. Seeberg, *Christliche Dogmatik,* I, pp. 299ff.
180. Loci 1559, *De Deo,* in *Loci praecipui theologici* (1559) (Berlin, 1856), p. 4.

the glory beyond all conceptuality or abstraction. I knew what I was doing when in the thesis I expressly added the word "God" to each attribute in either class. In neither class must any attribute be understood in itself but only as an attribute of *God*. But now to the point.

Worthy of being put first here is the concept of God's unity, which carries with it the two thoughts of his uniqueness and simplicity.[181] In absolute mystery there stands behind each relative attribute the truth that God is both unique *(unicus)* and simple *(simplex)*. He alone lives, he alone is mighty, he alone is wise, he alone is blessed; in his knowing and willing lies the reality of all things, of all that he is not. Alongside him there is no other god [Exod. 20:3], which means, no other life, power, wisdom, holiness, righteousness, love, or blessedness. All that can seriously be called these things, he himself is, and all that may lightly pretend to be these things is only a nonentity or idol[182] before him. Knowledge of God means *eo ipso* the most radical twilight of the gods. Olympus and Valhalla are emptied out and become secular. Their inhabitants become successively weaker as ideas, demons, ghosts, and finally comic figures. "Why do you ask me about the good?" *(heis estin ho agathos)*, the NT tradition has even Jesus say (Matt. 19:17). There is no good but *the* good, the one good, the supreme good, the only good. There is only one God. No statement is more dangerous or revolutionary than this for all mythologies and ideologies. When this truth is known, then the 450 priests of Baal at Carmel are called to account [1 Kgs. 18:40], and many other priests with them.

I will give Heidegger's definition of simplicity: It is the property whereby he has no part in any composition, coalescence, concretion, commixture, confusion, or diversity, so that no matter what may be thought, in God is God himself, and there is thus an absolute identity of the divine essence and attributes, and even of the attributes among themselves.[183] The whole series of divine attributes is thus set in a circle behind one another, and between each of them there is a sign of equality, and God's nature is not the sum of them, but their being ineffably one and the same.

We have seen already that we have here the problem of the whole

---

181. Marginal note: "Thom I, 11; Bartmann, I, 125, 128." (*STh* I, 9, q. 11: De unitate Dei; Bartmann, I, §§ 28-29, pp. 125-31.)

182. See above, n. 94.

183. Heppe, p. 43; cf. Heppe-Bizer, p. 47; ET p. 63. Marginal note: "Simplicity = spirituality, bodies being composite." See Heppe-Bizer, p. 59; ET p. 66.

doctrine of the attributes in brief. In the light of this simplicity, the Trinity does not consist of three divine essences, nor of three parts of the divine essence, but rather, as we saw,[184] of three persons of one essence, and of equal dignity within this essence, each person sharing in all the attributes. But this simplicity also means that God will not be combined or amalgamated with anything else. Thus one may not call him the world soul. One may not speak of a mutual permeation of the divine and the human, for example, in Christ. The detailed safeguards with which the older dogmatics surrounded the doctrine of the incarnation and the personal union of natures in the God-man were most appropriate. There are no emanations from God into the world in virtue of which what we might call divine islands or colonies can arise among what is not divine. We must also be careful how we handle the idea of a so-called intervention of the divine in the world, an idea which I myself used to like very much.[185] Again, we must not make any image or likeness of God. The Reformed were right to regard this prohibition [Exod. 20:4] as a separate commandment. Pictures of former pastors may be tolerable in church, and pictures of God or Christ may be possible in a museum or by way of adornment, but strictly speaking they are neither possible nor tolerable in church! The crucifix does not enable us to look upon the revealed God but presents only the human nature of Christ, and to contemplate this in isolation is almost inevitably confusing and misleading, since it is the revealed God who must be proclaimed and worshiped. Such depictions can only obscure the revealed God in the human nature of Christ. No wonder that the story of depictions of Christ is such a radically dubious chapter in the history of art. It would perhaps have been better if artists had never set their hands to this task.

But enough of that. I need hardly demonstrate that the unity of God as his uniqueness and simplicity is an incommunicable, absolute, negative attribute of God; that the concept of "one" is in fact a borderline concept. Every one known to us is a "one" alongside something else. It is one example of a species. God is *only* example, without species. He thus transcends every "one" known to us. He transcends our conceptuality. We can comprehend him only as incomprehensibly unique. Again, all that we know is made up of other things and may be combined and amalgamated

---

184. See above, pp. 99ff.
185. K. Barth, *Römerbrief,* 1st ed. (1919), ed. H. Schmidt (Zurich, 1985), p. 671 (Index).

with other things. But God is the quintessence of simplicity both inwards and outwards. In trying to think out the concept of God's unity, we are really dealing from the outset with God's aseity, with his independence, with his lordship on every hand. The concept of unity pushes God back into absolute mystery, removes him at a stroke from all competition or clumsy familiarity.[186]

But we must halt and do a right-about turn. It is of *God's* unity that we want to speak. Let us see to it that we do not just speak about unity in general. The "unique and simple" might be a fatal idol if it is not really a predicate of God. If we think through the concept of unity to the end we can come dangerously near to Islam's fanatical proclamation of the one God, alongside whom — how humorous! — it keeps a small place of honor for the baroque figure of his prophet. It was not a good moment when the discovery was made that Christianity and Islam at least have monotheism in common as compared with other religions. If by the uniqueness of God what is meant is so-called monotheism, the religiously clarified and embellished idea of the "one," the cult of the number 1, then the uniqueness of *God* is certainly not meant. Anything ending with "ism" has little or nothing to do with God. Note that! What one can just as well construct speculatively as believe may have value as an interesting hypothesis, but it does not come into consideration as an expression of the knowledge of God. A question mark must be set against the uniqueness of God no less than against his love.

Similarly, if we think through the thought of simplicity to the end, we naturally come dangerously close to a spiritualistic pantheism, to what is called panentheism, as it has usually been indulgently termed since the days of Schleiermacher.[187] If we reverse the statement and say that the simple is God instead of saying that God is simple; if we think the thought of the perfectly noncomposite or the noncompositely perfect, which is independent in relation to everything else, and then call this the most simple God, might it not be out of place reverently to offer a lock of hair to the shades of the holy, rejected Spinoza along with Schleiermacher?[188] Is God to be compared, then, merely with the sustaining note of a fugue, is he merely the unconditioned that confronts everything conditioned in its monotonous — let us say it openly, its boring, insignificant, and un-

---

186. This sentence was added in the margin.
187. In fact the term goes back to K. C. F. Krause (1781-1832).
188. Cf. Schleiermacher, *Reden*, p. 31 (54); ET *Speeches*, p. 30.

related unconditionality, because this is part of the concept? Is this really God the Lord with whom we thought we had to do in this attribute? Is this really the divine aseity?

In face of this caricature of the divine uniqueness and simplicity we must do a dialectical turn of 180° back, of course, to God's personality, recalling that the neutral "it," the one, the unique, the simple, has no meaning except as a predicate of the known He about whom we are talking here. What is the unity of God in the act of the knowledge of revelation? Obviously, what we read about in the Psalm, which tells us that if only we have him we ask for nothing in heaven or on earth [Ps. 73:25]. This is not an "ism." This is an encounter. This is the answer to a summons. This is the human result of the fact that a Thou has met the I, a Thou that has all the marks of the incomparable, of what cannot be united with anything else.

The incomparability of God in his revelation is his uniqueness, the fact that he cannot be united with anything else is his simplicity. We have here something that we cannot perceive or comprehend in God. No word that we use for it is adequate, not merely in the last analysis but at the very outset. It cannot as such be an object of our knowledge. We can describe only our awareness of this limit of our knowledge. But obviously this description of our awareness in the knowledge of revelation takes this form. The "If only I have thee" with which we here call God unique is not in any sense a general idea that we can form of him but a command that meets us: "You shall have no other gods but me" [Exod. 20:3] — this is the basis of the uniqueness — and: "You shall not make any image or likeness" [Exod. 20:4] — this is the basis of the simplicity. The basis of the divine unity lies in the Johannine I: "I am the way, the truth. . . . I am the resurrection" [John 14:6; 11:25].[189] God tells us that he wills to be known and worshiped as unique and simple, so that there is no reason for us to become intoxicated with our monotheism or pantheism. In God's Word in which he meets us as a He there is no basis for this type of uniqueness or simplicity, the Mohammedan or Indian. These bypass God's Word just as much as the crassest fetishism of Central Africa, and perhaps more so, for they are much more lofty and refined. God's Word does not allow us to yield to the demonism of the concept of the unconditioned. It opposes to monotheism the offense that God in his revelation, as the one God, is triune, and to pantheism the folly that in his simplicity he becomes man in Christ and calls us his children by the

---

189. This sentence was added in the margin.

Spirit.[190] The limit lies not in the concept, for such concepts as uniqueness and simplicity are unlimited, but in the thing itself, which is always God. The limiting concept is not itself the lord; it accompanies us like an unruly horse. God is the Lord, He is Lord over us even when we try to think of him as Lord, even over our very correct limiting concept. If this leads us to random speculations,[191] then it is time to issue to ourselves an intellectual *metanoeite*, to give ourselves a call to order, to go to the place where we know what that concept can do and what it cannot do, where it is clear to us not that God is *one* but that *God* is one. Then the concept becomes a tool that we may use strictly and joyfully — a tool that we theologians need and have to use at every point.

We must now discuss God's eternity and omnipresence.[192] What difficult, dark, ambiguous, and inexplicable thoughts we have to think in order to deal with God's incommunicable attributes, in order to think these borderline thoughts relating to our knowledge of God. We see this perhaps even more impressively now than we did in dealing with the word "unity," which does have at least a certain clarity. What do we mean by eternity? What do we mean by omnipresence? The reference is obviously to time and space. We have to discuss God's relation to time and space. Not merely from the days of Kant[193] time and space have been terms for the limits within which we are human. They are thus limits of what we call the world. If our humanity is constituted by knowing and willing, then we must say that as an act with at least two members in sequence this knowing and willing presuppose time, and as an act that is oriented to one or more objects they presuppose space. We know of no humanity outside time and space. And because we know and will (i.e., can be human) only in a sequence of acts and in relation to a sequence of objects, it may be added that we know of no humanity outside a specific time and a specific space, outside a specific stretch of time and space which in both cases we cannot think of as other than unending. What we call the world differs from the existence of both the race and the individual in that by it we mean the sum and epitome of what is possible and real in time and space, in infinite time and infinite space. A world outside time and space is equally unthinkable and indescribable.

---

190. The last two points are marginal additions.
191. Cf. Melanchthon, *Loci praecipui theologici,* p. 4.
192. Marginal note: "Thom. I, 10; Bartm. I, 134, 137." (*STh* I, q. 10: De Dei aeternitate; Bartmann, I, §§ 31-32, pp. 134-41.)
193. I. Kant, *Critique of Pure Reason,* Part I.

As regards the epistemological significance of this, philosophers, not we, must decide. In the first instance what has to be said about time and space in dogmatics has nothing whatever to do with the problem of idealism or realism — though here, too, subsequent agreement with our neighbors is not ruled out. No matter how they may be understood epistemologically, time and space are the limits within which we move, and with us what we call the world, our world. The knowledge of God, pressing on, as it must if it is the knowledge of *God*, to the granite rock of the divine aseity, does not come up against these limits (the fact that we come up against them, we recall, is not in itself the knowledge of God), but at these limits and in place of them and even *beyond* them, it comes up against God. God stands precisely where we cannot think of humans or any other creatures or the world as a whole. This is the general sense of the predicates "eternal" and "omnipresent." The fact that time and space are in a pregnant and unconditional sense the *limits* within which we move — that is the knowledge of *God*. One may vacillate on whether time and space are ideal or real, but one cannot vacillate on the eternity and omnipresence of God. Here we stand before *the* limit.

Let us look at this more closely. The older dogmaticians sometimes summed up eternity and omnipresence under the concept of infinity. God has no measure or end.[194] This definition is ambiguous. According to what we said above, there can be no question of understanding God's eternity as the infinity of time or his omnipresence as the infinity of space. If this were so, we would be describing only the limit and basic concept of the known and knowable world, and to the extent that the world is our world, in a monstrous concave mirror *ourselves*. God is not space and God is not time. Those who make this equation have not yet really trod the way of negation that we have to tread here. It is good that with the help of the fabulous numbers that astronomers can provide we see clearly what time and space are even in terms of our finite calculations, and it is good that taught thereby we try perhaps to think out the thought of infinity both on the large scale and the small. With this we will obviously describe not a finitude multiplied a million times but the presupposition, possibility, and measure of all finitude. But this presupposition that lies at the basis of all time and space, and is thus present in every time and space, is not the eternity and omnipresence of God. For as it is the condition of everything finite, it is also itself conditioned by the finite. As there are not times or spaces without the infinity of time and space, this fact stands or

---

194. Heppe-Bizer, p. 59; ET p. 65 (Wollebius).

falls with the existence of finite times and spaces. One might call it their primal basis, but also their gigantic and indescribable shadow. This is not God. This is finally humanity, which we can sometimes think of as the principle and measure of all things[195] and sometimes as a film fantastically played over on a white wall in a dark place.[196] We do not begin to conceive of God's eternity and omnipresence by infinitely extending time and space but by negating them. This, then, is how we must understand the definition "without measure or end." This is what it meant for the older theologians. God is he for whom the limit of time and space has no necessary meaning, not even as a necessary correlate, as one can hardly deny in the case of the concept of infinity. This is what we have to understand when the older dogmaticians used for "eternal" such terms as "interminable" and "indivisible" and "independent,"[197] or "alien to time," as Tertullian said already,[198] or "immune from all temporal succession,"[199] and also when they used for "omnipresent" such terms as "interminable,"[200] "impartible," and "nonlocal."[201] For this reason they could often even distinguish immensity from omnipresence as a separate quality.[202]

Schleiermacher defined eternity and omnipresence as the absolutely timeless and spaceless causality of God which with the temporal and spatial also conditions time and space themselves.[203] Absolute timelessness and spacelessness are the good things in this definition. More dubious is the concept of conditioning causality, which brings the matter close again to infinity. Biedermann says more soberly that eternity and omnipresence are the pure nonspatial and nontemporal being-in-itself of the absolute ground of the world.[204] I will adduce Wichelhaus here as a witness that this is actually what is meant in the knowledge of the revelation of God. He tells us that we ourselves cannot think of a God without the world, and that we call eternity an incalculable series of world-epochs. But where God reveals himself, time and space give ground, the foundations of the world sink, and a different being declares itself, namely, an eternal being which

195. Cf. Protagoras (Plato *Theat.* 151 E f.).
196. Cf. Plato's shadows (*Polit.* VII).
197. Mastricht, in Heppe, p. 56; Heppe-Bizer, p. 60; ET p. 65.
198. Nitzsch-Stephan, p. 409.
199. Hutterus, in Hase, p. 140.
200. Hase, p. 141 (Quenstedt).
201. Schmid-Pöhlmann, p. 94; Schmid ET p. 123 (Gerhard).
202. Heppe-Bizer, p. 60; ET p. 66 (van Riissen).
203. *CF,* I, §§ 52-53.
204. Biedermann, *Christliche Dogmatik,* p. 627.

rests in itself, which is self-fulfilled, and in which we can find perfect rest from all works and affairs and desires in a different being and becoming and having, because the temporal and visible have passed and an eternal has been found that is sufficient and lasting in itself.[205] Perhaps nowhere can we see so clearly as here how devastatingly negative are all these attributes of aseity. Where time and space are not simply extended infinity, that is, realized or idealized, but negated, everything comes to a halt. If I were the theologian of negation that I am rumored to be, I could hold a perfect orgy here. I will be content simply to recall Ps. 90, which tells us that a thousand years in God's sight are like a day that has passed, like a watch in the night, that is, like midnight when one day merges into another, and also 2 Chron. 6:18, which says that heaven and the heaven of heavens cannot contain God, and how then can the house which Solomon's hands have built?

But now, in keeping with our theme, we must continue at once in the words of Solomon's prayer, asking the Lord God to look upon the prayer and petition of his servant, that his eyes may be open day and night to this house where he has promised to set his name [2 Chron. 6:19-20]. This applies to both space and time. With a mere negation of time and space we have not yet thought the thought of God's eternity and omnipresence. God's freedom has to be God's lordship over time and space. It is lordship backwards only if he created time and space, and forwards only if he rules them, only if he is present every moment in them as the Lord. God is the author and Lord of time.[206] He is the fabricator of all times.[207] He is the ground of being of the bodily world that depends upon God for its being and upholding.[208] God is not contained in space, but himself gives space and the things that are in it their being.[209] This is what Schleiermacher meant to say with his conditioning causality if we take him in better part.

For the older dogmatics the first statement, namely, that God is the creator of time and space, was not so difficult as the second statement, namely, that he rules them. This means that even though he is nontemporal and nonspatial he stands in a positive relation to the limit of time and space and to what they enclose as his creatures, without himself being

---

205. Wichelhaus, *Die Lehre der heiligen Schrift*, p. 339.
206. Hutterus, in Hase, p. 140 n. 1.
207. Augustine, *De genesi contra Manichaeos* I, 3.
208. Van Til, in Heppe, p. 56; Heppe-Bizer, p. 60; ET p. 66.
209. Gerhard, in Schmid, p. 80; Schmid-Pöhlmann, p. 94; Schmid ET p. 123.

limited by them as the infinite is by the finite. They made the following attempts at explanation. To describe eternity they coined the term "coexistence."[210] Eternity constantly[211] coexists with time as the tree on a riverbank is with the river but does not flow with it, or as the polestar stands at the zenith but does not go round with the other stars, or as the ocean surrounds the land on every side but is not the land.[212] Yet this is not to be regarded as a mere standing alongside. Eternity is the quality of God in virtue of which he contains in himself the meaning of time.[213] Eternity is simultaneous duration.[214] We recall the biblical saying: "My times are in thy hands" (Ps. 31:15).

As regards omnipresence, it was stated in this regard that it is the ubiquity in which God cannot fail to be everywhere.[215] This being everywhere was explained as follows. God is everywhere in essence and not just in power and efficacy.[216] This was aimed at the Socinians and their mistaken doctrine that God is substantially only in heaven and that from there he exercises remote control, being only actively omnipresent.[217] As though his activity did not mean his presence! It was also stressed that God is present, not *synektōs,* as comprehended, but *synektikōs,* as comprehending and containing all things.[218] Hence we must not say that things coexist with eternity[219] but that eternity coexists with things — a rather different matter. A distinction is made: God is present as *God,* in a divine and not a circumscribed way (i.e., not as himself spatial in space like a hand in a pocket), not in a limited way (i.e., not under the limits of space as the soul is in the body), but in a repletive or relative way[220] (i.e., as the nonspatial God filling all spaces, containing all spaces in himself like a most minute point!).[221] Again, we are to think of God's omnipresence not

---

210. F. Burmann, *Synopsis theologicae,* p. 155.

211. Cf. *STh* I, q. 10, a. 2 ad 1.

212. Cf. Lipsius, *Lehrbuch der evangelisch-protestantischen Dogmatik,* p. 227; Nitzsch-Stephan, p. 410.

213. Hutterus, in Hase, p. 140.

214. Heppe-Bizer, p. 47; ET p. 65 (Polanus).

215. Quenstedt, in Schmid, p. 86. For this quotation cf. Hase, p. 141 n. 3.

216. Schmid-Pöhlmann, p. 94; Schmid ET p. 125 (Gerhard).

217. Nitzsch-Stephan, p. 457.

218. Schmid-Pöhlmann, p. 94; Schmid ET p. 125 (Gerhard).

219. Bartmann, I, p. 49.

220. Schmid-Pöhlmann, p. 94; Schmid ET p. 125 (Gerhard); cf. Nitzsch-Stephan, p. 457.

221. Gerhard, in Luthardt, pp. 77-78.

as *adiastasia* but as *energeia*.[222] It is efficacious and operative.[223] It is the presence of the Almighty.[224] Finally, our dialectical friend Polanus added in good Reformed style that God is omnipresent in such a way that he is totally in all things and totally outside all things.[225] God is not a prisoner of his omnipresence. Not as a denial but as a sharper interpretation of his omnipresence, Polanus said that God is outside the world, not in another world, but negatively, for all the space in the world cannot exhaust him; he is in himself and forever before the creation of the world.[226]

Please do not say that these are useless scholastic triflings! If we put them all together, we have a very serious and objective attempt to say what can be said about the positive relation of God to the world and us in loud and strong words such as we seldom hear in modern dogmatics and without betraying the mysteries of God, without surrendering, as often occurred later, the hidden No which in these attributes is the presupposition of the Yes. This attempt is a respectable one, and it will be rewarding to think it through in detail. It was a platform on which one could dare to take up in some intelligible way the great classical statements of the Bible: "I am the first and I am the last, and besides me there is no God" (Isa. 44:6); "Who was and who is and who is to come" (Rev. 1:8); "He is not far from any one of us, for in him we live and move and have our being" (Acts 17:27-28). God's antithesis and relation to the limits of our human existence are the great and solemn theme of the doctrine of his eternity and omnipresence.

But now we must make a sharp turn here again and recall that if this is not to be all up in the air, if this coexistent eternity and this omnipresence that contains things in itself as in a most minute point are not to be metaphysical ghosts, everything depends on this being *God's* antithesis and relation to the limits of time and space that are at issue in the doctrine. God is personality. God reveals himself. Eternity and omnipresence in themselves, as concepts, break apart. In these concepts we do not get beyond infinity unless we know them in a here and now in which we are known by God, in which we encounter his holy, righteous, and merciful will, in which we are the objects of his love. This is what is right in the intrinsically regrettable attempt of many modern theologians either

---

222. Schmid-Pöhlmann, p. 94; Schmid ET p. 126 (Hollaz).
223. Schmid-Pöhlmann, p. 94; Schmid ET p. 125 (Gerhard).
224. J. Gerhard, in Schmid, p. 86. See Schmid-Pöhlmann, p. 94; Schmid ET p. 125 (Gerhard).
225. Heppe-Bizer, p. 47; ET p. 66.
226. Heppe-Bizer, p. 61; ET p. 66 (van Riissen).

secretly or openly to rob these attributes of their force, for example, of Schleiermacher, for whom eternity and omnipresence are finally no more than other terms for spiritual omnipotence,[227] or of Ritschl, for whom eternity is the constant and immutable orientation of God's will to the Christian community in virtue of which God at every point, even centuries before Christ, experiences the actualization of his plan,[228] or of Seeberg, for whom omnipresence amounts only to the fact that as God wills all things, he is present to all things and all things to him.[229]

These are, of course, sorry dilutions of the strong wine of a doctrine that must be thoroughly and strictly maintained as the doctrine of God in the limit of time and space and not divested of its solemn universality by the unfortunate personalism and moralism that stand behind the reinterpretations. The limit of space and time is our limit, and the whole truth of the gospel and the law lies in the fact that in Christ time was fulfilled and the world was loved [Gal. 4:4; John 3:16]. Certainly we stand and move within other limits. I think of those of creaturehood and sin, which are not in themselves identical with that of time and space but must be distinguished from it. Nevertheless, all these limits come together materially, and there is thus good reason for having to speak about the limit of time and space, and not, for example, about that of sin, when we are looking at the divine attributes, at the conditions of our knowledge of God. It is only in the light of revelation, however, that we can speak meaningfully about these things. Our knowledge must be found at a place where all the knowledge of eternity and omnipresence in secular philosophy can find only offense and foolishness. The point here is that the eternal light has risen, and the circle of the whole world cannot contain what now lies in the virgin's womb.[230] We have to do what a D. F. Strauss could never cease shaking his head over when he spoke about such things.[231] We have to think of eternity and omnipresence together with personality. Things make sense only when there is this scandal. We must accept this as a particle of truth in all the confusion, and once again close with the thesis that it is God who is eternal and omnipresent, and that we cannot reverse this. The truth of the thesis lies in its irreversibility.

---

227. *CF,* I, §§ 52-53.
228. Ritschl, *Rechtfertigung und Versöhnung,* III, 1st ed. (Bonn, 1883), pp. 277-80.
229. Seeberg, *Christliche Dogmatik,* I, p. 408.
230. Quoting Luther's "Gelobet seist du, Jesu Christ."
231. Strauss, *Christliche Glaubenslehre,* I, pp. 561-62.

As regards the last two attributes, God's immutability and glory,[232] I will be brief. The doctrine of immutability is in some sense merely a compendium of all the attributes of aseity. God is always the same to all eternity with no shadow of turning.[233] He is necessarily what he is and such as he is.[234] This means that we are biting on granite if when we talk about God we want God and his Word to be other than they are. From the very outset God is the supreme court. There can be no bargaining with him. But God is also faithful. To protect this attribute against misunderstanding, against confusing it with Stoic fate or Hellenistic *heimarmenē,* we best explain it in terms of another attribute that is often adduced, namely, the veracity whereby he is known to be true in himself, true in his words and deeds, the author of all truth in creatures, and most foreign to all falsity, mendacity, dissimulation, or forgetfulness.[235] If there is any incommunicable attribute, this is it, for God is truthful and all we are liars [Rom. 3:4]. Finally, God's glory or majesty is the quality which according to the older theologians makes him the necessary object of our knowledge and worship. If you have understood what I have been trying to say in this whole section, then you have gathered that with each attribute I was trying to say: "*Thine* is the kingdom . . ." [Matt. 6:13]. If you have not understood this, then it is too late now to say anything specific about the glory of God.

---

232. Marginal note: "Thom. I, 9; Bartm. I, 132." (*STh* I, q. 9: De Dei immutabilitate; Bartmann, I, § 30, pp. 132-34.)
233. Heppe-Bizer, p. 47; ET p. 67 (Heidegger). Cf. Jas. 1:17.
234. Heppe-Bizer, p. 61; ET p. 68 (Heidanus).
235. Polanus, in Heppe, p. 50; Heppe-Bizer, p. 53; ET p. 98.

§ 18

The Election of Grace

If veiling is the content of God's unveiling and unveiling the point of his veiling, we are obviously set under a twofold possibility grounded in God himself. The hiddenness of God in his revelation might mean that with hearing ears we hear only offense or foolishness or nothing at all and therefore do not know God. In this case nothing special happens to us; without being aware of what it means we remain in contradiction, in guilt and need, and finally in the eternal perdition to which we have hopelessly fallen victim. Or else God's revelation in his hiddenness through the Holy Spirit becomes the basis of faith and obedience and therefore of knowledge of God. Something special then happens to us, for the darkness in which we find ourselves becomes the judgment of God, but we also participate therewith in the grace of God and the hope of eternal salvation. In the first case we are passed by or rejected by God; in the second case we are elected or accepted by God. In the either-or of this twofold possibility which is actual for each of us at this moment, God's glory triumphs no matter how the decision goes, and by each of us at each moment this decision is to be sought where it has been taken from all eternity, that is, in God's wisdom and mercy.

I. Introduction

We have dealt with God's knowability, nature, and attributes on the stretch of our inquiry that is now behind us. Starting with the presupposition of revelation, of God's address and our encounter with God, as this is made in Christian preaching or posited in the Bible as holy scripture, we attempted to look at all sides of the mystery denoted by the word "God" and to comprehend and describe it in human terms as though it were a static objective entity that we could contemplate objectively — the concept of revelation gave us the right to regard this assumption as legitimate. But in an unusually disruptive manner two things kept getting in the way: first, at every point the object was not willing to be an object, as it were, but confronted us forcefully, and completely forbade us in our conceptions to abstract away from ourselves as the one decisive presupposition of this conceiving, so that, because the matter was too pressing, we could never succeed in thinking through our concepts as we would have liked; then, the object was not willing in itself to be an object, but hardly had we begun to form concepts before it again wrapped itself in impenetrable obscurity and prohibited further approach, so that from this angle, too, we were left with strangely fragmentary concepts or conceptual fragments. All the same, we were not frightened off, but said to ourselves that in view of this great disruption, and its devastating consequences for any schoolmasterly understanding (and we have no other!), there is here an object that we must look into and give some account of. We thus moved forward and backward and forward again, and we now see before us a number of partly methodological and partly material conceptual fragments rather like the strange Cyclopian stone avenues in Britanny and other ancient dwellings of our oldest Europeans, which point to the place where the sun usually rises at the summer solstice, or once pointed to some constellation according to the earth's position at the time.

Once pointed! This brings us at a stroke to the whole problem and up against the realities that we have to deal with in this new section. Once pointed! Those stone avenues, 3,000 years later, no longer indicate today the constellation that was originally in view. They now point to a place where nothing in particular is to be seen. But how if it is the same with our conceptual fragments, which are in truth human work? Assuming that they have fulfilled their purpose for a moment, or more than a moment, and that they are not merely conceptual stumps, we have followed the best traditions of Christian scholarship and arranged and set them up in such a way that, as might have happened to even the most foolish workman 3,000 years ago, we see what we are doing and why we are doing it, and cheerfully forgetting the colleges and professors and manuscripts and Lutheran and Reformed scholastics and Schleiermacher and all the rest, we perceive that we are talking about God, that we can talk here because God has spoken once and for all, and that we must never forget that the strange wrinkles in our concept of God are tolerable, that we may even rejoice in them, because they are an expression of the reality of God that is concealed but that also declares itself in them.

Let us now assume that this is the happy situation. What we have said about God's knowability and nature and attributes is schoolmasterly, but for all that it is so tied to earth that it is still a true reflection of the knowledge of God *in actu*, both deriving from it and giving rise to it. But why should this be the only situation? The other situation is also conceivable that we have here only the flapping of a conceptual mill that does not help us; that we are not talking about the knowledge of God at all. And what was perhaps the situation for a person once might no longer be the situation for that person, not 3,000 years later but only a few hours later. We move away, other impressions claim our attention, the one incomparable recollection becomes one among others — it was just a concept of God and not the knowledge of God or the reality of God. If that is so, what a dubious matter dogmatic work becomes! How we must envy historians and those in other faculties who do not have to take such eventualities into account. And let us remember that the very same thing that we are talking about, the first situation and then along with it the second, that sinister Perhaps and Perhaps not, can apply just as well to the Christian preaching for which we are now in training. "Who believes our preaching, and to whom is the arm of the Lord revealed?" [Isa. 53:1]. In no Christian preaching is God's Word so proclaimed that we can exclude the second possibility, the possibility of the minister giving a fine and effective address but nothing else happening. And where and when does something else happen for everybody present, and where and when in such a way that it does so once and for all? One can certainly serve the Word of God with preaching, and that is why we theologians are here. But no one has yet found a way, and no one will, so to serve it that it is always heard and retained by all. The possibility of another situation seems to be intimately bound up with the matter itself.

Nor are things different with the Word of God in the Bible. One can obviously receive it or not receive it. One can receive it and then no longer do so. One can understand the Bible historically and spiritually, or one can think one understands it spiritually but in truth do so only carnally. All reading and exposition and circulation of the Bible stands under this caveat. What is true of the Bible is no less true of the revelation that stands in or behind or above it, of the Word of God in the primary sense. Look where you will, faith is not for everyone even at the source of all sources

[2 Thess. 3:2]. In a remarkably sober and natural way the Bible always reckons quite simply with the presence of disobedience, unbelief, hardness of heart, and obduracy. "Two will be grinding at the mill; one is taken and one is left" (Matt. 24:41; Luke 17:34-36). What the disciples saw and heard, Caiaphas and Pilate also saw and heard. What Peter and John saw and heard, Judas Iscariot also saw and heard. What was revealed to Peter at Caesarea Philippi, not by flesh and blood but by the Father in heaven, he could later deny in Jerusalem (Matt. 16:16; 26:69ff.). Some seed always falls on the path, some on stony ground, some among thorns, and some, but only some, on good ground [Matt. 13:4ff.]. The wind always blows where it will and we hear the sound of it but cannot tell whence it comes or where it goes (John 3:8). The Logos came to his own possession, but his own people did not receive him, yet to those who did receive him he gave the right to become God's children, even to those who believe in his name, of whom we then read in a puzzling saying that they were not born of blood, nor of the will of the flesh, nor of the will of man, but of God (John 1:12-13). Here already we have the positive side of our thesis for the section on predestination, namely, that belief in revelation, decision for the possibility of real knowledge of God, is exclusively the will and work of God.

The doctrine of predestination in its strict form — not the Roman Catholic or Lutheran but the Reformed form in which I propose to present it to you here (though with one incisive deviation) — both derives from and also aims at the truth that the twofold possibility that we have noted in practice relative to God's Word has its basis in God himself. The either-or that meets us in a rising curve and with increasing force as the human side face-to-face with preaching, the Bible, and revelation itself, is not primarily a human matter at all but the human and temporal shadow, manifestation, repetition, and outworking of a divine and eternal reality. The discussion that begins with the puzzling possibility that our concept of God can be simultaneously or successively both meaningful and meaningless compels us to give a new and wider turn to our concept of God. The obvious questionability of our knowledge of God, as it is set in the light of its object, must result in a basic enrichment of our knowledge of God. If it be assumed that the doctrine of predestination is correct and necessary, then what it says very generally is that at the point where the simultaneous presence and succession of faith and unbelief in different individuals or even in the same individual brings us up against what seems to be the riddle of the partial failure of the Word of God — at this very

443

point it may be seen in all truth that God's speaking is real speaking, that it replaces God's silence and can be broken off again by God's silence. What we encounter in a very vivid, concrete, and actual way in this simultaneity or succession is the fact that God is a living person — one of his attributes according to our general thesis and exposition.

When we have said what we can say about God as a static entity, then the first further word of dogmatics is this word *ad hominem:* Whether you know or do not know, understand or do not understand, believe or do not believe, all that we have said or him to whom all that we have said is pointing, either the one thing or the other, is already his work in you. You yourself cannot come up to this object, consider it, and decide what attitude to take to it. No, from all eternity this supposed object has considered you and decided about you, and no matter what attitude you take, you are his either for grace or for perdition. No matter what we may think about the doctrine of predestination, we have to let ourselves be told that in the context of the doctrine of God it means that the term "concept of *God*" is all the richer as a description of what God actually does. It is obviously one thing to say in a general sense that God lives, knows, or wills, and quite another, precisely under the pressure of the doubtful nature of what is said, to have to say further that he does this in particular, that he is the God of the election of grace, that he has mercy on whom he wills and hardens whom he wills (Rom. 9:18). This is the difference from painting and plastic art. It is as if a painting suddenly left its frame and came toward us. From now on we have to do with this God who acts concretely.

This is what is implied as we begin this new stretch of our work. We shall go on in the next sections to deal with creation and providence. But I think it makes sense to begin this new stretch with the doctrine of predestination in the Reformed fashion. In the usual Lutheran structure (though not in Luthardt),[1] predestination comes only in the fourth part either before or after the doctrine of justification.[2] On this view it is only a sparse construct or has only a shadowy existence. The Reformed order which puts it here[3] before the doctrine of creation tells us that the first and decisive thing that we have to know and say about the God who acts

---

1. Luthardt in his *Kompendium* puts predestination at the end of Part I before creation (Part II), sin (Part III), and christology (Part IV).

2. H. Schmid puts predestination in Part III (§ 30); cf. Hase, Nitzsch-Stephan.

3. Heppe-Bizer, pp. 120ff.; ET pp. 150ff.

concretely is that we with our faith and unbelief are in his hands and power. In us and our relation to the Word it must be demonstrated what it means that God's will is a Therefore! that brooks no Wherefore? Descending from this steep mountain we shall then see how far the same thing must be said in another way regarding the creating and governing of the world, then again in yet another way regarding our human fall and sin, etc. Thus, if the doctrine of predestination is correct, it may be said that it rightly belongs here as a continuation of the doctrine of God, both in relation to the dead point beyond which it leads us and in relation to what follows, which puts it in a proper light.

II. The Twofold Possibility

In view of our previous findings, the thought that God's revelation sets us in a crisis that is grounded in God and faces us with a twofold possibility can hardly take us by surprise. In § 15 we gave a definitely positive answer to the question of the knowability of God, but definitely in the sense of an indirect knowledge grounded in revelation, which meets us only in a mystery. In § 16, in opposition to mysticism, we gave a definitely positive answer to the question whether it is necessary and right to form a concept of God, but relying on revelation, and seeing that there is no revelation except in a mystery, we had to admit that beyond defining God's nature as personality and aseity we neither may nor can press on to an unequivocal concept. Then in § 17, again in opposition to a speculatively mystical theology, we definitely affirmed the reality of attributes in God, that is, of certain conditions under which he gives himself to be known by us in revelation, and which force us to give a material definition of the formal concept of his nature. But we saw that these conditions, in accordance with the knowledge and also with the nature that is known, fall into two groups: concepts of the conceivable and concepts of the inconceivable. In face of each of these conditions we had also to make it more or less clear that both the conceivable and the inconceivable that we were trying to state and formulate have their truth-content in the fact that they are the conceivable and inconceivable of *God* and not just a concept of God that we are presenting, that the whole amazing doxology of the Christian church and theology in no sense has its point in itself but in him alone by whom it is occasioned and to whom it applies, in the good pleasure with which he accepts it. It is not for us to say that he *must* accept it with good pleasure. He must if he *wills*, if *he* wills. He can say *Yes,* and does say Yes. But it is obvious that he can also say *No,* and does say No. In face of us clever theologians, who always try to do more than is fitting for us, and in face of the human race as a whole insofar as we have only representative significance, he has reserved it for himself to be the main thing in all the fine things that we think and will and feel regarding him, to be the head without which all things are at every moment nothing, absolutely nothing. "When thou hidest thy face, they are frightened; when thou takest away their breath, they die and return to dust" (Ps. 104:29). Christian theology and the Christian church live by the fact that God himself makes himself heard in free grace. They know and confess that we live by the Word that proceeds from God's mouth (Matt. 4:4). They know and confess that God can also take back this life-giving Word of his without being any the less glorious or divine or worthy to be praised. Grace would not be grace if things were different with God's Word. God would not be *God* if he did not have this freedom. Worship would not be worship if it were not addressed to God also and precisely in this freedom. But this freedom is the freedom of God's election of grace, of predestination.

Let us first look at the twofold possibility under which we are placed face-to-face with revelation. In the concept of revelation we continually came up against a diacritical element. This is to the effect that God's revelation always takes place in concealment. It is in the concealment of a hard, puzzling, by no means obvious objectivity that God's Word always meets us first, whether we are thinking of the human word of Christian preaching, the human word of the Bible, or finally the crucified man who is the object and focus of the biblical witness and in whom revelation took place according to this witness. Jesus Christ takes on a complete incognito here, *en homoiōmati sarkos hamartias* (Rom. 8:3). He is fully incorporated into the picture of weakness, questionability, relative significance perhaps, but perhaps also relative offensiveness which is the picture of all earthly things. The form to which the Christian church can point when it is asked: Where is your God? Where has he hidden himself? Where and what is his revelation? is a veiled form — veiled in the church's own present proclamation, veiled in the prophetic and apostolic witness, veiled even in that to which these first witnesses point. Now think again of our own dogmatic concept of God. Broken in all the dimensions with which it stands before us, it too is in truth a veiling.

But let us now turn to the positive side. This is God's revelation. Its possibility is that he enters into this concealment. God is directly and openly manifest only to himself. No one has seen God directly. It is for our good, in order that we might see and hear him, that the inalienable, nonobjectifiable divine I conceals himself in that by no means obvious objectivity, that he becomes a part of the human world and his Word a part of the human word. In this concealment God *is* revealed. Unveiling is the point of this veiling. It is Jesus Christ, God's Son, who enters into that incognito, then and there in Galilee and Jerusalem, then in the kerygma of his witnesses, then in the message of his church, miserable, no doubt, though that incognito often was. But the Crucified has risen. This was the power of the word of his apostles; this covers in advance the many signs of his church (cf. 1 Pet. 4:8). The Christian church knows very well what it is doing when it points steadfastly to that veiled figure, when it answers the questioner: There is not only *my* God and *our* God but also *your* God (Isa. 40:9), the God without whom we are eternally lost and by whom we are eternally saved. It is in relation to this *revelation* in concealment that we, fulfilling for our part the function of the one, holy, catholic church, have tried to present for this special purpose the concept of God, and ventured not to call our action foolishness, tempted though we might be to abandon its execution in detail. The diacritical element in the whole concept is clearly the relation between revelation and concealment even when we consider the matter on the positive side.

This relation is ambivalent, we now see. It might mean that here revelation is *hidden,* and it might mean that here *revelation* is hidden. In the first case the concealment is a great hindrance which makes the knowledge of revelation impossible. In the second case it is a gracious dispensation of God which makes such knowledge possible for us. In the first case we stand before a wall, find out that we cannot see through it, and complain that we hear the message but faith alone is lacking.[4] In the second case we stand before the same wall, still do not see through it, and say almost the same thing and yet not the same thing: "I believe, Lord, help my unbelief" (Mark 9:24). In the first case, on all sides we hear in it all only the No.[5] In the second case we also hear the No, but not without the deep secret Yes below the No.[6] In the first case the matter ends perhaps with serious perplexity regarding the improper, unfounded, and indeed in many respects religiously and morally dubious claim that is made there,

---

4. J. W. von Goethe, *Faust* I, v. 765.
5. J. W. von Goethe, *Iphigenie auf Tauris,* v. 451 (Act I, Scene 5).
6. Luther, WA, 17, II, 203, 39ff., on Matt. 15:21ff.

or with a resolve not to take it seriously since it is such an innocuous or irrelevant matter, or perhaps even with an indifference which has not been essentially dented from the very beginning. In the second case, face-to-face with the same fact, there is present what we call faith and obedience.

For the sake of caution and completeness, and remembering the possibilities envisaged in the parable of the Sower (Matt. 13:3-9), I will not omit presenting the either-or in a rather different form. In the first case we might have had some experience, we might have said Yes, Yes, we might have shown religious interest, we might have set out to preach to others, but in all this we might not have seen through to the mystery, the revelation might still have been concealed from us, more so than from the worst denier of God. In the second case we might have experienced nothing, we might have said No, No, we might have come to savage hatred of the theologians who think they know all these things, to the very end of life we might go about realizing only that we have here a question that will not let us be, and yet in all this we might have known that *revelation* is concealed here. But enough!

This is how the twofold possibility looks as it necessarily presents itself to us on the basis of that diacrisis. But we are anticipating. For us the first case, and only the first case, necessarily presents itself. The fact that revelation is concealed is easy to see and can be proved with cogent reasons that the church, if it is wise, will not try to refute. Where and when can revelation be seen in any way but incognito? Does not its denial have finally in its favor all the criteria and arguments of a quiet and self-possessed way of looking at human affairs? How then can those who by their own account know they are in the second case show that this is really so and that it is not all an illusion? Or where will they find criteria or arguments to show others that what these others think is only concealment and nothing more is really hidden revelation? The fact that the concealment is a hindrance to the knowledge of God is obvious. Not so obvious is the fact that it is a gracious dispensation of God to make the knowledge of revelation possible. Those in the first case would always reject it as a begging of the question if those in the second commit the folly of trying to make a proof out of what they can only assert. This has been so not merely in the modern period but as early as the days of Celsus, for by the nature of the case the chances of faith are as unfavorable as they possibly could be in conflict with unbelief. Faith has to assert, and its opponent need only stand by the fact that the revelation in which it believes is *hidden*. From this fact there is no way to the thesis that what is hidden is *revelation*. Faith confesses this, but it would itself inevitably become unbelief if it tried to prove it when for it, as faith, everything depends on there not being anything to prove here. If faith is really faith, then its proof is faith itself.

In relation to that twofold possibility, then, the first thesis is most necessary, the second is highly improbable. Who, then, can dare to step into the air and believe? Who can dare to say: I believe? But we are presupposing that this venture is being made. Let us not ask how far we feel that we share in this venture. It is enough if we say: I believe, or: We believe; with no proof, hopelessly exposed to all the protests and contradictions and suspicions, to all the winds, we still believe that it is revelation that is hidden here, that Christ is truly risen [Luke 24:34]. For the sake of discussion let us assume that those who say something of this kind are people whom we have to take seriously, whom we confidently believe know what they are saying when they say this, who do at least try to be clear about it, and let us then confront them with others whom we have also to take seriously but who for good reasons cannot or will not say it. What about these two possibilities? Why is it that some go to the right and others to the left? In a general sense, what happens is what Paul describes in Rom. 9:32-33 when, with a remarkable combination of the two prophetic texts Isa. 8:14 and 28:16, facing the unbelief of the Jews, he refers to the stone of stumbling and offense that has been set up in Zion, and then adds abruptly that those who believe in it will not be put to shame. This is the diacritical factor which is the parting of the ways. Why some go to the left is in the first instance at least understandable and needs little explanation. We have to admit that they have every reason in the world for doing so. But why do others go to the right? This is where the problem lies. If they are perspicacious, they will refrain from later supporting their faith with arguments, notwithstanding the fine victories won by Christian apologetics in every age. We have enough confidence in their boldness to think they they will make no efforts in this direction. But with the assured presupposition that there are those on the other side whom we have to take with equal seriousness, we have also blocked the path of saying that these others have not had such deep and penetrating experiences of conscience as they have, and hence have not come to the point where faith is unavoidable. If they are perspicacious, then even without our presupposition they will make no use of this point either. Nor will they say that we need a particular organ for faith that the others do not have or have not developed sufficiently, whereas they themselves enjoy it. Finally, they will not insist on special experiences that they have had even though they cannot say how or with what truth content. They will refrain from all these courses because if they took them they would be abandoning the presupposition on which they stand and which is the only thing that they have in common with those on the other side, namely, the presupposition that revelation is really hidden, so that it is not accessible to any secret human organ or unusual spiritual raptures. Do they not have to make a painful renunciation of all these things, and of all talk about their heart or mind or conscience, because they would be violating therewith their presupposition that revelation is *hidden,* and therefore their own thesis that *revelation* is hidden? Hence nothing seems to be left out but a simple *Credo,* I believe.

Or is there more that they ought to say? In description and elucidation of this *Credo* they might say: No matter what you think, rest assured that where you think you find only offense or foolishness (1 Cor. 1:23) or futility, we know God. We agree with you that at a first glance, and not merely a first glance, this is an unheard-of affirmation. But we believe that with what we say about ourselves we do not in any case have any advantage at all over you. We are so far from thinking this that we say that only God himself truly has knowledge of God. When we say about ourselves that we know God, the point at issue is not something that has developed or is spontaneous in us, or that has come about through the activity of our own spirit, though we cannot deny that our spirit is not inactive in this matter, for it is truly claimed in every respect. Yet it is only claimed. God knows himself, and he might be content with that, but he is not. Instead, through his Spirit he gives us a modest, human, earthly, fragile, but real share in his knowledge. Through his Spirit! We are not thinking of any experience but again of God himself, but of God himself as he calls us in such a way that we have to hear, that our whole person (we are not better than you or different from you) is converted to him. We did not find the hidden revelation, and therefore we cannot tell you how to do it. On the contrary, it found us. We did not elect God, and hence we cannot show you how we did it. God elected us. We did not rise up to faith and obedience in great piety, and consequently we cannot tell you about such matters. In all our impiety (yours can be no worse) our faith and obedience are there, not our work, but the impression made by God's seal ring in a wax that is poor enough but that cannot resist the impress. In all this we have told you no more than lies in the word *Credo,* but it should be clear now that we have nothing to boast about or to defend, that it is not because of deeper insight or more narrow-minded boldness that we have taken the right-hand path, but our eyes were opened and we were on this path which no one can enter, but on which one can only be born anew by the Word and Spirit of God.

We can still only turn up our noses at the helplessness of such a confession, yet we have to admit that where there is faith this is the only relevant answer that we can give to the question why one believes. God wills it.[7] He willed our faith and awakened it. That is why we believe. "I believe that I cannot of my own understanding or strength believe in Jesus Christ my Lord or come to him, but that the Holy Ghost has called me by the gospel, and illuminated me with his gifts, and sanctified and preserved me in the true faith."[8] Obviously denoted here is not a general or uniform action of God but a free and special action toward us. To this extent the basic thought of predestination is already attained and expressed in these words of Luther — how could it be otherwise? The choice or decision between the two possibilities does not lie in our hands but in God's.

III. The Shadow Side of Election: Reprobation

Faith would not be faith, faith in revelation, if it did not understand itself as willed, awakened, and effected by God the Lord. God is the primary subject of our knowledge of God. Only by God's free willing and doing can we become the secondary subjects. By the Holy Spirit, that is, by God himself, and not in any other way do we have a share in revelation. If these statements are true, and our Prolegomena and our doctrine of God have led us necessarily to them, then before we develop the doctrine of election positively, we must bring clearly to light its negative counterpart or foil. Election has to have a shadow side, that is, reprobation, just as the possibility of unbelief or offense corresponds to the possibility of faith and confronts it. If we can understand the possibility of faith only in terms of God's willing and awakening and effecting it, then obviously we can understand the possibility of unbelief only in terms of a divine nonwilling, nonawakening, and noneffecting, a planned and purposeful attitude of

---

7. Calvin, *Inst.* III, 23, 2; cf. Augustine, *De genesi contra Manichaeos* I, 2, 4; see MPL, 34, 175.

8. Luther's Short Catechism, 2, Art. 3.

God, a specific holding back, a presence and activity that produces a vacuum on the human side. Those who say A here must also say B. Those who say election seriously must equally seriously, with Reformed theology, say reprobation. Any basis for unbelief outside the divine will would *eo ipso* bring into doubt the fact that faith has its basis truly and solely in the divine will. If we could find a basis for unbelief in ourselves apart from God, at least in part, then we could find a total or partial basis for faith, for a faith that God did not will or awaken or effect, or did not do so totally, but that is totally or partially the result of our own piety or inspiration or conflict. But this faith would not be faith, faith in revelation. It would have no share, or only a partial share, in the promise given to faith in God's Word that in it we have fellowship with God. There are no half-measures here. There is no more or less. Faith is a Yes to God's Word with no ifs or buts, with no auxiliary reasons alongside God's Word. The fellowship with God that is promised to faith is either there or not there. It is not half there and half not. Hence we cannot talk seriously about any other disruptive basis for unbelief and disobedience outside God himself. We must grant to unbelief the same totality, originality, and transcendental character as we do to faith.

Obviously, we can properly appreciate the freedom of grace, in which it comes about that we may believe and obey, only if we realize that in the same freedom God might not be gracious but might let us walk in our own ways (Acts 14:16); only if, face to face with the factors of unbelief and disobedience in others and ourselves, we do not view them moralistically as a failing on our part, but as the working of God's withholding of grace, which can be reversed only at the source from which it comes, the free will of the holy, righteous, and merciful God. We do not properly appreciate the unheard-of thing that happens when we may believe if we interpret the situation of unbelief, whether it be that of others or of ourselves, as though God were passively neutral regarding us, letting us wait for him to grant us grace and faith or to restore it to us. Where, then, would be God's omnipotence and omnipresence? A God who is just an onlooker is not God. To be able to believe, to have to believe, is seen as grace only when we perceive that we are, as it were, passed from one hand of God to the other hand of the same God; that he who now receives us could with the same power reject us, hardening us instead of awakening us to faith and obedience; that the whole certainty and assurance of our acceptance rests in his freedom; that we are in his hands whether for grace or its opposite.

III. The Shadow Side of Election: Reprobation

I will first give you Heidegger's definition of reprobation: "Reprobation is the decree of God, by which out of the mere good pleasure of His will he has resolved to leave fixed men, whom He does not elect, in the mass of corruption and piling up sins on sins and, when they have been hardened by His just judgment, to visit them with eternal punishments, in order to display the glory of His righteousness."[9]

It will help to clarify matters if first in a little excursus[10] I touch at once on the point in this definition at which I feel compelled to deviate from the Reformed tradition, which in this regard is also the Roman Catholic and Lutheran tradition. It concerns the phrase "fixed men" (or "certain people") in Heidegger's definition. Reprobation, like election later, is supposed to apply to specific individuals, a fixed number.[11] Along with elect believers there are also rejected unbelievers. There are two separate groups like the blessed and the damned in medieval depictions of the last judgment, except that there the division is not apparent but is known to God alone. This is how Augustine understood the doctrine of predestination. This is how the Reformers understood it. This is how Roman Catholics, Lutherans, and Reformed (for all the distinctions in detail) understand it, unless they have completely dropped it. This is how all its opponents, both great and small, understand it.[12]

After all that I have said, you will not regard me as just a foolhardy innovator. And I for my part am fully aware that it is no secondary matter if I deviate here but that it will have the most far-reaching consequences. This is the rent in the cloak of my orthodoxy for which undoubtedly I would at least have been beaten with rods in old-time Geneva. Yet I can do no other. I regard this "certain people," this idea of two separated groups, as a secular error from which the whole doctrine, difficult enough in itself, suffers needlessly and irrelevantly. Having wrestled for years with Rom. 9:11, the *locus classicus* at this point,[13] I can only regard it as unbiblical. We cannot deny, of course, that this chapter teaches eternal, unconditional, twofold predestination. I have no intention of doing so. But eternal, unconditional, twofold predestination, God's free sovereignty over Jews and Gentiles that both has mercy and hardens, is precisely the theme and point of this chapter — not being predestined, not the different human states that result from predestination, as has been read off with remarkable obstinacy from some statements in the introduction (9:6-13) that are to be taken figuratively.

---

9. Heppe, p. 113; Heppe-Bizer, p. 113; ET pp. 178-79.
10. Barth put this excursus in brackets.
11. Cf. Heppe-Bizer, p. 140; ET p. 172.
12. Cf. the survey in Nitzsch-Stephan, pp. 705ff.
13. Cf. *Römerbrief*, 1st ed., pp. 356ff.; 2nd ed., pp. 316ff., ET *Romans*, pp. 345ff.

Naturally, specific people are catastrophically affected by the divine electing and rejecting, yet not some people as only elect and some as only rejected, but both as both. The Jews were elect, they are now rejected, and one day (11:25-26) they will be elected and loved again. Conversely, the Gentiles were once "not my people" but they are now "my people" (9:25), and yet, as the parable of the olive tree shows, they must be careful lest as presumptuous engrafted branches they are not broken off again as God broke off the natural branches. This means that God is free not only to elect and reject different people but also to elect or reject a particular individual at different times. It is in the eternal act of predestinating, as comes out in the different situations of a person face-to-face with it, that this divine freedom triumphs. It does not triumph in the situations as such, nor in their temporal definitiveness, which does not exist for God, for we have to re..iember that in relation to them God is greater than our heart (1 John 3:20). Predestination precisely as eternal predestination must not be confused with determination, with a decision regarding us whereby God has fixed his action for all time and is now the prisoner of his own decision for grace or its opposite. Precisely as eternal predestination, predestination is the divine decree in action, the divine decreeing concerning us in which at every moment God is free in relation to us and goes forward with us from decision to decision. As we see it, God's eternity means that "my time is in thy hands." It is not an ossified eternity but his living eternity, the eternity of his will, the eternity in which he is Lord. His unchangeableness is *God's* unchangeableness, which we know only in the inscrutability of his way with us, not in the comprehensibility of a fate which we can abstract from the givenness of a particular station on the way. In my view the traditional version of the doctrine must be rejected for this reason. It is an illegitimate abstraction. It anthropologizes or psychologizes a thought which strictly makes sense only as a concept of the knowledge of God. It mechanizes a truth which has its basis precisely in the inexhaustible life of God. It isolates an event in time from the event in the divine eternity instead of relating it to it. It stabilizes the divine either-or which is posited for us and which, precisely because it is the divine, inescapable, and serious either-or, must always be thought of as fluid.

This is not the time or place to go into the fateful consequences of this abstraction in church history or the history of doctrine. But it will be seen how precisely this "certain people," upon which the doctrine was thought to focus, and which aroused in the hearers an interest that was very understandable but just as passionate as it was irrelevant, necessarily raised the unhelpful question not of the living God but of his independent decree concerning particular people, and thus became the dead point, the sandbank upon which the doctrine of predestination continually ran aground. It is true that the passionate protest of modern Christianity, which was intimated already in the days of Calvin in a Bolsec or Socinius, and then at the beginning of the 17th century in the great movement of the Remonstrants, was not directed against this point but against the inconceivable mystery of God in his sharp, actual either-or. This protest was futile, and therefore the higher right was with orthodoxy in the conflict, for it upheld that which cannot be shaken, namely, the fact that predestination is eternal, unconditional, and twofold. The older Reformed church at the Synod of Dort (1618-1619) rightly struck down the protest, and did so with surprising force. It was right to do so because nothing lay behind the protest but the sighing of a semi-medieval, semi-humanist semi-Pelagianism such as Erasmus had defended against Luther.

But in its interest in the "certain people" orthodoxy had something in common with its opponents. These, too, were oriented to predestined individuals. They were abstracting. They were anthropologizing, mechanizing, isolating, stabilizing the relation of God to us in a more rational, understandable, and acceptable form, eliminating the element of the mysterious, the lofty, the majestic, and the free which they met in the orthodox insistence upon God's unconditional sovereignty. If only orthodoxy had met them more soberly, that is, simply with this insistence. The "certain people" was the worm in the timbers of Reformed orthodoxy. A hundred years after Dort the heresy that had been struck down was on the march into the church, and today, three hundred years later, even in the Reformed churches, not to speak of the Lutherans, there are few who do not honestly confess the semi-Pelagianism of the old Remonstrants. The "certain people," the perversion of the doctrine of predestination into a doctrine of predestined individuals, was the Trojan horse which was finally set up in the holy place in Ilion. If in truly classical proponents of the doctrine (e.g., Calvin)[14] it [the doctrine of predestined individuals] appears only as an occasional logical deduction, this becomes increasingly central in those who followed, and with its crass mythological arbitrariness it quickly made the whole doctrine unbelievable and untenable even for its most zealous champions.

Hence I could not espouse the doctrine of the election of grace, even in its Lutheran or Roman Catholic form, if it really were to stand or fall with that "certain people," if we were not permitted and even commanded, following trains of thought in Calvin and Augustine, to press back behind it to a better version which corresponds to the true intentions of these classical proponents, to objective exegesis of Rom. 9–11, and to the context of a Christian doctrine of God, and from which that "certain people" has been expunged, so that with elimination of this logically possible but materially absurd deduction, predestination becomes exclusively a basic description of God's dealings with us, of his free and actual use at every moment of the possibility of saying Yes or No to us, of electing or rejecting us, of awakening us to faith or hardening us, of giving us a share in the hope of eternal salvation or leaving us in the general human situation whose end is

---

14. *Inst.* III, 21-24.

perdition (cf. Phil. 3:19). I promised in § 12[15] that this would be a Reformed dogmatics but this does not have to involve mere repetition of the Reformed tradition. My conscience is clear that the dogmatics is Reformed in spite of my serious departure from the tradition and all its implications.

Having settled this matter, I will now return first to the doctrine of reprobation whose formulation by Heidegger was the occasion for the excursus. Having made the correction, and tacitly presupposing it in all that follows, we may confidently entrust ourselves to the older dogmaticians at every other point, though naturally we cannot hide the fact that all doctrine, and not just the doctrine of predestination, takes on a different appearance as a result of the correction.

What happens to people, then, when the hiddenness of God in his revelation causes them with hearing ears to hear only offense, or foolishness, or futility, and therefore not to know God? I said in the thesis that nothing special happens to them. We saw indeed in subsection II that the possibility of unbelief and disobedience is a very natural one. Over against that of faith it has every reason and probability in its favor. It is the authentic structure of human thought and consciousness. Faith cannot make its way into the human consciousness familiar to us. Those who believe are astounding to themselves. They are strangers to themselves. They can view their own faith only as a miracle that they can only affirm, to which they can orient themselves only because it is there and takes place, that they can derive from no other source than God. Faith comes into our orderly civil economy as *the* great extraordinary factor. It is as such that it maintains itself there. It does not legalize itself (either before or after) by asking for any residence permit or naturalization papers. This extraordinary factor, however, may stay away. The civil economy may go on undisturbed. Nothing special need happen. No alien guest has to knock at the door of the familiar human consciousness. We may be left to our own devices. This is our rejection by God. The older Reformed dogmaticians rightly described this as fundamentally a negative act. They called it preterition. God as the absolute Lord, as the *autokratōr,* passes us by.[16] He does not give us that which does not belong to us, to which we have no right or claim, for the giving or nongiving of which he owes us no account, which we cannot expect from him and do not in fact expect,

---

15. See above, p. 294.
16. Cf. Heppe-Bizer, pp. 144-45; ET p. 182.

namely, seeing and hearing him, knowing him, faith in his Word and obedience to it. Yet the Word of God still goes forth to us. The totally extraordinary thing is still close to us. The miracle is set before us, too, of not being able to stay alone but of knowing God and giving him the glory.[17] The concealment of revelation, even for us for whom it becomes a snare, is still the concealment of *revelation.*

Anticipating a main thesis of all antipredestinarians, both ancient and modern, we may say that God's will is that all people should not merely be helped (Luther) but *sōthēnai,* that they should be saved and come to a knowledge of the truth (1 Tim. 2:4). This is the evident, revealed, written, and proclaimed will of God as it comes in some way to all people at all times. But what if it does not find faith and obedience? Then people are again convicted of the inexcusable aversion with which they respond to God. They cannot complain that they were not told, did not hear, and could not know. Nevertheless, God's will is not broken but fulfilled in this form, as the will of sign or the revealed will, as we put it, in the seriously meant offer of grace, and as the will of decree or the secret will in the refusal of irresistible grace. The irresistibility or infallible efficacy of grace is what God owes to no one, though this does not provide an excuse. For, O man, who are you to call God to account (Rom. 9:20)? Accusing God or excusing oneself? And this apparently twofold will is still only *one* will, the will of *God,* though this one will of God is an incomprehensible will in face of which one can neither excuse oneself nor dispute with God. Naturally, it is not as a heavy fate or destiny that this fundamental reprobation takes place, nor as a mere absence of God. Full, sufficient, saving grace is present here as effective grace. This is the secret of this possibility of the divine will for us, and it is only when we see nothing of fate in it, whether against God or for us, that we understand this possibility of the will of God as such. We understand it only when we know that in this terrible situation we have fallen into the hands of the living God [Heb. 10:31], to whom our praise and worship belong even in this situation because he is God.

On the rest I may be brief. Older theologians differentiated preterition and predamnation.[18] The supposed ordinary human state into which faith and obedience come as something new and strange is in reality a state of guilt and need, of our flagrant rebellion against our Creator and

---

17. Heppe-Bizer, pp. 147-48; ET pp. 185-86.
18. Heppe-Bizer, p. 144; ET p. 181 (Wollebius).

therefore of the righteous divine wrath that falls upon us, of the rift that characterizes our whole temporal existence, though we cannot understand it as nature or destiny because in all its avoidability it is our own act, the act of our sin, that is, of our separation, parting, and isolation from God, of our independence over against him. As sinners against God we are *eo ipso* condemned and lost. We are judged by the righteousness of God. We cannot have fellowship with him. We are cut off from life. We are given up to the opposite of life, that is, death, and to the opposite of blessedness, that is, torment. We shall naturally have to speak more fully about these things in another context. Here it is enough to say that this is the situation in which nothing special comes to us from God inasmuch as God passes us by. It stays the same. "He who does not believe in the Son shall not see life, but the wrath of God *remains* upon him" (John 3:36).[19] As from our standpoint unbelief and disobedience are universal and self-evident, our only conceivable attitude, so from God's standpoint what corresponds to the ordinary rule of his righteousness is that those who turn from him should go their own way, and that everything should come upon them that has to do so on this presupposition. "Therefore God gave them up to the lusts of their hearts" (Rom. 1:24).

The mass of perdition[20] or universal corruption was what older theologians called this constitution of humanity that is in force apart from the efficacious grace of the Holy Spirit.[21] In it we are not necessarily serious offenders. On the contrary, morality, a good conscience, piety — subjectively honest and perhaps profound piety — are not excluded under the sign of this possibility. No, what we have here are simply people who are really on their own with their own ideas and powers and perspectives. They may not do or experience this or that bad thing. This is not the terrible aspect of the rejection under which they stand. No, the terrible reality is that they are so hopelessly left to do their own thing: To each his own.[22] Eternal damnation stands behind this "his." The reprobate can share the fulness of humanity, even of religious and Christian humanity. But under the shadow of the righteousness of God in virtue of which they are reprobate they heap up sin upon sin with their best thoughts and words

---

19. Marginal note: "Matt. 15:13."

20. Cf. Heppe-Bizer, p. 145; ET p. 181 (Leiden Synopsis).

21. Heppe-Bizer, p. 148; ET p. 185 (Waläus).

22. Cf. Domitius Ulpianus (170-228), *Corpus iuris civilis*, I/1, § 10; H. Martensen, *Die christliche Dogmatik* (Berlin, 1856), p. 349.

and works. As all things work for good to those who love God, who are called according to his purpose (Rom. 8:28), so all things that the wicked do and experience finally work for evil. All things stand under that sign that the reprobate is an *atheos en tō cosmō* [Eph. 2:12] — even his or her religion or prayers. The reprobate may twist and turn as they will, but they beat the air, they work for confusion and destruction, they are zealous for God but without understanding (Rom. 10:2). For them all things roll toward death. The biblical term for being left to oneself in this way is hardness, *pōrōsis*. Naturally, all that they do under this possibility that is grounded in God's will, they do themselves. They are not marionettes. They act on their own responsibility. They are not given up to a fate but to themselves. Their will is not psychologically unfree, but their heart is hardened. The older Reformed struggled with might and main against the logical deduction imposed upon them by Roman Catholics and Lutherans, namely, that according to their teaching God is the author of sin. Not at all, they replied. Sin, which rules in the circumscribed area to which the reprobate are banned, is not God's work, though it is certainly God's work that the reprobate are banned there and thus left to their own devices.[23] It is nothing but justice if God leaves people to themselves, for it is they who sin. It is nothing but justice if he condemns and punishes the hardened, for it is they who sin.[24] The fact that God passes people by and therefore condemns them adds nothing new to sin, which is not of God. Things just remain the same. The only point is that sin is recognized and taken seriously. Thus sin is the cause of ruin, not God.[25] We cannot complain against God and excuse ourselves. Our rebellion against God is a fact. If we really see the will of God in it[26] — but if we do, that is the beginning of the end of rejection and already a transition to election — then we justify God who has thrust us out as rebels, and we condemn ourselves.

Let us now turn to the second possibility, to election. We find in the canons of the Synod of Dort[27] the following complete and excellent definition (except for the one point): Election is the immutable decree of God before the foundation of the world, by the free good pleasure of his

---

23. Marginal note: "Rom. 9:20." (Cf. Heppe-Bizer, p. 148; ET p. 185.)
24. Heppe-Bizer, p. 148; ET p. 185.
25. Heppe-Bizer, p. 147; ET pp. 184-85 (Heidegger).
26. Marginal note: "*Inst.* III, 23, 8."
27. *BSRK,* p. 844.14-25; cf. Schaff, p. 582.

will, whereby in sheer grace he chose from the whole of the human race (which by its own fault had fallen from original perfection into sin and corruption) a certain number of people — no better nor more worthy than the rest but sharing the same plight — to salvation in Christ, whom from all eternity he foresaw as the Mediator and Head of the elect and hence as the presupposition of salvation, and thus resolved to give them to him for redemption, and to call them effectually and draw them by his Word and Spirit, or to endow them with true faith in him, to justify them, to sanctify them, and finally to glorify those who are kept by his power in fellowship with his Son, in demonstration of his mercy and to the praise of the kingdom of his glorious grace.

Regarding this we must say especially that we have to be clear that election and rejection are in no sense symmetrical. They do not stand alongside one another as equally true and real. None of the great champions of predestination thought this, though reprobation is also God's will. Predestination means neither fixed will of election and rejection nor vacillation between the two. Its point and goal are always election, not rejection, even in rejection. Rejection does not take place for its own sake but in revelation of the righteousness of God in order that God's mercy might be manifested in his election, and in order that in it all, though in this irreversible order, God himself might be known and praised. For God's electing the decisive point is that God's revelation, which has become possible through his incarnation in Christ and the gift of the Holy Spirit, should unequivocally proclaim our election. Those who are addressed in Christ by the Spirit are elect and not rejected. Rejection does not have the same significance. We cannot deny it. We must always remember it. We must insist upon it. Yet it is the shadow side of election. It arises in virtue of the hiddenness of revelation. This is unavoidable if revelation is to be revelation. But its point and goal are revelation in concealment. The concealment is not an independent truth. Hence rejection is not an independent truth either. It has to be recognized and acknowledged, because all recognition and acknowledgment of the truth of God comes about as God is on the way with us *from* here *to* there; because election would not be election if it were not the opposite of rejection, and would not be knowable except in this antithesis.

For the sake of this antithesis, even in the light of election we must also with fear and trembling[28] weigh the possibility of rejection. But the

---

28. Cf. 1 Cor. 2:3; 2 Cor. 7:15; Eph. 6:5; also Kierkegaard's *Fear and Trembling*.

way leads fundamentally from rejection to election, not vice versa. God has shut up all in disobedience in order to have mercy on all (Rom. 11:32), not vice versa. God wants to go forward with us, not backward. Hence I would not say that election and rejection are in a relation of tension,[29] nor that they are polar opposites or opposing centers. Treating them as equal or symmetrical may seem to be very illuminating and appealing, but it does not correspond to the fact that God turns to us in revelation. We certainly have to take into account his simultaneous turning aside, but this is only the ineluctable consequence of the circumstance that revelation without concealment would not be revelation. In himself and primarily, Christ is the Savior and Head of elect humanity, and only implicitly and secondarily is he also the Judge of rejected humanity. "God sent his Son into the world, not to judge the world, but that the world might be saved through him" (John 3:17; cf. 12:49). This is unequivocal, true though the secondary point is that those who do not believe are judged already (John 3:18). This balance or tendency in the relation of the two possibilities must not be sacrificed for the sake of pleasure in a logical parallelism. Thus the word "twofold" in the concept of twofold predestination has to be understood from a divine perspective, like all else in dogmatics. The divine to which we orient ourselves in it is the divine Word, without which we could do no dogmatics at all. But the divine Word does not say No. It says Yes, for the Yes constantly breaks forth out of the No. If this is not remembered, then we make an idol once again of the freedom in which God is to be worshiped, which is the point of the whole doctrine.

Let us now turn specifically to this second supreme and dominating possibility. In the definition of Dort that I gave you, the heavy emphasis hits us at once: This is of the most free good pleasure of his will, in sheer grace. Heidegger declares similarly that God alone is the cause of election.[30] This is obviously the core of the whole doctrine, and after what we said in subsection II above we need not elaborate on it. Heidegger is indulging in speculative though not unfruitful thoughts when he continues that what moved God to this stupendous work was the love of his glory, and especially the mutual love of the three persons in God in virtue of which they work reciprocally with great ardor for their mutual glorification.[31] If only

---

29. An allusion perhaps to the criticism in P. Althaus, "Theologie und Geschichte," *ZST* 1 (1923-24) 767-68.

30. Heppe, pp. 123-24; Heppe-Bizer, p. 134; ET p. 164.

31. Heppe-Bizer, p. 135; ET p. 165.

we were closer again to such a living and strict idea of God's eternity. But this "God alone" must be safeguarded by a number of critical negations. We follow here the vigorous Polanus: Not (1) the will of man, nor (2) a good use of grace, can cooperate as a basis outside God himself.[32] Such statements may be found at times in early and medieval writers, and they are not unknown in Roman Catholic theology. Yet we have to say that official Roman Catholic teaching, represented especially by Thomas Aquinas and his school, took over and maintained the basic thought of Augustine that the first grace is the pure, free grace of God, and that this is independent as such of any use that we might make of it.[33] No less resolutely than the later Calvin, Thomas finally writes that he could find in us no effective cause of predestination. The divine will is the only reason why some are elected to glory and others are reprobated.[34]

More important is the third point in Polanus: Not our foreseen faith.[35] This leads us to the difference between the Reformed doctrine of predestination and the orthodox Lutheran teaching. According to the latter we must distinguish between God's antecedent will in this matter and his consequent will. The antecedent will aims absolutely and universally at the salvation of the whole human race.[36] This will is conditioned, however, by the merit that Christ won for us.[37] It is fulfilled by the consequent will whereby God elects those who, he foresees, will make use in faith of the means of grace by which we come to share in Christ's merit, and who will persevere in this faith to the end of their lives.[38] The *prothesis* is thus defined by the *prognōsis*,[39] the divine *intuitus fidei* in Christ[40] which was defined also as the eye, as it were, of divine election.[41]

Against the natural protest that according to the Lutheran doctrine faith is a spontaneous act of ours that conditions divine grace, it was argued that they were thinking only of foreknown faith, or faith in correlation[42]

---

32. Heppe, pp. 124-25; Heppe-Bizer, p. 136; ET p. 166.

33. Barth is referring to a note in his edition of the *Summa theologica* on *STh* I, q. 23, a. 5.

34. *STh* I, q. 23, a. 5 i.c. and ad 3.

35. Heppe-Bizer, p. 136; ET p. 166.

36. Schmid-Pöhlmann, p. 188; Schmid ET pp. 278-79.

37. Ibid., p. 189; ET p. 278.

38. Ibid., p. 192; ET p. 282 (Hollaz).

39. Ibid., p. 192; ET p. 285 (Hollaz).

40. Ibid., p. 194; ET p. 288 (Hollaz).

41. Ibid., p. 195; ET pp. 289-90 (Hutterus).

42. Ibid., p. 194; ET p. 288 (Quenstedt).

(perhaps the best that can be said for the Lutheran view, but in this case it becomes Reformed), so that they regarded it only as an impulsive and not a principal cause.[43] We can only be astonished that a theology that bears the name of him who wrote *The Bondage of the Will* could accept such teaching,[44] and we can understand why in face of it the Reformed insisted at every point on their "God alone" and "sheer grace." Face-to-face with the common Protestant doctrine of the incapacity of fallen humanity, the Lutheran doctrine is intolerably defective. Instead, the Reformed said that our faith is not in any sense the cause of election, but we believe and persevere in faith because we are elected to eternal life.[45] Faith follows election.[46]

The fourth point of Polanus is: Not our foreknown merits.[47] What is rejected here is the teaching of the Jesuit Molina whereby God's decree follows his foreknowledge of the merits that are to be expected in us, a real caricature of the Lutheran idea of foreseen faith. More important is the next point: Not Christ's merit.[48] This is again aimed at the Lutherans. For, the Reformed said, the coming of Christ and his atoning death on the cross, like our faith, are an effect of divine election.[49] Who is elect? Not the individual, but the whole mystical Christ, that is, Christ with his own,[50] Christ as the Head and Redeemer of the church.[51] In this sense the Reformed wanted to recognize election in Christ. Election is understood as the act by which the church is created and in which at the same time the "God alone" and "sheer grace" triumph more than ever. The institution of Christ as Mediator and Head of the elect, their effectual calling and drawing to him, their justification, sanctification, preservation, and glorification — all are his work, as we heard already in the passage from Dort.

Finally, Polanus's sixth point, the ultimate end of election, that is, God's glorifying in his mercy, is not the determinative basis of election.[52]

---

43. Ibid., p. 194; ET p. 289 (Baier).
44. Schmid, pp. 206ff.; Schmid-Pöhlmann, pp. 188ff.; Schmid ET pp. 277ff.
45. Wendelin, in Heppe, pp. 125, 167; Heppe-Bizer, p. 136; ET p. 166.
46. Hottinger, in Heppe, pp. 127, 170; Heppe-Bizer, p. 138; ET p. 170.
47. Heppe-Bizer, p. 136; ET p. 166.
48. Ibid.
49. Heppe-Bizer, p. 136; ET p. 167 (Wendelin).
50. Ibid., p. 137; ET p. 168 (Mastricht).
51. Ibid. (Leiden Synopsis).
52. Ibid., p. 136; ET p. 166 (Polanus).

God does not need to glorify himself in this way. "The supreme good could not behold any object other than himself."[53] If he elects us, it is his good pleasure, his free love for us.[54]

If these points are good, then we have in fact to say that if God's revelation in concealment is by the Holy Spirit the basis of faith and obedience, and therefore of knowledge of God, then something special happens to us, *the* great special thing that can happen. We have to put the stubborn and exclusive Reformed "God alone" behind the fact of faith as the only basis for it — naturally, God alone in Christ — in the elect fellowship of his mystical body, with all the goods and graces that this means, yet precisely here and beyond all the goods and graces, God alone. We have to set before us once again that passage from Dort which tells us that the elect are not better or more worthy but share the plight of all.[55] If we do this, then we get some glimpse of that special thing. In the thesis, in order to make clear the material connection with reprobation, I said that the special thing is that in this situation the general darkness in which we find ourselves with all others, in distinction from the general non-noticing, becomes for us the judgment of God. I emphasize: the judgment of *God.* Without this emphasis it would be all wrong. Naturally, an insight into the questionability, fragility, and brokenness of existence, which one might also call a recognition of judgment, does not in itself have anything whatever to do with election. But a recognition of the judgment of *God* on our situation, the recognition of which we spoke in our discussion of reprobation, an acknowledgment of the factual state of rebellion in which we find ourselves, an acknowledgment of the fact that in this situation there is a hidden will of God who has let us fall into it, an acknowledgment that he was right to do so because we deserve no better, an acknowledgment finally that we are in the wrong — this has everything to do with election. We may now say that those who know that they are really rejected, rejected by God, also know therewith that they are elected, and in and with this knowledge, though not through it, of course, they are participants in the grace of God. For when God is known, even though it be in judgment, then he is known totally, and therefore also in his grace. When the divine No to us is truly heard, then it is broken through by the divine Yes, whose shell it is. Grace is not in itself the reverse side of judgment. But *God's*

---

53. Ibid., p. 136; ET p. 167.
54. Ibid., p. 136; ET p. 166.
55. *BSRK,* p. 682.22-23; Schaff, p. 582.

grace is the reverse side of *God's* judgment, we must say. Those whom God *loves,* he chastens [Heb. 12:6]. In his election the judged as such are also the elect. For within the general judgment in which they, too, stand, they are sought and found by the grace of God which is not merely offered but effectual, awakening them in their sinfulness to faith, just as judgment drives them, as those who are judged by the gracious God, to a posture of obedience.

In this regard it may be noted that the elect in Christ are not plucked out of the mass of perdition, out of rejection, in such a way that they are no longer sinners or mortal, or that they are totally or even partially lifted out of the darkness of human existence. Election does not give rise to any island of the blessed or Pharisaic corner of the righteous in the world. The special thing about the elect, so long as time endures, is the special thing that happens to them through God's Word, the forgiveness of sins that is promised to them, the demand that is addressed to them and that binds them, not their special possessing and fulfilling. The special thing is that, addressed in truth by God, and no longer left to themselves like the rejected, they can say that in both body and soul they are not their own, but belong to their faithful Savior Jesus Christ.[56] In what they possess and enjoy, in their possible piety and morality, they are in principle in the same situation as the rejected world around them. They are fully aware of sharing the burden of its curse and banishment. If they are wise, they will not want to alter one jot of the verdict passed on them, namely, that they are no better or more worthy than the rest but set in the common plight. It is as the judged that they are elected and gathered around their Head, Christ. They are rescued from the perdition that hangs over the rejected, not because they are better or more fortunate than others, but because within the world, beyond the condemnation under whose current woes they sigh, they have a sure and certain hope in God, who has received them, sinners and mortals, and written his promise upon their hardened hearts and blinded, foolish consciences. No one and nothing can separate them from his love [cf. Rom. 8:35] in a here and now in which everything seems to speak for this hiddenness and wrath and their own condemnation. This eschatological reality on the margin of their profane existence, this uncreated light whose broken rays shine on all things, this miracle, this new and inconceivable but also inexhaustible fact, is the special thing for them. The elect might also perish (i.e., on their own side), writes Riissen,

---

56. Heidelberg Catechism, Qu. 1; see Schaff, p. 307.

but they cannot fall away on the side of the decree, of God.[57] The Holy Spirit, through whose power our weak faith and obedience become the subjective possibility of revelation, is the special thing in the election of grace. His action is also the special thing, the last and proper thing, at which we see God aiming in his rejecting and electing — the God who precisely in his revelation shows himself to be the God of eternal, unconditional, twofold predestination.

IV. Special Questions in Reformed Theology

In conclusion, so far as is practicable, I would like to express my views on some special questions raised by the treatment of the doctrine in the older Reformed Theology.

1. I will begin with a few words on the famous inner Reformed debate on Infralapsarianism and Supralapsarianism. The issue here is the relation of predestination to the creation of the world and humanity and the fall of the human race. What is the first, primary, and original thing in the one will of God that we see in some way in all these acts? According to the usual view, what we have here is not, of course, a temporal *prius* but a logical and material *prius*. Are creation and the fall presupposed in predestination? Or is predestination the presupposition of creation and the fall? Is the object of predestination created and fallen humanity or humanity that may be created and may fall?[58] Have we to think that God first created humanity to his own glory, and then, again to his glory, to bring to light the incapacity of the unfree will (so the Leiden Synopsis),[59] permitted it to fall into sin, and only then, once again to his glory, brought into force the decree of election or reprobation in relation to this fallen humanity? If so, the revelation of God's righteousness and mercy that follows in the act of election and rejection is not God's final and absolute goal, but strictly it is subordinate to the revelation of his omnipotence, wisdom, and goodness in the act of creation. Does the election of grace refer only to God's glory in the governance of fallen humanity and not to his glory in relation to humanity generally and absolutely?[60] This is the

---

57. Heppe-Bizer, p. 141; ET p. 175 (Riissen).
58. Ibid., p. 131; ET pp. 158-59.
59. Heppe, p. 120; Heppe-Bizer, p. 130; ET p. 158.
60. Heppe-Bizer, p. 137; ET p. 159 (Heidegger).

Infralapsarian view, that of the majority of the Reformed theologians, as represented, for example, by Cocceius, Heidegger, Riissen, Wendelin, Wollebius, and the Leiden Synopsis.[61]

Over against it, the other view relied constantly on Eph. 1:4: *exelexato hēmas en autō pro kataboles kosmou,* "he chose us in him before the foundation of the world."[62] The Infralapsarians had to turn this statement into the platitude that predestination did not merely arise in time with the fall but belongs to God's eternal being.[63] But the Supralapsarians claim that God creates humanity immediately and originally with the destiny of manifesting his glory by manifesting mercy and righteousness. He thus created the human being as a rational creature in his own image, that is, as a being in which he might cause his own attributes to shine forth. The human was thus a creature that could fall, having a will of its own. Election and rejection are then the execution of this first and original decree, affecting created humanity.[64] This is the Supralapsarian view, that of the minority. In the Reformed confessions, and especially at the Synod of Dort, it finds no express recognition, though it was ardently represented at Dort by the Dutch under the leadership of Gomarus.[65] Hase calls it the esoteric orthodoxy of Reformed theology which fortunately never found a place in the German Reformed churches,[66] and Heppe calls it the private opinion of a few individuals.[67] But among these few were not only Bucanus, Gomarus, Trelcatius, Braun, Burmann, and Mastricht, but also above all Zwingli and Calvin.[68] Stricter logic and a higher material necessity are to be found on their side. The Infralapsarian idea of an indefinite general glory of God in creation and the fall, which is then followed by the glory of mercy and righteousness as a second factor,[69] is indeed very strange. It could at any rate be set in dangerous proximity to the idea of a general revelation outside Christ. The Supralapsarian view is a true barrier against any attempt to view with only partial seriousness the need to stand

---

61. Ibid., pp. 129ff.; ET pp. 155ff.

62. See *BSRK,* p. 844.14-25; Schaff, p. 582.

63. Heppe-Bizer, pp. 121, 134; ET pp. 151, 162 (Bucanus).

64. Ibid., p. 131; ET pp. 160-61 (Braun).

65. Cf. B. A. Schweizer, *Die protestantischen Centraldogmen,* II (Zurich, 1856), pp. 182, 186.

66. Hase, p. 224 (Hutterus redivivus); see Heppe-Bizer, pp. 120ff.; ET pp. 150ff.

67. Heppe, p. 122; Heppe-Bizer, p. 133; ET p. 162.

68. Heppe-Bizer, pp. 132ff.; ET pp. 160ff.; also Luthardt, p. 96; *CD,* II/2, pp. 127ff.

69. Heppe-Bizer, p. 131; ET p. 158.

within the act of revelation, the crisis of God's mercy and righteousness, against any attempt to view it with seriousness and yet at the same time to glance aside at another possibility of relationship with God, a relationship in which God's mercy, our being snatched out of the mass of perdition, the miracle of God's glory in his grace, alongside which stands his judgment as its shadow, is no longer the last word that we can say to ourselves about God's Yes.

I myself take the Supralapsarian position. As I see it, predestination is set at the *beginning* of God's ways. The decision before and under which we are set by God's Word in Christ is *so* decisive that we are not permitted to go back to an indecision, indefiniteness, or neutrality in God prior to this decision. The decision is always first and supreme. From and to all eternity we are simply the objects of the mercy and righteousness of the divine will. How can God's omnipotence, wisdom, and goodness be anything other alongside these? Predestination is the secret of creation *and* redemption *and* consummation. Even when God is all in all (1 Cor. 15:28), when the sun is at its zenith and the shadow of judgment will be merely under our feet, God will be all in all in the triumph of his mercy and freedom. It is in the light of this end, which it would be arrogant to bypass in defiance of the Word, that we are to think about the beginning. But in that case we can think only along Supralapsarian lines.

Other problems that arise for us, as they did for the older dogmaticians, out of the relation to predestination are (2) the problem of assurance (of truth and salvation), and (3) the problem of ethics, or, more generally, that of the relation of predestination to the human faith and obedience that are willed, awakened, and effected by the predestinating God. In regard to both issues the predestinarians have always aroused suspicion.

2. We turn first to the problem of assurance. Lutheran cartoons of Calvinists from as early as the 16th century depict a man on his deathbed with his Reformed pastor at his side, and this pastor can give him no better consolation than that Christ did not die for all, that some are elected and many are rejected from all eternity.[70] Where is the certainty of faith and salvation if behind what we can know and feel and grasp of God's love in faith stands his secret will with scales in hand, and we cannot say with apodictic certainty whether they will drop in favor of our election? This objection is even more difficult to answer, it seems, if you take my version

---

70. For an example cf. E. Doumergue, *Iconographie Calvinienne* (Lausanne, 1909), p. 200.

of the whole doctrine according to which the concept of predestination does not refer to a fixed number of elected or rejected people but according to its original sense describes the divine attitude to all people at all times: "God has concluded all under sin in order that he may have mercy on all" (Rom. 11:32). In the light of this twofold "all" it seems that in principle there can be no assurance of election and therefore no assurance of faith and salvation. That would mean the end of the crisis, the resolution of the actual "either-or" in favor of the "or," of election. In face of the older doctrine as well as this corrected Reformed doctrine, only assurance of God seems to be possible, and it may be noted that with our close relating of predestination to revelation even assurance of God, and along with it assurance of Christian salvation and therefore of Christian truth, no longer seems to be apodictic.

What am I to say to all this in the name of my worthy predecessors and in my own name? I would say that we must admit frankly that a serious, that is, Reformed, doctrine of predestination, either in the old style or the new, because it thinks out consistently the "God alone," sets the whole problem of assurance on a mountain peak where we might fail to hear or see it. If we are to speak about certainty here, then in no respect can we view it as anything but a human certainty, *in itself* relative, not apodictic, the reflection, with many question marks, of a certainty which is absolute, apodictic, indisputable, and self-resting, which I do not *have* in faith but in which I believe, so that paradoxically enough I am certain of it. Does this mean that *my* assurance as such is doubtful? Yes indeed, we must reply, so long as we view it as such, apart from the fact that as I constantly seek and find its object, as its object finds *me,* the object of this certainty of mine that is questionable in itself, my certainty can share in the self-certainty of the object and can thus be called adequate from an earthly standpoint, sufficient from day to day like the manna in the desert [cf. Exod. 16:14-21]. As Reformed, we cannot boast of the *absolute* assurance that Lutherans old and new always claim to have. For their own part the elect may be lost,[71] nevertheless — and we may be content with this — they may confidently expect that food for the journey from day to day and thus march on from the relative to the relative in a *reflection* of the absolute, though without having it in their pockets. Certainty is supreme in respect of God, writes Heidegger,[72] but in respect of us it is so great as to suffice for salvation and its consolation in this life.

---

71. Heppe-Bizer, p. 141; ET p. 175 (Riissen).
72. Heppe, p. 130; Heppe-Bizer, p. 142; ET p. 177.

The Reformed answer to the question where our assurance lies consists radically, then, in a reference to the place from which it comes, to the object in respect of which it is supreme. It consists radically of a reference away from the believer to the revelation of God which is the basis of faith in God. There is an analogy here to the religious psychological circle, as we said in the Prolegomena, but exclusively from above to below, so that it is not the same thing.[73] Calvin in particular had only one answer: We shall not find assurance of election in ourselves, nor even in God the Father if we think of him apart from the Son. Christ, then, is the mirror in which we must contemplate our election, and may do so without self-deception.[74] I know of no other reply to the question about certainty of God. This is first (subjective genitive) God's own certainty, and as ours it is to be sought in God's revealed, written, and preached Word whose content is Christ.

But with this answer Calvin and his followers were not merely setting forth the nature or source of their assurance of God but also the nature and source of their assurance of election, salvation, and faith. Do we have to renounce this if in the doctrine of predestination we speak only of God's action and not at all of a corresponding being in us? I firmly reject this conclusion, and remind you of what I said in subsection III above about the relation between election and reprobation, about their lack of symmetry, about the tendency, the *pollō mallon* in this relation. The predestinating God, known in his revelation, is not a double Yes and No, election and rejection, though in our poor theological heads, with which we constantly think past the matter, there may present itself the cheerless concept of an eternal up-and-down such as one might get in a cage of hyenas. In his revelation this predestinating God addresses us. This means that his Yes and No, his self-revealing and self-concealing, enter into a distinctly dynamic relation. The Yes breaks forth from the No, the message of the resurrection from the word of the cross, God the living Lord from aseity, from the absolute mystery of God, election from rejection — not, I say, as the end of the ways of God but as their undeniable goal in the light of Christ.

Our definition of certainty with regard to this object must take the same course. There can be no question of absolute certainty. Even the older Reformed with their "certain people" advised those who believed

---

73. See above, pp. 80ff.
74. *Inst.* III, 24, 5.

they could know they were elect to take up an attitude of fear and trembling before him who can cast both body and soul into hell [Matt. 10:28]. All that they say, with Calvin at their head, is impressively serious, as though the possibility of rejection were still open for the elect, as though the dark thundercloud of the divine wrath were on the distant horizon for *them* every day. One need only look at Calvin's face, which, as has often been objected against him, is not the face of a radiant child of God running clear in virtue of election. But Luther's face, too, has a very different look from that of Lutheran dogmatics. There was really no occasion for the anathema that Trent pronounced upon the supposed assurance of election taught by the Reformers.[75] No, there is here only a relative assurance for which they had to fight and pray each day, constantly going back to the sources. And I think I am simply drawing an inference from what the older dogmaticians taught about the gift of perseverance[76] if I say that the sources were in fact open on both sides. Naturally, I am not making the shallow statement that all are at every moment both elect and rejected. But I am saying that all are at every moment under the divine either-or and can be either elect or rejected. No one is hopeless, and no one is yet in port. All can and must seek the decision where from all eternity (but from God's living eternity) it has been made for time, and will now be made in time one way or another according to *God's* will. With reference to our actual situation I am simply saying herewith what the Christian church has always said.

There is, of course, a relative assurance of God, and therefore also of election and salvation, as surely as we know God in his revelation in Christ as the one whose will is to save and not to judge [John 3:17]. This is why Calvin insists so much on the fact that Christ is the mirror of election. In him we know predestination primarily as election, not without a sharp dialectical reference back to rejection, not ignoring for a moment the cross, the judgment, the condemnation in which we stand, yet by way of condemnation — indeed, by way of hell itself — to salvation and life. In this *teleology* of *God* that is revealed in *Christ* (we must stress all three words) there is the source of our certainty of election and salvation. Thus again, not in ourselves, not in an abstract idea of God, but in God's revelation, and there most certainly, we too, as we look there, can and should be most certain. We are not less certain because we must seek

---

75. Session VI, ch. 12, and *Can. de iust.* 15-16, in DS, 1540, 1565-66.
76. Cf. Heppe-Bizer, p. 461; ET p. 581.

certainty every moment. We do not seek it anywhere but above in Christ, to whose body, the church, we belong here below, the church in which the Spirit is at work, presenting Christ to us, the triumph of divine wisdom and mercy, as he speaks to us by the Word and makes us one with him as we receive food and drink in the Lord's supper and are strengthened and kept for eternal life. This is how it stands with the Reformed doctrine of assurance in this context. It is eschatological and, in the last resort, as indicated, it is churchly and sacramental. We cannot go into that now. It will be enough to say that this doctrine is not guilty of the charge that is often brought against it.

3. I can deal more briefly with the problem of ethics. The accusation brought against the doctrine of predestination in this regard from as early as Paul's day is so familiar that I hardly need formulate it. But naturally the fact that it crops up continually points to a misunderstanding that seems to be inevitably present. Why ask: What shall we do?, if we and all that we do are elected or rejected? If election and rejection mean determination, the fixing of the human will by fate or nature in a particular direction and form? If the act of predestination, the posing of an either-or to us, does not conversely free again the human will that has been set in specific forms and directions? If the divine freedom in which God turns to us is not a reminder of our own transcendental freedom? Certainly, it is only a reminder. Freedom does not come, even in election. But the *problem* of ethics, the problem of a pure will, is posed. How could it be posed more radically than by the fact that with our whole existence, which we will day by day, we are placed under the either-or of judgment in the grace of *God?* Calvin describes as the "grunting of swine" the unceasing and banal objection of anti-predestinarians with reference to ethics, and he boldly advances against it the fact that those who have ears to hear cannot speak of the ethical consequences of predestination in that way, but have to see that the goal of election is holiness of life.[77] The very last accusation that one can bring against Calvin's theology is that he does not find a proper place for law, penitence, obedience, sanctification, and the new life, that these are not deeply embedded in his thought. For him the work of the Spirit is from the very first twofold; justification and sanctification, divine sonship and penitence, gospel and law, faith and obedience are all correlates that cannot be separated for a single moment. The ethical consequences that he draws from predestination sound fully as though

---

77. *Inst.* III, 23, 12-13.

predestination is something quite different from determination. And rightly so!

But then, I conclude, from this angle, too, the "certain people" must be dropped, for that means determination. In its place we must put the pure, original, divine self-relating. Then everything is clear. For precisely in the terrible transition from judgment to grace, which is never a thing of the past, there arises that practical commitment to the will of God, the question: What shall we do?, the recognition of the eternal demand, the need for work and conflict in the world of the relative, the possibility of taking up in bitter earnest concrete tasks in the shadow of the transitoriness of all things earthly, the Christian life[78] which is lived with bowed head in meditation on the future life, which is unassuming but which is determined from within. Eschatology and ethics, predestination and ethics are totally inseparable from serious predestinarian thinking once we understand the first term in an actualist rather than a determinist way. The Reformed theologians even ventured to set the problem of ethics in dialectical relation to the problem of assurance. Thus Wollebius answered the question of assurance with the following syllogism: "Whoever feels in himself the gift of sanctification . . . is justified, called . . . and elect. But I feel this by the grace of God. Therefore I am justified, called and elect."[79] For Lutherans this is naturally an unacceptable and very dangerous statement, and one cannot deny that Pharisaism, the specific Reformed vice, couches at the door. Nevertheless, it was not meant in this sense. We have only to emphasize "*gift* of sanctification," to note that it is through God's grace, and to recognize that on the Reformed view obedience belongs to grace no less than faith, and we shall understand the point of the thesis: In those who are addressed by God not only is faith awakened, but *eo ipso* obedience as well, which is just as much a gift of grace as faith is. If we are no longer sure of our faith, then standing in obedience might be for us a sign that we are still standing in grace, in fellowship with Christ. We would not stand in sanctification did we not also stand in justification and therefore in election. One can, of course, find this train of thought questionable, and those who do not feel secure about the incontestable purpose with which Calvin himself could have stated it do best not to argue along these lines. But the statement shows, precisely as an extreme deduction, that serious objection cannot be taken to predestination in terms of ethics.

---

78. *Inst.* III, 6 and III, 9.
79. Heppe, p. 129; Heppe-Bizer, p. 142; ET p. 176.

4. The treatment of predestination begins in Calvin, and closes in most of the Reformed dogmaticians, with a twofold warning concerning the application of the doctrine in Christian preaching. The warning is against any audacity, temerity, or curiosity in the matter.[80] We must not attempt any Icarus flight.[81] We should observe biblical soberness, modesty, and moderation, writes Calvin; where God closes his mouth in sacred scripture, there we should call a halt.[82] We should not act speculatively as though we sat in the council of God. We should not work from above downward in the development of an a priori idea of God. We should proceed analytically rather than synthetically.[83] We should start with the visible signs of election or rejection as we see them more or less unambiguously in the different possibilities of human attitudes,[84] then refer back from these, then press on step-by-step to intimation of the final human secret that rests in God. In my view we must stand by the revelation in Christ and thus start with what predestination is in the first instance, that is, election.

The second warning is that we must not preserve a sacred silence regarding what we can and should know and say, an affected *tapeinophrosynē*.[85] How can election be proclaimed except in antithesis to rejection? Why do scripture and even Christ himself speak about the latter? Under a pretense of modesty and sobriety we must not be satisfied with brutish ignorance (Calvin).[86] Serious error lurks behind cautious silence.[87]

I can only underline these two warnings, the first even in relation to the older writers themselves. In my view the idea of a "fixed number" of the elect and reprobate rests on a palpable curiosity that we would do better to avoid. It is also illegitimate temerity to do as Schleiermacher did[88] and supplement the election of grace with a doctrine of apocatastasis which maintains that the election of all is the end of the ways of God. That election and not rejection is the goal of the ways of God is the most that we can and must say along these lines. Christian hope clings to the promise

---

80. *Inst.* III, 21, 1.
81. Heidegger, in Heppe, p. 136; Heppe-Bizer, p. 149; ET p. 189.
82. *Inst.* III, 21, 3.
83. Heidegger, in Heppe, p. 137.
84. Heppe-Bizer, pp. 149-50; ET p. 189.
85. Ibid.
86. *Inst.* III, 21, 3.
87. See Heppe-Bizer, p. 149; ET p. 189.
88. *CF*, II, §§ 118-20.

of the electing God. But it is the promise of the electing, free, and majestic God. The idea of apocatastasis, of the elimination of rejection, cannot derive from knowledge of this God. We must be content simply to say that he is on the way with all of us if we are not to go beyond the act of the knowledge of God. More than that is not theology but enthusiastic metaphysics.

Yet I would observe that we must handle my own version of predestination with the same prudence and restraint. There is truth in the judgment of Hase that in its strict form the doctrine of predestination is a bit of esoteric orthodoxy.[89] Its place is especially the theological school. It is there primarily for Christian preachers deliberately and quietly to consider in all that they say. They will say many other things better and more credibly if they say them with an eye on the God who can elect and reject and with whom alone is the power and freedom to know him truly. Once the doctrine of predestination is grasped, it is the death of all Pelagianism and semi-Pelagianism. It has always cropped up in church history when this foe has had to be resisted. Yet I would not advise that it be presented too often or expressly. It is best to show in some other way that what is at issue here has been understood. If we do present it, then we should do so analytically,[90] referring back, pointing to a final mystery, the mystery of the divine freedom under which we stand when we stand before God. Remember here too, and here precisely, that in the theses of dogmatics we have to do with the basic statements and presuppositions of Christian proclamation and not with material that we have to bring as such to the congregation. To these basic statements and presuppositions which we can and should sometimes present expressly in the pulpit, the doctrine of predestination belongs as one of the most important. Always and not just at times we must follow its compass. There can be no exoteric communication to the congregation that is not permeated by this esoteric doctrine of God's grace alone. All this is surely the point of the second warning of the older Reformed. The doctrine of predestination is a very sharply polished knife. It is good and it is also dangerous that this is so. It will undoubtedly do harm in the hands or on the lips of fools.[91] May we all have a good grasp of the matter and know how to handle it.

---

89. Hase, p. 227.
90. See Heppe-Bizer, pp. 149-50; ET p. 189.
91. Marginal note: "Prov. 26:9."

Index of Subjects

Absolute, the 369
Act 372, 403
Adam 147, 161, 166; new 161, 163-64
Advent 142, 151
Affirmation: divine 100, 128, 194, 461,
  464-65; human 154, 169, 171, 209;
  self 74, 209
Apocatastasis 474-75
Agnosticism 259
Analogy. *See* Revelation
Anhypostasis 90, 157, 163
Anthropology 191-92
Anthropomorphism 92
Anti-Moralism 62
Apologetics 24-25, 52-53, 64, 67, 79,
  106ff., 132, 161, 182, 221, 226, 271,
  289
Apostle 147ff., 233. *See also* Prophets;
  Witness
Aristotelianism 259
Art 33-34, 163
Assurance 47, 52, 67, 289
Astronomy 350
Atheism 64, 86
Attributes of God 88, 91, 375ff.; analogy
  397-98; aseity 371, 396, 406, 426,
  435, 445; blessedness 422ff.; communi-
  cable 375ff., 384-85; deduction 384ff.;
  division 384ff.: dialectical 390-91; intuitive 389-90; psychological 387; religious 387ff.; eternity 432ff.; freedom
  409, 415-16, 435; glory 439; hiddenness 426ff.; holiness 418ff.; incommunicable 375ff., 394-95; knowledge:
  natural 412; of vision 412; life 402-3;
  love 422ff.; majesty 439; mercy 420ff.;

and nature 377-78; objectivity 378ff.;
  omnipotence 404ff.; omnipresence
  428ff.; omniscience 410ff.; personality
  401ff., 428-29; power 404-5; righteousness 419ff.; simplicity 428ff.; subjectivity 378ff.; uniqueness 429ff.;
  unity 428ff.; way: of causality 398ff.;
  of eminence 398ff.; of negation 398ff.;
  will 414ff.; free 416; natural 416; revealed 417-18; secret 417-18; wisdom
  413
Authority 4, 15, 227ff., 256, 260, 270;
  absolute 248, 295; church 13, 202-3,
  219, 222, 229, 232, 245ff., 255, 260-
  61, 267, 296; confessions 239ff., 293-
  94; divine 16, 203, 266; fathers 237ff.,
  291; moment 243-44; relative 245ff.,
  291-92; scripture 53ff., 211, 215,
  219ff., 229ff., 248-49, 256-57, 260,
  291. *See also* Freedom

Baptism 68, 99, 233-34, 237, 240
Baptists 33, 211
Beginning 202, 255
Bible. *See* Scripture
Biblicism 65, 259, 288ff., 298, 300

Calvinism 173, 239
Calvinistic Extra 158ff., 172
Canon 15-16, 53ff., 99, 150, 212-13,
  231ff., 245ff., 257, 290. *See also*
  Authority
Catechism 39, 83
Christianity 5, 20, 23-24, 77, 145, 164,
  184ff., 206, 255, 280-81, 296; abso-
  luteness 150, 281; modern 207

476

Christians 35, 64, 266, 280
Christmas 151-52
Christocentrism 90, 120
Christology 132, 151-52, 294; apotheosis 115-16, 123; early 116-17, 153; kenosis 156; a posteriori 141-42, 151; a priori 140. *See also* anhypostasis
Church 4, 24ff., 33, 35-36, 40, 67, 100-101, 152, 154, 177, 189, 202, 237, 239-40, 242, 244, 252-53, 286-87; body of Christ 169, 202, 208; communion of saints 207; early 55, 99, 145, 153, 161, 233, 248; history 102-3; Lutheran 34, 54, 241, 247; medieval 207; Methodist 34; Protestant 31, 236, 242, 286; Reformation 240; Reformed 34, 54, 241; Roman Catholic 31, 34, 203ff., 219, 240-41, 248, 252; teaching office 243ff., 267, 295; truth 150; Union 34; unity 240; watchman 244, 261; and world 209, 248
Church history 55, 102, 203ff., 219
Celibacy 164-65
Certainty 47, 52, 67, 289
Comfort 83, 86
Command: and blessing 165, 179, 198, 243, 251, 272; of hour 244
Commandments, Ten 193
Confession 29, 40, 99, 103, 109, 123ff., 153, 169, 247, 312
Confessional writings 40, 239ff.; Lutheran 240; Reformed 17, 220, 233, 240-41, 294-95
Conscience 29, 50, 91, 172, 243, 252, 275. *See also* Heart
Consciousness 74, 137, 175, 216, 253, 284, 292; faith 26, 28, 81; God 82, 94; modern 66; religious 25, 28, 302; self- 98, 104, 174, 184, 186, 188, 190, 281. *See also* Theology
Contemporaneity 145-46, 148, 205ff., 210, 267
Conversion 25
Covenant 144ff., 303; new 144-45; old 144-45
Creation 76, 123, 155, 165, 176, 466
Creator 165, 169, 179, 187
Crisis 36, 46, 74, 148, 209, 246, 248, 281, 284, 435
Culture 25, 49, 70, 188, 216

Death 46
Dependence, absolute 47, 124, 184ff.

Despair 195, 197
Dialectic 65, 77ff., 83, 92, 100, 102, 120, 129, 140ff., 154, 160, 172, 182, 206, 241, 259, 272
Divine, the 153, 184
Doctrine, pure 30, 272ff., 296-97, 302
Dogma 13, 17, 28, 39-40, 132, 167, 193, 239ff., 247-48, 292, 294-95; fundamental 103, 105, 154. *See also* Authority
Dogmatics 47, 132, 167, 187, 194, 287, 290-91, 306, 309; actuality 295-96; autonomy 210-11, 231, 285ff., 304, 306; biblical attitude 288ff.; Christian 292-93; church 205ff.; confessions 292ff., 298ff.; dogma 13-14, 17-18, 26ff., 40; fundamental principle 300-301; goal 23ff.; loci 278, 303, 305; Lutheran 171-72, 241, 292-93, 300-301; medieval 21; modern 173; new 21, 40; norm 123, 280ff.; object 8ff., 133; penitence 36; presuppositions 13; principles 82, 132-33; prolegomena 23ff., 132-33, 279; Protestant 12, 39-40, 167, 237-38; Reformation 21; Reformed 171ff., 293ff.; regular 38-39; science 8ff., 38, 312; service 38; symbol 13; system 304-5; task 5-6. *See also* Formal principle; Material principle
Dogmatism 289
Doubt 64-65, 289

Election 440ff.; assurance 468ff.; absolute 469ff.; relative 469ff.; "certain people," 454-55, 473; Christ 454-55, 473; mirror of election 471; curiosity 474; ethics 472-73; foreseen faith 462-63; foreseen merits 463; freedom of grace 452; grace 459ff.; Dort 455, 459-60; infralapsarianism 466ff.; Lutheran 443, 453ff., 462-63, 466ff.; mass of perdition 458, 465; preaching 474-75; predamnation 457-58; predestination 443ff.; preterition 457-58; Reformed 443, 453ff., 466ff.; rejection 460-61, 470; Remonstrants 455; reprobation 451ff., 456ff.; Roman Catholic 443ff., 453ff.; supralapsarianism 466ff.; teleology 471; twofold 445ff.; will of God 457, 461
Enhypostasis 157
Enlightenment 59, 122, 246, 248, 252
Enthusiasm 115

Index of Subjects

Epistemology 126, 135, 271, 285
Eschatology 208
Eternity 50
Ethics 66, 258-59, 472ff.
Event. *See* Revelation
Exegesis 256ff., 290, 306. *See also* Method
Existence 4, 71, 77, 126, 179-80, 190, 230, 255, 261, 265-66, 269
Experience 6, 15, 28, 61-62, 67-68, 82, 86, 89, 126, 148, 170, 183, 196, 214ff., 223ff., 254, 281, 286ff., 290ff., 302-3; religious 47, 51-52, 94, 171, 185, 286ff., 290ff.

Faith 8, 27, 30, 46, 50-51, 64, 67, 147ff., 169-70, 214, 246-47, 269, 308, 335ff.; act 87, 172, 233ff., 242; certainty 86, 448-49, 472; decision 190-91; emotion 195; God 11; obedience 134, 152, 168ff., 202, 218, 222, 251, 292, 307ff., religious 94; venture 129, 218
Fall 29, 155, 162, 466ff.
Fathers 4, 215, 237ff., 245-46, 292
Feeling 28, 61, 82, 126, 153, 186-87, 254, 259, 273, 311; religious 26, 178-79, 186, 209. *See also* Dependence, absolute
Fideism 11, 171, 172-73
Flight from God 50
Forgiveness 89, 300
Formal principle 88, 248, 289, 291, 300-301, 303
Freedom 229, 243, 250ff., 268, 270; absolute 261-62; authority 232, 250ff., 260-61, 360; Christian 251ff., 257, 260, 262; relative 261-62

Gnosis 117, 154
God 88, 155, 275; action 12, 14, 24, 30; address 58, 60-61, 67ff., 80ff., 88, 126, 168, 192, 194, 203, 225, 251, 275, 285, 303; aseity 371, 396; authority 58, 78, 93, 135ff., 143; concealment 147ff., 335; deity 101, 135, 153, 312; encounter 137ff., 146-47, 150, 153, 161, 167, 179, 194; faith 11-12; Father of Son 99-100; Father God 100-101, 113; freedom 105, 176, 264, 294, 371; gifts 89, 128, 275; good pleasure of 180; He 179, 187; history 367; honor 76, 109, 172, 197-98, 202, 225, 278, 294, 312; immanence
112, 134; incarnation 78, 192, 203; incognito 138, 144, 184; inconceivability 58, 160; living 114, 119, 270, 325, 351ff., 402-3; Lord 96, 111, 124, 130, 146; over contradiction 113, 118-19, 125, 136, 180, 196; love 85, 89, 422ff.; majesty 134, 154, 176, 294, 439; mercy 208; mystery 93, 152, 216, 308, 420ff.; name 4, 110, 134, 327; nature 41, 93, 101, 119, 176, 351ff.; objectivity 11, 48-49, 57, 65-66, 101, 134, 160, 187, 267, 307-8, 327; person 113-14; 179, 185, 367; personality 369ff.; power 172, 189; predicates 89, 120, 307; problem(?) 289; proofs 48, 346ff.; reality 62, 122-23, 162, 176, 246, 266ff., 308; relation 120, 126, 129, 161, 172, 294; righteousness 67, 419ff.; subject 11, 57, 62, 65-66, 75, 78, 89, 101, 103, 120, 135, 138, 160, 185, 193, 205, 265, 307-8, 310, 332; time 160; transcendence 82, 112, 134, 186; unity 101, 240, 270; unknown 150; victory 118, 125; vision 337; voice 34, 91, 111, 222, 283; will 123, 172, 193, 198, 243, 414ff.; wisdom 119, 230, 413; with and in us 118, 268, 308; wrath 50. *See also* Trinity
God, concept of 119, 294
God, knowledge of 9, 12, 62, 65, 92, 113, 125, 130, 135, 194, 311, 331ff., 339ff. *See also* knowability of God
Godlessness 85, 246
Gods 49, 70, 106, 123, 166
Gospel 81, 259. *See also* Law
Gothic 71
Grace 78, 169, 172, 179, 190, 194, 310
Guilt 46, 77, 155, 164, 195

Hearing 24, 33, 73, 78, 110, 125-26, 192, 239, 253, 255, 259ff., 281
Heart 115, 225, 270, 308
Heathenism 123
Heaven 102, 109, 222, 312, 436
Heresy 100, 117, 211, 287, 302
Historians 108, 123, 257-58, 264
Historicism 218, 260
History 4, 33, 49, 53, 104, 148, 163-64, 202-3, 297ff., 231, 237, 248, 270, 292, 302, 305; apotheosis 60, 206. *See also* Moment
Holy, the 59, 62

Index of Subjects

Homiletics 29, 32, 276
Hope 50, 119, 151
Humanism 41, 251
Humility 305, 313, 359-60

I 50, 74, 255, 289; divine 135, 141-42; human 136-37; and Thou 46, 58, 62, 255
Idea 77
Idealism 115, 135, 139, 259
Idol 61, 89, 246, 257, 292, 302
Immediacy 25, 36, 155, 193, 207, 214, 232, 248-49, 262, 294
Incognito. *See* God; Jesus Christ
Individual 46
Intellectualism 153; anti-intellectualism 62, 103, 273
Inwardness 61, 215
Irrational, the 75, 196
Irvingites 34
Israel 147-48, 215

Jesus Christ 65, 79, 84, 152, 169, 270, 283-84, 292, 454, 471; *amētōr-apatōr* 165; baptism 123; birth 123, 148, 152, 161; conception 154, 160-61, 165; consubstantiality 124, 154-55; cross 111, 148ff., 197, 207, 214, 266; death 111; deity 62, 114ff., 138ff., 154, 156, 165, 310-11; divine likeness 119, 124, 154-55, 162; fact 142-43, 152, 156, 202, 212; God-man 90, 139ff., 162, 165; historical 79, 90-91, 215, 257; humanity 90, 156ff., 164ff.; incarnation 91, 131ff., 155, 173, 176-77, 196, 202, 222, 228; incognito 178; Jesus of Nazareth 60ff., 90, 110ff., 145, 157, 184, 190, 214; Kyrios 100, 102-3, 108ff., 116-17, 123-24, 146, 153; Logos 90, 92, 98, 105, 110-11, 115, 118, 154-55, 157-58, 166, 184, 269-70, 274; *ensarkos-asarkos* 160; Mediator 155, 160; Messiah 148; obedience 111; resurrection 123, 143, 149-50, 160-61, 164, 196, 233; return 108; Revealer 113, 117, 119ff., 143, 196; Son of God 99-100, 113ff., 152, 156-57, 176-77, 202, 214, 270; Son of Man 248; truth, 112
Judaism 123, 145
Judgment 37, 65, 197, 208-9, 254, 266, 308, 472
Justification 163, 172, 300, 472

Kerygma 16, 18, 24, 27-28, 63
Kingdom of God (Heaven) 111, 119-20, 155, 188, 194, 308
Knowability of God 325ff.; adequacy 329ff.; Holy Spirit 329; indirect 331; judgment 339ff.; limit 331ff.; mystery 331ff.; nature 328-29; subjectivity, divine 332; unknowability 328-29
Knowledge 8, 39, 87, 103, 151; of God 47ff., 87-88. *See also* God, knowledge of; Truth

Law 197, 248, 272, 368. *See also* Gospel
Liberalism 246, 264
Life 49, 62, 77, 162, 178, 246; élan vital 179; eternal 113; experience 215, 223, 281, 283; inner 25, 90, 178
Liturgy 31
Logos of situation 230
Lord's Supper 158, 169
Love. *See* God, love
Lutheranism 32, 171-72, 239, 469

Male 162ff.
Man, humanity 9, 69ff., 75, 131, 273, 277; alienated 72ff., 77, 119, 155, 174, 180, 184; before God 50, 80, 85, 127, 174ff., 284, 307; contradiction 73-74, 76ff., 95, 111-12, 118ff., 126, 139, 155ff., 174ff., 179, 311; creature 139, 164; divine likeness 74, 216; fallen 157, 311; home 73, 119, 155, 161; individual 53, 202, 229, 242ff., 251ff., 261-62, 270; modern 133, 182; nature 156-57; new 196; organ for God 61, 89, 135, 138, 173, 204; pious 281; plight 50, 77; prisoner 84ff.; problem, riddle 136-37, 155; relation to God 80-81, 84, 113, 125-26, 135, 177ff., 192, 281, 294; recipient of revelation 69ff., 127-28, 175-76, 251; religious 287; wanderer, pilgrim 74, 77, 125; will 74, 80, 192, 301
Man-God 82
Mary 274; God-bearer 152, 157; virgin birth 160ff.
Material principle 88, 287, 300ff., 319
Metaphysics 10, 12, 120, 154, 188
Method, historical 143ff., 216ff., 233, 236, 254
Middle Ages 274, 280-81
Miracle 77, 149, 160ff., 173, 176, 192ff., 269-70, 308

Moment 210, 230-31, 243-44, 248, 260, 270, 295
Monasticism 164
Monotheism 100, 188
Morality, morals 70, 73, 177, 188, 232, 273
Mysticism 130, 139, 177, 189, 193, 252, 259, 271, 352ff.
Myth 114ff., 165-66, 224

Naturalism 243, 274
Nature 33-34, 46, 49, 73, 91, 98, 144; philosophy of 166
Nature of God 351ff.; aseity 371, 396, 406, 426, 435, 445; conceivability 351ff., 359ff.; concept 351ff., 358; definition(?) 361ff.; He, divine 369; incomprehensibility 351ff., 356ff.; inconceivability 351ff.; mysticism 352ff., 362-63; mystery 361-62; personality 369ff., 445; speculation, 363ff.; Spirit 409
Neighbor, love of 193
Neo-Protestantism 7, 44, 105, 220, 238

Obedience 37, 54, 62, 233, 291, 472
Objectivism 126, 224-25
Offense 149ff., 192, 197, 209, 211
Office, ministry 52, 133, 243, 269
Organic 179
Origin 113, 118
Orthodoxy, Protestant 9, 13, 21, 30, 59-60, 65, 103, 130, 157ff., 166, 205, 235, 238, 273ff.

Pagan, paganism 91, 149-50, 302
Paradox 58, 64, 77, 86, 90, 116, 151, 153, 174, 198, 215ff., 273
Pastors 16, 32-33, 35, 38, 53, 64, 201, 248, 269, 275-76, 468
Pastoral care 67
Peace 50, 189
Penitence 36, 51, 112, 172
Person 123; Jesus 90ff., 117; religious 6, 90
Philosophy 12-13, 20, 46-47, 55, 60, 66, 72, 75, 82, 102, 106-7, 135, 216, 258ff., 289-90, 296
Pietism 9, 122, 211, 225, 259
Piety 70, 75, 85, 94, 100, 182, 184, 188, 194, 215
Pious states 11
Pious words 280ff., 298-99, 304, 312

Platonism 259
Possibility-reality 279
Prayer 3, 70, 151, 153, 172, 180, 193
Preaching 14ff., 23ff., 54, 81, 131, 153, 192, 212, 261-62, 295-96, 306-7, 312; act 17, 23, 267, 273ff.; modern 70-71; style 70-71; text 55; venture 201ff., 265ff.
Predestination 226, 443ff.
Primal history 148
Proclamation 4, 35, 40, 55, 192, 203, 280, 286
Progress 49
Promise 151, 194, 209, 234, 237; and fulfilment 145, 148-49, 217
Prophet 93, 124, 141ff., 243ff., 261ff., 312; and apostles 14-15, 24, 92-93, 146-47, 217, 222, 229, 248, 267-68, 280, 288; extracanonical 149-50
Protestantism 33, 36, 40, 57, 109, 169ff., 204ff., 251ff., 294; modern 211, 214, 248, 252
Psychology 124, 152, 196-97
Pulpit 71, 276

Question: divine answer 83-84, 94ff., 155, 162, 171, 179, 194, 308, 311; human 46, 67, 83, 85-86, 94. *See also* Response
Quietism 173, 189

Radicals 211, 262
Rationalism 71, 101, 211, 221, 224
Realism 135
Reality 162, 279, 295, 342ff.
Reason 19, 60, 94-95, 100, 197, 221
Reconciliation 79, 196
Redemption 155, 190
Reformation 5, 31, 33-34, 122, 169, 212, 219, 251, 296
Reformers 32, 41, 90, 195-96, 210-11, 215, 238, 251, 257
Regeneration 25, 28
Religion 9, 17ff., 30-31, 47-48, 66, 72, 81, 94, 106, 125, 145, 181ff., 215-16, 280, 285-86; disposition 91, 94, 183; genius 215, 217; history of 61, 105, 109, 123, 151, 181, 190, 216-17; of Israel 145-46; philosophy of 19-20, 47, 52, 55, 61, 181; psychology of 181
Religionism 11
Religions, founders of 107, 115
Remonstrants 4, 211, 455

Response: divine 92; faith 15; as question 171-72, 194. *See also* Question
Responsibility 50, 77, 252, 291, 312
Revelation 15, 24, 28, 35-36, 58ff., 86, 103, 117-18, 150, 153, 248, 255, 266ff.; act, event 58, 87, 93, 180, 187, 228, 248, 266ff.; analogies 91, 94-95, 109, 224; *autopistia* of 179, 187; church 202ff., 227; communication: direct 148-49; indirect 150ff.; concealment 59, 135ff., 143-44, 162, 164, 191, 197, 209, 248-49, 271; concept 107, 109, 131-32, 140, 144, 152, 154, 171, 212, 270; content 88ff., 99, 122, 138, 174-75, 303; faith 67, 154; history 13, 37, 59ff., 144, 148, 203, 205ff., 214-15, 248, 270; humanity 193; mediation 204, 207, 213-14, 220, 222, 225ff., 248-49, 253, 269, 288; mystery 65, 152ff., 160; natural 91-92; 109; object 95, 100; objectivity 193; possibility: objective 134ff., 192-93, 202, 275, 294, 303, 307; subjective 168ff., 202, 275, 294, 303; presence 36; reality 142, 151, 161, 176-77, 213ff., 229, 248, 305; reason 94, 197; scripture 15, 56-57, 192, 202, 213ff., 275-76, 286ff., 292-93, 299, 307; subject 57, 87, 95-96, 99-100, 134, 154, 174, 249; symbol(?) 60; time 128, 133, 152, 207, 209-10; witness 93, 142ff., 149ff., 203, 214, 216-17, 239, 261, 271, 275-76. *See also* Jesus Christ; Man
Ritschlians 11, 60
Roman Catholicism 31, 181, 251-52
Romantics 155, 207, 224, 297

Sacrament 24, 31, 168ff., 203
Salvation Army 33
Sanctification 163-64, 172, 301, 472-73
Scholasticism 162, 280-81, 295
Scripture 14, 35, 71, 81, 201ff., 264, 269-70, 287; *autopistia* 222-23, 249, 270; claim 254-55; inspiration 58-59, 217, 223ff., 235, 269, 275; *logos* 222; paper pope(?) 217; religious document 206; text 234ff., 244-45, 247, 257, 291-92; translation 234, 236. *See also* Exegesis; Holy Spirit; Method; Revelation; Word of God
Scripture principle 203ff., 238, 245, 248, 294

Self-knowledge 86
Sexuality 163-64
Silence 25, 51, 248, 277
Sin 78, 85, 157, 166, 172, 190, 266, 310; concupiscence 162; original sin 162ff.
Situation 84, 230, 242, 255, 267, 295
Skepticism 135, 246, 289
Socinianism 211, 247-48
Soul 63-64
Space 435
Spectators 5, 58, 77, 86, 103, 254, 269, 289, 312
Spirit 188; absolute 127; human 104, 248, 270
Spirit, Holy 61, 68, 78, 95, 113, 123, 125ff., 154, 165-66, 190, 193, 195, 215ff., 241, 247, 249, 264, 272, 307-8; deity 100, 130, 197, 313; of Father and Son 100, 125, 128, 165, 270; outpouring 128; personality 130; power 167; presence 12, 169, 208, 239; reality 177, 187, 225, 267; scripture 36-37, 58-59, 233-34; third person of Trinity 177-78, 186; work 128, 165, 173, 239
Spiritism 161
Subjectivism 224, 262, 302
Subordinationism 100, 192
Supranaturalism 61, 221
Symbol 17, 40, 60, 134, 171, 187
Symbolics 13, 30

Talk about God 6, 30, 88, 108, 153, 213, 267-68, 280ff., 359; and hearing 25, 33, 63, 93, 113, 193, 230, 248; permission 51ff., 62ff., 201, 271; venture 45ff., 63, 271
Testament: New 123-24, 145, 148, 151, 233; Old 142ff., 151, 233, 235; unity 143, 148-49, 213
Theology 4, 6, 12, 16, 35-36, 81, 109, 269, 273, 281; "as if," 182; consciousness 9, 283; early church 29, 108, 145; experience 67-68, 223; Lutheran 156, 170, 196, 300, 462-63, 468-69; medieval 67, 94, 104, 108, 162; modern 8, 10-11, 20, 48, 59, 61, 67, 82, 107, 181-82, 248; natural 92-93, 346; new 19, 30, 47, 78, 80, 83; Protestant 19-20, 182, 219, 238-39, 252; Reformation 29, 104; Reformed 36, 83, 92, 156, 192, 235, 300, 453ff., 459ff.,

466ff.; Roman Catholic 169ff., 182, 219, 237-38, 243, 462; science 5-6, 280-81

Thinking 27, 47, 188, 196, 218, 258-59, 304; after and with 151, 254-55, 257, 260-61, 292, 306; Christian 291; dialectic 309-10; dogmatic 39, 103, 279, 286ff., 296ff.; faith 307ff.; before God 307-8; religious 285ff., 290ff., 302; responsible 312. *See also* Revelation

Thou, divine 136. *See also* I

Thought, rule of 290-91, 294, 297

Time 147, 202-3, 277, 289, 435; eternity 112-13, 128, 144, 210, 243. *See also* God; Revelation; Word of God

Tradition 231, 237, 305

Trinity 37, 87ff., 145, 154, 169, 193, 303; analogies 101, 104ff., 123, 134; dogma 95ff., 117, 123-24, 138, 153-54, 205, 228; economy 101, 104; place in dogmatics 96ff.

Truth 14, 33, 46, 60, 62ff., 187, 190-91, 214, 244, 249, 261, 281; Christian 218, 305; of God 89, 92, 267, 271, 286, 313; knowledge of 8, 73-74, 255; of scripture 254-55; word of 295

Ubiquity 158ff.

Unbelief 50, 148, 215, 290, 449

Unconditioned 46, 60, 113, 299

University 49, 51; theology at 4-5

Witness 31, 103, 248, 261, 269, 288; Holy Spirit 222ff., 234, 261; preaching 36; prophets and apostles 16, 53ff., 62ff., 213ff.; scripture 223, 236, 239-40, 248-49, 253ff., 366

Woman 164

Word 186; human 79; and sacrament 169-70

Word of God 30-31, 118, 182, 195, 251, 277, 280; dogma 38ff.; freedom 277; glory 278, 284, 298, 304; and human word 24, 29, 36-37, 56ff., 99, 213ff., 229-30, 268-69, 281ff., 286-87, 294-95, 299; incarnate 115, 144, 212; Logos 62; preaching 24-25, 30ff., 265, 280-81, 283, 287, 298; presence 15ff., 35-36, 270, 274, 292; problem 3ff.; reality 270-71; scripture 33, 35ff., 55-56, 206, 215ff., 229ff., 242ff., 253ff., 283-84, 288; situation 230-31; time 36, 270; unity 194; unity and trinity 14ff., 270-71

World 60ff., 93, 105, 154, 162-63, 210, 262, 273, 276; contradiction 160; despising of 75; incarnation 144; two worlds 98, 118, 125

Worldview 49, 90, 154, 258

Youth movement 4

Zwinglians 239

Index of Names

Achelis, E. C. 140
Alsted, J. H. 98, 225
Althaus, P. 311, 334, 461
Amesius, W. 9
Angelus Silesius 424-25
Anglican Articles 233
Anselm 140, 142, 151, 348
Archimedes 85
Aristotle 135
Arius 100, 231
Athanasius 124, 231
Augsburg Confession 11
Augustine 31, 104-5, 108, 114, 129,
    214, 219, 238, 341, 345, 357, 364,
    379-80, 412, 435, 451, 455
Avancinus 424

Baader, B. F. X. von 258
Baier, J. W. 372, 391, 463
Barth, K. 60, 101, 107, 117, 134, 141,
    183, 243, 261, 300, 322, 395, 429
Bartmann, B. 239, 331, 337, 371, 378,
    404, 410, 414, 417-18, 428, 436, 439
Basil of Caesarea 27
Bavinck, H. 9, 12, 14, 18, 21, 97, 128
Beck, J. T. 9, 19, 25ff., 258, 290
Bergson, H. 179
Bernard of Clairvaux 355
Biedermann, A. E. 382, 387, 390, 422-
    23, 434
Biel, G. 379
Bismarck, O. von 244
Blumhardt, J. C. 6, 328
Bogatsky, K. H. von 270
Böhme, J. 258
Bolsche, W. 424

Bonaventura 5, 21, 73, 281, 365
Boniface VIII 202, 289
Book of Concord 240-41
Bornhausen, K. 357
Braun, J. 380, 394, 397, 467
Brunner, E. 353
Bucanus, W. 54, 128, 395, 467
Burmann, F. 408, 411, 436, 467
Buddha 5, 149-50
Bullinger, H. 32, 57, 355
Bultmann, R. 124

Calov, A. 9, 157, 238, 372
Calvin, J. 4-5, 9, 19, 21, 32-33, 54, 57,
    68, 83-84, 92, 96, 114, 143, 147ff.,
    156, 158-59, 162, 169, 172, 182,
    191, 220ff., 225, 239-40, 253, 259-
    60, 290, 294-95, 334, 351, 409, 427,
    451, 454-55, 462, 467, 470
Catherine of Siena 239
Celsus 448
Chemnitz, M. 96-97, 344-45, 356, 381
Cocceius, J. 9-10, 59, 67, 219, 355, 395,
    467
Cohen, H. 357
Confession: of Augsburg 24, 241, 300;
    Belgic 233; Gallican 33, 233; Hel-
    vetic I 220; Helvetic II 12, 32-33,
    219, 223-24, 240
Council of: Chalcedon 139, 141, 241,
    247; Ephesus 157; Florence 129;
    Toledo 114; Trent 170, 203, 471; Vati-
    can I 35, 343ff.
Creed: Apostles' 160, 260, 272; Athana-
    sian 15, 102; Nicene 16, 27, 102,
    112, 120-21, 128, 241, 294, 306

483

Cremer, H. 322
Cyprian 343

Danäus, L. 355
Dante 104
Descartes, R. 48
Dinter, A. 106
Dionysius the Areopagite 104
Dorsche, J. G. 238
Dort, Synod of 25, 247, 455, 459ff.
Dostoyevsky, F. M. 86, 235, 350
Doumergue, E. 468

Ebrard, J. H. A. 21
Eckhart 353, 364
Elert, W. 324, 334, 410
Emden Catechism 83
Erasmus 455
Eugene IV 129

Ferdinand I 421
Feuerbach, L. 11, 81, 358, 361, 399-400, 424-25
Fichte, J. G. 238-39, 350
Formula of Concord 25ff., 247
Formula of Consensus, Helvetic 223, 235, 247
Frank, F. H. R. 25, 28, 382, 422
Freystein, J. B. 181

Gellert, C. F. 148
Georges, K. E. 11
Gerhard, J. 32, 59, 96-97, 106, 158, 205, 238, 345, 351ff., 434ff.
Gernler, L. 235
Girgensohn, K. 324
Goethe, J. W. von 40, 110, 137, 178, 288-89, 357, 365, 376, 447
Gogarten, F. 353, 419
Gomarus, F. 467
Gorgias 25
Gregory of Nazianzus 105, 383
Grimm, C. L.W. 53
Grünewald, M. 151-52, 164
Gunkel, H. 146

Haering, T. 8, 20, 61, 97, 378, 391, 405, 420, 423ff.
Hafenreffer, M. 160
Hagen, O. 151
Hagenbach, K. R. 259, 347, 363, 378, 383
Haller, A. von 137

Handel, G. F. 21, 33
Harnack, A. von 91, 143, 163, 256
Hase, K. A. von 21, 57, 98, 349, 399, 423, 436, 467
Hegel, G. W. F. 76-77, 104ff., 135, 156, 166, 336, 364
Heidanus, A. 439, 453, 475
Heidegger, J. H. 59, 90, 225, 235, 344, 407-8, 411, 428, 439, 456, 459, 461, 466ff., 474
Heidelberg Catechism 83, 151, 159-60, 465
Heim, K. 48-49, 289-90
Heppe, H. 22, 57, 98, 324
Herder, J. G. 206-7
Herrmann, W. 8, 25, 28ff.
Hiller, P. F. 146
Holl, K. 183, 256
Hollaz, D. 112, 238, 372, 379, 437, 462
Homer 253
Horace 125, 384
Hottinger 463
Hugh of St. Victor 105
Hume, D. 41
Hutterus, L. 356, 381, 387, 418, 434, 462
Hyperius, A. 355

Ihmels, L. 237
Irenaeus 143
Irish Articles 233
Isidore of Seville 17

Jeremias, J. 237
John of Damascus 129
Jud, L. 83
Jülicher, A. 419

Kähler, M. 116, 423
Kaftan, J. 8, 14, 60, 240, 291, 301-2, 389-90, 404
Kant, I. 10, 20, 41, 135, 326, 345, 350, 356, 364
Keckermann, B. 57, 96-97, 104, 131, 158
Kierkegaard, S. 37, 50, 53, 77, 137, 143, 178, 332-33, 460
Kircher, A. 349
Kirn, O. 391
Kittel, R. 146
Kluge, F. 182
Knapp, A. 304
Knorr von Rosenroth, C. 306
Krause, K. C. E. 430

Kupisch, K. 244
Kutter, H. 339

Lagarde, P. A. de 182
Lang, A. 140
Lao-Tse 149-50
Leiden Synopsis 154, 157, 166, 425, 458
Leo XIII 238
Lessing, G. E. 37, 65, 203
Leydecker, M. 129
Lietzmann, H. 258
Lipsius, R. A. 7, 240, 390-91, 405, 436
Loofs, F. 147, 196, 300, 400, 414, 430, 432, 434
Lücke, F. 187, 306
Lüdemann, H. 324
Lulmann, C. 187, 306
Luthardt, C. E. 79, 196, 300, 436, 444
Luther, M. 5, 10-11, 54, 67, 93, 122, 147, 149, 170-71, 195ff., 208, 210, 212ff., 218, 230, 234, 237-38, 240-41, 246-47, 252, 256, 259, 300, 311, 335, 338-39, 389, 409, 427, 438, 447, 451, 455, 457
Marcion 76, 143, 163, 232
Maresius, S. 10, 159, 344, 385-86, 397
Martensen, H. L. 97, 353, 378, 390-91, 407-8, 411, 424, 458
Mastricht, P. van 156, 396, 409, 415, 424, 458, 463
Melanchthon, P. 21, 104, 196, 240-41, 372, 427, 432
Meyer, C. F. 276
Michaelis, J. D. 224, 226
Micronius, M. 83
Mirbt, C. 344, 355
Missale Romanum 308
Molina 412, 463
Mozart, W. A. 74
Müller, J. 103
Musculus, W. 57

Naumann, F. 296
Neander, A. 68
Nestle, E. 53
Nicholas of Cusa 357
Nietzsche, F. 74-75
Nitzsch, F. A. B. 7, 20, 301-2, 379

Occam, William of 374, 409
Oetlinger, F. C. 312, 395
Oettli, S. 146
Olevianus, C. 162, 303

Origen 76, 320
Otto, R. 419-20

Pascal, B. 83
Peter, Martyr 57
Peterson, E. 339
Piux X 238
Pius XI 203, 238
Plato 25, 135, 259, 434
Polanus 113, 121-22, 165, 346, 356, 372-73, 381, 397-98, 403, 418-19, 436, 439, 462ff.
Preiswerk, A. 295, 384
Protagoras 434

Quenstedt, J. A. 59, 90, 98, 113, 121, 156-57, 238, 285, 344, 372, 380, 411

Rabanus Maurus 127, 178
Rade, M. 97, 324, 347, 349
Reischle, M. 374
Riissen, L. van 90, 130, 156-57, 165, 219, 345, 416, 434, 437, 466ff.
Ritschl, A. 301, 348, 350, 365, 370, 394, 420, 424, 438
Röttger, K. 31
Rothe, R. 7

Sabellius 101
Salandra, A. 419
Schaeder, E. 322
Scheel, O. 98
Schelling, F. W. J. 59, 105-6, 258
Schiller, F. von 4, 54, 61, 79, 258, 420
Schlatter, A. 9, 19, 26, 28, 134
Schleiermacher, F. D. E. 5, 7, 9, 19, 28, 47, 59-60, 62, 76, 81, 90ff., 96, 98, 101, 104, 132, 143, 180, 182ff., 209-10, 238, 247, 270, 273-74, 281-82, 286, 306-7, 311, 322-23, 336, 348, 350-51, 364, 371, 379, 387-88, 401, 405ff., 413-14, 440, 474
Schlunk, R. 132
Schmalcaldic Articles 208
Schmaus, M. 202
Schmid, H. 324
Schmidt, W. 387
Scholz, H. 47ff.
Schwab, G. 6
Schweizer, A. 7, 10, 22, 26, 28, 57, 91, 344, 399, 467
Scotus, Duns 414
Sebastianus à Rostock 424

Seeberg, R. 324, 347-48, 387, 405, 414, 438
Servetus 96, 231
Socinius, F. 143, 454
Socrates 25, 149-50, 343
Söderblom, N. 107
Sohnius, G. 129
Spengler, O. 46, 71
Spinoza, B. 37, 430
Stage, C. 234
Stephan, H. 335-36, 339, 389, 391, 399, 405
Strauss, D. F. 225-26, 363-64
Stuhlfauth, G. 411
Suso 453, 478

Tauler, J. 353
Tertullian 434
Theresa of Jesus 239
Thomas Aquinas 3ff., 10, 12, 17ff., 39, 92, 112, 135, 149, 238, 333-34, 337ff., 346, 350, 380, 401, 404, 410, 412, 423, 439, 462
Thomasius, G. 322, 380, 382
Thurneysen, E. 86, 124, 132, 266
Tillich, P. 30, 46, 60, 365
Trelcatius 467
Troeltsch, E. 8, 28, 60-61, 97, 205, 210, 296, 301-2, 340
Turrettini, F. 235

Ulpianus, D. 458
Ullmann, C. 68
Ursinus, Z. 346, 355

Van Til, S. 401
Vergil 266
Vilmar, A. F. C. 132
Vincent of Lerins 241
Vitringa, C. 10, 46
Voetius 285

Waldensian Confession 233
Wegscheider, J. A. L. 320, 380, 382, 390-91
Weiss, J. 116-17, 258
Weizsäcker, C. H. von 234
Wellhausen, J. 146
Wendelin, M. F. 463, 467
Wendt, H. H. 8, 21, 60
Werenfels, S. 259
Westminster: Catechism 83; Confession 220-21, 233
Wichelhaus, J. 389ff., 399, 419-20, 434-35
Wobbermin, G. 47-48
Wollebius, J. 165, 433, 467, 473
Wolter, M. 321

Zanchius, H. 156-57
Zimmern, H. 107
Zinzendorf, C. R. von 90
Zinzendorf, N. L. von 90, 211, 247
Zurich Confession 233
Zwingli, H. 9, 13, 17, 21, 32, 76, 92, 118, 149-50, 182, 220, 240, 343, 405, 467

Index of Scripture References

Genesis
2:17 — 83
3:5 — 135
3:8 — 155
3:9 — 197
12:8 — 305
14:8-20 — 150
17:1-3 — 404
17:3 — 409
25:29ff. — 192
32:25ff. — 180, 189
32:27ff. — 426

Exodus
3:2ff. — 5
3:5 — 366, 399
3:14 — 88, 135, 308, 327, 368, 392
14:19-20 — 311
16:14-21 — 468
19:9 — 145
19:16 — 109
20:2-3 — 109
20:3 — 52
20:4-5 — 82, 385
20:5 — 96
32:20ff. — 140
33:20 — 292
33:21 — 332
33:22-23 — 366

Leviticus
19:4 — 402
26:1 — 402

26:12 — 144

Numbers
12:8 — 338

Deuteronomy
4:24 — 125

1 Samuel
4:10 — 32

2 Samuel
12:7 — 312

1 Kings
8:32 — 368
18:40 — 428
19:4 — 386
19:7-8 — 108
19:18 — 390

1 Chronicles
16:26 — 402

2 Chronicles
6:18-19 — 435

Job
38:1 — 366
42:3 — 414
42:7 — 350

Psalms
1:2 — 269
2:7 — 121
2:10a — 197
5:12 — 4
8:4 — 72, 174
9:11-12 — 4
31:15 — 436
36:19 — 126, 140, 162
39 — 146
51:10 — 127
51:17 — 127
66:1-2 — 366
69:34 — 366
73:25 — 431
90:12 — 86
96:5 — 402
97:7 — 402
103:1 — 313
103:4 — 411
104:29 — 446
116:10 — 67
116:11 — 271
119 — 63
119:18 — 180
139 — 146
139:1-5 — 411
139:5 — 101, 103-4
139:5ff. — 134
148 — 366

487

150	109	**Daniel**		**Mark**	
150:3-5	63	2:1ff.	40	1:15	119
		3:26	35	2:5	171
		7:13	115	4:4	446
Proverbs				4:11	366
26:9	475			9:23	245
		Amos		9:24	250, 447
		3:7	93	14:38	194
Ecclesiastes				15:35	349
1:9	407			16:15	54, 212
3:11	395	**Habakkuk**			
5:1	286	2:18	402	**Luke**	
				1:35	145
				1:37	404
Isaiah				1:48	271
6:5	175	**Malachi**		2:34	112
6:5-7	68, 271	3:10	4	9:62	109
8:14	449			16:8	4
28:16	449			17:10	35, 274
28:21b	197	**Matthew**		18:8	50
40:8	14	1:18	165	18:13	127
40:9	447	1:20	165	24:25	78
40:31	67	2:1-12	150	24:34	449
42:8	95	3:17	194		
44:6	437	4:17	155		
48:11	95	5:8	337	**John**	
53:1	442	6:2	178	1:1	114ff., 117
55:8	62	6:9	112, 327	1:3	119
55:8-9	291	6:10	418	1:11	155
58:1	306	6:13	439	1:12-13	443
		6:26	113	1:14	115, 144,
		6:33	108		166-67, 366
Jeremiah		7:6	109	1:18	328
2:8	402	7:13	63	1:29	118
2:18	402	7:14	86	1:47	146
2:20	402	7:16	102	3:4ff.	50
10:14	401	8:5-13	150	3:6	127
14:1	402	9:17	428	3:8	295
14:3	402	10:28	66, 471	3:10	239
23:18	366	11:12	308	3:16	423, 425, 438
23:28-29	366	11:27	328	3:17	461
23:29	304	13:3ff.	448	3:18	461, 471
31:7	402	13:4ff.	443	3:34	93
38:17-18	246	16:16	443	3:36	458
		16:17	335	4:24	180, 371, 409
		16:18-19	204	5:2ff.	38
Lamentations		17:20	64	7:17	224
3:23	59, 123	19:26	404	8:23	160
		25:18	194	8:56	143
		25:24	149	11:25	431
Ezekiel		26:56	149	12:49	461
2:3-4	146	26:69ff.	443	13:13	166

13:14	166	9:32-33	449	5:6-9	73		
14:6	113, 431	10:9	111	5:10	420		
14:9	427	10:12	459	5:16	158		
14:12	334	11:25ff.	454	5:16-17	335		
14:28	111	11:32	461	5:17	168		
16:13	234	11:33	371	6:9	53		
17:1	113	11:34	414	7:10	50		
21:7	112	12	25	7:15	460		
		12:6ff.	354	8:9	166		
		14–15	296	10:5	197-98, 291, 308		
Acts		14:8	296	10:13-18	53		
1:22	147	16:27	414	12:2	338		
2:32	147			12:7	75		
3:13	111						
3:15	147	**1 Corinthians**					
5:5	108	1:18-19	334, 413	**Galatians**			
5:10	108	1:23	354, 450	2:20	194		
10	150	2:3	460	4:4	160, 438		
10:40-41	147	2:7	335	4:9	4, 26, 118, 328		
14:15	401	2:9	183, 366	5:17	74		
14:16	452	2:10	93, 329	6:7	195		
17:22-31	150, 342	2:14	403	6:16	53		
17:23	150	6:14	111				
17:27	437	7:12	261				
17:28	126, 189	7:15	440	**Ephesians**			
26:19	34	8–10	296	1:4	467		
		8:2-3	352	1:10	160		
		8:3	328	2:6	161		
Romans		9:16	56, 290, 364	2:12	459		
1:4	128, 366	9:19	231	2:13	118		
1:16	81, 331	12	25	2:14	118		
1:19	365	12:3-4	125	2:15	155		
1:19-20	341-42	12:4-5	354	3:15	111		
1:20	344	13:9	93, 230, 332	4:6	112		
1:24	458	13:12	155, 328ff., 332,	6:5	460		
3:2	60, 235		334, 337				
3:4	439	14:43	386				
3:21	261	15:24	111				
3:23	46, 86	15:24ff.	337	**Philippians**			
4:24	111	15:28	156, 406, 468	2:6	138		
5:1	236	15:49	161	2:7	146, 157		
7:6	261	15:54	164	2:8	111		
7:24-25	349			2:9	111		
8:3	446			2:11	111		
8:11	111	**2 Corinthians**		2:12	35, 171		
8:28	108	1:22	126	2:15	146		
8:35	465	2:14	329	3:1	265		
9–11:32	468	3:17	128, 262	3:8	290		
9:6-13	453	4:4	112, 155	3:12	306		
9:11	453	4:6	225, 334-35, 349	3:14	306		
9:18	444	4:7	176	3:16	53		
9:20	457	4:13	27, 67, 123	3:19	456		
9:25	454	4:14	111	4:7	196		

Colossians

1:10	118
2:3	329
2:8	93
2:9	93
3:3	178

2 Thessalonians

3:2	123, 443

1 Timothy

1:17	414
2:4	457
2:5	118
3:16	453-54
6:15	370
6:16	93, 112, 143

2 Timothy

2:13	408

Hebrews

1:3	101
2:17	166
4:12	320
4:15	157
7:3	165-66
9:15	118
10:22	321
10:31	457
11:1	336
11:13	336
12:1	147
12:6	465
12:24	118
13:14	86

James

1:17	439

1 Peter

1:25	14
4:8	447
5:7	108

1 John

1:1	103, 118, 155
3:2	337
3:9	165, 330
3:20	454
4:2	148
4:8	16, 423
4:16	371
4:19	85
5:6	224

2 John

7	148

Jude 254

Revelation

1:8	437
1:17	370
21:5	414